KERNER

Liberty —
We hope you enjoy
this look back at
Chicago history.

Gene Schlickman

Bill Barnhart

Feb. '00

KERNER
The Conflict of Intangible Rights

Bill Barnhart and Gene Schlickman

University of Illinois Press

Urbana and Chicago

Publication of this book was supported by a challenge grant
from the Siragusa Foundation, which was matched by funds
from a foundation and individual donors who wish to remain
anonymous.

Library of Congress Cataloging-in-Publication Data
Barnhart, William E., 1946–
Kerner : the conflict of intangible rights / William E. Barnhart
and Eugene F. Schlickman.
p. cm.
Includes bibliographical references (p.   ) and index.
ISBN 0-252-02504-0 (acid-free paper)
1. Kerner, Otto, 1908–1976.
2. Illinois—Politics and government—1951–
3. Chicago (Ill.)—Politics and government—1951–
4. Governors—Illinois—Biography.
5. Judges—Illinois—Biography.
I. Schlickman, Eugene F., 1929–
II. Title.
F546.4.K47 B37   1999
977.3'043'092—dc21   99-6065
[B]   CIP

C 5 4 3 2 1

To our wives, Kate and Sherry,
for their contributions
measurable and
immeasurable

And don't make such an outcry about feeling innocent, it spoils the not unfavorable impression you make in other respects.
—Franz Kafka, "The Trial"

Contents

Preface

The task of writing the life and times of Otto Kerner began more than ten years ago when I recognized a void in Illinois history without such a book. Biographies of Henry Horner, Adlai E. Stevenson II, William G. Stratton, Richard B. Ogilvie, Daniel Walker, and James R. Thompson have been published, but none of Kerner, despite the richness of his family story and the widespread interest in his era. As a young Republican first elected to the Illinois House in 1964, when Kerner won his second term, I had no special feeling for the Democratic governor, but I came to believe that Kerner should be remembered for more than his conviction on criminal charges near the end of his life. I committed myself to the notion that a good biography must tell good stories in each chapter and reveal its subject's humanity, not just a chronology of facts.

Gene Schlickman, March 1999

Gene enlisted me in the Kerner project in August 1991. I had covered the Illinois legislature in the mid-1970s. I had never met Kerner and had no preconceived ideas about what Kerner's story might hold. The opportunity to write a life story from a clean slate, based exclusively on document research and interviews, appealed to my journalistic instincts from the start. Eventually I became absorbed in the obvious contradiction between a man whose name will forever be associated with superior public service—the Kerner Commission on the 1967 urban riots—and a man declared by federal pros-

ecutors to be a public enemy, unfit to live in free society. Exploring that contradiction required a detailed probe into the process by which public images
of men and women are created and destroyed—a process that is often tragically errant and unjust.

Bill Barnhart, March 1999

Acknowledgments

Many persons and organizations have assisted immeasurably in the production of this biography. We have elected to list them alphabetically while conceding that the assistance has varied in scope. We would be remiss, however, in not acknowledging the invaluable assistance of Anton C. Kerner. This biography would have been much poorer without his contributions, though we hasten to add that it is unauthorized and our sole responsibility.

The invaluable proofreading and editing by Catherine A. Eaton and Mary L. Rosner are especially appreciated. We offer special thanks to Richard L. Wentworth, director of the University of Illinois Press, and Bruce Bethell, manuscript editor, for their talent and support.

Arlington Heights Memorial Library, Arlington Heights, Illinois
Judge William J. Bauer, U.S. Court of Appeals for the Seventh Circuit
Brown University, Providence, Rhode Island: Sheila Cournoyer and Martha Mitchell
Chicago Historical Society, Chicago: Archie Motley
Chicago Tribune, Chicago: Joseph Leonard, associate editor; reference library staff
University of Chicago, Regenstein Library: Zdenek Hruban
Clerk of the Circuit Court of Cook County, Chicago, Ill: Phil Costello
Cook County Law Library, Chicago: John ("Jack") Foreman
The Czechoslovak Heritage Museum, Library, and Archives, Berwyn, Illinois: Dagmar Bradac

Ivan R. Dee, Chicago

Senator Richard Durbin and staff, Washington, D.C.

Fermi National Accelerator Laboratory, Batavia, Illinois: Adrienne W. Kolb, archivist

Alison LaBuy Foy, Wilmette, Illinois

Paul M. Green, director of the Institute for Public Policy and Administration at Governors State University, University Park, Illinois

Samuel K. Gove, director emeritus, Institute of Government and Public Affairs, University of Illinois at Urbana-Champaign

Harold Washington Library, Chicago

Historical Society of Oak Park and River Forest, Oak Park, Illinois: Anne Henders

Illinois Department of Military Affairs, Springfield: Kellie Hansen and Charles W. Munie

Illinois Legislative Reference Bureau, Springfield: Bernadine Gretzer

Illinois Legislative Research Unit, Springfield

Illinois Racing Board, Chicago: Joseph Sinopoli

Illinois State Archives, Springfield

Illinois State Historical Library, Springfield: Janice Petterchak, Cheryl Schnilling, Constance Holberg, and Mary Michals

Kenan Heise, Evanston, Ilinois

John Fitzgerald Kennedy Library, Boston: June Payne, research assistant

Anton C. Kerner and Helena Kerner Stern, Chicago

Lewis University, Romeoville, Illinois: Brother Bernard Rapp

Thomas Littlewood, Urbana, Illinois

Lyndon Baines Johnson Library, Austin, Texas: Linda Hanson

Museum of Broadcast Communications, Chicago

National Archives, Great Lakes Region, Chicago: Donald Jackanicz and Beverly Watkins

Newberry Library, Chicago

Northwestern University Law School Library, Chicago: Marcia G. Lehr

Oak Park Public Library, Oak Park, Illinois

Thomas E. Patton, Washington, D.C.

Fr. David F. Ryan, Des Plaines, Illinois

Professor Donald Lee Scruggs, Columbia, Missouri

Former senator Paul Simon and staff, Washington, D.C.

University of Texas Library, Austin

Dr. and Mrs. Richard Treanor, Long Grove, Illinois

Harry S. Truman Library, Independence, Missouri

Wilmette Public Library, Wilmette, Illinois

Introduction:
A Time Traveler

Andalusia, Illinois, lies snuggled where the Mississippi River flows un-conventionally east to west near the Quad Cities of Illinois and Iowa. The tiny village boasts an ambitious motto: "Volunteer Capital of the World." After the river overran its banks wildly in 1965, townspeople built a levee against the next deluge. Residents still take pride in the fact that their earthwork was not constructed by the U.S. Army Corps of Engineers.[1] When-ever other bootstrap levees give way to Mississippi rampages, the corps ut-ters predictable reproofs. But the unofficial Andalusia levee has held. Few people visit Andalusia, however, so the town displays its motto on a road sign along Illinois Highway 92, where motorists can glimpse it as they drive by, headed for somewhere else.

One warm, rain-threatening evening in late July 1967, a traveler arrived unexpectedly by boat—Otto Kerner, the governor of Illinois, in search of a telephone. Miles away, but brought close by the front pages of newspapers in nearby Rock Island and Davenport, fires of urban rioting smoldered in De-troit, where forty-three lay dead. Days earlier twenty-three had died in New-ark riots. In Washington Congress clamored for action to halt the violence that had frightened Americans for three summers in a row. Many in Congress and the country believed that a conspiracy of militant blacks was bent on destroying the country. President Johnson was going on television in a few minutes to address the nation about all this, and he needed some volunteers in a hurry.

Comfortably into his second term as governor, Kerner looked like a ma-turing matinee idol as he stepped off an excursion paddlewheeler called the

Quad-City Queen and onto the Andalusia levee. Fifty-eight years old and dressed impeccably in a dark business suit that was perhaps too formal for a pleasure cruise with fellow public officials, Kerner carried his five-foot-eight-inch frame erect in a perpetual military bearing that made him appear taller than he was. His naturally wavy dark brown hair swept backward from a firm, confident face that television cameras treated as favorably as that of any politician in the country. A national organization of press photographers named him the "most handsome governor." In his college yearbook, fellow students had called him "Adonis."

Asked to describe Otto Kerner, people first mentioned his piercing blue eyes and ruddy complexion, enhanced, it was said, by a sunlamp. Next they commented on his polished social manner. Some remembered the hint of English affectation in his speech from his days at Cambridge University, to which his proud Bohemian parents, despite the uncertainties of the Great Depression, had sent him for tutoring in the law. But there was more to him than good looks and correct manner. No politician better represented the ability of the Democratic Party of Cook County to promote individuals of obvious integrity for public office, at least when the occasion required it. In the years after World War II, the party's energetic chairman, Jacob Arvey, brought to the public stage Adlai E. Stevenson II and Paul H. Douglas, but before them Arvey had chosen Otto Kerner. Cynics in Chicago's Democratic machine nonetheless dismissed Kerner as a political version of Charles Van Doren, the suave, articulate, and high-class television quiz-show contestant who captivated audiences in the 1950s and made people believe the popular quiz programs were on the up-and-up.

Kerner saw his public role differently than did those who promoted his career. His success in winning elections fueled ambition, to be sure, but the primary influence on Kerner's public life was the military, not politics. The Illinois National Guard and combat duty as a regular army officer in World War II gave him a task-oriented structure based on a simple and direct sense of duty, and he applied that structure to his entire life. Former Illinois environmental official Clarence W. Klassen, who traveled frequently with Governor Kerner, recalled this essential element of Kerner's character in a 1981 oral history interview: "One time . . . we were talking about some complicated problems. He said, 'Clarence, I am basically a simple person.' He said, 'I like to solve one thing at a time and not get it all complicated by a lot of technical discussions.'"[2] Workers in Mayor Richard J. Daley's tightly run organization once called Kerner a "do-it-yourself" politician, a disparaging comment about his ability to find political support beyond the party machinery and his tendency to ignore the intrigue and complexity of political gamesmanship. They called him aloof.[3] His military colleagues, especially those he met in combat, would never have made such a remark.

Otto Jr. was born, in the words of Chicago newspaper columnist Mike Royko, with a golden ballot in his mouth, for his father, Otto Kerner Sr., was a respected figure in the prewar Cook County Democratic organization.[4] His wife's father (and his father's political sponsor), fellow Bohemian Anton Cermak, built the organization into the political machine that Daley later ruled. With such a pedigree Kerner could have enjoyed a successful private or public career in Chicago without much exertion. His dues to the Democratic organization had been paid early on by his father and Cermak. By the time he entered high school, his father had moved the family from the West Side ward that was Cermak's base, teeming with Eastern European immigrants, to the fashionable, WASPish, and largely Republican suburb of Oak Park. His parents sent him to an Ivy League college and an English university. As a young lawyer he enjoyed the company of Chicago's society elites, who did not speak in the "dees" and "does" of ward and precinct political dialect. Critics said he coasted on his pedigree and good looks, but his relatively easy passage to prominence gave him a clarity of vision and a freedom from convention that less secure public figures lacked, and combat duty gave him confidence. He was a private man of common sense and goodwill who believed those traits to be sufficient to accomplish his public endeavors and fulfill his duty.

The history of Bohemia, which was marked by bitter episodes of oppression over many centuries, created in the Kerners and other descendants of that region a deep skepticism about political maneuverings. Bohemians love individual liberty because for most of their history they have lived without it, and they distrust overbearing government because for most of their history they have had to accept it. No one needed to tell Kerner that the summer's inner-city strife could disrupt his state's always worrisome economic progress and social harmony. But no one should have expected him to be overawed by an appointment to examine urban unrest on a blue-ribbon panel in Washington, where so many good ideas were corrupted.

Andalusia was a fitting, though unscheduled, stage for Kerner to step into the hot national spotlight. He had boarded the *Quad-City Queen* that evening to do what governors do—in this case, to mingle with about three hundred local officials and explain how his administration in Springfield was looking after their interests. When the mayor of Rock Island, Illinois, gave him a key to the city, he responded: "It's very nice; I wish it were the key to the Senate,"[5] referring to the U.S. Senate's obstruction of funding for a major scientific project for the state. But images of protests in the big cities had intruded on such parochial interests. Just before Kerner's visit, the Federal Bureau of Investigation learned of possible African American protests in nearby Rock Island that might disrupt his appearance.[6] An editorial in the *Rock Island Argus* on the day of Kerner's visit reflected the general mood of the country: "It ought to be obvious to anybody in Washington that crime in general is rising and the chief cause is the softness in Washington, principally the misguided zeal of the U.S. Supreme Court to open loopholes for the escape of prisoners and the persistence of the White House in seeking a social cause for every crime, so more can be spent, instead of seeking a better way to crack down on it. . . . A constitutional amendment restoring the powers of police would be helpful."[7] America was scared and looking for answers.

In 1967, 128 American cities—from Boston to Los Angeles, from Peekskill, New York, to East Palo Alto, California—experienced civil disturbances in black, inner-city neighborhoods. When scholars and public policymakers looked for causes, they often began with words attributed to a former Republican state governor, Earl Warren of California, who, like Kerner, had grown in public life into a low-key liberal with a knack for seeing the nub of a matter. "We conclude that in the field of public opinion the doctrine of 'separate but equal' has no place. Separate educational facilities are inherently unequal," a unanimous Supreme Court under Chief Justice Warren ruled in *Brown v. Board of Education*. It was a judicial proposition that probably would not have won a national plebiscite. Once the breadth of the inequality implied in the mandate was realized fully, the country shrank from the job. Johnson's unprecedented Great Society programs, beginning in 1965, seemed like an ambitious attempt to match the federal government's revenue-raising powers with a national attack on poverty and discrimination. The results, however, were fiscally meager, politically overstated, and wholly unimpressive to urban blacks. Yet *Brown v. Board of Education* ignited African American aspirations.

Urban riots, sociologists discovered, were generally sparked by routine and therefore especially repugnant incidents of discrimination and abuse against blacks by white police officers. Isolated incidents exploded into generalized, random street violence in which blacks vented frustrations and expressed anger that came with unfulfilled expectations. They were not race riots, unlike the clashes between whites and blacks that the nation had witnessed earlier in the century in places such as Chicago and Detroit. They were riots by a race of people left behind, hopeless in urban ghettos. Nonetheless, the country would not stand for it, and those in charge knew it. Johnson, angered by what he considered to be ungrateful blacks and consumed by an unwinnable war in Vietnam, reached out to prominent Americans he believed he could trust to take the summer's urban heat off him. He wanted respected public figures outside his administration to exonerate him and his Great Society programs and to calm a fretful nation. They did not comply. Seven months later Johnson and the nation read an indictment of themselves in what became known as the Kerner Report.

"Our nation is moving toward two societies, one black, one white—separate and unequal," the commission unanimously concluded. A carefully drafted bill of particulars began: "What white Americans have never fully understood—but what the Negro can never forget—is that white society is deeply implicated in the ghetto. White institutions created it, white institutions maintain it, and white society condones it."[8] The pressure-cooker process of researching and writing a report on urban riots that showed every likelihood of resuming the next summer was rare alchemy. At a time when the generation gap was wide in America, the effort forced together venerable American leaders and zealous young social scientists. It forged viewpoints spanning the political spectrum into a unanimous statement of painful truth. Johnson's domestic adviser, Joseph A. Califano Jr., received an advance copy of the report at a breakfast in the White House mess with Kerner and the commission's executive director, David Ginsburg, a veteran Washington insider from the Franklin Roosevelt era. "As soon as I read it, I knew Johnson would erupt," Califano wrote in his memoir, *The Triumph and Tragedy of Lyndon Johnson.* Johnson refused to accept the report ceremonially or thank the commissioners publicly.[9]

February 27, 1968, was a devastating day in the Johnson White House. After breakfast with Kerner and Ginsburg, Califano and Johnson's advisers on the Vietnam War lunched in the private dining room of Secretary of State Dean Rusk. "It was the most depressing three hours in my years of public service," Califano wrote later. The war counselors "were beyond pessimism."[10] Johnson's nemesis, Robert F. Kennedy, calculating the odds of opposing Johnson for the Democratic presidential nomination, declared after learning the president's reaction to the Kerner Report, "This means that he's not going to do anything about the war and he's not going to do anything about the cities."[11] At the end of March Johnson went on television to tell the nation he would not seek another term.

Kerner certainly had no desire to embarrass or defeat Johnson. He and the president, born just twelve days apart in August 1908, had been Democratic Party colleagues since the end of World War II. He was loyal to the president's Vietnam policy and especially to its chief battlefield administrator, General William C. Westmoreland, who had commanded Kerner's artillery battalion in North Africa at the United States' entry into World War II. They remained friends. Moreover, after Johnson recovered from his initial anger over the Kerner Report, he rewarded its nominal author with the job he deeply desired, a seat on the U.S. Court of Appeals in Chicago, the bench where his father had served with distinction for fourteen years.

Nonetheless, in disappointing Johnson the Kerner Commission revealed the character of its chairman. Despite his central-casting appearance, Kerner did not always play the roles expected of him. Kerner did his duty, though not necessarily to Johnson. The Kerner Report, which sold in the millions as a paperback and continues to be quoted three decades later, shocked America's white establishment from its state of denial about the plight of ghetto residents. It caused police procedures throughout the country to be examined and improved. It prompted many corporations to reexamine their hiring and promotion policies long before affirmative action became a legal controversy. It sparked significant changes in the racial makeup of news media reporting and editing staffs, creating what writer Darryl Pickney called "the Kerner generation" of black journalists.[12]

This son of Chicago's white ethnic community was no stranger to the black struggle. During the 1963 annual convention of the National Association for the Advancement of Colored People (NAACP) meeting in Chicago, he saluted the black revolution as an extension of the American revolution, telling a South Side church congregation: "This is an undertaking in which we must not fail. Moderate men of good will must guide the powerful forces now at work into channels of effective, constructive, rapid action to remedy the ancient injustices that too long have oppressed so many in a land whose proud boast is to be free."[13] Four years before the riots that would lead to the creation of the Kerner Commission, he told his audience: "[White Americans] do not understand that the Negro ghetto far from protecting cities destroys them. They do not know that by walling people in and preventing their natural assimilation to the rest of society they create the very conditions of bitterness and despair that produce the crimes and violence they fear. They do not know that the only way to destroy the cancer they fear is to destroy the ghetto."[14] Later that week Mayor Daley was booed off a stage in Chicago's Grant Park when he attempted to address the NAACP delegates after assuring the press that there were no ghettos in Chicago.

After joining the federal judiciary, Kerner established himself as a defender of civil liberties for the poor and remained the Kerner Report's most ardent champion. In the *Chicago Daily News* he declared: "Racism, bred into our society for 300 years, is the underlying cause of the rioting in our cities. We must start by facing ourselves and admitting we have such feelings. If we are unwilling to do that, we can spend billions of dollars to overcome the racist system, and the money will go down the drain."[15] By 1968 the country had tired of the civil rights movement after it moved north from hard-fought victories in the South. But Kerner was one of the few mainstream northern politicians who persistently denounced the maintenance of ghettos in Mayor Daley's Chicago and other cities.

Kerner's confident advocacy on behalf of minorities and the underclass grew from his family background and blossomed with his political popularity. He was elected governor twice—only the second Democratic governor in the state's history to be reelected—with broad support from downstate voters, who instinctively distrust politicians from Chicago. His first victory for governor came in 1960, when the country narrowly chose John F. Kennedy over Richard Nixon for president. Kerner ran against a Republican seeking a third term and won easily, far outpolling Kennedy in Illinois and drawing traditional Republican voters into the Democratic column. His second victory was just as sweet. In the landslide election of Lyndon Johnson over Barry Goldwater, Kerner defeated Charles H. Percy, a man much like himself whom *Time* magazine had promoted gushingly in a preelection cover story as the great hope of the national Republican Party.

Kerner never received laudatory press treatment. But voters, including many who called themselves "Kerner Republicans," saw in him a man who looked and acted as they thought a governor should. He was the first governor ever chosen "First Citizen" by a newspaper in Springfield, the small midstate capital city where Abraham Lincoln honed his political craft. He was an elder in the Presbyterian church where Lincoln's pew is marked. He actively promoted the city's major undertaking, the restoration of the old state capitol where Lincoln served. He helped to raise funds for the local YMCA. After golf on Saturdays with Springfield businessmen, mostly Republicans, the governor bought drinks for the crowd in a workingman's corner tavern far from Springfield's capitol complex. During the week he did the family grocery shopping and often feigned surprise when fellow shoppers asked if he was the governor.

Kerner's public persona not only spanned the diverse geography and demographics of Illinois; it also reached across time. He was a time traveler in Illinois history, which was a blessing and a curse. The antecedents of Kerner's political acclaim and the source of his eventual vilification stretched back several decades to a time when no one knew the name Richard Daley. The names in the headlines were Democrat Tony Cermak, Republican Big Bill Thompson, and gangster Al Capone—men who wielded power for good and ill. Reformers condemning the synergy between Prohibition-era crime and politics drew few distinctions among these men. Kerner Sr., who never particularly liked politics, found himself in the thick of this roaring era. In a headline-grabbing charge, the Chicago Crime Commission accused him of "paltering with criminals" as a Cook County judge. He faced his accusers in a public hearing and prevailed resoundingly. People who knew father and son recognized in the younger man the same austere but gracious old-world manner his father had used to rise above the meanness of his time.

Four decades later old-world grace was out of style and a new meanness was abroad. Federal investigators bent on exposing corruption in the Cook County Democratic organization never believed the image anyway. They remembered the Kerner name for its place on the roster of Boss Cermak cronies. Investigators for the Internal Revenue Service, descendants within the federal bureaucracy of the men who jailed Capone, saw the younger Kerner as a legacy member of a corrupt fraternity of politicians, businesspeople, and syndicate criminals who operated brazenly in the Capone era and later burrowed deeply into Chicago's social and economic fabric. Investigators sprang into action when racetrack entrepreneur Marjorie Everett, seeking to ingratiate herself with the federal government, told them Kerner had obtained shares in her state-regulated enterprises. The IRS and Justice Department, laboring for more than two years with ambiguous laws and contradictory witnesses, engineered a criminal indictment of Kerner under the federal mail fraud statute. Amid widespread public cynicism in the wake of the Watergate scandal, a jury convicted Kerner in 1973, leaving many Illinois residents ashamed and angry. To the extent that they invested faith in any politician, many had invested in Kerner. Afterward they forgot his accomplishments and marked the Kerner name with the brand "corrupt."

Presenting Kerner as a public enemy made his prosecutor, U.S. Attorney James R. Thompson, into a public hero. Thompson's achievements as a prosecutor, which propelled him into the governor's office, depended on cleverly executing complex legal strategies dressed for public viewing in the simplicity of civic righteousness. Gentlemanly Otto Kerner seemed an unlikely target of this crusade. By August of 1974, when his appeals lapsed and he entered a federal prison, his immigrant mother, Rose, who outlived him by three years, finally spoke out: "I would like to know from you," she wrote to *Chicago Tribune* columnist Bob Wiedrich, "what my son has really done that is so wicked that it makes him, according to your article . . . , a worse criminal than stickup men, worse than Bonnie and Clyde, worse than Dillinger."[16]

What, indeed, was Kerner's crime? The government alleged—and the jury found—that in the racetrack stock transaction Kerner had defrauded the people of Illinois of an "intangible right" to honest government and faithful service by a public official. It was a novel idea, used by federal prosecutors until it was declared unconstitutional by the Supreme Court (but later codified by Congress) to justify their intrusions into Chicago's local affairs in the 1970s, much as they had used the federal income tax law in Chicago four decades earlier to jail Capone. Years later Samuel K. Skinner, a member of the government's prosecution team, called the Kerner case the most important federal prosecution in Chicago since Capone.[17] Many members of Daley's organization would follow Kerner into the government's artfully crafted net. Federal probes uncovered and punished pernicious corruption, to be sure, but in the process public affairs in Illinois suffered a coarsening and a dispiriting that persists to this day. Voters grew to expect the next scandal investigation rather than the next solution to public problems.

No one had ever asserted a right to Kerner's honesty and faithful service. As he journeyed through a public career, first in the military and then in government, there was no need. This "do-it-yourself" politician did much to achieve public esteem. In his conceit he believed he deserved the esteem, but he did not exploit it selfishly. He used his prominence to attract people to his message. He proved that a product of Chicago's midcentury Democratic organization, hardly a bastion of political progressives, could advance unpopular causes, such as civil rights and civil liberties for minorities and the poor.

In the end, whether through arrogance or naïveté, or both, he let down his guard; the ancient Bohemian wariness left him. Power brokers in the Democratic Party, which he had helped to rescue from widespread scorn, abandoned him. His clean image magnified his prosecutors' victory, and he was left alone to ponder how a life of public goodwill could end in public shame.

1

Schweiks No More

The most endearing character in Czech literature is the hero of the book *The Good Soldier Schweik*. Writer Jaroslav Hasek, a sometime anarchist, prankster, and Bolshevik, created Schweik more or less in his own image, an affable conscript in the Austro-Hungarian army who liked his beer and performed his duties with a supposed willingness yet determined incompetence that continually frustrated his superiors. Readers of the Schweik stories quickly grasped the subversive message in his feigned gullibility and witless dealings with officers and bureaucrats, not to mention the thinly disguised and often ribald satire that enlivened Schweik's rambling tales.[1]

Schweik was a national symbol for the passive resistance many late nineteenth-century Bohemians adopted toward their overlords, the decaying Hapsburg dynasty of Austria-Hungary. Hasek died in 1923, but Schweik endured. Later he became an icon of Czech resistance to Nazi and Soviet domination. "I am Schweik" was as much a battle cry as an oath of resignation for ordinary Czechs and other Central Europeans in the Soviet sphere. Today Schweik dolls are a popular souvenir for tourists in the Czech Republic and its magnificent central city, Prague.

✦ ✦ ✦

Rather than submit to the Hapsburg military draft, nineteen-year-old Karel Kerner, the eldest of Albert and Veronica Kerner's eight children, left his home in Bracic, a rural village about sixty miles east of Prague, and headed for Chicago. An unpublished family history recorded that his parents supported Karel's decision to avoid "service in the Austro-Hungarian Army, a nation and a service which was very distasteful to the Kerner family." They planned to follow him to his new home.[2] Karel set out in August 1871, the year in which Germany's Chancellor Bismarck handily defeated Napoleon in the Franco-Prussian War and the Hapsburg dynasty grew anxious about the reignited German Reich.

When young Kerner arrived in Chicago in October, much of the city smoldered in the ruin of the Great Chicago Fire that had swept a hellish flame-wind from the southwest to the northeast of the city just days earlier. The tragedy presented an opportunity for Kerner, who had no trouble finding work as a stevedore, unloading lumber for seventy-five cents a day on docks along the Chicago River. Karel alerted his family in Bohemia, who joined him in the summer of 1872. Albert also secured employment on the docks. The family history adds, "Joseph and Albert Jr., still being of school age, spent their playtime in searching through the ruins of the fire for salvage which they then sold, adding $3.00 to $4.00 per week to the family income for about one year."[3]

Two years later Karel married Josefa Schejba, a nineteen-year-old woman born in Milevsko, a Bohemian village south of Prague. She had journeyed on her own to Chicago in 1873 and was working as a housemaid. The couple set up housekeeping on DeKoven Street, in the heart of an early Bohemian enclave of poor frame houses and tenements just southwest of the central city. They called the ramshackle area Praha, or Prague, after Bohemia's beloved central city, which it resembled only in their imaginations. The nucleus of Chicago's Praha was St. Wenceslaus Church on DeKoven Street, the first Czech Catholic church in the city and a community edifice standing one block from the O'Leary barn, where the fire that engulfed Chicago began.

Soon after the fire the close-knit Czech community relocated further southwest, along Eighteenth Street, to a neighborhood that came to be known as Pilsen, after Bohemia's second-largest city. Karel and Josefa moved to a Pilsen apartment near Nineteenth and Fisk Streets in 1882. Karel became a knife-maker in a cutlery shop and a cabinetmaker. The couple had twelve children, four of whom died in infancy. Otto, the fourth child, was born February 22, 1884.

Not all young Bohemians migrated to America to escape conscription into the army of the failing Hapsburg empire. In 1888 a n'er-do-well named Frank Chmelik left the village of Lisov in southern Bohemia, bound for America at the insistence of his proud and locally prominent mother, who was annoyed and embarrassed by Frank's failure as a butcher. A year later Frank's wife, twenty-eight-year-old Anastasia, and their three daughters, Rose, Laura, and Mary, followed Frank to Chicago, where he had neglected to establish a home and was living as a bachelor with another family.[4] It was the year Archduke

Rudolf, the young heir to the Hapsburg throne, and his lover killed themselves in a tawdry affair that further tarnished the throne of Europe's most expansive dynasty. And it was the year of the birth of another Austrian, Adolf Hitler.

✦ ✦ ✦

Czech immigrants coming to America left behind an ancient and rich culture steeped in liberal traditions and a love of learning and music. Those traditions included the Czech language itself, which had survived religious and political repressions throughout history. Bohemia, a one-time kingdom bearing a Roman name but established by a Slavic tribe called Czechs, was the richest and most industrialized region of the multiethnic Hapsburg dynasty, which comprised elements of no fewer than eleven national groups, including Germans and Italians to the west, Poles to the north, Bosnians and Serbs to the south, and Romanians to the east. Bohemia had served as a punching bag for conquerors in Eastern Europe throughout many centuries. Czechs were forced into the Holy Roman Empire in the eleventh century. Germans from the west and Magyars, Huns, and Avars from the east overtook the land at various moments in history. Otto von Bismarck, the "Iron Chancellor" who joined German principalities and Prussia into an empire in the mid-1800s, once observed, "Whoever is master of Bohemia is master of Europe."[5] The Bohemian region of Austria-Hungary was smaller than South Carolina and heavily bordered by forests and mountains. It lay like a ball thrust into a socket at the southeast corner of Germany's body politic. Bismarck might as well have been speaking of the persistently independent Bohemian Czechs themselves.

Arriving in Chicago and other major American cities, Czechs enjoyed political and religious freedom and economic opportunity. But they found little awareness and less appreciation of their heritage, and America offered nothing like the splendor of Prague. Circumstances of geography and events of history brought to Prague and the rest of Bohemia lasting influences from France and Britain, to the west, and Hungary and Russia, to the east—influences that made Czechs the most cosmopolitan of Central Europeans. But their quiet preference for family, neighborhood, and homeland worked against Bohemians in America's cities. In the prejudiced popular parlance they were called "bohunks." Their inwardness, freethinker religion, and maintenance of Czech customs and language were derided as ineptitude and inability to assimilate. Czechs in turn grew even more self-reliant and disengaged. The very word *bohemian* suggested nonconformity.

Czechoslovakia: Twenty Years of Independence, an anthology edited by history professor Robert J. Kerner, a distant relative of the Otto Kerners, offers this insight into the Czech character: "The Czechoslovaks are industrious and thrifty. Their sense of humor and their idealism are above the general average, their criminality is virtually restricted to the mentally abnormal. They are not good money-makers, nor in general good politicians, or large-scale traders, having but infrequent inclination in this direction; but they excel in music, art and literature. They enjoy good living, but not luxury."[6]

The American political and cultural elite, almost exclusively comprising families of former British and Western European Protestants, had no interest in welcoming Czechs. Germans, another powerful immigrant group in American cities, openly disdained as racial inferiors their former neighbors from Slavic cultures, including Czechs. Few American political leaders, then or now, trace their antecedents to the proud, ancient kingdom of Bohemia that lay at the nexus of much of Central Europe's strife. The Czech Bohemian immigrants were few in number compared to the Irish, German, and Poles. In Chicago they established their own financial and community organizations; neighborhood taverns often served as headquarters for both. Czech youth organizations called Sokols provided community recreational and cultural upbringing, similar to the Boy Scouts and Girl Scouts of British origin. The South Lawndale neighborhood on Chicago's West Side became the center of Czech life in America after World War I. The area was isolated from the rest of the city by railroad tracks and factories. Few outside the community bothered to realize that the Czechs' seeming indifference toward American secular and religious conventions reflected a survival instinct deeply implanted over centuries of repression and betrayal by powers holding dominion over their tiny country.

World War I and the rise of Czech nationalism brought Chicago's Czechs out of their self-imposed political isolation. The charismatic leader of the nationalist movement was a handsome university professor in Prague named Tomas Masaryk. The son of servants to Austria-Hungary's Emperor Franz Joseph, Masaryk excelled in scholarship and politics. His first book was a treatise on suicide, which he described as the supreme act of selfishness. He was deeply religious and intellectual yet energetically engaged in politics. He married an American from New York, Charlotte "Charlie" Gerrague, whose father was an insurance executive of Danish birth and whose mother was a Chicagoan. As a young legislator in the Austro-Hungarian government, the commoner Masaryk was labeled by an Austrian nobleman as the best-dressed man in Parliament. Masaryk made a name for himself in Austrian and German academic circles by challenging conventional wisdom and the status quo. His notoriety grew when he wrote in defense of a Jew accused of murder. "Whosoever looks up to Jesus as a leader cannot be an anti-Semite," he declared.[7]

Masaryk studied the ways of the world and gained friendships and insights that served him well when the chance came to win independence for Bohemia as a new nation formed with its neighboring states, Slovakia and Moravia. Masaryk was in his midsixties when he and a small band of followers executed one of the most remarkable political maneuvers associated with World War I. They methodically guided the leaders of Western Europe and America to create Czechoslovakia from the wreckage of war. Although he recruited 180,000 loyal Czech soldiers from troops sent to Russia by the Austro-Hungarian army, Masaryk's nation building never required a shot to be fired. Instead he used the power of his popularity with Czech immigrants in cities such as London and Chicago to convince President Woodrow Wilson and other Allied leaders to grant nationhood for Czechoslovakia even before the war ended.

Masaryk employed a strategy of gradualism and indirection, courting journalists, especially the Jewish press, and other opinion makers instead of confronting the Allied leaders directly. Of all the ethnic groups of Central Europe, Czechs had the oldest tradition of desiring a national identity, and they knew how to control and focus their ardor. Nineteenth-century Czech writer Karl Havlicek advised, "A politician should act very much like a businessman."[8] Accordingly, "I did not go directly to the ministers," Masaryk recalled. "I would wait until they had been approached by others whom I had seen. I was in London for a whole year without catching a glimpse of Lloyd George."[9]

In May 1918 Masaryk, who had lectured at the University of Chicago twice since 1900, returned to a triumphant greeting from 100,000 supporters at the city's North Western train station and Blackstone Hotel. Although Chicago was the financial center of his campaign, Masaryk had his doubts about American Czechs, whom he described as "coarse" and "materialistic."[10] From Chicago Masaryk traveled to Pittsburgh, where representatives of Czechs and Slovaks agreed, despite their separate cultural and economic interests, to unite in a nation to be called Czechoslovakia.

The drive for Czech independence thousands of miles away helped to build Bohemians into a more confident and vocal political force in Chicago, home to the largest Czech urban population outside Prague. Czech newspapers in Chicago fanned the fires of nationhood and promoted the causes of various Czech politicians competing with larger ethnic groups for the services and spoils of city and state government. The other force in the political empowerment of Chicago's Bohemians was the war itself. When hostilities broke out in Europe in 1914, Germans constituted the largest group of first- and second-generation immigrants in Chicago. Out of a population of 2.44 million, nearly 400,000 were first- or second-generation Germans. Austrians were aligned with Germany in Europe's so-called Central Powers, and so were the 59,000 Austrians living in Chicago. Anti-British Irish, numbering about 147,000 in Chicago, counted themselves as Central Powers sympathizers.

Chicago's 102,000 Czechs were its largest ethnic bloc openly opposed to the German juggernaut, but most of the city and the Midwest was staunchly neutral, if not solidly in the German camp. Chicago buzzed with Teutonic patriotism. Huge gatherings, parades, and nighttime rallies created a frenzy of support for the German fatherland against the Slavic people of Poland, Russia, Croatia, Serbia, Slovakia, and Bohemia. Many Bohemians did not consider theirs a Slavic culture and identified more closely with Germans from the standpoint of culture and language. Nevertheless, the Bohemian press in Chicago denounced the German American attacks on Slavs and supported U.S. efforts to aid the Allied forces.

When the United States entered the war in 1917 on the side of Britain and France, the propaganda tide shifted quickly and dramatically against Germans in Chicago and elsewhere. Ironically, Bohemians and other Central Europeans long opposed to German expansion had to get out of the way. Suddenly they were lumped with the Germans as "hyphenated Americans," whose loyalty to Uncle Sam came under suspicion. Chicago's active Bohemian press and Bohemians themselves eagerly declared their allegiance to the United States and asserted the hope that an Allied victory would mean victory for Czech independence.

Before the United States declared war, Bohemians had enlisted in the Canadian and British armies, and others now rushed to enlist with the U.S. military. In cities such as Chicago, Americanization campaigns broke out to extinguish the powerful German influence in public education and culture. Chicago's Czechs, with their persistent and effective Czech- and English-language newspapers, excelled in the campaign, enthusiastically paying back Germans for their anti-Slav diatribes of a few years earlier. German-speaking Czechs infiltrated and undermined German organizations, not by the subtle foils of Good Soldier Schweik, but by direct counterintelligence. German culture in Chicago and other American cities never recovered from the Americanization campaigns that sprang up in 1918.

Chicago's Bohemians were Schweiks no more. They insisted on taking their place at the table when political favors were distributed among ethnic voting blocs. The anti-German campaign and the drive for an independent Czech nation awakened them to the rewards of political involvement in America that other ethnic groups—notably the Germans and Irish—had already reaped.

Not everyone in Chicago's Czech community viewed this development favorably. One critic, reflecting deeply felt Czech tradition, wrote: "Politics and politicians have their place and importance. . . . However, to every clear thinking individual it must be apparent that even importance may be carried to over-exaggeration and that the glamour of politics has been somewhat too strong in the community of Chicago Czechs. It has dimmed other accomplishments—science, religion, history, literature—all cultural considerations have taken a secondary position, while political prominence still holds the sway."[11]

Nevertheless, nationalism and anti-German fervor empowered Chicago's Czechs and provided a springboard for one of the most successful urban politicians America ever produced. Immigrant coal miner Anton J. Cermak was a Czech-American as coarse as any Masaryk ever encountered. They had little in common—one an intellectual, the other a political ruffian; one a smooth diplomat, the other a blunt administrator. But both men symbolized and nurtured Czech pride. In his 1918 race for Cook County sheriff on the Democratic ticket, Cermak opposed a Republican who claimed German ancestry. Cermak's vitriolic attacks against "the Hun"—campaign rhetoric many supporters warned him against—backfired, and he lost the election. His career as a Chicago politician prospered, however, bringing many fellow Bohemians out of their shells.

✦ ✦ ✦

A. J. Cermak's mother and father came to America a year after his birth in 1873. They settled in Pilsen, but Cermak's father soon sought work in the coal mines of Braidwood, a village sixty-five miles southwest of the city. Teenager A.J., with only about three years of formal education, became a muleskinner in the Braidwood mines, and after work he drank heartily with his colleagues in the taverns on Braidwood's Whiskey Row. At age sixteen he returned to Pilsen after he was fired by a mine operator on suspicion of being a labor agitator.

Alex Gottfried, in his biography of Cermak, described the young man who would construct the Democratic machine in Chicago: "Early in his stay in Pilsen, Cermak became a leader of his saloon gang, for reasons which are at least partially apparent. He excelled in the gang's two chief interests, fighting and drinking. Physically, he was extremely well adapted for gang brawls, being thick-bodied, broad-shouldered and heavily muscled. He delighted in combat. He had a great capacity for alcohol and could hold his liquor."[12]

In Braidwood, unlike Chicago and other big cities, Czechs were the dominant ethnic group. "This situation was of considerable importance in Cermak's orientation," Gottfried wrote.

> Instead of growing up as a member of one of many foreign groups living in a culture dominated by assimilated groups, as he would have in the city, Cermak grew up in an environment where his own culture was the dominant one. It was not merely in his home, his neighborhood, or a number of scattered neighborhoods that the acceptable mores and customs were Bohemian, but in virtually an entire town. It may therefore be conjectured that he was to an important degree left free of that sense of cultural inferiority which so often affects the less assimilated groups of a large city.[13]

Cermak later displayed remarkable skills in the complex administration of government, but he built his political career on a basic simplicity of urban life: the workingman's desire for drink. Well before 1919, when Prohibition made the "wet" movement into a national campaign, Cermak stridently promoted the unfettered sale of beer and liquor. To him and other wets, the open tavern represented an essential American freedom that immigrants had every right to expect as a salve for the harshness of their new surroundings. In an era before women could vote, drinking was an issue of "personal liberty," a civil right for the workingman. It was liberalism at street level and a surefire plank in the platform of an ethnic politician.

Chicago newspaper writer H. K. Barnard, in a biographical tribute to Cermak after his death, offered this rationale: "Cermak was as well aware of the evils in the abuses in liquor as any man. But he knew the pleasure that the working man, the foreign-born American particularly, derived from a stein of beer. He knew what it meant to a man to be able to go into a corner saloon and spend an enjoyable evening over beer mugs with his fellows. So, from the beginning he fought the prohibition forces in the Legislature, raising the banner of personal liberty years before other politicians had the courage to withstand the pressure of the dry and so-called reform elements."[14]

Cermak's youngest daughter, Helena, who inherited her father's aggressive disposition, held vivid memories of the antiprohibition campaigns her father led. As a pupil at Lawndale's Robert Burns Elementary School, Helena on one occasion wore a sweater festooned with antiprohibition patches reading, "Vote No." "The teacher told me to take them off," she recalled many years later. "I said, I will not. I said, it is a free country and I'll wear what I want to wear. My father is against Prohibition because it's depriving the working man and making millionaires out of other people. . . . It's the wealthy, the rich. They can buy it. Who are you helping? You're helping the bootleggers."[15]

Powerful commercial interests supported the wets. In 1907 Cermak got himself elected as the top official of the United Societies for Local Self-Government, a new coalition of Chicago ethnic groups formed primarily by Germans and dedicated to fighting restrictions on the operation of taverns. Brewers and distillers bankrolled the organization and the wet movement generally, a fact that did not escape the attention of the ambitious young A. J. Cermak, who was sitting as a representative in the Illinois General Assembly in Springfield. "When the Societies spoke, politicians and public officials listened," Gottfried wrote. "Not only did it claim votes, but it had money. The largest sums were supplied by brewers, some by distillers. The money was to be used to influence legislation and to elect favorable legislators, judges and other officials. It was collected by Cermak, and presumably he distributed it to candidates who were acceptable. Few of the members of the Societies were aware of this arrangement; no one questioned Cermak about the distribution of the money, not even the brewers who were footing the bill."[16]

Graft involving the promoters of drinking, gambling, and prostitution and the government officials supposedly keeping them in check was nothing new to Chicago. "Boodle," as it was called, was integral to the city's history and lore. But reform movements that had come and gone in previous decades gained new momentum in the early 1900s, after the 1893 Columbian Exposition on the city's South Side. The gaudy yet magnificent event was supposed to show the world how Chicago was bettering itself in architecture and sophistication since the fire. But the city failed utterly to restrain open gambling, drinking, and prostitution, which presented visitors a rough contrast to the fair's facade.

"You are gigantic in your virtues and gigantic in your vices. I don't know in which you glory the most," British editor William T. Stead remarked after his visit to the fair.[17] In his stinging book *If Christ Came to Chicago!*, which became a rallying cry of Chicago reformers for years after its publication in 1894, Stead wrote: "Chicago appreciates arguments that can be stated in percentages payable in dollars. Chicago is not yet sufficiently alive to arguments which relate to the administration of justice, to the prevention of crime and the repression of vice. These things are important, no doubt, but negligence in their enforcement does not entail an immediate money fine upon the respectable citizens. Were it so, they would make their police as non-political as their firemen."[18]

A new generation of business leaders, including the founders of the Civic Federation and Better Government Association watchdog groups, denounced the vice and corruption that profited many of their peers among Chicago's entrepreneurs and politicians. With appeals to civic pride and moralistic virtues, reformers refused to rationalize vice as part of Chicago's lusty appeal. They condemned the destructive consequences of drink and promoted liquor control as a means of curbing what they viewed broadly as socially repugnant and illicit behavior—behavior they closely associated with immigrant ethnic groups. Many of the respectables, as they were termed in the newspapers, drank no less than the average immigrant workingman, but they maintained that the immigrants' drinking habits displayed wantonness that went well beyond decent pleasure seeking. The massive figure of Anton Cermak embodied their prejudice.

"The liquor business not infrequently is insolent of speech, impertinent in demand, and dangerous in threat. Mr. Cermak is likewise," the *Chicago Tribune* declared in 1912, as Cermak's political ambitions emerged. "Let the dance hall wreck as many lives as it will; let the miserable drunkard go headlong into the deepest gulf of misery; let him drag his wife and children after him; let every atrocity which can flow in the wake of drink go undisturbed; but don't dare touch a single privilege of the business which sells liquor."[19]

Two decades later, on the eve of Cermak's election as Chicago's mayor, the Better Government Association issued a statement to Chicago voters recalling Cermak's stridency against liquor control in the years before Prohibition:

> The orderly use of liquor may be one question, but the debauching of boys and girls is quite another, and yet Cermak was the chief sponsor and defender for years of the special bar permit ordinance under which liquor was sold in several hundred public dance halls to young boys and girls until three o'clock in the morning in deliberate defiance of state law closing liquor resorts at 1 A.M. and forbidding liquor sales to minors. Cermak resisted every attempt of the Juvenile Protective Association and others to repeal this ordinance. Committees of leading citizens reported to the City Council that they had seen liquor freely dispensed by minors to minors in these places; girls laying drunk on the floors of main ballrooms, and they charged that the ordinance was responsible for the debauching of thousands of boys and girls. This made no difference to Cermak, and he determinedly fought on every occasion the repeal of this infamous ordinance.[20]

An effigy of the vice-addled immigrant underscored Chicago's reform movement. It suggested an alien force operating below the ostensibly respectable establishment, an underworld reaching up to ensnare vulnerable individuals and corrupt the legitimate structures of government and society. "The lords of the Kingdom of Graft do not live apart," wrote Charles Edward Merriam, a professor of political science at the University of Chicago who served in the Chicago City Council with Cermak. "They move among men, men of substance and affairs. They know magnates and powers in the world of efficiency and organization, and they do business with them from time to time, with some of them."[21] In his 1929 book *Chicago: A More Intimate View of Urban Politics,* Merriam described an unholy alliance between the "Underworld" and the "Upperworld," potent imagery that would forever define civic reform movements in Chicago. For many, Mayor Cermak symbolized the problem.

"As leader of an organization which assumed the misleading name of the United Societies, Cermak aroused and organized the underworld to enforce its demand for a wide open town," wrote Republican partisan Fletcher Dobyns in a scathing polemic titled *The Underworld of American Politics.* "For a quarter of a century, any politician, whatever his party, who dared to support any measure that would curb the license of those antisocial hordes was immediately confronted by Cermak, snarling and waving the club of the underworld vote."[22]

The Cermak name would forever be tied to public immorality and organized lawlessness, first in the rhetoric used by local reformers and later in the
rationale used by federal law-enforcement officials bent on attacking corruption in Chicago and dismantling the Democratic machine Cermak had built.

✦ ✦ ✦

Rose Chmelik and her friends held a picnic to celebrate their graduation from eighth grade, usually the last step in formal education for immigrant working-class girls, if they made it even that far. It was turn-of-the-
century Chicago, five years after the Columbian Exposition. Rose and her
sisters had toured the lavish fair tied to their mother by a rope so they would
not get lost.[23]

On arriving in Chicago, Rose's mother, Anastasia, had taken charge, rent-
ing an apartment in Pilsen for her husband and family. Like many immigrant
families from Central Europe, the Chmelik household was a matriarchy, paying only ostensible deference to the father. Rose and her sisters rode street-
cars to take Frank hot dinners at midday at his job in a South Side lumber-
yard, and mother and daughters treated him when he developed a serious case
of sunstroke. But Frank never amounted to much, and no one in the family
expected much of him. He was quiet around the home, except when he drank,
and he paid little attention to the children. Anastasia was in charge.

To supplement Frank's income, some of which was lost to gambling, Rose's
mother worked as a housemaid. She considered the duties below her station
in life and often became irritable at home when the girls were growing up. In
the sixth grade Rose decided she should contribute to the family income. She
skipped school for several days to hunt for a seamstress job in one of Pilsen's
many tailor shops. No one would hire such a young girl; she returned to the
Throop School and finished her grammar-school education.

At the graduation picnic Rose's circle of friends expanded when she met a
boy named Otto Kerner. For some time her girlfriends had talked about the
good-looking teenager, but what Rose saw was a small boy somewhat pale
and withered by a severe case of pneumonia. Otto had caught pneumonia
while working as a laborer in a picture frame factory by day and going to
school at night. After treating him, Dr. Frank J. Novak, the Kerner family
physician, arranged a job for young Kerner in the law office of his brother,
Alderman Joseph E. Novak. Otto took to the work and began studying law
at night. For the next several years, his social life would center on Rose's group
of friends, who met often at Bethlehem Church, a Protestant church in the
neighborhood. Otto played Rose's boyfriend in a skit the group enacted. Rose
wrote a poem about her teenage friends, giving each a nickname. Serious,

intense Otto was "the judge." In 1907 Otto, already two years into his legal practice, asked Rose's mother for permission to marry her. The service was performed in Bethlehem Church.

Through Alderman Novak young Otto Kerner entered the political constellation of fellow Bohemian A. J. Cermak. In 1902 Kerner helped Cermak defeat a challenge to nominating petitions he had filed to run for the state legislature. Four years later he moved into Cermak's South Lawndale ward. From then on Kerner's public image would be drawn in terms of Cermak, eleven years his senior. Cermak was Kerner's law client and political sponsor, but the contrasts between the two were more significant than the similarities.

In an unpublished autobiographic sketch written years later, Kerner praised Cermak:

> I confess that in my political background the power wielded by Cermak looms large. I owe much to him, perhaps I owe everything to him. His friendship, assistance and encouragement dates back to that fortuitous circumstance in 1902. . . . Cermak was strong, capable and powerful. Those who knew him as I know what I mean when I say he was powerful. He was not educated, but he had intelligence and common sense. He was not polished, but he had a determination which carried everything and everybody along. He was hard as a rock, but he could be and was often very kind. . . . The City called for a strong man, and he answered the call. Those close to him loved him for what he was. To him must go one credit. He consolidated the various national groups into a united cosmopolitan front and gave them their first taste of political strength. Under him these people participated in government. Before, these people had been willing to take a passive part in government. Under him they came to realize their strength, came to feel that after all they had something to contribute, came to know that they could belong to America.[24]

Kerner, who lacked Cermak's drive and physical prowess, was intent on bettering himself through education and a professional career. At this point, however, Otto and Rose had little material wealth and were forced to content themselves with simple activities. "We were both very poor, and our courtship was carried on in our daily morning walks downtown from the district of Eighteenth Street and Blue Island Avenue," Rose told an interviewer in 1932. "In those days, our existence was devoid of any good time that young people have nowadays. We never knew what it was to go to the theater or dance, and our amusements used to be taken once a week on Sundays when we gathered at the homes of our friends to sing and play pedro [a simple card game]. Mr. Kerner had no money to squander on pleasures."[25]

"I always have been proud and sensitive about my work," Kerner wrote in his personal sketch. "It means everything to me that I do my job well. I worry for fear that in my work I shall disappoint those who helped me and confided in me."[26] Cermak had few such sensitivities. He disdained the notion of "bettering" himself. He already had what he needed—raw determination, guile, and muscle—to prevail in the game of politics. Indeed, his appeal to the immigrant workingmen who supported him required that he remain at their level. Kerner, soft-spoken and austere, never participated actively in the United Societies or the wet campaign, although he attended Cermak rallies that nearly always included fiery rebukes of "dry" sympathizers. The dries were led by the wealthier, better-educated element of Chicago society—the Upperworld, in Merriam's term—into which Kerner aspired to bring himself and his family, distinct from the popular American image of low-class, beer-swilling Bohemian immigrants so repugnant to Chicago's elites and so delightful to pugnacious A. J. Cermak.

Kerner and Cermak were never close friends or confidants. Cermak's principal legal counselor and confidant was a Jewish Czech named Henry Sonnenschein. But the young Kerner became known as one of Cermak's "respectables," an essential supporting role in the entourage of many Chicago political leaders over the years. Meanwhile Kerner pursued his own legal career. Before finishing his law studies at Lake Forest College, he had driven to Springfield on his twenty-first birthday to take the state bar examination. He was admitted to the Illinois bar a few weeks later. Joseph Novak's promise of a partnership never materialized, so Kerner set up his own practice, working from a downtown office during the day and seeing clients in the neighborhood at night. He viewed his association with the Cermak political crowd primarily as a means of attracting clients.

The Kerners took their first step toward gentility shortly after their marriage. Following the Bohemian trail westward in the city, the Kerner and the Chmelik families moved out of Pilsen to the more agreeable neighborhood called South Lawndale. Their new neighborhood was known as "Czech California," a reference to its westerly location in the city and to California Avenue, which ran along its eastern edge. Rose Kerner had attended business college to study stenography. She held several jobs before the arrival of the couple's first child, Otto Kerner Jr., who was delivered by Dr. Frank Novak on August 15, 1908.

South Lawndale was a perfect venue for a close-knit ethnic group. To the west was the town of Cicero and the giant Hawthorne Works of the Western Electric Company; to the east stood the International Harvester Company factory. Once Czechs became dominant, South Lawndale took on the look of old Prague. Czech was taught in the high schools. Along Twenty-sixth Street, the principal artery, Czech shops carefully mimicked the Old World, and most shops employed at least one clerk who spoke Czech. One movie theater showed Czech films exclusively. Czech freethinkers built the John Hus Memorial Hall on Twenty-second Street, in honor of a Czech martyr to religious independence. Czech Catholics built St. Ludmila Church on Twenty-fourth Street and Blessed Agnes Church on Twenty-sixth Street.

Cermak had settled in South Lawndale in 1892, and by the time the Kerners arrived, he was a local political power broker in the Twelfth Ward. When Otto Jr. was born, Cermak represented the ward in the Illinois General Assembly and was a partner in the prosperous real estate firm of Cermak and Serhant on Twenty-sixth Street. He had long since given up his successful wood-hauling business that had made him a well-known figure in the neighborhood and had given rise to the future political epithet "Pushcart Tony."

By 1911 Cermak was an alderman and the Democratic ward committee-man from the Twelfth Ward. When Otto Jr. was three, his father's political activities in the Cermak organization drew the attention of newly elected Democratic mayor Carter Harrison II, who named Otto Sr. a city prosecutor. At this time in the history of Chicago and Cook County, politics was raucously bipartisan. Republicans tended to carry the county in national elections but jousted fiercely with Democrats in state and local contests. Harrison, the namesake of a popular Chicago mayor of an earlier era, narrowly defeated Republican council member Charles Merriam, the closest Chicago ever got to electing an intellectual reformer as mayor.

Bohemians, like Irish, Italians, and Poles, tended to vote Democratic, while Germans, Swedes, and blacks favored Republicans. The Jewish vote vacillated between the two major parties. Local party organizations were splintered internally by strident factions, creating opportunities for much cross-party wheeling and dealing, at which Cermak excelled. "Originally Republican, [Chicago's Czechs] were diverted to Democracy by the liquor issue and have remained in the fold since then," wrote Merriam. "When politically awakened they display political interest and capacity of a high order, with a talent for organization and administration, recalling the high level reached by Czechoslovakia in recent times under President [Tomas] Masaryk."[27]

Kerner Sr., one of Chicago's leading supporters of Masaryk and the creation of an independent Czechoslovakia, developed no reputation for agility in politics, nor did he appear to find any great joy playing in Cermak's game. But he was a loyal Democratic party worker, which kept him away from home a great deal. The family occupied the third floor of a three-flat building on Clifton Park Avenue (now called Drake Avenue) in South Lawndale. Rose's parents lived in the building's garden apartment a few steps below street level. Six months after Otto Jr. was born, Rose's father, Frank Chmelik, committed suicide by poisoning himself at age forty-nine. Rose's mother then joined the Kerner household, an arrangement that was supposed to be temporary but became permanent. In 1912 a second son, Robert, was born. That winter Kerner's father, who lived nearby on Clifton Park Avenue, was killed by a truck on a city street.

Cermak won his first citywide office—bailiff of the municipal court—and quit the city council in 1912. Kerner ran for alderman with Cermak's backing and won. The story told by some political analysts that he moved his family to South Lawndale just to run for alderman at Cermak's insistence was not true. But it is true that Cermak put up Kerner against an incumbent alderman of German heritage after a redistricting of the Twelfth Ward reduced its German voting strength. At that time each ward elected two aldermen every two years. Kerner's aldermanic colleague from the Twelfth Ward was fellow Czech and former law associate Joseph Novak, a well-worn cog in the Cermak wheel. Cermak also got a Czech of his liking, John Toman, elected alderman in the neighboring Tenth Ward, increasing his cadre of Czech public officials.

Kerner was regarded favorably by civic watchdogs during his tenure as alderman. When he ran for reelection in 1919, the Municipal Voters League, a reform group established after the vice wave that tarnished the 1893 World's Fair, declared of Kerner: "By reason of his high character, courage and experience, he is one of the most valuable aldermen."[28] Merriam counted Kerner among the "fine representatives" of Chicago's ethnic blocs.[29] One of Kerner's signature pieces of legislation was an ordinance requiring fenders on trucks like the one that killed his father.

Kerner held office during the first mayoralty of William Hale Thompson, a wealthy, bombastic politician who was virtually unknown when he first became mayor in 1915 but who soon came to embody the most ludicrous and corrupt behavior that Chicago politics had to offer. It was believed widely that Democrat Cermak helped to elect Republican Thompson as part of a scheme to subvert opponents within his own party, but Alderman Kerner often found himself aligned with progressive Republicans against "Big Bill." One incident remembered to this day occurred in 1917 when Thompson abruptly adjourned a city council meeting after shouting erupted from reformers, including Kerner, who demanded a role-call vote on his appointments to the school board.

"There was fierce mouth-to-mouth fighting, at the end of which No-Man's Land was covered with dead and wounded enemy cigars and tobacco juice," wrote Chicago journalist Ring Lardner.[30] As Thompson left the council chamber, Kerner, chairman of the council's judiciary committee, abandoned his well-cultivated reserve and joined others in pelting the towering, heavyset mayor with books. The council proceeded to conduct business without its presiding officer.

Such parliamentary revelry fit the personalities of Big Bill Thompson and

A. J. Cermak, but Kerner saw little point in it. He was not disappointed when Cermak, having lost the race for county sheriff, asked him to retire from the city council so that Cermak could resume his post as alderman from South Lawndale. As alderman Kerner not only was subject to the stress of the council itself but also faced constant demands from ward residents, who flooded his makeshift waiting room in the family dining room and bedroom aldermanic office. Unlike law clients, none of these constituents expected to pay a fee. When Cermak offered Kerner a slot on the Cook County circuit court, Kerner declined.

In 1916 he was appointed a master-in-chancery, a quasi-judicial role in which lawyers in effect worked as arbiters and consultants on behalf of the circuit court. Masters received no salary but collected fees from parties in disputes. The fees on average were four times the $15,000 annual salary of a circuit court judge. A Chicago Bar Association analysis found that in one case during this period, a master-in-chancery collected $159,000 in fees over eighteen months, a huge sum at that time. A study of the judicial system of metropolitan Chicago by University of Chicago researchers in 1932 concluded: "The fee system of compensation . . . reflects the commercial and financial aspect of metropolitan judicial work. Attorneys and authorities on judicial questions point out that the enormous fees received by masters-in-chancery in Chicago encourage bargaining with judges for appointments to these lucrative positions, lead to solicitation of business, and invite the use of the master's discretion in favor of those who have their proceedings assigned to him."[31]

The New York Times, surveying the situation in Chicago, commented, "Persons are asking why any man would want to be a judge if he has the pull to get an appointment as a master."[32] The private practice of law and the post as master-in-chancery were far more profitable pursuits than the job of alderman. Besides, Kerner suffered from severe headaches, a condition no doubt worsened by the obligations of an alderman in a burgeoning, low-income ward. Men like Cermak amassed wealth by staying in elective politics. Kerner became wealthy by getting out.

There was another reason Kerner did not hesitate to end his career as an alderman. By 1918 the Kerner family had four children: Rose was born in August 1916, and May, in May 1918. Otto Jr. was attending the Robert Burns Elementary School, two years behind Helena Cermak. A month after May was born, tragedy struck that changed the Kerner household forever. Robert Kerner, a beautiful child nearly six years old with glorious blond hair, was crossing Twenty-second Street with a friend when he was hit by a streetcar. The other boy ran away, leaving Robert lying at the curb alone. Passersby carried Robert into a drug store, but no one knew who he was. Within minutes, by coincidence, Robert's aunt Mary walked by the store and saw the unmistakable golden hair. Robert survived only until the next day.

More than sixty years later, Rose Kerner remembered vividly the accident and the effect it had on her. "For almost a year, I was mental," she told her great-grandson Anton C. Kerner in a tape-recorded interview. She recalled lapsing into a depression that virtually immobilized her. Speaking of Otto Jr., she said, "I didn't raise him. I can't take any credit for what he is. I don't know what Otto did, but he went through it. He must have felt out of everything."[33]

Before the accident one of Rose's friends had visited a spirit medium in Joliet who predicted that a little boy she knew would soon be killed in a traffic accident. Afterward Rose, who had studied and rejected Catholicism, became a devoted follower of spiritualism. She told of speaking with Robert and her father during sessions with mediums. Her belief in reincarnation and the ability to communicate with the dead became the essential fact of Rose's life, and she discussed it in a matter-of-fact manner with family members until her death in 1979 at the age of ninety-four.

"I don't know how people take it if they don't believe there is something beyond this life," she told her great-grandson. "Robert told me it was his mission to bring me into this knowledge."[34] Spiritualism was a subject Otto Kerner Sr. and his son never discussed outside the home. Kerner tried to spend more time with his surviving son after the tragedy. He belonged to the Bohemian Club in Lawndale, the neighborhood's most prestigious social club, where they participated in father-and-son bowling tournaments. Young Otto took up swimming at nearby Douglas Park. He also took up fighting, a decision that his younger sister May and a neighborhood friend from Lawndale attributed in part to his relatively small stature. "Kerner strove all of his life to be accepted, to be one of the boys—and never really made it," recalled the boyhood friend.[35]

✦ ✦ ✦

By the time young Otto was preparing to graduate from grammar school, Kerner Sr. was collecting the kind of income that enabled him to upgrade his family's status and at the same time demonstrate independence from his Twelfth Ward political sponsor, Cermak. The typical path for upwardly mobile Bohemians was Pilsen to South Lawndale in Chicago and then to the suburbs of Cicero and Berwyn. But Rose had her eye on the more prestigious, WASPish Oak Park, with its stately homes and superior high school, Oak Park and River Forest High School. Before she was married, Rose had worked in the leafy suburb of Oak Park, where she had been a secretary for a company that made typewriters. Later she worked for an executive of Sears, Roebuck and Company who lived in Oak Park.

Kerner Sr. somehow convinced officials at Oak Park and River Forest High School to enroll his son in 1922, while the family looked for a home in Oak Park but continued residing in South Lawndale. Leaving Chicago and South Lawndale was a significant political break with Cermak, to be sure, but that same year Cermak was elected president of the Cook County Board, bringing the Kerner family's new home in Oak Park once again into Cermak's political domain.

The Kerners' move to Oak Park was soon followed by a move in 1926 to River Forest, a smaller and even more exclusive suburb immediately to the west. At 1031 Ashland Avenue in River Forest, the family employed a housemaid, and Otto was allowed to have a dog, which he named Ado. Kerner Sr. took up golf at the exclusive Butterfield Country Club. The family bought a summer cottage in Pentwater, Michigan, where Otto attended summer camp and continued his swimming. Rose's grief over the loss of Robert subsided, but her devotion to spiritualism deepened. His mother, sisters, and female cousins showered Otto with affection, and he grew into a strikingly handsome, beloved young man.

In Chicago, meanwhile, the Prohibition era was in full swing under reform-minded Mayor William Dever. In his four-year term, beginning in 1923, Dever made things so uncomfortable for the beer-running gang led by Johnny Torrio and Alfonse Capone that they moved westward out of Chicago and set up operations in Cicero, an adjacent suburb whose population was 80 percent Bohemian working-class families. Oak Park and River Forest were only a few blocks from Cicero on the street grid of the Cook County "country towns," as the suburbs were known, but they were worlds apart for a Bohemian family of growing means and sophistication.

2

These Malicious Charges

Having withdrawn from the boisterous Chicago City Council and moved his family out of the city, Otto Kerner Sr. had every reason to feel aloof from the crime, corruption, and blaring newspaper headlines that told of Prohibition's lamentable effect on Chicago. He worked downtown, but at the end of the day he departed the congested, noisy central city for the broad lawns of suburban Oak Park and River Forest. His son became a popular student at stately Oak Park and River Forest High School. Too small for the varsity football team, Otto made his name as a swimmer. His classmates chose him treasurer of the senior class. His summers were spent at the family's retreat in Pentwater, Michigan. Like many of the senior boys, Otto Kerner Jr. was heading for an Ivy League school after graduation. He had left far behind, though just a few city blocks away, the gritty street life on the West Side that nurtured many young politicians and young criminals.

If Chicago needed another reason for graft and crime, which it did not, Prohibition provided it. Lawlessness and corruption found a new and for a while glamorous venue under the Eighteenth Amendment. In turn, crime fighting moved onto a new stage, with new public enemies emerging in the press. Despite its dubious premise, the nation's campaign against alcohol consumption under the Eighteenth Amendment created heroes as well as villains. For the first time a federal law, the Volstead Act, under which national Prohibition was to be enforced, placed the power of the government in Washington directly over the ordinary behavior of millions of American citizens. Previously federal law enforcement was limited largely to misdeeds that few Americans ever contemplated, such as counterfeiting or spying. The government had no national police force to pursue liquor violators, but the "Noble Experiment," as Prohibition was called, added heft to local campaigns for political and social reform and for the first time made the federal government a direct partner in those campaigns.

From the vantage point of the Kerner household, however, none of this appeared relevant. It seemed highly unlikely that father or son would ever stand accused by any of the zealous pursuers of corruption and vice or be portrayed as villains in any Prohibition-related drama. But the Kerners were not immune. Son followed father in many aspects of their lives, but in this unfortunate respect Kerner Jr. led the way.

✦ ✦ ✦

Young Kerner first confronted a professional crime fighter alone in a room in his high school a few weeks before his scheduled graduation. Hinton G. Clabaugh was an original G-man. A native of Alabama, Clabaugh headed the Chicago office of the Justice Department's Bureau of Investigation (later called the Federal Bureau of Investigation) from 1914 until 1918. Clabaugh, using Chicago police officers as spies, investigated tens of thousands of Chicago-area residents for possible seditious behavior or draft evasion during the Great War. "The [Chicago] bureau was credited with performing more war investigation work than any in the country," boasted the *Chicago Tribune*, reflecting no sympathy whatever for individual rights. "More than 250,000 were questioned by operatives under Clabaugh's supervision."[1] In a typical assessment the paper described Clabaugh as "the man who looked after the safety of the millions of Chicago's population, who has bared sedition plots and followed them up until the guilty were punished."[2]

Extending his bravado into purely local matters, Clabaugh confidently declared after the Great War that Chicago had been cleansed of vice and that no boy returning from the war need be tempted by it. When the war emergency ended, Washington's interest in prosecuting local crime on behalf of a tranquil home front waned. In November 1918 Clabaugh announced that his job was accomplished and resigned. He came out of retirement in 1922, however, when the Justice Department under President Warren G. Harding, a Republican, hired him to investigate charges of graft involving Prohibition outlaws, income tax violators, and corrupt agents in the department's own office in Chicago. A disgruntled assistant to the Democratic U.S. attorney in Chicago had brought ominous charges of internal corruption after his boss suspended him. Clabaugh, a Republican who later ran for lieutenant governor, took the headline-grabbing assignment seriously. Press accounts portrayed Clabaugh as digging deeply into corruption conspiracies involving the Chicago police department, the local office of the Bureau of Internal Revenue (later the Internal Revenue Service), and various Chicago politicians. Reports surfaced that he intended to enlarge his probe to encompass the Chicago offices of the Bureau of Customs, the U.S. marshal, and other agencies. At that point the Justice Department, sensing a loose cannon, quickly and quietly shut down the project.

Clabaugh's bombastic investigation of Chicago corruption never accomplished anything except some bureaucratic embarrassment and heightened cynicism within the local press corps. By 1926 he was back in the private sector, working for the legendary Chicago utilities mogul Samuel Insull. He continued sleuthing on the side, however, in the employ of his friend George Harvey Jones, president of the Oak Park and River Forest High School board.

Eleven years earlier the school's principal, M. R. McDaniel, known to students as "the fox," had expelled fourteen boys for organizing fraternities. Subsequently the Illinois legislature outlawed secret societies in public secondary schools. (The text of the law lifted entire phrases from a pamphlet McDaniel sent to his students' parents warning about secret societies.)[3] By the 1920s the law was generally ignored. High school fraternities were chartered by national organizations, just like college fraternities, but local chapters met clandestinely off campus, usually after Sunday school classes in the churches attended by members' families. When the annual fraternity recruitment drive led to a disturbance after the 1926 senior prom at McDaniel's school, he and Jones hired Clabaugh to expose the student violators, who included Otto Kerner Jr. Young Otto had traded the street gangs of the West Side for the snobbish cliques of the suburbs. Kerner was a "Geke"—Gamma Eta Kappa.

The behavior of Clabaugh toward Kerner and the other boys was, of course, far less noteworthy than his inquiries into wartime espionage and Prohibition-era corruption, but it made an indelible impression on the young man. Kerner was one of fifty-three boys—nearly all of them popular athletes in their senior or junior years—caught in Clabaugh's web and summoned one by one before him to confess. Kerner and the others were suspended for one year, which meant no spring graduation. "The general exodus takes away all the monogram men who won their letters last year on the gridiron; it wipes out the entire basketball quintet and it removes five men from the baseball team," reported the *Tribune*. "With them went the school's hopes for this year's baseball championship, next year's football title and a national oratorical championship."[4]

School board president Jones said he and the board showed leniency by imposing a suspension instead of expulsion. He said fraternities promoted cliques and snobbishness and diluted school loyalty. Worse, he said, fraternities encouraged drinking and gambling. "I am glad to say that nothing of that nature has come to my attention in this instance, but there is no knowing what might develop if the situation is not kept well in hand," he explained in an Oak Park newspaper. "On my request, Mr. Clabaugh interviewed the boys as a citizenship matter," McDaniel said. "He pointed out to them the mistake they were making in that they were in reality conspiring to break a state law, pointing out that this was certainly a very bad start for their business careers. I think Clabaugh rendered a distinct service in putting the matter up to them in that way and the boys acknowledged that they had done wrong and expressed regret on account of it."[5]

Faced suddenly with the prospect of being unable to ship their rambunctious offspring away to college in the fall, parents sued the school board, charging that their sons had been entrapped by the former G-man Clabaugh. According to parents and boys, Clabaugh had met with each student privately and assured him that if he confessed his membership in a fraternity and agreed to resign from the organization, the penalty would be a brief suspension of one or two weeks. Lawyers for the parents, in lengthy but strained arguments, also claimed that because the fraternities did not specifically bar membership by nonstudents, they could not be deemed high school fraternities under the law; that many more of the 2,800 students at the high school belonged to secret fraternities and sororities but only student athletes were targeted because McDaniel wanted to erase the image of the school as an athletic powerhouse; and, best of all, that the boys turned loose from school would be a menace to the community.

Superior Court judge William J. Lindsay, who heard the case initially, sympathized with the parents and boys. Agreeing that the school board had the power to suspend the students, he nevertheless took seriously one aspect of the parents' case. "It is charged that what amounted to a confidence game was practiced upon the boys by a paid informer [Clabaugh]," he asserted from the bench. "It is a question with me whether the morale of the school is lowered or raised by wholesale suspensions" he added.[6]

Twenty years later Kerner Jr. recalled the episode in a letter to Lindsay, who was still on the bench, having lost in 1928 as the Democratic candidate for Cook County state's attorney: "I often look back upon one of my transgressions when I was an interested bystander in the matter of the Oak Park High School hearing, when I, among a number of others, was asked to leave the school because of fraternity connections. Ever since that time I have felt I have known you well, and I have always enjoyed renewing your acquaintance." Kerner signed the letter "fraternally yours." Both men were members of the Phi Delta Phi law school fraternity.[7]

The suspensions and dispute between the parents and school board lasted through the summer. Kerner Sr. wanted the controversy ended quickly. Cook County Board president Anton Cermak had appointed him attorney for the county board, and he was about to end his sabbatical from elective politics to become a Cermak candidate for the Cook County circuit court in the 1927 election. Concerned for his son and mindful of adverse publicity, he joined other parents in promising to settle the matter by forming an organization dedicated to eradicating high school fraternities and promoting wholesome youth activities. He took another step independently. Just as he had enrolled Otto in Oak Park and River Forest High School before the family moved within the school's boundaries, he now had Otto admitted to Harrison High School back in the South Lawndale neighborhood in time for a June commencement. Young Otto thereby fulfilled the high school graduation requirement for admission to Brown University that fall.

The suspensions were lifted in the fall, allowing Kerner Jr. and the other seniors involved to receive diplomas. As a result, he graduated from high school twice in 1926. As was the case with the other offending seniors, however, his picture and accomplishments were purged from the senior class list in the school yearbook, which was published during the summer. The incident later perplexed Kerner's political publicists. His official vita did not mention Harrison High School but cited the Oak Park diploma. Yet his name appears only once, by oversight, in the Oak Park yearbook for his graduation year: he is listed among the members of the Burke Club, a debating society named after the great British political philosopher Edmund Burke, who once said, "All men that are ruined are ruined on the side of their natural propensities."

✦ ✦ ✦

Young Kerner had not met Clabaugh before the fraternity inquisition, but in his own troubles Otto Kerner Sr. knew his accuser well. Frank J. Loesch and Kerner were active members of the Chicago Bar Association. Kerner joined the association's governing board of managers in 1926 after heading its admissions committee. Loesch was a charter member of the association, which was formed in 1883 as the Law Club of Chicago, and belonged to several association committees over the years as well as its board of managers. A deeply religious man who taught Bible class on Sundays, Loesch had spent forty years as an attorney for the Pennsylvania Railroad. He had no formal background in criminal law. Nonetheless, at age seventy-six he became a freelance crime fighter and popularizer of reform movements that adressed the ironic tension between Chicagoans' craving for the latest colorful racketeer drama and their disgust for the growing illegitimacy of their own government. Charles Merriam, in his account of Chicago politics in the 1920s, described the gray-haired, handsomely stern Loesch as a "Cincinnatus type called from the plow to save the state."[8]

"Not a man of magnetism, or of wide group contacts, nor an organizer of political forces, he has the qualities of high intelligence, courage and an unconscious sense of the dramatic in public appearances," Merriam wrote. "There is a simplicity and directness in his courage and in his behavior that reflect a widespread general attitude toward a perfectly obvious situation. The masses speak frankly of crooks and thieves and so does he; have their opinion of feeble prosecutors and spineless judges and so does he; and thus Loesch is their voice—a voice their ears have been waiting to hear for many years."[9]

Loesch was named president of the Chicago Crime Commission in early 1928. The commission, one of several civic reform groups sponsored by wealthy Chicagoans, kept voluminous records of crimes and the prosecution of offenders, much of the material clipped from newspapers. Its data were considered reliable, but the commission was not a leading reform advocacy group until Loesch took over. His campaign to arouse the public shifted into high gear after the shootings and bombings that marked Chicago's infamous "Pineapple Primary" in April 1928.

As is customary in Chicago politics, the race for Cook County state's attorney was the principal focus of political operatives that year because the state's attorney held the power to impanel grand juries that could embarrass political opponents with strategically publicized investigations. Like the other leaders of the crime commission, Loesch was a dedicated Republican partisan who initially backed State's Attorney Robert E. Crowe, also a Republican, in his bid for renomination. Crowe campaigned against crime but was known to consort with racketeers. Under his leadership of Cook County's criminal prosecution machinery, Al Capone felt comfortable moving back to Chicago and setting up headquarters a block north of city hall, where another Republican, Big Bill Thompson, had returned to the mayor's office in 1927 after a four-year absence.

But Loesch and the crime commission abruptly abandoned Crowe after the homes of his GOP primary opponent, John A. Swanson, and Senator Charles Deneen, a leader of the Republican's anti–Thompson-Crowe faction, were bombed shortly before the primary. Loesch turned against Crowe with a vengeance and helped push Swanson to a surprising victory, thanks also to an electorate aroused by the preelection violence. Primary election day saw no respite from mayhem. In the worst incident, Octavious C. Granady, a black candidate for Twentieth Ward Republican committeeman running against Thompson-Crowe crony Morris Eller, was shot to death in his car. Eller was Thompson's city collector, and his son, Emanuel, was a Cook County circuit court judge.

The bloody primary prompted a senator from Nebraska to call on President Calvin Coolidge to redeploy to Chicago a contingent of U.S. Marines then stationed in Nicaragua, where they were supervising a national election.

But Congress reacted coolly to pleas by Vice President Charles Dawes, a leading Chicago reformer, for federal assistance against gangsterism. One senator said such assistance would represent "unwarranted interference" by the federal government in local affairs and "never-ending work" for Congress.[10]

Instead, self-styled prosecutor Loesch swung into action. The *Chicago Herald and Examiner* aptly called him the "septuagenarian battler for civic righteousness."[11] The phrase "civic reform" implies concerns for the process of government and the corruption of that process. "Civic righteousness" goes further, favoring morally driven outcomes of government action. The moralistic view of crime, popular at the time, held that a criminal justice system that coddled criminals encouraged antisocial behavior. This view competed with the determinist theory that criminals are genetically defective. Historian David E. Ruth, in his book *Inventing the Public Enemy: The Gangster in American Culture, 1918–1934,* stated the moralist perspective: "Criminals are essentially ordinary, and ordinary people are controlled by rational will that others could hope to persuade. Since would-be lawbreakers carefully calculate their deeds, the crime wave could be stemmed by improving the efficiency of law enforcement agencies and curbing the 'abuses' of constitutional protection of the rights of the accused."[12]

In this spirit the Loesch crusade targeted Cook County's criminal judges. Despite the image created by fictionalized portrayals of Chicago in the 1920s, crimes related directly to Prohibition and gangsterism constituted a small part of the county's criminal court docket at the time. But Prohibition's by-products—widespread corruption of local police and the erosion of public respect for law—nurtured a fecund social environment for petty street crimes, such as robbery and burglary. Any judicial system would have a hard time coping with the epidemic of wrongdoing Chicago was experiencing, but the courts produced by Cook County's political spoils system were particularly ill equipped.

Politics and elections were a major local industry in Cook County in the 1920s, with the judicial system serving as a vital subsidiary. The bewildering election process was designed by the captains of that industry to control the outcome. Voters faced an election on average once every five months. A Chicago Bar Association study of primary and general elections in the second half of the decade showed that over a six-year cycle a conscientious Republican voter in Chicago would have sorted through nearly 1,000 candidates for offices from president of the United States to ward committeeman; a Democrat, nearly 800. "The typical Chicago voter has been confronted with a ballot that is not only long but also wide and frequent," concluded the study.[13] More than half the elective offices were judicial—thirty-seven municipal court judges, twenty-eight superior court judges, twenty circuit court judges, a probate judge, a county judge, and a judge from Chicago for the Illinois Supreme Court.

Circuit court judges expected to impose society's will on lawbreakers were handpicked by political bosses and often had little schooling in criminal law. Bosses dictated judicial slates not to steer the outcome of criminal and civil cases toward their preferred judicial philosophies but to control the extensive patronage appointments judges were authorized to make, including masters-in-chancery, receivers in bankruptcy cases, and courtroom bailiffs. The Circuit Court of Cook County selected commissioners of the South Park System, Chicago's largest network of parks tended by more than one thousand patronage workers, who were hired by park commissioners acting by proxy for party leaders. Supervising such job appointments was far more important politically than influencing justice—too imporant to be left to the judgment of voters. Democrat Cermak and Republican Crowe, claiming to take politics out of justice, divided the judgeships scheduled for election and presented joint "fusion" slates of candidates intended to run unopposed.

The Chicago Bar Association believed it had a duty to leaven political party control of the judiciary and to assist voters in screening the dozens of judicial candidates. The association sought to negotiate with local Democratic and Republican leaders to fashion bipartisan slates of candidates deemed qualified by the legal community. In the 1921 election for the circuit court, however, Mayor Thompson put up his own Republican candidates and refused to participate in any fusion process that included competing interests in his own party, not to mention the bar association or the Democrats.

In the high-water mark for the bar association as a political agent, its slate, endorsed by Democratic leaders and anti-Thompson Republicans, scored a stunning victory over Thompson. A war chest of $61,000—a remarkable sum for a political reform campaign at that time—as well as the support of civic groups and newspapers brought out 60 percent of the county's registered voters, more than twice the number who normally voted in the June judicial election. It was a stinging defeat for Thompson and a major victory for the bar association and Chicago reformers. The victory gave the bar association a false sense of its power to influence Chicago politics. The association's monthly publication, *The Chicago Bar Record*, immediately proclaimed a new "militant policy" of reforming the courts.[14]

The Record of June 1921 claimed for the bar association the right of slate making: "By its successful fight in the June election, the Chicago Bar Association has advanced far towards the goal of leadership in this branch of its legitimate functions and has won the right to expect the people to look to it for guidance in future elections. It is our hope that the day is not far off when the nominees of the Chicago Bar Association for judicial office will be without opposition from any quarter and will be assured of election."[15]

The association attempted to increase its political influence for several years thereafter. In 1926 several prominent attorneys joined its board of managers, boosting its prestige. Among them were Frederick Ullman, editor of *The Record,* who had written fiery editorials in 1921 against political control of the judicial system; Weymouth Kirkland and William P. Sidley, lawyers whose names would mark two of the city's most prestigious law firms; and Otto Kerner Sr., a popular lawyer and master-in-chancery. But the association could not achieve dominance over the political parties.

In 1927 all but one of the twenty bar association–endorsed circuit court judges elected in 1921 sought reelection, and the association steadfastly supported the incumbents it had helped sweep to victory against the Thompson slate. But Cermak and Crowe reunited to resume control of the process. They dumped three bar association–supported incumbents from their coalition slate. Crowe instead slated Michael Feinberg and Stanley H. Klarkowski; Cermak slated Kerner.

In May 3,100 bar association members voted in an endorsement "primary" for the twenty circuit court slots. Early returns reported in an afternoon newspaper had Kerner, running without the association's endorsement, high among the top twenty vote-getters. By the next day, however, the final count showed Kerner in twenty-second place; Feinberg, twenty-fifth; and Klarkowski, thirtieth. Nonetheless, in a low-turnout June election, coming just two months after an exhausting mayoral race that saw the uproarious return of Big Bill Thompson, the bosses won the day. Kerner, Feinberg, and Klarkowski were elected.

In the wake of its loss, bar association leaders acknowledged that their campaign to "keep politics off the bench" had a curious result with respect to Kerner. *The Record* commented: "There are many who think the courts have always been in [politics] and at times the Bar Association itself seems engaged in activities strangely resembling politics. The last election saw it by vote of the membership opposing the election of a member of its own Board of Managers [Kerner] and supporting the election of a judge who in the opinion of the Association's Committee on the Judiciary in 1923 had 'by reason of his unjudicial and unethical conduct most seriously impaired his usefulness as a judge.' This is sufficiently grotesque to look almost like real politics."[16]

The association's zeal to supplant political leaders in judicial slate making irrevocably tainted one of its own, Otto Kerner Sr. Had the association moderated slightly its commitment to stand by its victorious 1921 candidates, Kerner almost certainly would have enjoyed his peers' warm endorsement. Instead Kerner took office marked forever by the stain of bossism, his link to Cermak overshadowing his stature in Chicago's legal community.

Kerner never wanted to be a criminal court judge. His speciality—and his livelihood—lay in the civil justice system. Nevertheless, the press of business required added manpower in the criminal division. He found himself there just as Loesch launched a probe of the criminal bench as a coconspirator in Chicago's system of corruption that, in the words of historian Ruth, "compress[ed] the distance between the lawbreaker and the upstanding citizen."[17] Hunting for those responsible for Chicago's crime spree, the crime commission's courtroom observers recorded proceedings, including the many occasions when an assistant state's attorney asked a judge to reduce gun-use charges and other felonies to lesser offenses. Based on these observations, the crime commission in April 1928 accused three judges: Kerner and Klarkowski, two of those who had won office without bar association backing, and Emanuel Eller, son of notorious Twentieth Ward Republican committeeman Morris Eller.

Loesch called their offense "paltering with crime," which meant taking it easy on criminals by reducing or dismissing charges. Loesch's indictment boiled down to a dry, statistical case based on the fact that the three judges reduced more charges than their peers. The specific cases cited by the commission related to ordinary street crimes, not the doings of Prohibition-era gangsters or corrupt politicians. But Loesch's rhetoric was anything but dry:

> These three judges, Eller, Kerner and Klarkowski, were put on the bench by the politicians against the protest and vote of the Chicago Bar Association. . . . It was politics in full swing in the State's Attorney's office and on the bench. Have the judges named and other complaisant ones no regard for the victims of the murderous criminals to whom they show such tender mercy? Have they no regard for the decent public opinion? Have they no regard to the laws which they are sworn to uphold in protection of the peaceable and law-abiding citizens? The record indicates that they have not. They ought not to sit a day longer in the Criminal Court. Common decency on their part should make them retire. But if they will not voluntarily do so, then the other judges of the Superior Court and of the Circuit Court who placed them in the Criminal Court should recall them and assign to the Criminal Court judges who will enforce the law against criminals.[18]

The normally reserved Kerner, who had never sought newspaper publicity, lashed back. He told reporters he wanted an immediate investigation by the circuit court and Chicago Bar Association of the charges against him:

> I want to say to the people of Cook County that the crime commission is dealing with statistics and numbers, while I am dealing with human beings. I was assigned to the criminal court last December. I had no desire to come, as I felt that I was better fitted to sit in chancery or common law. But as a good soldier I obeyed the order of the executive committee of the Circuit Court. Since that time, I have tried more cases than any other judge, which goes to prove that more felonies were tried in my court. I intend to ask the judges of the Circuit Court to take up this matter and to decide as a body whether I have ever done anything improper. . . . Mr. Loesch

and the crime commission have no idea, I am sure, of the injustice they have done to me and my family, and I am confident that if Mr. Loesch was sitting in my place he would have done exactly what I have done.[19]

Eller and Klarkowski also counterattacked. "Why doesn't [Loesch] compile the records of all the judges and not pick on three that he and his crowd don't like?" asked Eller. "I don't care about his opinion. I want the opinion of the people."[20] Klarkowski noted Loesch's professional background and said, "It is obviously unfair for a man who sits in his office serving corporate interests to pass judgment on the acts of others when he has no first-hand knowledge of the evidence in the cases involved."[21]

With newspapers bannering Loesch's charges and no established legal mechanism for dealing with Kerner's demand for a hearing, the circuit court executive committee named six judges, headed by appellate judge Thomas Taylor, to conduct a public hearing. The hearing became a venue for Chicago's corporate leaders, thoroughly disenchanted with the city's political structure under the ludicrous Mayor Thompson, to show their support for Loesch, the crime commission, and the whole notion of an elite, private crime-fighting campaign. On the first day prominent bankers and businesspeople, a University of Chicago trustee, and several wives of Chicago's business leaders ventured to the County Building to be in attendance. Julius Rosenwald, president of Sears, Roebuck and Company, joined the crowd of spectators packed into the Cook County Board's assembly room. He called the hearing "the most important thing that has happened in Chicago in many years."[22]

J. Hamilton Lewis, a once and future Democratic U.S. senator from Illinois and a man whose colorful and extraneous oratory matched his sartorial splendor, entered with a flourish and announced that he represented the three judges. With great rhetoric he demanded a bill of particulars from the crime commission. Kerner arrived on the second day with his wife and daughter Mary and immediately interrupted Lewis's elaborate plea for a continuance:

> These proceedings were instituted primarily at my request for an investigation. . . .
> I felt when Mr. Loesch made these charges, and coupled my name with them, that
> I stood to lose more than all the material wealth in the world—my good name. . . .
> I am sorry to say that I have never asked this honorable gentleman [Lewis] to represent me. I feel I need no representative. I have never asked that this investigation
> be stopped. Now I have nothing to fear, and I must insist that I be cleared or that
> I be transferred to the civil bench at once. I am only human, and it is interfering
> with my efficiency.[23]

In setting himself apart from Eller and Klarkowski and in demanding an expedited hearing on behalf of his name and his "efficiency," Kerner knew what he was doing. Unlike the others accused, he had kept copious notes of each criminal case he heard. He knew that neither Loesch nor the commission's courtroom observers could match his command of the facts regarding his rulings. One newspaper referred to Kerner's "Niagara of facts" to support his decisions.[24] In one armed robbery case cited by the commission, for example, the accusers were unable to dispute Kerner's notes that a cab driver who was robbed of six dollars by a twenty-three-year-old man sat in his cab with the robber and discussed who needed the money more. The robber, out of work for six weeks and suffering from tuberculosis, asked the driver for his card so he could return the money in thirty days. In court the cab driver had told Kerner, "Judge, I think that fellow is sick, that he is not bad, and I think this is a case where you ought to show mercy."[25]

Loesch and the crime commission fared no better in the other cases they cited against Kerner. In only one instance did Kerner admit regret, but the admission did nothing but enlarge his emerging public image as a hard-working yet caring jurist, the kind any citizen would hope to confront if called before the bar of justice. Kerner acknowledged that he placed on probation a boy named Stanley Thomas, who had been accused of stealing an automobile, after no evidence was presented linking him to the crime. Later the boy was accused of murdering a girl during a robbery in a Berwyn theater.

After the crime commission lawyer described the case, Kerner rose, his voice trembling, and addressed the judges:

> Yes, I put that lad on probation. And nothing has hurt me more than what he did afterward. I had no evidence against young Thomas. . . . But I wanted to help him— I felt he had been running in bad company. I talked to him and to young Frank Chmiel [another defendant in the car theft] as seriously as I have ever talked in my life. I thought what I could say to them might set them on the right track. I told them I rested my faith in them. I told them if they violated that faith, it would turn me against hundreds of other boys who might face me in my court. They promised me they would go straight. They thanked me for what I had said. And I believed them, your honors. I believed they were straight. I was glad because I thought I had helped them. Then Thomas went wrong. Nothing in my whole life, except the filing of these malicious charges against me, has hurt me so. I feel that boy's killing of the girl has taken years from my life. I have lived in Chicago all my life. I love Chicago. I would gladly do anything in my power to make Chicago a crimeless city. I have asked the Crime Commission to suggest methods for improving conditions—but the Crime Commission has done nothing in response to my invitation.[26]

If Chicagoans had been waiting for many years for the voice of Frank Loesch, as Merriam wrote, they responded with equal warmth to Otto Kerner's tragic story. Newspaper photos of Kerner and Rose attending the hearings showed a handsome, loving, and respectable couple caught up in a swirl of controversy. The *Chicago Herald and Examiner* called Kerner's emotional explanation of the Thomas incident "the greatest defense the accused jurists have had."[27] Amid the wrenching publicity about his father, Otto Kerner Jr. told his fraternity roommate at Brown University, miles away in Providence, Rhode Island, that he finally was beginning to feel close to his father, who had been absent and aloof for much of the younger man's life.[28]

In July the three judges were cleared by the judicial panel. It found that the crime commission's statistical case merely reflected a time-honored practice, dating back to early English law, whereby criminal court judges complied with requests by prosecutors to reduce charges when there was no compelling reason not to do so. The review panel found that the higher proportion of felony charges waived by the three accused judges was a random result of the cases they handled and did not stem from any inappropriate leniency on their part. As to Kerner, his fellow jurists were effusive in their praise: "We are of the opinion that the charge against Judge Kerner that he paltered with crime, in other words, was guilty of judicial misconduct, was in no way proved; that on the contrary, the evidence discloses not only a record of painstaking, industrious judicial service, but absolute integrity."[29]

Before he had seen the report, Loesch reacted with predictable indignation to its findings. "I think the Crime Commission sustained the charges absolutely," he told the *Tribune*. "Testimony was introduced substantiating the charge that politics played a large part in the waiver of felonies."[30] In fact, no such evidence was introduced, although the hearing did expose the supposedly nonpartisan judges Eller and Klarkowski as active campaigners for the Thompson-Crowe Republican slate in the April primary. The crime commission conceded two weeks after the judicial panel's report that Kerner "more or less made a satisfactory explanation of every felony waived by him." But the commission concluded that while the outcome of the hearing regarding all three judges was unsatisfactory, "it is satisfied that much public good has been accomplished as a result of the inquiry and that the public has been educated to a knowledge of the practice and meaning of felony waivers."[31] Indeed, the number of felony waivers dropped substantially after the inquiry began.[32]

In October a new crime commission report praised Kerner for "outstanding" performance on the criminal bench.[33] Shortly afterward Kerner was reassigned to the civil court, as he had requested. He returned to the criminal bench in 1929, again because of a swelling case load. Loesch welcomed Kerner's return, saying Kerner would "help materially in the crime clean-up."[34] In 1930 Kerner made headlines again, this time for sentencing to death a man named August Vogel, known in the newspapers as "the whim slayer." "Judge Kerner did not palter with crime today," one reporter observed.[35]

✦ ✦ ✦

The crime commission did not escape the paltering allegations unscathed. In late 1929 several officials of the Chicago Bar Association and other prominent lawyers as well as the judges of the circuit court denounced the crime commission for ignoring the rules of due process, creating a false impression of the judicial system in Chicago, and refusing to apologize to their colleague, Otto Kerner. Former state's attorney John J. Healy, one of the crime commission lawyers who brought the case against Kerner, joined in the rebuke. "Some judges probably deserve to be criticized, but I have no patience with an organization that has degenerated into a fault-finding, scolding body," he said. The crime commission, he said "ought to be required to fish or cut bait."[36]

But the demand by the Cook County judiciary to be treated with respect and fairness by the city's reformers rang hollow as Al Capone's efforts to solidify his control over Chicago kept the Thompson submachine guns blazing and bombs exploding. The St. Valentine's Day massacre in February 1929 established forever the city's reputation as a dangerous town and a haven for gangsters. Even Capone declared that the warfare was hurting business. Meanwhile, Chicago's blue bloods and entrepreneurs were in the early stages of planning another world's fair for the city, to be known as the Century of Progress Exposition. Although he could not interest Congress in tackling Chicago's crime and corruption, Vice President Dawes convinced President Coolidge to deploy federal authorities to root out Chicago's gangsters. Coolidge appointed straight-arrow prosecutor George E. Q. Johnson as U.S. attorney in Chicago. A young lawyer from the Bureau of Internal Revenue, Dwight H. Green, was assigned to assist him. In October 1928 Coolidge authorized the special intelligence bureau of the Bureau of Internal Revenue to investigate the income tax compliance of Al Capone. The longing of Chicago's business leaders for action against Capone and the gang war was being heard at the highest levels in Washington.

Civic righteousness was on the march. The Chicago Association of Commerce, under president Robert Isham Randolph, joined forces with Loesch. After *Chicago Tribune* police reporter Jake Lingle was assassinated in a downtown railroad station passageway in June 1930, *Tribune* publisher Robert R. McCormick declared war on gangsterism, grandly ignoring the fact that Lingle had been in Capone's pocket for years. Prominent business leaders and civic figures—Randolph of the commerce association, Loesch of the crime commission, Rosenwald of Sears, stockbroker George A. Paddock, utility chieftain Samuel Insull, and real estate executive Edward E. Gore—formed what became known as the Secret Six to direct and finance the activities of federal agents pursuing Capone.[37] Investigators such as federal agents Alexander G.

Jamie and his brother-in-law Eliot Ness were, in effect, employed by the Chicago business establishment. The powerful forces being arrayed against Prohibition-era gangsters were united in their belief that Chicago's legitimate political structure—including its policemen, elected representatives, and judges—was incapable of doing the job. The 1928 exoneration of Kerner, Klarkowski, and Eller strengthened their determination to find their own means for attacking Chicago's corruption and restoring the city's image.

A special grand jury authorized by the Illinois attorney general and directed by Loesch indicted Emanuel Eller and his brother, ward boss Morris Eller, on charges relating to the violence of the April 1928 primary election. The case against the brothers was never brought to trial, but several of Morris Eller's henchmen were convicted. Klarkowski later became a central figure in another highly publicized scandal involving judges who used their power to appoint receivers in real estate foreclosure cases as a way for political bosses to dole out favors while the nation sank into depression. Politically appointed receivers disposed of property in bankruptcy and skimmed off egregious fees, a vulture-like process that outraged Chicagoans and brought a new wave of negative national publicity to the city.

Meanwhile Kerner's public esteem rose in the wake of the paltering scandal. Cermak slated him for Illinois attorney general in 1932. After the election sweep by the Democrats that year, Kerner pushed legislation to end receivership abuses, and his overall record won widespread praise. Nonetheless, while names from the Loesch era such as Crowe, Eller, and Klarkowski faded, the name Kerner remained a prominent and inviting target for fighters against crime and corruption in Chicago.

3

This Job Is Much Better

In the mid-1920s America's military stood at parade rest, a self-satisfied pose befitting a nation that had extended its hand to help England and France defeat German aggression and established itself as a victorious global power. Calvin Coolidge was president. Nothing seemed amiss. Pomp and ceremony replaced military preparedness. Aging military bandleader John Philip Sousa composed "The Black Horse Troop" march in honor of a mounted unit of the Ohio National Guard in Cleveland. Like all Sousa marches, it was built on a disciplined, predictable musical structure that both inspired and soothed. When the Sousa band played the march for the first time in 1925, "the mounted troopers were dressed in the blue uniforms of 1877, complete with black fur busbies. They rode right up onto the stage with the band."[1] It was a glorious, innocent moment.

Across the Atlantic political rabble-rouser and Austrian misfit Adolf Hitler, just released from a German prison after serving eighteen months for treason, made an unlikely but ominous appeal to Bavarians. His Nazi Party promised to reestablish Germany's military might.

In 1927 Chicago lawyer and newspaper publisher Roy D. Keehn, who represented the interests of newspaper mogul William Randolph Hearst in the Midwest, was named commander of the Illinois National Guard by Governor Len Small, a Republican. Keehn, who owned an extensive estate in the exclusive suburb of Lake Forest on Lake Michigan's shore north of Chicago, decided that Chicago needed its own Black Horse Troop similar to units in Ohio, New York, and Pennsylvania. Prominent Chicagoans, led by utilities

magnate Samuel Insull, raised money to outfit the Chicago Black Horse Troop
and Mounted Band, and in 1929 the unit received official authorization from
the War Department as Headquarters Troop, 106th Cavalry. Maxwell Cor-
pening, a West Point graduate and well-known local polo player, was named
to head the unit.

The troop acquired one hundred matched black horses and began its colorful duty, escorting dignitaries, competing in polo matches, and performing at musical events in and around Chicago. The national guard soldiers wore
elaborate uniforms designed by wives of financial backers and modeled after
outfits worn by the army dragoons who manned Fort Dearborn during the
War of 1812.[2] Officers included Keehn's son, Roy Jr., a Princeton graduate,
and Paul Butler, a dashing young polo player and paper manufacturing executive from west suburban Hinsdale. The unit became known as the kin-
dergarten of Chicago's elite. Early supporters included Insull, bankers Charles
and Rufus Dawes, and Sears, Roebuck executive Julius Rosenwald—the same
men who financed the government's campaign against Al Capone. Individuals backing the ceremonial organization boasted names quite prominent in
Chicago, such as McCormick, Florsheim, Harris, Meigs, Pick, Blair, and
Swift.[3] Its members were sons of Chicago's upper class, far removed from the
rough-and-tumble world of Chicago politics.

One young man who bridged the gap was Otto Kerner Jr., who enlisted
in the Black Horse Troop as a private in 1934 while completing law school
at Northwestern University's downtown campus. The unit was stationed
conveniently in an armory on East Chicago Avenue, near the school. By sending young Otto to an Ivy League college, Cambridge University, and Northwestern University Law School, Kerner Sr. secured for his son what no other
ethnic politician in Chicago achieved for himself or his offspring during the
Great Depression, a place in the city's social elite based on something besides
pure expediency. Kerner had the looks and academic credentials, though not
the society pedigree, for admission into the circle of Chicago's blue bloods.
In his fancy black LaSalle ragtop roadster, purchased by his father in his junior year at college, young Kerner eased his way into the world of debutantes,
polo players, and lavish parties as if it were his legacy from generations of
family wealth and breeding. While his law school classmates worked nights
to finance their studies, Kerner enjoyed the high life available to very few in
the depression years. As one law school classmate remembered, "He seemed
to be enamored of the Lake Forest crowd."[4]

But the pomp and ceremony of the Black Horse Troop were more than a
dalliance for young Kerner. The National Guard placed him in a challenging
yet amenable military structure, and unlike the Good Soldier Schweik and
Kerner's ancestors in Bohemia, he readily took to it. The military life became

for him a worthy alternative to the political structure his father had known in the Cermak organization.

At Brown University, in Providence, Rhode Island, Kerner developed the suave, correct manner that throughout his career in public life set him apart from the stereotypically monosyllabic ward heelers and political fixers who were essential to the success of any Democratic candidate in Cook County. The quiet, austere pride that the elder Kerner had displayed in upgrading his family from its humble roots in Chicago's Pilsen neighborhood blossomed in his son. In a word, Kerner Jr. had style. In their yearbook fellow students in the class of 1930 named him a "society man" and "best dressed,"[5] a noteworthy achievement for a West Side boy in the elite Ivy League. Like many young people in the years after the Great War, however, Kerner felt the disillusion and absence of purpose that the horrors of the war inflicted on America and Europe.

It is unclear why the Kerners chose Brown University as the place to send Otto for grooming. Certainly the Kerner and Chmelik families had no prior association with the school. Upper-middle-class families in Oak Park and River Forest typically sent their sons and daughters east to prestigious colleges, however, and the newcomers from South Lawndale sought to do the same. In addition, William Kinnaird, Kerner's fraternity-house roommate from St. Louis, recalled that a young woman Kerner dated in high school had enrolled in a women's college nearby in Connecticut.[6] Academic competition for admission to Brown's all-male undergraduate college was somewhat less rigorous than that for Harvard, Yale, or Princeton, although Brown tightened admissions standards in 1926. Freshman Kerner had to attend summer school at the University of Wisconsin in 1927 after receiving failing grades in English and Latin in his freshman year. He was admitted to his sophomore year "on strict warning."[7]

Brown University, founded in 1764, sits high on a hill above Rhode Island's capital city, which had slumped into decline several years before the Great Depression. The state's historic textile industry had eroded, and nothing took its place as an economic generator. Up on the hill, however, Brown's faculty and administrators prepared young men for a life of financial success and social correctness, more or less oblivious to the harsher realities below. The college dean, Otis Everett Randall, insisted on well-starched dress and deportment as well as rigorous scholarship. With equal discipline he taught geometry and the proper way to carry a cane.

Though it was nonsectarian, Brown had deep roots in the Northern Baptist denomination, the chosen faith of the school's leading patron, oil tycoon

John D. Rockefeller. The Reverend William Herbert Perry Faunce, Brown's president from 1899 to 1929, had been the pastor of the Rockefellers' church in New York City, the Fifth Avenue Baptist Church. Faunce maintained an atmosphere of Christian discipline appreciated by parents, even those such as the Kerners who were not strict about formal religious observance at home.

Ivy League life was nevertheless an experience of sharp contrasts in the late 1920s. Schools conducted religious services fastidiously and structured student life carefully *in loco parentis* to achieve an outcome predetermined by upper-class traditions. At the same time, the hypocrisy of Prohibition and America's postwar aimlessness created a climate of disrespect and excess that frequently led to seriously destructive and self-destructive behavior by students. Riots, prompted as much by drunkenness as anything else, occurred throughout upper-class colleges in those years. In Kerner's junior year, an annual celebration by Brown freshmen marking their release from first-year dress codes turned into a melee in downtown Providence. Freshman John E. Kreps Jr., the son of a railroad executive from Cleveland and one of Kerner's fraternity brothers, was shot in the wrist, apparently by student gunfire. A town resident also was shot, and twenty-one persons were hospitalized.[8] The next year Brown officials suspended classes and other campus activities for two weeks—the first campus shutdown since 1891—"to allow carpenters and repairmen to mend the damage caused by rioting in several of the dormitories," according to the campus newspaper, the *Brown Daily Herald*.[9]

John D. Rockefeller Jr. attended Brown and belonged to the Brunonian chapter of the Alpha Delta Phi fraternity. Kerner joined the same Alpha Delta Phi chapter and lived in its richly paneled, leather-upholstered Brunonian chapter house just behind the university library. He was chapter president in his senior year, when many classmates were forced home by the nation's financial collapse. Three days a week the student body attended morning chapel services in cavernous Sayles Hall, at which time Faunce, known to the engineering students as "Willie Horse Power," lectured the young men on achieving a wholesome and useful life. Predictably Brown men regarded the aging Faunce as a pompous scold. "Dr. Faunce with firm conviction bellowed out the benediction," was a popular student slogan.[10] But a collection of Faunce's admonitions, published in 1928 under the title *Facing Life*, reveals a thoughtful and progressive mind, fully aware of the pressures and responsibilities imposed on upper-class young men in the Prohibition era:

> The World War was naturally followed by a period of unrestrained excess and all kinds of intemperance. During the War, all barriers were lifted, the Ten Commandments were abolished by Christian nations, and we went to the limit in meeting a foe that we thought recognized no law save the law of the jungle. Did we then dream that by signing the Armistice we would restore the commandments and

rebuild the fences? Everywhere we have seen intemperance—in violent, heated language, in glaring headlines, in extravagant expenditure based on unlimited profiteering, in the headlong plunge into pleasure, in the craze for savage syncopated music, in erratic, provocative costume, in reckless driving and a devil-may-care attitude toward life. . . . The social life in the American college today is thoroughly intemperate. It unfits our students for either work or play. It is exhausting to purses and nerves, devitalizing to mind and character. . . . Unlimited indulgence means merely ennui and boredom, and excessive pleasure is a form of pain.[11]

Upholding a senior class tradition, Kerner's class of 1930 created a "mascot," a molded plaster plaque intended to capture the essence of campus life. The mascot revealed no hint of the stock market crash or the gathering depression that would grip the nation and sap Brown's enrollment for years to come. The student newspaper described the plaque, saying it "depicts a grinding machine into which a stream of youth is flowing. A professor in cap and gown is turning the crank, and out of the end of the machine walks a senior in academic regalia. Three rejection slots open from the side of the instrument, out of each of which a boy is being thrown, one for wine, one for women, and one for week-ends."[12]

The *Brown Daily Herald* in April 1930 published a student essay titled "The Art of Drinking" that told the darker side of the privileged world Otto Kerner had entered:

Failing to become an art, drinking has become a religion. The religion of drinking is tyrannical, evangelist and intolerant. The ideal party begins with an attempt to make the home as like the roadhouse as possible. The estates of Long Island, the Spanish villas of Palm Beach and the apartments of Chicago and New York set out, in spite of their limitations, to rival the places arranged for drinking and drinking alone. In Westchester and on Long Island, along various lake shores and in all those communities to which the wealthy retreat from nearby cities, there is a choice between various formulas. They all begin with numerous cocktails before dinner—and dinner is scheduled late as the theater is excluded from the forms of entertainment. The cocktail hour here is distinguished from most others because it rigorously rejects fruit juice; gin and vermouth are prescribed elements and the point of variation is in the proportions used. The ratio of gin has gone up—four to one, six to one, eight to one, and I have a record of a charming hostess who was asked how much vermouth she had allowed into an extremely successful cocktail and who replied, "Oh, we just put in the gin and the ice and walk through the room with the vermouth bottle." The religion of drinking denies the right of any man to enjoy his bond selling, his book collecting (or reading), his squash games, his breakfast, his children—if his pleasure of any of these requires him to drink less. In this religion it is right to tear up tickets to the season's single performance of "Don Giovanni," and it is not right to throw one of ten thousand identical drinks down the sink. If someone answers that drinking is, after all, still optional in America, he had better leave the company, or he is in the presence of the profound illusion of our time.[13]

The "personal liberty" for which Anton Cermak had for years fought on behalf of the long-suffering workingman bore little resemblance to this bleak portrait of upper-class indulgence. Kerner Jr. tasted this life but did not succumb. His Brown years were congenial and balanced, and as with many young people of that time, the many opportunities for intemperance produced in him a longing for meaning and structure in his life. His grades improved, especially in his major, English literature. As a senior he was vice president of the Brown Christian Association, a leading campus service organization. He and roommate Kinnaird published *The Bear Facts,* the annual handbook that the association prepared for incoming freshman.

There was also time for fun. Kerner chaired the Senior Frolic Committee. He became an officer of a whimsical campus society called Owl and Ring, which apparently had as its sole purpose opposition to the joint commencement by men from Brown and women from the affiliated Pembroke College. His friends included two brothers named Jack and Walter Walsh, who came from a wealthy construction family in Davenport, Iowa. He dated their sister, Mary Jane, who was on Broadway as understudy to Ethel Merman in *Annie Get Your Gun.* Kerner took up the ukelele and pipe smoking and became a habitual cigarette smoker.

He contemplated becoming a doctor but decided to follow his father in a law career. His grades were unimpressive for either career. His C+ average over four years was insufficient for admission to the better law schools. The Brown yearbook of 1930 offered this prescient summation of the young man, known on campus as Adonis: "Sincere, sedate and serious. Ott has traversed his collegiate career untrammeled by convention. Without the ballyhoo of the athlete or the presumption of the scholar he has succeeded in attaining distinction rivaled by none."[14]

Lacking the presumption or the grades of a scholar, Kerner traveled to England in the fall of 1930 to be tutored in law at Cambridge University's Trinity College, known worldwide not for legal scholarship but for excellence in science and mathematics. Until June 1931 he lived in rooms near the Trinity campus and studied under the guidance of a historian named Sir James R. M. Butler.[15] He acquired a slight English affectation in his voice that annoyed his father. He abhorred the fledgling communist sympathizers he met among students and faculty. In the summer of 1931 he toured Europe and encountered Hitler's National Socialist movement, which was gaining momentum and visibility throughout Bavaria after scoring surprising success in German parliamentary elections in September 1930. Hitler was consolidating power and drawing support from German financiers and industrialists who anticipated his rise to dictator and wanted to be on the right side.

"At Munich that year I saw the students staging demonstrations, and the thunder of Hitler's words was already rolling across the land," Kerner told a newspaper interviewer a dozen years later. "The clouds of war were forming even then. The young men, the would-be fighters, were smarting under the decade-old peace terms of the First World War. . . . But, now, these students told me, America would learn it had not foreclosed on Germany's glorious future. They boasted that Germany had never been defeated on home soil. . . . What they said to me convinced me then, and that rumbling under ground convinced me that war was coming—and coming soon."[16]

Kerner never forgot the image of Hitler's black-shirted and brown-shirted private armies that numbered 100,000 men—more than Germany's national army—led by a man whose professed racism included hatred of Czechs and Slavs as well as of Jews, Poles, and Russians. His education finally brought him into contact with the realities that would shape his life.

✦ ✦ ✦

In the spring of 1931 events in Chicago as well as his father's unease with his son's experience in the rarefied atmosphere of Cambridge pulled young Otto home. After the Harding, Coolidge, and Hoover years, punctuated by the most serious stock market crash ever, Americans soured on Republicans. No international military conflicts threatened American tranquility, but the Great Depression brought the age of postwar innocence to an abrupt end. In Chicago the St. Valentine's Day massacre and the subsequent gangland shootings—in broad daylight in downtown Chicago—of *Chicago Tribune* reporter Jake Lingle and mobster Jake Zuta turned public fascination with Capone-era gangster violence into revulsion. Voters tired of the antics of the city's Republican mayor, Big Bill Thompson.

The chief beneficiary of the new public mood was Anton Cermak, who had built a diverse political coalition to challenge the Irish hold on the Cook County Democratic Party. Cermak's candidates dominated the nominations for congressional and local offices in the 1930 election year, and his slate scored a decisive victory over the Republicans in November. "This was the greatest Democratic victory in Illinois in a generation and perhaps the greatest since the Civil War," declared Cermak biographer Alex Gottfried. "Cermak had proved himself handsomely."[17]

Despite his poor health, which included chronic colitis, Cermak at age fifty-seven prepared to establish a Democratic organization led by Czechs, Poles, and Jews that would place him firmly in charge. He needed full support from friends such as Kerner Sr., by then on the state appeals court; Henry Horner of the probate court; Benjamin F. Lindheimer of the South Park Commission; Moe Rosenberg, the wealthy West Side Jewish political broker, and his right-hand man, Jacob Arvey; and Polish leaders such as Cook County judge Edmund K. Jarecki, who oversaw the city election process, and a young state legislator named Benjamin S. Adamowski. Cermak even had a few Irish allies, including Eleventh Ward alderman Joseph B. "Big Joe" McDonough, whose protégé was a stocky, energetic student at DePaul University law school named Richard J. Daley. In 1930 McDonough won the office of Cook County treasurer on the Cermak slate. Preferring horse-racing tout sheets to financial ledgers, McDonough turned the daily work of the treasurer's office over to his personal assistant, Daley. While Kerner Jr. climbed Chicago's social ladder, Daley studied the intricacies of government finance and political patronage.

In the spring of 1931, Cermak defeated Thompson to become mayor of Chicago. This time Cermak drew support not only from his broad ethnic coalition but also from the city's business interests and newspapers. Though its constituents were unsure of Cermak and his gruff demeanor, the city's economic and civic leadership—with the notable exception of the Republican-controlled Better Government Association (BGA)—was determined to unseat Thompson. The BGA urged Chicagoans to reelect Thompson out of fear that Cermak and his ilk would be worse. But Chicago's voters did not agree. The Cermak mayoral victory has been described by political scientists as the most effective display of coalition politics in the city's history until that point. Historian Roger Biles, in his biography of Chicago mayor Edward J. Kelly, wrote, "The strength of Cermak's nascent coalition and the importance of ethnic politics were evidenced by his campaign for the mayoralty. . . . Thompson erred egregiously in conducting a vicious nativistic campaign; his references to Cermak as 'Pushcart Tony' and 'Tony Baloney' served only to alienate the thousands of ethnic voters who saw the Czech as their champion."[18]

When Otto Kerner Jr. arrived home from England to enter law school, the Democratic Party in Chicago and Cook County was beginning an ascent that would be accelerated a year later by the presidential campaign of Franklin Delano Roosevelt. The 1932 Democratic National Convention in Chicago lured political activists to the city just as New York City's Broadway drew entertainers. While Cermak and other professional politicians shut themselves in proverbial smoke-filled rooms, hammering out the choice of nominees and the party's platform (Cermak was a last-minute supporter of Roosevelt), rank-and-file Chicago Democrats celebrated the dawn of their era and enjoyed the convention spectacle in Chicago's International Amphitheater. They packed the galleries and cheered for a "wet" plank in the party platform calling for the repeal of Prohibition, the central national issue of the day as far as Cermak was concerned. They held boisterous street marches on behalf of the party.

Living in suburban River Forest, Kerner Jr. was not called on for the kind of hands-on city precinct work that made Richard Daley a popular figure in his South Side neighborhood of Bridgeport. Neither young Kerner nor his father belonged to the meticulously disciplined city ward structure that Cermak was building. But Kerner was one of the many young people who, amid the pain of the depression, believed that Roosevelt would find a way out of the country's misery just in time for them to take up the responsibilities of adulthood.

Kerner Jr. lived in two worlds, represented by two of his closest law school friends. Lake Forest scion George B. Rogers, son of a wealthy corporate lawyer, provided Kerner access to high society and Chicago's business establishment. After law school the younger Rogers became general counsel for the First National Bank of Chicago. William A. Redmond, who had been a child actor in Milwaukee and lived in an Irish enclave in Chicago's West Side Austin neighborhood, kept Kerner close to his less affluent roots. Redmond rode to law school in Kerner's roadster. He entered Democratic politics and became the liberal and canny Speaker of the Illinois House in the 1970s.

Driving downtown from River Forest in Kerner's swank LaSalle convertible, Redmond recalled, "I was quite surprised that Otto was a Democrat."[19] The two young men joined the Young Democrats, an appendage of the party that in Chicago and elsewhere became an important training ground for New Dealers. Kerner's friends in the organization included Helena Cermak Kenlay, the youngest daughter of the mayor. As a student at the University of Illinois in 1926, she had eloped to Indiana to marry a handsome law student, Floyd Kenlay. The couple had a beautiful daughter, Mary Alyce. Kenlay became a lawyer in the Illinois attorney general's office and attempted to form a new statewide Democratic support organization. Another friend in this circle was Cermak's secretary, Helen Silhanek, a daughter of one of Cermak's Bohemian cronies and sister-in-law of a former Kerner Sr. law partner, Vernon Tittle. Helen, who married Irish music enthusiast Thomas McNamara in 1937, became secretary to every Chicago mayor from Cermak to Harold Washington. These young people from Chicago's proud Bohemian community saw a bright future for themselves with Cermak as mayor and Roosevelt as president.

Young Kerner's largest political role in 1932 was aiding his father's campaign for Illinois attorney general. He drove his father throughout the state for appearances at campaign rallies led by gubernatorial candidate Henry Horner. It was his first exposure to the breadth of Illinois's complex political interests, from the urban northeast that identified with other industrial areas of the nation to the southern Little Egypt region that held strong ties to the rural South. He met men who were to play important roles in his life, including Ben Lindheimer, Horner's campaign manager, who successfully marketed the

Jewish candidate in downstate counties where the Ku Klux Klan was active, and Joseph Knight, who at age twenty-one helped to energize downstate campaign rallies on behalf of Horner and who later won a job on the Illinois Commerce Commission under Lindheimer.

Kerner saw how Horner's membership in the Masonic order eased his acceptance downstate. Horner biographer Thomas B. Littlewood observed, "Advancement in the Masonic order has always been a requisite for political success in downstate Protestant counties."[20] Kerner would later join the organization and establish through it several powerful friendships in Chicago and downstate. The state's legacy from the Civil War and the sharp divisions between rural and urban interests created a fractured political landscape that existed in microcosm in the state legislature. For non-Catholic politicians, the Masonic lodge structure was one of the few common threads that bound the state together.

An article Kerner wrote for the December 1932 edition of the *Illinois Law Review,* compiled by the Northwestern law school, revealed Kerner's interest in statewide politics after his experiences campaigning with his father. He analyzed a contemporary U.S. Supreme Court decision that addressed a fundamental and recurring political problem, the apportionment of congressional and legislative districts after each decennial census. Power brokers in Springfield dealt with the rising ethnic and black population of Chicago by allowing disproportionate representation for downstate regions. Kerner cited Illinois's fifth congressional district on Chicago's West Side, represented by veteran Bohemian politician and Cermak ally Adolph J. Sabath, with a population of 541,785 in the map drawn after the 1930 census. He compared it to the fourteenth district in western Illinois, which included Rock Island and several rural counties along the Mississippi River, with a population of 211,848.

The Supreme Court ruled in a case arising from another state that a 1929 federal election law repealed the requirements of equal, compact, and contiguous congressional districts. The decision, Kerner pointed out, completely reversed the court's stance just a year earlier in an Illinois redistricting case, when the court threw out the legislature's congressional district map for violating equal, compact, and contiguous requirements.[21] Three decades later Kerner as governor would veto a legislative redistricting map he judged unfair, setting the stage for the first-ever statewide election of Illinois House members.

With Roosevelt leading the ticket, Illinois Democrats scored another stunning victory in November. Horner defeated former governor Len Small's bid for a comeback by the strongest statewide plurality ever recorded up to that time. Roosevelt carried Illinois decisively, but Horner outpolled Roosevelt by 100,000 votes, a clear indication of the Cermak organization's focus on local and state elections. The Cermak coalition in Illinois had all the marks of a political dynasty. It reached into all segments of the population, including Chicago's African Americans, who in the Roosevelt era were just beginning their historic migration from the Republican Party to the Democratic Party. Cermak's appeal arose from simple ideas that everyone understood, such as repeal of Prohibition and economy in government. Cermak promised a spectacular display of the city at the upcoming 1933 Chicago World's Fair, an extravaganza dear to the hearts of the city's business and civic elite. "Now he was truly boss of Chicago and Illinois," wrote Cermak biographer Gottfried. "Not only were Republicans completely demoralized but there was no threat of insurgency within Cermak's party. . . . Although some of the Irish leadership was still secretly unreconciled, and although a few were champing at the bit of Czech overlordship, there was little they could do."[22]

Cermak understood how to wield power. Although Henry Horner had a deep independent streak, there was no question that he was Cermak's man in the governor's mansion. Likewise, Kerner Sr. was Cermak's attorney general, despite his proud Bohemian self-reliance. Cermak's son-in-law Richey V. Graham was named president of the Illinois Senate. Horner's cabinet contained another Cermak son-in-law, Dr. Frank J. Jirka, as head of the Department of Health and Cermak ally Martin P. Durkin of the building trades union as head of the Department of Labor. Cermak plotted to get his share of federal jobs as well. He arranged a trip to Miami, Florida, in February 1933 to discuss patronage directly with the new president. If he had cared to, young Kerner could easily have obtained a place in the Cermak organization.

◆ ◆ ◆

Not everyone held an optimistic view of Chicago under Cermak and Roosevelt. To many midwesterners Roosevelt was the president from the corrupt New York City Democratic political organization known as Tammany Hall, even though New York City's Democratic leaders opposed Roosevelt's nomination in favor of Alfred E. Smith until the closing hours of the convention. To his critics Cermak intended to replicate the Tammany Hall structure in Chicago. His long-standing links to powerful saloon and liquor interests cast doubts on his independence from the crime syndicates that ran the nation's liquor-trafficking business during Prohibition.

Cermak was president of the Cook County Board when the criminal gang led by John Torrio and Al Capone operated drinking and gambling establishments virtually unfettered in such county suburbs as Cicero, Burnham, and Stickney. Cermak did nothing about gambling kingpin William R. Johnson's casino in Cermak's own West Side neighborhood. The Better Government

Association charged that Cermak had established a power-sharing agreement with organized crime. *The Nation,* a national magazine, spread the BGA view:

> This morning, with the election not yet twenty-four hours old, Chicago is already beginning to ask itself whether the price it paid to get rid of Thompson may not in the end prove too high, for the man elected in his place is A. J. Cermak, Democratic boss of Illinois and sole proprietor of a complex political machine built entirely along the lines of the Tammany organization in New York. . . . Perhaps Big Bill Thompson was as vicious as his defamers pictured him. To the practical and unprejudiced observer it appears that Chicago simply has swapped one evil for another. . . . The people of Chicago, by electing Tony Cermak, have made him the most powerful political boss in the United States today.[23]

Nonetheless, Cermak's administration eventually won praise from critics. As Chicago prepared to host a world's fair, memories of the crime and vice that had embarrassed the city at the time of the 1893 Columbian Exposition gave Cermak, his police chief, James P. Allman, and other city leaders every reason to crack down on criminal behavior. The Secret Six, the private crime-fighting force financed by the city's business interests, reported in the autumn of 1932 that "the old alliance between politics and crime, so flagrant under the former city administration, still exists and is strong," but it also declared, "There has been marked improvement in crime conditions in the city since Anton J. Cermak became mayor and James P. Allman commissioner of police."[24]

The voluminous record of organized crime activities in Chicago in the 1920s and 1930s leaves no doubt that Big Bill Thompson consorted with and was supported by the Capone gang. Evidence of illicit Cermak ties to organized crime, on the other hand, was largely circumstantial. Capone biographer Laurence Bergreen wrote, "Fueling the fear surrounding Cermak's elevation to the mayor's office was a considerable amount of ethnic prejudice and ethnic envy, for the new mayor was cut from a different cloth than William Hale Thompson. For all of his buffoonery, Big Bill came from an old, moneyed New England family, while Cermak had been born in Prague, son of a miner, and had immigrated to the United States as a child. To his opponents, a foreigner had become mayor of Chicago."[25]

Anticrime crusaders and Republican partisans needed little evidence to accuse the powerful new mayor of complicity in organized crime, and the allegations became part of Chicago's crime lore embellished liberally by journalists and reformers for years thereafter. A principal source for future authors matter-of-factly asserting Cermak's complicity in organized crime was journalist William H. Stuart's 1935 memoir of the Big Bill Thompson era, *The Twenty Incredible Years.* Stuart wrote:

The new city administration evidently had deferred any important re-adjustments in the underworld rule until after the [1932] state campaign was over. A new set-up was to be made, it had long been rumored—and report, too, had it that the new administration was going to get a new syndicate, one from New York. . . . Police Captain Allman had been made police commissioner but without direct responsibility for, or authority over, gambling. Allman was but a name, a shadow. Cermak in fact was head of the police department; he kept himself informed in phases touching gambling, liquor and other underworld branches. Mayor Cermak was a master of detail. He dealt closer with the mysterious, menacing line of the underworld than any mayor in Chicago's history. . . . It was apparent that Cermak had no conscientious aversion to the business of gambling and beer-running, yielding huge profits.[26]

Such influential writers as Virgil W. Peterson (*Barbarians in Our Midst*) and Ovid Demaris (*Captive City*) used Stuart's unattributed reporting to paint Cermak as an agent of organized crime and a symbol of an evil conspiracy between politicians and hoodlums. The characterization became embedded in law-enforcement attitudes. But Peterson, Demaris, and others failed to point out that Stuart spent his twenty "incredible years" as a writer for the staunchly Republican Hearst newspaper the *Chicago American,* where he was an unabashed publicist for William Hale Thompson.[27]

Cermak planned to rule indefinitely as Chicago's mayor and had little interest in sharing power with organized criminals. In fact, few of the hopes and fears about city hall under Mayor Cermak came to fruition: he died on March 6, 1933, in a Miami hospital. At a reception for Roosevelt in Miami's Bayfront Park on the evening of February 15, 1933, Cermak was shot by a thirty-two-year-old immigrant named Guiseppe Zangara as he attempted to kill Roosevelt. Cermak was rushed to Miami's Jackson Memorial Hospital, where his daughters held a vigil. He responded to treatment and spent days conducting city business from his hospital bed, but he never saw Chicago again. The coroner's jury ruled that Cermak died at the hand of Zangara, who was executed less than five weeks after the shooting.

Cermak's death certificate cited two causes of death: "gunshot wound of right lung (lower lobe) with atelectasis and gangrene" and "ulcerative colitis with perforation."[28] Several doctors who treated Cermak at the end later insisted that colitis, not the gunshot wound, was the cause of death, an assertion possibly designed to deflect criticism of their treatment of the bullet wound.[29] But it was too late to save Zangara, and Cermak was mourned as the "martyred mayor." Later considerable debate erupted over whether Cermak had in fact been Zangara's intended victim. Zangara could have been hired by the Capone organization in the wake of the Frank Nitti shooting, some journalists speculated. Nevertheless, Cermak is remembered in most history books as the man who took a bullet intended for Roosevelt.

A quotation that became legendary had Cermak telling Roosevelt shortly after the attack, "I am glad it was me instead of you." The remark was relayed to the world by Hearst newspaper reporter John Dienhart, who had covered Cermak for years, and later etched on Cermak's tombstone. Veteran Chicago news editor A. A. Dornfeld recalled in his memoir: "Everyone else who was near Cermak that day in Miami swore that Cermak had said, 'Where the hell was that goddam bodyguard.' But it was Dienhart's version that went out over the news wires and into the history books."[30]

◆ ◆ ◆

Cermak's death had a significant impact on the Kerner household. The man who had slated Kerner Sr. to various political posts and might have sponsored Kerner Jr. was gone. Kerner Sr.'s interest in politics became even more remote, but a new attachment to the Cermak name soon developed. When news broke of the shooting in Miami, Helena, the youngest and most politically savvy of the three Cermak daughters, was traveling by car with a friend to Florida to tell her father about her breakup with Floyd Kenlay, who had never accepted her primary devotion to her father. Four months after Cermak was buried in a classic Chicago-style funeral, Helena filed for divorce, accusing Kenlay of "repeated and extreme cruelty" and citing two beatings earlier that year.[31] According to family members one attack permanently impaired her hearing.

A year later Helena and Otto Kerner Jr. were married. They had known each other for many years, but Helena—called Helen by Kerner and his family—was more than two years older. Despite the political tie, the families never were close. The notion circulated in the newspapers of two prominent Bohemian political families forming an alliance was fanciful. After her stormy years with Kenlay, however, Helena saw in Kerner the stability and dedication she so admired in her father. She undoubtedly realized that Kerner would be a better father for her daughter, Mary Alyce. The recorded recollections of Otto's mother and interviews with Otto's younger sister May indicate that the Kerner family was not enthusiastic about the prospect of this marriage. Rose initially feared that Helena was after Otto's money and took pains to assure her there was no fortune in the Kerner household.[32] Helena by then was a heavy social drinker, behavior abhorred by the austere Kerners, and may already have been afflicted with alcoholism.

Kerner Jr. and Helena were married on October 20, 1934, by a Congregational minister in the lakeside Cermak family compound in Antioch, a village north of the city near the Wisconsin border. George Rogers was Kerner's best man. Afterward Rose attempted to make the best of it. "Everywhere I go, people seem pleased to know of your marriage," she wrote to Helena shortly after the wedding. "Of course, they'd say nice things to us, but I'm sure most of them mean it. Many have a . . . political career all planned for Otto—they work fast."[33] In 1940, on Kerner's thirty-second birthday, she wrote to him: "Time and events have made me gladder than ever that it was Helen you married. She has many strengthening influences over you and the experiences you have had must endear you to each other and cause you to have deep understanding of things and appreciation of each other."[34]

For his part, Kerner Sr. chose to view the marriage in terms of ethnic pride. "When my son married the daughter of Cermak, I was very pleased," he wrote in an autobiographical sketch many years later. He added, "I need not suggest that more reasons tha[n] that she was of Czech descent supported my pleasure in this regard. When my daughter Rose married a person of German descent, I was a little upset. Yet this upset was only of a temporary nature and I assign the past as the probable reason for this reaction. Later another daughter [May] married a person of Scotch-Irish descent. This time I suffered no upset whatever."[35] The couple was childless, although Otto adopted Mary Alyce as his daughter, apparently the result of a bargain struck with Kenlay in return for his relief from alimony and child-support payments.

If Helena imagined her new husband taking up the Cermak political mantle, she was mistaken. Kerner completed law school with distinction, being named to the board of editors of the school's law review, and then entered private practice. For a while the couple lived in the Cermak home on South Millard Avenue in Lawndale. They were active in the Young Democrats organization, but Kerner did not seek and apparently was not offered a place in the Kelly-Nash Democratic regime that succeeded Cermak. Cook County Democratic chairman Patrick A. Nash saw to it that the city council chose an Irish Catholic public official from Bridgeport, Edward J. Kelly, to be mayor, thereby restoring Irish rule over county Democrats.

The Kelly-Nash organization did not dismantle the ethnic coalition Cermak had been building. On the contrary, Kelly expanded it with relatively progressive policies toward Chicago's growing African American population. The Cook County Democratic organization provided structure and opportunity to many young men in Chicago. Obtaining a job with the city, county, or state in return for service to the party at the precinct or ward level was an attractive alternative during the depression years. The party, through various units of government, became the largest single employer of black residents on Chicago's South Side.

Affiliation with the organization meant more than a living wage. It meant membership in the most important club functioning in Chicago's working-class neighborhoods. The party's foot soldiers traded their fealty for the chance to rub shoulders with power brokers and maybe even rise in the ranks. Richard J. Daley followed that path. In the first of many legendary political maneuvers, he ran for the Illinois General Assembly as a Republican write-in candidate after the slated candidate died. He switched parties after he took office.

Surely a place in the organization could have been found for a young lawyer who was the son of the state's highly respected attorney general and husband of the martyred mayor's youngest daughter. But Kerner Jr., aware of the burdens that attended his father's entry into politics and mindful of his mother's scorn toward the profession, chose a different path.

✦ ✦ ✦

Kerner's enlistment in the Black Horse Troop represented more than social climbing. He was a competent horseman but had no affinity for horses or the sport of kings. Law school classmate Redmond recalled taking Kerner to a racetrack and finding him totally unaware of the rules and strategies of wagering.[36] More to the point, horses had lost their role in combat, except as beasts of burden. Cavalry units were being replaced by mechanized artillery units. After two years of his three-year stint with the 106th Cavalry, Private Kerner requested a transfer to the headquarters battery of the Fifty-eighth Field Artillery Brigade, "the reason for the . . . transfer being the desire to become informed in the types and uses of military pieces."[37] In 1937 Kerner reenlisted for a full three-year stint with the artillery unit. He was promoted to corporal and then to second lieutenant and was assigned as aide to the unit's commanding general, Samuel T. Lawton.

Lawton, a prominent Chicago lawyer and distinguished veteran of the Great War in Europe, was the same age as Otto's father. He exerted a strong influence on the young man. In 1940 Governor Henry Horner ousted Kelly loyalist Roy Keehn as head of the Illinois National Guard and appointed Lawton. Kerner was Lawton's aide from May 1937 until January 1941. "I have always felt that my interest in the military really began at the time I served under you in the Headquarters Battery of the Old 58th Brigade," Kerner wrote to Lawton in 1947.[38]

The Illinois National Guard, like its counterparts in other states, was a hybrid of state and federal authority. It was staffed and manned at the state level and available to governors for duty in the event of natural disasters or civil unrest, including floods, race riots, and labor strikes. But the units were part of the federal military structure and could be called up by the War Department. In peacetime guard units conducted weekly training exercises at armories throughout the state and engaged in annual summer camps. The guard provided a change of pace for many businessmen and professionals as well as an important network of social, business, and political contacts. Its officers were often chosen on the basis of prominence in those networks rather than proven military leadership ability. Kerner thrived in the guard the way others thrived in the Democratic Party. "I made military life a special plane of existence," he told an interviewer years later.[39]

In 1941, 12,000 men of the Thirty-third Division, which was the Illinois National Guard, mobilized as part of Roosevelt's effort to enlarge America's military power even though he had no authority to send troops against Hitler's advances in Europe. Lawton, Kerner, and the rest of the division traveled to Camp Forrest, Tennessee, a mud-soaked, thoroughly inadequate army installation that had just been named in honor of the Confederate cavalry general and slave owner Nathan Bedford Forrest. Lawton protested the name, saying it was offensive to soldiers from the Land of Lincoln. But the Camp Forrest name stood, and the Thirty-third Division coped with the name and the mud.

In the period before the Japanese attacked Pearl Harbor on December 7, 1941, Roosevelt's military buildup drew considerable opposition. Isolationism ran deep, especially in the Midwest. Robert R. McCormick's *Chicago Tribune,* the region's most influential newspaper, inveighed almost daily against U.S. involvement in Europe's struggle against Hitler. Few Chicagoans turned out to express their support when the Thirty-third Division left for Camp Forrest in March 1941. When the division returned to celebrate Armistice Day and paraded down Michigan Avenue, it met only a lukewarm public reception. The substitution of motorized vehicles for the flashier mounted horses and horse-drawn equipment was not the only factor in the muted public reaction to the parade. Several peace protesters demonstrated. Training and marching in a military unit during the months before Pearl Harbor offered none of the acclaim that a young man seeking a career in politics might desire.

As a married man with a child, Kerner would have qualified for exemption from military service. Richard J. Daley, for example, avoided military service by virtue of his family status. Several factors influenced Kerner's decision to seek active duty as the nation prepared for war. His year overseas broadened his perspective and made him sympathetic to the plight of Europeans, especially the Czechs, facing another expansionist German regime. His mother's antipathy toward politics no doubt influenced him, as it did his father, and made military service seem a more wholesome pursuit. In 1937 Governor Horner secured for the elder Kerner a lifetime appointment to the federal appeals court in Chicago. The Kerner family was officially and happily out of politics.

In 1956 Rose wrote to her son that in running for alderman and circuit court judge her late husband had always been a reluctant candidate for elective office. "You must notice that each time Dad was practically commandeered into the candidacy. . . . If ever anyone indicates that anyone did him a favor and through those favors he reached the heights he did, remember that it was Dad who did the favor. . . . The main thing for you to remember is that no one 'made' him."[40] In 1940 Horner, dying of heart disease, asked Kerner Sr. to be the Democratic candidate for governor in 1940. He declined. According to Horner biographer Littlewood, who interviewed Kerner Sr., he "told Horner, 'if I were governor it wouldn't be long until I'd be in the same condition you are,' referring to his own minor heart condition."[41] Rose Kerner's recollection expressed a similar view: "He went to Gov. Horner's room and asked his true opinion, as to how long it would be before he would be a physical wreck, and the Governor said, 'you are right, Otto, you would work yourself to death as I have done, don't do it.'"[42]

Two months after arriving at Camp Forrest, Kerner Jr. went for training at the army's artillery school at Fort Sill, Oklahoma. He returned to the Thirty-third Division but made a crucial decision shortly thereafter. In the spring after Pearl Harbor, Kerner, now a major, departed his Illinois National Guard unit to join the Thirty-fourth Field Artillery Battalion of the U.S. Army's Ninth Infantry Division. The Thirty-fourth Battalion was a regular army unit equipped with twelve 155-mm mobile howitzers, known as Big Toms, and manned by draftees and green officers from college Reserve Officer Training Corps (ROTC) units and Officers Candidate School (OCS). They were being whipped into shape at Fort Bragg, North Carolina.

Kerner's decision to join the regular army indicated that Illinois politics was not his abiding ambition. Quitting his state's National Guard unit after it had been called to active duty was the military equivalent of his father's decision to move his family out of Chicago as the Cermak ward organization was fighting for dominance in Chicago politics. Kerner sought a direct role in training men for combat. The Illinois National Guard, filled with inept political appointees, was a long way from seeing action. His mentor in the guard, Major General Lawton, had been transferred to a desk job in Washington. Raymond Stults, who had recruited Kerner into the guard's Fifty-eighth Field Artillery Brigade, died of pneumonia at Camp Forrest in January 1942. The division would not see combat until 1945, when it fought in the Philippines near the end of the war.

✦ ✦ ✦

In the lusty army town of Fort Bragg, Kerner became executive officer to the Thirty-fourth Battalion's new commander, a twenty-eight-year-old Citadel and West Point standout named William Childs Westmoreland. "Westy" was a dashing southern bachelor officer. He was everything the U.S. Army could hope to present in tackling its critical state of unreadiness. He stood ramrod straight and radiated a level of confidence that the army at this point had no right to claim. He embodied the spirit and composure of a professional fighting man. Kerner's place at the right hand of such a promising young military professional was extraordinary for someone who came to the army from the National Guard. Westmoreland was more than five years younger than Kerner, but the two shared the same rank of major. Each man benefited from the relationship, and they formed a life-long friendship.

George Connolly Jr., a Harvard graduate with ROTC training who served in the unit, recalled years later that officers from the National Guard typically were scorned by regular army officers, but Kerner was accepted as an equal. "He was quiet, firm, precise, neat in dress and appearance and cool under pressure. . . . The relationship between him and Westmoreland was ideal, the perfect commander–second-in-command relationship," Connolly recalled. "The commander who was the aggressive, perfect image of an officer desirous of ensuring that his command was training to the highest limit possible, and the second-in-command who was approachable, perhaps acting as a cushion at times between the commander and the battalion."[43]

Westmoreland demanded much from his officers and troops. He wore a fresh uniform each day and expected his officers to do the same. He had loved wearing uniforms since his days in the Boy Scouts. He regarded an officer's deportment as an essential form of communication to the troops and insisted that the message convey a positive, aggressive, can-do attitude. Kerner got to know the men under his command and demonstrated his willingness and ability to suffer each hardship imposed on them. Ernest B. Furgurson, who interviewed Kerner for his biography of Westmoreland, recounts one example: "On conditioning hikes out of Bragg, Westmoreland and Kerner would stand by the road and watch the battalion march past, then run up past the moving column, march with it a while, stop, watch it pass, run up again and finally get ahead at the end so they could review the troops as they filed past into their barracks area. The morale effect of the outfit's two senior officers dog-trotting while the men moved at route step was noticeable."[44]

In letters to Helena from Camp Forrest, Kerner had expressed typical frustration at the tedium of military life. His mood changed for the better serving in the regular army with Westmoreland: "Dearest, I spent my first days as a battalion executive, and it has been most interesting. . . . For a change I feel that it's fun to be in the army. . . . Had a conference with Major Westmoreland today. He does know his job and I think [is] very well based. I know I will enjoy working with him. It also presents many opportunities of learning command functions. This job is much better than my last, there's no comparison."[45]

During the Fort Bragg training, Westmoreland's unit was visited by a little-known senator from Missouri whose assertive demeanor in a life of public service had begun when he was a field artillery officer in the Great War in Europe. Harry S. Truman participated in a field "problem" with the Thirty-fourth Battalion's howitzers. Years later, in a letter congratulating Westmoreland, then a general, on his appointment as commander of U.S. forces in Vietnam, Truman wrote to Westmoreland: "If you will remember, that problem was presented to me in a manner that no field artilleryman could fail to make work. I was called on to fire, after another artillery officer had attained the bracket and filled in the necessary program for the purpose. All I had to do was to move the direction of the battery fifty mills and when that was done we were on target. It was a real field artillery officer's problem and those who were there were exceedingly kind to me."[46]

Operation Torch was the code name for America's initial entry into the war against Germany. Under the command of Lieutenant General Dwight D. Eisenhower, the United States landed in North Africa in November 1942. Most of the Ninth Division was there, but the Thirty-fourth Field Artillery Battalion stayed stateside until December. On Christmas Eve the brigade landed at Casablanca, in French Morocco, after a 4,000-mile sea voyage over twelve days in a former cruise ship. Disembarking and unloading their equipment under black-out conditions, the battalion—1,800 men and thirty-six 155-mm mobile howitzers—set up camp behind the Casablanca lighthouse. Kerner toured the area on Christmas Day looking for a holiday meal for the men, but he ended up with C rations "scrounged from a unit down the road."[47]

The battalion's soldiers sought refreshment among the Arab residents of the area before their unit joined the rest of the Ninth Division. Several were murdered or robbed outside the camp or made sick by Arab wine brought into the camp. Furgurson wrote that Kerner devised a solution that would have made Anton Cermak proud:

> Kerner thought the outfit could contain this trouble by taking orders for legitimate wine and letting the troops enjoy it while blowing off steam within their own camp—behind a triple guard, with the first sergeants in charge. He suggested this to Westmoreland, who at first said absolutely not, this is Army property and no alcohol is allowed. But, reminded of what already had happened despite orders to the contrary, he later listened to his executive officer's proposal that he simply busy himself elsewhere so he would not know regulations were being violated. So, for a few days wine was brought in, the troops held their own well-policed and organized drinking sessions, and then the novelty wore off and battalion life returned to normal.[48]

In mid-January Westmoreland's men, fully equipped with guns and ammunition unloaded from ships at Casablanca, joined the Ninth Division at Port Lyautey, one hundred miles to the northeast. The rest of the division had seen combat in the initial phase of Operation Torch, but Westmoreland's Thirty-fourth Battalion was still green, in more ways than one. An officer in one of the battalion's batteries cheated his fellow soldiers by exchanging dollars for French francs unfairly after a devaluation of the franc. "Major Otto Kerner discerned what the battery commander did, investigated the matter and preferred court martial charges," Westmoreland recalled years later. "The officer was tried and convicted and the soldiers got full return on the new exchange rate."[49]

Camp life ended abruptly in mid-February when Westmoreland's battalion was ordered to lead the entire division on a nearly eight-hundred-mile trek over four bitterly cold and snowy days to engage the enemy in mountainous territory 4,000 feet above sea level near Thala in Tunisia, where Field Marshal Erwin Rommel was advancing westward after having decimated U.S. and British units a few days earlier in the Kasserine Pass. Rommel's German and Italian infantry and tank forces had pushed through the pass and were poised to strike deep into Allied territory in North Africa. Eisenhower ordered the Ninth Division artillery units, under Brigadier General S. LeRoy Irwin, to aid British troops holding Rommel at Kasserine—the ground that proved to be the high-water mark of Germany's Africa campaign. On February 22, with the unit taking cover in a grove of trees, a 155-mm gun of C Battery in the Thirty-fourth Battalion fired the battalion's first shot in combat, the beginning of a three-day assault on a German Panzer division that turned the North Africa campaign in favor of the Allies. Despite little or no sleep during the long journey to the combat zone and notwithstanding persistent aerial attacks on the battalion by German Messerschmidts and Junkers, Westmoreland's battalion kept up an unrelenting attack.

"We had our first engagement with the enemy," Kerner proudly wrote to Helena a week later. "Tell Dad my birthday gift to him was the direction of our first round of the war on the evening of his birthday. We have no casualties but very interesting experience with our artillery having stopped a German breakthrough."[50]

Irwin's artillery assault convinced Rommel that the U.S. reinforcements had turned the tide on the German tank advance. Kasserine Pass, the site of Germany's initial victory in North Africa's desert and a major British humiliation, now was the beginning of Germany's retreat. "German tank formations emerged from the rocky defiles ahead of us no less than eight times, often in great numbers," Kerner recalled in a newspaper interview later. "Our guns spoke imperiously, and they withdrew each time. . . . Our . . . men played hell with the enemy, and after the eighth try he gave up and retreated south through Kasserine Pass and lit out for Gafsa, where he was beaten again. Rommel had begun his back-pedaling now."[51]

The Presidential Unit Citation awarded to the Thirty-fourth Battalion after the battle said:

> Although enemy forces were entrenched only 2,500 yards distant and there were only three platoons of friendly infantry in front of the artillery, the unit maintained constant and steady fire with such deadly effect that the enemy tank units were dispersed and driven back. The cold, determined manner in which the 34th . . . entered into battle after an almost incredible forced march contributed in great measure to the defeat of the enemy's attempt to break through the Thala defile. The gallant entry into battle and the heroism with which the volume of fire was maintained despite terrific enemy fire are in keeping with the highest traditions of American military service.

The battalion distinguished itself again in battles at El Guettar and the port city of Bizerte as Allied forces pushed Rommel out of Africa. "I, who had seen little action before Kasserine, was seeing plenty now," Kerner recalled later.[52] "Westy's instruction has done wonders of good, and the strict discipline we demand has paid great dividends—no doubt it is responsible for our not having any casualties of any sort," he wrote to his wife after the battle. "He is still the excellent officer I have always considered him to be. [I] still believe that he will go a long way if this keeps up for any length of time."[53]

By May Westmoreland's reputation as a combat leader in the Ninth Division was ascending. His battalion's next action came in Sicily, where Westmoreland, who had long desired an assignment to an airborne unit, volunteered his artillery to support an invasion near the port of Gela by the Eighty-second Airborne Division under Major General Matthew B. Ridgeway. The II Corps under command of General George S. Patton approved the transfer. Ridgeway's artillery commander, Brigadier General Maxwell D. Taylor, was impressed by the Thirty-fourth Battalion and invited Westmoreland and Kerner to dinner in mid-July. "It was the first meeting in a friendship that was to have an important influence on Westmoreland's later career," according to Furgurson.[54]

After the successful conclusion of the Sicilian campaign, Kerner earned his first individual medal. As fellow officer Leon R. Birum recalled years later, the battalion's enlisted men and officers were swimming in a cove of the Tyrrhenian Sea when one of the men ventured too far out and was being swept out to sea by the tide.[55] According to the citation of the Soldiers Medal, awarded for heroism in a noncombat situation, Kerner swam three hundred yards to the man and held him afloat until a boat could be dispatched for a rescue. "Major Kerner's prompt and courageous action was an example of heroism that reflects great credit upon himself and the Military Service and undoubtedly saved the life of the drowning man," the citation read.

Later Kerner received a Bronze Star for his service in North Africa. The citation read, "Throughout this period, Major Kerner performed his duties as Battalion Executive and Adjutant in an exceptionally meritorious manner. Displaying expert judgment and thoroughness in all his work, he supervised the administration of the Battalion competently and efficiently." These were heady days for Kerner. "Sicily is a long way from Czechoslovakia, the land of my fathers, and from Berlin, but it proved to be the first milepost on the bloody highway leading to victory," he told a reporter later in 1943.[56]

As the summer of 1943 continued, however, Kerner grew frustrated that he had not been promoted beyond the rank of major. He shared his complaint in letters to Helena, who offered support: "I know this merit system is unfair," she wrote in September. "Otherwise you would have had your promotion months ago, as you have always been so conscientious in your work, whether it was the law or the military. Why, even little me couldn't keep you from duty for even a second."[57] On the ninth anniversary of their marriage, Helena wrote: "This makes the second anniversary we will be apart. But the tenth holds more hopes, doesn't it? Honey, I must admit I love you more than I did in 1934, if that is possible. Darling, I love you very, very much."[58]

By then Kerner's absence had taken a heavy toll at home. Helena complained bitterly about feeling alone. Her relationship with Kerner's parents soured, and she frequently left Mary Alyce in the care of a domestic servant as she sought solace in parties and nightlife. Kerner tried to comfort her from afar. Writing from Fort Bragg in June 1942, he said: "Dearest, Received your very cold letter today. You know in your heart I love you, want you near and to see you at every opportunity I can get. You also know what the Army expects in the way of work. You have always said, and I know you meant it, that you wanted me to do a good job. You have been patient and have been a 'brick' about this way of life which has not been particularly to my liking. But we're apparently in it for the duration. Let's not let a misunderstanding break it up now."[59]

Rose also tried to console Helena. In an August 1943 letter she indicated the estrangement between the Kerners living in River Forest and Helena just a few miles away on Chicago's Gold Coast:

> I was very sorry to note your frame of mind Sunday. You seemed very discontented and disturbed. I don't know what I can say to relieve your nerve strain. . . . You've come along so greatly so far, I hope you will snap out of it and carry on with a stiff upper lip a little longer. It will soon be over and you still will have many years to enjoy living a normal life. These times are terribly hard for almost everyone. . . . It was Otto's choice to take the hard way to serve his country. . . . I wish we could be more helpful to you but you don't seem to want to bother us or something just doesn't click. It may be that the last couple of years and then events of the time that have made us too old and set and dull. . . . I hope you won't mind my writing like this but I know Otto would be very unhappy if he knew your state of mind.[60]

For a month near the end of 1943, as the Ninth Infantry went to England to begin preparations for what would be the Normandy invasion the following spring, Kerner returned to Chicago to take charge of his domestic situation, but without much success. In December he was reassigned to Fort Sill as a field artillery instructor, and he took Helena and Mary Alyce with him. In the summer of 1945 he shipped out again, however, this time to the Pacific theater as part of the Thirty-second Infantry Division. He served slightly more than four months with the rank of lieutenant colonel, but Helena could not accept her husband's decision to leave her for overseas duty a second time.

In October 1945 Kerner wrote from Japan: "Please, dear, don't be too upset too much about my not being home now. I will be. It was unfortunate that I came over, but let's try to make the best of it."[61] He returned to Chicago in December and left active service in March of 1946, rejoining the Thirty-third Division Illinois National Guard as a full colonel. Most men in National Guard units came home from World War II and fairly seamlessly resumed their civilian lives. The transition was not so easy for Kerner. Executing combat strategies with career military officers left a lasting impression on him and remained a defining period of his life. Military life was organized, challenging, and rewarding in a straightforward manner, like a Sousa march. Life in Chicago with Helena was nothing of the sort. He did his best to repair his marriage, but as he tried to resume his law practice, Kerner found himself still focused on military matters. Samuel Lawton was reassigned to head the Thirty-third Division and ordered to reorganize the Illinois National Guard. Kerner eagerly volunteered to help.

He was joined in the task by a clever National Guard war veteran, Theodore J. Isaacs. Now Kerner had his own executive officer, a man who seemed to display toward him the same kind of loyalty Kerner felt for Westmoreland but who was craftier than Kerner at accomplishing the tasks at hand. There was something appealingly devious about Isaacs, who was a lieutenant colonel. Combat situations had taught Kerner to appreciate unorthodox—if not necessarily crafty—means. Once in Sicily, when he was under orders to deliver some of the Thirty-fourth Battalion's trucks directly to General Maxwell Taylor, Major Kerner encountered one of Taylor's colonels blocking the road and, while brandishing a pistol, demanding to take the trucks for his regiment. As Furgurson told the story, "Kerner informed the colonel that he had a pistol himself and that General Taylor wanted the trucks and was going to get them."[62]

Isaacs and Kerner formed a bond in the Illinois National Guard that lasted the rest of Kerner's life, and Isaacs would invoke Kerner's name and reputation on many occasions.

4

The Welfare of the Child

The end of World War II left many American men, Otto Kerner Jr. among them, with an abiding sense of accomplishment and a void in their lives. The welcome-home celebrations, including the lavish reception Kerner's father held for his son in the Red Lacquer Room of Chicago's Palmer House hotel, were wonderful but brief. Soon the tedious work of rebuilding civilian lives began. Fighting men were expected to become family men, and the objectives and disciplines that brought victory to the Allies suddenly seemed out of place. The unique wartime combination of responsibility and irresponsibility was inappropriate. Career opportunities that blossomed later in the 1950s were not apparent when the troops came home.

Indeed, many economists feared the country would sink back into depression. With the government's massive war procurement machine winding down, it was a difficult matter to convert the munitions production that had sparked an economic boom in industrial cities such as Chicago into peacetime production that could employ all the men who needed jobs and wanted homes and automobiles. The end of armed conflict also exposed latent national tensions, notably within race relations. Americans, black and white, who had found employment and purpose in the war effort did not scale back their expectations when the fighting ended.

For Kerner Jr. the problem was not about fulfilling expectations but about defining them. At thirty-seven he resumed the private practice of law by joining his father's former firm, handling mostly civil cases. He spent a few hours a week working with Theodore Isaacs to reorganize the Illinois National Guard.

He lived with Helena and Mary Alyce in an exclusive East Lake Shore Drive apartment on Chicago's Gold Coast. A career in government and politics seemed no more likely than before the war. His only political job was as a Democratic poll-watcher on election days in his heavily Republican precinct. Two years after leaving active duty in the army, however, Kerner once again answered the call.

This time his commanding officer was not a rising star in the regular army reared in the South and dedicated to battlefield disciplines of honor and combat victory but a diminutive, energetic son of Chicago's West Side Jewish ghetto who was dedicated to the political disciplines of patronage and winning elections. Many veterans seeking to perpetuate the glory of the war years continued using their military rank in civilian life. Such vanity soon wore thin for most who tried it, but the military title stuck quite well to Colonel Jacob M. Arvey, the man who led the fight to rebuild the Cermak political organization. The Cook County Democratic machine, as it was known in later years, could easily have fallen victim to its own venality and to the anti–New Deal sentiment deeply embedded in the Midwest. Arvey almost single-handedly prevented the organization's demise, not only by resurrecting a vote-generating juggernaut second to none in the nation, but also by changing the face of Illinois's Democratic Party. Otto Kerner Jr., who looked as good in a white shirt and dark suit as he did in an army officer's uniform, would be part of Arvey's makeover.

✦ ✦ ✦

Jacob M. Arvey was born in 1895 in Chicago to Eastern European Jewish immigrant parents. His father, an orthodox Jew, died in an accident when Arvey was thirteen. He grew up poor on the streets of the West Side Jewish enclave. With only one year of high school, he studied law at night under William J. Lindsay, the liberal-minded lawyer who as a Cook County judge once expressed sympathy for some fraternity boys from Oak Park and River Forest High School. Arvey's mentor was Moe Rosenberg, a rough-hewn Jewish equivalent of Czech Anton Cermak. Rosenberg championed Eastern European Jews who settled in North Lawndale, just as Cermak represented Bohemians a few city blocks away in South Lawndale. Journalist Thomas Littlewood, in his biography of Henry Horner, wrote: "At Passover time Rosenberg and Arvey personally handled [sic] out matzoth, baskets of noodles, chickens and sometimes shoes from fleets of trucks. In return Rosenberg demanded votes and respect."[1]

Moe Rosenberg and his brother, Mike, had economic ties to Cermak. A major newspaper exposé of 1934, published after Moe and Mike were dead, centered on Moe's admission, under questioning by federal tax investigators, that Cermak had helped the Rosenberg Iron and Metal Company to obtain bargain-priced scrap metal from utility companies operating in the city. In return the Rosenbergs had funneled tens of thousands of dollars of their profits back to Cermak and other politicians in Cermak's coalition vying for power in the Democratic Party. John Dienhart, the Hearst newspaper reporter and Cermak confidant, explained to Cermak biographer Gottfried, "Cermak raised the money and bought the organization."[2]

Arvey was a political dynamo, standing just over five feet tall and weighing about one hundred pounds. He performed ably as a young city council ally of Cermak in the days after Otto Kerner Sr. withdrew from the council to make way for Cermak's return. "Like Cermak, Arvey and the Rosenbergs . . . smarted under what they felt were continual blows to their prestige and inadequate recognition by the Irish leadership," wrote Gottfried.[3] In an interview with political historian Milton Rakove late in his life, Arvey called Cermak "one of the most intelligent non-educated men I ever knew in my life."[4] After Cermak died, Arvey's name was mentioned for mayor, but instead he became chairman of the council's finance committee, the most powerful job in the council, under Mayor Edward Kelly. Arvey was smart, energetic, and charming, a man whose broad smile masked his sharp mind for details.

Paul H. Douglas, the University of Chicago economics professor who served with Arvey in the city council and was later elected to the U.S. Senate with Arvey's backing, called Arvey

> the ablest member of the council. . . . Arvey was . . . a fascinating man. He had come up the hard way, from the ghetto, and made his ward the strongest Democratic center in the nation. It polled some 25,000 Democratic votes at each election, to not more than a thousand Republican votes. Arvey was polished, lucid and conciliatory in manner, but underneath the surface he had a will of steel. His sympathies were basically on the side of the poor, and his acquaintance with the educated Jewish community gave him an insight into liberal movements that the average politician lacked.[5]

Arvey cemented his claim on the respect of the Cook County Democratic organization in 1936 when he went along with party leaders in their unsuccessful attempt to defeat independent-minded Governor Henry Horner's bid for a second term. Jewish voters, especially among Chicago's affluent South Side German Jews, criticized Arvey for opposing a fellow Jew, but he remained loyal to the Kelly organization. In return newspaper magnate and Kelly supporter Roy D. Keehn, the commander of the Illinois National Guard and the creator of the Black Horse Troop, gave Arvey a commission as captain in 1939. Although he was forty-four years old, Arvey wanted to fight for his country and his people against the Nazis. He became the division's judge advocate and was promoted to colonel in 1941 at muddy Camp Forrest, Tennessee.

Given the Illinois National Guard's poor state of combat readiness, Arvey never fought against the Jews' greatest enemy, but he saw combat against the Japanese in the Pacific near the end of the war. Like many U.S. fighting men in the Pacific, Arvey welcomed President Truman's decision to use atomic bombs instead of a potentially disastrous land invasion against Japan, but his appreciation of Truman lapsed when the theater of battle switched to domestic politics.

During four and a half years of active duty in the National Guard, Arvey learned the art and science of behind-the-scenes leadership. His success in politics drew heavily on that experience, which involved managing an organization so that others attained high office but he held power. He disdained the undisciplined bravado of men such as General Douglas MacArthur and admired less audacious heroes such as Dwight D. Eisenhower, whom he attempted to recruit into the Democratic Party as a presidential alternative to Truman. Arvey told Adlai E. Stevenson II biographer John Bartlow Martin: "When I was in the Army I was determined that when I went back into politics it would be on my terms—with good candidates. If I were selling beer and I wanted to sell it to Negroes, and a Negro would sell beer better, I'd hire him. If I were selling to Jews, I wouldn't send an Arab. It's the same with politics. The precinct captains have a better line to sell when they've got a good man on the ticket."[6]

Although his leadership of the Cook County Democratic organization was brief and ended in scandal, Arvey lifted the party banner and provided an unbreakable supply line of votes to a new regiment of Democratic officeholders recruited in Illinois. Adlai E. Stevenson II, Paul H. Douglas, Otto Kerner Jr., and Richard J. Daley followed Arvey's lead to become nationally recognized Illinois Democrats in the post-Roosevelt era. "I wanted to bring new blood into the party, and while I appreciated the services of the ward committeemen and old-time party stalwarts, I thought we ought to broaden the base of the party, bring new people in, especially young people, and the only way we could attract young people was by bringing new faces in," Arvey said in a 1967 oral history interview.[7]

After World War II the Democratic Party lay in disarray. Nationally the death of Franklin Roosevelt in April 1945 left the New Deal without an effective spokesperson and icon. Many voters distrusted Truman, who never escaped the taint of his association with the corrupt Pendergast political machine in Kansas City. In Chicago Mayor Kelly's scandal-ridden administration had lost favor with the voters after a dozen years. After the death of

Patrick A. Nash in 1943, Kelly also chaired the Cook County Democratic Central Committee, the assemblage of ward and township committeemen who ran the local party. But he was in poor health and spent a great deal of time outside the city. Among Kelly's greatest failings was a corrupt and incompetent city school system that the National Education Association denounced in a nationally publicized report.

As a Jew and a returning war veteran, Arvey stood aloof from the intra-party bickering among local Irish politicians. In their disarray the Irish made him chairman of the County Central Committee, but he could not prevent a major defeat for the party in local elections in 1946. Party stalwart Richard Daley, whom Kelly had convinced to quit the Illinois Senate and run for Cook County sheriff, lost to a war veteran—the only election defeat Daley ever experienced. In the wake of the 1946 losses, which the party suffered on a national level as well, Arvey vowed to reinvigorate the political organization that had meant so much to Jewish immigrants in Chicago and to Franklin Roosevelt in Washington. Columnist Mike Royko, in his biography of Daley, put it this way: "Several cuts above most ward bosses in intelligence and imagination, [Arvey] set out to save what Cermak created."[8]

The year of Arvey's rebuilding campaign, 1947, began with the death at the early age of forty-eight of another skillful organizer and political maneuverer. Al Capone had retired to Florida after his release from prison, but he remained an enduring presence in Chicago. After World War II the city was no more free of vice than it had been after World War I, when federal agent Hinton G. Clabaugh had declared Chicago safe for the soldiers coming home. Gambling, the principal illicit activity in the post-Prohibition era, thrived in Chicago and Cook County under the control of Capone protégés. When the inheritors of the Capone organization fought and won a battle to operate newswires that relayed racetrack information to bookies and gambling establishments, the shootings reminded the nation of Chicago two decades earlier.

Tolerance for wide-open vice and gangland violence reflected poorly on the city's image during the Kelly years, just as it had done during the reign of Republican mayor William Hale Thompson. The parallel between the two mayors was not lost on Chicago voters. Neither was another characteristic of the two men, the support they enjoyed among the city's African American population. In addition to crime, lax administration, and school board scandals, Kelly's tolerance toward blacks crowding in ever greater numbers into the city spelled his political doom. Roger Biles, in his biography of Richard J. Daley, wrote, "Most distressing to the South Side Irish, Kelly seemed to have fallen victim to the virus of racial egalitarianism, throwing his administration's support behind open housing and public school desegregation. Scandals of every stripe had surfaced over the years and the Democratic Party had always survived brief flurries of public indignation, but party insiders would not tolerate city hall's imprimatur of racial integration."[9]

Arvey recalled to Rakove:

> I told [Kelly] that, in my opinion, if he ran, he might win, but it would be by a scant margin as a result of what he had done when he took a stand on that Morgan Park [a Southwest Side neighborhood seeing a major influx of blacks to wartime jobs in its industrial plants] open housing controversy, where he said, "As long as I am mayor any person will be allowed to live where they want to and can afford to live." That was laudable, but we took a poll after the 1946 election and we lost the election partly because of resentment toward Mayor Kelly. The Irish and the Poles and the Bohemians were against him, and I told him so. I said, "Ed, you're being hurt by something I believe in, and I believe you were right in."[10]

Nonetheless, at Arvey's urging Kelly agreed to step down.

With Kelly discharged, Arvey emerged as the undisputed leader of the Cook County Democrats. He became the embodiment of all that local government was and was not doing on behalf of its citizenry and a lightening rod for critics and competing political interests. Arvey was called different nicknames depending on whether the speaker or writer was a supporter or detractor. To his admirers he was what he called himself, "Jack," a beloved name among the Irish. To his enemies he was the more alien-sounding "Jake." Anti-Semitism as well as race prejudice was as strong among Chicagoans, including many newspaper writers, after World War II as it was before.

After obtaining Kelly's withdrawal, Arvey needed a candidate for mayor in 1947. He selected civic-minded businessman Martin Kennelly, whose major assets were his good looks and his political distance from the Kelly organization. Kennelly, a native of the South Side Irish enclave who ran a moving and storage company, was "a white-thatched man who looked more like a pastor than a politician," wrote John Bartlow Martin.[11] He had opposed Kelly in a previous Democratic primary, but he was best known for leading the city's Red Cross chapter.

Kennelly's minimal political attributes mattered less to Arvey than the opportunity to demonstrate the effectiveness of his revitalized ward and precinct organization. Kennelly's decisive victory as a "respectable" candidate of the Democratic organization proved Arvey had done his job, and his power swelled. He kept an eye out for more such men to reshape the public face of his organization. At the same time, he paid close attention to less presentable precinct captains and patronage workers, soliciting their loyalty and rebuking their failings on behalf of the party. Arvey capitalized on the influence that only a successful vote-getter has in politics: he took a place among those shaping the ideals and strategies of the national Democratic Party, including its progressive stance on civil rights—a view quite opposite to Arvey's treatment of Kelly. What became known as the New Frontier and the Great Society under Presidents Kennedy and Johnson began with the confluence of lofty principles and pragmatic politics artfully merged by Arvey and others like him.

Arvey's reputation as a kingmaker and shrewd chairman of the Cook County Democratic Central Committee grew to legendary proportions after he selected the maverick liberal Paul Douglas to run for the U.S. Senate and the cerebral liberal Adlai Stevenson to run for Illinois governor on the 1948 ticket. Both men were supposed to lose, according to conventional wisdom. Instead, both won and went on to become icons of Illinois political history. In the spring of 1947, however, months before slating Douglas and Stevenson, Arvey made another high-tone selection for public office. He chose Otto Kerner Jr. to be the U.S. attorney in Chicago.

The U.S. attorney was a less well known, nonelected post, to be sure, but as any student of Chicago politics knows, the offices critical to local party leaders are not senator or governor but those with the power to impanel grand juries. Chicago's 1928 "Pineapple Primary," which created a public outcry that led to corruption charges against Otto Kerner Sr., proved how far incumbents in Cook County politics would go to control the post of state's attorney. The only other office in the city with grand jury power was the appointed post of U.S. attorney for the northern district of Illinois, a job filled by the president on the formal recommendation of the attorney general and the informal urging of senators in the president's party.

Since the early 1920s Chicago reformers have sought to engage the investigative and prosecutorial might of the federal government to root out local corruption. Their greatest achievement in the years before World War II came in 1927 when Vice President Dawes, a prominent Chicago civic activist, secured the appointment of George Emerson Q. Johnson as U.S. attorney in Chicago. Johnson, a product of the strict Scandinavian heritage flourishing in the rural Midwest, was an incorruptible lawyer and the right man for the job. But he is best remembered for hiring a fellow Scandinavian, Eliot Ness, to make life uncomfortable for gangland Prohibition violators. While Ness and his "Untouchables" conducted ostentatious raids on beer warehouses in Chicago and its suburbs, diligent intelligence agents from the U.S Treasury Department—Elmer I. Irey, Frank J. Wilson, and Patrick O'Rourke—quietly gathered evidence that enabled Johnson and his chief assistant, Dwight H. Green, to indict and convict Al Capone for income tax evasion.

The Capone tax case was a masterful attack by proxy on Chicago's criminal structure and a milestone in the federal government's intercession in the local affairs of a big city. The Capone prosecution convinced Chicago political leaders never again to ignore the office of U.S. attorney, but it left unscathed most officials who tolerated Capone and the organization that succeeded him. Although Green was later elected governor, Johnson displayed no political ambition and was rewarded by President Hoover with a federal judgeship. Treasury Department agents used the tax code and the techniques developed against Capone and other Chicago gangsters to nag politicians, including Kelly and Nash, but the probes did little to diminish their power. The Roosevelt administration was not likely to come down hard on the Kelly-Nash machine, which produced large numbers of Democratic votes.

In his memoir Roosevelt's secretary of interior, Chicagoan Harold L. Ickes, wrote: "Frank [Murphy, Roosevelt's attorney general] . . . said he wanted very much to clean up Chicago because he thought it was the worst mess in the country and that he hoped 'they' would let him go ahead. I found out that it was surmised that the president would not permit Murphy to go ahead with this investigation on account of Ed Kelly. . . . Murphy told me that the Department of Justice had all the goods that it needed on the Chicago crooks and apparently he is only waiting for the green light which probably will not flash."[12]

President Truman, with his tentative hold on the White House after Roosevelt died, had even less reason to offend the Chicago machine. Within the Justice Department, the Federal Bureau of Investigation under J. Edgar Hoover was far more interested in ferreting out labor organizers and communists than in attacking local political corruption. Moreover, no U.S. attorney in Chicago needed an anticorruption agenda to attract favorable headlines in the city's fiercely competitive newspapers. In the 1940s a conviction of a counterfeiter or a war profiteer garnered as much public acclaim as an investigation of gamblers and politicians on the take. U.S. attorneys had the ability to hand compelling crime stories to eager reporters. The 1939 federal Hatch Act precluded them from overt political activities, placing them ostensibly above the political fray and thereby helping to ensure coverage by newspapers across the political spectrum.

In 1947 the U.S. attorney in Chicago was J. Albert Woll, son of a prominent official of the American Federation of Labor (AFL). A native of Chicago and a six-year veteran of the Justice Department in Washington, Woll at age thirty-six had returned to Chicago to accept the post from Roosevelt in 1940. Shortly after being reappointed in 1945, Woll announced he had grown tired of government service, which on occasion required him to investigate labor leaders, including politically connected bandleader James Petrillo, on charges of labor racketeering. Postwar union organizing was akin to the communist conspiracy in the minds of many Americans, and swelling union bank accounts made organized labor an attractive target for infiltration by organized crime. Instead of following such trails, Woll joined the AFL's legal department in Washington.

Several local Democrats saw their names in the newspapers as possible successors, including Arvey's law partner, Barnet Hodes, state legislator Abraham Lincoln Marovitz, and defeated sheriff candidate Richard J. Daley. The man who most wanted the job was Stephen A. Mitchell, an energetic Democratic activist and adviser to Adlai Stevenson. But Mitchell, who saw the appointment as a springboard to his own political career, made the fatal error of promoting himself without first obtaining Arvey's blessing. Arvey said later, "If Mitchell had gone to Kelly or me it would have been all right. His credentials were good."[13] In reaction to Mitchell's disrespect, Arvey decided the post would go to anyone but Mitchell, and none of the others mentioned had much interest. Arvey told biographer Martin that he and an assistant U.S. attorney, under pressure from President Truman to come up with a name, "went back to my office and took down a Sullivan's directory [of Chicago lawyers] and started going through it. We got to the K's and found Otto Kerner."[14]

The story probably tells more about Arvey's lingering resentment toward Mitchell than about the obscurity of Kerner Jr. At the end of the war Kerner had joined Arvey's army unit in the Philippines and later played a role in the U.S. occupation of Japan. His earlier exploits in the European theater were well known to the public and to Arvey. Kerner's father, now on the federal bench, was an elder statesman of the party and represented the best the party organization could produce.

Kerner Jr. was not burdened by the pretense of Stevenson or the unpredictability of Douglas. He appeared to have no personal political agenda. He was fishing in Wisconsin when the decision about the U.S. attorney appointment was being made.[15] But his wife had inherited the political acumen and drive of her father, Anton Cermak. According to Kerner family members, Helena aggressively promoted her husband to Arvey as Arvey struggled to rebuild the Democratic machine her father had established. In the days when few women dreamed of aspiring to significant political office, Helena meant to see that her husband got one. The link between Arvey and Cermak, forged three decades earlier on Chicago's West Side, did not require searching the Sullivan's directory of lawyers as a reminder. Helena was reminder enough.

On Arvey's recommendation, President Truman received the name of a fellow artillery officer. The appointment certainly was not the result of any deep-seated ambition on Kerner's part. "I believe I was surprised as any one could be," Kerner wrote to a friend. "Even during the rumor stage there were so many names mentioned that I considered it an idle hope and made no plans concerning it."[16] To another friend he wrote, "I do feel the credit for this appointment is largely due to [Kerner Sr.] and his reputation, rather than anything I might have done."[17] To a Chicago banker and fellow Brown University alum, Kerner wrote, "The present District Attorney took part in one of the greatest freshman riots at Brown University. And that was among my lesser crimes."[18]

Kerner's virtually effortless entry into public life displayed no sign of political calculation, much less grasping for office. His war experience had made him more comfortable with himself. At the same time, home life with Helena made him—as well as his mother and father—leery about the consequences of political ambition. Cermak had worked day and night to be the champion of the drinking man, but Helena, his youngest daughter, was addicted to alcohol. This irony was not lost on Rose and Otto Kerner Sr. as their son enlisted in the second generation of the Cermak Democratic organization under Col. Arvey. Nevertheless, Arvey's charm quickly won over the handsome young lawyer. Kerner's telephone logs as U.S. attorney reveal almost daily calls from Arvey, who was grooming a man who had all the appearance of an outstanding political candidate and who was no threat to his power.

Shortly after Kerner became U.S. attorney, Arvey and the other party leaders began the process of choosing candidates for the 1948 election. Men were handicapped like racehorses in an attempt to pick winners. Joseph Sam Perry, a lawyer from suburban Wheaton and a member of the party's State Central Committee, was unable to attend the slate-making session in Springfield to choose a candidate for governor. Instead he put his thoughts in writing— something that was rarely done. "I take the liberty of making some suggestions," he wrote to the committee. Recommending that Senator Scott Lucas, though a good candidate for governor, should not be "sidetracked" from national office, Perry wrote: "The candidate should come from Cook County. The votes are there and besides they feel subconsciously that the only way that they can get proper representation is by controlling the governor's office." He added, "The candidate for governor must have a war record." Among his assessments of the contenders were these:

> Paul Douglas. Ideal candidate but needs some schooling by downstate politician who knows country voters. If Russian situation gets worse he would be still better.
>
> A. Stevenson. If he has a World War I record, O.K.—don't think his services in this war are the type to take votes from [incumbent Dwight] Green and other servicemen.
>
> Richard Daly [sic]. Short on war record, I think—maybe World War I, if so he would be good.
>
> Otto Kerner Jr. Name-color-ability-good speaker-war record-appeal to foreign elements-satisfy Catholics-Jews-Protestants.
>
> Benjamin Adamowski. Will fool you as to downstate votes he could garner— but will he stay hitched?

It is my thought that Paul Powell would be a good candidate but it might be better to reserve him for speaker or leader.[19]

In the end Arvey and the slate makers chose downstate Bloomington scion Stevenson for governor, ignoring his lack of World War II combat experience, the absence of Chicago roots, and Stevenson's thinly veiled disdain for the job. Perry's letter reveals that Daley, who had kept a low profile in the Illinois legislature during the war and had no recognized family name or important backing, was largely unknown to Democratic leaders outside Chicago at this time. On the other hand, party leaders quickly recognized the statewide appeal of Judge Kerner's son. But in a letter to Perry the young U.S. attorney demurred: "I consider your letter a great compliment and appreciate your interest," Kerner wrote. "I am, of course, very happy in my present position and hope that I may remain here. However, I am conscious of the fact that people in public life are sometimes called upon in the line of duty to present themselves to the people as a candidate. I hope this does not happen to me—certainly within the next few years—as you have no idea how much enjoyment and pleasure I am having as United States District Attorney."[20]

✦ ✦ ✦

Kerner's enjoyment and pleasure as U.S. attorney was in many respects an extension of his war service. In Chicago's classically styled federal building, which boasted a dome larger than the one atop the nation's capitol, he commanded a dozen able assistants, most of whom were fellow officers from the war. Lawrence J. Miller, a holdover from Albert Woll's tenure and an army major during the war, ran the office's criminal division, an area of the law where Kerner had virtually no experience. A man who thrived in the military culture and structure, Kerner remained active in the Illinois National Guard and joined the Chicago-area leadership of the Boy Scouts of America, the organization important to his wartime friend William Westmoreland. His assistants regarded Kerner as a supportive administrator, not a hard-charging prosecutor. He preferred being a team leader behind the scenes, but occasionally the lure of publicity led Kerner to participate in high-profile trials. He might have been better off not interrupting his comfortable schedule of golf, weekly National Guard duty, and the collegial administration of his office, for he lost his two biggest cases.

Some government lawyers seek controversy as stepping stones in a career. Others, including Kerner, have controversy thrust on them. On joining the hierarchy of the Justice Department, Kerner entered a world of intrigue he could not have anticipated. It was the world of J. Edgar Hoover, director of the Federal Bureau of Investigation. Officially the FBI was the investigative arm of the Justice Department, but unofficially it served Hoover as his personal agency. Its power and freedom from scrutiny depended on Hoover's extensive and ever-expanding files on politicians and other individuals who could threaten the bureau and its director. By 1947, as Hoover agitated for direct authority to expose communists within the federal government and elsewhere, Truman wrote that he feared a "gestapo" was in the making.[21] But like presidents before and after, Truman knew there was little he could do about it. Well on his way to fashioning himself into a national hero, Hoover was obsessed with controlling public perceptions of the FBI. No one in public life who criticized the FBI escaped Hoover's censure or ever was rehabilitated in his eyes.

Early in his tenure Kerner learned this lesson the hard way as he became one of hundreds of public figures watched and reported on by FBI agents for Hoover's files. In September 1947, shortly after Kerner was sworn into office by his father, an agent overheard Kerner agreeing with criticism of the bureau uttered by the U.S. attorney from Kansas City. Randolph Carpenter complained out loud about the slowness of FBI reports and referred to the reports as "lousy," according to Hoover's informant.[22] An FBI report on Kerner recounting the incident states, "Assistant Director [John] P. Mohr stepped up to the two just as Kerner was relating the fact that he had an impersonation case in which the impersonator traveled over virtually the entire United States and Kerner was pointing out the inadequacy of FBI reporting methods."[23]

Accounts of this trifling episode remained prominent in the many routine investigative reports written by the FBI on Kerner throughout his public life. Agents related to Hoover stories of Helena's excessive drinking, information typical of the contents of Hoover's files on public and private figures. Kerner's numerous public expressions of support for Hoover never were enough to blot out what to Hoover was an unpardonable offense—speaking ill of the FBI. After a 1948 newspaper article indicated Kerner's displeasure with FBI investigative procedures in clearing much-needed assistants for his office, Hoover wrote on an FBI field report about the article, "It looks as if we have caught Kerner off base. This is not the first time we have had to call his hand."[24]

Hoover again became annoyed with Kerner when Kerner took a personal role in a major organized crime case. In 1947 four Capone-era hoodlums— including Louis "Little New York" Campagna and Paul "The Waiter" Ricca, the apparent heir to the Capone leadership after the 1943 suicide of Frank "The Enforcer" Nitti—were paroled from the federal penitentiary in Leavenworth, Kansas, after serving barely three years of ten-year sentences for extortion in the movie industry. Investigations by the *Chicago Tribune* and other critics of the Truman administration alleged that the men won release through the influence of Truman cronies, notably Attorney General Thomas Clark.

While efforts were underway to revoke the paroles, Kerner targeted an underworld figure involved in the scandal who had a remarkable knack for staying out of jail, Anthony Joseph Accardo.

A burly former Capone bodyguard and Chicago's gangland chief after Ricca went to prison, Accardo once beat a gambling charge by telling a judge he was about to be inducted into the army. The army almost immediately declared him morally unfit for military service, and Accardo went on his way. Kerner directed a grand jury investigation of Accardo on evidence that he had made eleven illegal visits to the Leavenworth penitentiary with Chicago criminal lawyer Eugene Bernstein to discuss the parole process with Ricca and Campagna.

Accardo, whom Capone years earlier had belittled for having an easily identifiable image of a bird tattooed on the back of his right thumb, was indicted for conspiracy and for signing the name of Chicago lawyer Joseph I. Bulger to gain access to the prisoners, thereby falsifying government records and breaking prison rules against visits by persons other than family members or legal representatives of inmates. It was a minor violation of the law, but it was Kerner's chance to play in the big leagues of crime and punishment.

According to an FBI report at the time,

> The Chicago syndicate was reportedly displeased with Democratic Central Committeeman Jake Arvey's selection of Otto Kerner, Jr., for U.S. Attorney. The reason for this allegedly lay in Kerner's vigorous Grand Jury investigation which resulted in the indictment of Anthony Accardo and attorney Eugene Bernstein on charges of falsification of government records in connection with Accardo's visits to Paul Ricca at Leavenworth Penitentiary. The Syndicate believed that Kerner pushed this investigation on his own initiative rather than on orders from Attorney General Clark.[25]

Hoover also disliked Kerner's initiative, but for a different reason. An FBI report on the case states that Kerner "requested isolated and spasmodic individual items of investigation without apprising the Bureau of facts being developed by his individual grand jury investigation, thus putting the FBI in the position of being half in and half out of the case. At the Bureau's request, Assistant to the Attorney General Peyton Ford talked with Kerner who assured him he would cooperate entirely with the Bureau."[26] But Kerner persisted, according to the FBI report, to the point of asking Chicago-based FBI agents to drive him to "the farm of one of the subjects" [probably Ricca's farm in Kendall County, Illinois]. The agent in charge in Chicago, George R. McSwain, balked at Kerner's vague request.[27]

"Kerner would not tell [McSwain] the purpose of his visit to the farm or what the Agents would be expected to do, since it was 'on the Q.T.'" To this report Hoover responded in a handwritten memo: "McSwain should be commended for the way he handled this. The way Kerner acts would indicate he meticulously follows the radio program, 'Mr. Dist. Atty.'"[28]

Unfortunately for Kerner, a jury acquitted Accardo and Bernstein in November 1948 after a five-day trial before federal district judge Walter LaBuy. Accardo never testified, but Bernstein told the jury, "All that Accardo did was go to the bastille to visit a couple of friends."[29] LaBuy, a no-nonsense judge who had been a Cook County Democratic Party stalwart before his appointment to the federal bench in 1944, sent typewritten instructions into the jury room after three ballots had been taken without a verdict. The next vote was for acquittal.

Accardo soon thereafter moved from his first River Forest home, not far from the long-time residence of Kerner's parents, into a twenty-two-room walled estate elsewhere in the suburb that featured an indoor swimming pool, bowling alley, and gold-plated bathroom fixtures. Living in opulence and traveling freely around the world, Accardo taunted federal investigators with what appeared to be his immunity from the law.

Accardo's name and nicknames—"Big Tuna," for his reputed prowess at deep-sea fishing, and "Joe Batters," for his reputed viciousness in beating men with a baseball bat—took on legendary proportions in the fraternity of law-enforcement officials and crime reporters. But he never spent more than one night in police custody; his single night's stay occurred when he was picked up on Lincoln's birthday for questioning in a gambling matter and had to wait until the next day before a judge was available to release him.

Jailing the gangster who some believed (probably incorrectly) was a gunman in the St. Valentine's Day massacre would have made Kerner a civic hero on a par with George Emerson Q. Johnson, but it was not to be. Indeed, agents of the FBI and Internal Revenue Service working in Chicago never got satisfaction from Accardo. Their hunger after "the Outfit," as the post-Capone cabal was known, deepened accordingly. Hoover at this time was denying the existence of organized crime, but federal agents in Chicago believed otherwise. To them, "immunity" applied to Accardo was a dirty word, a slap in the face to their diligence and moral rectitude in maintaining the standards set by Johnson and Green of the Justice Department and Irey, Wilson, and O'Rourke of the Treasury Department, the men who jailed Al Capone.

Investigators in the 1940s and 1950s came to believe that criminals such as Accardo won their immunity from corrupt individuals in the legitimate worlds of Chicago politics and business.

✦ ✦ ✦

Kerner's most celebrated trial was not cast in the exciting and sinister glow of Capone-style gangsterism. Even more than the Accardo case, however, the indictment and trial of automobile promoter Preston T. Tucker placed Kerner in headlines as a government prosecutor directing the enormous power of the federal government against an individual. Whereas such advocacy and power held clear justification when applied against violent criminals and criminal organizations, its use against an inept, flamboyant entrepreneur and his ragtag company was a step at least to the edge of legitimate authority. Preston Tucker did not have immunity—but he did have a talent for salesmanship.

In the late 1940s Americans wanted to look forward and to move forward in automotive styles that the nation's auto industry could not supply quickly enough after years of building war materiel for European and, later, American troops. As Tucker publicist Charles T. Pearson noted in his biography of Tucker, America's auto industry was retooling from wartime production as quickly as it could. It needed more than a return to prewar assembly lines, however; it needed a car design that was distinctively new. No one wanted the car of yesterday, and there was no car of today. What Detroit sought desperately was the "car of tomorrow." Detroit "was buzzing with rumors," Pearson recalled. "Who would be the first to get back into production with a postwar dream car? What would it be like?"[30] In addition to the major prewar manufacturers, such as Ford and General Motors, several upstart entrepreneurs emerged with fresh ideas. One was a former police officer and automobile enthusiast with a robust ambition and a gift for gab.

Born in 1903 in Capac, Michigan, Preston Tucker worked briefly during Prohibition for the police department of Lincoln Park, Michigan, a small town just south of Detroit along the Escorse River that was a port of call for illegal liquor from Canada. "That two-mile stretch of riverfront along Escorse was one of the toughest areas in the whole country," fellow officer Floyd Crichton told Pearson. "It was the main port of entry for booze from Canada, and more money changed hands there in bootlegging days than anywhere else in the United States. It was a tough district and being a cop was a tough job. . . . There wasn't a damn thing [Tucker] was afraid of and he could spot a booze runner a mile off. He learned all the tricks of dirty fighting in the police and he could handle a gun. I don't think he ever started a fight, but if he had to he never hesitated."[31]

This small-town Eliot Ness took his tenacity in rousting Prohibition hoodlums and applied it to his true love, the automobile. His first idea for a design change was providing passenger compartment heat for the bulky touring cars then used by the police as well as the bootleggers they chased. Officer Tucker borrowed an acetylene torch from the Lincoln Park Department of Public Works and cut a hole through the dashboard of a police touring car to pipe in hot air from the engine. It worked, but the effort won him a demotion to foot patrol for damaging city property. In the late 1940s Tucker would be in trouble again—this time not for what he did to reshape an automobile but for failing to turn his design into reality.

Tucker made a name for himself as an automobile salesman, but he had much greater ambitions. He correctly perceived that cars with sleek, aerodynamic designs would be in heavy demand after the war and that established Detroit automakers would be slow in retooling from wartime manufacturing. He saw an opening for himself and gathered around him a group of designers and promoters—some from existing automakers and others from the less tangible world of business deal making and public relations—to form a new car company, the Tucker Corporation. An artist's sketch of a Tucker automobile concept called the "Torpedo" appeared in the national magazine *Pic* in January 1946. The article and drawing caused a sensation and made Tucker into an instant celebrity.

The sketch showed a sleek car with a rear-mounted engine, passenger doors that opened upward, bullet-like front fenders that turned independently of the body as the driver steered, and a driver's seat in the middle of three front seats. It looked like the embodiment of speed to an American car-buying public just becoming acquainted with jet propulsion. Pearson later acknowledged that the *Pic* article he authored stated falsely that the car had advanced "off the drawing board into the production stage."[32] In fact, the car never made it to the drawing board from the standpoint of engineering design. Nevertheless, widespread interest in the radical concept and Tucker's hearty assurances that he would create a new car company employing thousands gave him credibility among Washington officials and hopeful investors. One supporter was Walter Reuther, president of the United Auto Workers.

After strenuous lobbying and considerable controversy, Tucker obtained a lease from the War Assets Administration for a massive 475-acre assembly plant previously operated by Dodge on Chicago's Southwest Side. The plant had been taken over by the government and leased to the Ford Motor Company to manufacture B-29 aircraft engines. In February 1946 Tucker told an audience of Chicago business and civic leaders that he would build the largest assembly line under one roof, employing 25,000 workers to turn out 1,000 cars a day. What he actually did was sell $7 million worth of sales franchises to would-be Tucker dealers, $17 million of stock to eager investors, and $3 million worth of accessory packages to prospective Tucker automobile buyers. But he never put a car into mass production. In all, fifty cars called the "Tucker 48," which were far more conventional than the "Torpedo," were assembled by hand.

Struggling to finance his company, Tucker had several run-ins with the Securities and Exchange Commission (SEC), a Roosevelt-era agency established in the wake of the 1929 stock market crash to protect investors from fraud. By the time Otto Kerner got the case against Tucker ready for presentation to a grand jury, SEC officials in Washington had become convinced that Tucker was perpetrating a fraud on would-be dealers, prospective purchasers of his cars, and the investing public. Working with the FBI, SEC investigators put Tucker and his company under a magnifying lens. From his headquarters at the former Dodge plant, they carted off boxes of company records that revealed all sorts of questionable business practices. They collected evidence of numerous unfulfilled promotional statements about his proposed automobile.

A supposedly confidential internal SEC report on the Tucker operation was leaked to a Detroit newspaper in March 1949, severely damaging Tucker's ability to keep his company afloat. Three months later Kerner's grand jury indicted Tucker and seven associates on thirty-one counts of mail fraud, securities law violations, and conspiracy. The company was forced into bankruptcy, and the government reclaimed the former Dodge plant.

Despite the SEC's zeal, the case against Tucker was weak. In his opening statement to the jury, Kerner wisely sought to separate the formal charges from an evaluation of Tucker's automobile or his company: "The Tucker Corporation is not on trial," he said. "Whether it is a financial success or failure is not a matter to be determined in this case. It is not for us to determine whether the promised automobile was to be 'five years ahead of its time,' whether the promised engineering features were good or bad, whether it was to be 'the safest automobile in the world' or whether it would deliver thirty-five miles per gallon of gasoline. The matter to be determined by you is whether or not fraud was perpetrated by these individuals."[33] Kerner asked the jury to focus on the defendants' allegedly unsupportable claims to those who gave them money—a necessary but, it turned out, insufficient criterion for a conviction.

After a twelve-week trial with testimony from seventy-three prosecution witnesses, the defense declined to call any witnesses and rested its case. Contrary to the 1988 motion picture *Tucker*, produced by George Lucas and Francis Ford Coppola, Tucker did not address the jury at the end of the trial. Rather, it was the presiding judge, federal district judge Walter LaBuy, who had the last word. LaBuy, who earlier had instructed the government to "get to the meat" of its case,[34] told the jury that evidence of inflated product claims and shoddy business practices was not enough to convict Tucker and his associates.

> The fact that the defendants and those associated with them failed to mass-produce an automobile and accomplish what they undertook is not of itself proof of fraud. Erroneous judgment may be as consistent with good intentions as with bad intentions. You are dealing here with offenses which require specific intent. Unless there is proof that the particular defendant whose case is being considered was

acting in bad faith with intent to do wrong, he must be found not guilty. Good faith is a complete defense. In weighing the evidence as to a particular defendant, you are to view his act or his representation in light of the facts and circumstances as they appeared to him at the time he did the act or made the representation. It is one thing to look back on a transaction in the light of things that have since occurred and quite another to look at the transaction at the time it occurred.[35]

With that admonition and with virtually no evidence presented by the Kerner team showing an intent to defraud, the jury acquitted all defendants on all counts in January 1950, after just one day of deliberation. The *Chicago Tribune* reported that jurors wept and the two hundred onlookers in the courtroom erupted in "deafening, joyous confusion for nearly a half an hour."[36] Kerner thanked the jury but declined further comment. Tucker subsequently sued Kerner, Assistant U.S. Attorneys Lawrence J. Miller and Robert J. Downing, and several SEC officials for malicious prosecution. The case was thrown out of court. But Tucker and his company were ruined. After attempting unsuccessfully to restart with backing from Brazilian investors, Tucker died of cancer in 1956.

Because the Tucker investigation was instigated at high levels of the SEC, Kerner escaped criticism for losing the headline-grabbing case or bringing the charges in the first place. There is no record of Kerner commenting on the acquittal at the time or in later years, when his attitudes toward civil liberties evolved to an extent that probably would have made him less eager to engage the power of the government against another Preston Tucker.

"The government interference was monumental," Tucker's lawyer in the trial, William T. Kirby, told the *Tribune* in 1988, when the movie *Tucker* was released. "The SEC had more time to investigate Tucker than he did to build a car. When you go after someone to the extent that they did—such as asking for every possible record, relevant or not—then a crippling intent is clear."[37]

The Tucker auto plant on South Cicero Avenue was transformed into the city's largest enclosed shopping mall, called Ford City. As for Kerner, an apt footnote to the Tucker trial was Kerner's repeated objection to a defense lawyer calling him "prosecutor." Kerner insisted that was not his correct title.[38]

✦ ✦ ✦

Kerner was not destined for stardom in the role of "Mr. District Attorney," although his appearances in newsreels always brought compliments about his handsome looks. "You can step into your motion picture career if you ever tire of the law business," wrote one friend.[39] Despite his losses in the Accardo and Tucker cases, Kerner was reappointed to his post in 1951. Deputy Attorney General Peyton Ford notified Kerner of the appointment, assigning Kerner a salary of $10,750 per year.[40] The fates of Tony Accardo and Preston Tucker at the hands of federal prosecutors also mattered little to Democratic boss Jacob Arvey as he monitored Kerner's career. Kerner had not embarrassed the party through his trial work, nor had he launched any politically damaging investigations of local corruption or election fraud. Kerner remained a well-bred and well-mannered horse in Arvey's stable.

In 1950 Arvey's handicapping talent failed him. For reasons that still confound Chicago political historians, he picked Daniel A. Gilbert as the party's candidate for Cook County sheriff, an office poorly regarded by professional politicians and the one that Richard Daley had lost four years earlier. Gilbert, who was widely known as "Tubbo" Gilbert because of his size and sometimes called "Two-ball" Gilbert because of his habit of cheating at golf, began his career as a beat cop on Chicago's West Side in the early 1920s. He was an imposing, handsome policeman and later a detective with a flair for headlines and drama. He took leave from the Chicago Police Department to become right-hand man to State's Attorney Thomas Courtney during the Kelly-Nash regime. After Gilbert helped to indict small-time bootlegger Roger Touhy, Gilbert and Courtney won high praise. Chicago crime historian Richard C. Lindberg wrote, "Courtney and Gilbert were the men of the hour in Chicago. They were young, handsome men who had earned their stripes by putting away a vicious depraved kidnapper and rum-runner [Touhy]."[41]

But Gilbert, like scores of men employed in Chicago law enforcement, played on both sides of the street. He fraternized with Prohibition-era gangsters and enjoyed gambling on everything from horse races to elections. His gambling and heavy speculating in stocks and commodities earned him the newspaper label "the world's richest cop."

In 1944 the *Chicago Tribune* obtained and reproduced in its pages handwritten ledgers listing gangland payoffs to protect gambling enterprises. A payee listed as receiving one of the largest kickbacks was "Tub." "Another [individual] referred to as 'Tub' did something for which the syndicate listed him as getting $4,000," the *Tribune* reported.[42] Gilbert's boss, Courtney, was quoted in the article, grandly vowing to stamp out syndicate gambling in Cook County. But the *Tribune* failed to raise the obvious question: who was "Tub"?

In the wake of the Rica parole scandal, Tennessee Senator Estes Kefauver, attempting to build for himself a national profile for a presidential campaign, brought Senate committee hearings on organized crime and gambling to Chicago. Shortly before the November 1950 election, Gilbert testified to a closed session to answer charges of corruption being made against him by his Republican opponent for sheriff. Gilbert proved to be a candid and compelling witness. "I have been a gambler at heart all my life," Gilbert declared.

When asked by a committee lawyer whether his gambling was legal, Gilbert replied, "No, sir, it is not. Well, no, it is not legal. No."[43]

Kefauver—not unmindful of the importance of big-city Democratic machines to his presidential aspirations—had promised to sequester this and other politically sensitive testimony until after the November election. But *Chicago Sun-Times* reporter Ray Brennan obtained the transcript of Gilbert's testimony, which his newspaper published five days before the election. Gilbert was trounced by his opponent. Worse for Arvey, the tumult over Gilbert contributed to the defeat of Senator Scott W. Lucas, who as the Senate majority leader was a key Truman ally. The winner in the senate race was a verbose, long-shot Republican from the tiny downstate town of Pekin named Everett McKinley Dirksen. Gilbert got a job as security chief at Arlington Park racetrack, which was owned by long-time Democratic insider Benjamin F. Lindheimer.

"Obviously I blundered," Arvey said later.[44] He quickly stepped down as party chairman, citing his high blood pressure. He became the state's delegate to the Democratic National Committee on the death of Edward Kelly.

One Democrat who survived the public outrage over Gilbert was Richard J. Daley. After serving ably as state director of revenue under Governor Adlai Stevenson, Daley was appointed Cook County clerk on the death of the incumbent and won the office outright in 1950. Daley's victory in a bad year for Democrats locally and nationally elevated him in the party and set the stage for his election as Democratic county chairman in 1953 and mayor of Chicago in 1955. People in the party had begun spelling Daley's name correctly.

✦ ✦ ✦

If Kerner's conviction record as U.S. attorney mattered little to Arvey, so did Arvey's slate-making misstep make little difference to Kerner, who was retained in office by the incoming Republican Eisenhower administration. In the early 1950s, however, two events in his private life shook Kerner out of the well-structured and well-protected public life of a midlevel federal official and pushed him to a riskier step into the political spotlight. It was a period of redefining personal expectations for a man already in his early forties. Much of what Kerner had in life had been handed to him. In his 1947 letter to Joseph Sam Perry, he had written stiffly, "People in public life are sometimes called upon in the line of duty to present themselves to the people as a candidate. I hope this does not happen to me."[45] Now he recognized that his good fortune brought obligations to his political party as well as a chance to test his ambition.

In December 1952 Otto Kerner Sr. died of a heart attack at age sixty-eight while attending a Masonic dinner in Chicago's beautiful Edgewater Beach Hotel. Rose Kerner said later that she almost immediately began to communicate with her husband in the world of the afterlife. But Otto Kerner Jr. lost a close friend and link to old-world Bohemian values that were quickly disappearing in postwar modernism. Kerner Sr. had helped to lead Bohemian Americans in founding the independent nation of Czechoslovakia only to see it conquered by the Nazis and then by the Soviet Union. His service as Illinois attorney general was unblemished and, on several occasions, at odds with the Democratic organization in Chicago. His tenure as a federal appeals court judge reflected general support for the New Deal as well as progressive instincts in the area of civil liberties. Nonetheless, he was remembered in the newspapers primarily as a protégé of Anton Cermak.

The second event occurred in August 1953 on a country road near Milwaukee. A young man, drunk and driving at high speed, lost control of his car, which overturned, injuring himself and his three passengers. One of them, Mary Alyce Kerner, at twenty-two a woman of stunning, movie-star beauty, was injured fatally and for a month lay slowly dying in a Milwaukee hospital. Kerner's friends and associates in the U.S. attorney's office, the Chicago office of the FBI, and the Illinois National Guard donated blood for Mary Alyce, but to no avail. The driver and other passengers survived.

Mary Alyce Kerner, called "Dolly" by the family and "Mac" by her high school chums, was life itself to her mother. She attended the exclusive Latin School in Chicago, where her senior-year classmates voted her "sweetest," "best figure," and "best profile." The yearbook said she looked like a Dresden doll.[46] She was sent to various summer camps and boarding schools to limit her exposure to her mother's drinking, but the absences never diminished her mother's love. In 1947, following Helena's example, she eloped with the son of a Milwaukee furrier named Anders Christensen.

"Mary Alyce apparently didn't think much of parental consent," Kerner wrote to a former army friend.[47] By the time of the fatal accident, the couple had divorced, as her mother had done in 1933. There were two children from the marriage, five-year-old Anders III and Helena, age three. Her agonizing death was a severe shock to the family and a recurring nightmare for her mother, who fell into periods of deep depression on each anniversary of the senseless tragedy. Just as Kerner had adopted Mary Alyce as his daughter twenty years earlier, he and Helena adopted her young children. Christensen did not contest the adoptions and disappeared from the children's lives. Anders III became Anton C. Kerner and was called Tony.

Kerner at age forty-five took on the role of parent for a second time. This time there would be no overseas absences for war; there would be no surrender of the children to Helena and whatever live-in help could be hired. The Kerners at first took the children into their Astor Street apartment. Later they moved to the northern suburb of Glenview. The loss of his father, the death of Mary Alyce, and his sudden new responsibilities for two preschool children deepened Kerner's sense of privacy and might have turned him inward, away from the pressures and distractions of public life. Instead, it was at this time that friends in Chicago, including Theodore Isaacs, began to coalesce around the notion of promoting Kerner for elective office, and Kerner saw the chance to follow in his father's footsteps. When seventy-four-year-old Edmund K. Jarecki, a native of Poland and feisty Democratic ballot fixture for thirty-two years as the county judge for Cook County, decided to retire, the party slated Kerner for the job.

✦ ✦ ✦

The post of county judge in Illinois, created by the 1848 state constitution, was a catchall office for a variety of legal duties generally regarded as perfunctory, such as incorporating municipalities, appointing trustees of fire protection districts, committing mental patients to sanitariums, authorizing adoptions, and issuing judgments against delinquent real estate taxpayers. In a 1954 editorial supporting Kerner's Republican opponent, the *Chicago Tribune* declared, "The legal jurisdiction of the court isn't impressive."[48] To political professionals and civic reformers, however, the jurisdiction was enormously impressive for a single reason. The county judge of Cook County appointed boards of election commissioners and oversaw the elections in Chicago and ten suburbs. The judge thereby supervised the process by which political power in a city and county infamous for corruption was legitimized and, in the view of critics, immunized from proper accountability.

At least in his early years on the bench, Jarecki—an independent-minded jurist who sported a pince-nez and bow tie—took his responsibility for clean elections seriously.[49] One ill-fated incident demonstrated his zeal and became part of Chicago's lore. In 1924 Jarecki vowed to prevent the Capone organization from terrorizing voters in a municipal election in Cicero. The gang had moved into the working-class suburb adjacent to the city after Mayor Dever made Chicago too hot for Capone. Capone backed the Republican candidate for Cicero mayor and was not about to be overruled in his organization's new hometown. On election day Jarecki deputized seventy Chicago policemen and sent them across the Chicago border into Cicero dressed in plain clothes, armed with shotguns, and riding in unmarked automobiles. Chaos erupted. In one corner of town Capone's men shot dead a Cicero election official, and in another Jarecki's police squad literally mowed down Capone's brother Frank with bullets. Viewing the aftermath of the unprovoked hail of gunfire,

Cicero newspaper reporter Robert St. John recalled, "For the first time, I understood the newspaper cliche about a body 'riddled' with bullets."[50] The Capone-backed man won the race for mayor, and Frank's summary execution deepened Capone's intensity as a violent outlaw.

Thirty years later cries of vote fraud were a standard election-time headline as the Cook County Democratic Party's rigid discipline led many precinct workers to manufacture and buy votes to protect their jobs, even when victory was assured. The local Republican Party, whose appeal had all but evaporated, routinely lashed out with vote-fraud complaints. Jarecki drew much of the criticism, although he had clashed repeatedly with Democratic Party leaders in the 1930s and 1940s. Democratic Chairman Daley believed vote fraud was the inconsequential and predictable complaint of losers. When Jarecki finally said he would retire after eight terms, Daley worried far less about election irregularities than about finding a candidate who would appeal to the Eastern European ethnic voters Jarecki had attracted since he first ran for alderman in 1911—when Daley was nine years old.

Bohemian American Otto Kerner made an easy choice, even though he was not well known to Daley at the time. Arvey, in his capacity as elder statesman, strongly supported Kerner. At least as important to Daley as he prepared to run for mayor in 1955 was the fact that Kerner, though no political threat, appeared to have the beginnings of his own campaign organization and therefore would not be totally dependent on the party's bank account. The nucleus of the first Kerner campaign comprised men from outside the party organization: Roy D. Keehn Jr., a Kerner friend from the Black Horse Troop; Theodore J. Isaacs, the man who helped Kerner to restructure the Illinois National Guard after the war; and neighborhood newspaper publishers Michael and Leo Lerner.

All four major Chicago newspapers endorsed Kerner's Republican opponent, sixty-two-year-old William J. Mannion, citing the vote-fraud issue and the desire to put a Republican watchdog in charge of the county's election machinery. But Kerner won 994,636 to 765,757. In Daley's first test as county chairman, Democrats swept the county offices, led by Daley in his bid for reelection as county clerk. Daley established himself as an able slate maker in the closed-door sessions held in Chicago's Morrison Hotel, the center of gravity for the Cook County Democratic Party. He immediately began to prepare for his next step, the race for mayor. This time he would demand the loyalty of the Arvey organization not on behalf of any blue-ribbon candidate but for himself.

But Kerner was not thinking about a next step. Winning the post of county judge was an elixir for the man who had just lost a father and daughter and who now wanted to assert his own identity. Kerner dropped the "Jr." from his name. Political columnist John Drieske correctly sensed one aspect of the transition: "One of the principal objections to Kerner in the Democratic Party hierarchy hereabouts is that Kerner thinks that he, as County Judge, is a do-it-yourself project for which he doesn't have the party to thank. The committeemen, who have to keep the doorbell-ringing precinct captains happy, don't like this attitude one bit."[51]

Kerner did become a do-it-yourself project. He took a judicial office considered perfunctory and, building on something close to his heart, made it relevant to thousands of ordinary people, including many Democratic party bell ringers.

◆ ◆ ◆

When World War II ended, Americans wanted children as well as automobiles. In the previous decade the number of children available for adoption had increased, as families were broken up by death and separation caused by war. The supply-and-demand pressures reversed themselves in the late 1940s, however, and an international black market in babies for adoption grew in response. With newspaper ads, nights in hotels, and cash payments, adoption brokers induced unwed pregnant women, usually in their teens and without caring guidance of parents, to surrender their babies.

The children, many of whom came from Canada, like Prohibition liquor in days past, were made available at hefty prices to couples who did not ask many questions. Some young women entering hospitals to have their babies registered in the name of the would-be adoptive mother to avoid paperwork and expedite the transactions. Before the sexual revolution of the 1960s, when frank discussion of reproductive and family issues came into vogue, adoption was not a subject treated seriously in the newspapers or other public forums, especially when it involved the taboo of unwed mothers.

Concerned lawyers practicing legitimately in the field received little pay and less acclaim for their efforts. Judges in Cook County and elsewhere typically rubber-stamped adoption petitions, with hardly any inquiry regarding the interests of the natural mother and baby or the suitability of the would-be parents. Couples from outside Illinois seeking children came to Chicago because the standards of adoption proceedings were low and the number of available babies was high.

Adoption was an unpopular, largely administrative specialty that a few honest lawyers practiced more or less pro bono, subsidizing their time with other parts of their practice. Many of them had been adopted themselves or were the parents of adopted children. It was a small subculture of social service and law. No one thought to build a career or run for public office on the issue of adoption. As adoption petitions swelled after the war, however, adoption rackets became a serious abuse. Selling babies was a lucrative black market that depended on the indifference or corruption of the various courts administering adoption laws.

Edmund Jarecki said or did little about the growing problem. On a typical day in his court, as many as thirty lawyers representing would-be parents lined up in the morning and watched the judge nonchalantly sign adoption papers they put before him. He rarely interviewed adoptive parents or inquired about the intent of the natural mother. During his eight terms newspapers covered adoptions only when they involved celebrity parents. Gracie Allen and George Burns and Delores and Bob Hope found babies through a respected private agency in Evanston called the Cradle and adopted them in Jarecki's court. But black-market adoption rackets drew little interest. A three-page, single-spaced summary and tribute written anonymously about Jarecki's lengthy tenure on the bench did not even mention his responsibility for adoptions.[52]

After Kerner took office, the baby-selling racket began to receive public attention and priority. The *Chicago Tribune* in May 1955 recounted a typical story: a twenty-four-year-old woman from Kentucky, while unmarried and working as a secretary in Chicago, was impregnated by a rapist. Several social service agencies in the city refused her aid or counseling. A private doctor demanded $300 to perform an abortion, an amount the woman could not raise. Instead, "if she would give up the baby for adoption, he told her, he would pay her $30 a week until the birth, give her an additional $200 and pay medical and hospital expenses. She accepted." Shortly after the baby was born in a Chicago hospital, the doctor ushered the woman and baby into his car. "Two blocks away, they stopped at a filling station and gave the baby to someone else." The new adoptive parents, who paid $1,500 for the baby, took the child to their home in Detroit. The doctor told the woman who just surrendered her child he would pay her $500 for referrals to other women willing to give up a baby.[53]

Before Kerner took office, Chicago had become a haven for baby sellers from all over the country because there was no requirement that the child or adoptive parents be Illinois residents. The 1945 state adoption law required only that a baby be "found" in the county where an adoption petition was filed. Babies brought to Chicago for quick adoptions were said technically to be "found" in Cook County. Moreover, judges routinely waived a legal requirement that the child live with the prospective parents for at least six months before an adoption petition was filed. Amendments enacted in July 1955 at the urging of Kerner and Cook County state's attorney John Gutknecht removed the term *found* from the law and required the baby or the adoptive parent to "reside" in Illinois but set no minimum term of residency.

The amendments also prohibited anyone from accepting a fee for placing a baby with adoptive parents or with an adoption agency.

About 20 percent of the 3,000 adoption petitions that came before the county judge annually were what Kerner called "unsupervised," meaning they did not involve relatives of the natural mother as prospective parents or a licensed church-sponsored or private adoption agency. "I've heard that some adoptive parents pay $1,500, $2,000, $4,000 or $6,000," he said. "This is a business and the child is not getting the best home. Instead, it is going to the person paying the highest price."[54]

Kerner acted swiftly and unilaterally to take control of the adoption process in his court. He ordered background checks for all natural mothers and prospective adoptive parents. He refused to accept the consent of a mother giving up a baby until she was interviewed by state or county welfare officials outside the presence of lawyers and doctors. "I can block these cases simply by refusing to sign the [adoption] decree," Kerner said.[55]

He published in the *Chicago Law Bulletin* a notice to lawyers—and to fellow judges—that he would enforce the provision requiring a child to live with the would-be parents for six months before adoption proceedings could begin. Despite his misgiving about the law's stated preference for same-religion adoptions, Kerner used the language to deny adoptions he found to be unsuitable or unethical. He required child welfare agencies offering children for adoption to prove they were licensed by the state and sought to impose the licensing requirement on lawyers engaged in the adoption racket.

In one case receiving press coverage, he instructed a Chicago lawyer representing a Brooklyn couple seeking the baby of a Chicago woman to "get out of this business."[56] In another he publicly accused, though not by name, two Chicago hospital administrators of aiding in the selling of babies.[57] Kerner insisted on open, thorough court hearings concerning adoptions and often ushered would-be parents from the courtroom into his chambers for lectures on the obligations of parenthood. Lawyers seeking to avoid the rigor of Kerner's court often filed adoption petitions before other judges. "I consider that a compliment," Kerner said.[58]

With a new spotlight suddenly focused on adoption abuses, publicity-seeking Estes Kefauver once again traveled to Chicago to hold hearings. Instead of targeting crime syndicate figures, Kefauver, who had adopted two children through the Cradle in Evanston, summoned baby-selling lawyers and doctors, most of whom snubbed Kefauver and refused to appear. Kerner testified about the reforms he had implemented. "I felt it my primary duty to look out for the welfare of the child, and if the mother had signed her consent and knew of her situation, certainly the consideration of the emotion of the adoptive family was certainly secondary," he said. "Sometimes a judge sitting up there and acting on these matters practically finds himself in the position of God, to determine who shall and who shall not have children. It is a heavy responsibility. . . . A judge by insisting upon certain practices and procedures in his court can obtain, to a certain degree, what sometimes cannot be obtained by legislative effort."[59]

Chicagoans held mixed feelings about their city's worldwide reputation for gangsterism, but the stigma of baby selling magnified by the Kefauver adoption hearings was more than they would bear. Committees of the Chicago and Illinois Bar Associations, a citizens committee formed by State's Attorney Gutknecht, and a special legislative commission created under a bill introduced by state representative Paul Simon all took up the adoption crisis. The 1955 amendments to the 1945 state adoption act were not enough. "We . . . believe that the best interests of all concerned will be served by the introduction of a completely new act," said the legislative commission, reflecting the public mood.[60]

Commuting on the Skokie Valley train between Chicago and their north suburban homes, Kerner and attorney Richard L. Mandel discussed the tenets of a new law. Mandel, a lawyer who handled adoption cases in addition to his general practice, was vice chairman of the Chicago Bar Association's adoption laws committee. Once a week drafters met in Kerner's chambers to prepare a bill they would submit to the legislative commission created by Democrat Simon and chaired by Republican William C. Harris of Pontiac.

The new statute, enacted in 1959, for the first time split the formal adoption proceeding into two parts. At an initial court hearing the natural mother would give formal consent, and the investigation of the prospective parents would begin. A decree of adoption could not be issued until six months later, however, when the prospective parents would return to court for a hearing on the investigation. To end Chicago's reputation as a baby-selling haven, the new law retained the 1955 amendment outlawing fees and added a requirement that prospective parents be residents of Illinois for at least six months before petitioning for adoption.

The drafters scrapped the old law's requirement that a child live with the prospective parents for six months before an adoption petition could be made, a requirement that sometimes put a baby in an unfit home and then made it difficult to separate the child from the would-be parents. Instead the law required that the adoption petition be filed within thirty hours after the child becomes available for adoption, thereby beginning the review process quickly. The new law said a natural mother could not give consent to an adoption until at least seventy-two hours after the birth, a period during which she could experience motherhood before making her decision.

A controversial reform that pitted Kerner and the other drafters of the law against the Catholic Church was an admonition contained in the new act: "The welfare of the child shall be the prime consideration in all adoption proceedings." This seemingly innocuous statement codified a 1957 Illinois Supreme Court ruling that permitted a Presbyterian couple to adopt twin baby girls who had been baptized in the Catholic Church. The 1945 adoption law stated, "The court in entering a decree of adoption shall, whenever possible, give custody through adoption to a petitioner or petitioners of the same religious belief as that of the child." In a case closely watched by the Archdiocese of Chicago, a downstate court had upheld, under the "same-religious-belief" provision, a Catholic mother's repudiation of her consent. The Supreme Court reversed the ruling, siding with the Protestant parents.

The archdiocese's Springfield lobbyist, Claire Driscoll, prepared numerous amendments to safeguard the primacy of the same-religion preference. Kerner traveled to the capitol to lobby Driscoll in favor of inserting the sentence about the "welfare of the child" being the "prime consideration" in front of the existing language concerning "same religious belief." "Kerner went to Springfield and said he'd fight them on this," Mandel recalled nearly thirty years later. "It was his act."[61]

One of Kerner's former assistants in the U.S. attorney's office, state representative Anthony Scariano, sponsored the "welfare of the child" amendment and won approval. The final bill passed with overwhelming bipartisan support. Representative Harris came to Kerner's court to file, on behalf of himself and his wife, the first petition for an adoption under the new law.

Kerner's work on behalf of adoption reform and the visibility his court brought to the adoption process made Kerner into a popular news media figure. All four major Chicago newspapers, including the staunchly Republican *Tribune,* endorsed his bid for reelection in 1958 against Republican Charles R. Barrett. The *Sun-Times* led its endorsement with the view that Kerner "has kept his court free of the adoption scandals that have discredited similar courts in other sections of the country."[62] The *Tribune*'s endorsement emphasized the newspaper's Republican roots but bowed to the overwhelming endorsement of Kerner by the Chicago Bar Association.[63] Kerner was the biggest vote-getter in the county that year.

In addition to caring deeply about the serious campaign to reform Illinois adoption law, Kerner clearly enjoyed his role as overseer of adoptions. The press joked that as the county judge, Kerner "fathered" thousands of children a year. On one occasion proceedings in his court were halted while Kerner and a German immigrant sketched maps to confirm that they had been within five hundred yards of one another—on opposing sides—during Rommel's North Africa campaign. The two veterans became so involved in reminiscing that the

German's wife interrupted to remind them that they were in court to adopt her son by a previous marriage. "Oh, that—sure, I'll sign the adoption papers," Kerner said before he posed for photos with the happy parents.[64]

During these years Kerner also advocated popular election law reforms and began a campaign for reforming Illinois's mental health code. He cultivated the new medium of television, appearing in a series of public-service films demonstrating the mechanical voting machines that had come into widespread use throughout the county. His performance on and off the camera changed the view of many party bell ringers, who recognized Kerner as a proven vote-getter.

Apart from his official duties, Kerner quietly spearheaded a reorganization of Boy Scout districts on Chicago's South Side to eliminate an all-black district and integrate its scouts into previously all-white districts, a step taken with no publicity whatever.[65] But it was his attentive administration of adoptions that amassed for Kerner a lasting reservoir of bipartisan goodwill among ordinary residents of Cook County.

◆ ◆ ◆

Many years later one of those ordinary residents, Harold H. Harmet, was called to serve on a federal grand jury. He was not pleased by the interruption of his research work for a Chicago-based investment firm, but he served ably as the grand jury's foreman during months of on-and-off secret meetings—sometimes occurring five days a week, sometimes once a week, and sometimes not for several weeks at a time. Unlike the twelve members of a trial jury, who decide on the guilt of persons at a single trial, the twenty-three members of a grand jury, who are impaneled for a term, consider many often unrelated sets of evidence brought by prosecutors. Then they may be asked to vote whether to indict a variety of persons for crimes. One of Harmet's fellow jurors who worked for a nut-roasting company brought in samples while assistants to the U.S. attorney brought in the fruits of investigations for their consideration.

The most memorable, Harmet recalled, concerned a $6.8 million bank embezzlement allegedly staged by officials of a bankrupt Chicago discount store chain. U.S. Attorney William J. Bauer called it "the largest bank fraud and embezzlement in the nation's history."[66] The grand jury never got to hear from the president of the company, Louis Steinberg, who had absconded to Africa shortly after the money disappeared and was living lavishly, free from the threat of extradition. But prosecutors did manage to summon his wife and children as well as his alluring girlfriend and business associate, Yvonne Woo, a thirty-year-old divorcee whom the newspapers always described as "a Eurasian" and whom grand jurors called "the Dragon Lady."

A case involving a former governor of Illinois, Otto Kerner, and some of his associates made less of an impression. It had to do with complicated race-track stock transactions and income tax matters. Harmet recalled being annoyed by Kerner's "imperious attitude" and "ministerial tone" as a witness. But he remembered little of what Kerner said before the jury voted a nineteen-count criminal indictment against him. His clearest recollection of Kerner was from a happier time.

Harmet had married a widow whose husband had been killed in an accident. In 1956 he adopted his wife's three-year-old daughter in what was for him an unexpectedly moving ceremony before the county judge of Cook County. "This is a big responsibility," Kerner told the couple. "I can remember those words distinctly," Harmet said.[67]

5

The Shame of It

Kerner wore his judicial robe comfortably. As the decade of the 1950s ended, he enjoyed the contentment that came with professional accomplishment and a smattering of public acclaim. To this day lawyers recall the dignified temperament of Kerner's courtroom. But he was not destined, nor did he intend, to be another Edmund K. Jarecki, serving three decades as a reasonably popular judicial functionary and ethnic ballot presence for the Democratic Party. He believed he could win higher office, and many party professionals, though they held no particular fondness for Kerner, had to agree. He set his sights on the job his father had turned down twenty years earlier: governor of Illinois.

Kerner possessed proven voter appeal beyond his ethnic group. In his bid for reelection as county judge in 1958, he became the first Democratic candidate on the county ticket since Anton Cermak's victory as county board president in 1926 to carry the suburbs as well as the city. Political leaders throughout the state knew the name Otto Kerner thanks to his father's tenure as Illinois attorney general in the 1930s. "I never kid myself about that," Kerner told his son, Anton, many years later.[1] In addition, downstate judges whom Kerner invited to serve special duty for his court remembered fondly their trips to the big city and their host. They became his advocates in the clannish meetings of county Democratic organizations throughout the state.

Kerner was the state's first ready-made television candidate. His bright eyes, well-chiseled features, and resonant voice suited perfectly this increasingly potent medium for politics. He commanded no legion of beholden patronage workers. He was never a ward committeeman. "Therefore, I've never been part of the inner circle of the Democratic Party," he told his son.[2] His small group of political supporters consisted of his wife, friend and adviser Theodore J. Isaacs, publicist Richard C. Thorne, and a few political novices riding Kerner's well-tailored coattails. But the handsome Bohemian visage represented a blank page on which two larger groups—seasoned Democratic Party regulars and eager party reformers—hoped to write. After nearly a decade of Republican administrations in Springfield and Washington, Illinois Democrats—regulars and reformers—hungered for elective offices. Both wings of the party hoped Kerner would be more than a prominent name on a winning Democratic ticket in 1960; they believed he could be an instrument of their ambitions.

What they got instead was a man who followed his own, often intensely personal, public agenda. He would be a private man in the state's highest office. Daley and reformers opposed to Daley found Kerner difficult to understand, but they could easily count the votes he produced.

✦ ✦ ✦

Slate making for the 1960 election presented a critical test for Daley. In 1959 he had won a shoo-in victory for a second term as mayor of Chicago, and he seemed well ensconced in city hall. But he had yet to master his second title—chairman of the Cook County Democratic Central Committee, headquartered a few blocks away in the Morrison Hotel—and he was therefore insecure in both jobs. Being mayor was not good enough. Only the county chairman could amass the clout that Daley as mayor needed in Springfield and Washington, which explains why, after being elected mayor in 1955, Daley ignored his pledge to symbolically separate party politics from governing by resigning as the county chairman. The chairman commanded votes and dispensed spoils for an urban county growing faster in its suburban ring than at its city core. The chairman's fund-raising opportunities and slate-making powers linked Daley to the state and national Democratic Party structure, vital to city management. In turn the party chairman was expected to win offices outside city government and to carry weight on the state and national political scenes.

Republicans, once an equal party in Chicago politics, had become a virtual nullity as far as city government was concerned. As mayor, Daley had corralled freewheeling Democratic aldermen and other city officials, though many of them harbored resentments toward his deft and, in their minds, selfish grasp of city hall power. But the party chairman was measured by a broader test. Daley appreciated Arvey, although Arvey had proven vulnerable after the party's miscues in the 1950 election. But his model was Cermak, who battled for years to grab from the Irish the dual posts of mayor and party leader and never divorced the two roles. Richard Daley, the Irish heir to the Cermak organization, understood clearly the lasting contribution Cermak made in defining the role of party leader in Cook County. In a 1973 interview with Anton Kerner, Daley lauded Cermak's skills as a political organizer and builder of the countywide Democratic Party. He also recognized Cermak's ability to attract diverse ethnic groups under the party's tent, which was a principal factor in establishing the party's solid base of votes.[3]

Three decades later, with the Irish back in control, Daley had not yet achieved Cermak's power. The 1956 election, his first effort as mayor and party boss, had fallen far short—as unrewarding for Chairman Daley as the election of 1946 had been for his predecessor, Chairman Arvey. With Eisenhower even more popular than Truman had been unpopular ten years earlier, Republicans took the major state and local offices in contention that year. Governor William G. Stratton won a second term, despite a scandal centering on thievery by fellow Republican incumbent Orville Hodge, the state auditor of public accounts. In July federal and state grand juries indicted Hodge, a rising star in the GOP who had been slated for reelection, for embezzlement and forgery concerning the theft of nearly $1.3 million of public funds, an enormous sum in those days.

Whatever political benefit Democrats might have enjoyed from the Hodge scandal eroded when reporters discovered that Daley's slated candidate for governor, Cook County treasurer Herbert C. Paschen, had vacationed in Europe on money he collected from his employees through what was known as a flower fund—contributions supposedly earmarked to pay for bereavement and wedding flowers and other incidentals for an officeholder's employees and their families. Daley dumped Paschen from the ticket six weeks before the election, but Stratton narrowly defeated Paschen's replacement, Circuit Court judge Richard B. Austin. Austin, who became a federal judge, came to believe he had been set up as a sacrificial lamb by Daley.

On the national level, Adlai Stevenson's second half-hearted campaign against Eisenhower was doomed from the start. Stevenson, who opened the door to Stratton by his belated decision to run against Eisenhower in 1952, lost for a second time against the popular World War II general. Stevenson even failed to carry Chicago, the first time a Democratic presidential candidate lost the city since 1928, when the Catholic Alfred E. Smith fell to Protestant Herbert Hoover. The attempt by Stevenson's political strategist Stephen Mitchell to straddle the support of white segregationists in the South and urban blacks in the North had black voters in both areas fleeing the party in droves. Stevenson, whose civil rights views were not well formed, was slow to endorse the Supreme Court's *Brown v. Board of Education* desegregation ruling and was vague in eventually doing so. He displayed little awareness of the growing black resistance to racial discrimination.

According to Chicago political commentator Len O'Connor, Daley compounded the Stevenson debacle by pushing Senator John F. Kennedy as Stevenson's running mate at the 1956 Democratic National Convention. Daley's unsuccessful advocacy of the young Irish Catholic from Massachusetts angered anti-Catholic party regulars in the Illinois delegation and, just as important, annoyed the senator's wealthy father, Joseph P. Kennedy. The elder Kennedy did not want his plans for his oldest surviving son weighed down by the predictable Stevenson defeat. Nonetheless, Daley remained staunchly devoted to electing a Catholic president.[4]

The biggest calamity of the 1956 election, as far as Daley was concerned, was the election of Republican Benjamin S. Adamowski, a former Democrat and one-time ally of Daley in the Illinois legislature, as Cook County state's attorney. In 1955 Adamowski ran against Daley in the Democratic primary for mayor and later switched parties, still with the ambition of becoming mayor. A year later Adamowski defeated State's Attorney John Gutknecht, a credible Democrat who had helped Kerner to clean up the county's black market adoption rackets. The fiery Adamowski caused many long-time Republicans to wince, but he won not only countywide but also inside Chicago— a major embarrassment to Daley and a testament to the power of the Polish vote. Adamowski, as smart and ambitious as Daley, knew how to manage grand juries as state's attorney just as Daley knew how to manage the city council as mayor. Republicans in 1956 also won the patronage-rich county posts of clerk of the circuit court, trustees of the Metropolitan Sanitary District, recorder of deeds, and coroner.

Edmund F. Kallina Jr., in his analysis of the 1960 Cook County election *Courthouse over White House*, concluded: "In November, 1956, Daley had been party chairman for just three years and mayor for less than two. He had not yet consolidated his power, and he by no means had reached the invulnerable position that he achieved in the 1960s. A lesser fiasco in 1950 had led to the replacement of Jacob Arvey as county chairman, and Daley had to be concerned about the possibility of history repeating itself."[5]

◆ ◆ ◆

In the 1950s Illinois was a conservative, Republican state, and Governor Stratton was its superintendent. William Grant Stratton was known among his critics as "Billy the Kid," a reference to banditry in state government as well as to his youth and his relation to his politician father, William Joseph Stratton. But he excelled at the two things that mattered most in Springfield, fiscal austerity and Republican patronage. State government barely recognized the changes underway as a result of the urbanization and suburbanization of postwar Chicago, not to mention the implications of the swelling tide of African Americans moving into the state from the South. The progressive, liberal political movements found elsewhere in midwestern states were conspicuously absent in Springfield. Aside from undertaking highway construction, encouraged by the Eisenhower administration and politically connected road builders, state government entertained few public policy initiatives.

After winning statewide elective posts as congressman at large and state treasurer, Stratton easily was elected governor in 1952 at age thirty-eight, running against the Democratic lieutenant governor Sherwood Dixon. Dixon, a National Guard veteran who hailed from a town along the Rock River that bore his name (it was named after his grandfather), got a late start because Governor Stevenson did not abandon his reelection bid until the summer, when the Democratic National Convention nominated him to run for president. Popular Chicago Democrat Edward J. Barrett, who was Illinois secretary of state at the time, believed he should be the party leaders' choice for governor, and many party regulars agreed. But Stevenson held out for fellow downstater Dixon. Daley, still unsure of himself as a party leader, saw no reason to encourage a potential rival such as Barrett within his Cook County organization, so he supported Stevenson's man.

After this intraparty squabbling, the Dixon campaign did not begin until late summer, and it needed to raise money quickly. To that end a committee was formed outside the regular Democratic organization. Its treasurer was another National Guard veteran named Theodore J. Isaacs, a member of Dixon's Chicago law office. Dixon lost, but Isaacs's efforts were well-regarded by Democratic leaders.

Stratton ran an efficient administration, with a bare-bones staff, hands-on control of his departments, and generally good relations with the legislature. But Stratton's agenda for Illinois ignored the growing welfare needs of its citizens. His pragmatic, minimalist style rankled the small core of Stevenson's followers, who in Stevenson's single term as governor had tasted the power of managing a major industrial state. The professionals in Springfield disdained Stevenson's intellectual approach to governing, but his band of torchbearers in Chicago and downstate worked to keep it—and themselves—alive on the political stage. They formed the Committee on Illinois Government, a small liberal think tank that scrutinized the Stratton administration. Members included Daniel Walker, a former Stevenson aide and future Illinois governor, and several other aspiring Chicago lawyers, among them James W. Clement, James T. Otis, and Dawn Clark. "We were all Democrats, sort of excluded Democrats, but Democrats," Dawn Clark Netsch recalled in a 1992 interview.[6]

Noting the dominance of Republicans in state government for most of the century, the committee wrote a comprehensive, unprecedented position paper on state affairs called "A Democratic Challenge, 1958."

> Republican one-party rule has meant an inequitable, arbitrary and inefficient tax system; an inadequate effort toward more and better public education; the deterioration of our mental health program; the misplanning and mismanagement of our highway development; administrative weakness and poor financial management; an archaic and wasteful state and local government structure; and a low moral tone and cynicism which have been the marks of public administration under Republicans Len Small, Dwight Green and William Stratton. When it comes to tolerating Republican corruption and boodle, we Illinoisans certainly have been gracious.[7]

Joined by Paul Simon, a rare downstate progressive Democrat, the Committee on Illinois Government evolved into the Democratic Federation of Illinois, which sought to establish liberal Democratic clubs throughout the state using the Democratic club structure in California and New York as a model. In Chicago the Independent Voters of Illinois, a group formed in 1944 that became an adjunct of the national Americans for Democratic Action, similarly sought to influence statewide politics.

On a personal level Illinois liberals could not forgive Stratton for defeating one of their own, Emily Taft Douglas, to become congressman at large in 1946, in part by linking the wife of Senator Paul Douglas, a liberal, to the communist scare then rampant in the country. In 1955, although anticommunist hysteria was winding down and Wisconsin senator Joseph R. McCarthy was finished as a red-baiter, Stratton signed legislation requiring a loyalty oath of state employees. The Orville Hodge scandal and a guilty plea by top Stratton adviser William W. (Smokey) Downey on federal income tax charges provided the liberals with plenty of ammunition during Stratton's lackluster second term.

On a policy level Stevenson Democrats longed to recast state government after two decades of uninspired leadership, indifferent responses to pressing economic and social problems, and casual complicity in corruption by Springfield denizens whom veteran *Chicago Tribune* political editor George Tagge called "the money players"—politicians who literally sold their votes and influence for cash.[8]

Moreover, the Stevenson Democrats were political activists, and they wanted to reclaim a piece of the action. But they had little in the way of a following among Illinois voters or even a specific policy agenda. They were motivated abstractly by their fondness for Stevenson and Douglas, their chagrin at being excluded by the post-Arvey Chicago political machine, and their urge to reform state government. Aside from criticizing the Stratton incumbency, they mostly espoused causes that echoed national liberal concerns, matters of importance to organized labor, and issues raised by newspaper exposés. Underlying their efforts was their support for a state income tax, an idea so unpopular that few Illinois politicians dared mention it, let alone debate it openly. Ironically one lawmaker who proposed an income tax in Illinois was former state legislator Richard J. Daley, who in 1939 introduced a bill calling for a 2 percent income tax. Journalist F. Richard Ciccone wrote that Daley, in the spirit of the New Deal, proposed the tax "to protect the poor from the regressive sales tax." But by 1960 Daley realized fully the incendiary properties of an income tax and steered clear.[9]

One issue that energized reformers was the deplorable condition of the state's mental health facilities. Under Stratton's public welfare director, Otto L. Bettag, mentally impaired individuals and many persons who merely found themselves rejected by their families were warehoused in a few giant, overcrowded, and poorly staffed mental institutions that provided the single largest source of patronage jobs in state government. Journalist Thomas Littlewood, then a reporter for the *Chicago Sun-Times,* began what he later called a "nonending crusade to expose the horrible things that were going on in the mental institutions" and "to prove (Bettag) was corrupt."[10]

A statewide referendum scheduled for the 1960 general election to authorize $150 million in state bonds for mental health facilities—a measure Stratton as well as Kerner supported—focused public attention on existing conditions and raised the question of whether more money would improve those conditions or merely produce a greater patronage pie for Bettag and Stratton.

Fortunately for Democrats, by 1959 Stratton had lost favor in his own party. His tendency to keep tight controls on political and governmental affairs left many Republicans feeling excluded. His thin victory in 1956 encouraged other Republicans, notably Secretary of State Charles Carpentier, to seek greater influence. Stratton even managed to exasperate conservative downstate newspaper publishers by refusing to support the special-interest legislation they favored concerning the publication of highly profitable legal notices. Phil White, a political columnist for the *Tuscola Journal* in Tuscola, just south of Champaign, warmly endorsed Richard Nixon for president, but he spoke for many Republicans in assessing Stratton. "You can sum up the situation in Illinois like this," he wrote. "With the small bore politicians you have on the state level, you have to make a change once in a while or they'll start carrying off the state house. Stratton claims he can handle the Cook County politicians. Fooey. No one has played footsie with Mayor Daley more than Stratton."[11]

✦ ✦ ✦

With a heritage dating back to the Bohemian freethinkers of Central Europe, the Kerner family did not practice religion formally or regularly.

Kerner's mother rejected Catholicism as a young girl and later actively practiced spiritualism. Helena's mother, Mary Horejs Cermak, insisted on a Catholic upbringing for her three daughters and demanded a second wedding conducted by a priest after daughter Helena eloped with Floyd Kenlay. But Helena was not a practicing Catholic. Her father engaged in no active religious practice. In terms of congregational activities, Otto and his father followed the liturgy of the Masons. Masonic rites and collegiality, little known to people outside the organization, were for both Kerners a substitute for the traditional religious affiliations so important to Catholic and Jewish politicians.

It was ironic, therefore, that religious identities played a major role in Kerner's becoming governor. Daley, a devout and public Catholic, remained officially silent about his preference for John Kennedy for president until the first ballot at the 1960 Democratic National Convention in Los Angeles. But Daley and every other political observer knew during the slate-making process six months earlier that two Catholics at the top of the Illinois Democratic ticket would spell trouble in the fall. Of the nine or ten men, including Daley himself, mentioned as possible Democratic Party choices to oppose Stratton's bid for a third term, only Kerner was not a Catholic.

Expressing this point in the negative—not a Catholic—was important, because neither was Kerner an outgoing Protestant. The thousands of Catholic voters in Cook County, including Irish, Poles, Italians, and many Czechs, had found Kerner an acceptable ethnic candidate in 1952 and 1958 and presumably would do so again. Meanwhile voters in traditionally Protestant areas of the suburbs and downstate could comfort themselves with the fact that Kerner was not a Catholic. Former congressman Daniel D. Rostenkowski, a Daley loyalist and keen political observer, put it this way in an interview with Richard Ciccone: "We had a Roman Catholic at the top of the ticket, we had a Mason, Otto Kerner, for governor."[12]

Kerner also was not a politician in the sense of someone emerging from the vineyards of precinct work, commanding a wide base of patronage workers, or holding support within the party that could threaten Daley in Springfield. Kerner was no Adamowski, who would prove disloyal. According to the image portrayed in the news media, Kerner seemed a central-casting candidate, the neutral, good-looking, well-dressed, and well-spoken son of a popular Democrat whose clean reputation as U.S. attorney and Cook County judge helped to validate Daley's pronouncement that the Democratic organization had chosen a "blue-ribbon" slate for 1960.

Joining Kerner from Chicago were Daniel P. Ward, respected dean of the DePaul University law school and a surprise choice to oppose Adamowski for Cook County state's attorney; popular state representative William G. Clark for attorney general; and Michael J. Howlett, an Arvey protégé who had exposed the Hodge scandal, for state auditor. Downstate selections included state representative Samuel H. Shapiro of Kankakee, a leader in the fight to reform the state's mental health system, for lieutenant governor; and James R. McLaughlin from Mt. Vernon, a former professional basketball player in St. Louis and member of the State Democratic Central Committee, for the long-shot challenge to Secretary of State Charles Carpentier.

The relationship between Daley and Kerner was professional and distant. Kerner—who lived in the suburbs, had attended Ivy League and British schools, had extensive wartime experience in Europe and Japan, and counted many friends among the Gold Coast and North Shore upper-class—would never break into the small, clannish world of Chicago's mayor from Bridgeport. Kerner owed his political career not to Daley but to Arvey, with whom Kerner shared a more cosmopolitan view of public affairs and an interest in liberal causes. Years later Kerner told his son that as Democratic county chairman in 1954, Daley had sought out Kerner to run for county judge. "I didn't know much about the job," he said. "I felt I was better qualified to be probate judge [the job that launched Henry Horner's political career]. He said, no, that had been promised. I asked mother [his wife, Helena] and she said that was all right."[13]

Contemporary commentators and political historians maintained that Mayor Daley could have tolerated a third term for Stratton, who shared with him a solitary demeanor and single-minded mastery of public administration. After the 1956 election fiasco, however, county chairman Daley needed as many victories as he could get to protect himself against rivals within his own organization. Despite the journalists' consensus characterization of Kerner as a lightweight, Daley could not afford an amateur in the number-two ballot position as he turned his efforts toward his primary goals: winning Illinois' electoral votes for John Kennedy and eliminating Benjamin Adamowski. But he knew that Kerner would have a skillful man as his campaign manager.

◆ ◆ ◆

Daley rarely traveled outside Bridgeport and his city hall environs. But he beamed with pride when the world came to him. In 1959, after his sweeping victory for a second term, the world did just that. He hosted a visit by Queen Elizabeth and Prince Philip; sponsored an international trade fair; celebrated the opening of the St. Lawrence Seaway, which strengthened the trade link between Chicago and the rest of the world; and saw his favorite team, the Chicago White Sox, play in baseball's World Series.

He also hosted a lavish, eleven-day athletic spectacle, the third quadrennial Pan-American Games. The games, which the *Chicago Tribune* proclaimed to have "the greatest entry list of any international sports event ever held in the Western Hemisphere," established Chicago as a worthy contender for the Olympics.[14] Daley, a detail-oriented administrator who left little to chance, wanted the visiting 2,200 athletes to go home singing the praises of his city. To manage their accommodations in the more than ninety-degree heat of a Chicago August, Daley chose a man who had distinguished himself at logistics—Theodore J. Isaacs.

Isaacs grew up in Chicago learning to play the game. The game was chess, and his father, Lewis J. Isaacs, was an internationally recognized master. The 1926 National Chess Tournament, held in the LaSalle Hotel, was the main event of what is regarded as the Golden Year of Chicago chess. The tournament featured Lewis Isaacs playing the Hungarian national champion. The *Illinois Chess Bulletin* of May 1968, in a retrospective on 1926, described the match: "Maroczy gradually outplayed Isaacs, building up an apparently overwhelming position, but his opponent fought back hard and kept his cool. On his 30th move, Maroczy went after the enemy queen but was forced to pay too much for the lady and could only draw!"[15]

In a 1994 interview Isaacs recalled his father sitting alone in the library of their home while Ted's grandfather had the game's chessboard in front of him on the dining-room table. "Grandfather would call in his moves" as his father played entirely from memory, Isaacs said proudly. "I've seen him play three boards at one time blindfolded," Isaacs said.[16]

Lewis Isaacs was born in Lithuania. He operated his own real estate brokerage and management company at Halsted Street and Roosevelt Road on Chicago's Near West Side. In addition to being devoted to chess, he was an ardent Zionist since meeting Austrian writer Theodor Herzl, the founder of the Zionist movement, in London in 1900. His only son, Theodore, was born August 15, 1911—Otto Kerner's third birthday—and attended Northwestern University, Columbia University, and Kent College of Law.

Lewis was not pleased when Ted, at age thirty, announced he was enlisting as the nation prepared for war in 1941. But Ted shipped out to Tennessee with the Illinois National Guard, Thirty-third Division, quartermaster's office, and rose in the ranks to lieutenant colonel, a title he continued using well after hostilities ended. A pamphlet written in English and Spanish for participants in the 1959 Pan-American Games lists "Colonel Theodore J. Isaacs" as the village manager for the principal event site at the University of Chicago campus in Hyde Park.[17]

The skills Lewis Isaacs displayed at chess carried over to his son's life, though the games were different. Isaacs's talent at chess never rivaled his father's, but his task-oriented and strategic mind fit perfectly with the requirements of military logistics. "Generally, when there was a logistics problem, I got it," he recalled.[18] The series of problems Isaacs tackled in the postwar era began with the reorganization of the Illinois National Guard, a project that placed him under the command of Otto Kerner, a decorated combat officer who was elevated to brigadier general by Governor Stevenson. Isaacs and Kerner helped to reshape the statewide Thirty-third Division into a new unit drawn just from the Chicago area.

Years later Illinois political observers and members of Kerner's family wondered about the Kerner-Isaacs association. Many warm-hearted friends of Kerner as well as hard-bitten political professionals believed that Isaacs was a Rasputin- or Svengali-like character in Kerner's life who exploited his undue influence over the governor and led him astray. There can be no doubt the relationship was deep and trusting. An Internal Revenue Service investigator who questioned Kerner in 1970 about Isaacs's close involvement in Kerner's financial affairs wrote in his report of the interview: "I then asked if he (Kerner) had that kind of relationship with Isaacs and Kerner replied, 'Yes, I would have trusted him with my life, and I still would trust him with my life.'"[19]

In a 1992 interview May Carter, Kerner's sister, expressed the doubts common among Kerner's family and friends regarding Isaacs. She recalled an incident that occurred after Kerner was released from federal prison and shortly before he died. The brother and sister were shopping in a grocery store near Kerner's home in Lake Geneva, Wisconsin. "I know one of the last times I talked to Otto, after Otto was out of all this, that's when Otto and I got close. . . . I brought Ted Isaacs up to him, which I had never done before. And I said, 'Otto, I don't understand Ted Isaacs.' I said, 'What is this? Everybody is talking so against him and saying such terrible things about him and that he is the one who caused all your problems, and this and that and the other thing.' He said, 'May, Ted Isaacs is a good man.' So, I don't know; to this day, I can't understand it."[20]

Isaacs explained the basis of his friendship with Otto Kerner by relating an episode during the two men's National Guard service after World War II. Kerner and Isaacs had disagreed over the solution to a problem concerning the artillery unit, Isaacs told Anton Kerner in 1973. Isaacs did not recall the nature of the dispute, but, in typical fashion, he did recall that he was right. Isaacs told Anton that despite his superior rank, Kerner smiled and acknowledged the correctness of Isaacs's view. Isaacs said that the incident, in which Kerner complied with Isaacs's wishes, established what Isaacs called his admiration for Kerner.[21]

In July 1951 U.S. Attorney Kerner wrote to Isaacs after he joined the Chicago law firm of Dixon, Dixon, and Wynne: "Congratulations on your new association and best wishes for a successful career. I know that if you apply yourself to law as you do to your military duties there can be no question of your future."[22] Isaacs became a frequent caller and visitor to Kerner's office in the federal building.

At his 1973 trial Kerner testified that he and Isaacs became close associates after he selected Isaacs to manage his campaign for county judge in 1954 because of Isaacs's impressive work on behalf of the Sherwood Dixon campaign two years earlier. "By that time, I got to know Ted Isaacs intimately and well and had great confidence in him, not only in his integrity but in his ability," Kerner said.[23] In 1973 Kerner elaborated in a conversation tape-recorded by his son:

> As you meet people, Tony, you appraise them, and I found him to be an able fellow who was thorough in his studies in the National Guard, and because of the experience he had with Sherwood Dixon I thought he would be a good man who knew something about running a campaign, even on a county level. . . . He did a fine job as attorney for the [Chicago] Board of Election Commissioners [which was governed by Kerner as Cook County judge]. Because of some of his business experience, we set up a new process of bidding for contracts for paper and printing, things of that nature, and saved the Chicago Board literally hundreds of thousands of dollars a year.[24]

On the other hand, Isaacs was not motivated entirely by public spirit. Since his work for the Dixon campaign in 1952, Isaacs had been an effective troubleshooter for Democrats, but he had precious little to show for it. Isaacs saw others enriching themselves through the opportunities presented by service to the Democratic Party and feared that "he was letting the brass ring go by," said Abner J. Mikva, a former Democratic state legislator, congressman, and federal appeals court judge who led many reform fights in Springfield.[25] Isaacs's job as attorney to the Chicago Board of Elections under Cook County judge Kerner kept him close to movers and shakers but provided few side benefits. He had been rebuffed in a bid to join the politically connected law firm of Hyman B. Raskin, a Chicago lawyer and intimate operative for the Kennedy family in Illinois.[26]

Isaacs had another characteristic, which political scientist Milton L. Rakove mentioned during a 1973 conversation tape-recorded by Anton Kerner. "You were a pretty abrasive guy, too, Ted," Rakove told Isaacs. "You're not the most tactful, diplomatic guy I ever met."[27]

Kerner and Isaacs were never friends in the sense of enjoying social activities other than such incidentals as playing cards in the evenings at National Guard summer camps. Kerner did not have many social friends, and they were mostly people outside government and politics. Kerner's wife, who was jealous of anyone who commanded his time, disliked Isaacs. Years later Isaacs acknowledged that Helena caused difficulties for him and his wife, Lillian.[28] Political scientist and former Kerner gubernatorial aide Norton E. Long saw

Kerner in the historical role of prominent Eastern European gentiles, who frequently retained Jewish counselors for business, banking, and legal affairs. In that sense Isaacs acted for Kerner as Jewish lawyer Henry Sonnenschein had done for Anton Cermak. Sonnenschein was Cermak's secretary and intimate adviser for thirty years.[29]

As director of revenue in Governor Kerner's first cabinet, Isaacs saw no ethical dilemma in having the State of Illinois as his public client and soliciting private clients who had substantial business entanglements with the state. Respected business lobbyists in Springfield, including Joseph T. Meek of the Illinois Retail Merchants Association and Maurice Scott of the Taxpayers Federation of Illinois, lauded Isaacs's work as director of revenue. While he artfully devised ways to collect more state taxes, however, Isaacs actively represented taxpayers seeking to pay fewer taxes. His clients included Marjorie Everett, the mercurial heir to the Lindheimer horse-racing empire, whose tracks were regulated and taxed by the state almost like a public utility, and Sears, Roebuck and Company, a major state sales and property taxpayer and employer with an important voice in state affairs. None of this was illegal, despite appearances. But Isaacs was forced to resign as revenue director in 1963 after newspaper stories charged that he owned stock in a small company selling envelopes to the state.

Although he told Kerner he had merely done a favor for the company's president and was unaware the stock had been awarded to him, Isaacs was indicted by a Sangamon County grand jury in Springfield. The case was dismissed before trial by the Illinois Supreme Court, in a mind-bending ruling authored by Justice Ray I. Klingbiel. Klingbiel asserted, among other things, that Isaacs's ownership of stock in Cook County Envelope and Lithographing, Inc., did not constitute a "direct pecuniary interest" in the company's supply contracts with the state and therefore did not violate the conflict of interest law governing state officials.

Klingbiel and Roy J. Solfisburg Jr., the chief justice of the state's high court who also ruled in Isaacs's favor, later resigned in disgrace over the Isaacs affair. A special investigative commission appointed by the court and assisted by Chicago lawyer John Paul Stevens (now a justice of the U.S. Supreme Court) concluded that Isaacs had influenced the judges with offers of stock in a new bank he was organizing, Civic Center Bank in Chicago.

Isaacs, who died in 1998, spent a career in the law and public service that wove a tapestry of complex and risky gambits, befitting a chess master's son. He was an eager problem solver, always in search of a new angle, a new deal, although the result often brought him new trouble. After he and Kerner were convicted in the racetrack stock scandal, *Chicago Daily News* columnist Mike Royko dubbed him "the bungling bagman."[30] A different epigram was wo-

ven into a sampler pillow resting on the living room sofa in Isaacs's tidy suburban home twenty years later: "If all else fails, ask Grandpa." Over the years,
many people did.

✦ ✦ ✦

Daley expected Isaacs to run a respectable, independent campaign for
Kerner that would not sap the party's resources dedicated to helping John
Kennedy and Daniel Ward. To make sure, Daley arranged a June 10 breakfast meeting in the Morrison Hotel for himself, Kerner, and William S. Miller,
a flamboyant entrepreneur and member of the Illinois Racing Board since
1951. Miller, a native of Indiana, was a prosperous businessman in downstate Ottawa, Illinois. His association with Illinois politicians dated to 1938,
when he and fellow downstater Joseph E. Knight joined the successful campaign to reelect Governor Henry Horner against the opposition of the Kelly-
Nash machine. In 1948 Miller and Knight helped to elect fellow downstater
Adlai E. Stevenson in his gubernatorial race against former G-man and incumbent Republican Dwight Green. Stevenson appointed Miller to the racing board, and Stratton retained Miller in the post.

The day before their breakfast, Daley, Kerner, and Miller attended the
funeral of racetrack kingpin Benjamin S. Lindheimer. Miller was busy helping Lindheimer's adopted daughter, Marjorie Everett, sustain the near monopoly on Chicago-area horse racing that Lindheimer had built. Lindheimer
had been a friend of Otto Kerner Sr. and Henry Horner and was a long-time
supporter of Illinois Democrats. Daley asked Miller to pledge $120,000 in
U.S. Treasury securities as collateral for a bank loan to the Kerner campaign
to pay for billboard advertising. Miller, who had known Daley since the two
men worked together in the Stevenson administration, readily agreed. Years
later he told writer Hank Messick that he never knew why Daley picked him
for the financial assistance to Kerner.

"It had been a favor, nothing more, a favor a hundred men in Chicago
would have been eager to supply if asked," Messick wrote in *The Politics of
Prosecution*, a book based largely on Miller's account of the racing scandal
that resulted in Kerner's conviction. "Indeed, Miller felt a bit flattered to have
been selected."[31] Noting that those who rented billboard space to political
candidates did not extend credit, Kerner told his son, "He (Daley) . . . realized I had not had time to raise funds to pay certain bills that were going to
come due very quickly, and he asked Miller to see whether he could put up
some security so I could borrow money." When the younger Kerner asked
his father whether he had initiated this help from Daley, his father replied,
"No, he was much more sophisticated in those things than I at that time."[32]

Given Daley's pragmatic approach to solving municipal and political problems, the involvement of Miller early on in the Kerner campaign for governor—a circumstance that figured prominently in the federal indictment of Kerner and Miller more than a decade later—may have been purely coincidental. Since Kerner and Daley met only occasionally, it is not too speculative to theorize that Kerner mentioned the cash-in-advance demands of billboard operators to Daley at the Lindheimer funeral and Daley spotted a quick solution standing nearby in the person of Miller, who made no secret of his wealth and his connection with the Lindheimer estate. Later Marjorie Everett made a $45,000 cash donation to the Kerner campaign.

For his part, Kerner was confident of his statewide appeal and, in particular, his ability to overcome the characterization of being a Daley patsy. During the Democratic National Convention, when reporter Jack Brickhouse of WGN-TV in Chicago asked Kerner whether having Kennedy on the ticket would help him in his race for governor, Kerner replied sternly and, it turned out, accurately, "I will help him."[33] The Kerner campaign delivered for Daley more than the mayor could have hoped, and at virtually no cost to the party coffers. The loans collateralized by Miller's Treasury bills were repaid fully.

◆ ◆ ◆

In organizing Kerner's first campaign for governor, Isaacs studied Henry Horner's second campaign in 1938. Horner had energized young Democrats throughout the state against the Cook County organization's effort to unseat him because of his refusal to toe the organization line. Unlike Horner's campaign aides in 1938, Isaacs knew he could rely on Democratic doorbell ringers in Chicago's precincts. Outside the city, he realized, Stratton had problems in his own party. But Isaacs wanted a Horner-like groundswell of votes to counter the Republicans' historical advantage in suburban and downstate areas. To that end he planned to present Kerner as a welcome, virtually nonpartisan alternative to bleak status quo Illinois politics, much as the Horner campaign had done twenty-two years before.

As the 1960 election year began, the status quo of Illinois Democrats under Daley's rule looked particularly unappealing to suburban and downstate voters. In 1959 Cook County state's attorney Adamowski sparked headlines about bail bond corruption in Chicago's municipal court and accused employees of the city's traffic court of stealing money paid as fines. In the fall a Chicago police lieutenant was spotted accompanying crime syndicate chief Tony Accardo on a European jaunt. The most damaging story erupted just after the Democratic slate was announced in January: revelations of a burglary ring inside the Chicago police department. The case became known as the Summerdale police scandal.

Whatever upbeat publicity Daley and Chicago had enjoyed in the national press in 1959 with the queen's visit, the World Series, and the Pan-American games evaporated. Alderman Leon M. Despres, a lonely reformer in the city council, put the dirty linen before a national audience in a scathing article in *The Nation*, a liberal political journal. Recounting the police burglary ring scandal, Despres wrote: "Today, the mayor and his associates find themselves fighting for their political lives. Already some important 1960 county election contests seem lost to them; the state election is in jeopardy and even the city precincts are running scared."[34] With the zeal that typified Illinois's struggling Democratic reform movement, Despres went further, exposing for the first time in a national forum issues that would haunt Daley later in the decade:

> The city is falling behind in the war of neighborhood decay; an inefficient Building Department is failing to provide decent enforcement of a housing code so modest that it does not even meet the minimum standards set by the American Public Health Association. Without any internal checks, and with incredible confusion and a good deal of "payola," the department limps along to the great benefit of Chicago's multi-billion-dollar slum industry. . . . Residential segregation is Chicago's number one problem, yet the machine scarcely even talks about it, much less tries to solve it. . . . The Daley administration has helped Chicago become the "most residentially segregated city in America" [Despres quoted a finding of the U.S. Commission on Civil Rights].[35]

The April 12 primary presented a ripe opportunity to challenge Daley and Kerner, whom Despres called "the machine designee." True to their independent spirit, however, reformers in the Democratic Federation of Illinois, the Independent Voters of Illinois, and like-minded activists backed not one but two candidates against Kerner: Steven Mitchell, the former Stevenson aid and national Democratic party chairman whose quest for the job of U.S. attorney had so irritated Arvey in 1947, and Joseph D. Lohman, a sociology professor at the University of Chicago who had been elected Cook County sheriff in 1954 and Illinois treasurer in 1958 as what Chicagoans used to call a "respectable" candidate on the party's slate.

Kerner and Isaacs, along with most political observers, guessed correctly that the reformers were too few and too divided to pose a problem, given the Daley organization's vote strength and Kerner's statewide name recognition. Kerner received 55 percent more votes than Mitchell and Lohman combined. Taking nothing for granted, however, the Kerner campaign knew it needed to win over the reformers as well as Republicans in the November general election.

Stevenson and his political operatives and wealthy North Shore friends mostly snubbed the Kerner campaign. Stevenson noticeably absented himself from Illinois during the campaign, as he maneuvered for a federal appointment in a possible Kennedy administration. Nor could Kerner count on Kennedy's coattails. Party liberals, including many Stevenson supporters in Illinois and elsewhere, were lukewarm toward Kennedy. His charisma in campaign appearances around Illinois was dulled by deeply embedded anti-Catholic sentiment in many parts of the state and by doubts centering on his youth and elite upbringing. "I was primarily concerned about how Kennedy would do," Kerner told his son. "He was a Catholic, and there are certain areas of the state that are anti-Catholic; so, I spent an inordinate amount of time in areas where Catholics are not welcome."[36]

William G. Clark, the Democratic candidate for attorney general, recalled that Southern Illinois power broker Paul Powell, who had opposed Kennedy's nomination, came to the rescue. In stump speeches downstate Powell would remind voters of Kennedy's soon-to-be-legendary experience when the Japanese sank his patrol-torpedo boat (PT-109) in World War II. As Powell told it, Kennedy rescued a drowning sailor by grabbing the man's belt in his teeth and swimming to safety. The sailor "didn't ask Kennedy if he was a Catholic, because he'd open his mouth and he'd drown," Powell would say. When Powell asked Clark what he thought of the speech, Clark told him, "It's pretty good, but you ought to throw in some sharks." Soon afterward Kennedy was rescuing the sailor in shark-infested waters.[37]

Daley insisted that the Kerner campaign operate independently from the Kennedy campaign—a tactic Kennedy's people in Illinois never fully understood or appreciated—and from Daley's campaign to oust Adamowski in Cook County. Following the Horner strategy, Isaacs also wanted the word *independent* to dominate the Kerner message to voters. But he did not intend *independent*—whether dictated by Daley or his own instincts—to mean "irrelevant." Isaacs wanted his man to speak with authority about current public policy challenges in the state. The campaign would present Kerner as what one internal campaign memo called the "designated governor of Illinois, pushing for the needs of the state."[38]

Richard C. Thorne, the public relations agent for Judge Kerner who later became Governor Kerner's first press secretary, recalled that billboards and other images of Kerner were deliberately muted, avoiding traditional red-white-and-blue colors.[39] Journalist Littlewood remembered the "magnificent" billboards with the distinct lettering "OK" and "the candidate's exquisite facial profile, which had set many a female heart aflutter."[40] The campaign portrayed Kerner as a serious and thoughtful alternative to the normal bombast that characterized election-year politics. To develop the necessary talking points, Isaacs chose as the campaign's research director an energetic, temperamental education administrator named Marvin W. Mindes, who managed the University of Chicago's evening study program in the Loop. Chicago labor lawyer and former state representative Harold A. Katz, who was one of the men Mindes recruited, later recalled the single-minded intensity of Mindes's efforts.[41]

Mindes urged University of Chicago faculty members in Hyde Park to replicate the intellectual task force recruited in 1958 at Harvard University and the Massachusetts Institute of Technology in Cambridge, Massachusetts, to boost John Kennedy's quest for the Democratic presidential nomination. The Kennedy brain trust included Arthur M. Schlesinger Jr., John Kenneth Galbraith, and Walter W. Rostow. In June 1960 Mindes wrote to Kennedy speechwriter Theodore C. Sorenson: "On behalf of Otto Kerner, Democratic candidate for governor of Illinois, I am presently engaged in setting up the local equivalent of a 'Cambridge Group.' Judge Kerner is extremely popular here among the faculty members of the University of Chicago and other institutions, and it is from these groups that I am gathering advisors and soliciting memoranda. . . . Any suggestions concerning procedure and functioning of an advisory operation which you could supply me with would be very greatly appreciated."[42] There is no record of a reply.

The group Mindes assembled never became a Kerner brain trust or "kitchen cabinet," but it did plant intellectual seeds that helped to set Kerner apart from traditional Illinois politics for the rest of his public career. Among those submitting confidential background papers were George P. Shultz, who later became U.S. secretary of state; Arnold P. Weber, who became chancellor of Northwestern University; James Q. Wilson, who became a leading scholar in sociology; Harold Katz, who became one of Illinois's most progressive legislators; Anthony Downs of Real Estate Research Corporation, who played leading roles in economic development in Chicago and elsewhere; and reform-minded Chicago lawyer Morris Wexler, who after the 1960 general election enraged Daley when, as special investigator of vote fraud in Cook County, he accused 650 individuals, nearly all of them Democrats, of voting irregularities.

Of the research papers submitted to Mindes, two by Wilson were the most significant. The first, "Civil Rights in Illinois,"[43] was a strong indictment of current practices:

> Illinois is considered, by almost all concerned parties, to be the least advanced industrial state in the nation in the field of civil rights legislation and conditions. Fair employment practice (FEPC) laws have been enacted in 18 states. In 16 cases, these laws equip state agencies with enforcement powers. Illinois has no law of any kind on this subject. Almost all northern states have created state commissions to enforce existing civil rights legislation. The Illinois Commission on Human Relations has no enforcement powers. . . . The 20 members are appointed by the governor for two-year terms. Gov. Stratton has appointed many men who have no knowledge of or interest in civil rights. Some are known to be hostile to many civil rights programs.

Wilson described the enforcement of Illinois's law against discrimination in places of public accommodation as "a dead letter." Citing widespread illegal segregation in public schools, especially in Southern Illinois, Wilson wrote, "The withholding of state aid has not been used as a means of compelling school district compliance with the law and the 1954 ruling of the U.S. Supreme Court."

Regarding housing discrimination, Wilson was especially prescient in suggesting what a Kerner administration might do: "Most discrimination in housing will require new remedial legislation. However, it is possible that the licensing power exercised by the state over the real estate brokers can be used to eliminate the grossest discriminatory practices. This licensing is performed by the State Department of Registration and Education. The leadership of the department, appointed by the governor, has shown little inclination to use those powers."

Stating that "housing is the most acute problem in the field of race relations," Wilson described the process of racial steering by real estate speculators and lenders, which resulted in the fact that "Negroes are denied access to housing in all but 'Negro' neighborhoods." He reported that Colorado, Massachusetts, Oregon, and Connecticut had laws forbidding discrimination in the sale and rental of housing. "Such laws are known as 'open occupancy' laws," he noted. "There is no more explosive issue in Illinois politics. It is most unlikely that a state-wide open-occupancy bill could pass both Houses of the legislature, even with strong support of the governor." Instead of urging the pursuit of such legislation, Wilson advised Kerner to use the existing executive powers to attack panic peddling by realtors and discriminatory practices by mortgage lenders.

"A strong governor can place the prestige of his office behind efforts to deal with these matters from within the real estate business," he wrote. Kerner should consult privately with leaders of the real estate industry, seeking voluntary cooperation in curbing unethical sales practices and warning them "that their failure to take their leadership could leave the state with no alternative but to employ sanctions at its disposal [the licensing power] to eliminate unprincipled actions."

Wilson advised similar closed-door negotiations with mortgage lenders, leveraging the state's licensing power. To conclude, Wilson urged Kerner to name qualified black individuals to prominent state jobs.

In a second paper, titled "Campaigning in Negro Areas,"[44] Wilson recommended reliance on the Democratic organization, especially the South Side organization of Congressman William Dawson. "Attempts to by-pass or go above the organization will create some resentment and will not pay off in additional votes sufficient to offset the cost." Nevertheless, Wilson instructed the Kerner campaign on protocol in black areas. By 1960 African Americans in Chicago had awakened to the civil rights struggle in the South. Militancy had not yet developed, but sensitivity to racial issues and racial pride were high, Wilson observed. Among his pointers were these:

> Negroes are very sophisticated in detecting the precise shade of commitment to civil rights and Negro issues. Any equivocation or doubts will be quickly noted and redound to your disadvantage. It is necessary to speak with some feeling on these matters. A dispassionate analysis is best saved for university classrooms. Certain phrases should be avoided at all costs. NEVER refer to Negroes as "you people," or to whites as "my people." Make use of no phrases which imply natural distinctions. Don't speak to Negro leaders in terms of "their people" or "your people." Avoid the word "colored." The word Negro, or Negro-American, is usually preferable.

Wilson's observations and admonitions about civil rights and Illinois's growing black population represented an effort, almost certainly for the first time, to guide a white candidate for statewide office in Illinois toward acknowledging black social and political sensitivities and anticipating what in a few years would become the flowering of black assertiveness.

Kerner followed Wilson's advice about letting existing political leaders in black areas represent him to the voters. But in even more alien territory for a white Daley Democrat—the Republican suburbs—Kerner campaigned for votes directly and extensively, employing simple appeals to equity and integrity that would have played well in black neighborhoods as well as in white ones. James T. Otis, a member of the Committee on Illinois Government and a supporter of Steve Mitchell in the 1960 primary, recalled years later the handsome, well-dressed candidate snapping his shirt cuffs inside his neatly tailored suit coat and urging North Shore voters to support a fairer, broader sales tax base for Illinois. Noting that the state sales tax was not levied against the services of a tailor for "us fellows," even though the tailor's work constituted the bulk of a custom-made garment's cost, Kerner reminded his well-heeled listeners that "the fellows who buy their suits off the rack" were taxed fully on their purchase.[45]

To Stratton's charge that Kerner had too little experience to be governor, Kerner replied matter-of-factly that Stratton had too much. Republicans as well as Democrats remembered the tax-evasion indictment of Stratton aide Smokey Downey and understood Kerner's meaning. Even in heavily Republican Winnebago County, northwest of Chicago, the *Rockford Morning Star,* whose publisher had served with Kerner in the National Guard, endorsed Kerner over Stratton. Later voters in such areas would refer to themselves as "Kerner Republicans."

Another voter segment pointedly developed by Isaacs was the women's vote. Kerner had a magnetic appeal to women. In his 1973 interview with Anton Kerner, Isaacs explained that in addition to Kerner's good looks and charm, his loyalty to his ailing wife made a deep and favorable impression. Although reporters, following the custom of the time, carefully avoided mention of Helena's alcoholism, many people around the state knew she was impaired for some reason and recognized that Kerner was a supportive husband, Isaacs said. Kerner's good looks and debonair manner enabled him to have any woman he wanted, but the women of Illinois knew that Kerner was faithful to his wife, Isaacs told Anton.[46]

On election day Kerner beat Stratton by 524,252 votes—2,594,731 to 2,070,479—by far the largest plurality among statewide candidates. Kennedy carried the state by just 8,858 votes, well short of the 500,000-vote margin Daley had promised Kennedy. In voting outside Cook County Kerner beat Stratton 1,139,057 to 1,132,854. Suburban Lake County, Stratton's birthplace, immediately north of Cook County, voted 59 percent to 41 percent for Nixon but supported Kerner. Among other major counties—Will, Peoria, Tazewell, Kankakee, Macon, and Winnebago—all carried for Nixon for president and Kerner for governor.

Stratton biographer David Kenney concluded, "Richard Nixon was a victim of Stratton's insistence on running for governor in 1960."[47] Kenney reasoned that a more popular GOP candidate for governor—such as Secretary of State Charles Carpentier, the party's only statewide winner—would have not only defeated Kerner but also helped Nixon to carry Illinois. Ticket splitting by those disenchanted with Stratton clearly favored Kerner. But it is not unreasonable to speculate that Kerner's well-executed campaign as a respectable Democrat convinced at least a few thousand Republicans to give the nod to the Democratic candidate for president as well.

Nixon forever suspected the Illinois vote had been stolen for Kennedy, but no evidence has emerged that he blamed Kerner personally for his 1960 defeat, a charge frequently made by Kerner family members and friends after Kerner was indicted during the Nixon administration. Soon after the election Nixon surprised even close associates by opposing a formal challenge to the vote count in such key electoral states as Illinois and Texas. In his memoirs Nixon said he had no desire to impair the nation's global standing by throwing a cloud over Kennedy's presidency, nor did he wish to risk establishing himself as a sore loser, a characterization he was convinced would destroy his future in politics.[48] Winning Illinois would not have given Nixon a victory, and Nixon almost certainly was aware of Stratton's poor standing in the Illinois GOP.

In any case, Kerner's landslide victory greatly aided Daley, especially in the

Cook County suburbs. Kerner, while purposefully emphasizing his independence from the Daley organization, captured 1,455,674 votes in Cook County.
Daniel Ward, aided by as much pressure as Daley could apply to his
organization's precinct workers, received 1,205,553 votes in beating Adamowski. Like Kennedy, Ward benefited greatly from Kerner's presence on the
ballot. Illinois Republicans, who for years had sought to retain control of state
government in part by demonizing the Cook County Democratic organization, were shaken deeply when a product of that organization beat them in
their strongholds, especially the emerging suburban counties surrounding
Chicago. In addition, Daley's hopes for a relatively cheap gubernatorial campaign were realized, for Kerner's campaign under Isaacs's leadership spent just
$475,000 statewide to bring thousands of new voters into the Democratic
column, an unexpected bargain that cost the mayor virtually nothing.

◆ ◆ ◆

In 1836 a crafty country lawyer and state legislator named Abraham
Lincoln introduced a bill to relocate Illinois's capital from Vandalia in the
southern part of the state to the more centrally located city of Springfield,
not far from his home in New Salem. Vandalia residents responded by tear-
ing down the capitol building and building a fresh one for $16,000, hoping
to show the legislature their commitment to hosting state government. The
effort failed, and in 1837 the capital and Lincoln himself moved to Springfield.

It took sixteen years to complete the new capitol, at a cost of $260,000—
twice the initial estimate. Two years later Governor Joel A. Matteson and his
family moved into the new governor's mansion, a grand, early Victorian-style
brick home a short walk from the capitol and Lincoln's home. A century later
the capitol had long since been replaced by a massive $4.5-million limestone
edifice on the other side of railroad tracks west of downtown, but the
governor's mansion served on, badly deteriorating. It was the third-oldest
executive mansion among the states and the largest. It stood patched and
retrofitted here and there to shore it up for the twenty-seven governors and
their families who had called it home.

In the 1930s the floor of a room holding Governor Henry Horner's Lin-
coln-related books had to be braced to hold the weight of the collection. State
workers installed an elevator to carry the ailing Horner upstairs. Plumbing,
heating, and electrical systems were outdated and inadequate. Fire safety and
security were major concerns. Governors could not comfortably entertain
more than thirty guests for dinner.

The Kerners—Otto, Helena, and their children, Anton and Helena, who
was called Babe—moved into a house needing major renovation in the pri-

vate rooms upstairs and the public rooms downstairs. Portions of the floors were weak and tilting. Anton recalled stepping through a lower floor to the dirt below while playing hide-and-seek with his sister. Portions of the house were rarely used. Anton remembered a visit by former governor Stevenson during which Stevenson invited the Kerner children up to the attic. To Stevenson's surprise and the children's fright, they found undisturbed behind a closet door a shroud-draped mannequin that Stevenson had installed as a Halloween prop many years earlier.

Like the governor's mansion, the office of Illinois governor needed modernization. Secure incumbency, even after a much-needed legislative reapportionment pushed through by Stratton, had swelled the power of veteran senators and representatives. But the office of governor, a captive of the legislative process, was starved for resources and overly dependent on the state's bureaucracy, which was just as entrenched as the legislature.

Legislative leaders kept the governor's staff too small to accomplish the planning, budgeting, and oversight necessary for a major industrial-agricultural state. The veto power, including line-item veto power for spending bills, and the power to appoint job seekers to departments and agencies under his domain gave the governor potent tools to keep the legislature in line and accomplish his goals. Nevertheless, the role was largely a function of the personality and political prowess of the job holder rather than an established, sustainable system of authority and responsibilities.

"There is no 'model' or accepted way of being governor in Illinois," University of Illinois political science scholars Gilbert Y. Steiner and Samuel K. Gove wrote in 1962. "Governors are individuals, they have achieved an important degree of political success, and they play their roles according to their individual perceptions of what constitutes success."[49]

Springfield was the seat of Sangamon County, the home of thousands of state employees who, like voters in other Republican strongholds, voted decisively for Nixon but carried narrowly for Kerner. Despite that showing of support, Kerner and his small band of advisers arrived to begin the new state administration only to discover that campaigning as the "designated governor" was much easier than being governor. William H. Rice, an assistant to Stratton who joined the Kerner team and provided vital help in the transition of power, confidentially told Kerner's people shortly after the election that the state appropriation for the governor's office had for years been insufficient to hire an adequate staff.

The staff totaled seventeen people: four assistants, ten secretaries and clerks, a driver, a receptionist, and a general errand runner. Many of them drew their paychecks from other departments and were "borrowed" by the governor's office because the governor's budget could not afford them.

Stratton rarely used his Chicago office and had assigned just one staff person there. Rice urged Kerner to expand his staff and boost their salaries, a politically risky move given the tight constraints on state spending and the desire of state Republicans and their mouthpiece, the *Chicago Tribune*, to clip the new governor's wings.

A product of well-stratified and established military command, Kerner was unprepared for the logistical void he faced after his election. In the glow of the election victory, he and his family departed on a Caribbean vacation, unmindful that the post he had just won was effectively undefined. Having barely tolerated Stevenson for four years, the Springfield power brokers rolled their eyes at the prospect of another aloof outsider in the governor's chair. The Illinois Senate was run by Republican war-horses such as Senate president Arthur J. Bidwill of suburban River Forest, who was first elected to the chamber in 1934. The Illinois House was controlled by Speaker Paul Powell, first elected in the same year from Vienna in far Southern Illinois.

Although he had no ties to Stevenson, Kerner seemed destined for the same strained relations Stevenson had experienced. Despite his lobbying efforts as Cook County judge on behalf of reforms in the state's adoption and election laws, Kerner knew almost nothing about how the legislature and the state bureaucracy worked. Stratton had swept his office bare of files and papers, leaving Kerner no background on the job of governor. In a 1962 interview with University of Illinois political science professor Thomas J. Anton, Stratton explained, "When I came in I didn't ask Stevenson for anything but the key to the mansion and the key to the office. I wouldn't expect to do any more than that for any other governor."[50]

Kerner aide Norton E. Long described the incoming Kerner administration in an article for the *Midwest Journal of Political Science* titled "After the Voting Is Over":

> The madhouse of the campaign is viewed as a confused hurly burly by its more orderly minded participants in which nobody knows what is going on, everybody is in everybody's way, and everything is a moment to moment reaction to the day's press and the hour's crisis is a significant interval in the social process in which mutation can occur. The soft, plastic state of the campaign organization is transferred to the top echelons of the government for a considerable period after the electoral transfer of power. The newly elected executive is like an assembly hand at a conveyor belt with forced options constantly coming up to which he must respond. While it would be carrying the figure too far, perhaps, to compare this situation to that portrayed by Charlie Chaplin in Modern Times, the image it conveys has a point.[51]

The *Modern Times* imagery accurately describes the initial experiences of Kerner's staff, but Kerner did not see the job that way at all. He took immediately to the ceremonial aspects of being a modern governor but was slow to grasp the immensity of the tasks he faced. Professor Anton, who studied the first Kerner term exhaustively, described Kerner's early performance:

> Though it would be stretching a point to assert that Kerner campaigned as a "reformer," it was clear that he viewed political activity as instrumental to the achievement of good works for the public interest, and that without those larger purposes, political office was barren of meaning. This stance obviously was an effective campaign device, but it did little to prepare the governor-elect for the specific problems he would face upon assuming his responsibilities. Indeed, it very probably hindered Kerner's ability to deal with those problems, for he was sufficiently unaware of the rules of the game to assume that others shared his beliefs and would cooperate with him in every way to ensure their realization.[52]

Kerner had ambition enough to play the game. He may have been a novice in Springfield, but his career in the military and government acquainted him well with the tricks of exercising political and bureaucratic power. His impressive victory in the election gave him confidence and credibility that his critics could not disregard. Helena's intimate knowledge of her father's political skills, absorbed throughout her young adulthood, made her an able and essential adviser. But the couple's intensely private lives, reflecting among other things Helena's alcoholism and the death of Mary Alyce, plus their ancestral Bohemian distrust of political maneuverers, magnified their newcomer status in a town that thrived on bold scheming and audacious behavior. To make matters worse, Helena disliked Springfield and resented the demands the role of governor placed on her husband. The daughter of Anton Cermak regarded many of the capital's movers and shakers as second rate, a view she on one occasion expressed frankly to an embarrassed audience of legislators until Kerner, calm and dignified as always, coaxed her away from the podium.

Despite Kerner's slow start, the times were on his side. The election of John Kennedy marked the emergence of a new class of technocrats, educated after the war and eager to try new solutions to public policy challenges. Despite widespread doubts about the ability and integrity of Kennedy himself, government in the early 1960s attracted skillful and well-meaning individuals captivated by Kennedy's youthful image. Kennedy and, to a lesser extent, Kerner symbolized a new beginning. State representative Mikva, an anti-machine Democrat from Hyde Park, remained dubious of Kerner's credentials as a political independent, but he saw nothing wrong with priming the pump. In a letter to Kerner days after the election, Mikva congratulated him on his "tremendous victory," which he called "a clear mandate for you to do in Illinois what Senator Kennedy has to do in the country—get us moving again. I look forward with great anticipation to serving under the dynamic and progressive leadership you will provide our state."[53]

The nation was in recession. The economic and spiritual boom of the postwar years declined into rising unemployment and a national malaise in the face of Soviet advances in space. Since the enactment of national urban renewal legislation in 1954, the federal government's involvement in shaping state and local affairs had been gaining momentum, despite resistance by many officials in Illinois and elsewhere. By the time Kerner took office, state relations with the federal government had become a crucial part of the governor's job description. Despite constitutional guarantees of states' rights, federal grant programs of various kinds were shaping fiscal priorities at the state and local levels and enabling Washington officials to rationalize an increasingly direct interest in those whom voters elected to city halls and state houses around the country. In February 1961 Kennedy sent the following telegram to Kerner and other state and local officials:

> I urge prompt consideration of specific action at every level of government in this country to invigorate our economy, including acceleration of state and local projects that are genuinely useful and will provide immediate jobs and business help. I also personally want to emphasize the fact that the federal government has released for obligation this month $724 million for the federal aid highway program and $350 million in appropriations for direct federal construction and construction grants primarily for hospitals, schools in federally affected areas, and waste treatment facilities. Use of these funds is now largely dependent on state and local action. I will appreciate your cooperation to speed these and other needed public programs to strengthen the economy of your area and throughout the nation.[54]

In May Kennedy launched the U.S. space program, a monumental undertaking promising billions of federal dollars to space-related industries. Such presidential initiatives for countercyclical federal spending plus the $345 million approved by Illinois voters in the November election for mental health facilities and schools appeared to give the incoming Kerner administration instant momentum for positive accomplishment.

"Only last week, we saw a Russian soldier as the first man in space—a result of policies that gauged themselves according to the past—policies that have put us in second place in the race for outer space," Kerner said in his first budget message, delivered April 19 to a skeptical General Assembly. Illinois legislators were not accustomed to being lectured about international affairs as they set to work dividing up the state's largesse, which by 1960 had been deeply eroded by the recession and the state's outmoded reliance on sales and personal property taxes. "Why is it necessary to listen to announcements of cosmonauts or sputniks to shock us into action?" Kerner asked. "When are we going to recapture that characteristic American initiative that in the past would have meant that we were making the announcements of achievement?"[55]

The key word was *action*—a word that inspired a new breed of public officials in Washington and elsewhere around the nation but held an especially cynical meaning in Springfield. When Adlai Stevenson was elected governor in 1948, Paul Powell remarked, "The Democrats smell the meat a-cookin'." He and other state leaders eagerly awaited clues about how the game would be played with Kerner.

The first appearance of Kerner's executive staff raised eyebrows and left the question unanswered. Isaacs, named revenue director but in reality Kerner's closest adviser, preferred to spend most of his time in Chicago, where his law practice continued. Professional politicians in Chicago and Springfield respected Isaacs's quick mind on matters of public finance, and they did not object to his private conflicts of interest—many had their own that were equally unprincipled. But they disliked Isaacs's attempts to insinuate himself into their inner circle without paying any dues. His request for a floor pass for the House and Senate chambers beyond the single pass already permitted to a member of the governor's staff was greeted with scorn.

Isaacs could be charming, witty, and persuasive. "Ted is a delight—a buttoned-up, smart, relaxed guy, with humor and a sense for social progress," Kerner adviser Long recorded in his diary in February 1961. But not too far below the surface lay Isaacs's feeling of superiority toward most politicians and their mundane obligations to the "yokums," as he told Long, who wanted only state road contracts and jobs.[56] According to Long's diary, Isaacs admired Kerner but was frustrated by the man Isaacs called "more Eisenhower than Eisenhower," referring to both men's tendency toward simplistic thinking and aloofness from stimulating and profitable political byplay.[57] Isaacs enjoyed the byplay, and he liked mixing with powerful individuals. He did not like public exposure and criticism, however, and he did not view a public servant's salary as the best source of income for his family.

In 1959 Isaacs had used his press contacts to start a whisper campaign on behalf of Kerner's bid for governor. He retained good relations with certain reporters who shared his fascination with the game of politics and his condescension toward many of the players. He was especially fond of George Tagge, the longtime ear and voice of the *Chicago Tribune* in Springfield. Tagge in turn used his relationship with Isaacs to impress on Kerner the *Tribune*'s conservative positions on state issues, especially the paper's opposition to any form of income tax.

Daley kept an eye on the fledgling Kerner administration through James A. Ronan, the son of a Chicago meat packer and the chairman of the Illinois State Democratic Central Committee. Kerner named Ronan to head the Illinois Department of Finance. His astute political skills and widespread popularity among political professionals in both parties provided crucial ballast to the Kerner team. It was sorely needed.

Kerner's first press secretary, Richard Thorne, was a former Chicago radio announcer and public relations agent whom Isaacs had hired to publicize the work of Chicago Board of Election Commissioners and its overseer, Judge Kerner. "My job was to get him good press, and that wasn't hard to do, because he was a good judge," Thorne recalled years later. Thorne was instrumental in creating Kerner's public image in the campaign for governor but acknowledged he was "a virgin" in Springfield.[58] Kerner steadfastly refused to accept Thorne's coaching about the way to behave in press conferences and frequently lost control of the largely theatrical events. Thorne recalled that he urged Kerner to slam the table and say "hell" and "damn" on occasion, but Kerner could not bring himself to do it.[59] A golf outing for reporters proved awkward when ragtag press duffers showed up at Springfield's Lincoln Greens public course to play a round with the fashionably dressed governor outfitted with his kangaroo-skin golf bag and matched set of clubs. Thorne was eventually replaced by Christopher Vlahoplus, a reporter for United Press International who, unlike Thorne, had good relations with the legislature and the Springfield press corps. Vlahoplus, who did not hesitate to use profanity loudly and often, became a devoted aide.

Another early recruit was Dawn Clark, a bright, petite, and intense antitrust lawyer who was a core member of the Committee on Illinois Government. Clark had graduated first in her class at Northwestern University Law School in 1952 and had worked for a high-powered Washington law firm whose leading partner was Dean Acheson, formerly Truman's secretary of state. Clark was the only active member of the Committee on Illinois Government who was unencumbered by a spouse or children, so the others chose her to assist Kerner as full-time legal adviser in Springfield while the men tended to their families and law careers in Chicago.

Unlike Isaacs and Thorne, Clark had no association with Kerner before he became governor. But Kerner admired her drive and trusted her instincts, naming her deputy governor, an unofficial title. It was the first time a woman held such a high post in Illinois, and her arrival caused considerable comment in the capitol. Helena took an immediate dislike to Clark and would not permit her to attend meetings in the executive mansion. Many legislative leaders, some of whom openly engaged in extramarital affairs while in Springfield, were unwilling to deal with a woman on a professional basis.

Female secretaries and other women on the governor's staff, many of whom were longtime Springfield residents and well versed in the culture of the state capitol, were not sure what to make of an ambitious female lawyer who used a rakish cigarette holder and spoke in a formal voice as alien to them as Kerner's. Virginia Morris, a former secretary to Paul Powell who was one of several capitol regulars recruited in early 1961 to rescue Kerner's office from near chaos, recalled thinking, "Is this for real?" when she first saw Clark.[60] Clark made headlines the first time Kerner left the state, when reporters said a woman was in charge of the governor's office.

Norton Long, a prolific and creative thinker who peppered anyone who would listen with ideas and opinions, held a three-day-a-week job as a speechwriter and policy consultant while he retained an academic post at Northwestern University. Long had a Ph.D. from Harvard and had worked in the federal Office of Price Administration after the war. He first met Kerner in May 1960 at a campaign dinner for Chicago-area academics in the University of Chicago Quadrangle Club. He became known within the Kerner staff as "snortin' Norton" because of his constant barrage of suggestions and program initiatives. In his daily diary, written late at night in small spiral notebooks, Long recorded the efforts by the staff to force Kerner to define his role and take charge.

"My problem is to get the governor to recognize that however he feels about himself he must build up the office of governor as a central symbol of restoring and creating a sense of honor to government service and beyond," he wrote in February 1961.[61] Long believed Kerner's closest advisers had to "persuade Kerner that if he is to do his best to bring Illinois public life out of the mire of jobbery and sordidness he must dramatize another conception to which people can rally by his own conduct and role playing. The most effective way I can see of conveying this to him is through his military experience. Ted Isaacs and Dick Thorne agree with this."[62]

But efforts at such role playing and symbolism took a back seat to the daily crises flowing into the governor's office: the question of whether to permit the sale of beer at the summer's state fair, the ancient ritual of distributing free passes to Illinois racetracks to legislators and others, and the fact that the state literally was running out of cash to pay its bills. Kerner's staff agonized over them all, sending mixed signals to the governor, the legislature, and the public. On one occasion Long gave a speech in Chicago calling for a special session of the legislature to deal with the fiscal crisis, a call Kerner immediately rejected. Meanwhile Kerner gave his own speeches, welcomed visitors, established himself as a well-liked citizen of Springfield, and kept up remarkably copious correspondence with the public through his Dictaphone machine. But no one knew what kind of governor he would be.

"So, we have our work cut out for us," Long told his diary.[63]

✦ ✦ ✦

To the uninitiated, Cook County Psychopathic Hospital in the 1920s could easily have been mistaken for a police station. Paddy wagons came and went twenty-four hours a day at the building, an adjunct of Cook County Hospital on Chicago's Near West Side. The heaviest traffic was at night. Alcoholics picked up on the streets, unruly children and elderly parents, and persons involved in family fights or acting violently for no apparent reason were carried to the hospital to remove them from society. Nine thousand persons a year came to the admittance desk and were processed in a manner more akin to a criminal proceeding than medical diagnosis and therapy.

"It was rough and tumble," recalled Dr. Francis J. Gerty, who was appointed administrator of the hospital in 1922 by Cook County Board president Anton Cermak and held the job for nineteen years. At Cermak's request Gerty testified before Congress about the failure of Prohibition. Based on those he saw being brought into his hospital, he "didn't think Prohibition did any good," he said later. "The numbers went down, but in six months they popped back up again."[64]

State law required that those admitted to the Psychopathic Hospital be granted a formal hearing within three days. About once a week the Cook County judge or a judge designated by him would make the rounds of the four floors housing patients and hear diagnoses from attending physicians. The judge would then move into a small hearing room, where a clerk would call the cases for the day. At least two doctors would testify, followed by relatives and friends of the patient, if any could be found. "It was really pressure work," Gerty said. "Sometimes, a patient from out of town would be found wandering around the streets. If patients didn't know their names, they would be given a *nom de plume*. They might be committed, and no one would know who they were. Doctors were paid $5 a case. Some people liked the work and became pretty proficient at psychiatric examinations."[65]

The process went on throughout Illinois. Once a judge signed the commitment order, the patient would likely be sent to one of the state's giant mental hospitals in such towns as Jacksonville, Anna, Galesburg, Kankakee, and Elgin, as well as Chicago. The word *hospital* was a misnomer, because the institutions were little more than asylums, custodial facilities where people were hidden away and rarely treated. Press accounts and general public discourse about the state's mental hospitals frequently used the phrase "snake pit." Housing and feeding the patients—or "inmates," as they were more commonly known—created the state's single largest public payroll, charged to the Illinois Department of Public Welfare. Certain hospitals operated large, profitable farms that exploited inmate labor. The department employed nearly 15,000 workers, including 2,500 who were not covered by civil service protection and were strictly political appointees.

In 1960 Illinois had 48,000 persons judged to be mentally ill or mentally retarded and housed in seventeen state hospitals designed for no more than 35,000. The state ranked forty-third in terms of its ratio of professional staff to patients and thirty-ninth in per-patient spending, despite being eighth in the nation in personal income. The legal process of commitment provided few rights for patients. There was no opportunity for short-term institutionalization for observation and early treatment without the shattering stigma of formal commitment proceedings unless the patient voluntarily agreed to commitment.

As county judge Kerner had presided weekly at commitment hearings and knew what outcomes his commitment orders produced. He regarded mental health reform as a major item of unfinished business from his tenure. He took pride in the enactment of a new state adoption law but told his son in 1973, "I felt I had not accomplished too much as far as mental health was concerned, so that one of the major thrusts of my campaign in 1960 was to improve mental health and establish a mental health department."[66]

He first raised reform of the state mental health code in his campaign for reelection as county judge in 1958: "I feel that many people are wronged and their futures impaired because of the requirement that a legal petition must be filed in court before a medical commission can determine whether the individual actually should be committed to an institution or discharged. Once a petition is filed, it becomes a matter of public record. On many instances this has brought embarrassment to individuals who are later discharged after the hearing. This could be construed to be an invasion of the rights of privacy of the individual." He advocated a medical evaluation first and a judicial proceeding second. "In this way, no public record is made unless the individual is actually proved to need mental treatment at one of our institutions."[67]

In his campaign against Stratton, Kerner charged that Illinois had become merely a training ground for psychiatrists, many of whom earned degrees at state universities and took brief internships in state hospitals only to flee into private practice or leave the state altogether, leaving behind staff with inadequate training and pay. State hospital superintendents were not required to have professional training in the field of mental health. At the pleasure of state politicians, they ran taxpayer-financed fiefs. As director of public welfare under Stratton, Otto L. Bettag made sure the system worked for the superintendents and their political sponsors but not necessarily for the patients. At one hospital in Manteno, the superintendent installed a putting green for his amusement. "We need a man at the head of the welfare department who is

interested in somebody else's welfare, not his own," Kerner said on the campaign trail. It was one of his most effective themes.[68]

It came as no surprise to Bettag, therefore, that Kerner's first appointment,
made within days of the November election, was a new director of the Department of Public Welfare. (Kerner's second appointment was William Miller,
to be chairman of the Illinois Racing Board. Marjorie Everett and Theodore
Isaacs assured Kerner that Miller could cleanse and modernize the state's
horse-racing industry.) Kerner's choice was a surprise, however. Francis Gerty
was sixty-seven years old and awaiting retirement as chairman of the Department of Psychiatry at the University of Illinois's College of Medicine, a post
he had held since 1941. He had just completed a one-year term as president
of the American Psychiatric Association. Three months before the election,
Kerner called and asked Gerty to postpone his retirement from public service.
Kerner offered to make Gerty his first appointment when he won the election. Gerty, who knew he had only a few years left to make money in private
practice, demurred. As Gerty recalled, however, Kerner said, "I'll put you
down as favorably disposed. I can't often get a man with such qualifications
as yours, so I'll call you."[69]

Shortly after the election and a few days before Gerty's sixty-eighth birthday, Kerner called again. Illinois voters had just approved $150 million in
bonding authority for state mental hospitals after a bipartisan campaign under
the theme "The Shame of It." Gerty wanted to play a role in deciding how
the money would be spent and believed he had a better idea than merely dress-
ing up existing hospitals. "I knew these hospitals," he recalled years later. "I
did not think the referendum was going to do the good they thought it was
going to do. I had been working on another plan. I thought they'd do much
better with a different kind of hospital, one that takes a maximum of 200 or
250 patients, spread across the state where they'd be handy for quick admission of patients."[70]

Gerty had developed his concept of what became known as zoned treatment centers while working as a consultant for the State of Texas in 1956.
"State hospital patients are immigrants from the communities," Gerty told
the Welfare Council of Chicago in a 1958 speech. "Too few of these immigrants can get back to the local communities which lack the facilities to care
for them even in rehabilitation and re-establishment. . . . Our plans should
channel our activities by the most direct route possible to the point where they
should go, that is, to the patient and the community of which he is a part."[71]

But after nearly forty years in the public sector, Gerty knew he was proposing a political bombshell. Concentration of the mentally ill in a few large
hospitals meant a concentration of political power in the hands of legislators

in whose districts the hospitals operated. Certainly Paul Powell would not eagerly surrender his control over the hospital in Anna. Remembering his days at Cook County Psychopathic Hospital, Gerty wanted to try a decentralized system emphasizing early intervention and offering, when appropriate, brief institutionalization instead of a virtual life sentence. "At least we would be better prepared for what could be done for patients before admitting them to the state hospitals," he said later. Kerner agreed and authorized Gerty to implement his plan.[72]

Bettag did not go quietly. Kerner was forced to oust him from a new state job that Stratton had arranged carrying a 33 percent salary increase and the prospect of civil service protection. Once in office Gerty wasted no time. Legislation creating the Illinois Department of Mental Health and authorizing his zoned treatment center plan was drafted quickly for Gerty by Lowell E. Sachnoff, a Harvard Law School graduate and member of the Committee on Illinois Government. An enthusiastic worker in Kennedy's Illinois campaign, Sachnoff was one of many smart and energetic liberals from Chicago who saw Kerner's decision to hire Gerty as the glimmering of reform in state government. He turned down a job with the Kennedy administration in Washington and traveled instead to Springfield, postponing the start of what became a prosperous legal career in Chicago.

"I had three kids at the time, and I was flat broke," Sachnoff recalled. "Kerner said [to Gerty], 'I'll give you free rein, and I'll support you in every way.' And, to his credit, he did. I remember vividly Otto Kerner's pledge to Gerty. He made a commitment to Gerty and myself that was extraordinarily impressive, in fact unbelievable."[73] Gerty not only energized political reformers. He boosted the morale of the professionals working in the state's mental hospitals. Here was a doctor who over four decades had seen the best and the worst that Illinois could offer for the mentally impaired. Sachnoff recalled one visit he and Gerty made to the state school for retarded children in Lincoln. Gerty approached an eleven-year-old boy who sat apart from other children in his ward. He requested the boy's chart and saw that he was from a large family and had been institutionalized after poor performance at school. Gerty walked behind the seated child and snapped his fingers. Then he asked Sachnoff to strike an iron bar behind the boy. The boy showed no reaction either time. An attendant told Gerty the school had no equipment to test for deafness, which turned out to be the boy's primary difficulty.

Gerty and Sachnoff soon tested Kerner's pledge to protect their independence. In drafting the mental health legislation, Sachnoff purposely sidestepped language in the mental health bond referendum proposal that appeared to require bond proceeds be spent exclusively to enhance existing state mental hospitals. His bill allowed existing facilities to be "enhanced" by construction of new facilities elsewhere. The loose interpretation held, despite its politically risky consequences, largely through Gerty's force of will. At one point during legislative debate, the Republican caucus in the Senate gave the Democratic appointee a standing ovation. Despite a state fiscal crisis that sparked fistfights among legislators on the floor of the Illinois House, lawmakers granted a 79 percent increase in the appropriation for Gerty's department from the previous Department of Public Welfare budget. Gerty also demanded and won from Kerner a pay raise for his department's employees far beyond what budget makers knew the state could afford for all state workers.

Kerner's pledge to Gerty also withstood a primal political test. Gerty threatened to resign unless Kerner fired the number-two appointee in the department, Herbert M. Lowery, who was also the Democratic chairman of Rock Island County. Kerner had appointed Lowery to reward him for bringing in a heavy Democratic vote in November, and he hoped Lowery would be an effective go-between for Gerty and the legislature. But the doctor neither wanted nor needed such assistance, and the match failed. Partly at the instigation of Sachnoff, newspaper articles appeared suggesting a battle royal between professionalism and politics. Lowery was accused of firing Republican workers at the East Moline State Hospital in Rock Island County and installing Democratic minions in the non–civil service jobs, moves Lowery willingly acknowledged as his right and duty. Other stories accused Lowery of demanding that workers pay a Democratic organization four dollars a month to keep their jobs and of conspiring with Paul Powell to subvert Gerty's insistence that directors of state mental health hospitals be psychiatrists, accusations Lowery denied.

Lowery in turn accused Gerty of seeking to cover up wrongdoing that Lowery said he had discovered. He accused Sachnoff of aiding a union organizer agitating in state mental hospitals. Gerty persisted in his threat to resign, forcing Kerner to weigh the importance of Rock Island County's votes against his pledge to Gerty. Kerner sided with Gerty and fired Lowery. "We congratulate Kerner for swinging his own ax," wrote the *Chicago Daily News*. "His prompt action bucks up faith in his sincere intentions."[74] Politically bygones became bygones. At a Democratic rally later that year, Lowery praised Kerner and Gerty. After the dust settled, the bond issue meant more contracts throughout the state for construction firms and architects—including Dawn Clark's future husband, Walter Netsch.

The Kennedy administration praised the Illinois mental health program as a model for the nation. "Illinois . . . has been a leader in the development of community mental health programs and its centers concept has had a profound influence on the national mental health program," Robert H. Felix, the director of the National Institute of Mental Health, wrote in 1963. "There are high hopes . . . that talented young people will be attracted to positions in the new centers by the excitement of trying new methods and techniques in this frontier of psychiatry. With all sincerity, I say that full implementation of this program will make possible what we fully intend to be a new day for the mentally ill."[75]

The creation of a nationally recognized mental health program was a highlight of Kerner's first two years. During that time the state also enacted the Fair Employment Practices Act and managed to squeeze enough money out of existing revenue sources to pay its bills. But Kerner's inability to control the game in Springfield led politicians and reporters to view him as a one-term governor, despite the expectation that Kennedy would be a strong leader to the Democratic ticket in 1964. In December 1962 journalist Littlewood assessed the governor in a magazine article titled "Otto Kerner of Illinois: The Problems of Being a Nice Guy."

"Possessed of plentiful intentions of the highest order, Kerner has nonetheless been thus far a disappointment," Littlewood wrote. "The Kerner administration has been content to coast through two years without anything resembling a 'crash program' to solve the state's financial problems or any other problems, save possibly the deplorable conditions of mental institutions."

Calling Kerner a "complicated man," Littlewood described the governor's disengagement from much of Springfield's political hurly-burly and noted that the governor had failed to take full advantage of his widespread voter appeal to write a larger record of accomplishment. "But perhaps one day he will wake up with fire in his eye—as another governor named Horner did in the 1930s—and suddenly be inspired by the fact that he is the governor of Illinois."[76]

As one explanation for Kerner's early performance, Littlewood alluded briefly to Helena. "A series of personal tragedies in their lives, beginning with the assassination of her father in 1933, must be considered in understanding Kerner."[77]

✦ ✦ ✦

In July 1962 Charles Witz, a twenty-seven-year-old assistant Cook County state's attorney, was assigned to help supervise commitment proceedings at the mental health unit of Cook County Hospital, formerly the Cook County Psychopathic Hospital. The work was like being stationed in traffic court, he recalled. Not much had changed in the forty years since Dr. Gerty ran the facility, but the amendments to the mental health code just adopted required attention to the civil rights of patients being recommended for commitment. One morning he received a phone call he would never forget: "This is Otto Kerner. Would you be able to come and see me this afternoon?"[78]

When Witz was ushered into the governor's Chicago office, Kerner said matter-of-factly that he needed to discuss a delicate matter and hoped Witz would keep the information confidential. During the next ninety minutes Kerner unburdened himself to the young lawyer, whom he had not met previously. He discussed frankly the effects of his wife's addiction. He spoke primarily out of concern for his wife, not his public position, Witz recalled. Helena's life, at one time filled with so much carefree glamour and fun, had plunged down a steep slope. Her disastrous first marriage had ended at the same time her beloved father lay dying in a Florida hospital. Her marriage to Kerner, which might have restored her, had been strained by his wartime absences. The shocking death of her only child, from which she never recovered, magnified the burden of putting on appearances in behalf of her husband's career.

Kerner told Witz of an incident a few days earlier when he, Dawn Clark, and Norton Long were attending a governor's conference in Hershey, Pennsylvania. Helena had made repeated harassing phone calls to Clark and attempted to order a state airplane to take her to Hershey, where President Kennedy was the keynote speaker. In her tantrum she had threatened to kill Clark. It took four attendants to restrain her in her Glenview home. The Hershey incident convinced Kerner that his wife's condition, which had been monitored by numerous doctors and explained in public as illness or accidents, required a radical step. Kerner told Witz that Helena refused to seek institutional treatment. He wanted Witz's assistance in seeking a court order that would allow Helena to be evaluated for treatment without the publicity of a formal court commitment proceeding—one of the major reforms of the new mental health code.

In August, the always traumatic month of Mary Alyce's death, Helena agreed to check into a hospital on the North Shore for evaluation. According to Long's diary, *Chicago Sun-Times* editor Milburn P. Akers told Norton Long, "'The domestic situation is going to be remedied.' He advised [Kerner] it would be a one-day story."[79] A hearing was held in the hospital. Witz, who was present, recalled that Helena fought against her husband's plan and the proceeding quickly became chaotic. In the end, however, Helena agreed to thirty days of voluntary hospitalization. There is no record of the hearing in court files. Kerner kept all this to himself, but at a cabinet meeting in mid-July he surprised his subordinates by becoming demonstrably angry. "The governor was much more profane than I've ever seen him," Long recorded in his diary. "Joe Knight [director of financial institutions] said he was glad to see his dander up. They all seemed to get a charge out of the boss being mad."[80]

The staff attributed Kerner's mood to the public pressure building around the scheduled electrocution of murderer Paul Crump, whose story of reha-

bilitation into a model prisoner in the Cook County jail had become a nationwide cause célèbre. Only later did they learn the deeper source of Kerner's
uncharacteristic irritability. One man who knew everything was Dr. Gerty.
Kerner had sought his advice about Helena since early in their association as
governor and department chief in reforming the mental health code. At his
one-hundredth birthday party in 1992, Gerty lamented that he never was able
to treat Helena successfully and relieve the burden the couple carried.

In a 1962 speech about the role of the governor, Kerner said: "It is for each
governor in each administration to determine whether he will conduct his
administration as a creator or curator—whether he will see the problems of
his state as those his administration can help solve—or whether he views
existing conditions as those which right themselves in the day-to-day workings of the various elements that go to make up the state."[81] Kerner saw himself as a creator, not a curator. But he also defined his public role in a uniquely
empathetic manner, not the transactional manner of conventional politics. In
accomplishing adoption reform and mental health reform, he transformed
intensely private burdens into significant public priorities. It was a style of
governing that appealed intuitively to ordinary voters but confused professional politicians, journalists, and many of his closest advisers.

6

The Ultimate Decision

Kerner frequently shaved with an electric razor in the private bathroom just off his capitol office. One of his press aides, Mary Butterfield, recalled daring to ask him a difficult question above the whir: "Why don't you just call them up and tell them not to electrocute him?"[1]

Vincent Ciucci, thirty-five, shot to death his wife and three children with a rifle late on a Saturday night in December 1953. More than eight years later, when Butterfield spoke up, he was a few hours and seventeen steps from his scheduled execution at 12:01 A.M., March 23, 1962, in the dank basement of the Cook County jail. Butterfield never was shy about expressing her views on political and social issues to her boss or anyone else. Her chief worry at that moment was that Mrs. Kerner would find out she was so close to her husband while he was engaged in such a personal activity as shaving. Nevertheless, she pressed her point. On many occasions Kerner had declared his opposition to the death penalty, and Ciucci was the first capital offender to come to him for a reprieve.

Kerner answered matter-of-factly that he was obliged to uphold the law, regardless of his beliefs, Butterfield recalled. Ciucci had exhausted his appeals to state and federal courts, including the U.S. Supreme Court. Two days earlier Kerner had denied a petition for executive clemency. But this would be a long night, as he and his staff, as well as the rest of the nation, struggled with the morality and efficacy of capital punishment.

Controversies confronting politicians usually involve constituency groups seeking attention and favor in an unending cycle of solicitation and resolution. Skillful politicians engage in complex calculations around competing interests, mixing their private knowledge and beliefs with their assessments of opposing political forces, in the hope of satisfactory outcomes for themselves at the next election. One decision nearly always leads to fresh confrontations, often overlapping and conflicting. But the process becomes stark, personal, and often final when a solitary constituent makes a simple plea to the lone politician assigned the last look at a death-penalty appeal. Governors responsible for executions, commutations, and reprieves employ the same political calculus that they apply to other decisions, but the consequences are stripped of ambiguity. Illinois's capital punishment law in no way restricted Kerner's power to commute or delay an execution for any reason and, when a clemency petition was filed, allowed no escape from the obligation to decide. In this matter the power of the state rested entirely in the person of the governor, one to one with the convict.

The Reverend Dismas Clark, the well-known "hoodlum priest" of St. Louis, pleaded for Ciucci's life and warned Kerner, "Whoever takes a life—whether lawfully or unlawfully—lives with this decision for the rest of his life."[2] Kerner concurred in a letter to his former minister in Glenview, the Reverend Robert A. Edgar: "I find in this position there are so many people who know the answers to my problems. But they do not have the responsibility of the decision nor do they have to live with their consciences."[3]

The Ciucci case was the first of three capital punishment decisions coming before Kerner in 1962. After that year there would be no state executions in Illinois for nearly three decades, as judges and legislators tested public sentiment and tinkered with procedures for litigating capital crimes. By 1990, when executions resumed, the passion for the debate had cooled. Politicians found little advantage even in raising the issue. Voters had become hardened by the viciousness of big-headline murders and the seeming casualness of street crime. During the moratorium Illinois replaced electrocution with lethal injection as the means of state execution. The lawmaker who sponsored the new technique called it "energy conservation legislation."[4] The governor who signed the lethal injection bill was James R. Thompson, elected in 1976 by this more callous electorate. Kerner and Thompson first interacted over the issue of capital punishment in the watershed year of 1962, when the governor determined that two men should die and one should live.

◆ ◆ ◆

In 1928 an electric chair called "old smokey" was installed in the former Cook County Jail at Dearborn and Illinois Streets just north of the Loop. A year later Anton Cermak, president of the Cook County Board, built a criminal court and jail complex at Twenty-sixth Street and California Avenue in

South Lawndale, closer to his Bohemian constituents who wanted jobs. The chair was moved to the new facility along with other furniture. By the time Kerner took office, sixty-five men had paid the ultimate price in the wood, metal, and leather contraption. The most recent prior to Kerner's election was twenty-eight-year-old Richard Carpenter, who killed a police detective in 1953. "Get it over with quick," Carpenter told his guards as they strapped him in just after midnight on Dec. 19, 1958.[5] After that the chair stood empty.

In the early 1960s public sentiment was intensifying on both sides of the national capital punishment debate, and a resolution seemed anything but quick. Seemingly interminable arguments were framed mostly as emotional appeals. America's postwar optimism toward science was noticeably muted in this debate, observed criminologist Hans W. Mattick. "A paradox of our modern world lies in the ambivalence we exhibit toward scientific methods when they are applied to political affairs," he wrote in a 1963 report for the John Howard Association, a Chicago-based prison watchdog group. "We have applied them to the material world and achieved a remarkable level of control over nature. Our accomplishments in these respects tend to beguile us into the conceit that man is a rational animal. When we view the relations between men and the social order, however, we are confronted with the cold war, contemporary race relations and a host of continuing social problems that must make us qualify the degree of rationality that men have achieved. . . . This is particularly the case in the area of social problems related to crime and punishment."[6]

Statistics gathered by Mattick supplemented the debate but gave little guidance toward a resolution. In 1961 forty-four states authorized the death penalty. The annual number of executions had declined to 42 in 1961 from a peak of 199 in 1935. From 1930 through 1961, 55 percent of the 3,766 prisoners executed nationwide were nonwhite, during which time nonwhites constituted about 10 percent of the population. In the same period Illinois executed 88 prisoners, 34 percent of whom were nonwhite, while the state's nonwhite population grew from 5 percent in 1930 to 11 percent in 1961. The odds against a convicted murderer in Illinois being executed, based on statistics from 1945 through 1958, were eighty-three to one, Mattick calculated.[7]

Opponents argued that executions had no effect on reducing crime and were carried out primarily against the poor and racial minorities. In particular, African Americans newly asserting themselves in the arenas of civil rights and economic justice noted the disproportionate number of their race being killed. With equal fervor death-penalty proponents charged that indecisiveness and delay in carrying out executions made a mockery of the nation's system of justice and thwarted the will of the public, which by majority supported state executions as the ultimate response to crime. Each side believed the moral authority of the state was at stake.

Beneath the data and beliefs lay a patchwork process developed over decades by politicians and judges in various states for determining and implementing capital punishment. The death penalty was a technical labyrinth of political and legal accommodations. During the 1950s many states, including Illinois, empowered juries to levy death sentences at the same time they ruled on guilt. This system allowed ordinary citizens to deliver swift and rough justice to society's accused. It was a flawed, arbitrary process that invited injustice and error. For one thing, prosecutors routinely excluded from murder trial juries any individuals who opposed the death penalty. As a result juries were often biased in favor of prosecutors, because jurors willing to return a death sentence were also more likely to convict on the underlying charges. Capital case defendants who exercised their constitutional right not to testify in the underlying trial thereby surrendered their chance to plead for their lives and offer mitigating evidence explaining why they should not be put to death. Partly for this reason, by the early 1960s most death-penalty states required automatic appeals when the sentence was imposed. Appeals usually multiplied. This process, which often included repeated execution-night vigils and last-minute reprieves, made celebrities out of some death-row inmates and gave the debate a human face.

In March 1960 the face of small-time thief and ex-convict Caryl Chessman, sentenced to die in California's gas chamber, made the cover of *Time* magazine. His first date of execution was March 25, 1952, for a crime spree in early 1948. Americans had long since forgotten, if they ever knew, what capital crime Chessman had committed. He was sentenced to death after a string of robberies along so-called lovers lanes in and around Los Angeles. His capital offense under California law was harming the victim of a kidnapping—specifically, forcing two female robbery victims into his car and sexually assaulting them. The campaign to save Chessman through eight execution dates had become an international spectacle that only California could produce, including poetry readings, hunger strikes, a documentary movie, and a folk song. A film, *Justice and Caryl Chessman,* played in theaters across the country. "The Ballad of Caryl Chessman" spun in American jukeboxes. Another song on the subject, "The Death Song of Chessman," was produced in the Netherlands. Chessman wrote four books in jail, including a best-seller, *Cell 2455 Death Row.* But he did not have nine lives. He was put to death on May 2, 1960. His execution sparked an even more intense debate over capital punishment in America.

Part-time truck driver Vincent Ciucci never achieved such notoriety. Like Chessman, however, Ciucci became a symbol in the capital punishment debate. Weighty national legal and moral issues as well as the prurient allure of a state execution lived for a while in his slender person. Newspapers, always finding a way to make criminals more colorful, had dubbed Chessman the "Red Light Bandit" because of a flashing red light he displayed in his car to make his robbery victims believe they were being pulled over by police. Ciucci was the "Grocery Romeo." With his engaging smile and bright eyes, he did not look like the defiant or downtrodden souls who normally appeared in press photos of convicted killers. He had lived with his wife, Anna, and their children in a West Side neighborhood known as Little Italy. Their home was an apartment in back of a grocery store, a business Anna's brother had given her. Ciucci sometimes helped Anna in the store, but he usually was away from home, gambling and carrying on an affair with another woman who had borne him a child four months before the murders. He wanted to take up with her permanently. After he killed Anna and the children in their beds, Ciucci set fire to the apartment to cover up the crime. A pathologist for the Cook County coroner's office found bullet holes in the charred heads of Anna and the children, ages nine, eight, and four. He found twenty-two-caliber bullets in three of the heads.

Like Chessman, Ciucci received eight stays of execution. Even Justice William O. Douglas, the leading liberal on the Supreme Court, had no sympathy for such delays. Concerning the California case Douglas wrote in 1957: "The conclusion is irresistible that Chessman is playing a game with the courts, stalling for time while the facts of the case grow cold. . . . Chessman has received due process over and over again."[8] Not surprisingly State's Attorney Daniel Ward quoted Douglas's words in a letter to Kerner opposing a reprieve or commutation for Ciucci. Ward had known Kerner since they worked together in the U.S. attorney's office. He had been recruited into politics by Mayor Daley and joined Kerner on the victorious Democratic ticket in 1960. Citing the Chessman case was Ward's attempt, one elected official to another, to remind Kerner that California governor Pat Brown, a fellow Democrat who also opposed the death penalty, had been widely ridiculed for his indecisiveness in disposing of the Red Light Bandit.[9]

But Ciucci's case presented an important difference that did not escape Justice Douglas's attention. In this case the state itself had delayed justice— not to postpone an execution, but to obtain one. Ciucci was tried four times essentially for the same crime before the state won a death sentence from a jury. In March 1954 a jury sentenced him to twenty years for killing Anna. Four months later another jury in a separate trial gave him forty-five years for killing daughter Angeline. (The second trial was the first time in Illinois that lie-detector results were admitted as evidence in a criminal trial. Ciucci had sought the test, and administrator John E. Reid testified that he failed.) In both trials the gruesome details of all four deaths were portrayed to the jury. A juror in the Angeline trial said the panel would not impose death in a case built on "circumstantial evidence."[10] Judge Richard B. Austin, who conducted the trial, complained later that the jury lacked "intestinal fortitude."[11] Assistant state's attorney Irwin Block said: "Nothing short of the death penalty is enough for Ciucci. We definitely will try the other cases. We hope that someday a jury will realize the enormity of this crime."[12]

Next up was a trial for the murder of nine-year-old Vincent Ciucci Jr., but a mistrial was declared because of prejudicial statements by Block. A new jury was shown evidence of all four killings. Late at night on January 11, 1955, the nine men and three women deliberated just over two hours and convicted Ciucci of murdering his son. They gave him the electric chair. No trial regarding daughter Virginia was held. The government was satisfied.

In his letter to Kerner citing Douglas's frustrations with the Chessman delays, Ward did not cite Douglas's later words condemning the Cook County prosecutor's tactics in the Ciucci case. In a dissent to a five-to-four Supreme Court ruling denying Ciucci an appeal, Douglas wrote:

> The case presents an instance of the prosecution being allowed to harass the accused with repeated trials and convictions on the same evidence, until it achieves the desired results of a capital verdict. . . . In my view, the Due Process Clause of the Fourteenth Amendment prevents this effort by a State to obtain a death penalty. No constitutional problem would have arisen if the petitioner had been prosecuted in one trial for as many murders as there were victims. But by using the same evidence in multiple trials the state continued its relentless prosecutions until it got the result it wanted. . . . This is an unseemly and oppressive use of a criminal trial that violates the concept of due process contained in the Fourteenth Amendment, whatever its ultimate scope is taken to be.[13]

Chief Justice Earl Warren and Justice William J. Brennan concurred in Douglas's dissent. Justice Hugo Black dissented in a separate opinion, saying simply, "The Fourteenth Amendment bars a State from placing a defendant twice in jeopardy for the same offense."[14]

During the Illinois General Assembly's chaotic 1961 session, lawmakers reacted with surprising rationality to Douglas's criticism. They enacted legislation that expressly barred future Ciucci-style prosecutions. In the same series of bills recodifying the state criminal code, the legislature abolished the power of a jury to pronounce a death sentence simultaneously with a conviction. A capital sentence could be imposed by a judge only after a hearing in which fresh testimony for and against execution was permitted. The new criminal code went into effect January 1, 1962, over Kerner's signature.

Among the law's drafters was a young assistant Cook County state's attorney named James R. Thompson. Thompson, just twenty-five years old, was a lanky, close-cropped lawyer from Oak Park who had impressed the Northwestern Law School faculty. He joined the state's attorney's office after graduating from law school in 1959, the year of Kerner's twenty-fifth graduation anniversary at the school. At the urging of his law school mentor, Professor Fred E. Inbau, Thompson sought a job under State's Attorney Benjamin Adamowski. After Ward defeated Adamowski in 1960, he kept Thompson on the advice of another Thompson mentor, Judge Austin.

On March 19 Kerner called an emergency meeting of the five-member Illinois Parole and Pardon Board to hear the Ciucci matter. Ciucci's lawyer, George N. Leighton, a brilliant young black attorney of prodigious energy and determination, argued for an hour on behalf of his client. He attacked the state's use of "dry-run" prosecutions. But he detoured from this well-grounded civil liberties argument to present a weak, bizarre new theory of the case that had been headlined in newspapers a few days earlier: yes, Ciucci had shot and killed his wife with the rifle he had borrowed to hunt rabbits, but he killed Anna only after she had used the weapon to kill their three children. Anna had said that Ciucci might leave her but that he would never take the children, Leighton asserted.[15] This provocative eleventh-hour declaration invigorated the tawdry press sideshow that characterized the case until the end, but it overshadowed the substantive issue of multiple prosecutions, which received scant attention in the newspapers.

Thompson addressed the board, urging the state to carry out the will of the jury, and Kerner sided with Thompson. On Wednesday, March 20, he denied Ciucci's commutation with a brief, perfunctory statement. He made no mention of the civil liberties issue. He implied that his role was obligatory, with no room for compassion. "Our courts have held that the evidence was sufficient to sustain a verdict of guilty. The facts and circumstances of this case are that the punishment—death by execution—is consistent with the gravity of the crime. The sole question for decision at this time is whether or not this is an appropriate case for the exercise of executive clemency. I feel that it is not."[16] The next day Leighton sought and was denied another court appeal. Thompson, receiving the first significant press coverage of his career, called Leighton's plea "an example of scandalous delay" and a "good reason" why the public holds lawyers in contempt.[17]

On Friday evening Ciucci refused his last meal. Kerner headed home from his capitol office. Dawn Clark stayed behind to handle phone calls, mostly from death-penalty opponents. Where were they, she wondered alone, when a bill suspending the death penalty and supported by Kerner was defeated by the legislature in its previous session?[18] Her aggravation was compounded by Kerner's inwardness. It was hard enough to engage him in constructive argument on far less serious matters. The emotional barriers he kept around himself would never give way to her on a question of this magnitude. Kerner aides William H. Chamberlain and Richard Thorne were with the governor in the executive mansion, where the coffee was black and stale and the lights of the telephone blinked with callers seeking a last-minute plea or a last-minute quotation. Parole and Pardon Board chairman James C. Craven arrived from his farm less than five miles west of Springfield. Craven, Chicago newspaper publisher Leo A. Lerner, and Theodore A. Jones, an African American accountant and Democratic activist, constituted the liberal majority of the board. They had emphasized to Kerner Douglas's opinion in the Ciucci appeal. Surely the dubious process of this conviction required leniency, Craven said. Kerner listened as Craven beat on him with an emotional plea. He was a good listener, Craven remembered.[19] But on this matter he was not a dissenter, and he told Craven so.

From Chicago Warden Johnson called the mansion and asked whether there was any reason not to proceed with the execution. There was none. Cook County sheriff Frank Sain, who had fortified himself and Ciucci with a few shots of liquor, invited reporters into Ciucci's cell for an unprecedented death row press conference. Ciucci smoked a cigar and told once more his new version of the crime. He asked for "truth serum, a lie box or anything to substantiate [his] story."[20] Ed Baumann, a reporter for the *Chicago Daily News* who was there, wrote: "At 11:28 P.M., after the medical contingent departed, a jailer entered the cell, unscrewed an overhead light bulb and plugged in an electric razor. Ciucci obediently pulled off his tee-shirt, sat down and continued to chatter above the buzzing while the dark, curly hairs of his head tumbled into his lap."[21] Minutes before midnight Thorne called the newspapers and said there would be no stay of execution. With a black hood over his head, Ciucci received alternate bursts of 1,900 volts and 900 volts for two minutes. Thirty-five witnesses observed the execution, which was declared accomplished at 12:09 A.M. Craven drove home exhausted and depressed. He wondered whether he should resign from the board. Otto Kerner, he decided, was no John Peter Altgeld, Illinois's first liberal Democratic governor who unexpectedly and courageously pardoned three of the eight anarchists convicted for the 1886 Haymarket Square bombing in Chicago. Altgeld denounced the judicial process that had led to the convictions and did not win a second term as governor.

The next capital case of 1962 contained none of the civil liberties themes of the Ciucci matter, but it nonetheless presented Kerner a rationale for choosing life over death and this time put him at odds with Thompson.

✦ ✦ ✦

Paul Crump, a handsome black man from Chicago's South Side, had been convicted and sentenced to death twice for killing a white security guard, Theodore Zukowski, during a robbery on March 20, 1953. Crump was twenty-two years old at the time of the killing in the Libby, McNeil and Libby plant in Chicago's stockyards, southwest of the Loop. His first conviction was reversed by the Illinois Supreme Court, but the second one stuck. By the time Kerner took office, Crump's lawyers had ceased arguing that Crump was convicted wrongfully. They had failed to convince juries or courts that Crump, an ex-convict and former Libby employee, was not one of the five holdup men who stole more than $20,000, the weekly Libby payroll and credit union cash, and the one who, left stranded by the others, assaulted five employees and shot Zukowski.

Crump's defense team had also dropped its plea that police beat him into making a false confession to first assistant state's attorney Richard B. Austin. Crump steadfastly refused to admit guilt, but his lawyers and a growing cluster of supporters maintained he was a new man, different from the one who had committed the crime. As Crump's appointment with the electric chair approached during numerous appeals, the rehabilitation story gained widespread attention and credibility. Warden Jack R. Johnson and other staff members and counselors working in the jail became convinced that the prisoner was not the same man who had committed the crime.

In 1953 Crump, one of thirteen children, was the youngest person ever condemned to death in Cook County. By 1962 he was the senior convict awaiting execution. By one count he had been close to execution fifteen times as various appeals came and went. He became a "barn boss," the leader of his tier of cells, after Johnson, a surprisingly compassionate man in the cynical patronage bureaucracy of Cook County justice, abolished the "death row" cluster of cells. Johnson frequently put his most difficult inmates in Crump's tier so that he could minister to them. Crump read extensively and developed remarkable eloquence in speaking about his circumstances. He was befriended by Chicago artist Eddie Balchowsky, who during a stint in the jail on a minor conviction introduced Crump to writers Nelson Algren and Felix Singer when they came to visit. Hans Mattick, then an assistant warden in the jail, assisted in Crump's education.[22] With this inspiration, Crump authored a mostly autobiographical novel, *Burn, Killer, Burn,* published by the Chicago-based Johnson Publishing Company. He dedicated the book to "Mama, who gave so much and got so little."[23]

The book did not sell as well as Chessman's *Cell 2455,* but it helped to establish Crump as a suitable symbol of the anti–capital punishment crusade. He became a cause célèbre among the Chicagoans known as Lake Shore liberals, including several news media personalities and members of Chicago's literary set. The unofficial head of this group was lawyer Lois Solomon, publisher of a progressive journal called *The Paper.* Members included attorneys Donald Page Moore and Elmer Gertz, both of whom would represent Crump;

writer Studs Terkel and journalist John Justin Smith of the *Chicago Daily News;* and celebrity gossip columnist Irv "Kup" Kupcinet of the *Chicago Sun-Times.* Solomon, Kup's sister-in-law, hosted parties where a frequent discussion topic was the burgeoning national campaign against capital punishment.

The story of Crump's transformation and his efforts on behalf of fellow inmates appeared in a *Life* magazine photo spread in July 1962.[24] Kup, the host of a popular television talk show, broadcast a sympathetic interview with Crump. Several other newspaper columnists took up the cause. After his nearly ten years in jail, the rage had gone out of Paul Crump. He gave every indication of being at peace with himself and finding meaning in good works. He was a far better subject for a national anti–capital punishment campaign than the unrepentant Ciucci or the arrogant Caryl Chessman. Crump became the thinking man's Chessman. Despite the sincerity of Crump's defenders, however, the public relations campaign to save him almost went horribly awry.

✦ ✦ ✦

One young member of Lois Solomon's salon was William "Billy" Friedken, a brash writer-producer-director at Chicago television station WGN who had been adopted by Chicago's literary and media elite as a rising star. Eager to accelerate his career and ingratiate himself with Solomon and her friends, Friedken decided to make a documentary film in defense of Paul Crump as a moonlighting project for a competing television station, WBKB. But Friedken was a storyteller, not a journalist. He had learned his craft from his loquacious uncle Harry Lang, the proprietor of a North Side tavern called the Sip 'n' Bottle, which according to Friedken's biographer "attracted a crowd of cons and cops that entranced young Friedken."[25]

Friedken's uncle was a genuine figure in Chicago crime lore. He had been a Chicago police detective assigned to a special unit reporting directly to Mayor Cermak and under orders from the mayor to roust gangsters. In December 1932 Lang led a raid on Al Capone's Loop headquarters at 221 N. LaSalle Street, a block north of city hall. The apparent target was Louis "Little New York" Campagna. Lang testified later that Cermak feared Capone had imported Campagna from New York to assassinate him. In the raid Lang shot and nearly killed Capone's "enforcer," Frank Nitti. At first Lang was hailed as a hero. But in the trial of Nitti, who was charged with shooting Lang, a police officer present at the raid testified that Nitti had been found unarmed just before Lang shot him three times in the neck and chest. Lang then shot himself in the finger. Lang subsequently was convicted for assaulting Nitti and for perjury. Afterward he vowed to "blow the lid off Chicago politics and wreck the Democratic Party" if he was sent to jail.[26] He was granted a new trial, and the charges were dismissed in 1934. He retired to the Sip 'n' Bottle and never collected the $300 award he won for his bravery in the raid on Capone's headquarters.

In his quest for Harry Lang–style drama, Friedken scripted his film, *The People versus Paul Crump,* around the discredited and discarded notion that Crump was innocent. In the sixty-minute black-and-white docudrama, Crump willingly followed Friedken's plot line, as did actor Brooks Johnson, who played Crump in scenes reenacting the incident. When reporter John Justin Smith, appearing in the film, asked Crump whether he had anything to do with the killing of the plant guard, Crump replied, "I most certainly did not . . . positively nothing. . . . I was with a woman. I was in a woman's bed at the exact time this thing was happening."[27] Crump, who was articulate and composed on camera, insisted for the teleplay that his confession was beaten from him.

Luckily for Crump *The People versus Paul Crump* was not aired in the summer of 1962, when his fate lay in the hands of Governor Kerner. Attorney Moore realized the film was too inflammatory and would create a backlash against clemency. Moore, a dedicated but emotional and erratic lawyer who often drank excessively, knew whereof he spoke. He had appeared in the film, vehemently denouncing the Chicago police. Asked by reporter Smith about Crump's charges of police brutality, Moore, emphatic in a camera close-up, responded:

> I would say that the overwhelming probabilities in this case are—I may be wrong, and this is my opinion, and this is what I think—the overwhelming probabilities, based on the record of the Chicago Police Department for the last thirty years, are that Paul Crump was beaten within an inch of his life. And if I had to bet on it that's what I'd bet, because that's what I think, because this is what the Chicago police have been doing to get confessions, the memory of man runneth not to the contrary. . . . The history is disgraceful. . . . I'm not talking just about Paul's case, now. I'm talking about the beaten and battered people I've seen with my own eyes fresh from police stations.[28]

Friedken later claimed Moore was drunk at the time.[29] With the execution date of August 3 quickly approaching, no one in the Crump camp except Friedken wanted to risk airing the film. Moore's charges and the film's chilling enactments of police brutality would have enraged Mayor Daley and probably made clemency a political impossibility for Kerner. Nonetheless, for years thereafter Friedken said his film helped to save Crump's life. *The People versus Paul Crump* may not have helped Crump, but it did help Friedken. The film won a major award later that year in California and brought Friedken to the attention of major moviemakers. His Hollywood directing career included *The French Connection,* which also was based loosely on actual events, and *The Exorcist,* which was not.

✦ ✦ ✦

Crump's advocates were reading from a different script—more than two hundred pages of affidavits sworn by well-seasoned observers of prison behavior inside Cook County Jail. Petitions based on successful rehabilitation rarely worked in defeating the executioner. What prisoner facing death would not claim to be rehabilitated by the experience? In Crump's case, however, the record was compelling and authentic. When Moore applied to Kerner in early July for executive clemency for Crump, he took a position diametrically opposed to that of the Friedken movie. He affirmed that Crump "accepts the judgment of the courts that his confession was voluntary, his trial under the then existing law of Illinois was fundamentally fair and that there was substantial evidence to support the verdict."[30]

Crump's supporters made no attempt to deny he had been a vicious criminal and rebellious prisoner when he began his journey toward the electric chair nine years earlier. On the contrary, the best case for demonstrating rehabilitation depended on dramatic change. "Upon admission to the jail, Paul was a frantic young man," said Episcopal priest James G. Jones in an affidavit supporting Moore's clemency plea. Jones ran a prisoner rehabilitation center and ministered in Cook County Jail for the Episcopal Diocese of Chicago. He was the single greatest influence on Crump's life at that time. Jones recalled Crump as "bitter, explosive and certainly in an advanced stage of delinquency orientation."[31] He went on to describe Crump's metamorphosis, how Crump nursed sick prisoners, educated himself, and became a force for good inside the seething jail. "When I would run into potential suicides, representing a goodly number out of 20,000 men a year, I would request their transfer to [Crump's] wing and put Paul on the case. Only once did he fail." Jones also told how Crump helped him through his own personal crisis, when his wife was in critical condition with a difficult pregnancy. "I always think gratefully of Paul when I see my caesarean-born daughter growing older."[32]

Fifty-seven persons submitted affidavits supporting clemency. Most were guards or police officers who worked at the jail. Joseph Lohman, the former Cook County sheriff who opposed Kerner in the 1960 Democratic primary for governor, wrote on Crump's behalf. Two other letters to Kerner, both handwritten, shaped the issues clearly. Veronica Zukowski wrote on July 18:

> To My Regret, we have to meet this way: In 1953, Paul Krump [sic] Killed my Husband. He was sentenced by the People of the Jury, not me; and everything went on according to the Law, which I approved: Because I believe in Law. He was supposed to get the chair Aug—20—1953. After that, I was dropped out of the picture and Krump was taken care by the Law. And Now All of a sudden, I'm on Top just to be Stabbed at: I feel the Law had him in his hands so Let them keep him

and be responsible for him. To make the story short—I do not want Paul Krump
to get the Electric Chair—For Many Reasons.[33]

On July 23 Kerner replied by letter: "Your letter is most moving and I deeply
appreciate the fact that you took time to express your thoughts to me."[34]

The second handwritten letter, dated July 27, was addressed to "Honorable Sir":

> As I stand on the threshold of eternity, with malice toward no one and fully rec-
> ognizing the contempt God has for the sin of deceit and not desiring to tempt His
> wrath and loss of the heavenly balm of salvation, I am completely devoid of ill
> human motives except the desire to live so that I may justify my life and the faith
> of those who have done so much for me. I humbly pray that the dictates of your
> inner convictions will justify your mercy toward me, as I prayerfully wait with my
> life in your hands, and the faith that God will guide your judgment. Humbly and
> Respectfully Prayed, Your Sincerely and eternally Indebted—Paul Crump.[35]

Organizing the affidavits and letters was a production no less elaborate
than a Friedken movie. A big part of the job involved keeping Crump's case
in the press, which tends to tire quickly of a story. Moore, Solomon, and other
local supporters worked tirelessly, but for the last act they turned to an outsider, New York lawyer Louis Nizer. Sixty-year-old Nizer had an international
reputation for high-profile, long-shot cases. He found irresistible the chance
to enter the Crump case at its climax, although he had scheduled a rare vacation for late July. A few days before the July 30 Parole and Pardon Board
hearing, Moore and Crump sent separate telegrams urging Nizer to volunteer to speak for Crump. "Need older and wiser head to assist," said Moore.
After the telegrams came phone calls and the affidavits supporting Crump.[36]

In his 1966 book *The Jury Returns*, Nizer's self-aggrandizing was in full
flower as he recalled reading the affidavits: "The words were flames which
leaped from the paper and enveloped me with zeal. I never went to sleep.
Before dawn broke I knew I would be in Chicago the next day fighting for
Paul Crump. . . . The law said rehabilitation was 'not a basis for clemency.'
It was a law which had to be reformed, and I was burning to make the attempt."[37] Nizer believed that, despite the well-orchestrated campaign on
Crump's behalf, public sentiment was against commutation. "Governor Kerner would be risking his career if he yielded to entreaties for clemency in so
shocking a case. He would have to be courageous beyond the call of duty to
commute the sentence," he wrote.[38]

Actually the media campaign already had accomplished much, and
Crump's story had won him considerable public sympathy. As of July 27 the
Parole and Pardon Board had received 140 petitions, bearing 6,933 signa-
tures, and 1,035 letters all favoring commutation of the death sentence. Just

166 letters opposed commutation. Among those writing for Crump was evangelist Billy Graham. In a June 16 letter to Kerner, Graham said he had gone to Cook County Jail "quietly and without any publicity" to talk to Crump. "I was deeply impressed by this warm and intelligent man," Graham wrote.

> There is no doubt that he has been rehabilitated in a most remarkable way. Therefore, although this is the first such letter I have ever written, I would like to add my voice to those of many others to ask you to consider commuting his sentence. In the first place, he has already died a thousand times in the 10 years he has been in prison. In the second place, he is not the same man who committed the crime. It seems to me the object of the penal system is rehabilitation, and in Paul Crump I believe you have Exhibit A. . . . Please forgive my boldness to inject myself into this matter, but I have come to feel rather strongly about it. I am not sure whether I believe in capital punishment or not. Be that as it may, in this particular case I do not believe in it.[39]

Kerner's June 22 reply to Graham indicated that Kerner had not yet joined the rally to Crump's cause:

> I . . . am expressly against the death penalty. I do not believe that it serves as a deterrent to crime. Above all, it is morally unjust. . . . However, I am an elected public official of the State of Illinois, sworn to uphold its statutes. The decision rendered in our courts was that of death. As Governor of the State of Illinois, it is my duty to uphold this ruling of the judiciary even though it is against my personal philosophy. I spent many wretched hours earlier this year when I was faced with a similar decision in the case of Vincent Ciucci. I cannot, in good conscience, grant executive clemency to Crump when it was not granted to Ciucci. In both cases the crime of murder was involved. Both men had been rehabilitated.[40]

The sweltering sixteenth-floor hearing room in the State of Illinois Building at 160 N. LaSalle was jammed with television cameras, press photographers, and eager spectators. Somehow a courier for WGN television managed to get his motorbike up the elevator to the room so that he could race film back to the station. The Parole and Pardon Board had considered closing the Crump hearing to the public but knew it would get stiff opposition from the two ambitious lawyers on either side of the case: Nizer and assistant state's attorney James Thompson. Craven was the most vocal advocate of open hearings. "Mushrooms are the only things that grow well in the darkness," he said later.[41] Nonetheless, it was hard for board members to hear witnesses above the din of the crowd and the noise of electric fans trying unsuccessfully to cool the room.

In his book Nizer recorded his initial impression of Thompson: "He was very tall, and his blond hair was closely cropped. He was young enough for his bespectacled face not yet to register the sternness and cynicism of his professional work. On the contrary, he had a pleasing look. Moore had told me of his reputation as a skilled advocate. It was not easy to detect whether supreme confidence or poise accounted for his manner."[42]

Nizer gave the opening statement. He made no effort to attack the institution of capital punishment. Following the agreed strategy, he stressed that "Crump was a vicious animal at the time he was convicted." He said Crump had undergone a "miraculous" transformation that could not be said of other murderers. "Crump's rehabilitation is unique. Granting him clemency will not commute the death sentence of every murderer."[43] To establish some legal basis for the rehabilitation theory, he quoted a delegate to Illinois's 1870 state constitutional convention that adopted the constitution still in force at the time: "Pardons are sometimes given as a reward to furnish new and better life. . . . The whole scheme of salvation is based upon the idea." He cited Abraham Lincoln's clemency rulings and examples of Lincoln's mercy toward condemned soldiers. "If rehabilitation is not a basis for clemency, what is?" Nizer asked. "Is not the entire objective of all punishment, if not the hope of the world, to rehabilitate the criminal? This is the only civilized objective. It is the vital issue for this board and the governor."[44]

Nizer knew he was on thin ice here. There was no basis in Illinois law or prior clemency rulings for the notion that rehabilitation is "the entire objective of all punishment." Nizer concluded, "The only thing we ask is that his life not be snuffed out and that he be confined to jail for the rest of his life." He then called several witnesses, including Father Jones.[45]

Thompson called only one witness, his friend and now federal district judge Richard B. Austin, the 1956 Democratic candidate for governor and former assistant Cook County state's attorney who had received Crump's confession. He testified that what prison officials and others supporting Crump's plea had seen was not a transformation but the guile of a chameleon cleverly changing appearances to fit his circumstances. He agreed there were two Crumps, evil and good, but said both lived in the man facing execution. In his summation Thompson condemned Crump and Nizer's case. He quoted passages from the affidavits that expressed doubts about Crump's rebirth. He ridiculed the publicity campaign mounted on Crump's behalf and the idea that Crump should escape execution merely because time and his condition in jail permitted him to feign an improved attitude and demeanor. In closing Thompson pointed attention directly at Kerner, who was in Springfield awaiting the results of the hearing. He said the board should not substitute its collective conscience for the conscience of the governor. "That awesome power [clemency] is left, as it should be, to the Governor of this State. . . . You gentlemen are no more than ministers to the governor's conscience."[46]

The board retired to a room across the street in the Bismarck Hotel. For several hours the five men harangued each other in private. Kerner had told the members he wanted the Crump matter ended quickly, but each of the five members had to state his position. Craven said the testimony of Father Jones was the most persuasive. The board regarded Nizer as an out-of-town brain surgeon brought in for a quick operation after local physicians had painstakingly evaluated and prepared the patient. They found Thompson to be an effective advocate who, in Craven's words, "could (do) with a more generous serving of humility."[47]

They prepared a confidential recommendation that summarized the history of the case and Crump's journey through the court system. It included the letter by Billy Graham and reminded the governor that Zukowski's widow favored commutation. "The presentation of this case was by a rather novel approach," the board wrote.

> Neither the fairness of the trials nor the competency of the witnesses nor any error in the judicial proceedings were suggested. This case was presented entirely upon the basis that, notwithstanding the validity of the proceedings, the change or rebirth of the inmate was such as to make him a different person than the one who was originally incarcerated. The inmate was described as a unique and classical instance of the positive response, changing from an asocial to a social person. It was urged that the rehabilitation of this inmate was a symbol of that which could be accomplished and that the symbol should not be destroyed.[48]

In a unanimous decision the board concluded: "We recommend this case as proper for the exercising of the constitutionally given powers of the governor to extend clemency while also persuaded by the established fact of rehabilitation. Our consideration were [sic] not limited to the fact of rehabilitation alone. Unquestionably Paul Crump has become a symbol. His execution as now scheduled would be destructive of something that could be turned to useful purposes."[49] The statement pointed out that three of Crump's four accomplices received sentences of 199 years and recommended that Crump get the same, thereby "incarcerating the prisoner for such time as will permit him to be separated from the free community as surely as if his life were taken." The formal recommendation called for Crump's sentence of death by electrocution to "be commuted to imprisonment in the Illinois State Penitentiary for a term of one hundred ninety-nine years, without parole." The last two words were extraordinary. The board knew that Kerner could not restrict the authority of a successor to grant parole and that Illinois required that after twenty years' imprisonment a felon must be eligible for a parole hearing. Craven recalled years later that the words probably were appended to the recommendation simply to bring the board's debate to an end and get a unanimous decision.[50]

Craven volunteered to carry the board's statement and recommendation down to Springfield. He took time to pick up his wife and children, who were staying with Craven's parents in Chicago. His somewhat leisurely drive to the state capitol did not please Kerner aide Chamberlain, who was on the phone looking for the statement while Craven and his family were driving down Route 66. State police were called out to find the courier and hurry him along.

Two days later Kerner adopted the recommendation of his Parole and Pardon Board. He said he had the power of clemency "in exceptional cases" and declared,

> This is such a case. I am personally opposed to capital punishment. My personal convictions, however, will not predetermine my actions in a request for commutation in a capital case. It does not follow, however, that every request for clemency must be denied. To take that position would be to abrogate the power which was consciously and deliberately invested in the Governor. The most significant goal of a system of penology in a civilized society is the rehabilitation of one of its members who, for a variety of complex reasons, has violated the laws of the society. If that premise were to be denied, solely because it is a capital case, a great disservice would be done to what we hopefully embrace as the ultimate goal of the system. What has troubled me is how the concept of rehabilitation can be judged and evaluated in a case where the process of law, after the extensive review permitted every defendant by our concern for justice, has determined that a man committed a crime so repugnant as to merit a sentence of death. I do not suggest that by my decision in this case I have totally resolved this dilemma, nor that I can set forth standards so universal as to lead to an inevitable conclusion in the next case. We must, however, be able to hold forth to others the hope that they can look forward to a useful life—to life itself—if they will make the necessary effort to face squarely their past actions and the alternatives.

Kerner said that the evidence in favor of Crump was "virtually unanimous that the embittered distorted man who committed a vicious murder no longer exists. . . . Under these circumstances, it would serve no useful purpose to society to take this man's life. . . . This consideration, however, can never be entirely free of doubt, for the real test for Paul Crump lies ahead. The years he must face in prison will serve as a true test of his willingness and ability to be of service to his fellow man." Kerner ordered the recommended 199-year sentence, "without parole."[51]

The factors behind Kerner's decision go beyond the record assembled by Crump's supporters and the deliberations of the Parole and Pardon Board. Aide William Chamberlain, a highly skilled administrator who had transferred from Paul Powell's staff to rescue Kerner's first term from near disaster, was a friend of Donald Page Moore from their days as classmates at the University of Illinois Law School. Moore had lobbied Chamberlain directly. Kerner

aide Dawn Clark, who wrote the statement on Crump, was under considerable pressure from the liberals in the legislature and back home in Chicago
because of the Kerner administration's failure to follow a progressive agenda
to their liking. She did not know how to shift the blame to where she believed
it belonged—on Ted Isaacs, Kerner's wheeling and dealing confidant. A decision in favor of the national campaign on behalf of Crump would put Kerner and herself back in the good graces of liberals and at least temporarily
lift the spirits of his staff. "This will give him some mileage," Kerner aide
Norton Long wrote in his diary.[52]

Chamberlain told Craven the decision was never in doubt. There was no
organized pressure favoring Paul Crump's death. Nevertheless, Chamberlain
wanted the board's statement delivered as quickly as possible to prevent anyone from getting to Kerner and changing his mind. In the same week Governor Pat Brown, campaigning for reelection amid widespread criticism of his
handling of the Chessman case, found no mercy for convicted murderer Elizabeth Duncan and two male accomplices. "I am unable to find circumstances
to warrant commutation," Brown wrote.[53]

Kerner, as usual, kept his views to himself, leaving Chamberlain and other
anxious staffers unsure how wedded he was to the rehabilitation theory. But
there is no doubt that the evidence of Crump's transformation resonated with
Kerner. In his letter to Rev. Robert Edgar, which he wrote two days after the
Crump commutation, his attitude had changed from the letter written to Rev.
Billy Graham. He insisted he had remained aloof from the media clamor and
focused singularly on the question of rehabilitation and the individual's power
to transform himself: "There are many, as you can imagine, who still believe
in the eye for an eye and tooth for a tooth philosophy, and there are those
who believe that even a slight show of rehabilitation ought to excuse all of
an individual's past actions. These are the two extremes and I have always
tried to remain more on the right, in favor of rehabilitation."[54]

✦ ✦ ✦

There was no constituency on behalf of Jesse Welsh, thirty-seven, after
he was sentenced to die for the 1956 street-fight shooting of a Chicago police detective. Nor was there much case to be made that Welsh had become a
different man, although he once had tried to become one by taking a new
name—James Dukes—when he was being sought for questioning in the
murder of a Chicago woman in 1947. Just twenty-one days after commuting Crump's sentence, Kerner refused clemency for Dukes. The decision angered both sides in the capital punishment debate, but there was a certain
symmetry to the logic.

Dukes was a "bad man," recalled Craven.[55] He had served time on two armed robbery convictions. Outside a tavern near Forty-seventh and Wells Streets, shortly after midnight on June 15, 1956, Dukes was beating a woman in a drunken rage when three men from a nearby church attempted to intervene. He pulled a revolver and shot two of them. Two police detectives in plain clothes, John Blyth Jr. and Daniel Rolewicz, heard the shots and jumped from their unmarked car, approaching Dukes along opposite sides of Forty-seventh Street. Dukes fired at Rolewicz and ran into an alley, where he encountered Blyth. Rolewicz followed and testified he saw Blyth fall with a gunshot wound.

Like Crump, Dukes had won a second trial but was twice convicted. On three occasions the U.S. Supreme Court refused to hear his appeals. Seeking leniency from Kerner, Dukes relied on three claims: that Blyth was killed by a bullet fired by Rolewicz; that he was intoxicated and had no premeditation of a crime; and that the prosecution, at both of his trials, had excluded blacks from the jury. After the Crump clemency decision, Dukes's attorney, Jason Bellows, sought a reprieve. Bellows described Dukes as a good prisoner who was baptized a Catholic in jail. But he did not claim rehabilitation. In a six-page handwritten letter to Kerner, Dukes separated himself from Crump: "I would like to say this about the big howl regarding rehabilitation. In the case of Paul Crump your decision was just and humane. He was a good example of a man's ability to change from one extreme to another. But my case is entirely different because I don't see how a man can be rehabilitated from normal man to normal man! I am not saying that I have been perfect, which no one is. What I want to stress is, the crime I'm accused and convicted of could have happened to anyone. A fight! Pursuing a few drinks and unfortunately an individual was killed. The fact that he was a police officer does not change the naturalness of mass confusion." Dukes maintained, "I haven't done anything to be rehabilitated for" and repeated his claim that Rolewicz accidentally shot Blyth.[56]

Kerner called a hearing of the Illinois Parole and Pardon Board for Monday, August 20, in the State of Illinois Building in Chicago. The board adjourned to Cook County Jail to hear from Dukes himself. There was little to be said for Dukes on the basis of his crime or the theory of rehabilitation. But the liberal majority on the board—Craven, Jones, and Lerner—believed the Crump decision strengthened their hand in making a bolder recommendation. In a private communication to Kerner, they asked him to overlook the particulars of Dukes's crime and clemency plea and to concentrate instead on the state of capital punishment in Illinois.

Dealing with clemency petitions case by case, "we deal in symptoms and not substance," they wrote.

We would be remiss in our duties if we did not report to you on the social and economic relationship of this case and other pending cases. Eight of the next ten persons under sentence of death are Negroes. It was alleged in this case that no Negroes served on the jury. . . . It was true in this case and it was represented to the Board that in other cases no Negroes served upon the jury. We cannot but conclude that this goes beyond the possibility of mere coincidence. The facts of the matter are that the social structure is such that Negroes are most likely to receive the death sentence because, in the opinion of this Board, they are more often involved in serious crimes of violence. This is not due to excessive criminal propensities but rather to the facts of social and economic life here to be found. To decide this case and leave untouched the challenge to society is to ignore reality. James Dukes, whether dead or incarcerated, is but a symbol of the problem. To execute James Dukes can serve no useful purpose and to commute his sentence without reference to the obvious and complicated environmental factors that contributed to his crime would compound the injustice.[57]

The three board members indicated they would likewise recommend nullification of other death sentences. They asked for a private meeting with Kerner to discuss the broad issues they raised. In separate remarks Lerner added that he believed Dukes's crime was a crime of passion and deserved leniency, especially compared to Crump, who killed as part of a well-planned holdup. Kerner did not follow where Craven, Jones, and Lerner were leading. He held no special meeting with his Parole and Pardon Board, as they had requested. On August 22 Kerner denied Dukes's petition. Without mentioning his Crump decision or the extraordinary appeal by the board majority, Kerner returned to the perfunctory language of the Ciucci decision: "James Dukes has received every possible consideration in our courts. The conviction and sentence have been consistently upheld. Further consideration was given to all of the petitioner's contentions in an extraordinary session of the Parole and Pardon Board held last Monday. I do not feel that it is an appropriate case for the exercise of executive clemency."[58] Dukes was executed shortly after midnight on August 24. Detective Rolewicz sat on a wooden bench with other witnesses to see Dukes die. "I've been waiting a long time for this," he told a reporter.[59]

Reflecting the views of many death-penalty opponents, an editorial in the liberal *Chicago Sun-Times* bitterly attacked the contrasting outcomes in the Crump and Dukes cases:

What should have been a solemn proceeding intended only to determine whether Crump was or was not entitled to clemency became an emotional binge. . . . The type of campaign carried on in Crump's behalf to influence the pardon board and the governor is as out of place in our society as would be trial by fire. . . . These persons exerted themselves in Crump's behalf. But few of them were heard from in Duke's [*sic*] behalf. Their sympathies were played upon masterfully in behalf of Crump. Emotionally exhausted, as a consequence, they didn't overly exert themselves in behalf of Dukes. . . . If their dedication to the repeal of capital punishment couldn't survive the interval between the Crump case and the Dukes case, it would appear to be founded on little more than emotional involvement."[60]

Supporters of capital punishment complained as well. Claude R. Sowle, a conservative Northwestern University law professor whom Kerner had asked to observe the Crump clemency hearing, had recommended against clemency. After Dukes died, he accused Kerner of holding a double standard. Having established a precedent in the Crump case, Kerner immediately ignored it, he said. "A cynic might say that Dukes is to die because he was never vicious enough to win the attention, time and support of those whose stature and advancement are enhanced by the working of miracles in the area of criminal rehabilitation," Sowle said. "I hope this is not the case, but there is certainly reason to wonder."[61]

The enormous publicity surrounding the Ciucci, Crump, and Dukes cases in the first nine months of 1962 provided a solid test of the claim that awareness of the death penalty deters murder, one of the principal arguments of death-penalty proponents. The answer, according to Hans Mattick's analysis, was no. "The Crump case became an international *cause celebre* with more local news coverage than any commutation case since the Haymarket rioters of 1886 were commuted by Governor Altgeld," Mattick wrote. But Kerner's score was two-to-one in favor of execution. "According to the tenets of the deterrent theory of capital punishment, one would expect that such overwhelming public discussion of the relation between murder and the death penalty should have penetrated the minds of any potential murderers in the Chicago area," Mattick wrote. "The facts . . . , however, do not support the theory." Except for a decline in April, the murder rate in Chicago that year remained essentially constant—about thirty killings per month—throughout the period of newspaper headlines concerning the three cases.[62]

✦ ✦ ✦

In commuting Crump's death sentence, Kerner suggested a new course for the state's relationship with its most serious offenders and lent the prestige of his office to an airing of important doubts about capital punishment. But the Crump case set no precedent in either regard. Rehabilitation never became a ground for commuting a death sentence in Illinois or other death-penalty states. Crump failed to blossom as a rehabilitated man. Later diagnosed as a paranoid schizophrenic, he was a troubled and often troublesome prisoner until his release on parole at age sixty-two in 1993. Nor did Illinois voters undertake a fresh examination of the issue as a result of the Ciucci,

Crump, and Dukes cases. On the other hand, Kerner suffered no political repercussions from rendering separate justice to Crump on the one hand and Ciucci and Dukes on the other. Despite considerable clamor created by the three cases, a public opinion survey conducted for Kerner in December 1962 made no mention of capital punishment as an issue affecting perceptions of the first-term governor. Capital punishment did not become an issue in his 1964 bid for reelection, and Kerner never sought public sympathy for his ambiguity on the matter. As did his father's, Kerner's advocacy of civil liberties evolved over many years.

Unlike Kerner, James Thompson displayed no ambiguity whatever. His performance was never affected by doubt. Like Kerner, he made no bid for political benefit from his position. "He was restrained. He hurt us for just that reason," Crump attorney Donald Page Moore told *Chicago* magazine. "And I think he cared a lot more about the case than he ever showed. He was the very model of a great prosecutor. He didn't do any of this low-down rabble-rousing. He was a gentleman. A merciless gentleman."[63]

Mayor-elect Anton Cermak (right) visiting Tomas Masaryk, Czech president, after a hero's welcome in Prague in the fall of 1932. Masaryk was called the father of his country after he achieved the formation of Czechoslovakia following World War I. Courtesy of Anton C. Kerner.

Otto Jr., eight years of age, his mother, Rose, and his brother, Robert, five years of age, in 1916. Later, after Robert was struck and killed by a streetcar, Rose fell into an extended depression, causing her to wonder years afterward how Otto Jr. got along without her. Courtesy of Anton C. Kerner.

Rose and Judge Otto Kerner Sr. in court in 1928 during hearings on charges that he and other judges were soft on crime ("paltering with crime"). Representing himself, Kerner was exonerated without qualification and went on to be elected Illinois attorney general. Courtesy of the *Chicago Tribune*.

Helena Cermak Kenlay visiting with her father, Anton Cermak, president of the Cook County Board, in the hospital. Following her mother's death, Helena increasingly aided her father in his political career. Courtesy of the *Chicago Tribune*.

Shirley Kub and Alexander Jamie waiting to be called before the special grand jury investigating charges concerning law-enforcement corruption in 1933. Jamie was a federal prohibition agent and brother-in-law of Eliot Ness. Described as an investigator, detective, stool pigeon, spy, and undercover agent, Kub influenced IRS special agent Jack Walsh, who presided over the investigation of Otto Kerner Jr. thirty-five years later. Courtesy of the *Chicago Tribune* (photo retouched). .

Major Otto Kerner Jr. studies a map of Sicily after helping to defeat Field Marshal Erwin Rommel and his Afrika Korps in Tunisia (photo taken in 1943). Kerner received the Bronze Star for meritorious service and the Soldier's Medal for rescuing a drowning soldier along the Italian coast during World War II. Courtesy of the *Chicago Tribune*.

Mary Alyce Kerner Christensen, daughter of Helena Cermak Kerner, with Kerner Sr. and Rose. Mary Alyce died from injuries in an auto accident outside Milwaukee in 1953. She had previously divorced Anders J. Christensen II and was survived by her son, Anders III (now Anton), and daughter, Helena. Just as Mary Alyce had been adopted by Otto Jr., so were Anton and Helena. Courtesy of the *Chicago Tribune*.

Richard J. Daley points to Joseph Lohman and Otto Kerner, both gubernatorial candidates in 1960. To Daley's right are Jacob Arvey and Abraham Lincoln Marovitz. The occasion was a party at the home of politically connected Chicago police officer Martin Joyce on the northwest side of Chicago. Courtesy of Lou Joyce.

Governor Kerner (right) with his aide Chris Vlahoplus (left) and state revenue director Ted Isaacs, who served with Kerner in the Illinois National Guard and was Kerner's campaign manager. Illinois State Historical Library.

Paul Crump, convicted of murdering a guard at a plant in Chicago's stockyards during an attempted robbery in 1953, talking with a reporter about his petition of commutation in July 1962. His execution was scheduled for August 3, 1962. UPI photo.

Cook County assistant state's attorney James R. Thompson (seated, center) awaiting completion of New York attorney Louis Nizer's (standing, center) opening statement in support of Paul Crump's petition for commutation of his death sentence. The hearing was before the state's parole and pardon board July 30, 1962, just days before Crump's scheduled execution. Courtesy of the *Chicago Tribune*.

President John F. Kennedy, Senator Everett Dirksen, and Governor Kerner at the White House on the eve of the departure of Illinois's European trade delegation in the fall of 1963. Weeks later Kennedy was assassinated. Photograph by Abbey Rowe; courtesy of the John Fitzgerald Kennedy Library.

Kerner and Republican gubernatorial opponent Charles H. Percy at the
Du Quoin State Fair in 1964. The "casual" confrontation was arranged
by Percy forces. AP/Wide World Photos.

Governor Kerner and
Illinois secretary of
state candidate Paul
Powell with former
president Harry S.
Truman, who came
to Springfield to sup-
port Powell in his bid
for election in 1964.
UPI Telephoto.

Atomic Energy Commission chairman Glenn Seaborg (left) visits
the proposed accelerator site at Weston in April 1966. To his left
are Governor Kerner, Weston mayor Arthur Theriault, and Senator Paul H. Douglas. Courtesy of Fermi National Accelerator
Laboratory.

Governor Kerner (right) and General William Westmoreland going over a map in Vietnam in 1965. During World War II Kerner served as Westmoreland's executive officer.
Illinois State Historical Library.

President Lyndon B. Johnson with the Kerner Commission at its initial session in 1967. Second row, left to right: James C. Corman, U.S. representative; Herbert Jenkins, chief of police, Atlanta; I. W. Abel, president, United Steel Workers; Fred R. Harris, U.S. senator; Vice President Hubert H. Humphrey; Katherine Graham Peden, Commerce Commission member, Kentucky; Charles B. Thornton, chairman of the board and CEO, Litton Industries; Edward W. Brooke, U.S. senator; (unidentified). First row, left to right: Roy Wilkins, executive director, National Association for the Advancement of Colored People; Chairman Otto Kerner, Illinois governor; President Johnson; Vice Chairman John V. Lindsay, New York mayor; William M. McCulloch, U.S. representative. Photograph by Yoichi R. Okamoto; courtesy of the Lyndon Baines Johnson Library.

Kerner meeting with President Johnson in January 1968, less than two months before the issuance of the Kerner Report. Photograph by Frank Wolfe; courtesy of the Lyndon Baines Johnson Library.

Marjorie Lindheimer Everett with Mayor Richard J. Daley in 1966. George Schaller, a Daley law partner, was one of her attorneys. Courtesy of the *Chicago Tribune*.

"Brass Knuckles," a political cartoon by Bill Maulden appearing in the *Chicago Sun-Times* in 1973. Kerner supporters saw the hand of President Richard Nixon in the government's decision to indict Kerner. Reprinted with special permission from the *Chicago Sun-Times* © 1998.

BRASS KNUCKLES

U.S. Attorney James R. Thompson (left) and first assistant Samuel K. Skinner at news conference after Kerner was convicted on April 19, 1973. Courtesy of the *Chicago Tribune*.

Otto, Anton, and Helena Kerner after Otto's sentencing on July 9, 1973, to three years and a $50,000 fine. Courtesy of the *Chicago Tribune*.

Kerner's room at the Federal Correctional Institution in Lexington, Kentucky. Courtesy of the *Chicago Tribune*.

Kerner and his mother, Rose, at a 1975 welcome-home party in Springfield attended by friends and supporters, including former governor Richard B. Ogilvie. Kerner observed: "There is nothing like personal contact, like seeing people again." AP/Wide World Photos.

7

The Giant Ring

In the early 1960s, when federally funded expressways extended Chicago's reach westward into Du Page County, a down-and-out subdivision stood alone amid farmland on the county's western edge, suggesting none of the neatly clipped upward mobility that suburban home builders were promoting to city dwellers. The tract of one hundred prefabricated single-story frame rental houses, assembled near a former Native American refuge called Big Woods, had been marketed unsuccessfully as "affordable housing." The builder was long gone, however, and the development languished in receivership under the Federal Savings and Loan Insurance Corporation. The houses looked like a remote emplacement of gunnery pillboxes waiting for an enemy that was engaged elsewhere.

The nearly four hundred residents—most of them from Chicago—held high hopes for their community. They called it Weston, although downstate Illinois already had a whistle-stop town by that name. In May 1963 they incorporated as a village, with an eye toward expansion and respectability. One resident, a Hungarian shoemaker who had suffered under communist repression in his native country, proudly raised the American flag each morning in the center of town.

✦ ✦ ✦

Weston attracted a second real estate entrepreneur, William G. Riley, who like the town's optimistic souls dreamed of better days. Riley had constructed several single-bedroom apartment complexes—each named "King

Arthur Court"—throughout Chicago's near suburbs. In January 1964 he threw a cocktail party in a downtown Chicago hotel to unveil an elaborate 1,600-square-foot model of a massive residential project he hoped would enhance his respectability and bring him quick cash. It would be a city of 50,000 residents on 4,700 acres, offering homes in a wide price range and such amenities as golf courses, bridle paths, an airport, and a polo field. In terms of area, the base of Riley's model was bigger than the houses then standing in the fledgling community. He called his project New Weston and explained grandly to his cocktail party guests "what is involved in the birth of a city and why this city is vital to America's future growth."[1] Weston Village president John Lowe, standing with him, declared, "Within three years Weston will be one of the ten largest cities in Illinois."[2]

The members of the Du Page County Board were not impressed. They disdained Weston's cookie-cutter houses that government receivers were unloading for $200 down, a sum buyers could forgo in return for cleaning up and redecorating the forlorn property. "They really did not want a blue-collar community developing on the west side of the county," recalled one former Weston resident. "There was one already in Addison forming in the east."[3] Du Page officials were all too familiar with Riley's King Arthur Court apartment project in Addison, a suburb on the eastern edge of the county that was an enclave for singles and low-income workers at the light industrial plants expanding around O'Hare International Airport. Riley and his Addison tenants were not what Du Page's old-family farmers and entrenched politicians had in mind for Weston or anywhere else in their domain, which was fast becoming one of the wealthiest and most Republican urban counties in the nation. They had their eyes on Weston as a site for a garbage dump. To gain the upper hand, the county board sued to overturn Weston's incorporation, claiming it was not "a village in fact" under an ambivalent phrase in Illinois law.

But there was more to Riley than either Du Page politicians or the people of Weston knew. One resident of Addison's King Arthur Court apartment complex was a convicted rapist named Joseph Amabile, known in law-enforcement and organized-crime circles as "Joe Shine" and "The Freak." In 1962 Riley made the mistake of siting an apartment project in Northlake, a blue-color suburb directly east of Addison in Cook County. The crime syndicate, which lived on well past the death of Al Capone, ruled Northlake. "What do you mean you're going to build in Northlake?" Amabile asked him, according to Riley's later testimony in federal court. "Nobody builds in Northlake without my permission. I'm the man in Northlake. With my permission you can build in the middle of the street. Without it, you can't turn a shovel."[4] The government charged that Amabile and his underworld boss,

Salvatore "Teetz" Battaglia, made themselves Riley's silent partners in a scheme to loot savings and loan associations.

The residue of the Capone organization, accommodated by Chicago-area politicians and local law-enforcement officials for three decades, was known as "the Outfit." Among true aficionados it was called "West Side," a reference to the fact that ever since Capone established headquarters in Cicero, on the city's western border, crime chieftains kept a hand in the city's West Side wards and chose to live in the swanker near-west suburbs, such as Oak Park, River Forest, Riverside, and Oak Brook. After West Side crime leader Momo Salvatore "Sam" Giancana, an associate of Capone lieutenant Anthony Accardo, fled to Mexico to escape the federal government's heat, the Chicago press and Chicago Crime Commission identified Battaglia, who lived in Oak Park, as Giancana's successor. Amabile was a Battaglia henchman. Northlake was their town. They demanded money from Riley for allowing his King Arthur projects in Addison, Westmont, and Lansing, as well as Northlake. In the face of this extortion, Riley's company went bust, taking with it hundreds of gullible investors—Riley called them "armchair investors"—who had helped to finance his apartment-building enterprise.[5]

Four months after Riley unveiled his model of New Weston, he abandoned the project. He blamed his troubles on the Du Page County Board's lawsuit. The litigation questioning the town's legal status made it impossible to obtain utilities and other public infrastructure, he said. But Riley told an entirely different story after he entered the Justice Department's witness protection program. Seeing how the government had chased Giancana out of Chicago, Riley explained, he felt safe to be singing to law-enforcement officials. His new partners were Internal Revenue Service criminal investigators, including a particularly skillful and dogged special agent named John M. "Jack" Walsh. Walsh and fellow IRS agents used Riley's testimony to build criminal cases against Battaglia, Amabile, Northlake mayor Henry Neri, and others under the federal extortion statute known as the Hobbs Act, one of the government's principal weapons against organized crime. Riley, who at one time had reveled in his underworld associations and in syndicate-controlled nightclubs, proved to be one of the best courtroom witnesses the IRS ever had against the Outfit. With tears in his eyes, he described threats with baseball bats and told how a lighted cigarette was held to his eye as part of the extortion. "I was afraid for the personal safety of myself and my family," he told a jury.[6] Riley helped the IRS convict Battaglia once and Amabile twice before federal district judge Julius J. Hoffman. The Northlake convictions were major victories for the IRS in Chicago. Jack Walsh won his stripes as a genuine Chicago crime fighter.

Meanwhile, Weston looked like a loser, a pothole on the road to suburban sprawl. Du Page County persisted in its lawsuit, and federal thrift regulators pushed to sell the houses in receivership. Fifteen remained vacant. Efforts to get paved sidewalks and sewers stalled. Riley's grandiose model community was forgotten. But some who had seen it remembered its most distinctive feature: a doughnut-shaped civic center and shopping complex, 1,300 feet in diameter, forming the center of New Weston, a giant ring that was supposed to be the heart of the community.

✦ ✦ ✦

In November 1964 Otto Kerner handily won a second term, but his victory margin of 179,299 votes over Republican Charles Percy paled in comparison to his 524,252-vote margin over William Stratton. This time Kerner could not claim that he helped to carry the Democrats' national ticket in Illinois. Lyndon Johnson swamped Barry Goldwater by nearly 900,000 votes in the state. Nonetheless, his victory over the attractive media darling to become the first two-term Democratic governor since Henry Horner gave Kerner new clout with the General Assembly.

Moreover, he faced a refreshingly new and progressive Illinois House as a result of his decision in July 1963 to veto a Republican-drafted redistricting plan for the fifty-nine Illinois House districts. In a vestige of the bitter divisions in Illinois left after the Civil War, each of the fifty-nine legislative districts elected three representatives to the House. Bullet voting, whereby a voter could cast three votes for a single House candidate, virtually guaranteed minority representation from each district. Republicans had estimated that their new map would have swelled their majority in the House by more than three members. Chicago's population declined sharply between 1950 and 1960, reducing the city's share of state population from 42 percent to 35 percent. Southern Illinois, another traditional stronghold for Democrats, also lost population absolutely and relatively. Growth was concentrating in the suburban ring around Chicago. The Republican redistricting map transferred two of Chicago's twenty-three House districts from Chicago to the suburbs. The map enlarged the representation of heavily Republican Du Page County by giving the county two districts instead of one. But Lake County to the north, which had a growing Democratic population in and around Waukegan, retained a single district, despite its own significant population growth.

Kerner's remap veto, urged by Mayor Daley and Lake County Democrats, set in motion an at-large statewide election of Illinois House members in 1964. Both parties slated 118 candidates for 177 seats, seeking names with the biggest statewide appeal. The Democrats slated Adlai E. Stevenson III, son of the former governor and presidential candidate, as their standard bearer. The Republicans chose moderate Earl D. Eisenhower, a brother of the former president, and dumped from office several disreputable Chicago legislators who belonged to the infamous West Side Bloc, which was linked to organized crime. With the Lyndon Johnson landslide, the so-called bedsheet ballot election shifted control of the House decisively to the Democrats, 118 to 59. It brought to Springfield many first-time legislators and gave the House an energetic, progressive composition. The first serious look at the operation of the General Assembly of this period, the Commission on the Organization of the General Assembly proposed by freshman legislator Harold Katz, a former Kerner aide, was enacted, although similar measures had failed three times since the late 1950s. Legislation requiring a "fiscal note" to be attached to legislation, addressing a proposal's likely impact on taxpayers and the state budget, finally won approval after numerous failed attempts. For his part, Kerner found the Seventy-fourth General Assembly more receptive to his proposals for reforming state government.

Like Illinois governors before him, Kerner had a department of agriculture to promote the farmer, a cabinet-level department of labor for the worker, and even a department of conservation for the angler and hunter. What he did not have was a department for business. When Kerner took office in 1961, the unemployment rate had climbed above 6 percent in Illinois and had surpassed 10 percent in nearby Michigan. New jobs emerging in the suburbs required workers who were more skilled than did jobs tied to urban industrial plants or farms. Moreover, the new breed of employer did not require access to rail and water networks that had made Chicago the heart of the Midwest. These jobs could and did migrate around the nation to locales judged most favorable by employers unencumbered by tradition. In New York Governor Nelson Rockefeller was promoting his state aggressively to attract new business. The governor of North Carolina on one occasion traveled to Chicago to brag about the number of Illinois companies he had lured to his state. Meanwhile, the influx of poor African Americans from the South was beginning to register on the unemployment rolls of midwestern industrial states. The influx of unskilled workers from the South and a brain drain of highly skilled workers to the coasts threatened the state with economic and cultural poverty. Illinois risked going broke trying to support a growing welfare population on a declining income and industrial base. A 1964 study by the Illinois State Chamber of Commerce put the problem in stark terms: in the previous ten years, Illinois on net lost 64,000 white residents and gained 189,000 nonwhites. This evidence of racial change carried clear and unsettling economic implications.

Shortly after his inauguration in 1961, Kerner asked forty-one officials of industry, labor, and government to find solutions to unemployment. Illinois's diverse economy, which included farming, mining, transportation, services, and manufacturing, made the state an ideal setting to study employment trends. The Cassell Committee, named for its chairman, Frank H. Cassell, who was head of personnel at Chicago's Inland Steel Company, concluded that the state must grow its economy. Specifically, Illinois needed to expand its export of manufactured goods and its import of employers, including employers engaged in high-technology development. The committee's proposals, issued in January 1963, met with skepticism and indifference in the Republican-controlled General Assembly. No one in either party was prepared to embrace the committee's recommendations for affirmative action on behalf of unemployed black youth.

The 1964 election improved political sentiment for the Cassell proposals. Kerner's bill to create the Illinois Department of Business and Economic Development passed with bipartisan support after the at-large election. Cassell recalled that Kerner, in his typically introspective manner, had been developing the idea quietly for two years: "He never said anything to me, but one day I discovered he was working on it."[7] Dismissed by a justifiably jaded Springfield press corps as a public relations agency for tourism and launched with only half the funds Kerner requested, the department nonetheless was in Kerner's view a major achievement of his second term. He called it an important step in modernizing Illinois state government, enabling Illinois for the first time to compete in the intensifying national contest for business and jobs. Kerner named Gene H. Graves to run the department. A native of Kentucky, Graves was an affable, imaginative, and persistent super-salesman who was popular with the legislature. He had been the chief promoter in Springfield for Southern Illinois University, the favorite institution of the state capital's most powerful politician, Paul Powell, the newly elected secretary of state.

Kerner instructed his new department to arrange trade missions to Europe and Japan, the first overseas trips by an Illinois governor to solicit business. But he also wanted to incubate and retain business within the state and to obtain federal dollars to help pay for his efforts. The substantial proceeds of the postwar federal income tax, much of which Congress recycled back to state and local governments as economic development aid, justified concerted state strategies to win the cash. "Back in those days, money was flowing out of Washington," Graves recalled.[8] Expanded federal oversight of state and local political affairs—which many state and local politicians saw as an onerous consequence—did not deter the money chase. Graves immediately opened an office in Washington to be close to the source grants and to unify Illinois's appeal within the state's congressional delegation, which was almost evenly split between Republicans and Democrats. To get the federal money, state and local governments danced to tunes Congress played. Old-style pork-barrel spending requests for water conservation projects, highways, and bridges were redubbed "economic development" programs.

The newest theme, reflecting the space race and nuclear preparedness imperatives, was "research and development." R and D had become the mantra of business and government during World War II, as vital achievements in radar, jet propulsion, and atomic energy spun off from basic scientific research. With an apparent postwar Soviet threat, no one questioned the federal government's authority and responsibility to continue financing scientists and others engaged in solving important peacetime security problems and reaching new vistas of knowledge. Scientists, especially physical scientists, enjoyed a political stature they had never before known. In the Eisenhower administration grantsmanship under the R and D banner was akin to similar maneuvering in the interstate highway program—in prestige value though certainly not in dollars. Physicists increased their clout during the Kennedy administration and early years of the Johnson administration.

R and D spending differed from traditional government largesse in that the recipients were scientists, not politically connected contractors or trade unionists. Scientists worked at universities, including state universities that had previously enjoyed influence in state legislatures mostly because of their football prowess or the patronage potential of their payrolls, not because of achievements in scientific research. Intensely political within their own academic ranks, scientists were alien creatures in the world of party politics. They often held no regard for politicians and offered little of the traditional political currencies—namely, votes and campaign contributions. Nevertheless, rich political and economic payoffs beckoned at the end of the R and D rainbow. Communities that became successful centers for scientific research, with the inevitable commercial spin-offs, could transform themselves or hold off economic decline. They became magnets for America's best and brightest. It was one thing to get a new highway or military base in your state, but without R and D projects, a state would become a backwater. Technology-based industries in California and New England drew the best scientific talent out of Illinois's colleges and universities. Federal spending to harness the atom, compete in the space race, and develop the power of electronic computers flowed to the coasts.

Kerner told a congressional hearing: "We are a brains development center as a whole. Other states produce automobiles and vegetables or scenery; in Illinois we develop minds. And we ship our finished products to all states of the nation to help them develop their intellectual and economic potential.... If we do not maintain and, in fact, increase research in our geographic region, we will find that population will move in the same direction as the movement of the brains and we cannot allow this to happen in the Middle West."[9]

From 1955 to 1965 total spending on research and development by government, industry, and other sources tripled from .007 percent of America's gross national product to 0.02 percent. As political scientist Anton G. Jachim noted, "Any sector of the economy that grew as fast as this was bound to attract attention, positive and negative."[10] Of the dollars awarded to the top twenty university recipients of federal R and D money in 1963, 60 percent went to eleven schools on the East or West Coasts, led by the Massachusetts Institute of Technology.[11] Grants came from the Atomic Energy Commission (AEC), the National Science Foundation, the National Aeronautics and Space Administration, the National Institutes of Health, and the Department of Defense. In the two highest-profile research areas—aerospace and atomic energy—the Midwest was a loser. Thanks largely to Johnson, Texas would become the center of America's adventures in space. And although the University of Chicago was the cradle of basic atomic research, the Lawrence Radiation Laboratory of the University of California at Berkeley and the Brookhaven National Laboratory in Long Island, New York, seemed destined to carry that work into the future.

Sociologist Robert K. Merton, who studied the behavioral aspects of science, proposed the "Matthew Effect" in scientific research, basing the name on a verse from the Gospel according to Matthew: "For whosoever hath, to him shall be given, and he shall have more abundance; but whosoever hath not, from him shall be taken away even that he hath."[12] The verse concerns faith in God, but another meaning was quite evident to high-energy physicists not at Berkeley or Brookhaven and to politicians who were not from New York or California. Simply put, the rich were getting richer and the poor were getting poorer in the R and D game. Money was not the only issue. Physicists' access to the machines that split the atom, thereby making possible their probes into the basic particles of the universe, became a crucial problem. The researchers called it "beamtime." Scientists not associated with universities or other facilities equipped with state-of-the-art particle accelerators found themselves supplicants to proprietors of the available machines. In their own way, physicists outside the existing centers of basic atomic research expressed genuine affinity for the civil rights movement and the struggle by African Americans for access to public accommodations.

In the spring of 1963 a commission formed by President Kennedy recommended that America construct the world's biggest particle accelerator, capable of generating 200 billion electron volts (BEV). The Brookhaven accelerator, by comparison, generated 33 BEV, and U.S. officials believed the Soviets were building a 70-BEV accelerator. The commission recommended that the design work for the project be awarded to particle physicists at Berkeley, with the clear implication that the accelerator would be built nearby in

California. In January 1964 the AEC issued a press release that appeared to endorse that outcome. At the same time the AEC, despite early indications to the contrary, said it would not support construction of another accelerator proposed by a team of midwestern scientists organized as the Midwest Universities Research Association (MURA). Physicists at universities in Illinois, Michigan, Minnesota, and Wisconsin felt betrayed. The loss became a rallying cry for unusual—some said unseemly—political activism by the midwestern scientific community. The tradition of scientific meritocracy, in which those with the most successful research and the most Nobel prizes expected to get the bulk of federal funding, began to erode. Prompted by have-not scientists, midwestern politicians, including Vice President Hubert Humphrey of Minnesota, complained about "intellectual incest" among a handful of high-energy physicists on the coasts.[13] The debate over splitting the atom turned to a debate about splitting the federal pie. The words *fairness, equality,* and *redistribution* entered the scientific lexicon.

Members of Congress from have-not states challenged the very credibility of the physics elites who previously had kept politicians in awe by promising to solve the mysteries of the atom. As one congressman crudely put it, physics research was a pork barrel, and the pigs were in charge. In July 1964, taking a page from the nonviolent protest textbook of Martin Luther King Jr., Senator Gaylord Nelson of Wisconsin told midwestern governors and senators: "When we refuse as a unit to support east- and west-coast projects until a sensible policy governing spending is established, then we'll get a hearing. . . . We aren't going to support the others and make a wasteland of the Midwest."[14]

Throughout the country, physicists not associated with Berkeley or Brookhaven insisted that the new accelerator proposed by Kennedy be a "truly national laboratory," in the words of Columbia University physicist Leon M. Lederman. Lederman, who had won fame for helping to confirm the existence of two subatomic particles called neutrinos, believed that Brookhaven and the Lawrence Radiation Laboratory denied access to legitimate experiments. He said scientific cooperation in probing the atom would be broken unless "it is clear that the new facilities are accessible as a right to any physicist bearing a competitively acceptable proposal."[15]

The 200-BEV accelerator was a far cry from a research project involving a handful of scientists in a cramped laboratory with a few beakers and test tubes. It would be a nearly four-mile-long ring of magnets, more than one mile in diameter, built under a mound of earth. The magnets would propel protons at nearly the speed of light before diverting them and crashing them into target atoms or particles, thereby producing other particles. In 1965 the accelerator was estimated to cost $375 million to build, with an annual operating budget of $60 million supporting a staff of 2,000 scientists, technicians, and support personnel.

Despite its earlier statements about Berkeley, the AEC insisted that the location of the 200-BEV accelerator had not been decided. Responding to political pressure, the AEC established a national competition for what became known as the scientific prize of the century. Kerner and his new Department of Business and Economic Development quickly entered the race. Graves called the early stages a "cloak and dagger operation" because Illinois wanted to push its cause without offending Midwest neighbors or arousing real estate speculators.[16]

Whereas he had disliked the absurdities of state budget fights and the agony of death-penalty decisions in his first term, Kerner relished the campaign to win the accelerator. It represented what being governor meant to him in the new era of expanding federal involvement in state and local affairs: rallying competing groups from business, labor, and politics behind a common mission; addressing the state's burgeoning revenue needs by enlarging its industrial base; broadcasting the story of Illinois to the world; and building political unity in the Midwest to keep the nation's heartland prominent on the national political agenda—all without politically unpalatable tax increases. These and other benefits would surely radiate from the great proton ring, enabling Illinois to take a leading role in federal-state affairs.

In the fall of 1962, long before the accelerator project had surfaced in Washington, Kerner hosted a dinner in Chicago for physicist Frederick Seitz of the University of Illinois, shortly after Seitz became chairman of the National Academy of Sciences (NAS). The academy was formed in 1863 to help direct federal spending toward basic scientific research. The dinner, the brainchild of Kerner adviser and political scientist Norton Long, brought together for the first time a large number of Illinois scientists, business leaders, and politicians to promote the state as a center of research and development. The conversation was awkward. Long's diary entry suggests Kerner felt uncomfortable with men of science. But Kerner and his staff eagerly sowed goodwill among Seitz and his peers, who were influencing an increasing amount of federal spending.

Faced with demands for fairness and access in nuclear research, in the spring of 1965 the AEC chose Seitz and the NAS to screen potential sites for the accelerator. Illinois congressman Melvin Price chaired a subcommittee of the Joint Congressional Committee on Atomic Energy that oversaw the selection process. Seitz and Price gave Illinois an edge. The man at the center of the site selection was AEC chair Glenn T. Seaborg. Seaborg, a Michigan native who died in February 1999, shared the 1951 Nobel prize in chemistry for identifying five radioactive elements, including plutonium. During World

War II he worked at the Metallurgical Laboratory of the University of Chicago, where the first wholesale production of plutonium was undertaken. His brilliance was not isolated to the atom. A tall, imposing man with a big, soft face, Seaborg was "a romantic at heart," in the words of a physics colleague.[17] He was also a scientist with remarkable political skills.

Kennedy named Seaborg chair of the AEC in 1961, and Johnson, who enthusiastically admired his political instincts as well as his scientific credentials, retained him in the post. Seaborg advanced the idea of a national competition for the accelerator in part to lessen the complaints among university presidents, physicists, and their politician friends about favoritism in federal R and D funding and the lack of access to research facilities. But there was another reason, which he did not express publicly until much later: "One result . . . was the sought-after shift, as a result of the nationwide competition for the accelerator, from the question of *whether* we should build such an accelerator to the question of *where* we should build it," he wrote in 1987.[18] With the budget squeeze suddenly facing all federal agencies as the escalating war in Vietnam stifled a decade of federal largesse, Seaborg knew he had to act quickly. Placing the 200-BEV particle accelerator at Berkeley, which had the deepest scientific team, or any other site determined exclusively by scientific merit would raise protests that easily could delay and even scuttle the project. But as long as every region of the country thought it had a chance, no one on Capitol Hill would want to see the project canceled.

In an interview in 1995, Seaborg was still delighted by his scheming. "We got the whole country behind it. By the time we made the final choice, nobody was in a position to oppose it successfully. It was skillful execution of the game plan." Backers of the superconducting supercollider—a project in Texas that was to be the next generation of high-energy research until it was canceled by Congress in 1993—"were rank amateurs compared to us," he said.[19]

✦ ✦ ✦

Arthur J. Theriault, a Marine veteran who worked nights as a printer in Chicago in the early 1960s, is a compact man of unflagging energy and dogged determination. Theriault always conveys an air of enthusiastic expectation. He is not easily discouraged or put off. Troubled by the decline of their neighborhood near Chicago's beloved Riverview amusement park, Theriault, his wife, and his three children packed up and resettled thirty miles west in the far reaches of Du Page County. In an audacious move for city dwellers, they rented a modest home in an unincorporated subdivision named Westfield Unit 1. The developer of the project, Wolfson Development Corporation, had abandoned the eighty-one-acre site. There would be no unit 2. The 100 houses were modest, and Theriault worried about living so far away from his job.

At that time it was stretching a point to call this outskirt a suburb, but the area showed promise, and driving to and from Chicago for his night job proved to be no problem.

"I had time during the day to be involved out in the community," he recalled.[20] Theriault started a community newspaper and with other residents began promoting the lonely community in the cornfields—Weston—as a site for industry. After Wolfson defaulted and the blue-sky dream of William Riley disappeared, Theriault realized the townspeople were on their own. He bought his house from the government and was elected mayor. Working to obtain natural gas service to the tiny municipality, he met the head of industrial development for Northern Illinois Gas Company, Howard Etchison. "I said, what can I do to get something going out here in the cornfields?" Theriault recalled.[21] The utility official told him about the "super atom smasher" that his company and other Chicago-area corporations were trying to win for the state. The area around Weston was being discussed secretly as a possible location, Etchison revealed.

Though he knew almost nothing about atomic energy, Theriault began writing federal officials, saying the farmland adjacent to his town seemed ideal for the project. There was plenty of flat acreage, abundant water, good schools, and easy access to O'Hare Airport; moreover, Theriault wrote to the AEC in June 1965, it was "out of the initial impact area of a direct atomic attack on Chicago." He added, "We are small in size but big in ambition and want to be part of this large undertaking and promise to work hard to improve our community."[22]

◆ ◆ ◆

In 1965 the racial justice campaign of Martin Luther King Jr. and the Southern Christian Leadership Conference (SCLC) came north to America's big cities. King's hard-fought nonviolent protests against discrimination had brought national attention to himself and his movement. For the first time his organization was adequately funded, largely through contributions from northern liberals. Against the advice of many associates, who feared that agitation in northern cities would turn away northern contributors, King declared, "This is where our mission is; we have received a calling to come north."[23]

SCLC workers and a handful of indigenous civil rights leaders in Chicago, led by Albert A. Raby of the Coordinating Council of Community Organizations, pinpointed the best target for a King-led campaign in Chicago: the city's West Side. The dynamic center of assimilation and dispersal of European immigrants in the first half of the century by the early 1960s had become a deteriorating dead end for the newest immigrants arriving from the

South. Unlike the longer-established African American neighborhoods on the South Side, the West Side was populated by newcomers with far less of a stake in the status quo. There were fewer entrenched leaders, and living conditions were worse than on the South Side. West Side communities such as North Lawndale and East Garfield Park would be more amenable to a grass-roots protest movement sparked by outsiders, Raby and SCLC leaders believed. Organizing on Chicago's West Side would be similar to organizing in Mississippi or Alabama, SCLC staff members up from the South reasoned.

But the objectives had to be different. Daley officially barred discrimination against blacks in city hiring. In 1963 Daley's city council passed an open-occupancy ordinance for Chicago, although it was under attack in the courts by realtors and unenforced. Daley stood by while his candidate Kerner, in his first term as governor, overcame years of legislative opposition and enacted a state fair employment practices law aimed at curbing racial discrimination in hiring. Discrimination against blacks was less apparent in Chicago than in the South. In the South racism revealed itself in buses, lunch counters, and other conspicuous places of general public accommodation that were part of the aggregate community. Racism in the North meant splitting the aggregate community into black and white enclaves through the creation and maintenance of black ghettos. Southern whites may have opposed the black struggle for civil rights, but at least they understood what it was about. In the North, King discovered, whites had grown unaware and indifferent to black grievances by simply removing themselves from city neighborhoods and leaving behind African Americans living in nearly total estrangement.

King's people decided that the organizing issue in Chicago would be the West Side ghetto's deplorable living conditions, not segregation itself. Improving the community certainly was an urgent need. But the campaign sidestepped the more intractable issue of how the West Side—and black ghettos like it in every large northern city—came to be that way. Forming unions of West Side residents to protest slum conditions, as the SCLC planned, seemed feasible and sensible, but it meant organizing against an elusive enemy. Many blacks prospered as slumlords. Apartment building owners, white and black, hid their identities behind secret land trusts. African American politicians in the Daley organization as well as most black bankers and business leaders who could have energized a slum improvement campaign saw King as a meddling opportunist and preferred that he wage his fight somewhere else. Daley, who endorsed civil rights and antipoverty policies on a national basis, especially if they meant federal dollars he could distribute in Chicago, had an official city program for virtually every complaint that could be raised against slum conditions. Few of them worked or were meant to, but Daley had an immediate retort to King's message.

The SCLC strategists knew well the root cause of slum conditions in the West Side ghetto, though at first they hesitated to address it. It even had a name: the cycle of poverty. Congested urban neighborhoods such as Chicago's West Side previously functioned as stepping stones for European immigrants, as succeeding generations moved on to better lifestyles and surroundings. In Chicago and other northern cities, however, this mobility was denied to African Americans because of their skin color. For them, the traditional stepping stone was a pit where succeeding generations could look forward only to worse conditions and less hope.

Ironically, nowhere was the cause of the urban poverty cycle more apparent than in prosperous Du Page County, not far from Chicago by expressway but quite distant in terms of opportunity. The boilerplate contracts that Du Page real estate brokers handed to property owners seeking to sell or rent contained what was called the "M clause." It instructed the broker, as agent for the owner, not to show the home or apartment to minorities. The M clause allowed brokers to insist, and perhaps even to believe, that property owners, not themselves, were discriminating. It also allowed white areas to remain white with hardly a word spoken about it. Blacks knew about the M clause as well as whites did, a grim process of self-selection.

In the Illinois legislature a handful of dedicated black and white liberals, led by Representative Cecil A. Partee of Chicago, were repeatedly defeated in their efforts to break this system, making Illinois the only major industrial state without some form of open-occupancy law. In the spring 1965 session of the General Assembly, Kerner's open-occupancy bill, sponsored by Partee, passed the House, which was far more receptive after the at-large election of 1964, but failed in the Republican-controlled Senate.

A year later King's Chicago campaign to improve the West Side ghetto was foundering. It had produced few results and had provoked little sympathy outside the immediate area. Meanwhile, the rise of a more militant black power movement under men such as Stokely Carmichael undercut King's stature nationally. To reenergize his northern crusade King and his followers shifted their focus from improving conditions in the West Side to exposing the reality of northern segregation, the true cause of the problem. Their new protest target would be not landlords but the real estate brokerage business. They would attack discrimination in the sale and rental of housing by staging protest marches in white neighborhoods and white suburbs. Challenging prevailing real estate practices in Chicago and its suburbs meant challenging white people in their private homes, not at public lunch counters and in voting booths. It was a risky move by King and his followers. The civil rights movement was already tarnished by riots in northern cities. New York suffered a major disturbance in 1964. Violence broke out in black ghettos in Los Angeles and

Chicago in the summer of 1965. King was taking a major gamble as he prepared to march into white-only neighborhoods in and around Chicago.

✦ ✦ ✦

In the mid-1960s America's scientific establishment came under the influence of two essays by a British molecular physicist and novelist named C. P. (Charles Percy) Snow titled "The Two Cultures" and "The Scientific Revolution." In "The Two Cultures" Snow argued persuasively that practitioners of science and the humanities did not understand each other and were not even talking to each other. He described the perils of this estrangement and observed that the West's cold war competitor, the Soviet Union, was not so encumbered. In "The Scientific Revolution" Snow narrowed his critical focus to the community of Western scientists. A corrosive split had evolved between pure science and applied science, he observed. Atomic energy, space exploration, and other technological marvels convinced postwar Americans of the seemingly endless bounty of science. But many of the theoretical scientists who benefited richly from generous public acclaim and funding believed they should be revered and held aloof from the practical concerns of society as well as from their less distinguished peers.

"Pure scientists have by and large been dimwitted about engineers and applied science," Snow wrote. "They couldn't get interested. They wouldn't recognise that many of the problems were as intellectually exacting as pure problems and that many of the solutions were as satisfying and beautiful. Their instinct . . . was to take it for granted that applied science was an occupation for second-rate minds."[24] Snow believed that "the point where pure science turned into applied" in current times was the moment when nuclear physicists at the University of Chicago created the first sustained nuclear reaction. The destructive power of the nuclear bombs dropped on Japan and the buildup of nuclear arsenals in the United States and the Soviet Union made the small community of atomic physicists keenly aware of Snow's admonitions and the broader context of their work.

No one was more aware of this than Glenn Seaborg. Speaking to the American Philosophical Society in April 1966, Seaborg said that even the purest form of atomic research must address the immediate public interest:

> We must temper, adapt and redirect the enormous technological forces we have created to the end of serving the individual human being—an end for which the forces were created but which has begun to elude us as we have become more and more taken with the power, the momentum and the "open sesame" fascination that our modern science and technology have provided. . . . We are developing an imbalance in our national personality, one which is arising from a well-intentioned emphasis on technological gain but one which is weakening our framework of

values nevertheless. Being a nation founded on concern for the individual—his freedom, his welfare and his pursuit of happiness—it is all the more ironic that today our concern with the techniques for achieving many of these goals has somehow pushed the individual into the background. And sometimes he feels sorely neglected as a human being. This is becoming more evident on our college campuses, in our big cities and in our industries, where people, living and working together in large numbers, are reacting to the strange combination of the pressure of competition yet the lack of meaningful human contact.[25]

Echoing C. P. Snow, Seaborg spoke of the need for a "symbiosis" between science and broader human aspirations, and he told his Philadelphia audience of one outstanding example: the search then underway for a site for the 200-BEV accelerator. Records of the AEC's site selection process, including Seaborg's personal diaries from the period, make clear that Seaborg and his colleagues had a larger purpose than just building a giant ring of magnets to propel particles and fracture atoms. They realized that obtaining funds for the accelerator within tight and highly political federal budget constraints meant the ring must encircle more than the desires of a few elites in the world of nuclear physics.

"As you well know, the possibility of having a scientific laboratory of such importance and economic impact in their area has created keen competition among many communities. What is less well known—but has even greater significance—is the unexpected effect of this competition on the various communities," Seaborg told his Philadelphia audience. He spoke of the "unprecedented self-appraisal" underway in localities competing for the accelerator.

> As local resources were being mustered, it suddenly dawned on community leaders that the overall attractiveness of an area must be measured by factors which transcend economic considerations. . . . This local self-appraisal brought a greater interest in racial harmony. It brought renewed support for education at every level. It brought a greater appreciation for the public library, the symphony and even children's ballet classes. . . . It has helped change the public image of the scientist from a cold, detached individual to that of a very human person with a deep interest in his family and his community.[26]

Whether or not he understood the sincerity of atomic scientists' social concerns, Kerner undoubtedly recognized the political pressures on the AEC from Congress and the have-nots in the physics community. Kerner, Graves, and the other political and business leaders working to win the 200-BEV project for Illinois may not have appreciated C. P. Snow's "two-cultures" hypothesis, but they fully grasped the task at hand. Their self-appraisal, as Seaborg put it, first and foremost concerned developing a successful strategy to win the project. Whatever social benefits the project might bring to Illinois, none would materialize if it went to another state. Kerner could not dispute Seaborg's wider perspective, but in the intensely political world he occupied, such thoughts were a diversion.

The AEC's ambitious and progressive social goals, expressed by Seaborg in his Philadelphia speech, did not favor Illinois. Other states in the running had far more progressive social records. Moreover, victory for Illinois required keeping extraneous social issues off the table, because raising them could stir the ever-present reactionary instincts of Illinois's political establishment. Such instincts were stirred nonetheless. Kerner's immediate problem was that wealthy and influential constituents living near the Illinois site that atomic scientists most favored did not want it.

✦ ✦ ✦

The earliest overtures to obtain the accelerator came from Colorado, California, Washington, and Missouri. Members of Congress, seeking political cover from disgruntled losers, instructed the AEC to make the selection, and for much the same reason the AEC turned to the National Academy of Sciences. Johnson, having helped to make Texas the headquarters for the National Aeronautics and Space Administration's space program, was an intensely interested spectator but publicly stood aside in the early going. By early July 1965 the AEC had received 126 proposals concerning 200 sites in forty-six states. Four general site proposals came from Illinois: the Chicago area, which comprised five locations offered as a single site by the Kerner administration, Mayor Daley, and Chicago's major utilities and business interests; the town of Princeton, ninety-five miles southwest of Chicago; Shawneetown, in far southern Illinois near Kentucky; and Morgan and Scott Counties, west of Springfield. By the end of July the commission, working with the National Academy of Sciences site selection committee, narrowed the field to thirty-four sites in thirty states. All the Illinois proposals outside the Chicago area were eliminated. The number of potential sites quickly rebounded as President Johnson bargained for votes among members of Congress on unrelated legislation. The number magically expanded to eighty-five sites in forty-three states.

In late November 1965 AEC staff members visited the five Chicago-area sites: 4,200 federally owned acres known as the Joliet Arsenal in Will County; 2,800 acres in Will County, near the Argonne National Laboratory; 5,500 acres near far northwest suburban Wauconda in Lake County; 5,000 acres north of the Northwest Tollway in the Cook County suburb of South Barrington; and 5,200 acres near Weston in Du Page County. After this visit only South Barrington and Weston remained in the running.

The land around Weston was unpretentious rural acreage for corn farming, and it was not particularly good for that. By contrast, the northwest suburban Barrington area, which comprises several municipalities with

"Barrington" in their names, featured rolling hills and scenic lakes and was the AEC's preferred Illinois site. It is one of the Chicago area's most exclusive residential enclaves. Corporate executives such as Harold Byron Smith of Illinois Tool Works and the Northern Trust Bank and Robert W. Galvin of Motorola—two leading Republican fund-raisers—owned large estates in the area. Horse farms with white rail fences added to a forbidding elite image. Despite its Republican politics and idyllic appearance, South Barrington had one attribute that none of the other Chicago-area accelerator sites—indeed, no other site in the nation—possessed. It was in Cook County, the domain of the decidedly nonidyllic Richard J. Daley. Daley had heard about "research and development," too. He once proposed Chicago's abandoned, desolate stockyards, not far from his bungalow in the South Side Bridgeport neighborhood, as the site for a major research and development installation.

Daley controlled Cook County politics, but he did not control the Barrington area. Two weeks after AEC inspectors visited the South Barrington site, the village board in neighboring Barrington passed a resolution "earnestly request[ing] that the South Barrington area not be considered for the location of the Atomic Energy installation." The resolution, which other Barrington-area communities and school districts quickly matched, complained that the project would take land from the tax rolls and "would require the addition of many apartments and other facilities for the additional people that would be needed in the facility and such facilities would not be of the type that would substantially increase the tax base in the school districts." The resolution added, "The development of apartments and other mass housing is not in accordance with Barrington's long-range planning for the Village and the surrounding areas which is directed toward an increased tax base and the preservation of a healthy balance between village residential developments and countryside multi-acre homesites."[27]

Barrington-area residents protested individually to Kerner and other state officials and to John A. Swartout, the AEC staff member who led the site inspection team in November. Nevertheless, in January 1966 the National Academy of Sciences site selection committee informally told members of the AEC that South Barrington and Weston (considered as a single selection) were among six finalist sites nationally. The others were Brookhaven on New York's Long Island; Sacramento, California; Madison, Wisconsin; Ann Arbor, Michigan; and Denver, Colorado.

By now President Johnson was micromanaging the process. At one point he asked Seaborg to postpone for twenty-four hours a scheduled statement on finalist sites "because of the vote on the rent subsidy bill in Congress" scheduled for the following day. Seaborg complied.[28] Once the statement was issued, complaints erupted from Texas, Washington State, and Indiana. Senator Birch Bayh of Indiana said the decision put Indiana "back in the Dark Ages in the Middle West."[29]

Meanwhile, the objections of Barrington-area residents could no longer be ignored. As U.S. attorney in Chicago, Kerner had confronted similar not-in-my-backyard protests when the government claimed land in southwestern Du Page County for the Argonne National Laboratory. Kerner knew that the AEC, which planned to visit finalist sites in April, would not go where it was unwanted. Seaborg would not risk delays in the light of the tenuous federal budget outlook. Seaborg knew that wealthy residents near the site of the Stanford Linear Accelerator Center in California had tied up the AEC in legal battles for years. He made it plain he would never tolerate another such delay.

On April 1 leaders of the campaign for the Chicago-area site, including Kerner and Senator Paul Douglas, confronted Barrington-area residents at an invitation-only dinner meeting in the Argonne National Laboratory. Kerner knew well the tenacity of the South Barrington protesters and their leader, attorney J. William Braithwaite. As Cook County judge in 1959, Kerner had signed municipal incorporation papers for South Barrington presented by an aggressive Braithwaite-led group of residents who favored a minimum residential lot size of five acres. On the morning the incorporation papers were filed, Braithwaite and a member of his contingent physically blocked an attorney for a rival group favoring a one-and-a-half acre lot size minimum from posting his documents ahead of Braithwaite. Kerner opened his remarks to the Argonne meeting with a joke that few beside Braithwaite understood. It was unfortunate, he said, that Illinois law allowed only thirty days to challenge a judicial ruling of municipal incorporation.

Some of Kerner's aides privately mused about building a state prison in the recalcitrant Barrington area. But Kerner's eye was focused on the accelerator prize, and he had no intention of pushing against what he knew from experience would be well-organized South Barrington activism. Their opposition, standing in sharp contrast to the eager solicitations by dozens of communities around the country, had made the national news. Kerner did not need further embarrassment on this score. But Douglas, apparently unconcerned that he was up for reelection in November, did not let the matter rest. After the Barrington delegation said their community was "most unusual" and did not wish to be "downgraded," Douglas responded that it was, indeed, most unusual that any community would feel downgraded by the presence of some of the best-educated people in the country. He mocked fears of "alien Ph.D.s lowering the intellectual and moral atmosphere" of the Barrington area.[30] Douglas chided the protesters, saying that they might have doomed Illinois's chances of winning the project for any site. Braithwaite and other Barrington residents came away respectful of Kerner but resentful of Douglas.

✦ ✦ ✦

Art Theriault would have his say a week later. After fairly routine visits to finalist sites in Ann Arbor, Michigan, and Madison, Wisconsin, Seaborg and several other AEC members and staffers bypassed Barrington and came to Weston. Kerner economic development aide Raymond R. Becker greeted them at O'Hare Airport. Becker had asked Kerner how to pick out the eminent nuclear scientist Seaborg. "He's the one who glows in the dark," Kerner replied.[31] Seaborg recorded in his journal for that day that he found Kerner to be "capable" and "liberal."[32] He also noted: "The town of Weston is a prefabricated housing development in obviously deteriorating condition. Many houses are vacant and posted with signs indicating the government had foreclosed on previous owners."[33]

Theriault, who earlier had been advised by an aide to Mayor Daley not to engage in any freelance campaign for the accelerator, was now fully on board. He arranged for a high school band to play "Hey, Look Me Over" as the AEC team arrived. Local fire departments brought their equipment to the festivities. Hand-lettered signs held by Weston parents and their children greeted the AEC delegation. Weston resident Carol Miolli gave Paul W. McDaniel, the commission's director of research, her picket sign, which had been autographed by Kerner and read, "I Want an Atom Smasher." Kerner promised tax incentives for the project. A representative of Commonwealth Edison, the local electric utility, guaranteed that electrical power would be readily available for the accelerator, though not at discounted rates.

To offset Weston's somewhat bleak appearance, state officials sent the AEC motorcade on a tour of the nearby Morton Arboretum to show its splendor especially to Seaborg, an avid tree fancier. But Seaborg was not interested just in trees. Before leaving for the next finalist site, he read to the Illinois officials a carefully drafted question that he asked at every stop on the tour:

> Would there be any problems in obtaining assurances from persons and organizations in the communities—such as local government units, heads of community educational and recreational bodies, labor unions, professional societies, cultural groups, chambers of commerce and those who can speak for particular categories of business establishments, including commercial lending and housing organizations and real estate associations—that there would be individual and common undertakings to prevent discrimination as a community problem and to deal with it fairly and promptly should it occur?[34]

Kerner promised to respond fully at a later time. With that, Seaborg and his associates flew to Denver.

The short answer to Seaborg's long question had to be yes, there would be problems. The M clause was used routinely in Du Page County, and chances for a state open-occupancy law remained doubtful. Although the leaders of Illinois's political and business establishment embraced Kerner's campaign to win the accelerator, few believed it was important enough to alter the status quo in race relations, a subject that seemed distant from splitting the atom. "Who needs Weston?" asked Du Page Republican state representative James "Pate" Philip.[35]

✦ ✦ ✦

At age sixty-seven, attorney Oscar C. Brown was a senior statesman among Chicago's African American real estate brokers. He built his career on the South Side during a time when blacks were unwelcome on the Chicago Board of Realtors and thus founded a separate group called the Dearborn Board of Realtors. Brown also was active in the Chicago Negro Chamber of Commerce, an organization parallel to the white Chicago Association of Commerce and Industry. During World War II he was president of the Chicago chapter of the National Association for the Advancement of Colored People (NAACP). Brown's son, Oscar Brown Jr., had tried politics but turned his broad talents to creating theatrical musical productions that celebrated the spirit of the civil rights movement and black pride.

In March 1964, while the General Assembly was out of session and unable to take political revenge, Kerner named Oscar Brown Sr. to the largely perfunctory Illinois Real Estate Examining Committee, a low-profile state agency that administered tests to those wishing to become licensed real estate brokers and agents. He was the first black ever named to the board. Kerner's opportunity to place unobtrusively the first African American on the committee that oversaw Illinois's 37,000 real estate brokers and agents came after the legislature in 1963 expanded the committee to five members from three, reflecting an increased workload. Despite its stark implication for the open-occupancy debate, Brown's appointment barely received mention in the newspapers.

Not all Kerner's groundbreaking but low-key appointments of African Americans to state regulatory posts avoided the limelight, however. George Leighton, the Chicago lawyer who in 1962 had implored Kerner to spare murderer Vincent Ciucci, made headlines after Kerner picked him to be a hearing officer for the state's new Fair Employment Practices Commission. In the spring of 1964 Leighton ruled that an employee testing procedure used by electronics manufacturer Motorola discriminated against blacks. It was a major story in the press and the first test of the commission's authority. Robert W. Galvin, Motorola's chief executive officer, was the finance chairman of Charles Percy's campaign for the Republican gubernatorial nomination in the upcoming fall election. Galvin and Percy denounced Leighton's action, and Motorola officials refused to attend a commission hearing on the matter. Kerner stood by Leighton and the commission. The matter remained unresolved until the Illinois legislature passed a bill in 1965 validating Motorola's test procedure.

In 1963, as he began his reelection bid, Kerner issued an executive order barring racial discrimination by any agency of state government under his control. The real estate examining committee was one of the few that had failed to adopt rules implementing the order. Nonetheless, the order helped Kerner with liberal Democrats who believed he lacked assertiveness and was too subservient to Mayor Daley to be considered one of their own. The small but energetic band of civil rights advocates in Chicago did not look on Kerner as a kindred spirit. They were annoyed that the real estate examining committee had failed to implement his executive order. But they sensed that Illinois's eager pursuit of the giant particle accelerator was an opportunity to break up more than atoms.

In early 1966 the Illinois Human Relations Commission, a group appointed by Kerner to offer whatever support the state could muster on behalf of racial harmony, pressed Kerner to link the campaign for the atomic accelerator to direct administrative action on open occupancy. The Chicago Conference on Religion and Race, composed of leaders from every major religious denomination in the city, reported in a letter to Kerner that black employees of Bell Laboratories from New Jersey who were being transferred to Naperville, a Chicago suburb not far from Weston, "received poor service from Du Page County real estate brokers." The group's executive director, Eugene J. Callahan, warned the governor, "We believe that protest demonstrations might begin if and when the selection of Weston is announced." And he advised Kerner to extend his executive order to real estate brokers and sales agents under the state's licensing power. Citing Title VI of the 1964 Civil Rights Act, which bans racial discrimination in any federally financed program, Callahan said Kerner must act "to assure the [Atomic Energy Commission] that you have taken constructive action to provide equal opportunity in the federally assisted program proposed for Weston."[36]

In June Clarence Mitchell, national executive director of the NAACP, put Illinois's dismal fair-housing record in a national spotlight. He wrote to Seaborg that Illinois "has a long history of extensive housing discrimination on the basis of race."[37] Mitchell called to account the AEC's stated intention to promote civil rights as a by-product of the national accelerator selection process. Suddenly the civil rights issue was paramount.

On July 13 Kerner acted. Just as James Q. Wilson had recommended during Kerner's 1960 campaign, the governor conferred with leaders of the state's real estate brokerage lobby, meeting with them in Springfield for forty-five minutes, and then announced that the real estate examining committee, now chaired by Oscar Brown Sr., had adopted "Regulation V." This rule denied a license to any real estate broker or agent who participated in discriminatory real estate listings or acted as broker or sales agent "with respect to any property the disposition of which is prohibited to any person because of race, color, creed, religion or national origin." Brokers and agents who followed the wishes of sellers not to show homes to minorities would lose their licenses.

Kerner effectively outlawed the pervasive and longstanding M clause with an administrative order by a state agency unknown to nearly all Illinois residents. It was a stunning move. W. Russell Arrington, the Republican president of the Illinois Senate, declared that Illinois no longer needed an open-occupancy law.[38] Chris Vlahoplus, Kerner's press aide, called the decision "a very important tool."[39] Kerner immediately sent a letter to Seaborg announcing the action. "It was my thought that you would appreciate being informed of this action," Kerner wrote.[40] The *Chicago Weekly Defender,* noting the link between the atom smasher and Kerner's real estate licensing move, declared in a short, insightful headline, "Money Talks: Housing Bias Banned."[41]

Realtors in Springfield and Du Page County quickly filed suit to block the order, charging that the committee's action was unconstitutional and that Kerner had exceeded his power. But Kerner achieved a major breakthrough in his campaign to win the national accelerator. In the process, he accomplished an end run around the legislature and broke the logjam on open occupancy. Callahan recalled years later that his organization never heard from Kerner regarding his letter until a month after the licensing board adopted Regulation V, but they rejoiced nonetheless. The *Bloomington Pantagraph* declared, "By his actions Governor Kerner continues to erase his image as a weak governor which he earned in his first administration. In fact he is moving in the direction of becoming a defiant governor."[42]

Yet Kerner, focused on winning the accelerator, straddled the issue. He did not want controversy over this historic step in civil rights to divert Springfield support for the atom smasher campaign and all that it promised Illinois. In a response to the *Pantagraph* editorial, Vlahoplus wrote gingerly to the newspaper: "Governor Kerner did not issue an open-occupancy decree. . . . The Weston site did not motivate the freedom of residency action by the Illinois Real Estate Licensing Committee."[43] Vlahoplus insisted that the committee and the state's human relations commission had been developing a fair-housing policy well before civil rights protests to the Weston site began.

Kerner revealed the scope of his dilemma in a reply to a letter from Julius W. Butler, one of the wealthy Butler clan of suburban Oak Brook, who, quoting Abraham Lincoln's views on wealth and property, had denounced the examining committee's action as an attack on the fundamental principles of

America. Kerner wrote: "The recent discussions, I believe, have misled the public in that I did not issue any executive order concerning real estate brokers. Regulation V was adopted by the Real Estate Licensing Board and does not affect the right of any owner to sell his property as he individually desires."[44] Surely Kerner did not expect Butler or anyone else to believe that Oscar Brown Sr. and the real estate licensing committee acted unilaterally or that the ruling would not significantly change the nature of residential property transactions in Illinois. Implying as much gave Kerner some political slack with conservatives in both parties, but it kept him from enjoying acclaim from civil rights leaders, who concluded that Kerner acted out of expediency rather than principle.

Yet Kerner, whose family—like many other Czech, Jewish, and Irish immigrants—had moved from rental apartments on Chicago's West Side to home ownership in the suburbs, revealed a deeper part of himself in his reply to Butler: "There are individuals, who as Lincoln said, 'wish to enjoy the fruit of their labor and the ownership of property,' but are denied that opportunity because of belonging to some group that others may not consider desirable in the area. If they are denied an opportunity to upgrade themselves, they will remain forever in an area in which no opportunity can be achieved. This, generally, is defined as the poverty cycle."[45]

Kerner's attempt to break that cycle came at a time that long will be remembered in Chicago, though not because of anything he did. The day before the real estate licensing committee acted, rioting broke out in the West Side ghetto after police turned off open fire hydrants cooling the streets as temperatures soared above ninety degrees. The day the committee acted, eight student nurses were slain brutally in Chicago by an unknown assailant. Newspaper headlines the morning after screamed about the riots and murders and ignored Regulation V. Two days later Kerner responded to a request by Mayor Daley and ordered Illinois National Guard troops to active duty to deal with the West Side rioting. Civil rights leaders marched in the all-white Chicago neighborhoods of Marquette Park, Gage Park, and Chicago Lawn to the southwest. Citing the Kerner administration's new antidiscriminatory real estate licensing rule, King declared, "We want that thin paper to turn into thick action."[46] King's followers sought to provoke white retaliation to their marches, and they succeeded. Ugly incidents of racial hatred ensued. The Kerner campaign to win an atomic particle accelerator ring for Illinois seemed a triviality.

Kerner would be accused of exploiting the accelerator campaign to advance a left-wing civil rights agenda, but his strategy was more complex. He used his civil rights sympathies to win the accelerator contest, which had mandated that Illinois demonstrate progress toward social justice. In turn, the accelerator prize enhanced Illinois's stature in the national contest for jobs. The real estate licensing ruling achieved concrete but largely ignored success toward both goals. In contrast, King's more highly publicized efforts to ignite a national reaction to white racism in Chicago backfired. "In Chicago, the old formula applied to new problems did not work," wrote historian James R. Ralph Jr. in his detailed study of King's Chicago campaign, *Northern Protest.* "Carefully staged nonviolent protests were now as likely to stir the forces of reaction as to trigger groundswells for reform," Ralph wrote. "In an ironic, tragic twist, the Chicago Freedom Movement contributed to the broader flow of events that was shifting the center of gravity of American public life to the right."[47]

◆ ◆ ◆

The civil rights component of the AEC's deliberations also moved in Illinois's favor. William L. Taylor, director of the U.S. Commission on Civil Rights, undertook a survey of civil rights policies and practices in each of the finalist locations. In a letter to Seaborg, he wrote, "Since almost all of the communities have significant civil rights problems, one of the most important tests to be applied in determining the location of the installation is, in our judgment, the willingness of the community to commit itself to specific steps which will create conditions of equal opportunity for all persons potentially affected by the project."[48] In other words, the AEC could make its choice based on indications of future progress rather than evidence of past achievement in civil rights. Taylor's position appeared to violate the spirit, if not the mandate, of Title VI of the 1964 Civil Rights Act, which banned discrimination associated with federal programs. But it gave Seaborg and the AEC the opening they needed to pick Weston.

The AEC informally chose Weston on December 7, 1966, and officially ratified its choice on December 15. The announcement came the next day, a Friday. Weston mayor Art Theriault, now working as a manager for a mobile check-cashing service, was out monitoring his trucks when the news broke. It was payday. In a remark welcomed by scientists but sadly ironic to Illinois's open-housing advocates, the AEC declared "Weston has no equal in terms of accessibility." Regarding civil rights, the commission stated, "Information received pertaining to the Weston area reflected a progressive attitude toward equal employment opportunity, efforts to provide equality in suburban public school systems, and a number of community human relations councils devoted to eliminating discrimination." Regarding housing, the commission was even more vague. It "noted differing views with respect to existence of nondiscrimination in housing . . . but will expect that with the leadership of the state and local governments and with the cooperation and support of citizens and community organizations in the Chicago area, a broad satisfactory record of nondiscrimination and equal opportunity will be achieved."[49] The test of nondiscrimination was, in effect, waived in favor of good intentions.

Shortly after Christmas Seaborg flew to the Johnson ranch in Texas to review his annual budget request with the president and budget chief Charles L. Schultz. Johnson approved the $10 million Seaborg wanted to design the new accelerator. In his diary Seaborg wrote, "In connection with my handling of the site search for the 200-BEV accelerator, [Johnson] said it was an example of how a professor, who is not supposed to understand such things, handled the politics of the situation in a very knowledgeable and effective manner."[50] Nevertheless, belief persisted that Johnson had made the choice himself—perhaps to win the support of Everett Dirksen, the Senate's Republican floor leader, for a civil rights bill or to satisfy Mayor Daley, Vice President Humphrey, and other midwesterners who wanted their share of the R and D pork barrel.

The political fight over Weston was just heating up in Congress at the beginning of 1967. Loud protests were voiced by civil rights supporters in the delegations from New York and nearby states, including Senators John O. Pastore of Rhode Island, chairman of the Joint Committee on Atomic Energy, and Jacob Javits of New York. Newly elected California governor Ronald Reagan urged his state's congressional delegation to overturn the decision. Scientists at the Lawrence Radiation Laboratory in California denounced the selection. Director Edward McMillan told Seaborg that nuclear physicists would not go to Chicago. He complained about potentially threatening "glacial till" in the Chicago area's geology.[51] Others made rude remarks about doing science in cornfields[52] and said they "could not conceive of moving [their] lives and . . . families to the dismal Chicago area."[53]

An unsigned memorandum that was circulated in the legislature by members of the Illinois Senate who supported the Weston project declared, "We are hanging by our last thread." The objections by eastern senators were damaging the state broadly, the memo stated. It summarized the situation in early 1967: "Illinois is portrayed as lacking in truth; Illinois is losing face throughout the country; [the AEC] is embarrassed; the Chief Executive Officer of our state is embarrassed; we will not only lose the accelerator but we will lose major private and federal projects. Already two major companies have indicated their desire to locate manufacturing plants in Du Page County but will not do so because of our inaction on open occupancy."[54]

Against the advice of Senator Dirksen, who warned him about the irascibility of Illinois state legislators, Seaborg and several other members of the AEC flew to Springfield in April to confront legislative leaders and community officials from the Weston area. Seaborg said bluntly that the Weston site was in jeopardy if the legislature did not adopt an open-occupancy law. "Enactment of an effective open housing law by the Legislature of Illinois would go a long way toward ending any question of change of location of the accelerator site," Seaborg said. "We are not in a position to say what Congress will do with regard to the 200-BEV Accelerator Project if such a law is not enacted."[55]

In late April Pastore went too far. He vowed publicly to exclude the initial $10 million design appropriation for the accelerator from the AEC's authorization bill if Illinois failed to pass a fair-housing law. Pastore gave Kerner ten days to come up with an answer. The ultimatum crossed the line between proper and improper political debate, and Pastore aroused a formidable opponent who until then had taken only scant interest in the Weston project. Everett Dirksen, the flowery orator from downstate Pekin and the Senate's Republican leader, went on the offensive. He and the full Illinois congressional delegation laid aside the merits of the accelerator and the worthiness of Illinois to be its home. Pastore had attacked the sovereignty of their state. In tones that few other men could muster and no senator could ignore, Dirksen called Pastore's demand "blackmail."[56] He and Republican congressman John N. Erlenborn from Du Page County vowed to block federal projects in other states without pristine open-occupancy records, a threat members of Congress took seriously because Dirksen could enforce it.

Meanwhile, many Republicans in the state legislature were by now aiding Kerner's cause in Springfield. In floor debate William G. Barr, a freshman Republican from Joliet, not far from the Weston site, acknowledged that as the owner and manager of rental housing in his district he had discriminated against blacks: "I am ashamed to say I have turned them down in fear—fear of my competitors." Barr said mortgage lenders in his community refused to back his effort to end discrimination. "I want to end this type of economic fear," he added. Speaking of the open-housing bill then before the house, Barr said: "The only fault with this bill is that it doesn't go far enough. Let's get on with the business of dealing with each other as human beings regardless of race or creed or color."[57] On May 10 the Illinois House passed a timid open-occupancy bill sponsored by Republican Lewis Morgan of Wheaton, the Du Page County seat.

In late June civil rights pressure came from a new source, Robert Rathbun Wilson, a fifty-year-old nuclear physicist from Cornell University selected by the AEC to manage the new accelerator. Wilson, whose lanky, youthful looks were enhanced by wire-rim "granny" glasses popular among young people at the time, was no ivory-tower scientist. He was a maverick in the high-energy physics community who had few supporters at the University of California at Berkeley. He had a national reputation as a tough administrator dating from his years as mayor of Los Alamos, New Mexico, the town at the center of America's development of nuclear bombs.

Wilson is a descendant of John G. Fee, an abolitionist minister and a founder of Berea College, an integrated college established in pre–Civil War Kentucky. On the twenty-fifth anniversary of the National Accelerator Laboratory, Wilson wrote: "It was a family obligation to be involved in the civil rights movement of the sixties, and becoming Director of Fermilab (as the accelerator came to be known) offered an opportunity for me, as well as for my comrades, to do something other than just talk."[58]

As Wilson was setting up a temporary office in Oak Brook, a handful of civil rights demonstrators established a "tent-in" on the grounds of a Catholic retreat two miles from Weston. The night before the protesters marched briefly and peacefully to Weston, Martin Luther King addressed them in what would be the final speech of his Chicago campaign. Most of his staff had already relocated to Cleveland, where a smaller effort was underway. King told the Weston protesters that federal funding for building the accelerator in an area where housing discrimination persisted would further weaken the 1965 Civil Rights Act. But he acknowledged to a *Chicago Tribune* reporter that his campaign in the North had failed to attract much support."I don't know how much support we are losing, but I will say the vast majority of Americans are against us."[59]

The scientists coming to Weston were with him, nonetheless. Two days before the march on Weston, Wilson sent a telegram to King: "We scientists now designing the 200-BEV accelerator to be located at Weston strongly support the struggle for open housing in Illinois. Science has always progressed only through the free contribution of people of all races and creeds."[60] The next day Wilson wrote to Kerner, saying that because of Illinois's nationally tarnished reputation on the fair-housing issue and the legislature's failure to improve it,

> we are having great difficulty in attracting physicists to Illinois. . . . Many of them, although welcome themselves in the area, feel that they would lose the respect of physicists elsewhere in moving to an area where some of their respected friends and colleagues might be rejected. This is not an imaginary difficulty—I have already been turned down a number of times by people who have given the uncertainty due to this racial problem as their principal reason for not coming. Of course, the very real danger that the accelerator may not be authorized by Congress this year because Illinois has not implemented open housing is another reason that makes it almost impossible for a family man to decide to leave his present position.[61]

Wilson's concern was well founded. By July major northern cities had suffered the most serious rioting the United States had ever seen. The *New*

York Times, which in keeping with the East Coast campaign for the Brookhaven site had opposed strongly the selection of Weston, turned its editorial guns on the accelerator project itself. After the Senate voted, over Pastore's and Javits's objections, to authorize the project for Weston, the *Times* remarked: "The nation is engaged in a bloody war in Vietnam; the streets of its cities are swept by riots born of anger over racial and economic inequities. It is a distortion of national priorities to commit many millions now to this interesting but unnecessary scientific luxury."[62] This was the viewpoint Seaborg feared the most. Celebrated black historian John Hope Franklin, chairman of the history department at the University of Chicago, drew an analogy between building the accelerator in a "lily white" community and the plight of America's black soldiers facing racism in towns near U.S. military bases in the South.[63]

Days after Lyndon Johnson named Kerner to head a blue-ribbon commission investigating the causes of urban riots in the summer of 1967, Senator Philip Hart of Michigan, which had lost its Ann Arbor bid for the accelerator, sent Kerner a telegram saying: "Placing the accelerator in Weston would I believe be tragic. While this particular [authorization] vote did not set off a Detroit riot, symbols are important at this moment: symbols of indifference, symbols of lack of understanding, symbols of lack of hope. Clearly this is not a symbol of hope." Hart, whose home state was a finalist for the project, vowed to oppose the project when the appropriations bill including $10 million for the accelerator came up for a vote.[64] But Dirksen's pledge to defeat other federal projects if money for Weston was denied proved unbeatable. In addition, many members of Congress soured on taking progressive civil rights stands that might appear to be rewarding rioters and looters. By August even Pastore had withdrawn his objection, and the Weston appropriation won approval quietly.

Kerner was able to undertake a new mission that would address more broadly the nation's civil rights conflict—as chairman of the National Advisory Commission on Civil Disorders—with initial funding for Weston secure. He did not possess the "key to the Senate," as he mused during a political cruise on the Mississippi River when Johnson named him to head the commission. But Everett Dirksen did.

✦ ✦ ✦

The federal appropriation to begin designing the national atomic accelerator marked the beginning of the end for the Village of Weston, which had worked hard to win the project as the best hope for its future. After important fights to enhance scientific egalitarianism and civil rights generally, Weston could not save itself. Several ambitious but ultimately abortive proposals, surpassing C. P. Snow's fondest hopes, were made to surround the accelerator with a model community similar to Reston, Virginia. But physicists heading for Weston opposed the delays and distractions such an undertaking would generate and had no interest in living in a sociological fishbowl. The town's existing prefabricated houses as well as several barns and other farm structures in the area were converted quickly into housing and office space for engineers and designers. The legislature authorized acquisition of 6,800 acres, including the village, to donate to the AEC. For several months in 1967 and 1968, the daily lives of Weston's unassuming residents were entwined with busy scientists and engineers surveying and preparing the site for the giant atom smasher ring. But residents were excluded from participation and simply urged to leave.

Theriault's dreams for his community to grow with the accelerator were dashed, and he felt betrayed. Seaborg insisted that no one ever misled Weston officials. But Theriault, who at a critical moment in winning Senate funding had appeared on NBC's *Today* show to announce the village's passage of an open-occupancy ordinance and give the mysterious accelerator a sympathetic face, remained bitter. He refused to surrender his house and instead had it lifted and placed on a foundation in the nearby suburb of West Chicago. In 1967 the Illinois Supreme Court threw out the Du Page County lawsuit and upheld the village's incorporation, but a year later Weston's families were gone. Houses were picked up and clustered into a community center for the project, which in 1972 was named after the Italian nuclear physicist Enrico Fermi. All that remains of Weston is a bronze plaque near the center of the Fermilab village, "Dedicated to the residents of Weston who desired local government and unselfishly worked to improve the economy of Illinois by promoting this site for the accelerator laboratory."

Under Wilson's creative and insistent direction, the accelerator was constructed on time and within budget. Its central laboratory towered over cornfields that eventually became suburbs. Wilson and his staff proved to be equally effective in encouraging the employment of minorities at Fermilab. Kennard Williams, an African American who as head of the Du Page County NAACP chapter had opposed bringing the accelerator to Weston, was hired by Wilson and Deputy Director Edwin L. Goldwasser to direct an ambitious minority hiring program. In 1968 Williams and other staff members went into Chicago to recruit young black men, many of whom were gang members with police records, to enter a novel training program. They were sent to Oak Ridge, Tennessee, for training as technicians for the project. Within a year twenty-one of the twenty-four recruits were working as technicians on the site and one young man took a job with the state. Only one washed out of what was probably the most ambitious affirmative action program underway in Du Page County at the time. Separately, unemployed young black men were trained at Argonne National laboratory in using earthmoving equipment. Seventy-two were later employed as operating engineers on the Weston site.

By the end of 1969 20 percent of the nonprofessional employees at the accelerator project were black. The melding of two cultures—those of the particle physicists and inner-city black youths—was not without friction. In a January 1970 speech, Goldwasser recalled one incident:

> A few months ago Bob Wilson came to me and said he was deeply disturbed by the fact that most of our young black employees were carrying large knives sticking out of their pockets. He asked if I had noticed it. I had not. We agreed first that it was dangerous, second that it was not our idea of the way we wanted people to behave in our laboratory or feel about it. Bob felt that he would have to issue an order banning the knives, while I preferred that we wait to see if, as the men acclimated and began to feel more secure, the knives would just disappear by themselves. As of a few weeks ago the knives had not yet disappeared. Bob had preferred not to raise the subject with Ken Williams yet, but by a devious path Bob's concern about the knives did reach Ken's ears. The next day he came to Bob's office, and of all things not out of his back pants pocket but right out of his jacket breast pocket prominently stuck one of the vicious-looking knife handles. "Dr. Wilson," said Ken approaching Bob, "there is one matter that I simply must discuss with you." He leaned over so the handle was only a few feet from Bob's face, reached up, grabbed it decisively, pulled out an Afro-comb and proceeded to comb his hair. That was the pleasant end of the Case of the Pocket-Combs.[65]

As the turbulent 1960s came to an end, no other employer in Du Page County was encouraging racial integration and welcoming inner-city black culture with the same dedication as the National Accelerator Laboratory. As Glenn Seaborg had promised, the presence of the proton accelerator had accelerated the cause of racial harmony and equality. By 1970 about thirty municipalities around the former village of Weston had their own open-occupancy ordinances. That same year Illinois voters approved a new state constitution with a strong civil rights article.

Had Kerner sought an unprecedented third term as governor in 1968, his administration's victory in winning the National Accelerator Laboratory for Illinois would likely have been a major theme of the campaign. The accelerator's unique contribution to promoting civil rights and race relations might have been more widely noted. Instead, Kerner sought and received from Johnson an appointment to the U.S. Court of Appeals for the Seventh Circuit in Chicago, and Fermilab's scientists became absorbed in basic research that few outside the boundaries of the laboratory understood.

The compelling story of Weston faded from history. But one minor player in the drama later reentered Kerner's life. In 1969 federal appeals judge Otto

Kerner threw out, on the grounds of double jeopardy, the second extortion conviction of West Side hoodlum enforcer Joseph Amabile in the Northlake case. It was a ruling on behalf of the constitutional rights of a mobster that earned Kerner the unrelenting enmity of Chicago-based special agents of the Internal Revenue Service.

8

The Sadness of Our Time

A remnant of Prohibition in Detroit's black ghetto was the "blind pig," informal social clubs that provided after-hours drinking and minor gambling. In the 1920s whites called them "speakeasies." In the 1960s Detroit's blind pigs were inner-city versions of the American Legion halls found in middle-class suburbs and small towns, refuges where men felt free to complain among themselves about the social and political ills of the day. But the early-morning boisterousness in Detroit's blind pigs often involved African Americans denouncing the white establishment and its primary agent in their lives, the police.

On the morning of Sunday, July 22, 1967, a vice squad officer, unaware of what was going on inside but convinced by an ex-convict informant that "it's getting ready to blow," invaded a blind pig in a second-floor office on Twelfth Street.[1] The club, sponsored by a new organization called the United Community and Civic League, was the last of five such establishments raided that night along Twelfth Street, a congested, vice-ridden strip of apartment buildings and shops where poor blacks crowded together after urban renewal had pushed them out of other neighborhoods.

Seven months later white Americans who knew nothing about blind pigs were shocked when eleven representatives of the nation's "moderate and 're-sponsible' Establishment," as journalist Tom Wicker called them, reached their verdict about the deadly, charred aftermath of the Twelfth Street police raid. "When they first met they seemed an unpromising group," Wicker wrote in the introduction to the Bantam edition of the report of the National Advisory Commission on Civil Disorders.[2] But the commission chaired by Otto Kerner laid at the door of white America responsibility for the 1967 Detroit riot and scores of inner-city uprisings over three summers that had left 225 dead and more than 4,000 wounded—the greatest domestic unrest since the Civil War. Wicker called the document, which quickly became known as the Kerner Report, "an indictment" of white Americans who made life in the northern cities hopeless for black immigrants from the South.[3]

At its initial publication the report was dismissed by America's emerging radical left as a bland affirmation of failed government policies and upper-class hegemony. Conservative commentators accused the authors of pandering to rioters and proposing to bankrupt the country through welfare programs. Much of the condemnation fell on Kerner himself as the public face of the commission in countless press conferences and other public appearances. But he never backed away from its controversial findings and recommendations. On the contrary, his public statements after the report was published went beyond the commission's carefully drawn language concerning racism in America. Well into his tenure as a federal judge, Kerner stumped like a political campaigner for the report that bore his name.

Many of the report's recommendations were undertaken immediately and achieved demonstrable, lasting success. These included improved procedures for police departments and National Guard units facing the threat of mass disorders, more conscientious hiring and promotion of minorities by major public and private employers, and greater sensitivity to minorities and inner-city concerns by the national and local news media. Others—including effective reform of the nation's welfare system, stiffer gun control laws, relevant job training, and incentives for private home ownership in low-income areas—remain on the nation's agenda three decades later. Still other recommendations—that the nation spend massive amounts of federal dollars to create millions of jobs, rebuild America's cities according to master plans, and provide guaranteed incomes for the poor—never attracted popular support and virtually disappeared from public debate.

But the greatest contribution of the Kerner Commission went beyond its published findings and recommendations. The commission, through the process of its investigations and deliberations, took one of the most intractable issues in U.S. history—race prejudice—to a higher plane and, despite deep national fear and division, for once allowed goodwill to conquer defensiveness and negativism. Ten men and one woman—nine whites and two blacks—plus twenty-two principal staff members and dozens of advisers, researchers, and consultants confronted more closely than even they expected the uniquely intangible as well as the tangible problems of race, poverty, and urban decay. They found and exposed what most Americans had ignored or insisted on denying: an existing rationale for violent revolution in America's cities. They met in charred ghetto neighborhoods and in ornate Washington hearing rooms. They heard from rioters and police and from many city dwellers who were neither. It was an urgent, often contentious passage over seven months that began in crisis and ended in unanimity even as police departments in many cities were arming themselves for escalated violence in the summer of 1968. Material eliminated from the final report was in many cases as important as the final draft. What began as a diversionary tactic by a White House embroiled in Vietnam ended as a statement to the nation that went against the interests of President Johnson and the political establishment. When summers in America meant burning cities and armed violence among citizens, the Kerner Commission and its staff embarked on a search for truth—truth that could be found only in cities such as Detroit—and insisted that it be told.

✦ ✦ ✦

At nearly 4 A.M. on that Sunday morning, the undermanned Detroit police department was not equipped to arrest and quickly process the eighty-two individuals gathered in the blind pig to welcome home friends and relations returning from duty in Vietnam and to send off others to the war. Weeks earlier an African American soldier had been slain by white youths for daring to have a picnic with his pregnant wife in Detroit's Rouge Park. Newspapers in the generally prosperous but racially changing city downplayed the story for fear of inciting a riot. The vice officer who entered the social club first on the explosive scene insisted on making arrests. Emptying the club took more than an hour, during which time the crowd inside loudly denounced the police and a new crowd began to form outside. One unidentified young man, who came to be known as "Mr. Greensleeves" because of the color of his shirt, shouted, "We're going to have a riot!"[4] Someone threw an empty bottle through the rear window of a police car. A litter basket was hurled through the window of a nearby store. Rumors circulated that the police had used excessive force in making the arrests.

Over the next four days and nights, Detroit exploded in the worst violence of that long, hot summer. City and state police, the Michigan National Guard, and eventually federal troops failed to restore order until the rioting, looting, and sniping spent itself. Forty-three people died, thirty-three blacks and ten whites. Among the dead were seventeen looters, including two whites; one National Guardsman; one white firefighter; and one black security guard. The army, National Guard, and police killed twenty-eight persons. Fires destroyed or damaged 682 buildings. Nearly 300 families were rendered homeless.

In the early stages Detroit police stood by as looters emptied stores. Untrained, ill-equipped, vastly outnumbered, and to some extent indifferent to destruction in the ghetto, the police at first seemed content to stand back and let the several thousand residents spilling onto Twelfth Street and nearby commercial areas have their way with the mostly white-owned shops. A few weeks earlier Detroit police had staged a "blue flu" strike to demonstrate their own plight, prompting Mayor Jerome Cavanaugh, a progressive and competent public official, to put police on twelve-hour shifts. City officials, knowing the sullen attitude of their police force, hoped that a passive stance by police on Twelfth Street might stem the ardor of the crowds. That view was tragically mistaken.

The Kerner Commission staff reported the result: "Bantering took place between police officers and the populace, some still in pajamas. To some observers there seemed at this point to be an atmosphere of apathy. . . . A spirit of carefree nihilism was taking hold. To riot and destroy appeared more and more to be ends unto themselves. Late Sunday afternoon it appeared to one observer that the young people were 'dancing amidst the flames.'"[5] Firefighters radioed to their command center from several fire scenes that they had no police protection. As the turmoil spread, many black residents aided the fire department, which on a per capita basis was one of the smallest in the nation. "In some areas residents organized rifle squads to protect firefighters."[6] There was no mutual aid pact for the Detroit department to summon fire departments quickly from the suburbs.

The passivity of the police eventually transformed into aggression. The commission staff later described what happened:

> With a major police effort in the late morning to re-establish control of the streets, violence entered a new and ominous phase. An elite riot squad, equipped with bayoneted rifles, was brought in to sweep the streets. From a permissive inaction, the police policy suddenly changed to vigorous and aggressive control tactics. In full view of hundreds of people, police bayoneted a drunken man who was too slow to move out of their way. Photographs later showed his intestines coming out of his mouth. As word of the incident spread, the crowds became furious. Further, the sweep tactic was ineffective in that the crowds were so large they continually filled in behind the police. The response of Negro youth activists to the attempt to re-establish police control was aggressively competitive rather than obedient and submissive. They saw the police as an occupying power and viewed the tough stance of the police as a challenge. Great numbers of fires were set by roving bands, false alarms were turned in, fire hoses were cut. Police riot training had prepared them for controlling street crowds of limited scope contained within limited geographical areas. It had not trained them for the possibility of highly generalized and purposive attack against authority and property by bands of intensely motivated youths.[7]

The chaotic and escalating violence in Detroit, which a generation later many Americans, both black and white, find incomprehensible, was just the latest of that summer, and that summer was just the latest of three summers scarred by major urban violence. In 1967 alone 150 separate episodes of inner-city disorder were reported. By July even minor incidents were being labeled "riots" in the news media. Before Detroit, outbreaks were handled— or at least contained—by local and state police powers.

A telephone call by George Romney, the Republican governor of Michigan, to Attorney General Ramsey Clark asking for federal troops put the problems of America's cities in a historically momentous context as far as the Constitution and the Johnson presidency were concerned. Americans had fought a war with Britain over issues such as the right of national authorities to dispatch troops within the states. Except during the Civil War, federal troops had been deployed to suppress a domestic uprising only about a dozen times in the nation's history, and it was a step no president welcomed. Constitutional interpretations and federal law required a state governor to request federal troops and to specify their purpose. "The reasons for such elaborate certification are deeply imbedded in our constitutional history," Johnson observed in his memoirs. "Our forefathers wanted to prevent abuse of federal authority."[8] Federal troops had been sent to Detroit once before, by President Franklin Roosevelt, to put down a race riot in 1943.

Johnson felt more than a constitutional constraint in considering the deployment of troops against a domestic disturbance. He recoiled at the admission of failure such a step would represent. When the first major riot of the 1960s broke out in the Watts neighborhood of Los Angeles in August 1965, shortly after Johnson signed the Voting Rights Act, the president refused to deal with it. "He just wouldn't accept it," White House domestic policy adviser Joseph A. Califano told historian Doris Kearns. "He refused to look at the cable from Los Angeles describing the situation. He refused to take the calls from the generals who were requesting government planes to fly in the National Guard. I tried to reach him a dozen times. We needed decisions from him. But he simply wouldn't respond."[9]

Romney's call again put Johnson on the spot. Romney was an undeclared candidate in the GOP's moderate wing seeking to oppose Johnson in 1968. According to Califano, "LBJ considered Romney a more potent rival than [Richard] Nixon."[10] There was no sympathy for Romney in the White House. Romney realized what Johnson was thinking and was livid. At the same time, several key members of Congress—where Johnson's efforts to expand his Great Society programs and broaden U.S. involvement in Vietnam were in serious trouble—demanded committee inquiries into urban riots. Democrats as well as Republicans pushed to hold hearings. "In short, there was developing a struggle for national leadership of major proportions," Donald Lee Scruggs wrote in his doctoral dissertation on the Kerner Commission. "Congress was clearly attempting to challenge the President in the area of domestic policy and was showing increasing signs of rejecting the means if not the ends of the Johnson foreign policy."[11]

Presidential aide Cyrus R. Vance, in Detroit to assess the situation for the White House, phoned the president Monday night: "The situation is beginning to deteriorate. There were twelve hundred persons now being detained in felony court. Reports of incidents are increasing throughout the area. Conditions are worse than ever; I am ready now to recommend the deployment of federal troops. I believe you should sign the Executive order to federalize the Michigan National Guard. I urge this action."[12] Johnson and his close adviser Abe Fortas and other White House strategists crafted a plan to make Romney bear the brunt of the responsibility for the necessity of federal action. "I'm concerned about the charge that we cannot kill enough people in Vietnam so we go out and shoot civilians in Detroit," the president said, according to Califano's memoir.[13]

Shortly after 11 P.M. Johnson signed an order authorizing federal troops to put down the riot. He immediately went on national television to read a statement, citing "undisputed evidence that Governor Romney of Michigan and the local officials in Detroit have been unable to bring the situation under control. . . . The federal government in the circumstances here presented had no alternative but to respond, since it was called upon by the Governor of the State and since it was presented with proof of his inability to restore order in Michigan."[14]

Johnson's order federalized the exhausted Michigan National Guard in Detroit, but it did not improve their readiness or their discipline in using firearms. The Kerner Commission later reported the following episode:

> Employed as a private guard, fifty-year-old Julius L. Dorsey, a Negro, was standing in front of a market when accosted by two Negro men and a woman. They demanded he permit them to loot the market. He ignored their demands. They began to berate him. He asked a neighbor to call the police. As the argument grew more heated, Dorsey fired three shots from his pistol into the air. The police radio reported: "Looters, they have rifles." A patrol car driven by a police officer and carrying three National Guardsmen arrived. As the looters fled, the law enforcement personnel opened fire. When the firing ceased, one person lay dead. He was Julius L. Dorsey.[15]

Army paratroopers numbering 2,700 entered the city. On orders from Johnson, General John T. Throckmorton, who was in command of the military units, ordered all troops to carry unloaded weapons. He also ordered street barricades be removed. But the mayhem continued. Machine-gun-equipped Huey helicopters, the kind used in Vietnam, circled above, hunting for snipers. National Guard units roamed the streets in Patton tanks. The Kerner Report illustrated the results:

> At approximately midnight [Tuesday] . . . a machine gunner on a tank, startled by several shots, asked the assistant gunner where the shots were coming from. The assistant gunner pointed toward a flash in the window of an apartment house from which there had been earlier reports of sniping. The machine gunner opened fire. As the slugs ripped through the window and walls of the apartment, they nearly severed the arm of twenty-one-year-old Valerie Hood. Her four-year-old-niece, Tonya Blanding, toppled dead, a .50 caliber bullet hole in her chest. A few seconds earlier, nineteen-year-old Bill Hood, standing in the window, had lighted a cigarette.[16]

By late Tuesday firebombing and looting had subsided, but sniping continued. "Of the twenty-seven persons charged with sniping, twenty-two had charges against them dismissed at preliminary hearings, and the charges against two others were dismissed later," the Kerner Report found.[17] Only two stood trial. By Thursday, July 27, the riot activity was over. Exhaustion defeated rebellion. Fire had consumed several inner-city commercial streets, forty-three persons were dead, and institutions of government from Detroit's city hall to the White House were crippled by their ineffectiveness.

As in any war, truth was the first casualty of the urban riots of the 1960s. Neither government authorities nor ghetto residents understood how isolated, albeit tragically routine, police incidents degenerated into riots. No one was even sure who the rioters were. Lessons that should have been learned in one city never made it to the next. Black and white civic leaders who had lobbied successfully for civil rights laws were confused and bewildered. The fear among whites and blacks caused by this gulf of ignorance reached crisis proportions during the week of the Detroit riot.

A widespread view in Washington and throughout the country was that the riots were caused by a conspiracy among black militants, probably inspired by communists from Cuba and elsewhere. *Newsweek* magazine, in its initial coverage of the Detroit riot, reported that the FBI "spotted Negroes using walkie-talkie radios to report movements of police, firemen and soldiers. Agents told . . . Cyrus Vance . . . that the communications were precise enough to indicate previous drills and central organization. FBI men made recordings and movies of ring-leaders during the four-day rioting."[18] Many in Congress and the administration suspected communist influence. One of the most popular pieces of legislation under consideration was a bill to make it a federal offense to cross state lines to incite a riot. Another popular view insisted that rioters were petty criminals and urban riff-raff, undeserving of any sympathetic hearing of grievances, let alone taxpayer-financed aid. Conspirators or riff-raff, the rioters were seen by Johnson principally as threats to his Capitol Hill agenda and personal legacy. As he did with nearly everything else, Johnson interpreted the urban riots in terms of their effect on his ability to win congressional approval for his legislative program, in this case domestic spending bills known collectively as the Great Society.

In a telling sign of the times, Johnson's bill to spend federal dollars for the eradication of rats in inner cities, called the Rat Extermination Act, had become an object of derision on Capitol Hill. Republicans and southern Democrats called it the "Civil Rats Bill" and refused even to debate it on the House floor. An outraged Johnson complained that thousands of ghetto babies were being bitten and killed by rats while the federal government spent taxpayer dollars to control predators that attacked farm and ranch animals. (The urban rat control measure was enacted later that year.) Johnson saw the riots in intensely personal terms. He condemned urban blacks as well as congressional opponents. "It simply wasn't fair for a few irresponsible agitators to spoil it for me and for all the rest of the Negroes, who are basically peace-loving and nice," he told Kearns, calling them "a few hoodlums sparked by outside agitators who moved around from city to city sparking trouble. Spoiling all the progress I've made in these last few years."[19]

The great achievements of America's industrial revolution, its big cities, looked like terrible mistakes in the summer of 1967. The fabled urban melting pot of racial and ethnic assimilation boiled over. Because of race prejudice, one ingredient was not blending into the mix. The heat was forging a black urban underclass into an irreducible weight that grasped and tore society's fabric as it fell. In the process Americans' most elemental and tangible rights—to be free from assault, theft, and willful destruction of property—seemed under attack. The nation was on trial. Naming the criminals was a matter of perspective, however, seen much differently from the bottom of the melting pot than from the top. Even the president could be cast as a victim or a perpetrator. But he alone selected the jury, and Johnson chose carefully from among his peers. On the evening of Thursday, July 27, Johnson again addressed the nation by television, this time to announce Executive Order 11365, creating the National Advisory Commission on Civil Disorders.

✦ ✦ ✦

"Tomorrow, I go to Washington to help organize this group of citizens for the saddest mission that any of us in our careers have been asked to pursue—why one American assaults another, why violence is inflicted on people of our cities, why the march to an ideal America has been interrupted by bloodshed and destruction," Otto Kerner told a community organization in Chicago on the eve of the riot commission undertaking. "We are being asked, in a broad sense, to probe into the soul of America," he said. He deplored the failure, once again, of the Illinois legislature to enact a statewide open-housing law, which he knew could be a safety valve against inner-city frustrations. "We must be sure as Americans that the full resources of our government are . . . at the disposal of our people to wage war against poverty and discrimination. There must be no holds barred in this war, a war that is truly a continuation of the American revolution."[20]

In a remarkable moment in the evolution of federal-state relations, the same White House strategists who advised blaming a governor, Romney, for the necessity of sending federal troops to Detroit selected a governor, Kerner, to chair a national commission intended further to absolve Johnson of responsibility. To give the strategy a bipartisan appearance, Republican mayor John V. Lindsay of New York City would be vice chairman. Califano said later he feared that the commission would prove unruly, but there was no sign of dissent at the start. Kerner initially saw his role as responding to a temporary national emergency and shoring up the rule of law, as represented capably by the president of the United States. No one expected that Kerner and the others would grind a new lens through which America would see its problems with race relations for decades to come.

Kerner, just about to turn fifty-nine, was the only Democratic governor of a major industrial state. He had pushed hard for fair employment practices and open-housing laws. He was a decorated combat veteran of World War II and had become a general in the National Guard. The Illinois National Guard under Kerner's leadership had a higher percentage of blacks than did any other state's guard, although the level everywhere was small—just 5.3 percent in Illinois, 1.3 percent in Michigan, 1.7 percent in New Jersey, 2.5 percent in New York, and 1.9 percent in California.[21] The Illinois guard had performed with restraint and professionalism during Chicago's West Side riot of 1966. Johnson knew that Kerner was a former U.S. attorney who had prosecuted many criminals. He was a liberal on civil liberties and civil rights issues and popular among Illinois's black voters. He hailed from the political organization of Mayor Richard J. Daley, the most powerful Democrat in the country next to Johnson. He supported Johnson's Vietnam policies, then being executed by his former battlefield comrade, General Westmoreland. Well into his second term in Springfield, Kerner wanted Johnson to appoint him to the federal appeals bench in Chicago, where his father had served. There was no warning that Kerner would stray from the Johnson corral.

On the other hand, Kerner had just completed his most successful session of the Illinois General Assembly and was finally coming into his own as

Illinois's chief executive. When Kerner's appointment to the riot commission was announced, *Chicago Sun-Times* political columnist John Drieske, a frequent critic of Kerner's capabilities, wrote: "Kerner used to be a mousy sort. . . . The 75th General Assembly changed Kerner. . . . Kerner began to register with the legislators and party colleagues as a man who liked being governor and was born to command, not merely sit back and judge."[22]

John Lindsay, forty-seven, a popular New York politician with an enviable following in the national press corps, seemed a riskier choice in the necessarily bipartisan undertaking. Lindsay was a handsome, lanky (six-foot-four), and ambitious product of Manhattan's silk-stocking Upper East Side. He would be more likely than Kerner to use this national forum for his own political ends. But Lindsay was an anomaly within his own party. He stood closer to Johnson and Kerner than to the GOP on the importance of civil rights legislation and was more adamant than either Johnson or Kerner, not to mention his fellow Republicans, about the need for massive federal spending on behalf of cities and the urban poor.

The other members of the commission were drawn from similarly elite backgrounds. None had a large national reputation, but all were admired for their diligence. Johnson believed each would be sympathetic to his predicament as well as to the plight of urban blacks.

I. W. Abel, fifty-eight, of Ohio was ending his second year as president of the United Steelworkers of America. In his first major decision as head of the union, Abel had helped to prevent a potentially crippling steelworkers strike by accepting a compromise fashioned in White House negotiations in August 1965.

Herbert Jenkins, sixty, had been police chief of Atlanta, Georgia, since 1947. His open-minded, progressive approach to police work had won praise from Attorney General Ramsey Clark. In 1967 Atlanta was not considered one of the nation's major cities, but it was a stronghold of both the Black Power movement and the Ku Klux Klan.

Katherine Graham Peden, forty-one, directed the Kentucky Commerce Commission. She was a nationally prominent businesswoman and a candidate for the U.S. Senate. Johnson earlier had appointed her to a national commission dealing with small-business issues. Peden owned a radio station in Kentucky and for that reason was somehow thought to represent the news media.

Charles B. "Tex" Thornton, fifty-four, was a native Texan and former associate of Defense Secretary Robert McNamara when they both worked at Ford Motor Company. He was the chief executive officer of Litton Industries in Los Angeles. He was a conservative on law-and-order issues but believed along with Johnson in the necessity for better jobs, education, and housing for the nation's African Americans.

Roy Wilkins, sixty-five, led the National Association for the Advancement of Colored People. He was one of the establishment black leaders who, Johnson and his advisers knew, had a greater following among white Americans than among black Americans. Nevertheless, he brought to the commission the urgently needed perspective on being black in America.

The remaining commissioners were members of Congress whose committee assignments and political leanings counted more than their seniority or clout in the House or Senate.

Edward K. Brooke, forty-seven, a liberal black Republican from Massachusetts, was one of the senators calling for the creation of a commission on the riots. He would help to balance the conservative views of Thornton and others but was absent for much of the deliberations. At one point during the work, Johnson sent him on an unrelated mission to Africa.

James C. Corman, forty-six, of California was in his fourth term as a liberal Democratic congressman from suburban Los Angeles, an increasingly conservative area that had been a key factor in the 1966 election of Governor Ronald Reagan. He admired Johnson and had won a seat on the powerful House Ways and Means Committee. Corman, a Kansas native, was married to a liberal southerner from Atlanta whose family had courageously advocated integration in the South throughout the 1950s. Corman believed strongly that segregation—not poverty—was the principal cause of urban riots.

Fred R. Harris, thirty-six, of Oklahoma was a young, liberal member of the Senate who was pressing for hearings on the riots. To some Harris seemed a young Lyndon Johnson. Just as important to Johnson, however, Harris sat on the Permanent Subcommittee on Investigations headed by John McClellan of Arkansas. McClellan, with the support of Republican leader Everett Dirksen, planned to hold hearings on the riots, focusing on criminality and conspiracy theories and explicitly rejecting economic and social causes.

William M. McCulloch, sixty-five, a twenty-one-year veteran of the House and ranking Republican on the Judiciary Committee, was a long-term civil rights advocate who nonetheless subscribed, as did Johnson, to the criminality theory of the riots.

Johnson did not permit the commission to select its executive director, the person who would oversee the work of the staff and guide the deliberations of the commissioners. After Johnson's appearance at the first commission meeting in the Cabinet Room on July 29, Kerner short-circuited any debate about an executive director by announcing that Johnson would make the appointment himself. It would be veteran Washington insider David Ginsburg, whose career in the Washington establishment began during the first term of Franklin Roosevelt. Ginsburg, a prosperous lawyer, was one of Johnson's most trusted unofficial advisers and troubleshooters. Recent assignments on behalf of the White House had taken him all over the world. He was on the West Coast vacationing with his family during the Detroit riot, when Abe Fortas called him and put the president on the line.

Ginsburg had no special expertise regarding urban problems or race relations, but as a Jew he understood the handicaps faced by minorities. He welcomed the job as a chance to make a contribution to what he had come to see as America's historic contradiction: its global image as a free society and its oppression of blacks. He found Johnson convinced that a conspiracy lay behind the riots, but he demanded a free hand in pursuing a broad investigation. In the end he struck a course that embarrassed and angered his beleaguered client.

Kerner set off to Washington for what he called "our investigation of the sadness of our time" in America's cities,[23] but he found much sadness in the White House. Lyndon Johnson was under siege and reacting with even more than his usual level of suspicion bordering on paranoia. At the commission's initial meeting, held on a Saturday morning in the Cabinet Room of the White House, Johnson tried hard to steer the commission in the direction he intended. He asked seventeen precise questions covering three general themes: "What happened? Why did it happen? What can be done to prevent it from happening again and again?"[24] The questions focused narrowly on issues related to rioting. This was a calculated attempt by the White House to limit the scope of the commission. Only one question posed by Johnson opened the door to the broader agenda the commission ultimately pursued: "What is the relative impact of depressed conditions in the ghetto—joblessness, family instability, poor education, lack of motivation, poor health care—in stimulating people to riot?"[25]

Frank Cassell, whom Kerner had appointed to study unemployment in Illinois and who in 1967 was working for Johnson's secretary of labor, Willard W. Wirtz, tried to show Kerner the ropes in Washington. "You can get chewed up," he told Kerner. Cassell recalled the prevailing Washington prejudice: "Anytime some guy comes in from the states, he doesn't know anything."[26] In an attempt to stake out a leadership role, Kerner aligned himself with Johnson. He told the commission he intended to proceed deliberately to accomplish the task, strictly as Johnson had assigned it, within the twelve months allowed by the executive order. But he resisted Thornton's advice that the commission go public quickly in endorsing Johnson's efforts to end the riots. Lindsay, Harris, and McCulloch, on the other hand, wanted immediately to launch a wider investigation of social ills and the problems of the cities. Kerner stated that the commission would establish offices in Chicago as well as Washington to facilitate his other job as Illinois governor and to extricate the work from an exclusive Washington venue, where he was a virtual stranger.

He told the commission he would be available for the probe seven days a week once he had disposed of the batch of bills passed by the Illinois General Assembly in its 1967 session.

He urged low-key, unpublicized visits by commissioners to cities where riots occurred. He favored allowing press coverage, though not television coverage, of commission hearings and emphasized the commission's responsibility to educate the public through its deliberations. "My concern all the time about this commission has been that at the conclusion our greatest problem is going to be to educate the whites rather than the Negro," he told a commission meeting in September.[27] Fred Harris agreed, telling fellow commissioners, "The worst problem we have in America today is that nobody is talking to each other about this problem and nobody really understands it."[28] Other members, notably Peden and Thornton, as well as the White House, preferred a secret, grand jury-style process to elicit a more candid search for facts and viewpoints and to deliver a fait accompli report. Donald Lee Scruggs noted two principal reasons for the decision to close the hearings and deliberations from public view: the White House distrusted the press generally, and the commission was unwilling "to provide a public forum for particular public figures, including persons from the Negro community, whom they knew they would be forced into hearing if the sessions were opened."[29]

At Kerner's side in the earlier meetings sat Theodore A. Jones, Illinois's revenue director and the highest-ranking African American in the Kerner administration. Shortly after coming to Washington, Jones and Kerner had dinner with Ginsburg. Ginsburg found Jones amiable, but he was annoyed a few days later when Johnson named Jones to be the commission's staff director, the number-two staff position. Ginsburg wanted blacks in key staff positions, but he did not believe Jones was up to the job. Moreover, the appointment was a major concession by the White House to Kerner, who, like the other commission members, had no say in the selection of Ginsburg as executive director.

Jones was unknown to the close-knit community of social scientists and urban policy experts whom Ginsburg hoped to tap for the commission's investigation and report. His responsibilities would include hiring and supervising the researchers and writers who would develop factual background and outline recommendations. Ginsburg knew that finding qualified researchers would be difficult enough as it was. Many in academia would refuse to serve because of Johnson's policy on Vietnam, and Johnson would not abide any appointees to the commission or its staff who opposed his war policy. Ginsburg saw Jones as a mere political appointee who could not bring the commission the prestige he wanted.

In fact, Jones was a successful Chicago businessman who brought at least two important attributes to the work ahead: an intimate understanding of power politics as practiced by the nation's leading urban politician, Mayor Daley, and a deep sympathy for poor, urban blacks. As a child he had witnessed Chicago's race riot of 1919. He had direct experience in urban unrest in the 1960s as Midwest regional director of Johnson's Office of Economic Opportunity. He had been one of the members of the Illinois Parole and Pardon Board who supported clemency for killer Paul Crump and who opposed on principle the execution of killer James Dukes. Johnson wanted a black man in a key staff position and was willing to accept Kerner's choice. At the urging of Kerner, Harris nominated Jones and the commission approved the appointment unanimously on August 1. At the same meeting Kerner unsuccessfully proposed Joseph Lohman, a well-known Chicago liberal and one of Kerner's opponents in the 1960 gubernatorial primary, as deputy director.

Jones's appointment ended abruptly one week later, however, and with it went Kerner's hope for primary authority over the commission's work. An FBI check (routine checks were done on all commission members and principal staff members) revealed that Jones was under investigation by the Internal Revenue Service in Chicago for tax evasion. The IRS at the time was pursuing several prominent Chicago blacks for criminal income tax violations, including future Chicago mayor Harold Washington. (Jones was indicted in 1968 and convicted of a misdemeanor tax violation in 1970.) Years later Jones recalled that Kerner knew about the IRS investigation when he recommended him for the riot commission post and did not consider it a serious matter. It was a serious matter to Daley, however, that Chicago newspaper headlines had quoted Jones pledging to hold riot commission hearings in his city, providing a forum his critics certainly would use to air their complaints before the national press. Daley, who had more influence with Johnson than did any other Illinois politician, wanted no mention of Chicago in the riot commission's investigations and report. Chicago's West Side riot occurred in 1966 and therefore was technically not part of the commission's purview. Daley wanted to keep it that way, and he largely succeeded.

Word of the IRS probe clinched Ginsburg's opposition to Jones. Jones wrote formally to Ginsburg that his obligations as Illinois revenue director prevented him from continuing on the riot commission staff. Explaining Jones's sudden resignation was awkward and embarrassing. Kerner's chief of staff, Chris Vlahoplus, put out a false story that the governor was angered that Ginsburg had expropriated the Illinois revenue director, depriving Kerner of a key state cabinet member in Springfield who would thus be preoccupied with the riot commission. The press reported that Kerner forced Jones's resignation as a way of asserting himself in an early confrontation with Ginsburg. In fact, the opposite was true. Ginsburg opposed Jones from the start. The loss of Jones reinforced Kerner's position as a Washington outsider.

Kerner's appointment of trusted adviser Dawn Clark Netsch as a consultant to the commission also ended quickly. In a thank-you letter to Netsch on September 10, after she had departed, Ginsburg acknowledged that she had been "isolated" in Washington. "Nevertheless the work you did is now embodied in how the commission is organized," he said.[30] With Jones and Netsch gone, there would be no women, no blacks, and no Kerner allies in top staff positions. Kerner had indeed been chewed up.

Ginsburg was determined not to let the Jones resignation unsettle the commission. He quickly and instinctively took things into his own hands. To replace Jones Ginsburg took the advice of a Justice Department official named Warren Christopher, who had been the executive director of a California investigative commission formed after the 1965 Watts riot. On Christopher's recommendation the commission selected Los Angeles real estate entrepreneur Victor H. Palmieri, a tough administrator who had attended Stanford University Law School with Christopher.

Palmieri had a low opinion of Johnson, whom he regarded as mentally unstable. As he recalled years later, Palmieri had gone literally "nose to nose" in an argument with Johnson in the Oval Office in 1966, when Johnson demanded that Palmieri accept an appointment as assistant secretary of the Department of Housing and Urban Development.[31] Palmieri refused, and Johnson loudly accused him of being an ally of the Kennedy family. Palmieri feared the president would physically attack him. Nevertheless, Palmieri hit it off with Ginsburg, who knew that Palmieri had close ties to the urban research establishment, which desperately was needed to inform and validate the commission's work. With the appointment of Palmieri and the start of commission hearings and staff work, Kerner's diminished role was settled. Ginsburg took charge of the critical relationship between the commission and the White House. Palmieri managed the staff. Kerner assumed the job of spokesperson and became the commission's smooth but persistent presiding officer.

The closed hearings in the historic, ornate Indian Treaty Room of the Old Executive Office Building began with Lindsay and Harris urging that the commission quickly make a preliminary statement about the riots. The White House meanwhile began working, as Califano put it in a memorandum to Johnson, to "keep the commission from shooting from the hip, which we believe would be damaging."[32] Kyran M. McGrath, a former administrative assistant to Senator Paul Douglas and a man who understood Washington's venomous culture, became Kerner's special assistant. McGrath kept detailed notes on commission meetings and briefed Kerner on political and substantive developments.

Kerner's participation became a duty, not an ambition. He and Ginsburg shared a vision of the commission's potential contribution to public understanding. The two men, who had not known each other before, formed a bond centered on the unenviable task of keeping the commission unified and the White House mollified while at the same time making an important statement about race relations that might avert another long, hot summer in America's cities.

✦ ✦ ✦

Five years after the Kerner Commission report was published, a mild-mannered social psychologist named Robert Shellow entered a federal courtroom in downtown Chicago to speak with the man on trial, Otto Kerner. He was not one of Kerner's many character witnesses in his trial for fraud and tax evasion—Shellow lacked the celebrity of broadcaster Jack Brickhouse and General William Westmoreland. He came, as he recalled years later, merely to tell Kerner "that the nation should be grateful to him for the service he rendered."[33] Shellow was grateful to Kerner for the opportunity, as research director for the Kerner Commission, to inject into the national debate about race a new way of thinking that went beyond static liberal/conservative perspectives. The work of Shellow's research team never was recognized publicly. Privately it was denounced by Shellow's superiors on the commission staff and by many of the commission members. Most of his team was fired in an economy move before the commission concluded its work. But their views were clearly visible in the final Kerner Commission report and were surprisingly compatible with the views of the chairman.

The news media carefully followed initial commission hearings, reporting leaks from the closed meetings and public statements by witnesses in connection with initial testimony. J. Edgar Hoover made headlines by stating at the August 1 meeting that his agents had found no evidence of conspiracy or coordination in the summer's riots. Not publicized was Hoover's provocative endorsement of rigorous gun ownership controls. "You have to license your dog," he told the commission. "You have to have a license sometimes to go hunting in various communities. Why should you not have to have a license to have a gun and be checked out by the local police department before a gun is issued to you?"[34]

Behind the scenes the commission's staff proceeded simultaneously along two paths. First, they gathered evidence to answer Johnson's questions about what happened and why. At the same time, they began organizing a report that would have findings and recommendations to address Johnson's third principal question, how to prevent urban riots. The press of time and resources—funds for the commission's work were not appropriated by Congress but had to be siphoned from several agency budgets—did not permit a more logical progression from fact gathering to report writing. Both were underway almost from the start. There were pressures and opportunities, therefore, to skew fact gathering to support conclusions and recommendations already being conceived and drafted.

The process of creating Great Society legislation, which had been more popular in happier times just a few years earlier, formed the template that the White House expected the commission to employ in examining the 1967 riots: begin with a description of a social ill, preferably using impressive-sounding economic and demographic statistics gleaned from experts; weave in compelling anecdotal evidence, such as rats attacking inner-city babies; and prescribe a new program of federal expenditures and controls to address the problem. This was the essence of transactional domestic politics that had shifted to the federal government from the state and local level during the Great Depression and remained firmly entrenched, thanks to the Internal Revenue Service's ability to raise large sums of money efficiently during the economic expansion of the 1960s. Typical liberal-versus-conservative debate focused on how much taxpayer resources to spend for what problems and how much to hand back as tax cuts. Much of the Kerner Commission work reflects this enduring transactional model. Indeed, Johnson hoped the commission would simply restate and affirm his domestic policies, but without raising the fiscal ante, as he struggled to finance the military buildup in Vietnam.

But Shellow and his research team tried to take the commission in a radically different direction, a more intangible one. Shellow, who was no celebrity even in his chosen field, was hired from the National Institute of Mental Health. His special interest was police-community relations. Unlike some of his fellow researchers on the commission staff, Shellow was not biased against the police. His search for common understanding and a middle ground between police and inner-city residents was based on extensive street-level study and was expressed in several articles on police training. In 1970 he became director of a pilot police district in Washington, D.C., that hoped to demonstrate ways to improve police service in the nation's capital.

To Palmieri's chagrin, Shellow lacked a national reputation in social science. In a 1970 article in *The Journal of Social Issues*, Shellow described his initial reception at the riot commission. He divulged a conversation between himself and "one of the staff directors" who he later confirmed was Palmieri. "You realize that it's going to be awfully difficult to mount a study of riots using social science methodology and compress it into four or five months," Shellow told Palmieri. The staff director replied, "That's not important . . . [;] what's important is that you've got that Ph.D."[35]

While Palmieri and the consultants he employed developed a statistically based economic and demographic snapshot of conditions in the inner cities, following the conventional Great Society transactional template, the Shellow team tried to fathom what rioters had actually been doing. In the fall of 1967 they became the center of the commission's energy. "We slept in our offices—they brought in cots—and we never left," team member David Boesel told journalist Andrew Kopkind. "It was crazy. We'd be found in our underwear darting across the hall in the mornings, just before people came to work. But we were really excited. We thought our case studies would be the guts of the report."[36]

After extensive interviews Shellow's researchers drew two conclusions: first, the urban riots of the 1960s lacked uniform causes and effects from city to city; second, several of the worst riots, including those in Detroit and Newark, were positive and overdue expressions of emerging political will among young black men. These men had rightly asserted themselves in a revolutionary manner against an embedded, hostile white authority, especially the police, just as colonists in many parts of the world had rebelled against their oppressors. The riots weren't a reaction; they were an action.

Martin Luther King Jr., addressing the commission in October, said: "People who are completely devoid of hope don't riot. Progress tends to whet the appetite for more progress."[37] Harvard University economist John Kenneth Galbraith, after President Johnson had called for a national day of prayer at the same time he established the presidential riot commission, quipped that the country might be better off with a national day of riot and a presidential commission on prayer. These, more elaborately stated, were the Shellow team's essential findings. The team wrote a 172-page report titled "Harvest of American Racism: The Political Meaning of Violence in the Summer of 1967." It was the "other" Kerner Commission report that never was published but nonetheless influenced the commission greatly and helped to form the backdrop of the final report. Two features of the "Harvest" document that distinguished it from the published report were its focus on the political character of black inner-city youth and its emphasis on grass-roots solutions instead of Great Society programs.

> In terms of both numbers and initiative, Negro youths constitute a profound social force in the ghettoes. This fact cannot be overemphasized since there is a radical break in continuity between today's Negro youth and their parents. . . . Negro youths are rejecting the compromises and subservience of their elders and developing a racial pride which at this point probably has become self-sustaining. Consequently, they make greater demands upon the larger society and press them with more vigor. And, on the whole, society has not responded. Despite their importance as a social force, Negro youths have almost no access to the established political system.[38]

Needless to say, this was not the perspective the Johnson White House, justly proud of its accomplishments in promoting civil rights laws, wanted broadcast. In assessing the struggles of oppressed races throughout history, however, the Shellow team did not shrink from provocative statements: "A central question to emerge from the study of disorders in American cities in the 1960s is not why there has been so much violence thus far, but why there has been so little. . . . To be blunt, a stable civil society requires that the monopoly of legitimate violence rest in the hands of the government. That monopoly is now being threatened in a way that it has not been since the Civil War."[39]

Perhaps the most provocative aspect of the report was its suggestion that "under certain conditions, violence can have positive consequences, especially for improving communications between the contesting groups and for the establishment of a climate in which bargaining can more readily take place. . . . While poor blacks don't have many votes, much money or extensive political skills, they do have the power to disrupt society."[40] Evidence for this cause-and-effect perspective on the 1967 riots was sketchy, the Shellow team found, in large part because of social and political inertia and hopelessness in many cities. Nevertheless, "In Milwaukee, Plainfield (New Jersey) and Detroit, the militant Negroes' presumed ability to control violence and to speak for the poor has thrust them into positions of leadership. In all three cities, militants have been included on committees of the establishment concerned with change, sometimes—as in Detroit—over the protests and resentment of more moderate Negroes who feel they are the real leaders of the Negro community."[41]

Finally, "Harvest" dealt directly with the issue of racism:

> Five years ago racism in America was widely regarded as a Southern problem; today, it has become evident that racism is a national problem. In degrees of greater or less intensity it is manifest in a substantial majority of the white population. It pervades our major institutions—some to a greater extent than others—and is one of the chief determinants of action in our society, economy and polity. For Negroes, it is an ever-present force, a fact of daily life which infuriates, annoys, humiliates and harasses. There is no need here to offer proof that Negroes in America—North and South—are second-class citizens in fact, if not in law. Common sense observation and hundreds of volumes on the subject make that abundantly clear.[42]

Racism is manifest, "Harvest" found, in the white majority's failure in many areas to endorse open housing, to create civilian review boards for police, and to abolish at-large elections for local offices. Yet the Shellow team found little evidence of a black separatist reaction. "Urban, industrial and affluent America is being confronted violently by a growing number of Negro youth who have been raised in this setting, have accepted its basic values and want their share. In demanding to be taken seriously, they are simply demanding that America live up to its ideals."[43]

In its recommendations the "Harvest" report optimistically saw young black men as the principal entrepreneurs of positive social change in America's cities and saw the federal government ideally as their champion and venture capitalist, not as a benevolent plantation master under the traditional system:

> The well-being of the whole community requires the recognition of Negro youth as a major power bloc. Since local government has shown no willingness to do this, then the federal government must. . . . We can expect to see Negro youths resort less and less to violence if their aspirations for power and development of their own areas can find fulfillment in extensive and expanded poverty programs which they direct. . . . To get out of the present crisis requires a willingness to invest in groups within the Negro community who can find the answers, who will develop the programs, and who will create organizations, an effective and coherent force for government to deal with. . . . How willing white America will be to share the power of the society with Negroes, to allow those powers to be used for Negro advancement, is the major problem.[44]

Reaching to the political heart of the matter, the Shellow group denounced the practice, demanded by Mayor Daley and others, of giving local political incumbents veto power over federal antipoverty programs. "Permitting such veto power is tantamount to taking sides in a community between entrenched political groups and a new social force; the latter, unless it is politically incorporated, will continue to use violence as a rational tool or as a nihilistic substitute for other kinds of power."[45]

"Harvest," taking up Kerner's principal ambition for the riot commission, also called for "a massive educational effort directed toward the white community of this nation to bring home to them the realities of Negro life. The gap of ignorance that stands between white perceptions of reality and what the real situation is among Negroes is phenomenal," even among white liberals in cities such as Detroit. "Group stereotypes must be broken and people seen as they are in daily life."[46]

Palmieri angrily rejected the "Harvest" report as an inflammatory and impressionistic statement that lacked statistical rigor. He believed it was a rhetorical bombshell. Ginsburg feared the report would undermine the commission's increasingly tenuous relations with the White House. Kerner, while speaking at several commission meetings about the legitimacy of the black revolution, agreed that the "Harvest" document needed to be contained within the commission, lest it damage the critical goal of keeping the commission unified. Nonetheless, chapter 2 of the final report reflects considerable influence by "Harvest," and the report's overall sense of urgency expresses the Shellow team's passion. Its statements concerning white racism, although diluted and confined largely to a brief summary, acknowledge the "Harvest" report's basic premise.

Shellow and his researchers succeeded, more than they may have realized at the time, but not on their own merits. Commission members needed to experience its essence. At the outset most commissioners had little or no personal exposure to the young black militants in whom the Shellow team found so much legitimacy and hope. The White House did not want the commission to become a platform for leading black militants, such as H. Rap Brown and Stokely Carmichael. Their testimony was taken by staff members much later, as an afterthought. King testified late in the process. The only black radical invited to testify formally before the commission's initial hearings was a thirty-year-old bearded professional barber from Omaha, Nebraska, named Ernest Chambers. Chambers, who later was elected to the Nebraska legislature and became his state's resident black radical, did his best to shock the commission into paying attention. Addressing the governor of Illinois, he called Abraham Lincoln "one of the most pious hypocrites of all time." He suggested that black militants were in league with the North Vietnamese, planning to bring the Vietnam war directly to America's cities. "We have exhausted every means of getting redress, and it has not come. The only thing left is violence, because that's the only thing this country understands," Chambers said. "We have tried through what you call extra-legal channels to get the Vietcong to airlift some guerrillas into this country, but they don't have the means."[47]

Despite Chamber's best efforts, the predispositions of the Kerner Commission members were not transformed by any of the formal testimony. Their minds and hearts were changed on the streets of U.S. cities, where Kerner and the other commission members heard firsthand from the people whose experiences and attitudes the "Harvest" report revealed.

✦ ✦ ✦

A month after the national commission on civil disorders began its work, Michael Butler, a son of millionaire paper magnate Paul Butler and a friend of Otto Kerner, accompanied Kerner and his assistant John Taylor to New York City. Kerner and Taylor were on their way to an unannounced tour of Newark, New Jersey, the site of a major riot in July. Butler stayed in New York to attend the theater with friends. The off-off-Broadway production he saw was a musical called *Hair*. The show, staged by a financially destitute production company, celebrated the antiestablishment themes of free sex, peace, hippie tribalism, outrageous appearance, and rock music. It portrayed middle-class young whites who, like young black militants, were bent on shocking America's older generation.

Butler was looking for a way to invest part of his energy and wealth in the antiwar movement. Later, he recalled, "I saw this play, and I fell in love with it." He bought the rights and put the show on a national tour. "My reason for getting into it was political," Butler said. "The nude scene got them into the theater," but in the second act the young performers communicated honestly with their elders, he said.[48] Butler donated some of performance proceeds to finance peace demonstrations.

Frank language about racism was the "nude scene" of the Kerner Commission report. As in *Hair*, it was not contrived or gratuitous. Nor was it theoretical. It reflected the experiences of the commission members in formal and informal visits to riot areas. Ginsburg and Kerner were united on the need to send commissioners, not just staff personnel, on the so-called field trips to riot cities. Lindsay and Harris faced open hostility when they met with militant young blacks in the Avondale Community Center in the riot-torn area of Cincinnati. A staff member recorded that the young men refused to shake hands with the mayor of New York City and the U.S. senator from Oklahoma. They became personal targets for bitter hate and distrust, something neither had witnessed from their own constituents. "It was the city visits, more than any other factor, which moved the commissioners to construct a report to President Johnson which he regarded as unacceptable," wrote Donald Scruggs.[49] As the commissioners' work intensified, the field trips gave them an independent understanding of the riots and emboldened them to step beyond the intentions of the White House and the Great Society's transactional model of urban problem solving.

Isaac Hunt Jr., a commission staff member, recorded Kerner's September 27 trip to Newark:

> We took a walk for three blocks down Prince Street, an area of small shops and stores almost all of which had been gutted during the riot and most of which had not re-opened. . . . From Prince Street, directly across land which had been cleared under an urban renewal program two or more years ago, we could see a group of Newark public housing units. These are brick, high-rise buildings that are some of the dreariest and most depressing housing units any of us had seen. Near these housing units was an uncompleted swimming pool for the neighborhood which had been promised for the summer. This pool, and the general lack of outdoor recreational facilities, were obvious sources of resentment in the neighborhood from our conversations with Prince Street merchants.
>
> We next stopped to talk to area residents around the corner from Prince Street. These people mentioned three problems which they regarded as important: (1) extreme police brutality; (2) the difficulty of obtaining jobs in the area or close enough for area residents to get to them by use of public transportation facilities; and (3) the lack of any effective relocation program for people displaced by various public works projects which do not house all of the people formerly living in the area. One of the young men to whom we were talking stated to Governor Kerner that he had not had a job in eight years.[50]

The group visited the United Afro-American Association in Newark and its president, Willie Wright.

Mr. Wright conveyed to the Governor his strong feeling that unless Negroes were admitted into the mainstream of American society, more and bigger riots would be forthcoming. He emphasized his definition of mainstream participation encompassed not just well-paying jobs for Negroes but also more instances of important Negro-owned contracting and manufacturing firms, etc., and Negro ownership of large retail establishments. Except for a discussion between Governor Kerner and Mr. Wright on the use of the term "Afro-American" instead of Negro, which wasted some time, I thought this was the most useful discussion of the day. Mr. Wright is an intelligent and articulate man and expressed well the bitterness and alienation felt by many Negro militants today.[51]

John Lindsay—through his own force of will and the prodding of his assistant assigned to the commission, Jay R. Kriegel—sought to become the dominant force on the commission and clearly was the favorite of the news media. Califano and Johnson worried that Lindsay's big-spending sentiments were providing political grist for Richard Nixon, who was well into his 1968 campaign for the presidency. Other commission members resisted Lindsay and resented what they believed was an effort by the liberal commission staff to keep them on the sidelines. Nonetheless, it was the Lindsay Commission as far as most journalists were concerned.

Lindsay had run for mayor of New York City on a platform of rebuilding the "Empire City" with massive help from Washington. He insisted that New York City should forever be the wellspring of American culture, and he believed his city deserved to be not only made safe from rioting but also perpetually subsidized and aggrandized as a national monument. "Together, we can make New York the Great Empire City again," Lindsay vowed in his 1965 campaign.[52]

In his autobiography, published in 1967, Lindsay declared: "The nation must make an extraordinary investment in its sagging, often debilitated cities. This will require Federal talent as well as Federal billions."[53] Lindsay saw himself not as a traditional big-city mayor, balancing the competing demands for essential service and favors within the limited fiscal resources of a city, but rather as an "urbanist" who would bring in "a whole new world, a world of Washington, of large and complicated programs, of science, design and planning. It is a world almost wholly foreign to the precinct power broker."[54] Lindsay's objective was even more foreign to young black men in the ghettos of New York, Detroit, and Chicago who never had a chance to be precinct power brokers or, for that matter, to better themselves and their families by escaping the nation's big cities.

Kerner, by contrast, was skeptical of the federal government's ability to renew America's cities through massive spending programs directed from Washington. He was not convinced that urban renewal as practiced in the 1960s was wise or necessary. His vision of America's cities reflected the history of pragmatic Central European immigrants, whose notion of urban progress was moving out of congested urban centers to better neighborhoods in the suburbs as soon as they could afford to upgrade. His father had done so, leaving the bosom of the Cermak political machine.

A week before the Detroit riot brought him into the national spotlight, Kerner recorded his forecast of urban evolution—as opposed to urban renewal—in a tape recording placed in the cornerstone of the new First National Bank of Chicago building. Asked by a reporter what he foresaw in Illinois in one hundred years, Kerner said: "There will be little distinction between farm and non-farm people, although Illinois will remain an agricultural products producer. Many workers one hundred years from today will commute over one hundred miles to their employment in urban and semi-urban areas and return home to cities in green fields."[55]

For Kerner, the key to domestic tranquility was not glorifying cities but bringing African Americans into the urban stepping-stone process by breaking down the attitudinal barriers by which whites kept them confined in ghettos. He was wedded to the immigrant model, as he wrote in a letter to a California journalist after the riot commission report was released:

> The immigrants from abroad who came to the United States, came of their own free will and volition and many of them brought their wives; if not, at least they were allowed to marry once they arrived and they brought their own culture. The Black Man did not. He arrived involuntarily, separated from family if he had one, and prohibited by law from marrying and raising a family. In addition, those who made it economically are still prohibited from mingling in white suburbia and owning property there because of the color of their skin. Therefore, they have two additional strikes against them not experienced by any of the white immigrants who came to the United States.[56]

In the same letter Kerner noted a similarity between certain European immigrants and African Americans.

> I was particularly impressed with the statement that is often made to me that the Negro should get off welfare and go to work. . . . A number of employers have indicated they would be pleased to hire the Black Man; however, a prospective employer then immediately establishes certain criteria of education and skill which consciously he may know Negroes do not have in quantity, or unconsciously may

not realize. . . . I am old enough to remember reading employment advertisements "No Irish Catholic need apply." But this is also true of Italian and Southern Europeans. The experience of the Black Man is not unlike the immigrants who came here with the additional burdens we have placed on him.[57]

Chances that the commission might irreparably split along these lines loomed large in early 1968. Memos by Lindsay and Corman written four days apart in January reveal the tension. Commenting on a draft report, Lindsay wrote to his fellow commissioners: "The major failing of the report is the lack of a sense of urgency. In both tone and content, the report has a static quality. . . . This is the most serious domestic crisis we have faced in the past century. There can be no delay. We need action. Our program must call for an unprecedented commitment for a national program. The challenge is equal to any we have ever had from outside. And we need no lesser level of response—a wartime level of resources and commitment with a full domestic strategy."[58]

A few days later Corman responded in an uncharacteristically emotional letter to Kerner:

The potential for significant national service has virtually slipped from our grasp. Meeting our responsibility does not lie in an indiscriminate and unstudied attack on every problem of American society, but rather in a careful weighing of evidence from the disorders, a development of understanding for the frustrations and limitations of human beings in these conflicts, and a judicious setting of program priorities that respond directly to the immediate causes of riots. . . . I am not aware that this Commission has the responsibility of setting forth a detailed program to renew our cities, especially when no convincing case has been made that a total restructuring of American cities is an absolute prerequisite for effective solutions to disorder and its cause. . . . I am not prepared to turn principle into profligacy. I am not prepared to state with certainty that a wide variety of detailed, experimental, and, in some cases, plain silly programs are the proper direction for the American government. . . . A sudden zeal for unrealistic and unrealizable recommendations has brought us to this crisis. I devoutly hope that, under your leadership, we can return to unity in our direction and to the national service that the President called upon us to perform.[59]

In this debate Kerner was much closer to Corman than to Lindsay. In the late 1960s many Americans, especially in the media and intelligentsia, started to lose confidence in America's ability to solve long-standing social problems through expert analysis and federal government expenditures. Lindsay left office with his city near bankruptcy.

In September 1967, early in the commission's deliberations, Kerner spoke to 2,500 local-government officials in Springfield. In his prepared text Kerner declared:

The eventual success and the future of our state's cities lie with the state rather than the federal government. I do not make this statement lightly. . . . Each state and each community has its own particular strengths and weaknesses, and its own assets and liabilities, its own traditions and needs. It is difficult and often impossible for the federal government to take these unique needs and requirements into account as it tries to draft a universal program for all the cities in this huge and varied nation of ours. . . . The federal government, by nature, tends to be weighty, cumbersome and sometimes slow—too slow.[60]

Kerner laid this text aside, however, and spoke candidly on behalf of the intended beneficiaries of federal aid to cities. He startled his audience by addressing what he called "an unpopular subject." The burning ghettos were a product of the "dry grass" of frustration and broken promises to inner-city blacks, Kerner said. Nothing the commission on civil disorders had heard in its preliminary hearings was news to him, and he pointedly rejected the conspiracy theory of the summer's riots. "How long would you and I control our tempers under the same circumstances?" he asked.

Just because it is Labor Day, don't think that it is over. Don't relax, because it is a year-round situation. Many affluent people are not aware that these conditions exist. If something is unpleasant, you put on blinders or you refuse to see what is immediately in front of your face. If we are going to maintain law and order, if we are going to eliminate crime in our state, and if we are going to be the United States of America we believe we should be, we must look, we must see, and we must take action. If we refuse to accept this, we are an immoral nation. Our legislature has refused to recognize this. I will continue to insist and work for freedom of residence for those individuals who live within that invisible wall and live on top of each other in filth, vermin and unhealthy conditions with no opportunity. This is the problem in our cities, in our organized communities.[61]

Ironically, the common ground that brought the Kerner Commission's liberals and conservatives together was also its most controversial message— Shellow's message—that white racism was the root cause of urban violence. The Lindsay and Corman viewpoints could and did unite on this assertion. In a pragmatic sense, it required no price tag and indeed no solid definition. Coming from America's establishment, however, it offered the hope of changing attitudes as well as economic distributions. It was the essence of Kerner's message, not Lindsay's.

In addition to being moved by recollections of their field trips to riot cities, commission members from the left and right were prompted to their conclusion by a lengthy and emotional statement made near the end of their deliberations by Roy Wilkins, who spoke about what it was like to be a black man in America. Wilkins's voice was powerful in no small measure because it came from one of the commissioners themselves, one who was chosen by

Johnson to allay public fears yet who was able to speak of the personal fear of being a black man in white America.

The commission knew that terms such as *racist* and *racism* would be explosive, and members debated at length the style and semantics of this aspect of the final report. The phrase "two societies, one black, one white, separate and unequal" first emerged in a draft summary offered by Lindsay in mid-February. But the Lindsay draft neither used the terms *racism* or *racist* nor blamed the problems of the ghettos specifically on whites. It instead spoke generally of "pervasive discrimination and segregation in all aspects of American life which has had corrosive and humiliating effects on the lives of our Negro citizens resulting in the deepest bitterness."[62]

Five days later Palmieri offered his own draft summary, which was much stronger on the racism theme and put Lindsay's "two societies" phrase in the first sentence of the report's leadoff summary. Palmieri also inserted the summary's second-most controversial phrase, which appeared in altered form in the final report: "What the American public has never fully understood—but what the Negro can never forget—is that white society is deeply implicated in his plight. White institutions created it, white institutions maintain it, and white morality condones it."[63] In the final version of the summary, "his plight" was changed to "the ghetto" and "white morality" was changed to "white society."

The Palmieri draft went on: "Past efforts have not carried the commitment, will or resources needed to eliminate the attitudes and practices that have maintained racism as a major force in our society. Only the dedication of every citizen can generate a single American identity and a single American community."[64] This paragraph was rejected, but stronger language was adopted in chapter 4: "Certain fundamental factors are clear. Of these, the most fundamental is the racial attitude and behavior of white Americans toward black Americans. Race prejudice has shaped our history decisively; it now threatens to affect our future. White racism is essentially responsible for the explosive mixture which has been accumulating in our cities since the end of World War II."[65]

The final report expressed many of the Shellow research team's findings and opinions regarding the political aspirations of young black men in the nation's ghettos. While generally condemning violence and incitement to violence, chapter 4 states:

A climate that tends toward approval and encouragement of violence as a form of protest has been created by white terrorism directed against nonviolent protest [and] by the open defiance of law and federal authority by state and local officials resisting desegregation. . . . The frustrations of powerlessness have led some Negroes to the conviction that there is no alternative to violence as a means of achieving redress of grievances and "moving the system." . . . A new mood [has sprung up] among Negroes, particularly among the young, in which self-esteem and enhanced racial pride are replacing apathy and submission to "the system."[66]

These words, as well as the entire report, were read aloud to the commission and agreed on unanimously. But the commission did not specifically recommend empowering the frustrated and powerless or welcoming them into the political and social mainstream, as Kerner and Shellow advocated. Instead, its recommendations fell back to the more conventional transactional solution offered by Lindsay—massive federal spending in urban areas: "Only a commitment to national action on an unprecedented scale can shape a future compatible with the historic ideals of American society. The great productivity of our economy, and a federal revenue system which is highly responsive to economic growth, can provide the resources. The major need is to generate new will—the will to tax ourselves to the extent necessary to meet the vital needs of the nation."[67]

Without calling directly for an end to the Vietnam War, the commission was banking on a massive peace dividend to be spent in the cities. Johnson was struggling to get Congress to approve a surtax on the income tax to finance the Vietnam War. A peace dividend was nowhere in sight, as far as he was concerned. And he knew the financial demands of the commission's report could not be met. The president never received the report formally and managed to be out of Washington when it was issued on March 1.

In his memoirs Johnson wrote,

> The commission called for a substantially increased outlay of resources, doubling or tripling each ongoing program. . . . That was the problem—money. At the moment I received the report I was having one of the toughest fights of my life, trying to persuade Congress to pass the 10 percent surtax without imposing deep cuts in our Great Society programs. I will never understand how the commission expected me to get this same Congress to turn 180 degrees overnight and appropriate an additional $30 billion for the same programs that it was demanding I cut by $6 billion. This would have required a miracle.[68]

Johnson was more blunt when White House assistant Harry C. McPherson Jr. asked him to sign letters of thanks to the commission members on completion of their work. "I can't sign this group of letters," he told McPherson. "I'd be a hypocrite. And I don't even want it known that they got this far . . . otherwise somebody will leak that I wouldn't sign them. Just file them . . . or get rid of them."[69]

Roy Wilkins concluded that Johnson displayed an uncharacteristic lack of courage. "Mr. Johnson need not have balked at the acceptance of this report," Wilkins told an interviewer in 1972.

It was perfectly in line with his actions as President and with the accomplishments of his administration. I think probably, maybe the word racism, white racism, frightened him. He didn't want to go down in history as the President who had pointed his finger at his own people. This I think is understandable. . . . I feel that Mr. Johnson should have taken the same position that his commission took, that honesty compelled—the whole 670 pages—compelled the conclusion that it was the attitudes of white Americans toward black Americans that have brought us to this place. And I think the President might well have said that, although he is the best judge of all the forces that were at work on him and that he had to consider in his position as President of the United States.[70]

The risks of endorsing the findings of the Kerner Commission, not to mention its expensive recommendations, were enormous. Johnson aide McPherson saw them clearly. A native of Texas who had worked for Johnson since the mid-1950s, McPherson understood and appreciated the political calculus Johnson used in making every decision. In a 1969 oral history interview, he correctly described the hardening public mood as he bluntly explained one effect of the Kerner Commission report:

Johnson was extremely negative about the Kerner Commission for two reasons. One was because it hurt his pride. There wasn't enough said about what had been done in the last few years. The Civil Rights Act, the poverty acts and all the rest of it. The second was a much more hard-nosed and much more valid reason to oppose the Kerner Commission report. . . . It was to the effect that the only thing that held any hope for the Negro was the continuation of the coalition between labor, Negroes, intellectuals, . . . big city bosses and political machines and some of the urban poor. In other words, it required keeping the Polacks who work on the line at Rouge River in the ball park and supporting Walter Reuther and the government as they try to spend money on blacks. That's the only way they'll ever make it, because the people in that office building over there . . . don't give a damn about them. They're scared of them, always have been; they're middle-class whites; they don't want to live around them; they don't want to go to school with them; they don't want anything. But there is a coalition that just barely is a majority in this country if it's held together sort of loosely, and that is the coalition for progress, and it has supported such progress as we have made. The riots came along and scared the be-Jesus out of a lot of members of this coalition. The response of the federal government first . . . was to express the deepest concern about the well-being of the very race that was rioting, not so simply expressed as "reward the rioters," but saying it will continue to be this way until we do something about the conditions in the cities. This telegraphed to the other members of the coalition that nobody really gave a damn about their concern—that the city was going to be burned down; that you couldn't walk in it at night anymore, and all the rest. . . . Then a Presidential commission is formed and goes out and comes back, and what does it say? Who's responsible for the riots? "The other members of the coalition.

They did it. Those racists. . . ." And thereupon, the coalition says . . . "we'll go find ourselves a guy like George Wallace or Richard Nixon. At any rate, we'll vote this crowd out of office. They don't care about us anymore, and now they've indicted us, which is even worse."[71]

The interviewer asked McPherson, "And you think this is the way Lyndon Johnson saw it?" "You bet I do," he replied. "It's the way Bayard Rustin saw it, and it's the way Pat Moynihan saw it, and it's the way Lyndon Johnson saw it."[72]

Time proved McPherson *and* Kerner correct. Richard Nixon and others subverted the liberal alliance of blue-collar union members in the North and black Democrats in the South through what became known as Nixon's Southern Strategy. Meanwhile, no one ever came up with a better solution than Kerner's—for white Americans conscientiously to look past their history of racial bigotry and simply do the right thing, through neighborly interaction with African Americans as well as vigilant enforcement of antidiscrimination laws.

◆ ◆ ◆

Anniversaries of the Kerner Report have been national occasions for reviewing many nagging issues and the progress, or lack thereof, since 1968. "In the teeming ghettos that persist in our cities, the lot of their children is little changed," Tom Wicker wrote in the 1988 edition of the report.[73] The *Wall Street Journal* declared on the twentieth anniversary of the report: "In the Kerner Commission's study, a torrent of statistics and testimony detailed the isolation and despair of the nation's mostly black central cities in 1968; many of those same statistical measures paint a depressingly similar picture today." The headline on the *Journal*'s article read, "We're Having Quiet Riots Today."[74]

The report surfaced again when Los Angeles erupted in riots following the 1992 acquittal of police officers charged in the beating of Rodney King. This time the unrest involved mostly Latinos. On the twenty-fifth anniversary of the report, *Chicago Tribune* columnist Clarence Page noted the multicultural aspect of urban frustration today: "Two nations? We should be so lucky. America has become subdivided into several nations defined by ethnicity, class and, most significantly, economic opportunity."[75]

In a 1997 speech on racism, President Bill Clinton likewise extended the dimensions of the Kerner Report to include America's multicultural society. Over time the work of the Kerner Commission passed from being a shocking indictment of America's establishment to being a respected but tragically perennial statement of social challenge. Kerner left elective politics and became a strong advocate of civil rights and civil liberties on the federal appeals court in Chicago. He continued to use the notoriety of the Kerner Commission to speak frankly but hopefully to the American coalition of goodwill that McPherson saw eroding.

"Racism, bred into our society for 300 years, is the underlying cause of the rioting in our cities," he wrote in a newspaper series published in the summer of 1968 after the assassination of Martin Luther King. "What can be done about these racist prejudices? How do we cleanse our hearts of them? We must start by facing ourselves and admitting we have such feelings. If we are unwilling to do that, we can spend billions of dollars to overcome the racist system, and the money will go down the drain. All the federal money in the world will not help under these circumstances. From every American it will require new attitudes, new understanding and, above all, new will."[76]

In 1969 Kerner and his two children went with Michael Butler to see the Chicago premiere of the play designed to shock his generation, *Hair.* "He liked it," Butler recalled.[77]

9

Law and Order

A frustrated Lyndon Johnson snubbed the Kerner Commission report. Nevertheless, he fulfilled Otto Kerner's dream of a lifetime appointment to the U.S. Court of Appeals for the Seventh Circuit in Chicago, where Kerner's father had served ably for fourteen years. Kerner's liberal politics and loyalty to the president—attributes Johnson noted in selecting Kerner to head the riot commission—made him an acceptable candidate to succeed venerable Du Page County Republican Winfred G. Knoch, an Eisenhower appointee who at age seventy-two unexpectedly retired to senior status. With Johnson's popularity plunging, many Illinois Republicans had hoped Knoch would postpone his retirement until after the November 1968 election, when they expected one of their own to capture the White House and be empowered to appoint Republican judges. But Knoch stepped aside in December 1967. Johnson announced Kerner's nomination on March 8, a week after the Kerner Commission delivered its report and three weeks before Johnson shocked the nation by declaring he would not seek reelection.

The Senate readily consented to the Kerner nomination by a voice vote. The American Bar Association's Committee on the Federal Judiciary and the Federal Bar Association found him "well qualified." The Illinois Bar Association called him a "most outstanding choice."[1] Illinois's two Republican senators, veteran Everett Dirksen and freshman Charles Percy, supported Democrat Kerner's appointment without reservation. "I am extremely happy to have him out of partisan politics," Percy joked at Kerner's Senate Judiciary Committee confirmation hearing, referring to his defeat by Kerner in the 1964 race for governor.[2] He praised Kerner's accomplishments as governor to such an extent that Republican senator Strom Thurmond of South Carolina interrupted to ask "whether the Democratic and Republican Parties have merged in Illinois."[3] Percy, who later would recruit many Republicans to the federal courts in Illinois, concluded, "I cannot imagine that we could come up from our state with a more qualified citizen, a more qualified lawyer—a man who has been of greater distinction and will be to the federal bench than Otto Kerner."[4] Dirksen did not attend the hearing because of a leg injury. In a statement read by Nebraska Republican Roman Hruska—the only senator of Bohemian decent—Dirksen praised Kerner's father as a brilliant lawyer, excellent Illinois attorney general, and distinguished judge. "His son, Governor Kerner, follows in a great tradition," Dirksen said. He commended Kerner for "having the requisite ability as a lawyer and the temperament to make a good judge."[5]

Despite its pro-forma nature, Kerner's confirmation hearing before the Judiciary Committee featured a cameo debate on the issues of civil rights and law and order. On one side stood the former Democratic governor of South Carolina Strom Thurmond, who joined the Republicans rather than adopt the Democrat's platform on civil rights. On the other was Otto Kerner, the Democratic governor of Illinois who often quoted a Republican icon, Abraham Lincoln, on behalf of civil rights. The interchange between the southern conservative, with his distinctively high-pitched drawl, and the northern liberal, with a deep resonance still echoing his Cambridge tutoring, reflected the country's ambiguity. After saluting Kerner's military record, Thurmond quizzed him intently on the Kerner Commission report.

Thurmond: I have recalled the names of people who have gone from state to state and in their wake have followed riots, serious riots—Stokely Carmichael, Rap Brown, Martin Luther King—riots which have resulted from their work. You name me some white people in a similar situation.

Kerner: I could not name you any white people in a similar situation.

Thurmond: Then, why do you say "white racism" caused these riots?

Kerner: I beg your pardon.

Thurmond: Why do you want to blame the white people, then, for this trouble?

Kerner: Because we say this has developed over a period of time, and the people in the Negro ghettos indicated that the rebellion was against the white establishment. They have indicated that.

Thurmond: Well, there is a difference, if you want to call it the white establishment and white racism. What is the term? What does that term mean? What did you think it meant when you put it in this report or approved of it?

Kerner: I thought that it meant this—that over a period of years that the Negro was kept within a certain area economically and geographically and he was not al-

lowed to come out of it. And my reasoning was that, intentionally or unintentionally—I think primarily unintentionally—by the white people of this country.
Thurmond: How could it be white racism then?
Kerner: Because it is a term that is used to describe intentional or unintentional
action on the part of the white community.

[Taking another tack, Thurmond asserted that the Kerner Commission wrongly
exonerated individuals for their criminal behavior and instead blamed society.]

Thurmond: Do you place the cause of crime on the individual, or do you blame it
on society?
Kerner: Let me say this, Senator. I believe there has been a growing permissiveness,
and this is not isolated to any race or religion or any culture. It has generally
affected the entire United States. And I point my finger to every group, every
school, every church, every individual, for this permissiveness that we have
enjoyed that has caused this crime in the United States. And this is a local matter that is strictly a local and home matter.
Thurmond: Is not the individual responsible for his own acts?
Kerner: He certainly is.
Thurmond: How do you blame society then?
Kerner: I am not blaming society. I said the cause belonged with each individual,
the head of each family, et cetera.
Thurmond: You stood for law and order, but you blame it on the white racism and
insinuate in not so many words that society was responsible, did you not?
Kerner: We did not indicate that in any place in the report—we did not.
Thurmond: Do you favor the arrest and imprisonment of a person who incites riots,
as in 1967?
Kerner: That is presuming something that I cannot presume, in answer to your
question. We did not have any indication that these riots or disorders were in-
cited by anybody, but if any evidence can be found that anyone did incite, of
course, obviously, they should be indicted and severely punished.[6]

◆ ◆ ◆

The appellate courts of the eleven federal circuits are commonly seen
as cloisters, purposefully distant from the pressures that weigh on legislators,
who write laws, and public administrators, who implement them. Removed
from the obligations of politics and settled into the subdued, collegial environment of judicial review, appellate court judges occupy a world of their own.
The theatrics of trial courts unfold below, and the controversies of the Supreme Court loom above. In between, the task of reviewing how the law is
applied to criminal and civil cases requires deliberate, cooperative, and largely
secret efforts by appeals court judges and their law clerks. The news media
rarely cover these activities, except for occasional reporting on written opinions issued at the end of private deliberations. The contrast to the job of

governor was as obvious as it was attractive to Kerner. Frank M. Coffin, a former chief judge of the U.S. Court of Appeals for the First Circuit, in Boston, wrote in his 1980 book *The Ways of a Judge: Reflections from the Federal Appellate Bench*:

> Appellate judges exist in a special limbo. Trial judges, after all, are on the firing line. Their conduct in presiding over trials, their every decision and jury instruction are visible and audible to all. But appellate judges, excepting only the justices of the Supreme Court of the United States, are often no more apparent or visible than the vapor-inhaling priestesses at the Oracle of Delphi. The judges sit in a phalanx behind their elevated bench, listen to argument, ask a few questions, and, weeks or months later, issue an opinion. Exactly what goes on, if anything, between argument and decision is veiled in mystery.[7]

In a speech to fellow lawyers after he joined the seventh circuit court, Kerner noted the common impression of the appellate bench: "The image . . . might leave one with a picture of appellate courts as cold, in cloistered marble halls inhabited by tonsured types, scratching opinions on parchment with quill pens. . . . Frequently, in social and legalistic conversations, many questions are put about the basic operation of the Court. Not infrequently, the questions are asked in the hushed, whispered tones of a secret agent."[8]

Behind the prestige and mystique of the circuit court, where the law and not direct evidence forms the basis of rulings, federal appeals court judges hold enormous and often final power over the lives and property of those who enter the judicial system, voluntarily or otherwise. The Supreme Court's broad and unassailable discretion in deciding which cases it will review puts the circuit courts, usually meeting as panels of three judges, at the end of the line for most litigants appealing federal and state trial court outcomes or federal administrative agency decisions. The constitutional provision giving judges lifetime appointments, barring impeachment by Congress, protects and enhances that power.

Over the years court reformers, academics, and editorial writers have persistently demanded that the judicial selection process be purged of political patronage, but these calls have never come close to reality, leaving intact one of the greatest and least recognized responsibilities of presidents, the power to nominate federal judges. No president understood that power better or became more engaged in exercising it than Lyndon Johnson. Johnson realized many of those he placed on the bench would hold office well beyond his tenure, enabling him to extend his reach into the next decade, even as the mood of the country shifted to the right. Johnson made forty-one appointments to the U.S. Circuit Courts of Appeal. Neil D. McFeeley, in his 1981 book *Appointment of Judges: The Johnson Presidency*, noted that seventeen years after Johnson left office, thirty-five of his circuit court appointees remained on active or senior status, ruling on cases. "Those appointments remain a reflection of and a reflection on the presidency of Lyndon Johnson and the man himself," McFeeley said.[9] Kerner at age fifty-nine was seven years older than the average Johnson appellate court appointee. Nonetheless, as the last of three Johnson appointees to the seventh circuit court, Kerner showed every promise of fulfilling the president's expectations through the decade of the 1970s.

Johnson's record of judicial appointments in the months after the assassination of John Kennedy was spotty. In 1964 three of his eighteen appointments were rated "not qualified" by the American Bar Association's Committee on the Federal Judiciary, an embarrassingly high proportion. Several of the less well regarded nominees were selections initiated by the Kennedy White House whom Johnson pushed forward. After Johnson trounced Barry Goldwater to claim the White House on his own, however, he developed his own method for the appointment process, involving a rigor that depended greatly on Johnson's White House advisers and Attorney General Ramsey Clark. Johnson frequently met with prospective judicial nominees. According to a memo by White House aide S. Douglass Cater Jr. cited by McFeeley, Johnson offered two pieces of advice to one nominee for a district court: "[1] Don't get arrogant, [2] Get off the bench when you reach retirement age. The President said that he had detected a tendency toward arrogance among those whom he had helped appoint to judgeships over the years. There is something about the nature of the job with everybody saying 'Your Honor' which seems to cause this."[10]

Though Kerner enjoyed the attention and perquisites of the governor's office and believed he had accomplished much for Illinois in the areas of mental health, education, economic development, and fiscal management, he craved a less hectic life and probably regarded the judicial appointment as a well-deserved reward for his riot commission service. His wife's alcoholism and his adopted children's need for a capable parent at home made the demands of the governorship untenable. His mother, Rose, who nearly three decades earlier had urged her husband not to abandon his seat on the seventh circuit to run for governor, undoubtedly influenced her son. Kerner announced on February 7, 1968, that he would not seek a third term as governor. His close associate, Theodore Isaacs, told *Chicago Tribune* political reporter George Tagge, "I didn't tell him to run or not to run. But I probably told him a hundred times that I doubted he had the physical stamina to take four more years of what he had to put up with."[11] Speculation immediately arose that Johnson would appoint Kerner to some post. Kerner's friends touted him for the U.S. Supreme Court. Newspaper stories had him being appointed secretary of the U.S. Department of Health, Education, and Welfare or ambassador to the United Nations. But Kerner had his eye on the appeals court. He wanted to be called "Your Honor."

◆ ◆ ◆

The seventh circuit appeals court, like any American court, is an organism that evolves through time according to the succession of individuals who occupy its seats. Known today as a conservative Republican court, most of its history reflects Democratic and progressive influences quite compatible with Kerner's leanings. In addition, as urban problems mounted in the nation, Kerner's appointment renewed the court's outreach to urban ethnic groups that began with his father's appointment in 1938. He lacked the pedigree of scholarship and legal experience held by many of his predecessors and peers on the bench, but Kerner was a fitting heir to his particular seat, which dated back to 1895 as the third seat Congress created for the court. Kerner was the eighth appointee to the seat, whose history was endowed richly with personalities who shaped the judicial system for nearly three-quarters of a century.

The court's jurisdiction comprises Illinois, Wisconsin, and Indiana. The appointment to succeed Judge Knoch rightfully belonged to Illinois. Johnson's only other appointees to the seventh circuit took office in the same month, August 1966: Walter J. Cummings of Chicago, a former U.S. solicitor general, filled a newly created eighth seat on the bench, and former Wisconsin Supreme Court justice Thomas E. Fairchild succeeded Truman appointee F. Ryan Duffy, a one-time Democratic senator from Wisconsin. Win Knoch, a sixth-generation resident of the Naperville area in southwestern Du Page County, had been named by Eisenhower to the federal district court in Chicago in 1953 and then to the seventh circuit appeals court in 1958 after a career as a state court judge. Knoch inherited the seat from another Republican, Walter C. Lindley of downstate Danville, Illinois, who died in January 1958 after nine years on the appellate bench and twenty-seven years as a federal district judge. Lindley was the only Republican on the seventh circuit court when he was appointed in 1949. (There had been only one Republican on the court since 1919.) But he was a Truman appointee who had been endorsed for the federal bench by organized labor as well as many fellow judges and lawyers as far back as 1932. Lindley enjoyed a national reputation among jurists "for both outstanding legal ability and rapidity in deciding complicated cases," according to seventh circuit historian Rayman L. Solomon.[12] Truman appointed Lindley after elevating Judge Sherman Minton of Indiana to the Supreme Court, making Minton the first of two seventh circuit judges to receive that honor. (John Paul Stevens, a 1970 Richard Nixon appointee, was named to the Supreme Court by Gerald Ford in 1975.)

Minton was an ardent New Dealer and one of President Franklin Roosevelt's strongest congressional supporters during Minton's single six-year term in the U.S. Senate, from 1935 through 1940. Roosevelt's impact on the seventh circuit was substantial as the court reviewed and in the main endorsed the letter and spirit of the New Deal and its new federal agencies, including the National Labor Relations Board and Federal Trade Commission. Minton, nominated to the seventh circuit court in 1941 to succeed fellow Hoosier Walter E. Treanor, was the last of five Roosevelt appointees to the court over eight years. The others were Louis FitzHenry and J. Earl Major (both of downstate Illinois), Treanor, and Otto Kerner Sr.

In taking Win Knoch's seat, Otto Kerner Jr. might have inherited his father's seat had it not been for a political fight between Chicago mayor Edward Kelly and Illinois governor Henry Horner in the mid-1930s. After Horner beat the Kelly machine to win a second term as governor in 1936, he remained at odds with Kelly and Cook County chairman Patrick Nash. The feud extended to the issue of federal judicial appointments. When the liberal Samuel Alschuler of Aurora retired from the seventh circuit court in May 1936, Horner urged Roosevelt to appoint his friend, Illinois attorney general Otto Kerner Sr. Aside from being upset with Horner, Kelly and Nash had no reason to oppose Kerner, who had remained loyal when they tried to unseat Horner in the 1936 Democratic primary. Nonetheless, Kelly and Nash supported Chicago congressman Michael Igoe for Alschuler's seat. Roosevelt refused to take sides and instead chose Indiana Supreme Court justice Walter E. Treanor to fill the court vacancy. Kerner Sr.'s appointment to the seventh circuit court would have to wait until 1938, after Congress added a fifth seat on the court and created an additional district court judgeship in Chicago. Kerner Sr. got the new seventh circuit judgeship, and the district court seat went to Igoe.

Treanor was one of the most learned and least political men ever to serve on the seventh circuit court. He was a liberal Democrat but, as Solomon put it, "had only peripherally been involved in party affairs and Democratic campaigns when in 1930 he decided to seek one of the seats in the Indiana Supreme Court. . . . Although his liberal philosophy often clashed with the views of the Republican majority on the court (he wrote a large number of dissenting opinions), he was highly regarded by the Indiana bar as a legal scholar and a judicial craftsman."[13]

Judge Samuel Alschuler, whose seventh circuit seat Treanor took, was a 1915 Woodrow Wilson appointee and one of Illinois's leading progressive politicians at the turn of the century. He was the first Jew named to any federal appeals court. He campaigned actively in 1892 for progressive Democratic governor John Peter Altgeld and won election to the Illinois House in 1896. Alschuler never introduced a bill in the legislature because he believed

sponsoring bills "invited trading and log-rolling whereby undesirable legislation was at least facilitated."[14] He ran unsuccessfully as the Democratic
candidate for governor in 1900. Alschuler's twenty-year tenure on the seventh circuit court was marred in 1935 when a second-term Republican congressman from Pekin, Illinois, named Everett Dirksen attempted to have him
impeached. Dirksen alleged Alschuler had shown favoritism toward a political ally in a patent case. The House Judiciary Committee rejected Dirksen's
charge and rebuked the young congressman for having a personal link to the
other side in the case. Fellow congressman Michael Igoe speculated that
Dirksen, thirty-nine years old, sparked the controversy primarily to broaden
his name recognition for a possible campaign for Illinois governor.

Dirksen's charge against Alschuler was the second time that the seat Otto
Kerner would take was exposed to public controversy. The initial episode concerned Peter S. Grosscup, one of the most colorful and outspoken men ever
to serve on a federal court in Illinois. In 1899 Grosscup, a progressive Republican and prominent figure in the Chicago bar, was appointed to the seventh
circuit appeals court by President William McKinley. A native of Ohio and
political ally during McKinley's years as an Ohio congressman, Grosscup had
joined the federal bench in 1892 as an appointee to the federal district court
in Chicago.

In 1907 Grosscup became the first sitting federal judge to be indicted for
a crime. Grosscup and other officers and directors of a railroad Grosscup
owned were charged with criminal negligence after a fatal train wreck in
Charleston, Illinois. Grosscup's attorney, noted Chicago lawyer Levy Mayer,
successfully argued that his clients and the other defendants could not be held
criminally liable unless they were involved directly in the operation of the
train. But the charges deeply wounded Grosscup. "The prosecution was the
sorest thing that has ever befallen me," he wrote to Mayer after the trial. "It
touched me where I was the most sensitive. And it dragged in—exultingly it
seemed to me—the greatest trust I hold. I have always felt towards my Judgeship as a bridegroom feels toward a bride—a jealousy almost passionate of
its good name."[15] Grosscup remained on the seventh circuit court until 1911,
when he resigned to campaign for Teddy Roosevelt, leaving a vacancy until
the Alschuler appointment.

Grosscup's predecessor and the first occupant of Kerner's seventh circuit
chair was John W. Showalter, whom President Grover Cleveland, a Democrat, appointed to the newly created third seat on the court in 1895. Born in
1844, Showalter was not active in Democratic Party politics, but he was the
Yale University roommate of Wilson Bissell, who would become Cleveland's
postmaster general. Showalter served just three years. He died of pneumonia in December 1898 after hearing cases for weeks in a drafty courtroom in

Chicago's Monadnock Building, the early skyscraper where the court was housed from 1894 to 1905 during construction of a new federal building in Chicago.

✦ ✦ ✦

Never before had a son been named to the same federal appeals bench as his father. Two seventh circuit judges, J. Earl Major, appointed in 1937, and F. Ryan Duffy, appointed in 1949, served with Kerners senior and junior. Major and Duffy had attained senior status by the time the younger Kerner joined the court, but both reviewed cases on judicial panels with Kerner. They undoubtedly saw much of the father in the son.

In April 1953 seventh circuit judges held a special session to memorialize the life of Otto Kerner Sr., their colleague on the bench from November 1938 to his death the previous December. Supreme Court justice Sherman Minton sent a remembrance of his former colleague:

> If I were to sum up my impression of Judge Kerner in one word, I would choose "courtly." Everything he did was done in a courtly manner, without being pompous. Those who have seen him on the bench will remember him as a courageous, pleasant, interested and attentive judge. Those who have seen him outside the courtroom will retain the same impression of a real gentleman. He was always the soul of courtesy and affability, with a pleasant remark for everybody, even when he himself might be in some discomfort. A man like that is not soon forgotten.[16]

Judge Ulysses S. Schwartz of the Illinois Court of Appeals, a friend of Kerner Sr. over four decades, recounted Kerner's heritage and life in Chicago:

> This was his native city. Here he lived, was educated, married, raised a family, did his work, and died. He was the child of immigrant parents. Bohemia, the land from which they came, was in the early part of the seventeenth century the scene of a great struggle between the Emperor and the people that resulted in an agreement guaranteeing full liberty of religious worship to all groups. This was 180 years before the adoption of our own constitution, and thereafter, the freedom-loving citizens of that small country never ceased to battle for their liberty. They are a sturdy, realistic people who have developed great skill in industry and commerce. In our own time, it was their proud and well-justified boast that under Masaryk and Benes, both of them friends of Judge Kerner, they had established a judicial system which, in the administration of fair and equal justice, compared well with the Anglo-Saxon system. Before the sad days of Munich and the later Hitler and Communist tyrannies, they were known as the Yankees of Europe. Otto Kerner was not without heritage for his judicial career.[17]

The Bohemian legacy was one of Kerner Sr.'s two unique contributions to the court. Liberalism tempered by austerity and wariness toward the power of government—all historical features of the Bohemian character—were especially useful traits for a federal appeals court judge during the Great Depression. Under Roosevelt the government in Washington flexed its taxing and regulatory powers to respond directly to the needs of individuals in communities throughout America, widening its reach and expanding its power significantly—well beyond what the Founding Fathers intended, in the opinion of many.

As to his second contribution, Kerner Sr. was the first member of the modern Cook County Democratic organization to win a seat on the seventh circuit court, though he hardly had functioned as an active cog in the political machine. "Politics held no charm for me," Kerner wrote in an autobiographical essay about his initial association with the party. "It meant more acquaintances, more business connections and experience in public speaking. I never really liked it, for it is too exacting and compels compliance with many unreasonable requests."[18] His chief political sponsor, Anton Cermak, was long dead. His friend Governor Horner died in 1940. He was far from being a Kelly-Nash crony. As Illinois attorney general, he worked to abolish a particularly onerous mechanism for political meddling in courts, the Depression-era spoils system for naming receivers in bankruptcy proceedings. Other Kerner decisions clashed with the Kelly-Nash agenda, especially on the issues of legalizing off-track betting and slot machine gambling. After Horner died, Kerner refused the party leaders' request that he quit the seventh circuit appeals court and run as the organization's candidate for governor in 1940.

Nonetheless, Kerner Sr. was the first to bring the street-level sensibilities of an urban politician to the cloistered atmosphere of the seventh circuit court. He knew firsthand the rigors and satisfactions of precinct politics—the picnics, weddings, and wakes where politicians press the flesh and receive instant feedback on their performance. He was the first judge on the court ever to have won election to a statewide office, an experience that gave him insight and confidence unknown to most of his peers and predecessors on the bench. "His was no academic citizenship," the Bar Association of the Seventh Federal Circuit said in its tribute.[19]

Kerner Sr. participated in approximately seven hundred decisions in his fourteen years on the seventh circuit bench, which during his tenure was headquartered in a former life insurance company office building at 1212 North Lake Shore Drive, miles from the federal building at the south central end of Chicago's Loop. (Lawyers and judges later remarked that the separation of the seventh circuit's chambers from the rest of Chicago's federal complex in the central city nurtured the court's critical independence and constructive collegiality. The precious aloofness ended in 1964, when the seventh circuit court moved to the top floor of the new steel-and-glass Federal Center, designed by Ludwig Mies van der Rohe, at Dearborn and Adams Streets, coming under the same roof as the U.S. District Court for the Northern District of Illinois, a trial bench notorious in the Richard J. Daley years for judicial ineptness and political influence.)[20]

Like many individuals who spent careers in the legal system, both Kerners allowed their views to evolve, especially in the area of civil liberties. As Illinois attorney general in the 1930s, Kerner Sr. spoke out sternly against what he called "loopholes" and "technicalities" in the law that permitted criminal defendants to abuse the system, burden taxpayers, and escape justice.[21] He favored abolition of the rule that a jury's verdict must be unanimous. He urged tightening the rules governing the writ of habeas corpus, a fundamental individual right dating back to seventeenth-century England by which prisoners may seek their release on the basis of incarceration without a fair trial. "A prisoner who is serving a sentence should have no more privileges than any other litigant," he wrote in 1936 amid public outrage over the release of two notorious criminals.[22]

Ten years later, however, appeals court judge Kerner overruled a district court judge in Indiana and ordered a hearing on a habeas corpus motion that the lower judge had denied to Charles W. Potter, who was serving a life sentence for rape. Potter, an indigent, claimed that his confession had been forced and that the state had failed to appoint a lawyer to represent him. In a lengthy dissent Judge Earl J. Major, a fellow Roosevelt appointee from downstate Illinois, lamented that Kerner's opinion "marks the dawn of a new era of federal jurisdiction in *habeas corpus*. More than that, so far as the State of Indiana is concerned, the floodgates have been lifted and the federal courts will be deluged with petitions making every character of scurrilous attack upon the judiciary of that state. . . . If we pursue the direction we are now headed it will not be long until the Indiana judges will be on trial in federal courts."[23]

In an annotated paper on habeas corpus written after the Potter opinion, Kerner called the writ one of the greatest institutions "sanctified by law and custom designed to bulwark" individual liberty. While acknowledging that judges and lawyers must guard against abuse of the writ by disgruntled convicts, Kerner said, "If there is any principle more deeply imbedded in our jurisprudence than that no man shall be illegally confined, I, for one, do not know what it is. No plea to expediency should cloud this principle. Both bench and bar have a duty to see that each man's rights are protected."[24] The federal district judge whose denial of Potter's petition Kerner reversed was Luther M. Swygert, a popular thirty-nine-year-old former Notre Dame football player who had been an assistant U.S. attorney in Hammond, Indiana. Like Kerner Sr., Swygert's judicial temperament would evolve. Twenty-five years later he was one of the great civil libertarians of the federal bench. He and Kerner's son became allies on the liberal wing of the seventh circuit court in the late 1960s.

Crucial points of legal controversy during the depression years concerned public law issues, especially the federal government's powers to tax and regulate economic behavior. Aside from handing down several rulings that diminished the authority of the National Labor Relations Board, Kerner generally supported the expansionist trend of the Roosevelt government. In particular, Kerner supported the tendency of the Internal Revenue Service to interpret its powers broadly. On civil liberties issues concerning criminal defendants, however, Kerner Sr. consistently favored protecting the individual from the power of the state.

In his memorial tribute to Kerner, Chicago lawyer Thomas L. Marshall cited a typical Kerner decision, one that anticipated the groundbreaking *Escobedo* and *Miranda* rulings by the Supreme Court at the end of the 1960s:

> A man was arraigned before a district court upon a charge of stealing an automobile and transporting it across a state line. The district judge asked if the prisoner had a lawyer and he said no. The judge asked if he wanted a lawyer and he said no. After such conventional procedure, the prisoner pleaded guilty and was duly sentenced. The opinion of Judge Kerner reversed. He was not clear that the prisoner understood that the judge would appoint a lawyer if the prisoner's reason for not having a lawyer was that he could not afford one. The unquestioned principle of law was not to be applied in such conventional or routine manner that by any possibility a prisoner could be uninformed as to his rights.[25]

✦ ✦ ✦

The fifteen-year interval between the two Kerners saw significant changes in the work of the seventh circuit court. By 1968 the court, like every other federal court, faced the public's bitter reassessment of national authority, which had become ensnared in deadly conflicts in America's cities and Vietnam's countryside. The assassinations of Robert Kennedy and Martin Luther King gripped Americans with a sense that things were unraveling. For the federal courts the years of digesting the Roosevelt New Deal in depression times, arbitrating money issues in the postwar boom, and introducing Americans to a new standard for civil rights had given way to fundamental questions about the legitimacy and competence of the government. Americans asked where one ought to draw the line between the preservation of civil liberties and the goal of law and order. Many believed the legal system had shifted too far in favor of the rights of the accused. Court rulings favoring criminals hobbled effective law enforcement, they believed. National prohibition of alcohol was long forgotten, but cases involving narcotics trafficking swelled. The constant menace of organized crime spread into legitimate business and seemed to draw strength from the public's disillusionment about legal authority.

Not long after Kerner Jr. took his lifetime appointment, "law and order" asserted itself as an effective political message, scripted and delivered skillfully by Richard Nixon, Spiro Agnew, and others. The nation in search of answers moved sharply to the right with the election of Nixon. But the seventh circuit court, with Kerner as its junior member, moved the other way. Kerner's appointment in May was followed in June by the resignation of Eisenhower appointee John S. Hastings of Indiana as the court's chief judge. Latham Castle, a former Illinois attorney general and a less-conservative Eisenhower appointee, became chief judge. In September Elmer J. Schnackenberg, a former Speaker of the Illinois House and the most conservative of the Eisenhower appointees on the court, died. In February 1970 Luther Swygert, a liberal Kennedy appointee from Indiana, became chief judge after Castle accepted senior status. With Swygert as the chief judge, by early 1970 the makeup of the court was decidedly Democratic and liberal. Other judges included Roger J. Kiley, who was a product of the Cook County Democratic organization appointed to the bench by Kennedy, and the two other Johnson appointees, Thomas E. Fairchild of Wisconsin and Walter J. Cummings of Chicago. The leanings of the court did not go unnoticed in Washington. Nixon eventually made his mark, beginning with the appointment of former FBI agent Wilbur F. Pell Jr. of Indiana in April.

The well-documented American neuroses of the 1960s reflected in no small part a generational conflict that, to use Judge Minton's word, was anything but "courtly." The youth counterculture that impresario Michael Butler promoted in the musical *Hair* disdained successful men in public life who came from an earlier era and had not rebelled against their fathers. The graybeards could become aging cranks or slide into complete irrelevance as far as the disaffected youth and urban blacks were concerned. Remarkably, the aging white men serving on the seventh circuit appeals court managed to avoid that outcome. One reason was their careful attention to the ever-renewing Constitution, especially the Bill of Rights. Another was the smart and energetic law clerks who brought the next generation into the inner sanctum of the court and helped to keep the judges young.

Each appellate judge could employ two law clerks at a time. Justice Learned Hand, one of America's greatest jurists, called law clerks "puisne judges," meaning younger and inferior judges but judges nonetheless.[26] The word *clerk* is nearly as incorrect as the word *judge* to describe their role. Beyond performing the roles typically attributed to them, such as legal researcher, confidential sounding board, and intellectual backstop, law clerks make widely varying contributions in drafting opinions. Writing in a 1973 law review article, Judge Eugene A. Wright of the U.S. Court of Appeals for the Ninth Circuit, in Seattle, explained that the writing assignment varies from judge to judge. Sometimes a judge will instruct his clerks very broadly: "See what you can do with this one." The clerk is expected to work the case out for himself and submit a memorandum for the judge's use in drafting an opinion. . . . If a judge chooses, he may rely on talented clerks for even more writing. Indeed, he may have to because the case load of the eleven federal courts of appeal has increased massively from 4,200 appeals in 1962 to 14,500 in 1972. . . . Clerks with prior experience in legal writing who measure up to their judges' expectations will, at this stage, have the opportunity to produce material which can be used verbatim in an opinion.[27]

A few federal judges, asserting pride of authorship, ban or severely restrict their clerks' involvement in opinion writing. According to his clerks, Otto Kerner was not one of those. Interviews with former Kerner clerks revealed a judge who preferred conversation and story telling to legal scholarship and writing and who encouraged clerks to take initiative in drafting opinions and to follow their instincts. He approached adjudication in the same manner as successful military officers or political party leaders approach their jobs, rallying troops around simple, well-established norms of conduct rather than challenging conventional thinking and providing the leeway necessary to accomplish the mission rather than sticking to the book. Kerner was not a deep questioner of the law or seeker after new truths and nuances in the minutia of legal scholarship. Neither was he inattentive nor indifferent. He preferred to listen and balance views expressed conversationally by his fellow judges and the law clerks in combination with his own straightforward outlook on the world. He wanted to draw out consensus, not challenge it. While he occasionally dissented, he believed strongly in the importance of unanimous decisions by the three-judge panels on which he served.

In a speech to lawyers practicing before the seventh circuit judges about the working procedures of the court, Kerner said that the seventh circuit court was known among its peers as a "'hot' bench, rather than a 'cold' bench," meaning that its judges and law clerks studied appellate briefs before hearing oral arguments, not afterward. "Personally, I prefer the 'hot' approach, in order that I may have some concept of the setting, the *dramatis personae* and the issues involved," he said.[28] Though fully engaged in the court's ever-increasing workload, the junior member of the bench trusted his clerks to find and communicate correct answers from the law books and briefs.

His clerks, many of whom sought employment with Kerner because of their appreciation of the Kerner Commission report and Kerner's progressive views on race, recalled their surprise and amazement at the latitude Kerner gave them in developing opinions. "Kerner was the least active of the judges in modifying or writing decisions," recalled former clerk Stephen M. Cooper, who was twenty-seven years old when he worked for Kerner. "I don't think he had any desire to be a great legal scholar. Clerks for him wrote the drafts. It used to scare me. . . . He was less concerned with procedure than getting the result he wanted."[29] "Otto expressed very few opinions of his own," recalled former clerk Joel D. Rubin. "He listened more than he talked. He was very inward."[30]

In his speech about the workings of the seventh circuit, Kerner said, "I find the work of the court most interesting and stimulating—albeit the development of blisters on occasion. . . . Within the Court itself, I find a delightful interchange of ideas and frequently much humor in the intra-court memoranda."[31] His father was fifty-four when he was named to the bench; Kerner turned sixty shortly after his appointment. He intended to spend his time on the bench passing on the collected wisdom of his many years in public service. He frequently spoke publicly about the Kerner Commission report and its prescriptions for American society—prescriptions quickly losing public support as the 1960s drew to a close. "The only thing he was passionate about was defending the Kerner Commission Report," recalled Rubin.[32]

In a 1971 letter to a college professor from Massachusetts, Kerner said the Kerner Commission remained a work in progress. Calling reform of the state's mental health system his major accomplishment as governor, Kerner said: "I would presume that most people would state that the work of the Commission on Civil Disorders would bring satisfaction. This was most interesting work and my name is known more nationally for that work than for the work I accomplished solely within the state. The Report, however, is ongoing. It has caused some people to be very much disturbed about the socio-economic and racial conditions within the United States."[33] Against the tide of public opinion, Kerner intended to keep that disturbance energized.

Kerner enjoyed the quiet collegiality of the seventh circuit bench but missed the contact with the more rough-and-tumble world of politics. Well-wishers from Kerner's past frequently visited his chambers. They paid their respects, shared a few stories, and left. Kerner enjoyed these visits as a way to keep in touch and to avoid feeling forgotten. One of the most frequent visitors was Theodore Isaacs, his former campaign manager and confidant. Another was Mary Sethness, a socialite and longtime friend. Helena did not visit but would telephone the chambers often, sometimes only to ask where her husband was at the time. Kerner's law clerks were aware of Helena's disease but chilled by the calls. Taking the first phone call from Mrs. Kerner was a rite of passage for a new clerk.

Though always meticulously dressed and correct—courtly—in his manner, Kerner was remarkably tolerant in dealing with his young clerks. Long hair on the male clerks was permitted. Occasional unexplained absences were ignored. Youthful exuberance was welcomed. Law clerks were encouraged to test new ideas, although Kerner himself seemed little inclined to do so. His fellow judges, especially Swygert and Kiley, formed a supportive environment for Kerner's judicial style. His most loyal and hard-working ally was his secretary, Mary Banzhaf, whom the clerks regarded as a third law clerk in the chambers. "She was a very special person," recalled Eliot A. Landau, an especially precocious clerk for Kerner. "We would do things in rough form, and she would whip them into shape."[34]

Like his father, Kerner was not a doctrinaire liberal. Many of his opinions in commercial civil cases could best be described as conservative. He was grounded firmly in a belief in simple ideals and cherished the American establishment that he and his father had worked to join. But he shared an immigrant's love of individual liberty and the right to have a chance. The Kerners' stamp on the court appears most clearly in the area of civil liberties. The opinions of both men reflected learned appreciation for the rights of defendants in criminal cases, a temperament under concerted attack during the late 1960s. Earlier in his career, Kerner Jr. prosecuted Preston Tucker, overlooked the dry-run trials of Vincent Ciucci, and seemed unsympathetic to the racial and economic factors in death penalty cases. But when clever and determined individuals in the ranks of politics, law enforcement, and legal scholarship fought under the law-and-order banner against the rising tide of rebelliousness threatening the nation's economic and social establishment, Kerner refused to join the campaign.

✦ ✦ ✦

First-degree murder suspect McKensie Davis sat anxiously in his seat next to Milwaukee police detective Rudolf Schneider on an airplane ride from Pittsburgh, where Davis had been detained on a twenty-year-old charge. Davis's lawyer for the extradition proceedings, who stayed behind in Pittsburgh, had advised Davis to go back to Milwaukee and tell the truth. As the plane fought against the westerly headwind, Davis started talking. "Can you tell me what is going to happen to me?" he began.[35] Before the plane landed, Davis had made a self-incriminating statement to Schneider that, along with two other comments to police at a later time, helped to convict him. Schneider testified that when Davis started talking, the detective said:

"Before we go into that, I want to tell you that I am interested to know what actually did happen, but you don't have to tell me anything, and any statement that you might make to me could be held against you in any criminal trial. . . ." I told him that in my opinion the best way would be to tell the truth; and I impressed upon him that if he didn't care to tell me anything he didn't have to. And I informed him that we did have a witness to the act of murder, and if he didn't care to tell me anything he could wait and discuss things with an attorney that might be appointed for him by the court, if he didn't have money to hire his own attorney.[36]

On appeal to the seventh circuit court, Judge Knoch and Judge Castle affirmed Davis's conviction. Knoch, then on senior status, wrote:

> We cannot adopt any general rule that voluntary statements freely given by an accused must be suppressed merely because he has retained counsel, when he voluntarily elects to speak in the absence of that counsel. . . . The petitioner here had been advised by his counsel to tell the truth. He and not Detective Schneider opened the conversation concerning his case while aboard the airplane. From the evidence, the Trial Judge was amply justified in finding not only that there was a complete absence of coercion but that the petitioner was adequately warned that he need not speak and that he could wait to consult counsel.[37]

"I respectfully dissent," declared Kerner in a lengthy rebuttal that helped to establish his place on the seventh circuit bench.[38]

The *Davis v. Burke* decision, dated March 7, 1969, came after several years of widespread public debate about court leniency in favor of criminal defendants. Police and prosecutors as well as defense lawyers engaged in a delicate game of strategies to achieve their aims within the bounds of the Bill of Rights. One of the nation's leading coaches on the side of the police, Fred E. Inbau of the Northwestern University Law School, published pragmatic techniques for police interrogations designed to win confessions. Inbau's disciple, assistant Cook County state's attorney James R. Thompson, at age twenty-eight argued his professor's views before the U.S. Supreme Court under Chief Justice Earl Warren in *Escobedo v. Illinois,* the first landmark case of the period setting rules for the game. Thompson maintained the validity of the confession that murder suspect Danny Escobedo had given the Chicago police officers who had questioned him in an interrogation room without his lawyer present—a common practice at the time. Inbau, who died in 1998, called Thompson's presentation to the high court "his finest oral argument."[39] As Thompson biographer Robert Hartley put it, however, "the Supreme Court disagreed, and in a five-to-four decision against Thompson and in behalf of Escobedo, fired the first shot in a revolution that altered all practices in questioning suspects and obtaining confessions."[40] Justice Arthur Goldberg, writing in the June 1964 opinion, said a criminal defendant has a right to an attorney not only at formal arraignment and trial proceedings but from the beginning of his involvement with the police as a criminal suspect.

Two years later, in *Miranda v. Arizona,* the court extended the *Escobedo* ruling by declaring that whatever an arrested person says without a lawyer present may not be used against him unless he expressly waived his right to a lawyer before saying it. Shortly after the *Escobedo* case and the national acclaim it brought Thompson throughout the law-enforcement community, he left the Cook County state's attorney's office to join his mentor Inbau at Northwestern. Two years later he, Inbau, and former Chicago police commissioner O. W. Wilson organized Americans for Effective Law Enforcement, which was intended to be a counterweight to the American Civil Liberties Union. Hartley writes: "Decisions of the Warren Court, civil unrest in the cities, growing discontent with Vietnam involvement, and the discordant notes of a society in turmoil had prepared the nation for Richard Nixon's comeback and created a demand for persons in high office who would work to strengthen the nation's 'peace forces,' as Nixon called them. James R. Thompson's emergence in Illinois and in the nation as an important member of these 'peace forces' was about to begin."[41]

Kerner believed national peace would not result from police tactics that trampled the protections of the Bill of Rights. His opinions consistently pointed out that the most aggressive behavior of police and prosecutors focused on the least advantaged individuals caught up in the system. Davis's fateful plane ride took place in February 1964, before the *Escobedo* and *Miranda* decisions became the law of the land, but the prisoner rights asserted in those decisions applied no less to Davis, Kerner found. "I feel that Davis' rights were seriously imposed upon with the deliberate eliciting of confessions from him after he had been arrested," the Kerner dissent stated. "The first statement was blatantly elicited from [Davis] by Schneider with the standard misleading police approach that 'it would be better' or 'go easier' on the arrestee if he confessed. Such a nebulous statement is frequently used by a great number of police forces throughout the United States."[42] Kerner's opinion noted inconsistencies in Schneider's testimony and said Schneider and the other police involved in questioning Davis appeared to have collaborated on "a well memorized litany" that would conform to the Escobedo ruling, even though the incident occurred four months before the ruling was issued. "I for one am not willing to accept such patterned, self-serving testimony as determinative of Davis' rights," the Kerner dissent read.[43]

Ironically, Kerner cited no less an authority than Inbau to enforce his opinion:

Also compelling is the rejection of "it would be better for you" by the leading author of widely followed police texts on interrogation. Professor Fred E. Inbau has been criticized by various writers as an advocate of harsh and improper police practices, especially in the areas of interrogation and detention. The most authoritative criticism of his methods of interrogation was undertaken by the Supreme Court in *Miranda v. Arizona*. In that able opinion, many examples of Inbau's stratagems are quoted and criticized for their coercive effect and the Court expressed its fear over "this interrogation atmosphere and the evils it can bring." It further pointed out that Inbau's caveats against methods which may make an innocent person confess are of little avail to an innocent person who is so compelled. Yet, even Inbau states that "It would be better for you if . . ." is not to be used.[44]

Kerner then commented that, despite public concerns about the *Escobedo* and *Miranda* rulings, "the 'damage' is much more imagined than real, especially when weighed against the overarching Bill of Rights protections against unjust prosecutions and overzealous police work." Moreover, "many recent empirical studies have shown the impact of these decisions to be very small."[45]

Kerner's dissent arose from a consistent judicial philosophy that revealed itself in numerous seventh circuit opinions bearing his name as author or as participant, often to the chagrin of the court's conservative members. A review of those opinions leaves no doubt about Kerner's push against the tide of law-and-order dogma rising in the nation. He was especially firm on the obligations of the state to provide counsel for indigent defendants. In *Rini v. Katzenbach,* a Kerner opinion, the court reversed the conviction of an accused bank robber who was not provided with a lawyer before he signed a guilty plea and later during his sentencing. "Appointment of counsel for an indigent is required at every stage of a criminal proceeding where substantial rights of a defendant may be affected," Kerner wrote.[46]

In *United States ex rel. Pennington v. Pate,* convicted burglar and rapist Charles Pennington appealed Illinois's refusal to provide him with a state-appointed lawyer for an appeal to the Illinois Supreme Court. Kerner concurred with his colleagues Swygert and Castle that in this case the state had no obligation to fund the second appeal. But Kerner wrote that under other circumstances "a further appeal to the Illinois Supreme Court would merely be another portion of the 'one and only appeal an indigent has as of right.'" He added: "As to the institutional difficulties involved in implementing such a decision, having been governor of Illinois when [two U.S. Supreme Court rulings mandating state-appointed lawyers for indigent appellants] were rendered and having dealt with the budgetary and manpower problems involved, I, perhaps more than my brethren, am aware of the practical problems in this area. Yet, I am unwilling to sacrifice a major constitutional right solely because its implementation may be difficult and expensive."[47]

In *United States ex rel. Worlow v. Pate,* Kerner joined in an opinion by Judge Castle that criticized district court judges Julius J. Hoffman and Joseph Samuel Perry for failing to obtain the record of the original trial of two burglars in which errors were alleged to have been made. Judge Major dissented, saying the result of the majority's opinion was "calculated to be a mischief maker as a precedent" that would "cast an additional burden on district judges in this and perhaps other cases, for which . . . there is no logical or legal basis."[48] James Thompson, who had returned to public life as an assistant Illinois attorney general, was a member of the team opposing the prisoner's appeal. Although there was virtually no public discussion of the liberal drift of the seventh circuit court at the time, Thompson was one of many prosecutors who encountered its widening diversion from the public mood known generically as pro law and order.

In *United States ex rel. Townsend v. Twomey*, Wilbur Pell, Nixon's first appointee to the seventh circuit and the successor to Hastings, attempted immediately to steer the court to the right on the issue of prisoner rights. In a lengthy and acerbic opinion, Pell lamented the frequent appeals on behalf of death row inmate Charles Townsend. Townsend claimed his confession for a 1953 South Side murder was induced by drugs administered by the police. Federal district court judge Perry denied Townsend's first appeal but in a subsequent appeal ordered a new trial. The state brought Perry's second ruling to the seventh circuit, and Pell reversed Perry. "The itinerary of the subsequent court proceedings has been elevator-like between Cook County and the United States Supreme Court with intermediate stops at the Illinois Supreme Court, United States District Court and this court . . . the net effect of which has been to give Townsend the dubious distinction of national seniority on death row," he wrote. "It appears to the writer of this opinion that sometimes courts lean toward the belief in words of one who stands as a convicted criminal rather than the words of law enforcement officers."[49]

In his dissent Kerner attacked Pell's argument that Townsend's appeals were a burden on the law-enforcement and judicial systems. He cited a Supreme Court ruling in *Sanders v. United States* that "conventional notions of finality of litigation have no place where life or liberty is at stake and infringement of constitutional rights is alleged."[50] Kerner also delved into the basis for the original conviction. He painted a detailed and troubling picture of Townsend as a nineteen-year-old African American prisoner in the hands of Chicago police. Townsend had been a heroin addict since age fifteen, he was illiterate and had an I.Q. indicating mental retardation, and he was not allowed to contact anyone for nineteen hours after his arrest. Kerner recounted the fact that Townsend had been given an injection containing phenobarbital, a tranquilizer, and hyoscine, a so-called truth serum. The use of hyoscine violated Chicago Police Department rules. "Within minutes of this injection, however, Townsend was interrogated" and confessed to six crimes, including three murders, Kerner recalled.[51] He reiterated the testimony of a psychiatrist who explained the power of hyoscine to make a person, especially one with Townsend's history, confess to police. Townsend was convicted on only one of the crimes, the murder of Jack Boone Sr. The state withdrew four of the charges, and he was acquitted on one. He also cited evidence that the state's chief witness against Townsend had lied to get out of jail. In short, Kerner looked beyond the expense and inconvenience of Townsend's many appeals and concluded that his conviction deserved to be overturned on its merits. "These facts, I believe, support the conclusion that the confession in the case at bar was unreliable and involuntary," he wrote.[52]

Kerner's antiestablishment rulings extended beyond cases involving suspected street criminals and convicts. In 1969 he overruled Judge Julius Hoffman and permitted radical leader Rennie Davis, free on bond after his arrest for conspiracy to incite riots during the 1968 Democratic National Convention in Chicago, to travel to Hanoi to obtain the release of three American prisoners of war. The same year Kerner headed a three-judge federal panel that ordered the State of Indiana to reapportion its legislature to end discrimination against black voters in Marion County, which included the state capital, Indianapolis. In 1970 Kerner and Swygert authorized a Chicago doctor to perform an abortion on a sixteen-year-old rape victim, contrary to Illinois law.

In *Breen v. Kahl* Kerner came to the defense of high-school boys in Williams Bay, Wisconsin, who were expelled in 1968 for violating the school's regulation mandating that "hair should be washed, combed and worn so it does not hang below the collar line in the back, over the ears on the side and must be above the eyebrows." Citing numerous precedent cases as well as the Bill of Rights and perhaps remembering his own high-school expulsion, Kerner found "the right to wear one's hair at any length or in any desired manner is an ingredient of personal freedom guaranteed by the United States Constitution. . . . The Constitution protects minor high school students as well as adults from arbitrary and unjustified government rules." He found no reasonable basis for the hair requirement and concluded, "Discipline for the sake of discipline and uniformity is indeed not compatible with the melting pot formula which brought this country to greatness."[53]

Senior judge Duffy dissented, expressing the reasoning that typified the elder side of the generation gap. He argued that the case had less to do with personal freedom of expression than with an individual's defiance of legitimate authority. "Suppose Breen required extra time each morning to comb and train his long hair. Could he demand, as a constitutional right, and to show his individuality, that morning classes commence at 10 A.M. instead of 9 A.M.? Where is the line to be drawn? Who is the final arbiter?"[54]

✦ ✦ ✦

Federal officials carrying badges of the Internal Revenue Service (IRS) and Federal Bureau of Investigation (FBI) exercised considerable autonomy in drawing the line against organized crime in Chicago. After decades of neglect the IRS and FBI in the 1960s operated righteously and creatively against the Outfit, as it was known, with moral support from eager local news media. Newspapers and television stations vied for colorful stories about the remnants of the Capone crime syndicate and voiced the public's indignation toward thugs who muscled into unions, businesses, and local governments. Federal judges asserting the Bill of Rights on behalf of indigent blacks withstood the rebukes of law-and-order advocates, but they risked severe condemnation when they protected the rights of crime syndicate hoodlums.

The compelling story told by suburban apartment complex developer William G. Riley exemplified the Outfit's contemporary modus operandi. The government charged that Salvatore "Teetz" Battaglia and his associate Joseph "Joe Shine" Amabile had invaded Riley's business and threatened him with bodily harm unless he assisted them in looting savings and loan associations through the guise of construction loans to his company—a form of bank robbery slightly more sophisticated than confronting a teller with a gun. For most of the 1960s Battaglia, Amabile, and corrupt local officials and contractors in league with them were major targets of the IRS's intelligence division in Chicago. Before the cases landed at the seventh circuit bench, no one challenged the government's methods in pursuing these men with powerful federal laws and sophisticated investigative and prosecution techniques.

In February 1967 Battaglia and Amabile were arrested by federal agents on twin indictments. They were charged with conspiracy to violate the federal Hobbs Act in connection with Riley's apartment complexes in suburban Lansing and Northlake, which were marketed to young singles. The Hobbs Act makes it illegal to interfere with interstate commerce through extortion. The arrests followed an eighteen-month investigation by special agents of the IRS intelligence division. A jury in the courtroom of district judge Julius Hoffman convicted Battaglia, Amabile, and one of Riley's business associates of conspiring to extort money from Riley in connection with the Lansing project. Hoffman sentenced the two reputed mobsters to fifteen years in prison each.

A year later and several months before Kerner joined the court, Judges Schnackenberg and Cummings upheld the convictions. But Swygert, the third member of the appeals panel, issued ringing dissents on behalf of Battaglia and Amabile. He insisted that the government had not demonstrated a Hobbs Act conspiracy by the men and cited numerous trial errors by Hoffman. He tried, notwithstanding the substantial momentum of government strategy and popular opinion in the "war" against organized crime, to limit the scope of the Hobbs Act and conspiracy statutes. Simply put, he found that the government had failed to do its job under the law. "On this record [of the trial], there is absent any evidence, direct or circumstantial, that Battaglia knew that money was to be extorted from Riley or that threats were to be made to Riley by Amabile," Swygert wrote in his first dissent. "Nor is there any evidence that Riley feared Battaglia or that Battaglia received any of the money extorted from Riley. . . . There can be no doubt that Amabile and Battaglia associated together, but . . . a mere association is insufficient evidence of guilt to support a conviction."[55]

In other words, organized crime, as defined by IRS investigators and the newspapers, might not have been very organized after all, at least as far as Teetz Battaglia was concerned. Swygert issued a highly provocative statement of the constitutional rights of mobsters:

> Instead of the traditional assumption of innocence with which criminal defendants are ordinarily clothed, the record in this case suggests a presumption of criminality attached to these defendants because of their infamous reputations and notoriety. The defendants may have been guilty of nefarious conduct for which they deserve imprisonment, or they may have had such bad reputations as to be considered menaces to society. Such facts alone, however, cannot warrant a blinding of eyes, permitting a conviction to stand that is based on surmise rather than evidence. This kind of difficulty is present in this case because the charge on which the defendants were convicted and imprisoned, an agreement to extort money, was not sustained by the evidence. No person should be punished under our criminal laws unless he has been proved guilty of a specific offense by competent evidence in a fair trial. Due process of law demands nothing less.[56]

When Amabile lost his appeal, also at the hands of Schnackenberg and Cummings, Swygert once more dissented. He again rebuked the government's overzealous reliance on the Hobbs Act, saying, "I do not believe that the Hobbs Act was intended to have such broad reach."[57] He also faulted Judge Hoffman for not permitting defense cross-examination of Riley concerning facts that might have deflated his credibility in the eyes of the jury. Riley for a time enjoyed his association with the syndicate men and was a regular patron at their nightclubs. He had his own problems with the law. He was under indictment in Illinois for forgery, but the case had been suspended pending his cooperation with the federal government. The IRS, following standard operating procedure for reluctant witnesses, had Riley under investigation for tax evasion. Hoffman had refused to permit defense lawyers to question Riley on the stand about any of these matters or what Riley hoped to gain by cooperating with the government. In grand jury testimony that the trial jury was not permitted to see, Riley had testified that Amabile threatened him regarding the IRS investigation. "Don't tell them anything," Riley quoted Amabile as saying. "You know what happens to guys who talk, don't you?" Riley told the grand jury that he replied: "What is the matter with you guys? On one hand you tell me you will kill me if I don't pay you the money; on the other hand, those guys [Internal Revenue agents] tell me they will put me in jail."[58] Swygert concluded, "I believe that Amabile's efforts to question the credibility of Riley by showing his relationship to the Government and the reward he hoped to gain by reason of his testimony was entirely proper and should have been permitted."[59]

Despite Swygert's dissents, the government prevailed in its initial case against Battaglia and Amabile. Indeed, Riley's testimony was so persuasive that the government obtained a separate conviction against Amabile in Judge Hoffman's courtroom in connection with corruption in Northlake. Also convicted in the two-month trial were Nick Palermo, head of Melrose Park Plumbing; Henry Ed Neri, mayor of Northlake; Leo Shababy, an alderman of the suburb; and former alderman Joseph Drozd. But with Kerner on the seventh circuit bench, government prosecutors of the Outfit began to lose. In February 1969 Kerner, with Kiley and Cummings concurring, voided the convictions of thirteen reputed underworld figures in a highly publicized truck hijacking case. In April, following Swygert's lead and with Schnackenberg and Cummings concurring, Kerner threw out the Northlake convictions. (Schnackenberg participated in the oral argument and conference of the judicial panel but died before the opinion was written.) Kerner wrote that the government, having alleged a Hobbs Act conspiracy charge against Amabile in his dealings with Riley in Lansing in 1964 and 1965, could not indict Amabile for similar crimes in Northlake in 1962. Kerner noted that an agreement between Amabile and Melrose Park Plumbing to loot Riley's business was integral to each episode of the alleged conspiracy.

Kerner said the government "is not free to arbitrarily decide whether there is one agreement or several. . . . To convict a party severally for being part of two conspiracies when in reality he is only involved in one overall conspiracy would be convicting him of the same crime twice. . . . Since Amabile has already been tried and convicted of conspiring to extort money from Riley, Amabile's fifth amendment rights were violated by placing him in jeopardy twice for the same criminal act."[60] The Kerner ruling was the mirror image of Swygert's in the Battaglia case. Swygert suggested an absence of conspiracy. Kerner said that if the government sought to prove a conspiracy, it could not win guilty verdicts in discrete criminal cases to swell its conviction count. In both instances Swygert and Kerner disputed, on the basis of civil liberties, essential techniques of the government's campaign against the Chicago crime syndicate.

In the same decision Kerner reversed the convictions of Amabile, Palermo, Neri, and Alderman Leo Shababy (former alderman Joseph Drozd did not appeal) on the grounds that Judge Hoffman had failed to question the jury individually, as defense lawyers had requested, about whether they had seen any of the mountain of news reports about the trial. Kerner cited a 1962 ruling by his seventh circuit colleague Judge Kiley in a government case against mob boss Anthony Accardo. Kiley ruled that each juror must be questioned regarding adverse publicity. "Warning a jury without questioning them is insufficient," Kerner wrote.[61]

Finally, Kerner ruled that the government had failed to present to Hoffman concrete reasons for barring defense questions about Riley's current address and occupation. Riley and Wayne Seidler, a former Northlake official and an unindicted coconspirator, were in the government's witness protection program. At the government's mere request, without demanding a full explanation in his chambers, Hoffman had refused to allow defense questions about Riley's and Seidler's most recent addresses and occupations—questions normally considered routine in trial testimony. "The court agrees . . . that where there is a threat to the life of a witness, the right of the defendant to have the witness' true name, address and place of employment is not absolute," Kerner wrote. "However, the threat to the witness must be actual and not a result of conjecture." No evidence of an actual threat against Seidler was apparent, although it was for Riley, Kerner found. And "in neither case was the relevant information disclosed to the trial judge in order that he could make an informed decision," Kerner ruled.[62]

Threatening the sanctity of the government's witness protection program, criticizing the zealous use of federal conspiracy and extortion statutes, and seeking to expose the government's questionable tactics in obtaining testimony from disreputable witnesses such as Riley put Kerner and Swygert at odds with the government's latest crusade against organized crime in Chicago. In a rare editorial comment on a seventh circuit court ruling, the *Chicago Tribune* put Kerner's opinion in the context of the national law-and-order debate. Saying Kerner had acted on "the flimsiest of technicalities," the *Tribune* alluded to civil liberties rulings by the U.S. Supreme Court, including the *Escobedo* and *Miranda* rulings. The editorial was titled "Justice Impossible without Wisdom:"

> The appellate court's decision is regarded by some lawyers here as a shocking miscarriage of justice which could upset the convictions of many notorious characters in this circuit whose trials were subject to news reports. It is a rule of criminal procedure in United States courts that convictions by a jury may be reversed only upon substantial questions of law, and not for "harmless" technicalities. In view of recent decisions by the United States Supreme Court, it would not be surprising if that tribunal, when it has an opportunity, should uphold the position of the appellate court here. However, it is the responsibility of appellate judges to follow established rules of procedures and not to anticipate what the Warren court will say. Because of the appellate court's action, the three defendants must be tried again, at great expense and inconvenience to the government and with no assurance that justice will be done.[63]

Amabile, who sometimes was called "The Freak" because of his reputation in the company of prostitutes, never was tried again. It took IRS investigators two years to rebuild the case against his associates in politics and business, Neri, Palermo, and Shababy. Special agent Jack Walsh, the leader of the IRS probe in Northlake, assigned the job to an especially capable intelligence division colleague, William Witkowski. The three pleaded guilty in 1971 rather than face another trial. By then Walsh had become convinced that Kerner, now operating under the immunity of a lifetime federal appointment, was part of the Outfit's pernicious web.

10

To "CRIMP" Is to Hinder

Of the many underworld characters who survived the Capone era to play important roles in Chicago's organized crime and politics, none was more colorful than William R. Skidmore, a bail bondsman, gambling entrepreneur, and busy political fixer whose career began on Chicago's West Side in the early part of the century. Ovid Demaris, in his extensive rendition of Chicago's organized crime lore, *Captive City,* called Billy Skidmore "a saloonkeeper-gambler and junk yard operator who was to become the foremost political fixer and underworld bagman during the Kelly-Nash regime" in the 1930s and 1940s.[1] In 1941, when the *Chicago Tribune* published ledger sheets said to belong to former Capone accountant Jack "Greasy Thumb" Guzik, one name marked as receiving payoffs was "Skid." Another was "Tub," probably policeman Dan "Tubbo" Gilbert, Jack Arvey's unfortunate choice to run as sheriff of Cook County in 1954. Skidmore was a principal character in the 1952 book *Barbarians in Our Midst,* the disturbing and authoritative portrayal of midcentury vice and corruption in Chicago by Virgil W. Peterson, a former FBI special agent and operating director of the Chicago Crime Commission. The book was an updated version of the classic polemic *If Christ Came to Chicago!* by British journalist William T. Stead, who exposed vice and corruption in the city at the turn of the century.

Peterson, whose anticrime zeal was second to none, related several Skidmore escapades, including events routine to the operation of his junkyard:

The headquarters for the payoffs for political protection was located in Skidmore's junk yard known as the Lawndale Scrap Iron and Metal Company, 2840 South

Kedzie Avenue, Chicago. At appointed times gamblers and politicians from all parts of Chicago and Cook County lined up outside the junk-yard office and awaited their turn to make the required payments for the privilege of violating the law. A former investigator for the state's attorney's office acted as Skidmore's master of ceremonies. He would call out, "you're next." The gambler indicated would then enter Skidmore's office, give the address of his gambling establishment, which was duly recorded, pay the necessary protection money and depart—assured of continued immunity from police interference.[2]

But Skidmore's immunity, like Capone's, ended at the door of the U.S. Treasury Department. In March 1941 a jury convicted Skidmore of income tax evasion and sent him to the federal prison in Terre Haute, Indiana, where he died of heart failure in February 1944. Skidmore's partner in several gambling operations, William "Big Bill" Johnson, was convicted on income tax charges in October 1940 but remained free during numerous appeals that ran out in 1946. Unlike Skidmore, Johnson donated ostentatiously to churches and other charitable organizations; this created clear evidence of net worth and income beyond what he reported to the government but also produced a list of respectable supporters who extolled his civic virtues during his lengthy court appeals. This hypocrisy prompted Peterson to write, "Perhaps it was to the credit of Skidmore that neither he nor his supporters made any serious attempt to hold him out as anything more than a member of the underworld, a racketeer and a social parasite."[3]

Nevertheless, Skidmore was not without a certain quantity of human warmth. As youths who played baseball on the West Side, Skidmore and his Irish friends adopted into their circle a girl badly disfigured in a fall down a flight of stairs. She was stunted and hunched over, unable to play like other youngsters. Her name was Shirley Elizabeth O'Neil, born in 1890 to a family in the construction business in Chicago. She took up with the Skidmore street gang and became a sort of mascot. They protected her, and she amused them with a sparkling personality and a gift of gab. After her first marriage failed, O'Neil married a businessman named William E. Kub and lived on West Adams Street in Chicago's Austin neighborhood during the Roaring Twenties. She made headlines in 1922 when her husband shot and nearly killed the nineteen-year-old son of a wealthy California doctor after the boy had fallen in love with Shirley while she was on the West Coast seeking treatment from his father. The lurid incident was reported widely in Chicago newspapers.

Shirley Kub's name reappeared in headlines nearly a decade later during the hotly contested race between Republican mayor William Thompson and Democratic challenger Anton Cermak. A few days before the April 1931, election, the *Chicago Tribune* published officially secret testimony Kub had delivered to a special county grand jury investigating police corruption. The newspaper called Kub an "undercover investigator" for Thompson's acting police commissioner, John H. Alcock. Alcock denied he employed Kub for more than a few days, and grand jurors told reporters her testimony amounted to hearsay. But her story, as told by the *Tribune*—which staunchly opposed Thompson's reelection—further damaged the mayor's already low repute among civic-minded Chicagoans.

Kub testified that Daniel Serritella, a long-time Capone associate who held three public jobs in the Thompson organization—city sealer, state senator, and Republican ward committeeman—was the "boss" of vice in the Loop and, acting on orders from the mayor, kept gambling and drinking "wide open" downtown. She reported that Serritella and James W. Breen, another Capone associate and first assistant corporation counsel under Thompson, had warned Willard Malone, the police captain in charge of the Loop police district, against raiding gambling parlors and speakeasies. "I have known Capt. Malone all my life, was raised with him and his people," Kub told the grand jury. "I went to see Capt. Malone. He told me in confidence, which must be protected, that Serritella came to him and told him the administration wanted the First District . . . to go along [with lax vice enforcement]."[4]

Kub's report was hardly news to Chicago's crime reporters or to those who followed tales of the Capone era in the newspapers. Nonetheless, coming from a fashionably dressed woman who was barely four feet tall and who had married a black man after divorcing her second husband, the story of the "police spy," as headline writers called her, was too sensational to ignore. Privately journalists debated Kub's credibility. An unpublished memo written by a *Tribune* reporter in January 1931 states: "The woman is obviously screwy, according to [William C.] Dannenberg [a veteran Chicago police officer and source for many crime stories], who, however, does not deny the possibility that she was collecting [payoffs] for the coppers and maybe for others. He says he doesn't believe she was ever really connected with the police department." Elsewhere in the memo the reporter writes, "Geo. Wright [the criminal courts reporter who obtained Kub's grand jury testimony], who knows, says the Kub woman is not crazy."[5]

In either case, Kub remained loyal to her friends from the West Side days of her youth, and they remained loyal to her. When she faced jail for contempt of court after initially refusing to testify before the police corruption grand jury, no fewer than seven prominent criminal defense lawyers represented her. "When counselors stepped forward they stood in a group completely hiding their client," the *Chicago Herald and Examiner* reported.[6] Among them were Thomas D. Nash and Michael J. Ahern, who at the same moment were engaged in a last-ditch effort to derail the federal income tax indictment of their principal client, Al Capone. Pleading on behalf of Kub, Ahern told Judge John P. McGoorty, "Too much publicity has been given to this poor, unfortunate woman who has been an invalid most of her life."[7]

Kub's notoriety as an investigator, detective, stool pigeon, spy, and undercover agent—among the appellations newspapers used to describe her—grew during a bizarre contretemps between Cook County state's attorney John A. Swanson, the Republican reformer nominated in the Pineapple Primary of 1928 after his home was bombed, and fellow Republican Robert Isham Randolph, the zealous civic leader and founder of the Secret Six. Randolph's armchair posse of prominent Chicago business leaders and self-appointed crime fighters had helped to finance the booze-busting operations of federal Prohibition agents Alexander G. Jamie, Jamie's brother-in-law Eliot Ness, and the rest of the "Untouchables." But with Prohibition thoroughly discredited, Capone in prison, and Big Bill Thompson out of office, operations of the Secret Six had deteriorated badly.

In late August of the pivotal 1932 election year, news broke that the Secret Six, led by its chief investigator, former G-man Alexander Jamie, and his agent, Shirley Kub, had been probing Swanson's office for wrongdoing and that Swanson had in turn installed a telephone tap in the office of the Secret Six operatives. The *Tribune* reported that Jamie had uncovered what he called a "political-criminal cabal," but Jamie declined to elaborate.[8] Swanson, who was up for reelection in November, charged that Kub had virtually taken over the Secret Six operation and was using the organization, which Swanson once took credit for forming, as a tool for blackmail.

Randolph, an engineer whose revered father had saved Chicago's Lake Michigan water supply by designing the Sanitary and Ship Canal, was the former president of the Chicago Association of Commerce and the newly appointed director of operations for the 1933 World's Fair in Chicago. He tried to defend his unofficial crime-fighting organization while distancing himself from the embarrassing telephone-tapping affair. He told reporters that he was unaware of Jamie's investigation of Swanson and knew little about Shirley Kub. As the fall election drew near, Swanson became more strident in his rhetoric against his fellow Republican Randolph, labeling Randolph, Jamie, and Kub "reform racketeers"—a potent turn of phrase that put a new perspective on Chicago's legendary struggle with the underworld.

"I am grateful for the enemies I have made," Swanson said in a statement to the *Tribune,* which warmly endorsed his candidacy. "Among them are a number of individuals who have tried to make a racket out of reform. These racketeers have gone on the public platform denouncing the city that has given them a living and made some of them rich. . . . They have held Chicago up to the scorn of the world in speeches and magazine articles, as a paradise of racketeers, thus gratifying an insatiable desire for self-advertising at the expense of their home city's good name."

Swanson complained that the relentless outcry of corruption "has not only injured business and aggravated the Depression in Chicago but has made this city seem to be a mecca for criminals from all parts of the country. . . . These reform racketeers in good times were able to solicit large sums from the public ostensibly to fight racketeers but apparently expended in the manner that would do them the most good. They hope and pray that we will never have a crimeless city for in that event sources of large revenue would disappear." Regarding Shirley Kub, Swanson said: "The Secret Six started out along the lines suggested by me, which at first were effective. Then it fell under the malign influence of Mrs. Shirley Kub, whose reputation as a police stool pigeon is well known."[9]

Swanson kept the issue alive by launching a headline-grabbing investigation of Kub's marriage to determine whether she had been married to two different men at the same time. For his part, a few days before the election Randolph accused Swanson's brother of illegal activities. Swanson lost in the November Democratic landslide that ushered in the Franklin Roosevelt era. But Mayor Cermak had heard all he cared to hear about Shirley Kub. In January 1933 Cermak ordered his new chief of police, James P. Allman, to end the department's cooperation with the Secret Six. "I never want to see a policeman talking to Mrs. Kub, and I don't want to see Mrs. Kub around the city hall," Cermak commanded.[10] Randolph responded that he already had fired Kub, and the Chicago Association of Commerce and Industry officially disbanded the Secret Six a few months later.

As far as Chicagoans were concerned, that was the end of Shirley Kub. She was in her forties and had three daughters by her first two marriages. In 1935 her third husband, against whom she had sought an annulment, died in Cook County Hospital. Kub became an avid collector of antiques and knickknacks. In 1945 she took in as a boarder and companion a young X-ray technician named James Hetterman, whom she called her nephew. The two lived in suburban Park Ridge and Barrington in the 1950s. In 1962 they moved to a large apartment at 20 East Cedar on Chicago's near North Side, which Kub jammed with thousands of antiques and bric-a-brac, filling tables and cabinets throughout the apartment. Hetterman died in 1963. Kub was a lonely old woman going blind with glaucoma. Her name had all but disappeared from Chicago crime lore. But she still had friends in the crime syndicate, and she still enjoyed telling stories to crime fighters. Perhaps the most remarkable story of Shirley Kub's long and curious life was the pivotal role she played in the downfall of a federal appeals court judge, Otto Kerner.

◆ ◆ ◆

In Chicago as in the rest of the country, organized crime emerged from World War II eager to stretch its wings and fly. Hoodlums shared with law-abiding citizens the urge to put behind them the privations of the Great Depression and the rigors of the war. Opportunity knocked in the postwar economic boom. With Prohibition a distant memory, gambling reemerged as the social habit that America's upper class sought to prohibit to the lower class and organized criminals sought to provide to all. As they had with beer and liquor during Prohibition, criminal syndicates took huge profits from the scarcity value of gambling opportunities created by a double standard. Chicago elites, many of whom came to prominence gambling audaciously on business ventures and Chicago's commodity exchanges, enjoyed recreational gambling inside their private clubs while they endorsed the deep-seated midwestern prudishness that condemned gambling among the masses. The Chicago-area workingman, unwelcome in swank lunch and golf clubs, took his business to bookies and numbers racketeers. For the more daring, there were sleazy vice parlors, such as the nightclubs along Mannheim Road running south from O'Hare Airport through working-class suburbs Northlake, Schiller Park, and Stone Park. Legal and illegal cash receipts from these operations flowed upward to a criminal plutocracy headed by men who in many cases were far better known than business and civic leaders.

Sam Giancana, head of the Chicago Outfit and a gambling kingpin, was a national figure, quite conspicuous in his power and prestige. He dressed well, lived well, and cultivated ostentatious friendships with famous entertainers, such as Frank Sinatra. He even dabbled in international intrigue. The Central Intelligence Agency solicited his help in plotting to assassinate Fidel Castro in the closing days of the Eisenhower administration. He appeared to enjoy absolute immunity from criminal prosecution.

FBI director J. Edgar Hoover, whose circle of friends overlapped Giancana's, barely acknowledged the existence of organized crime in America, even after a police officer happened on a conference of crime bosses from throughout the nation that took place in Apalachin, New York, in 1957. In the 1950s the Treasury Department's Bureau of Internal Revenue, which could have been a counterforce to Hoover's recalcitrance, displayed little of the ingenuity or diligence it had employed in the 1930s and 1940s to jail big-time gangsters and put fear in the hearts of local politicians. The bureau had lost interest in the effective but time-consuming process of building what were called net worth or net expenditure cases against high-profile hoodlums—the strategy used against Al Capone, Billy Skidmore, and William Johnson, among others, in which meticulously assembled evidence of a subject's wealth and lifestyle was compared to reported income to prove income tax evasion.

In the 1940s and 1950s the Bureau of Internal Revenue struggled under corruption scandals of its own. District revenue chiefs often were politically appointed tax collectors beholden to the party in power. They were not selected for competence or integrity. Internal Revenue officials were caught skimming cash from taxpayers, including Senator John J. Williams of Delaware, who promptly held hearings. In 1953 the agency changed its name to the Internal Revenue Service (IRS) in an effort to improve its public image. Congressional hearings, forced resignations, and a major reorganization shook the agency and severely tarnished the crime-busting reputation that Treasury agents had created in Chicago twenty years earlier. Journalist David Burnham, in his portrait of the IRS, *A Law unto Itself,* concluded: "One casualty of the restructuring of the IRS was apparently the highly touted but extraordinarily shallow drive to round up the nation's gangsters."[11]

The mission and culture of the IRS changed dramatically with the 1960 election of John F. Kennedy and Kennedy's appointment of his thirty-five-year-old brother Robert to head the Department of Justice. Robert F. Kennedy had never secured an indictment from a grand jury or tried a case in court. Since 1954, however, as counsel to the Senate Rackets Committee, chaired by Democrat John L. McClellan of Arkansas, Bobby Kennedy had jousted in Capitol Hill hearing rooms with labor leaders, including James R. Hoffa, and gangsters, including Giancana. His efforts to jail Teamsters boss Hoffa, which became known as the "get-Hoffa campaign," made him a more public figure than was even his brother John, the junior senator from Massachusetts, and helped to build national recognition of the Kennedy name in advance of John's presidential bid.

The McCarthy era, with its politically effective appeals to nativism and fear of foreign radicals, had run aground, to be replaced with what Robert Kennedy called "the enemy within," a phrase that formed the title of his 1960 book. After the 1960 election, "Subversion was out. Organized crime was in," wrote Robert Kennedy biographer Arthur M. Schlesinger Jr.[12] Knowing Hoover's indifferent attitude toward organized crime, Robert Kennedy centered his campaign not in the FBI, which under Hoover was part of the Justice Department only in a pro-forma sense, but rather in the department's organized crime section. He called into action all the other federal investigative agencies, including two Treasury Department units, the Narcotics Bureau and the Internal Revenue Service. Mortimer H. Caplin, the IRS commissioner appointed by President Kennedy, had been one of Robert Kennedy's law professors at the University of Virginia. Caplin, who fancied bow ties and enjoyed the limelight, agreed that "as long as we were making real tax investigations—not sham ones—there was nothing objectionable" to Kennedy's antimobster campaign.[13] He assigned a special IRS team to work with the Justice Department on organized crime projects under the heading of the Organized Crime Drive.

Robert Kennedy told an interviewer shortly after his appointment: "We are going to take a new look at the income tax returns of these people, to spot the flow of crooked money. I have been criticized on the ground that tax laws are there to raise money for the government and should not be used to punish the underworld. I think the argument is specious. I do believe that tax returns must remain confidential. But I also recognize that we must deal with corruption, crime and dishonesty."[14] Journalist Victor S. Navasky, in his book *Kennedy Justice*, reported that "60 percent of all organized crime cases from 1961–1965 turned out to be revenue cases."[15] After meeting with Kennedy, Caplin instructed the IRS investigators:

> I cannot emphasize too strongly the importance I attach to the success of the Service's contribution to this overall program. . . . The tax returns of major racketeers to be identified by the Department of Justice will be subjected to the "saturation type" investigation, using such man-power on each case as can be efficiently employed. In conducting such investigations, full use will be made of available electronic equipment and other technical aids as well as such investigative techniques as surveillance, undercover work, etc.[16]

Schlesinger noted the dark side of Kennedy's zeal against organized crime: "In singling out Hoffa or Sam Giancana . . . , he was abusing the prosecuting power. He was deciding that people were guilty and then looking for something they could be found guilty of. He was convicting them not for real crimes but for slips that anyone could have made. Beginning with the criminal rather than the crime was selective justice."[17] Schlesinger observed that the Bobby Kennedy approach to fighting organized crime appeared to turn law enforcement on its head. Instead of proceeding from a known crime to capture and convict a perpetrator, federal officials started with persons they identified as criminals and attempted to find a crime for which these individuals could be convicted.

In the 1920s civic righteousness crusader Frank Loesch and the Chicago Crime Commission revived a forgotten 1874 state antivagrancy law to harass men they judged to be "public enemies." Under Kennedy federal customs laws, the U.S. Migratory Bird Act, rules governing applications for Veterans Administration home mortgages, and Federal Communications Commission radio licensing procedures were among the statutes and regulations used to indict men the Kennedy government decided were members of organized crime. Navasky quoted one source as saying Kennedy's head of the criminal division of the Justice Department, H. Jack Miller, "would not hesitate to indict a man for spitting on the sidewalk if he thought that was the best he could get."[18]

The biggest weapon by far in the federal government's arsenal was the income tax code, along with the enormous and statutorily endowed power of the IRS. Bobby Kennedy and Caplin rekindled a flame that had been sparked in the Capone era in Chicago. Schlesinger dates the beginning of the Kennedy style of intrusive federal law enforcement to March 1929, when Frank Loesch traveled to Washington with a group of civic-minded Chicagoans to urge President Hoover to bring down the power of the federal government on Al Capone. Hoover agreed, later writing in his memoirs, "I directed that all the federal agencies concentrate upon Mr. Capone."[19] Repeatedly Hoover would ask Andrew Mellon, secretary of the Treasury, "Have you got that fellow Capone yet?"[20] The problem, as Schlesinger pointed out, was that targeting individuals first and crimes second could bring about unconscionable violations of civil liberties in the hands of undisciplined investigators and unscrupulous prosecutors.

✦ ✦ ✦

To jail Sam Giancana, in May 1965 the government used a ploy based on the very thing that federal investigators in Chicago found most annoying about the city's prominent mobsters, their apparent immunity from the law. This time immunity was not an abstract state of affairs but a concrete ruling by federal district judge William J. Campbell. As former FBI agent William F. Roemer Jr. explained in his book *Man against the Mob*, after years of openly tailing Giancana's every move, the government decided to let Giancana put himself in jail. Federal prosecutors, including an imaginative former seminarian named David P. Schippers, hauled the gangster before a grand jury and listened while he invoked his Fifth Amendment right against self-incrimination in response to every question. They then ushered Giancana before Judge Campbell, who granted Giancana absolute immunity from prosecution for any and all crimes he had committed up until that moment. Campbell explained that this immunity meant Giancana no longer had Fifth Amendment protection, because he was absolved of any and all crimes.

Giancana was returned to the grand jury room, where he answered a few inconsequential questions—his name and address—but took the Fifth on the first substantive question. Campbell declared Giancana in contempt of court and ordered him locked up in Cook County Jail. "You have the key to your own cell," Campbell told him. "Whenever you decide to obey the lawful order of this court, notify the U.S. Marshall and he will bring you before the grand jury."[21] Giancana never did. He waited out the term of the grand jury in jail and fled the country on his release a year later, turning leadership of organized crime in Chicago over to Sam Battaglia. But the ingenuity of Giancana's incarceration, however brief, brought to public acclaim a new generation of federal crime busters. One was Schippers, an architect of the immunity ploy. Another was an IRS special agent named John M. Walsh.

Schippers was a thirty-five-year-old graduate of Chicago's Loyola University Law School and an assistant U.S. attorney who had investigated labor racketeering in the Bobby Kennedy era. In January 1965 he was named head of special prosecutions under U.S. Attorney Edward V. Hanrahan. Schippers later tested the waters in Chicago politics but became instead a successful lawyer. Jack Walsh, armed with an accounting degree from St. Joseph College in Rensselaer, Indiana, became a revenue agent in the Chicago district office of the Internal Revenue Service in July 1958, shortly after his graduation. Two years later he was promoted to special agent assigned to the IRS intelligence division, now called the criminal division, which was charged with uncovering and proving willful violations of tax laws.

Contrary to the popular image of accounting majors, Jack Walsh, who today lives in Cincinnati, is a man of action. Short and powerfully built but with small hands, he is an avid duck hunter and dog fancier. He belongs to Ducks Unlimited, a conservation organization of bird hunters, which once counted Otto Kerner among its members. In an energetic, piercing tenor voice Walsh expresses strong, conservative opinions about the Catholic church, politics, and right and wrong in general. His career was influenced profoundly by Virgil Peterson's *Barbarians in Our Midst*. Walsh still holds the book in deep regard and sees dark implications in the fact that it is not widely available today. Like all 1,750 special agents of the intelligence division in the mid-1960s, Walsh was trained in surveillance techniques, the martial arts, and use of firearms as well as tax law and bookkeeping. Journalist William Surface, in his 1967 book *Inside Internal Revenue,* wrote, "The skill that special agents learn—or develop themselves—is to collect evidence, not excuses that it can't be done. Some agents' techniques are ingeniously original."[22] Walsh was a model special agent.

Schippers worked with local IRS agents in his investigations of organized crime, but in the early 1960s the IRS's Chicago district, under District Director Eugene C. Coyle Jr., a former bookkeeper and long-time civil servant, lacked the killer instinct. Coyle, who like Mayor Daley was a product of Chicago's South Side Irish enclave and an avid White Sox fan, was regarded within the service as a genial official who would not rock the boat in Chicago. Audits that might have opened the door to high-profile criminal tax cases languished.

Walsh's first big organized crime case involved working with the Justice

Department and the Better Government Association to rescue suburban Northlake from domination by mobsters. His first gangland quarry was Rocco Pranno, who according to legend once spit on Robert Kennedy and who was described by Ovid Demaris as "a wild and vicious hood, quick with threats and baseball bat."[23] The Northlake police chief was Pranno's cousin. With Walsh's help a federal jury convicted Pranno of extortion and conspiracy, and he was sentenced to fifteen years in prison. But the Outfit's intimidation of legitimate business and its corruption of public officials in Northlake, Stone Park, Schiller Park, and other near-in western suburbs continued. Joseph Amabile took Pranno's place as a brutal shakedown operator for Giancana's successor, Sam Battaglia.

The communities along either side of Mannheim Road provided plenty of work for crime fighters, and Walsh was in the thick of it. He helped to convict Battaglia and Amabile along with the mayor of Northlake after building contractor William G. Riley, who was impressed by the government's ability to jail Giancana, brought his story of extortion and intimidation to Schippers. As Walsh's efforts began to be noticed within Chicago's mob-fighting fraternity, he moved into the heart of organized crime intelligence circles. He developed a close relationship with former FBI agent George E. Mahin, who as director of the Better Government Association, a private civic watchdog organization, had worked since 1963 to cleanse Northlake of organized crime influence. In late 1967 Schippers arranged for Walsh to meet a person who was a living link between the Capone era and organized crime of the 1960s. That person was Shirley E. Kub.

✦ ✦ ✦

"Mr. Schippers introduced me, because he said Shirley Kub had information concerning the hoodlum element in Chicago," Special Agent Walsh testified in a U.S. Tax Court case involving Kub.[24] Walsh met with the elderly woman on average once a week in 1968, usually in the Greyhound Bus station at Randolph and Clark Streets or in Loop restaurants or hotels. Like Alexander Jamie in the 1930s, Walsh became intrigued with Kub's apparent inside knowledge of organized crime figures and their connections to politics and business—the "political-criminal cabal," as Jamie had called it. She regaled Walsh with stories of the old West Side gangs and spoke intimately of current mobsters and politicians. Kub convinced Walsh that organized crime in Chicago was much broader than a handful of brutes with Italian surnames.

Kub confirmed to Walsh what he already suspected: organized crime and corruption in Chicago encompassed not just notorious crime bosses, such as those Robert Kennedy had targeted for special prosecution, but also a much larger sphere of wrongdoers; in fact, there was a sinister triad. In addition to the Outfit, the other two legs of the stool were public officials of both parties and business leaders from many industries and professions. Kub said Chicago was ruled by a "true syndicate" comprising these three elements. Kub told Walsh that Anton Cermak, the mayor who had banished her from city hall shortly before his death in 1933, had created the three-headed "true syndicate" in Chicago.

Historically speaking, Kub's "true syndicate" hypothesis in the 1960s would have been no more a revelation to Chicago crime buffs than her grand jury testimony had been in the 1930s. Ever since it rose literally out of the swamp where the Chicago River met Lake Michigan, the city had been defined by the confluence of the best and the worst of human instincts collaborating in a quest for money and power. Writing at the turn of the century, British journalist William Archer said of Chicago, "More than any other city of my acquaintance, [Chicago] suggests that antique conception of the underworld which placed Elysium and Tartarus not only on the same plane, but, so to speak, around the corner from each other."[25]

Kub's idea of Chicago's "true syndicate" bore a close resemblance to what reform-minded Chicago alderman Charles Merriam in the 1920s called the "Underworld" and the "Upperworld"[26] and Virgil Peterson thirty years later called "the criminal-political system."[27] The imagery persists, sometimes to the point of paranoia and absurdity. In 1993 popular conspiracy theorist Peter Dale Scott employed the duality in his book *Deep Politics and the Death of JFK* in asserting, with no evidence whatever, ominous connections among prominent Chicago political figures, businesspeople, and local gangsters in the assassination of President Kennedy nine hundred miles away in Dallas, Texas. "Beneath the open surface of our society lie connections and relationships of long standing, virtually immune to disclosure, and capable of great crimes, including serial murder," Scott wrote.[28]

To Walsh, imbued with the spirit of Virgil Peterson, Kub represented an invaluable, top-secret source who spanned decades of corruption in underworld and upperworld Chicago and was eager to talk. He wrote hundreds of memorandums on his interviews. "She was very elderly, but one of the sharpest gals I ever met," Walsh recalled in 1995. "We had never heard the difference between the Syndicate and the Outfit. We did a lot of work to find out if this broad was for real."[29]

To gain Kub's confidence, Walsh pretended he was corruptible. The more he talked to Kub, however, the more he came to believe she was not as forthcoming as she might be and seemed to be steering him toward certain targets and away from others. Having helped to bring headline-grabbing indictments in Northlake, Walsh was then busy in nearby Schiller Park, which his sources

told him was under the control of Anthony Accardo, the Outfit's senior statesman. Kub seemed anxious to protect Accardo, a former Capone bodyguard,
Walsh recalled. "This informant was trying to get me off of the Accardo case
and onto the English brothers [lesser hoodlums named Chuck and Sam]," he
said.[30]

Walsh had gone deep into the underworld. In March 1968 he was "scared
shitless" when a massive hoodlum named Joseph Arnold, a North Side gambling operator who stood six-foot-two and weighed nearly 250 pounds, visited Kub's North Lake Shore Drive apartment one evening while Walsh was
present. In Kub's 1973 tax trial, Walsh gave this chilling account:

> It was approximately 7:10 P.M. [March 27, 1968] when the doorbell rang in Mrs.
> Kub's apartment. Mrs. Kub got up from her sitting room/bedroom, and said to
> me that might be Joe, went to the door of the apartment, rang the buzzer for the
> downstairs door and left the front door of the apartment ajar. . . . A few moments
> later, an individual known to me as Joe Arnold came into the apartment. Mrs. Kub
> said, "Hello, Joe." And I believe Mr. Arnold said something back. I don't recall
> exactly what it was. Mrs. Kub then brought Joe Arnold into her bedroom/sitting
> room and said . . . , "Joe, I want you to meet my friend, Jack Walsh. Jack, I want
> you to meet my—I want you to meet Joe, my closest buddy." I stood up, shook
> hands with Joe Arnold. And I returned to my chair in the sitting room. And Joe
> took the chair immediately to my right. And Shirley Kub sat on the edge of the
> bed. Shirley Kub immediately raised her voice, almost at times to the screaming
> point, and asked me why I had not told the Better Government Association and
> George Mahin [that] Sid Smith [Mayor Daley's building commissioner] was a good
> guy, since he had turned over some records to me. She asked if my office had any-
> thing on Tony [Accardo] or Joe and pointed to Joe Arnold. I believe I replied no.
> She then stated—I shouldn't say stated, in a loud voice asked me, or told me that
> if anyone touched a hair on their people's heads, certain things would happen. She
> said that if anything happened to her good friend Joe Arnold, certain things would
> happen; if anyone touched Tony or Sid Smith, or any of their people, my throat
> would be slit, I would be hanged, and generally that she and Joe Arnold would
> take care of me. Every time she mentioned some forceful act, she would say, "Isn't
> that right, Joe?" And Joe Arnold would nod in the affirmative. During this con-
> versation, if you want to call it that, I noticed Joe Arnold had moved to the right,
> or reached to the right. And when I finally looked at him, he had a gun in his hand.
> It was a .22 or a .25 calibre automatic, blued, and he immediately ejected the clip
> and the—the live shell, what appeared to be a live shell from the chamber. So, I
> knew the gun was on empty. He then proceeded to clean the gun. And after a few
> moments of cleaning the gun, he began to cock the gun, aimed it at the ceiling,
> and would pull the trigger and it would click. He continued to do this. And each
> time the gun was cocked and aimed at the ceiling, it came down closer to the top
> of my head. He aimed it closer to the top of my head. This was while Shirley Kub
> was doing her routine. I then pulled my service revolver, cocked the gun and aimed

it at Joe's head. I said, "Joe, if you aim that gun any closer to my head, I'm going to put a hole in your head the size of that gun." With that, Shirley Kub reacted very violently and slipped off the bed. Joe Arnold took the unloaded gun and the clip and put it in the cabinet to his right. I said, "What are you trying to do to me, Shirley? I'm up here trying to help you. What are you trying to pull?" Shirley Kub said, "Gosh, Jack, we didn't mean anything. We know you were all right; otherwise you wouldn't be here. Loyalty is the only quality that you need. If you are loyal to the party, the party will be appreciative." With that, I holstered my weapon, told Shirley Kub that if I received any additional information I would give it to her. I told Shirley Kub and Joe Arnold I had an eight o'clock appointment, stood up, kind of slapped Joe Arnold on the knee, said, "Joe, it's been nice meeting you," shook his hand and left the apartment.[31]

Walsh continued meeting with Kub after this bizzare encounter. To his surprise, she told him things he did not know about his own agency, the Chicago district office of the Internal Revenue Service. "It hit me one day that this source had information from inside the Service that I hadn't mentioned," he recalled.[32] He soon learned that Kub was having her income tax returns prepared by the second in command of internal security for the Chicago IRS office, Leonard Charles, and Charles's wife. Believing that the Chicago district office was untrustworthy, he took what he had learned about Charles higher in the ranks, to IRS Midwest regional director Alvin M. Kelley. The service had promoted Kelley, a boxer turned hard-hitting tax collector, to Midwest regional director in 1965 after his tenure as head of the Boston district office was marked by controversies over improper use of electronic listening devices. Based on Walsh's evidence, IRS officials in Washington launched a full-scale investigation of corruption in the Chicago district office. Leonard Charles was transferred out of the district.

Engaging in gunplay with a mobster and exposing internal corruption within the service without causing public embarrassment gave Walsh considerable prestige inside the IRS. As Walsh's star rose, so did Kub's, although Walsh kept her to himself. Walsh and his team of special agents, pursuing Kub's assertions, presented to Kelley detailed accounts of the "true syndicate" web. Kub told Walsh that Francis S. Lorenz, the former director of the Illinois Department of Public Works in the Kerner administration and later a rumored candidate for a federal judicial post, had received payoffs from a host of contractors doing business with the state. She claimed a politically connected Chicago law firm, O'Keefe, O'Brien, Hanson, and Ashenden, handled payoffs to Lorenz. She said Cook County assessor P. J. Cullerton was receiving payoffs in connection with real estate tax assessments.

Based on this and other Kub intelligence, Walsh and his team constructed two elaborate charts to show connections among mobsters, politicians, and business officials in Northern Illinois.[33] One of the charts used a hub-and-spoke design. The hub was a small circle labeled "SYNDICATE." Spokes radiating out from the hub connected to names of organized crime figures on the right side of the wheel and names of political figures on the left. At the top, connected by a line to the circle below, was the name Shirley Kub. To the right were such names as Alphonse Capone, Frank Nitti, Jack Guzik, William Skidmore, Anthony Accardo, Sam Battaglia, and Joe Arnold. To the left the names included Mayor Richard J. Daley; George W. Dunne, president of the Cook County board; P. J. Cullerton, the county assessor; Governor Otto Kerner; Sidney J. Smith, former Chicago building commissioner; Neil F. Hartigan, chief counsel of the Chicago Park District and later lieutenant governor; Jake Arvey, former chairman of the Cook County Democratic Party; Chicago fire commissioner Robert J. Quinn; Henry Crown, Chicago business tycoon and founder of Material Services Corporation; Republican U.S. senator Everett Dirksen; Sidney R. Olsen, Cook County recorder of deeds; Francis S. Lorenz; and attorneys James L. O'Keefe and James F. Ashenden.

The second chart, drawn like a business hierarchy chart, began at the top with the Illinois Department of Public Works and the names Francis Lorenz and Norbert J. Johnson, Lorenz's deputy director. Lines connected these names to those of several dozen architectural, engineering, construction, electrical, and plumbing firms.

Both charts were colored-coded to indicate the level of investigative activity and to differentiate presumed facts from suspicions. The charts represented Special Agent Jack Walsh's constellation of corruption. Each name recorded was suspect; each name was connected, no matter how indirectly, to the embedded illegality and corruption that for him defined life in Chicago and Illinois. Shirley Kub, a woman unknown to most Chicago historians and criminologists and dismissed as thoroughly disreputable by the few who remembered her, was the muse of Agent Walsh's elaborate vision.

In August 1969 the IRS in Washington followed its internal investigation of the Chicago office by sending a new chief of the district's intelligence division, Robert J. Bush, a veteran Washington IRS administrator who as an agent in New York had worked cases connected with the Apalachin crime syndicate meeting. Bush, a career IRS official of superior integrity and ability, represented the best the agency could put into the field. A few months after he arrived in Chicago, Bush brought Walsh's team back into the district fold, ending Walsh's freelance association with Kelley. He also hired additional intelligence agents to work in Chicago on underworld and political corruption matters.

In the early days of the new Nixon administration, resources flowed freely to federal law-enforcement agencies. The IRS and the Justice Department in Chicago benefited handsomely. Bush transferred Special Agent John Foy, a retired New York police officer and expert on illicit gambling, from the IRS office in Springfield, Illinois, to head a special task force to investigate public officials, including Mayor Daley, and the Cook County Democratic organization. In February 1970 the district's compliant director, Coyle, was replaced by a more aggressive administrator, Edwin P. Trainor.

These were halcyon days for the Chicago district office of the IRS and dangerous times for Chicago and Illinois politicians. Despite his narrow loss to Kennedy in 1960, Nixon deeply admired Mayor Daley, and Daley respected Nixon. But investigating public corruption in Illinois—a perennial endeavor of federal officials, both Republicans and Democrats, over many decades—inevitably turned the spotlight on the Daley organization. Walsh's team, called the Chicago Special Project, received favorable reviews among Chicago IRS officials and within the Nixon administration in Washington. In April 1970 Kelley urged Walsh to come up with a better name for his work. Revenue agent and team member Paul V. Berwick proposed the name "Project CRIMP." In a memo to Bush, Walsh explained what the acronym meant:

> C—CONSPIRACY—If the premise of the "True Syndicate" is true then naturally there is a conspiracy between legitimate businessmen, politicians and the hoodlum element, both as an organization and to commit crimes against the United States;
>
> R—RACKETEER—The racketeer or hoodlum element is certainly a part of the defined "True Syndicate" and allegedly is controlled and directed by legitimate businessmen and politicians;
>
> I—IMMUNITY—To date the legitimate businessmen and politicians identified to us as members of the "True Syndicate" appear to have been immune for all investigative agencies;
>
> M—MONEY—The only reason for the existance [sic] of any syndicate is to make money and this would be especially true of the alleged "True Syndicate";
>
> P—POLITICIANS—These individuals identified to us as members of the alleged "True Syndicate" are for the most part elected or appointed federal, state or local politicians and the legitimate businessmen identified to us as members of the alleged "True Syndicate" are the financial backers of these politicians.

Walsh continued: "The slang definition of crimp is to hinder and one of the objectives of the project is to hinder and naturally through criminal prosecution to destroy the alleged 'True Syndicate' as defined to us, or to prove that the alleged 'True Syndicate' does not exist."[34] Thanks to Kub, the legacy of Alexander Jamie, Eliot Ness, Frank Wilson, and Pat O'Rourke lived on under a new name, Project CRIMP. Bush never met the woman and never asked to meet her.[35]

✦ ✦ ✦

Nowhere did Chicago's Elysium and Tartarus intersect more fully than in the sport of kings: horse racing. Historian Donald L. Miller, in his depiction of early Chicago, *City of the Century*, noted that horse racing was one of the first entertainments and profit centers of Chicago's pioneering entrepreneurs. In 1832, when Native Americans and white men gathered in Chicago to sign a treaty that would force the former out of Illinois, Mark Beaubien, a tavern operator and all-around hustler in Chicago's sleazy Wolf Point hotel district, organized horse races on a track studded with booths selling liquor. Miller describes Beaubien as "a representative figure in the precapitalist community that flaunted progress and prided itself on its disdain for proper public conduct."[36]

The horse-racing business in the 1960s remained essentially unchanged from the spectacles staged by Beaubien, despite the elaborate traditions and regulations of the sport, the trappings of wealth and gentility among horse breeders, and the beauty of the animals. Unlike lotteries, which were unconstitutional in Illinois for most of its history, horse racing offers the amusement of selecting from among several contenders for prizes based on such presumably rational factors as a horse's past performance, the jockey (or driver, in the case of harness racing), and track conditions, as well as whatever irrational factors the bettor fancies, such as the color of the jockey's uniform. It was a short step up from a pure game of chance, but a big enough step to win the blessing of respectable individuals and government while in many cases drawing precious dollars out of the pockets of those least able to pay. William Stead of London, in a turn-of-the-century rebuke of Chicago's morals, wrote: "The great gaming hell of England is the race course, and I have never been able to understand the nicety of the distinction which damned the gaming table and upholds the race course."[37]

One distinction, of course, was the racing animal itself. Southern horse breeders in the 1800s discovered bone-building qualities in the grass growing in the limestone-rich soil of central Kentucky, a region known simply as "the Bluegrass." From then on other states could never compete with Kentucky in the number and quality of thoroughbred racehorses produced. When it came to providing capital for breeders and venues for racing, however, Illinois always has been equal to Kentucky, which shares Illinois's southern border along the Ohio River from Cairo to Shawneetown. The nation's premier harness race for trotting horses, which are not bred to the strict bloodlines of thoroughbreds and which run races in which they pull a two-wheeled sulky with a driver, was the Hambletonian, run each year at the Du Quoin State Fair in Southern Illinois.

Harness racing in Illinois was associated historically with the quaint image of country fairs. It became big business, however, when racetrack operators in urban settings, encouraged by downstate political dynamo Paul Powell, realized that harness races could be run at night, in all seasons and in almost any weather, if they simply erected lights and kept their doors open to the working man looking for after-hours entertainment. An ex-convict named Irwin Sam Wiedrick, from Buffalo, New York, teamed up with Powell and William H. Johnston, a protégé of the Capone interests in horse and dog racing, to exploit what they correctly foresaw would be tremendous public interest in night harness racing in the Chicago area. To create a statutory context for expanding harness racing—for example, a 1949 law to allow harness races on so-called flat tracks used by thoroughbreds—this trio set about to grease the Illinois General Assembly. Organizers of racing associations offered stock to legislators at ten cents a share, and even that amount did not need to be paid upfront. Racing operators simply allowed politicians to pay for their shares out of subsequent dividends. Those making the laws that governed the racing industry collected a share of the industry's profits at no cost or risk to themselves.

No other private industry so successfully aligned the competing interests of downstate Illinois and Chicago, and no other enjoyed such a symbiotic economic relationship with the political denizens of Springfield. *Chicago Tribune* reporter Ronald Koziol, in a 1971 article, described a typical transaction: "One of the legislators recently recalled how Wiedrick offered to sell him stock. The legislator, his wife and Wiedrick were dining when Wiedrick suggested they purchase stock in Chicago Downs (a racing association controlled by Johnston). The legislator said he told Wiedrick he couldn't afford to buy stock but Wiedrick offered to sell the stock to the legislator's wife for 10 cents a share. She bought 100 shares for $10. Three months later, a dividend check for $100 arrived at the legislator's home."[38]

Unlike in Kentucky, where the bloodlines of horse breeders were nearly as important as the bloodlines of the horses, horse racing in Illinois was pursued by self-made men, the nouveau riche of business and politics. One of the legendary boodlers of early twentieth- century Chicago, "Bathhouse" John Coughlin, demonstrated his initial rise out of poverty by purchasing a racehorse. The greatest of the horse-racing entrepreneurs in the early part of the century was Chicago businessman William Monroe Wright, who had founded Calumet Baking Powder Company in the late 1800s. In 1910, wealthy beyond his dreams and with a second wife who loved horses, he built Calumet Farm in Libertyville, Illinois, north of Chicago, to raise trotting horses. Journalist Ann Gaedorn Auerbach, in her book chronicling the rise and fall of Calumet Farm, *Wild Ride*, called Libertyville "then the nation's center for training trotting horses."[39] Later Wright moved Calumet Farm to the Kentucky Bluegrass, where it became the country's premier developer of racing champions.

Wright's son, Warren, a more able businessman than his father, sold the baking powder business for $32 million in 1929 and became active in Chicago politics. He and John Hertz, owner of the Yellow Cab Company, became the principal investors in Arlington Park racetrack in suburban Arlington Heights, northwest of Chicago. According to Auerbach, Wright and Hertz were urged to acquire the racetrack "in the late 1920s at the request of the Illinois governor, who was concerned that a potentially mob-controlled syndicate of investors was scheming to do so."[40] Throughout horse racing's history, the constant tug by "undesirable" elements of society seeking to wrest control of the sport from the upper classes ensured friendly regulatory environments and monopoly profits for those who promised to keep the industry in "respectable" hands.

Warren Wright became head of the Lincoln Park Board in Chicago and was touted as a possible Republican candidate for mayor, in part because of his stern denunciations of organized crime's influence. When Illinois elected Democrat Henry Horner as governor, however, Wright's days as park board chief— a gubernatorial appointment—were numbered. After the newspapers broke the story of a minor scandal involving a shortage of funds at the park board, Wright resigned and moved to Kentucky to assume control of Calumet Farm, where his father had died in 1931. "What Wright and his son brought to Kentucky was far more impressive than Roman numerals following a name," wrote Auerbach. "Both men possessed the hard-driving middle-class attitudes of making it on their own. Neither the elder Wright or his son, who would move to Lexington in the 1930s, had ever depended on luck or family fortunes. Theirs was a legacy of sweat and ingenuity, dogged determination and devotion. Their way was to aim at the things they wanted and never stop until they got them."[41] In other words, they were Chicago businessmen.

Auerbach's description of the Wrights applies well to another intergenerational team that would dominate Illinois horse racing for nearly four decades: Benjamin Franklin Lindheimer and his adopted daughter, Marjorie. Just as Warren Wright was moving south, Ben Lindheimer, a local businessman closely aligned with the new Democratic governor, had his eye on building a horse-racing empire. Ben was the son of Jacob Lindheimer, a Jewish saloon operator in Chicago's Bridgeport neighborhood who had ingratiated himself to Chicago's Irish political leaders to the point of obtaining a key job in the county treasurer's office and becoming an alderman.

Jacob Lindheimer promoted Henry Horner's political career. When Horner became governor, the important state post of Illinois Commerce Commission

chairman went to the man who was virtually Horner's brother, Benjamin. Ben
Lindheimer was born in 1890 in Bridgeport. According to an official biography issued by the Arlington and Washington Park Jockey Clubs, Ben's parents "were great horse race patrons and greatly interested in horse shows.
They always took young Ben with them to old Washington Park [at Sixty-
third Street and Cottage Grove Avenue], where he first learned to love the
sport."[42]

Building on Jacob's political ties, Ben Lindheimer became a prominent
Chicago real estate developer and property manager on the South Side and
in the Loop. At the height of the Roaring Twenties, Lindheimer joined with
Chicago's leading entertainment providers, the Balaban family, to open movie
theaters. He controlled the State-Lake Building and the Franklin-Jackson
Building in the Loop. In the process, the official biography states, "Ben was
developing the same exceptionally keen political judgment which made Jacob
a city power."[43] His civic activities included service on the executive committee
that managed philanthropist Julius Rosenwald's Michigan Boulevard Garden
Apartment project on the South Side and membership on the patronage-rich
South Park Board of Commissioners.

Like William and Warren Wright, Benjamin Lindheimer had no pedigree
in horse racing's genealogy, but he brought his acute entrepreneurial and
political skills to the sport. As head of the state commerce commission, he
pushed legislation to create the Illinois Racing Commission and to enact a
law that denied ownership or operation of racetracks to "persons engaged
in illegal business, bookmakers and any other types of undesirables." In 1935
he joined a group of prominent businesspersons to acquire the Washington
Park thoroughbred track in south suburban Homewood from John J. Lynch,
a prominent gambler and former associate of Moses L. Annenberg in the
General News Bureau, one of the national wire services for racetrack gamblers and bookmakers that were the object of bloody gangland warfare.
Lindheimer's associates in the Washington Park Jockey Club, by contrast,
included such respectable Chicago individuals as Laurence H. Armour of the
meatpacking family and Leonard S. Florsheim of the shoemaking family, as
well as Warren Wright and John Hertz.

Suburban Washington Park was the successor to the racecourse of the same
name built in Chicago's Washington Park, one of two great South Side parks
developed at the turn of the century. Mayor Carter Harrison II closed the
original Washington Park track in 1904 amid rising public outrage against
the evils of gambling and the escalating wars between competing racing operators, who liberally bombed or burned one another's establishments to keep
patrons inside their gates. Harrison's act of prohibition, to no one's surprise,
expanded the business of illegal bookmakers as well as wire service opera-

tors feeding betting odds and race results from tracks outside Harrison's jurisdiction. Chicagoans continued to bet on horses, but whatever tax receipts Chicago tracks might have generated for the city were lost. Without meaning to, Harrison helped to expand the foundation for modern organized crime in the city.

When horse racing was again legalized in 1922 under Mayor William Thompson, tracks were by then being built or renovated in the suburbs. With no racetracks in Chicago and the city mired in the depths of the Great Depression, Lindheimer and Chicago mayor Edward Kelly pushed for state legislation authorizing Chicago to license handbook operators, largely as a means of raising revenue desperately needed to pay Chicago's schoolteachers—the same fiscal crisis that had taken Mayor Anton Cermak to Florida to discuss federal relief with President Roosevelt. Handbook betting, the process by which bookies extend credit and gamblers do not have to visit the track betting windows, was allowed on the grounds of racetracks, but the proposed legislation would permit bookmaking to be licensed at 2,500 locations in Chicago. "Compared with this proposal for a vast system of legalized gambling dens, with its invitation for control by the remnants of the Capone mob and their political partners, the gang warfare during Prohibition might have resembled Sunday school musical chairs," wrote Henry Horner biographer Thomas Littlewood.[44]

The respectable owners of racetracks, where the odds on races were determined only by the amount bet on each horse at betting windows, did not oppose the presumably competitive business from even the most unsavory bookmakers. Bookmakers frequently carried bets directly to the track, thereby lowering the odds on favorites and reducing their risk of a big payoff. Legalized off-track bookmaking would stimulate public interest in horse racing, which was always good for track owners. And the system would enable breeders and track operators to exploit the gambling propensities of the working classes, especially African Americans migrating into Chicago, while not tarnishing their facade of gentility by having these people show up at the tracks.

Horner found himself wedged between emotional opposition to the bill in the Protestant strongholds of Southern Illinois (where, ironically, state legislators Paul Powell and other powerful advocates of harness racing ruled) and Kelly's threat of political retaliation if Horner did not sign the revenue-rich measure. He waited for several weeks before taking action just four hours before the bill would have become law in the absence of a gubernatorial decision. Horner vetoed the legislation, House Bill 1045, despite Attorney General Otto Kerner Sr.'s ruling that the measure was constitutional because it did not establish a lottery, which was prohibited by the constitution. Horner's veto message was unequivocal:

Changing conditions do warrant changes to customs and habits, of thoughts and action. But if we have fallen into conditions which are not what we may think they ought to be, this does not justify the lowering of standards. The principal argument for House Bill 1045 seems to be that it cannot be suppressed or eradicated and therefore it should be permitted, regulated and legalized with a portion of the profits accruing to government. It is readily admitted that the desire to gamble is found in most persons—perhaps in some form and to some extent in all persons. Its prevalence, however, does not stamp it as a virtue. Nor do I concede that public and commercialized gambling cannot largely be suppressed; even if it cannot be entirely eradicated. Because there are violations of a law, it does not follow that a law should be repealed. If there is any justification in legalized bookmaking, there is equal justification in legalizing all other forms of public gambling now prohibited. . . . So far as I know, legalized bookmaking has been proposed for no other state or city in the United States. No such law has been adopted for any other state or city. It will be without my aid if our state becomes the pioneer in legalized public and commercial gambling such as proposed in this bill. It is a hazardous experiment for a state to legalize a business which is now illegal everywhere in the country.[45]

Horner's stern, morally grounded rebuke of bookmaking caused the Kelly-Nash Democratic organization to bitterly oppose his 1936 bid for reelection. Ben Lindheimer quit the Horner administration and turned his attention to his private business affairs. In 1940 he followed in the footsteps of Warren Wright by forming a group of prominent businesspeople to acquire the Arlington Park thoroughbred track. Other stockholders included John D. Allen, president of Brinks and Company; John G. McCarthy, president of the Chicago Board of Trade; Daniel F. Rice, a major grain broker; and commercial radio magnate Ralph Atlass.

In 1941 the legislature created the Illinois Racing Board and placed a tax on pari-mutuel betting at racetracks, making the state a direct partner in the racing industry. From then on state complicity in the horse-racing industry was rationalized on the basis of generating public revenue, although much of the tax found its way back into state programs benefiting only horse racing. Lindheimer cooperated with the new state-racing partnership, spending millions of dollars to improve his two tracks and paying nearly half the $195 million in state taxes collected on pari-mutuel horse-track gambling between 1941 and his death in 1960.

Lindheimer also struggled to keep his racing operations free of organized crime figures. In 1953 Jack Guzik, the aging former Capone bookkeeper who became a figure of mythical proportions in newspaper coverage of the post-Capone Chicago crime syndicate, bought three hundred shares of Arlington Park Jockey Club, the Lindheimer-controlled entity that owned and conducted racing meets at Arlington Park. Lindheimer vowed to bar Guzik from the track, prompting Guzik to file suit and demand an audit of Arlington's records. Guzik, almost always referred to in the newspapers as the "brains behind the Capone organization," acknowledged he was a gambler and called Lindheimer a hypocrite who at one time had willingly accepted Guzik's bets. Guzik told reporters he wanted to challenge the state law that permitted gambling inside the fences of racetracks but not bookmaking outside them.

Sounding like Anton Cermak in his populist campaign against drinking laws decades earlier, Guzik said: "I'd like to see the handbooks get going again, because then a poor working guy didn't have to lose a day's pay to go to the track. And he didn't have to pay admission price and all of those other expenses besides having to make a minimum $2 bet."[46] Lindheimer fought back against Guzik's encroachment, and the two old men battled each other in court, enriching their lawyers, until Guzik died at age sixty-nine in 1956. Lindheimer's law firm, Kirkland, Fleming, Green, Martin, and Ellis, mourned the passing of the "Guzik that laid the golden eggs."[47]

Although Lindheimer controlled the Arlington Park Jockey Club and Washington Park Jockey Club, he did not own all the stock, which, as is the case with thousands of closely held corporations, was not traded publicly. Lindheimer sought to keep the illiquid stock in friendly hands, and when existing shareholders died or wanted out, he searched to find appropriate buyers. On October 11, 1950, after shareholder Emil Schwarzhaupt died, Lindheimer offered an option to buy 3,000 shares of both Arlington Park Jockey Club and Washington Park Jockey Club from Schwarzhaupt's estate to Jacob Arvey, chairman of the Cook County Democratic Organization. "You stated you might be interested in purchasing said block of stock for some of your friends or yourself," Lindheimer wrote. The option agreement bears the signatures of Arvey and Lindheimer.[48] Arvey told a reporter in 1972: "There were some people who thought I had influence over the Illinois Racing Board, but I never did and I never had anything to do with the board. Mr. Lindheimer apparently thought he was doing me a favor, and I guess he was, because I did make money on the later sale of the stock."[49]

At Lindheimer's side throughout this period was the youngest of his three adopted children, Marjorie, born in 1921, his only child to take an active interest in his racing empire and the first woman in America to hold a top administrative post in a horse-racing enterprise. She signed the Lindheimer-Arvey option agreement as a witness. Marjorie's relationship with her influential father was similar to Helena Cermak's relationship with her father, Anton Cermak. Both men doted on their youngest daughters, as many fathers do. Unlike many men in business, however, they also shared with their daughters the intimate details of their working lives and brought them into their occupations as if, in the more traditional family process, the daughters had been sons.

In the 1930s there was no chance for a woman like Helena Cermak to carry on her father's political ambitions. But Marjorie Lindheimer, who stood five-foot-nine and weighed 150 pounds and gave her birthplace as Albany, New York, was determined that nothing would stop her from someday gaining control of her adoptive father's racing enterprise and running it in Lindheimer's image. Journalist Hank Messick, in his book about Illinois's racetrack scandal of the late 1960s, *The Politics of Prosecution*, described Marjorie Lindheimer as a "tall, gangling teenager" who had stayed close to Ben Lindheimer's side when he built his racing enterprise: "Marjorie became Lindheimer's pet, was permitted to accompany him everywhere and sit in on conferences with trainers, lawyers and politicians. . . . By April, 1940, when Arlington Park was acquired, Marje, as the press and racing industry knew her, had become an official assistant to Lindheimer."[50] In 1957 she married Web Everett, a man twenty-five years older than herself.

Despite her best efforts, which included continuing her father's practice of drawing on a track slush fund to lavish cash and gifts on politicians, journalists, and others, Marjorie Everett believed she was constantly under siege. A woman of mercurial disposition and single-minded toughness in business, she cast herself as a victim of those who would do her—and therefore Illinois racing—wrong. Given the questionable backgrounds of Wiedrick, Johnston, and other Illinois racing entrepreneurs, Everett's claim had considerable legitimacy.

After Lindheimer died in 1960, his political instincts lived on in Everett. On the advice of William S. Miller, a long-time Democratic operative and Stevenson appointee to the Illinois Racing Board, Everett correctly sensed a shift in Illinois's political wind. She fired the Kirkland law firm, which was allied closely with Republicans and the Midwest's powerful Republican newspaper the *Chicago Tribune*. Weymouth Kirkland, a founder of the influential law firm whose partners at one time included Capone-era prosecutor and Republican governor Dwight Green, had been one of Warren Wright's investors in Arlington Park. She gave the largest single cash gift, $45,000, to Otto Kerner's 1960 campaign for governor and made it clear to Kerner that she represented the best interests of Illinois horse racing and its partner, the state. She hired Kerner's closest associate, Theodore Isaacs, to help resolve her father's estate. When Democrat Otto Kerner, believed by many to be a puppet of Mayor Daley, assumed the governor's chair, she retained Daley's former law partners, William J. Lynch and George J. Schaller, as her legal counselors.

In the 1960s Illinois racing and Everett's racing empire flourished, as she quietly salted the state legislature with shares of stock in her racing enterprises and earmarked shares for Kerner and Isaacs. The Illinois legislature enacted bills favorable to Everett's interests—including bills permitting her to create a new, out-of-state corporation for her racing enterprises that consolidated her harness racing and thoroughbred businesses. To achieve regulatory efficiency and, not incidentally, to solidify her friend Miller's regulatory power, the legislature merged the Illinois Harness Racing Commission into the Illinois Racing Board, with Miller as chairman.

Bills detrimental to her interests, including several sponsored by South Side reform legislator Abner Mikva, were shelved. Mikva recalled years later that one of Everett's lawyers, Joseph Zoline, offered him private legal business, an offer that Mikva assumed to be a bribe and rejected. Whatever enthusiasm Mikva held for Kerner evaporated when the governor called him in during a debate on racing reform legislation and complained that he was being too hard on Everett. "It was as stern as Otto has ever been with me," he recalled.[51] Kerner argued that Mikva's attempt to increase the state tax on pari-mutuel betting would diminish track patronage and lower state revenues. Dawn Clark, his assistant, sided with Mikva in the argument.

Politicians were not the only ones Everett sought to influence. She showered track reporters and columnists with gifts. Only a handful returned them. Two of her former publicity writers recounted their experiences in a November 1971 article in the *Chicago Journalism Review:*

> Marje Everett handled the press as she handled politicians, wooing them not with stock profits but with gift certificates, Christmas presents, sumptuous luncheons, cash payments for participation in promotional events and summer jobs for reporters' children. . . . She made life easy for them however she could, even writing their stories for them. The prose of your favorite turf columnist might have come from a 22-year-old publicity writer. We know, because during the four seasons we worked for Everett, from 1965 to 1968, we personally wrote many columns that appeared under the by-lines of well-known Chicago sportswriters. . . . All Everett demanded in return was the reporters' loyalty.[52]

During this time many of the men who had become shareholders in Washington and Arlington Parks during the Lindheimer era grew restless with Everett's management style and the lack of liquidity in their stock, most of which Everett had pledged to the First National Bank of Chicago as collateral for loans she took out to buy Arlington Park and Washington Park stock from her family members and to renovate Washington Park for winter-time harness racing. The minority shareholders grew anxious about Everett's habit of spreading shares of a newly formed racing association, Washington Park Trotters Association, around Springfield. Nevertheless, attendance and gross receipts at Illinois racetracks, which had stagnated during the 1950s, grew steadily during Kerner's years as governor, enriching the state treasury and owners of stock in Illinois racing corporations.

The state collected a percentage of the total amount wagered, the "handle," on a progressive tax-rate system; the state also collected an admissions tax on racetrack patrons and received half of the "breakage," the amount collected simply by rounding a bettor's winnings down to the nearest ten-cent increment. Annual horse-racing revenue to the state more than doubled, from $18 million in 1960, when Kerner defeated Stratton, to $40 million in 1968, when Kerner left office. In Stratton's two terms annual state revenue had ranged from $16 million to $18 million. During the Kerner years track attendance and total racing handle grew much more rapidly in Illinois than in the other major horse-racing states.

Illinois politicians from both parties and from one end of the state to the other had a stake in both sides of the partnership as public overseers of the industry and as stockholders of horse-racing associations. A legislative investigating commission reported in 1974 that Illinois racing had been "a forum for three vested interests—the State, the racing associations and the horsemen. Each . . . followed a course of self-enrichment."[53] It could have added a fourth vested interest, many individual legislators and state officials. Assessing the situation in 1972, *Wall Street Journal* writer Frederick C. Klein wrote, "No state . . . surpasses Illinois in the variety and mischievousness of political involvement in horse racing."[54]

By the late 1960s Illinois racing was ruled by a seven-member racing board appointed by the governor that each November assigned licenses to racing associations, allowing them to conduct racing meets on certain dates. Because of the bombings and arson that went on when tracks competed for patrons early in the century, state law required the board to grant exclusive dates to racing associations in the Chicago area and, separately, downstate. Most of the racing associations receiving dates were "paper associations"—they owned no racetracks or anything else but merely leased track facilities for racing meets on the dates they were awarded. Their only asset was the license issued by the racing board, which in terms of economic reality was nothing more than the right to collect the "handle" of 8 percent of the total amount wagered at Chicago-area tracks and 9 percent at downstate tracks. Racing associations also picked up the other half of the "breakage." Although some paper racing associations invested in track improvements, most did not. Washington Park Trotters Association and Chicago Harness Racing, Incorporated, were paper associations established after Ben Lindheimer's death to run harness races at Washington Park. Two of the most notorious paper associations were the Egyptian Trotting Association, run by a downstate legislator named Clyde Lee, and the Fox Valley Trotting Club, operated by William Johnston.

Newspaper publishers and editors in Chicago, many of whom were unabashed bettors and racing enthusiasts, overlooked substantial conflicts of interest when it came to covering the Illinois Racing Board and the state's racing
industry, a fact that helps to explain why for decades the transparent corruption in the industry was the subject of casual bragging in Springfield saloons
but not crusades in newsrooms. The *Tribune, Sun-Times,* and *Daily News* all
owned paper racing associations on behalf of publicity-generating charity racing
meets held on choice dates awarded every year by the Illinois Racing Board.
Newspaper officials, including *Chicago Sun-Times* editor Milbourne P. Akers,
were investors in the sure thing of Illinois racing enterprises.

Although they could not compete with the speed of the racing wire services, Chicago's newspapers built circulation by offering racing tips as seriously as they could and publishing racing results as quickly as they could.
Fiercely competitive afternoon newspapers were called the "turf edition"
because they carried the latest track information. In 1951 the *Tribune's* political reporter, George Tagge, who for years performed double duty as the
newspaper's Springfield lobbyist, won legislative approval of a measure to
finance the McCormick Place lakefront exposition center from taxes collected
on pari-mutuel wagering at thoroughbred racetracks. Like the state, the news
media were intimate partners in the racing industry.

Because racing dates were awarded annually each November, Marjorie
Everett and other racetrack owners who needed to borrow for capital improvements often found banks unwilling to lend without knowing what, if
any, racing dates the tracks would receive for themselves and for the paper
associations that would lease their tracks in the coming season. The process
of awarding dates was the critical variable in the business of being a track
owner or a racing association stockholder. Unfavorable dates meant fewer
quality horses, reduced fan attendance, and a smaller handle. The racing board
faced a difficult balancing act in awarding dates fairly and objectively, yet the
men appointed by Illinois governors to serve on the board often had no direct experience in the industry. Many were horse-racing dilettantes and rich
businesspeople who fancied themselves in the horsey set; others were well-
meaning but naïve political appointees who were no match for shrewd entrepreneurs such as Marjorie Everett, William Miller, and William Johnston
and politicians such as Paul Powell and Clyde Lee.

The individuals appointed to serve on the racing board may not have been
reputed gangsters, but they were hardly more likely to improve the sound-
ness of Illinois horse racing. "The state's system of regulation is outdated,
inefficient and fraught with potentialities for mismanagement and abuse," a
legislative investigating commission concluded in 1973. "Since its inception,
the Illinois racing board has ruled racing in Illinois with an iron hand. Un-

fortunately, the board has never possessed the requisite degree of racing experience to temper its positions and to plan its own actions."[55] Illinois racing was a well-entrenched and systematic realm of corruption, and Marjorie Lindheimer Everett was its queen.

◆ ◆ ◆

Internal Revenue Service agents in Springfield had nosed around the edges of the racetrack stock scandal for years, but the broad-brush IRS investigation called the Chicago Special Project did not target the state's horse-racing industry. Shirley Kub had not gossiped about the racing industry to Special Agent Jack Walsh. In the early days of the Chicago Special Project, there were plenty of other targets for Walsh's core team of a dozen special agents.

Project member William Witkowski, an intense, crew-cut special agent whose memory for details was legendary among his peers, suspected that Walsh levered his knowledge of internal corruption in the IRS to "build his own little empire" within the IRS bureaucracy. "I don't know if that's true or not, but that's my feeling," he said in an interview.[56] Witkowski, who joined the IRS in 1966, met Walsh when the two worked on the Northlake investigation involving Sam Battaglia, Joseph Amabile, and William Riley. When Walsh took his suspicions about internal corruption in the Chicago district office to Regional Director Kelley, Witkowski went along. "No one within the district knew what he was working on," Witkowski recalled.[57]

After Bush brought Walsh's team back into the district domain, Witkowski watched the Chicago Special Project expand. He was twenty-seven years old when Walsh put him on the multiphase Chicago Special Project team. Witkowski said that CRIMP, the acronym adopted in the spring of 1970, came to mean among his colleagues "Conception, Refinement, Implementation, Manpower and Promotion."[58] In the spring and summer of 1970, thirty-five special agents were detailed to Project CRIMP. Shirley Kub's theories and anecdotes were either unknown or incidental to the fact that Walsh's zeal brought the team members many intriguing cases and what seemed like carte blanche to pursue them, Witkowksi said.

"One area was state highway construction, which you can do anytime," Witkowksi recalled blandly. The probe included a host of construction contractors doing business with the state under the domain of public works director Francis Lorenz. "One area was the assessor's office," he said.[59] Investigators believed the office of Cook County assessor Patrick Joseph "Parky" Cullerton, a former alderman and close ally of Mayor Daley, routinely demanded payoffs for underassessing real estate, especially commercial real estate. Cullerton's head of real estate assessments was another member of Daley's inner circle, the Democratic committeeman from west suburban Proviso Township named Ralph "Babe" Serpico, better known to many as a former University of Illinois football star. Another target was Daley's Democratic committeeman from northwest suburban Wheeling Township, James Stavros. Shirley Kub had told Walsh that brothers James and Gus Stavros and their bootlegger father, Harry, all had ties to the Chicago Outfit.

Walsh's team produced a batch of indictments against functionaries in the Democratic Party. The project struck hardest at the office of the Cook County assessor, where more than a dozen former officials were indicted and convicted on income tax charges in connection with taking bribes to lower assessments. Many, including Babe Serpico, chose to plead guilty. Cullerton, though, escaped untouched by Project CRIMP. In 1974, at age seventy-six, he retired after Daley slated a younger man for the job. In the suburban corruption probe, James Stavros pleaded guilty to tax charges relating to extortion of builders for zoning changes. Francis Lorenz was never charged with a crime or linked publicly to any government investigation. Lorenz, a prominent Polish public official in Mayor Daley's always ethnically balanced organization, ran unsuccessfully for Illinois attorney general in 1968. After Republicans won the White House and the governor's mansion in 1968, outgoing Democratic governor Samuel Shapiro appointed Lorenz to the Cook County Circuit Court. In 1970 he was elected to the Illinois Court of Appeals.

Ironically, one person punished was Shirley Kub. At age eighty-five, the former mascot of West Side gangster Billy Skidmore and source to investigators Alexander Jamie and Jack Walsh over a three-decade span was found guilty by the U.S. Tax Court of failing to report income obtained, according to sworn testimony at her trial, as her share of political payoffs. The seemingly inconsequential case against Kub, who was too ill to attend her trial, was fought in the United States Tax Court over more than six years, with senior officials of the IRS from Washington representing the government against her, even though the final amount of tax delinquency found was less than $10,000 over six years, 1962 through 1967. William A. Barnett, a former IRS agent and Chicago lawyer who represented Kub, told the tax court that it was clear Kub was being harassed for failing to cooperate more fully with IRS investigators. In a 1996 interview Barnett added, "There wasn't any doubt that she was something of a bag lady."[60] In 1977, long after Project CRIMP had faded into the files of the IRS and Kub was nearly ninety years old, a three-judge federal appeals panel, including William J. Bauer, who was the U.S. attorney for Chicago during much of the CRIMP era, upheld the Tax Court decision against Shirley Kub and ruled admissible the evidence of Lorenz's alleged involvement in the payoff scheme.

The list of CRIMP indictments was long but shallow. Supervisor Robert Bush recalled years later, "We walked away from the whole project never

having proven the three-legged thing," the overarching "true syndicate" conspiracy among hoodlums, politicians, and businesspeople that the voluble
Shirley Kub had impressed on Jack Walsh.[61] Project CRIMP might have passed
quietly into history as a late vestige of Robert Kennedy's federal crime-busting campaign of the early 1960s had it not been for another talkative woman:
Marjorie Everett.

◆ ◆ ◆

Just as she had ingratiated herself to the Kerner administration eight
years earlier, Everett eagerly sought to make friends with the newly elected
Republican administration of Governor Richard Ogilvie in 1969. Moreover,
she wanted friends in the IRS, which was raising questions about her claim
of a capital loss on her 1966 tax return regarding the sale of Chicago Thoroughbred Enterprises, the Delaware-based corporation Everett formed as the
successor to Ben Lindheimer's Arlington Park and Washington Park Jockey
Clubs. Everett had disposed of the nagging minority shareholders in Chicago
Thoroughbred Enterprises, many of whom were friends of her father, by selling her controlling interest to a New York conglomerate called Gulf and
Western Industries, with the understanding she could stay on as chief executive officer. But politicians were becoming a bigger headache, despite her
previous generosity with racing association stock. Springfield constantly
threatened to draw more state tax revenue from the racing industry, and demands mounted for racing reforms.

Even more urgent was Everett's bitter fall out with William Miller, her one-
time mentor and the former chairman of the Illinois Racing Board under Kerner. For most of the 1960s, Everett and Miller had been friends and allies in
expanding the former Lindheimer racing empire. Miller coyly referred to their
association as a father-daughter relationship based on his solemn promise to
the dying Lindheimer to help maintain the racetrack business in his family.
Miller had operated on the inside as chairman of the Illinois Racing Board,
and Everett had done so on the outside as the "Queen of Illinois Racing." But
Everett went to war against Miller after he quit the racing board in 1967 and
began to fulfill his ambition to be a racing entrepreneur, even at her expense.

Seeking new allies, in 1969 Everett made it her business to meet George
Mahin, the former Better Government Association crime fighter who headed
Ogilvie's transition team and later became Illinois director of revenue. Mahin
listened to Everett's story of being oppressed by ruthless, powerful men and
quickly introduced her to his friend from Northlake days, Special Agent Jack
Walsh. At a meeting in Mahin's North Michigan Avenue apartment in Chicago, Everett spelled out what Walsh later described as a classic "Hobbs Act
extortion" case, in which Miller had forced her to pay tribute to political

figures in return for the suitable racing dates she needed to sustain her late father's business and keep her tracks in clean hands.

The Hobbs Act is a federal statute enacted in 1947 against labor racketeering. It became a favorite weapon of federal prosecutors fighting organized crime. The law makes it a crime to inhibit interstate commerce by extortion, defined as "the obtaining of property from another with his consent by wrongful use of actual or threatened force, violence, or fear, or under color of official right." According to Everett, the despicable William Miller coerced her to sell stock to state politicians who held life-and-death power over her business through the state's taxing and regulatory powers. Miller engineered the shakedown and pushed her unwittingly into the cesspool of Springfield corruption, she said. To Mahin and Walsh, Everett's story differed from William Riley's only in the details, including the idea that state regulations had replaced baseball bats and burning cigarettes as tools of extortion.

But there was more, a bombshell disclosure by Everett that instantly gave the Chicago Special Project the stature Walsh had dreamed of but not yet achieved. Everett said that Miller had forced her to influence Governor Otto Kerner by issuing to him and his associate Ted Isaacs fifty shares of her precious Chicago Thoroughbred Enterprises stock. The shares were pledged as collateral at the First National Bank of Chicago against loans Everett had secured with Miller's help to upgrade her tracks. Transferring them to Kerner and Isaacs was a major sacrifice, Everett implied.

Until that moment Kerner's name had been on Walsh's "true syndicate" charts solely because he had appointed Lorenz as Illinois director of public works. Kerner seemed an unreachable star in Walsh's constellation of corruption. The charts contained nothing about Miller, Everett, or other names in the Illinois racetrack scandal that would soon erupt. Walsh realized he had been handed dynamite. He and his superiors immediately took Everett's testimony to Washington and solicited the interest of the highest levels of the Justice Department and Internal Revenue Service.

The Chicago Special Project was authorized under President Johnson and continued under President Nixon as one of the occasional federal law-enforcement incursions into local political corruption in Chicago over many decades. Now the IRS aimed its sights on a national figure: the upstanding and sincere Cassandra of America's cities, federal judge Otto Kerner. This was no Parky Cullerton or other functionary of the Daley machine, little known outside Chicago. This was the square-jawed war veteran and Mr. Clean governor of network television fame, whose best-selling report on the 1967 urban riots gave white Americans a warning that they did not want to hear and largely refused to believe. In his 1968 campaign for the White House, Nixon had denounced the notion that white Americans should blame themselves for black protests and had seen this rhetoric resonate effectively in the North as well as the South. Except for Senator Strom Thurmond, however, who objected to Kerner's appointment to the U.S. Circuit Court of Appeals, no one in authority, including Nixon, had publicly questioned Kerner's standing as a model of exemplary public service.

There was no rush to judgment in Washington after Walsh first presented Everett's story, contrary to the suggestion in Messick's book of a Nixon administration campaign dedicated to "getting Otto's ass."[62] Nixon had cavalierly ordered investigations of the tax returns of organizations and individuals who opposed his policies, but investigating the returns of a respected federal appeals court judge from Mayor Daley's organization would not be undertaken casually. It required long, disciplined work and had to be held in strict secrecy, lest Nixon find himself accused of unconstitutional interference with the federal judiciary. IRS officials in Washington left the case in the hands of the special project team, a decision that probably made Walsh's barrel chest swell with pride but also revealed the instinctive wariness of Washington bureaucrats facing a potentially explosive problem. "This became another phase of CRIMP," Walsh recalled.[63]

Walsh discussed the case and the theory of CRIMP directly with an anxious Randolph W. Thrower, Nixon's first appointee as IRS commissioner and a man not cast in the mold of Robert Kennedy or Mortimer Caplin. Thrower believed the primary mission of the IRS was to collect taxes, not to pursue expensive, high-profile cases against organized crime and public corruption that yielded the Treasury little in the way of cash receipts. For many months, "whatever CRIMP needed, CRIMP got," Walsh recalled.[64] But it was up to Walsh and his team to confirm or reject Marje Everett's story.

In Chicago the wariness was even more intense. U.S. Attorney William J. Bauer, who at the time was seeking a seat on the federal district court, was kept in the dark for months about Project CRIMP. When he was summoned to a top-secret meeting at the Justice Department in Washington in October 1970—well after the Kerner investigation began—he listened skeptically for the first time to Special Agent Walsh's story of the "true syndicate." The meeting was conducted in code, with letters instead of names, and no one was allowed to take notes, Bauer recalled. A veteran of suburban Du Page County Republican politics who had to swim in the same pond as the Cook County Democrats, Bauer had no sympathy for the Washington cloak-and-dagger theatrics. He demanded to know the names of the Project CRIMP targets on his turf, and when he heard the name Otto Kerner, he turned to Johnnie M. Walters, an assistant attorney general in charge of the tax division, and said,

"I told you you were full of shit before, and now I think you're crazy." Bauer's main concern was to keep his eye on the probe. "I'm not that enamored of the IRS," Bauer said years later. "Their general theory is we're all crooks."[65]

Walsh and the other post–Robert Kennedy G-men on his IRS team fully subscribed to that theory, especially where Illinois political figures of either party, including Bauer, were concerned. But Walsh knew he was on thin ice in targeting a pillar of the Chicago political establishment and a nationally admired federal judge. Already Kerner had thrown out the second Amabile conviction from the Northlake investigation on the grounds of double jeopardy. "You never shoot at a sitting judge and wound him, because if he comes up wounded he's going to tear you apart," Walsh said later.[66]

Walsh assigned two of his men to what then became the racetrack phase of Project CRIMP, William Witkowski and a special agent about as different from Witkowski in appearance and demeanor as can be imagined, Oliver Perry Stufflebeam. The new partners could easily have stepped out of John le Carré's George Smiley spy novels. Witkowski was a quiet, lunch-bucket investigator, a diligent civil servant who did not mind drinking his coffee cold and spending hour on hour examining the recorded minutia of Illinois's racing industry and the tax filings of Illinois politicians. He had a marketing degree from Chicago's DePaul University, where the dean's secretary, a relative of his wife, passed him job notices from the IRS as well as from the Central Intelligence Agency and the FBI, each of which seemed more exciting than the insurance company job he quit to join the IRS in 1966. Walsh called him "the best investigator I've ever come into contact with."[67] He had turned to Witkowski to rebuild the Northlake case after Judge Kerner threw out the convictions.

Stufflebeam, known as "Pete" or "O.P.," a lanky, gregarious all-American boy, stood six foot four. He hailed from a well-to-do family in downstate Danville. His great-grandfather, the first of three Oliver Perry Stufflebeams in the family, had been mayor of Rossville, a town just north of Danville. He received an accounting degree from the University of Illinois in 1965. After graduation he dabbled in real estate investing on Chicago's trendy Near North Side and patronized the Four Farthings, a popular Near North Side tavern for young professionals. Stufflebeam, who never married, had no intention of remaining a career government employee. When the Kerner case began, he was considering several career options outside the federal service.

Stufflebeam was known to leave his paychecks in his drawer for months at a time. Fellow agents delighted in his low-key, aw-shucks style of interrogation, an effective combination of seeming indifference and vulnerability that put many interviewees at ease, usually to their peril. Stufflebeam had probed contributions to Kerner's 1964 campaign as a part of Operation Snowball.

"He was one of the original free spirits; he was really out of place in government. You don't see too many people like Pete in the government bureaucracy," recalled Darrell McGowen, a Justice Department official from Washington assigned to the Kerner case. "He walked like a farm boy who was walking through plowed ground."[68] Most important, he made a friendly and engaging witness on the stand before juries usually inclined to be intimidated or put off by stern, exact government tax investigators. Together "he and Witkowski would not be satisfied untying the Gordian knot; they would unravel the rope," said Paul J. Schaeffer, a Justice Department official who worked on the Kerner case.[69]

Stufflebeam was thinking of quitting the IRS when he and Witkowski began poring over the tax returns of Otto Kerner, Theodore Isaacs, and numerous state politicians named by Everett as acolytes of her nemesis, William Miller. In the countless hours they spent interviewing Everett, she turned on the charm and solicited their sympathy. "You have to understand Marje Everett," Witkowski said later by way of acknowledging that he did not. "I spent a lot of time with her, I mean a *lot* of time. I won't want to guesstimate how many hours I spent with her—both in Phoenix [where Everett had a home], and her apartment in Chicago. Wherever she was going, it was, 'come along guys, I'll pay everything, we'll meet down there,' and away we'd go. I think most of the time the G [government] picked it up, but she would always make the offer, and I'm sure she would have paid it. I don't know how to explain her. She's a very different woman."[70]

Witkowski and Stufflebeam never experienced the hard side of Everett, a side that employees at Arlington Park and many business associates saw daily. "She was very nice to us, because we kept her out of jail and everything," Witkowski said.

> Marje came through George Mahin; she wanted help and figured she could use the G to get a lot of help. She didn't want all the politicians messing around with Arlington Park, and she figured it would be nice to be able to call [and say], "Hey guys, lay off or I'll call IRS, and I know these eight guys." I think that's the way it actually started. She felt guys really owed her a lot, and she could pick up the phone and get what she wanted, and that wasn't happening. So to bring them in line and to show, "Hey, guys, if you don't, I'll have the government get you," she went to Mahin, who came to us.[71]

IRS investigators sensed immediately that Everett would make a convincing trial witness. She had the ability to mask her ruthless core completely. *Chicago Sun-Times* columnist Jack Griffin put it this way: "For all her rigid will, there has always been a certain strange shyness about her. By her own admission, she was a wallflower. 'I wasn't a particularly popular girl,' she said once."[72] In depositions and later in trial testimony, she peppered her responses to male inquisitors with the word *sir,* suggesting anxious solicitude and even subservience, a feigned attitude that would play well to a jury. Like Shirley Kub, however, Everett failed to recognize the hard side of IRS agents. Jack Walsh's Project CRIMP team was out to build cases, not friendships.

Witkowski said Everett did not intend to be the snitch who would get Kerner, Isaacs, or even Miller indicted. "Oh, never, never, never, no; she did not. I don't think she meant to do anything. She wasn't very forthright as far as making stock available to people. We found all that, but it took hours of work, a *lot* of hours of work. I think she thought like you can do many times if you're friendly with the local police chief and you've got problems and you can call him and he'll send somebody over."[73]

Despite the arresting details of her story, the agents knew Everett's testimony would not be enough. "There was grave concern on the part of Stufflebeam and Witkowski that we were going up a blind alley, and it was going to be the end of their careers," Walsh recalled. The demanding process of matching Everett's testimony with documents, including Kerner's and Isaac's tax returns, had to reveal a crime. "You never take a witness at face value," Walsh said.[74] The breakthrough came one night in the spring of 1970 when Walsh, Witkowski, and Stufflebeam scrawled on a blackboard in their office the key features of Everett's story and the 1968 tax returns from Kerner and Isaacs. "We said, shit, they've got capital gains treatment on a payoff; there really is a criminal violation here," Walsh recalled.[75] The agents believed they had discovered what would come to be the cornerstone of the IRS theory of the case: Everett, threatened by state officials' power over her livelihood, had sold Kerner and Isaacs stock in Chicago Thoroughbred Enterprises at a below-market, bargain price. The two men, in disposing of the stock, had declared a capital gain on what should have been reported as ordinary income from their extortion of Everett.

"Washington notified somebody in Chicago, and we were given the go-ahead to open up the [criminal] investigation," Walsh said.[76] Serious bureaucratic tension quickly developed between Walsh and his superiors in Washington as Walsh's "true syndicate" suspicions shifted into high gear. While steering clear of instructing Walsh—orders that could expose them to responsibility—officials in the Justice Department were demanding constant updates on his work, including the required initial interview with Judge Kerner that would have to be conducted shortly. Walsh did not trust anyone beyond his own team, including higher-ups in Washington and Chicago. "We had Kerner under surveillance. Washington kept wanting to know the results of the interview. We wanted, out of respect for the position, to talk to the judge without anyone else finding out we were interviewing him. No one in the Justice Department was forewarned."[77] On Wednesday, July 15, 1970, a day when

Witkowski was off work on personal business, an agent tailing Kerner alerted Walsh that the judge was alone in his office. Stufflebeam and a substitute special agent, Robert F. Campbell, rushed to Kerner's chambers and arrived at 10:30 A.M.

As Stufflebeam wrote later that day, in a memorandum that would be vital to the government's case: "We asked the receptionist if we could see Judge Kerner. She asked who we were and we identified ourselves as Special Agents of the Internal Revenue Service and stated that we wanted to see Judge Kerner on a personal matter. The receptionist went into Judge Kerner's private office and returned and told us we could enter. We entered the private office and were greeted by Judge Kerner. We introduced ourselves as Special Agents of the Internal Revenue Service and showed the judge our credentials."[78]

◆ ◆ ◆

It would not be stretching a point to describe that morning as the defining moment in Otto Kerner's life. It was a warm and blustery day in Chicago, with winds gusting to forty miles an hour, knocking trees into power lines and causing power outages. Until then Kerner, at age sixty-one, was heading for a place in the Illinois history books as a good governor, a good appellate judge, and a good husband and father. He was out of the political fray. As far as he knew, no one wished him ill, nor did he wish anyone ill. He possessed little clout, as they say in Chicago, but neither was he bothered by the political supplicants and hangers-on that power attracts. He had achieved an honorable and comfortable seat on the federal appeals court in Chicago, where his father had served ably until his death and where he advanced the cause of civil liberties and spoke out convincingly on the content and recommendations of the Kerner Commission Report through two anniversaries. Independent of politics and his new judicial role, Kerner believed in the report and used his stature to keep it before the public.

Privately he continued to shelter his wife, Helena, who despite frequent rambling phone calls to his law clerks and secretary was pretty much under control. His private life at last was his own. He enjoyed the professional collegiality of the appeals court and the interaction with his young law clerks, who in turn enjoyed remarkable freedom in writing opinions on cases assigned to him. He was welcome in Chicago high society and had time to enjoy his access. Like many other veterans of politics, the military, and other high-profile public service careers, Kerner believed he had earned respect and deference, but he had lost none of his quiet charm and gentlemanly warmth toward others.

What he had lost, if he ever had it, was the base instinct of fear, without which no one can survive the rigors of politics, with or without a lifetime judicial appointment. Fear is a primitive, animal instinct that in politics means constant vigilance, constant distrustfulness, constant calculation of the odds, and constant second-guessing of the motives of close associates as well as strangers and one's self. It means wanting never to be surprised by anyone or anything. Mayor Daley had it; Presidents Johnson and Nixon had it. Otto Kerner did not. Critics later called him naïve, stupid, and arrogant. Outside politics he might just as accurately have been called normal. But there is no doubt that he was off guard when the door closed behind Agents Stufflebeam and Campbell and he began to talk.

He could have, and should have, listened politely and silently to their overtures, including Stufflebeam's formal recitation of the Miranda warning against self-incrimination, and bid them adieu, leaving Walsh with nothing to tell his demanding Washington overlords and requiring weeks of additional investigation to establish a case that Washington wanted to be nailed down quickly or abandoned quickly. At the very least, Kerner could have asked the agents to return for a formal interview after he retained legal counsel, as Mayor Daley had done—along with hiring a stenographer—when the IRS called on him. But Kerner apparently did not feel the need to put up his guard or to seek legal advice. He may have believed his high office and reputation demanded that he cooperate with fellow officers of the justice system and that they would trust and respect him in return.

The morning's newspapers carried front-page articles concerning the ouster of Cook County Circuit Court judge Richard A. Napolitano by a panel of fellow judges for "conduct unbecoming a judge" and for violating the canons of judicial ethics. Napolitano, an Illinois legislator in Kerner's first term, had evoked his Fifth Amendment privilege when first questioned about a scandal involving the Illinois State Fair that bore an eerie resemblance to what soon would be front-page news about political influence in awarding Illinois racing dates. The judicial panel, following newspaper exposés, accused Napolitano of acquiring rights to well-situated concession stands at the annual fair in Springfield and selling them at hefty profits. He was charged with accepting two $1,000 bribes from a local dairy to influence state fair officials to award a favorable location for its concession. As part of that morning's front-page banner-headline coverage of the Napolitano affair, the *Tribune* published in full the fourth canon of judicial ethics—undoubtedly the first time most Chicagoans had seen it: "A judge's official conduct should be free of impropriety and the appearance of impropriety; he should avoid infractions of the law; and his personal behavior, not only upon the bench and in the performance of judicial duties, but also in his everyday life, should be above reproach."[79]

Kerner may have nodded in agreement as he read the article that morning, satisfied that his life was indeed beyond reproach. More than five months before he had been informed of an IRS audit of his 1968 tax return. This was no surprise. The IRS had audited Otto and Helena's tax returns many times since their marriage. After Helena's father died in 1933, Kerner recalled, an IRS agent questioned Helena's purchase of a car, based on a tip that Anton Cermak had left millions of dollars in unreported income that his daughters spirited from a safety deposit box. Kerner told the agent the family would gladly pay whatever tax was owed if the Cermak cash horde could be found. It never was. The Kerners lived well but frugally, in the best Czech tradition.

He had not spent campaign contributions for personal purposes, which was the basis of a so-called net worth case the IRS had brought in 1964 against Kerner's Springfield predecessor, Republican governor William Stratton. Stratton had cooperated with the IRS and had employed as his lawyers two former IRS agents, William D. Crowley and William A. Barnett, who would later represent Shirley Kub. Stratton was acquitted after his friend Senator Everett Dirksen won the jury over with an eloquent and convincing explanation of a politician's need to spend campaign money between elections to maintain a proper image of himself and his office.

Kerner probably recognized that morning the curiously disarming Special Agent Stufflebeam, who during Operation Snowball in 1968—not long after Kerner became a federal judge—had interviewed him and Isaacs in Kerner's chambers about campaign billboard financing in 1964. Stufflebeam and Isaacs developed a mutual dislike at the time. Kerner may have suspected that Stufflebeam and his new partner, Agent Campbell, were up to more of the same. With a Republican in the White House, investigations of Democrats were to be expected. He could not have expected that his inquisitors were following a lead from Marjorie Everett, whom he hardly knew, that had nothing to do with past audits, vague distinctions between personal and campaign spending, or the sources of dollars for his political billboards years earlier. He never could have known, and never did know, of the secret twenty-seven-point dossier on himself prepared many months earlier by Jack Walsh that began with the following chilling bits of intelligence:

1. Per Shirley Kub—Stated that one of the sets of Waterford crystal in her apartment was a gift from Governor Kerner's father.
2. Per Shirley Kub—Kerner is "syndicate" and is "high." Kerner is not from the old West Side "syndicate" but like Syd Smith [Chicago building commissioner] is "syndicate."[80]

Special Agent Campbell, thirty years old and a fresh recruit to the public corruption campaign, was called to the interview to comply with standard operating procedure requiring two special agents to be present and take notes whenever a suspect in a criminal case is interviewed. Campbell later disagreed with Walsh's recollection of haste or surprise in interviewing Kerner, although Witkowski's absence suggests a last-minute decision. He said Stufflebeam had called Kerner and made an appointment. In either case, Campbell, who hailed from a family of Chicago Democrats, had nothing invested in the Kerner inquiry and said he began the meeting with no preconceptions. "An awful lot of care had been made; we didn't want to drag his name through the mud," he recalled.[81]

The two agents sat on a couch while Kerner sat on a chair on the other side of a coffee table. Campbell recalled being surprised by Kerner's aloof and condescending manner, which seemed unnecessary and suggestive. Kerner was insulted by Stufflebeam's reading of the Miranda warning, reminding the agents that he was an ardent defender of the rule. He called Stufflebeam "young man," Campbell said. "I asked Judge Kerner if he fully understood his rights and he said, 'I certainly do,'" Stufflebeam wrote in his report.[82] "He got a little hot and a little indignant," Campbell recalled.[83]

Kerner acknowledged a cryptic entry on attachments to his 1967 Schedule D return, "C. T. Co. for Balmoral," related to sale of Balmoral racetrack stock that had been accepted in exchange for other racetrack stock of equal value. As to another entry on Schedule D attachments, he described "Chicago Co." as a Chicago-based financial institution among whose officers was a friend named Isidore Brown. He repeatedly denied that "Chicago Co." had anything to do with racing stock, according to Stufflebeam's memo. He expressed absolute confidence in Ted Isaacs and the role Isaacs played in arranging for his involvement in C. T. Company and Balmoral as a passive investor.

He said that Isaacs had arranged a loan from Kerner's director of financial institutions, Joseph Knight, to help pay for his C. T. Company shares and that Knight was the "nominee" masking his secret ownership. "He got really huffy" when Campbell asked him whether he had ever used his mother as a nominee, Campbell recalled, saying he quickly apologized to Kerner for the question.[84] Kerner spoke at length about his personal spending habits and financial lifestyle, insisting that he accepted no outside payments for speaking engagements and did not use credit cards. "He even mows his own grass," Stufflebeam wrote in his report. "As we were leaving, Kerner stated that he would like to see this investigation over as soon as possible so that this air of suspicion could be removed."[85]

Within minutes the agents were at Isaacs's office three blocks north in the Loop. Isaacs elaborated on his and Kerner's purchase of stock in Chicago Thoroughbred Enterprises (expressed as "C. T. Co." on Isaac's tax return as well as on Kerner's), financed by the Joseph Knight loan, and their later exchange of that stock for an equal value of Everett's shares in another racing entity, Balmoral Jockey Club, which was not encumbered as collateral by a bank. He also acknowledged having made another joint purchase, through William Miller, of shares in another paper racing association, Chicago Harness Racing. "Isaacs replied that he had made a joint purchase of this stock with another party but could not remember if this other party was Joe Knight or Judge Kerner," Stufflebeam wrote in his report later that day.[86]

July 15 saw a sweep by special agents probing racetrack stock deals. Several prominent businesspeople and investors in Everett's racing organizations were interviewed, including Harold H. Anderson, a prominent Republican contributor who was the nominee for *Sun-Times* editor Akers's racetrack stock holdings, and Modie J. Spiegel, heir to the mail-order establishment, who claimed that former Daley law partner William J. Lynch threatened him into selling his Chicago Harness Racing stock to Everett as she struggled to gain control of the association. When agents regrouped with Walsh, the day's events left them confused. Campbell remembered his late father's fondness for Kerner. "Are we screwed up, or is this guy lying?" Campbell had asked himself.[87] Stufflebeam told Walsh the "Chicago Co." entry was not racing stock. That meant the $22,400 long-term capital gain entered on Kerner's 1967 tax return could not be part of Everett's story. "When I came back, I thought we were wrong," Witkowski said.[88] The team worked until 9 P.M. sorting out their notes. The next day investigators went to see Isidore Brown, who flatly denied any knowledge of "Chicago Co." or any association with the private investment firm with a similar name, Chicago Corporation. Using his own words, and probably not Brown's, Witkowski recalled: "We went over and talked to this guy, and the guy told us, 'bullshit.' Brown told us Kerner is full of shit. Then we knew that something was wrong."[89] "I was convinced that day," Campbell said. "It was these fabrications that fueled the investigation."[90] "We knew Kerner had lied," said Walsh.[91]

Lying to an IRS agent is a federal crime in itself, but Kerner set the IRS on a much bigger hunt when he told the Isidore Brown story. Despite his years as "Mr. District Attorney," as J. Edgar Hoover disparagingly called him in 1947, and despite whatever he may have recalled about the hounding of automobile promoter Preston Tucker by the Securities and Exchange Commission, Kerner was not equipped for what would happen to him when relentless IRS investigators such as Witkowski and Stufflebeam got the scent of a lie. Kerner later swore that he had told the agents on July 15 that he was uncertain about the "Chicago Co." entry and had not lied. He said it was his word against theirs. Nonetheless, with their juices flowing, the two special agents worked throughout the summer and fall to establish a case. What they found was a maze of interrelated stock dealings, loans, and elaborate concealments that few minds, possibly except Ted Isaacs's and William Miller's, could have conceived. It looked as though Kerner and Isaacs had obtained racing stock at a below-market bargain price and sold it at a hefty profit, all the while keeping their transactions secret through the use of intermediaries and misleading tax return notations. "Chicago Co." was Chicago Harness.

But had the team established a case that could be brought to a federal grand jury under the Hobbs Act, as Walsh anticipated when he first met Marjorie Everett? The short answer was no. Indeed, the harder the CRIMP investigators worked to uncover intricate details of Everett's racetrack empire and the involvement of politicians in it, the more they lost control of their case. Nothing in the meticulously drafted CRIMP reports suggested an ordinary and legitimate business transaction in the acquisition and sale of stock by Kerner and Isaacs, as the two men claimed. But the legal system requires an indictment based on law, not on a self-serving story told by Marjorie Everett or the circumstantial evidence of cryptic tax return entries and suspiciously complicated investment schemes. The IRS's straightforward theory of the case, based on Hobbs Act extortion, simply would not hold water. A much more elaborate legal rationale needed to be found. Prosecutors in Washington and Chicago never warmed to the "true syndicate" conspiracy theory that Jack Walsh's private source, Shirley Kub, had provided. Inspired by Kub's legends, Walsh had flushed from the thicket of Chicago politics a trophy of historic proportions, to be sure. But it would take a bigger hunter to bring down Kerner. The CRIMP team assumed a supporting role, and a new cast of characters took the stage.

11

Intangible Rights

Andy Griffith portrayed him as a federal prosecutor in the chilling television miniseries *Fatal Vision,* based on the best-selling book about army doctor Jeffrey R. MacDonald and the gruesome bludgeon and knife murders of his pregnant wife and two young daughters. Try as he might have, however, the actor who starred on TV as a comic sheriff and later a wily defense lawyer was simply too charming to convey the imposing presence of Victor Charles Woerheide. When Woerheide died of a heart attack in Virginia in 1977 at age sixty-seven, he rated only a tiny death notice in the *Washington Post,* an oversight that proved even the *Post* can be uninformed about important people in its town. Woerheide was an invaluable troubleshooter for the Justice Department, a larger-than-life career government trial lawyer on whom superiors—political appointees in both Democratic and Republican administrations—relied to resolve sensitive, intractable criminal cases. When he pursued Otto Kerner, he marched the federal government deeply into Illinois's political system, an incursion that would have long-running implications for politics in America.

Woerheide stood six foot three, weighed 250 pounds, and put Tabasco sauce on nearly everything he ate. "Other than strawberry shortcake, there were very few things in the world he thought could not be improved with Tabasco sauce," said Justice Department colleague Paul J. Schaeffer. His shock of white hair "stood up almost like a white broom," Schaeffer recalled, and he spoke in a slow, booming voice that sounded "like a subway train."[1] He enjoyed big cigars and dry martinis and wore a Panama hat in Chicago during the summer of 1971. He was known to be absent-minded. Legend had it that his long-time Justice Department associate Francis Lloyd Williamson accompanied Woerheide on his many assignments around the country to make sure he did not get lost.

A native of St. Louis, he studied economics and obtained a law degree from the University of Missouri in 1939. Woerheide joined the Labor Department and in 1941 transferred to the Justice Department as an antitrust lawyer. His interests in traveling and international law and his ability to speak German and French enhanced his career during the war. When the war ended, the government dispatched Woerheide to Germany to investigate the "Axis Sally" treason case, which involved expatriate Americans who had broadcast Nazi propaganda from Berlin, Munich, Vienna, and Paris to English-speaking Allied troops. He received exemption from competitive civil service requirements in the late 1950s and qualified for top-secret clearance as a lawyer in the Justice Department's internal security division. His cases included bribery of federal officials and obstruction of justice. A 1965 letter of commendation cited Woerheide for his diligence during long criminal cases requiring extended absences from his wife, son, and daughter, who lived in Alexandria, Virginia. "Mr. Woerheide is in every sense of the term a 'career professional,'" the commendation read.[2] By the late 1960s he was a grizzled senior attorney, a "Justice lifer" who had seen it all, as one colleague put it. He reported directly to Will Wilson, the assistant attorney general in the criminal division.

In late 1969 he led a San Francisco grand jury probe of the Black Panther Party, a self-described revolutionary group whose rhetoric became louder and whose gun toting became more threatening as public sympathy for the civil rights movement waned. FBI director J. Edgar Hoover called the Black Panther Party "the greatest threat to the internal security of the country."[3] David Hilliard, the Panther's chief of staff, said in a November speech, "We will kill Richard Nixon. We will kill any m—— who stands in the way of our freedom."[4] Shortly afterward Woerheide became the senior attorney in a special Black Panther task force created by Attorney General John Mitchell and reporting directly to the heads of three Justice Department units, including Jerris Leonard of the civil rights division. Woerheide began his work on December 1, and Hilliard was arrested two days later for threatening the life of the president. The next day Chicago police raided an apartment occupied by Black Panthers and shot to death party leaders Fred Hampton and Mark Clark. The incident prompted moderate black leaders, including Roy Wilkins of the National Association for the Advancement of Colored People, to wonder aloud whether the Nixon administration was staging a vendetta against the militant group.

But many prominent Americans, including Nixon, said the nation was through coddling extremists. They often cited the 1968 Kerner Commission report as giving aid and comfort to the enemy. "One of the major weaknesses of the President's commission is that it, in effect, blames everybody for the riots except the perpetrators of the riots," Nixon said when the report was released. "I think the commission has put undue emphasis on the idea that we are, in effect, a racist society, white racists vs. black racists."[5] Woerheide remained on the Black Panther probe well into the spring of 1970, but the Hilliard indictment was the only one brought. He acknowledged in April that the government was "having a hard time developing evidence" for federal prosecutions of the Panthers.[6]

His next stop was Chicago. In 1971 Woerheide applied for a career upgrade, describing his work as follows:

> My work consists of heading up projects to develop and prosecute cases involving special problems, such as particularly sophisticated or complex crimes. These projects sometimes involve close cooperation with other agencies. I now head a team of attorneys from the Criminal Division, the Tax Division and the Internal Revenue Service developing cases involving corruption on the part of high political figures. Earlier, I was chief of a group of Criminal Division and Internal Security attorneys working on cases involving militant terrorists. Cases developed have included bank robbery by militants, hijacking by organized crime figures, threats to kill the President, murder, extortion, bribery, SEC fraud, mail fraud, conflict of interest, etc.[7]

Woerheide, who was months if not years behind in filling his travel vouchers, liked coming to Chicago because he could find the German magazine *Der Spiegel*. The highest political figure Woerheide was investigating at the time was Otto Kerner, and his job was to figure out which federal laws fit the facts of the Illinois racetrack stock allegations brought to Washington by Project CRIMP investigators. "He normally worked on cases that were more smoking guns and dead bodies than all the little minutia you run into in a tax case," Special Agent Stufflebeam of the CRIMP team told an interviewer in 1978. "He just wasn't a detail guy. . . . Just his background and experience and lack of experience in tax stuff was a little difficult to deal with."[8] But deal with Woerheide and an entire contingent from Washington they would.

◆ ◆ ◆

Project CRIMP trudged forward through the summer of 1970. Stufflebeam, Bill Witkowski, and team leader Jack Walsh worked hard to build a Hobbs Act extortion case against Otto Kerner. Their belittling code name for Kerner was "Zero," derived from the first letter of his name and their opinion of the judge's intelligence. Though no stories appeared in the press, word was around among reporters that a federal judge in Chicago was under investigation. Some reporters suspected, incorrectly, that the target was federal district judge William Campbell, who had jailed Sam Giancana. Meanwhile, the Kerner probe expanded into far-flung allegations from IRS sources that Isaacs and possibly Kerner had received payoffs in connection with state supervision of savings and loan associations and insurance companies and that an Outfit-connected contractor had done plumbing work at the Cermak compound in Antioch for Kerner and his wife. CRIMP continued to pursue other cases based on the Shirley Kub intelligence. On October 10, 1970, however, Jack Walsh's neatly structured universe of conspiracy among hoodlums, politicians, and business officials in Illinois experienced what might be called the Big Bang.

In the Kahler Hotel in Rochester, Minnesota, where he had gone with his personal secretary to seek treatment at the Mayo Clinic, Illinois secretary of state Paul Powell died. His body was returned to Springfield and laid in state in the Capitol rotunda on the same catafalque used for the coffin of Abraham Lincoln. In his eulogy Mayor Daley called Powell "a natural leader who never lost the common touch and who was proud to be called a politician."[9] Republican governor Richard Ogilvie said, "He was above all a man who demanded of himself a sense of honor that stood the test of service spanning four turbulent decades."[10] A few weeks later the public learned that investigators probing a mysterious fifteen-hour delay in the disclosure of Powell's death had discovered in his two-room suite in Springfield's St. Nicholas Hotel a hoard of cash, more than a half-million dollars stuffed in shoe boxes, shirt boxes, and a bowling bag. Tens of thousands more in currency turned up in safety deposit boxes.

The Paul Powell "shoe-box" story broke in the national press like the dawn of a blazing sun, shining directly on the IRS's intelligence division. The IRS, it seemed obvious, had given a pass to one of the most corrupt state or local officials anywhere in the country in the midcentury era. Subsequent investigations revealed that Powell had collected cash kickbacks from many corners of state government, ranging from contractors remodeling the Capitol to companies making license plates, giving an ironic meaning to Daley's praise about "the common touch." Investigators claimed he even retained a percentage of the coins fed into statehouse vending machines. His estate was estimated at $3 million on a $30,000 annual salary.

Paul Taylor Powell was born January 21, 1902, in a frame house in Vienna (pronounced Vy-an-na), Illinois, a community of a few hundred souls just fifteen miles from the Kentucky border and 380 miles from Chicago. His father, a native of Tennessee, operated a drug store where Powell worked as a youth. After graduating from Vienna High School, he became a traveling salesman, but he returned home to run an auto dealership and a cafe before entering politics. He dropped his middle initial because he thought voters would like the alliteration of his first and last names. He served on the school board, was elected mayor at age twenty-eight, and in 1934, at age thirty-two, he ran successfully for the Illinois House. His official residence for his entire life was the modest house where he was born, to which he would return on weekends to meet job-seekers and other well wishers. But his home away from home was the St. Nicholas Hotel. His suite had previously belonged to Orville Hodge.

Powell did nearly as much as Daley for the Kennedy presidential campaign in Illinois, even though he had opposed Kennedy's nomination at the 1960 Democratic National Convention. In the 1964 Democratic landslide following Kennedy's assassination, he was elected secretary of state, the most patronage-rich post in Illinois government, with 5,000 jobs at his disposal. Daley gave Powell a wide berth. A heavy-set, jowly man, Powell enjoyed uttering crude rural aphorisms that disarmed critics and endeared him to Springfield insiders, including the press corps, which twice named him "Outstanding Legislator of Illinois." Besides his remark "the Democrats can smell the meat a'cookin"[11] on the election of fellow Democrat Adlai Stevenson as governor in 1948, Powell's most memorable quip was "If you can't get a full meal, take a sandwich."[12]

United Press International reporter Chris Vlahoplus, in a 1961 profile of Powell, observed that he bore "a striking resemblance to Wallace Beery," the 1930s film star who won an Academy Award for his portrayal of a washed-up prize fighter in The Champ.[13] He had an encyclopedic mind about Illinois government, especially its cash-flow aspects. Behind his heavy, dark-rimmed glasses, his eyes continually twinkled with the knowledge that he knew the score. Another infamous Powell remark was "There's only one thing worse than a defeated politician, and that's a broke politician."[14] Stevenson biographer John Bartlow Martin wrote: "Powell was a man of great native ability and intelligence. He knew every highway and byway in Springfield, especially the byways. He was a fearsome alley fighter, a slashing, devastating debater. He knew every pressure point in the Illinois legislature, knew what made each vote turn. He sought power, and it flowed to him. He was, in a sense, a dishonest Lyndon Johnson."[15] To reform-minded legislators who criticized him for flaunting his ownership of stock in state-regulated horse-racing enterprises, he responded, "The only thing wrong with it is they don't have any."[16]

The Paul Powell disclosures in late 1970 had two dramatic effects on the flagging Kerner investigation. On the scales of chronic and large-scale corruption of government for personal gain, the Powell scandal by comparison reduced Marjorie Everett's self-serving allegations involving Kerner nearly to zero. Whatever Project CRIMP was up to, the IRS had let Powell get away, a major slipup that looked a lot like incompetence. At the same time, the shoe-box story suggested an enormity and venality of political wrongdoing in Illinois that must reach, the government reasoned, all the way to the U.S. Court of Appeals for the Seventh Circuit, where former governor Kerner still sat and ruled. On January 15 the *New York Times,* in a front-page profile of Powell, declared, "Paul Powell was not a bizarre aberration, but a skilled practitioner of Illinois-style politics."[17] The CRIMP "true syndicate" theory, with its intriguing connections to Al Capone and his criminal offspring, became irrelevant and even ridiculous. Nevertheless, career law-enforcement officials in Washington would now see the targets of the CRIMP project, including Kerner, in a different light, as part of a much larger picture of deeply embedded official wrongdoing in Illinois that cried out for federal intervention more loudly than at any time since the Capone era.

The embarrassment of the Paul Powell scandal made its way quickly to the upper levels of the Nixon IRS and Justice Department. The dogged but undisciplined investigative drift in Illinois needed to be brought to heel. Four days after the *New York Times* article, the Justice Department assigned Victor Woerheide to the northern district of Illinois. With him came Paul Schaeffer of the criminal division and Darrell McGowen of the tax division. Francis Lloyd Williamson of the criminal division and Thomas E. Fontecchio of the tax division followed in April. McGowen recalled that he was sent to Chicago to make sense of the CRIMP political corruption probe in general and the Paul Powell debacle in particular. "The Kerner case was not what brought me to Chicago," he said.[18] During this time IRS investigators fanned out well beyond the CRIMP targets to probe possible income tax violations within the entire hierarchy of Illinois politics, from members of Congress and federal judges to second- and third-tier state and local bureaucrats.

Woerheide's Washington team set up a war room in a building used by the IRS at 17 North Dearborn Street, two blocks north of Chicago's Federal Building, with some old file cabinets and metal desks arranged in a bull-pen fashion. They worked independently, although U.S. Attorney William Bauer assigned Richard A. Makarski, the chief of the criminal division in his office, to keep an eye on Woerheide's work. The Justice Department team was in Chicago "to get as many cases as they could on what they viewed as a serious issue of political corruption in Illinois," Makarski recalled. But Bauer wanted to be sure public officials would not be "sandbagged" by the Washington investigators and would be treated with courtesy.[19]

By April nearly a year had passed since Stufflebeam and Campbell first had read Kerner his rights, and nothing had happened. Walsh and the CRIMP team, always suspicious of corrupt motives even among their government peers, were doing a slow boil. The May 1971 grand jury was about to be formed in Chicago. In the light of the Powell affair, however, government lawyers disparaged Walsh's "cocky scheme," Makarski recalled later.[20] Personnel, including Walsh himself, were being diverted from CRIMP projects to Springfield. On May 6 Woerheide's superiors in Washington expanded his jurisdiction to the southern district of Illinois, which included Springfield and the Powell cash. Kerner was CRIMP's biggest catch, but nothing could move forward on the case until government lawyers decided what federal law or laws he had broken. Nearly the entire Washington team—Woerheide, McGowen, and Fontecchio—as well as Bauer's man Makarski and Special Agents Walsh, Stufflebeam, and Witkowski traveled to Dallas in mid-May once again to interview Marjorie Everett. Again she put the onus for illegality on former Illinois Racing Board chairman William Miller and portrayed herself as the victim of Miller's extortion. But a Hobbs Act extortion charge, the perennial favorite of IRS investigators, was not in the cards against Miller or Kerner. Another legal route had to be taken to jump start the Kerner case.

♦ ♦ ♦

An unsigned, handwritten legal memorandum in the U.S. attorney's case file for the Kerner prosecution put the extortion theory to rest. The Hobbs Act employed the popular view of extortion that required a perpetrator, including a public official, to have "obtained" or "induced" the payoff, words that connote effort. This "fine distinction," as the memorandum's author put it, meant that a Hobbs Act extortion charge against Kerner required the government to prove "threats, force or the oppressive exercise of official position." Witkowski and Stufflebeam had uncovered a great deal, but they found no evidence that Kerner had threatened or demanded anything from Everett or oppressed her in any way. The governor and the racing entrepreneur essentially agreed in efforts to expand Illinois racing and the state taxes it generated. There was no evidence that Kerner had declared himself a tollbooth on Everett's road to a bigger racing dynasty. Receiving racetrack stock passively as a gratuity, which is all CRIMP investigators could suggest Kerner had done, was inappropriate, but it did not qualify as Hobbs Act extortion. "It seems clear that there is almost no support for the argument that a public official is guilty of extortion by merely passively receiving money or property. The position seems wholly untenable," the legal memorandum concluded.[21]

The finding presented Woerheide's team with a major roadblock. Extortion's fraternal twin, bribery, was not an element of the Hobbs Act, which was written to attack strong-arm tactics by labor organizers but did not address sweetheart deals by employers bribing union officials. Bribery was unavailable to them as an independent charge because there was no federal bribery offense that could be cited against a state official. The constitutional protection of states' rights once again, as it had in the 1920s, seemed to stand as a barrier to federal assaults on corruption in Illinois.

Criminal charges against Kerner of income tax evasion or conspiracy to evade income taxes and file false tax returns—based on Kerner's capital gains treatment of his sale of racetrack stock—lacked legal weight. These essentially technical charges almost certainly would look inconsequential and politically motivated, given Kerner's national public stature and the relatively small amount of money involved (the government eventually alleged that Kerner evaded $84,129.58 in income taxes) compared to the government's enormous expense in building the case. A technical tax charge might have worked against a recognized public enemy, such as Al Capone, but it would not against a popular, exemplary public figure such as Kerner. Moreover, a simple tax charge would appear timid in the light of the government's belated sweep of widespread racetrack corruption in Illinois, most of which had nothing to do with Kerner.

Extortion or bribery allegations would be concrete and compelling. Extortion failed to fit the facts. Bribery was the answer. But the public and a jury would demand specific answers to specific questions: Who was the briber? What was the purpose of the bribe? Gulf and Western had fired Everett from her position as chief executive officer of the former Chicago Thoroughbred Enterprises, but her severance included the conglomerate's shareholdings in the Hollywood Turf Club, which owned the Hollywood Park racecourse in Inglewood, California. As the largest shareholder of Hollywood Turf, the newly arrived California businesswoman quickly needed friends among that state's racing regulators and law-enforcement officials. As she sought a license to engage in California horse racing, she was less likely than ever to admit bribing a politician back in Illinois. Miller, now seeking to build his own racing empire in Illinois, also refused to acknowledge bribing anyone.

Everett and Miller had conspired to influence Illinois racing regulation, the IRS agents had proven. With their evidence Woerheide was developing a presentation to a grand jury under the enormously pervasive federal conspiracy statute, a powerful prosecutorial tool he understood well. The federal conspiracy law permits the government to indict certain participants in a scheme while leaving others—in this case, Everett—untouched and available to become friendly government witnesses. A conspiracy indictment allowed Woerheide to present to a grand jury circumstantial evidence that would be barred in other prosecutions. The evidence uncovered by Stufflebeam and Witkowski reeked of a conspiracy in which, as the eventual indictment charged, Kerner, Isaacs, Miller, Joseph Knight, and even Miller's secretary and presumed mistress, Faith McInturf, "did unlawfully, knowingly and willfully combine, conspire, confederate and agree together, with each other, and with divers other persons to commit offenses against the United States."[22] ("I do not believe anyone related to a race track scandal could be named Faith McInturf," one government lawyer wrote in his analysis of the case.)[23]

Conspiracy can be charged as an independent offense under federal law, but it must relate to a substantive federal crime. Again, what "offenses against the United States" had Kerner and his coconspirators committed? Having determined they could not bring an extortion charge directly, prosecutors could hardly bring it indirectly under the cover of a conspiracy charge. The facts relating to Kerner's apparent income tax violations were incidental to the complex web of racetrack stock dealings the IRS agents had uncovered. The answer had to be bribery—not a federal bribery charge but a bribery charge based on Illinois law and brought derivatively into the indictment.

One federal statute that could achieve this goal was the 1961 Travel Act, or ITAR (Interstate and Foreign Travel or Transportation in Aid of Racketeering Enterprises), which made it a federal crime to use "any facility of interstate or foreign commerce, including the mail, with the intent to distribute the proceeds of any unlawful activity." This sweeping statute enacted in the Robert Kennedy era greatly expanded federal powers against the organized criminals and union racketeers whom Kennedy had vowed to defeat. The Illinois bribery law could define an "unlawful activity" covered by a Travel Act indictment. The government knew that three checks drawn on a Southern Illinois bank by Joseph Knight, a principal financier of the Kerner-Isaacs stock dealings, had briefly crossed the Mississippi River into Missouri to be cleared through the Federal Reserve Bank of St. Louis before being sent on to Kerner and Isaacs.

But the evidence supporting Travel Act charges was woefully insubstantial and barely relevant to the alleged conspiracy. (In a November 1971 memorandum on the case, Henry E. Petersen, acting assistant attorney general for the criminal division of the Justice Department, raised doubts about Travel Act allegations against Kerner. After the trial a federal appeals court dismissed all three Travel Act counts in the indictment and rebuked trial judge Robert L. Taylor for his "erroneous and highly prejudicial view" in allowing the charges to go to the jury.)

Another "offense against the United States" available as the underlying crime of a conspiracy was mail fraud. The federal mail fraud statute, first enacted in 1872, was a product of the post–Civil War era, when Americans suffered a rash of swindles by con artists using the U.S. mail. An Illinois congressman who sponsored the measure said the law was needed "to prevent frauds which were mostly gotten up in the large cities . . . by thieves, forgers, and rapscallions generally, for the purposes of deceiving and fleecing the innocent people of the country."[24] The law initially prohibited use of the mail for "any scheme or artifice to defraud," but in 1909 the following phrase was inserted after the word *defraud:* "or for obtaining money or property by means of false or fraudulent pretenses, representations or promises." Despite the use of the critical conjunction *or,* mail fraud cases nearly always relied on evidence that the perpetrator received something of tangible economic value— property or money—from his or her victim and thus deprived the victim of some right to the future benefit of tangible property.

Many legal authorities regarded the phrase in the 1909 amendment as clarifying and extending the preceding phrase, not dividing the two phrases. Under this interpretation Kerner had defrauded no one. Bribery, however wrong it may be, does not suggest fraud in any way. On the contrary, the essence of bribery is that the bribe giver and the bribe taker each know exactly what the other is doing and why. There are no pretenses in a bribe. But the judicial history of the mail fraud statute included a handful of cases that relied on the momentous word *or* inserted in 1909. A few courts had distinguished between infractions involving "money or property" and the broader 1872 language, "any scheme or artifice to defraud." The 1872 phrase, being isolated by the word *or,* seemed to some to open wide the prosecutor's door, covering acts of deception or false pretenses in which the victim is not deprived of any tangible monetary or property right and the perpetrator receives nothing of tangible economic value from the victim.

Traditionally a fraud charge required at least the second element, that whoever committed a fraud must have obtained something of tangible value from the victim. But in 1941 a federal appeals court upheld the mail fraud conviction of several Louisiana men, including a member of the Orleans Parish Levee Board appointed by Governor Huey Long, in a scheme involving fees for refunding bonds. The appeals court held that the defendants arranged an exorbitant fee, which they shared among themselves. But the court found separately that the levee board member and his confederates breached the board member's fiduciary duty to the parish taxpayers. "No trustee has more sacred duties than a public official and any scheme to obtain an advantage by corrupting such an [*sic*] one must in the federal law be considered a scheme to defraud," the court said.[25]

A year later a federal appeals court in Massachusetts upheld the mail fraud conviction of a private company, Procter and Gamble Company, which had been found guilty of bribing employees of a competitor to hand over trade secrets. The appeals court rejected Procter and Gamble's contention that the secrets had no tangible economic value and therefore did not encompass fraud. The court ruled that the company had defrauded the competitor of its "lawful right" to the "honest and loyal services" of its employees.[26] More contemporary to the Kerner case, a federal district court in Louisiana had ruled in 1969 that the federal mail fraud statute had been violated when the executive secretary to the governor of Louisiana received kickbacks from banks where he arranged for state funds to be deposited. There was no monetary loss to the state in the scheme, but the secretary was found to have deprived the people of Louisiana of their right to his loyal and faithful services as a public official.[27]

The legal phrase "intangible rights," a shorthand expression of these theories of law, originated not in Louisiana but in the northern district of Illinois. Around the time Victor Woerheide was cranking up his investigation of Illinois political corruption, Matthias Lydon, a twenty-nine-year-old assistant U.S. attorney in Chicago, was building a case brought to the government by an investigator for Chicago-based Zenith Radio Corporation. A Zenith purchasing agent had been discovered taking kickbacks from the supplier of the popular "Surround Sound" radio cabinets. But the price being charged by the cabinetmaker was a low bid, lower even than a bid by a Zenith subsidiary that made cabinets. Lydon, knowing it therefore would be difficult to prove that Zenith suffered a tangible economic loss, was contemplating a Hobbs Act extortion charge against the purchasing agent. Further research, however, aided by Justice Department lawyers in Washington, led him to propose a mail fraud charge based on the theory that the purchasing agent had defrauded Zenith of its right to his loyal and honest services.

"It wasn't universally accepted," recalled Lydon, now an attorney with the Chicago law firm of Winston and Strawn. U.S. Attorney William Bauer "didn't think it should be prosecuted as mail fraud." Lydon remembered Bauer asking rhetorically, "Do you mean to tell me if some guy sends a love letter to his mistress he's defrauded his wife of his loyal services?"[28] But Bauer's first assistant U.S. attorney, James R. Thompson, favored Lydon's aggressive tactic. Also in the meeting were assistant U.S. attorneys Samuel Skinner and Richard Makarski, Bauer's man in the Kerner probe. A vote was taken in favor of using Lydon's theory. Bauer "was pretty democratic about that," Thompson told his biographer, Robert E. Hartley.[29] "There was an awareness that if this theory of prosecution flew, it would have ramifications beyond just that case," Lydon recalled later.[30] Convictions in the Zenith case under the intangible rights theory were upheld by the seventh circuit appeals court, but not until 1973.

The intangible rights theory of mail fraud might seem analogous to federal civil rights laws, which empower the government to intercede to protect the intangible rights of minorities to nondiscrimination in voting, public accommodation, employment, housing, and other matters that cannot be denominated strictly in dollars and cents. When Lyndon Johnson proposed the

Civil Rights Act of 1964, he said civil rights went well beyond economic rights. But civil rights are established as a federal jurisdiction by the Thirteenth, Fourteenth and Fifteenth Amendments to the Constitution. "There is no issue of states rights or national rights," Johnson said in 1965. "There is only the struggle for human rights."[31]

On the other hand, there is no moral absolute or constitutional right in regard to the faithful and honest performance by state and local public officials in a democracy, where voters may freely choose their leaders in periodic elections. Indeed, Florida senator Claude Pepper, speaking on the Senate floor about a federal probe of official corruption in Louisiana in 1940, said, "I proclaim it is the privilege of a state in a democratic government even to have bad government, if its people want it to be bad." With Germany and Italy engulfed in fascism, Pepper asked, "At this time in American history, at this period in world history, do we want to admit to the world that democracy in America has so broken down that sovereign states cannot conduct their own elections?"[32] Nevertheless, in the 1941 Louisiana levee board case, the appeals court stated, "A scheme to get a public contract on more favorable terms than would likely to be got otherwise by bribing a public official would not only be a plan to commit the crime of bribery, but would also be a scheme to defraud the public."[33] This point of view slowly emerged to grant to the federal government enormous power over state and local governments—good and bad—through the federal mail fraud statute.

The intangible rights theory has been compared to the federal government's recognized power to seek criminal prosecutions as an auxiliary to state law enforcement, according to Ralph E. Loomis in a 1978 *American University Law Review* article. But even that explanation is controversial, he wrote. "Proponents argue that expanded federal jurisdiction is necessary to root out organized crime and other white collar corruption," Loomis wrote. "More moderate voices caution that enlisting the federal government in the battle against essentially local crimes hazards federal prestige, creates federal administrative problems and weakens the enforcement efforts by local officials. Critics argue that federal auxiliary jurisdiction is being extended to dimensions of a national police state."[34]

W. Robert Gray, writing in a 1980 *University of Chicago Law Review* article, similarly questioned the application of the intangible rights theory to the federal mail fraud statute.

> Analysis of the legislative history of section 1341 [the mail fraud statute] . . . demonstrates that the section's reach should be limited to fraudulent conduct that results in the acquisition of money or property from the victim. The meaning of fraud in the nineteenth century, when the mail fraud statute first was enacted, bolsters such a reading. Moreover, the Supreme Court and lower court decisions that have

been cited for an intangible rights construction of section 1341 do not provide support. The use of section 1341 against politically corrupt politicians thus remains contrary to Congress' original intent. Unless Congress amends the section, such use should not receive the imprimatur of the courts.[35]

Nonetheless, in Illinois's rich history of crime and corruption, the intangible rights theory of criminal prosecution would descend like a stealth bomber on the crude bagmen and boodlers scurrying about the political stage. It gave the federal government a powerful new tool, based however obliquely on the government's duty to safeguard the integrity of the mail, to accomplish in Chicago a law-enforcement intrusion that Congress specifically refused to authorize in 1926. At that time Chicago civic reformers had sought federal intervention against the city's long-running gang wars and political corruption. The Senate Committee on Immigration nevertheless rejected such intervention, which was requested by Vice President Charles Dawes, a Chicago banker and civic reform leader, and the Better Government Association, as an "unwarranted interference" in Chicago's affairs that lacked "an all-compelling federal question."[36] The committee's view of limited federal prosecutorial authority was discussed and endorsed widely around the country at the time, leaving Chicago to solve its own problems.

Agents of the Treasury Department's Bureau of Internal Revenue eventually unsheathed a potent federal weapon against the city's crime spree, the income tax code. Though few Americans applauded the federal income tax, fewer questioned its legitimacy. It was a well-known statute, debated thoroughly and authorized by the states in 1913 as the Sixteenth Amendment to the Constitution. The income tax—like the Hobbs Act, the Travel Act, and other statutory powers enabling the federal government to reach into state and local law-enforcement matters—was forged by open legislative and political processes in accordance with the general rule of law. The intangible rights theory of mail fraud was not. Instead, it was an ad hoc legal tactic, conceived by government lawyers from incidental judicial rulings without public notice or legislative debate. It was barely recognized in the federal judicial review process and bore no stamp of the U.S. Supreme Court. No opinions on the tactic had been written in the northern district of Illinois or the federal appeals court in Chicago at the time the Kerner prosecution unfolded.

Moreover, the income tax law and other federal statutes used against organized crime and official corruption achieved their validity not only from their rigorous legislative pedigrees but also from the public's sense of fairness and its outrage over the chronic and often violent wrongdoing being prosecuted. The intangible rights theory, on the contrary, would get its first major test in Illinois not against career criminals but against a gentlemanly, respected federal judge who by all accounts led a faithful life of public service;

who courageously had made himself a national spokesman on a major concern of the day, the scourge of racism; and who on several occasions over four decades had been audited under the income tax code without a penalty. The Paul Powell scandal energized the CRIMP investigation and sparked sweeping new IRS probes of official corruption in Illinois, which to federal prosecutors looked a lot like Louisiana. New law was made in the process. The federal presumption that Illinois stank of political wrongdoing provided a broad justification for asserting mail fraud jurisdiction in a way that, despite its tenuous origins and unlikely target, made the intangible rights doctrine a fitting weapon against an available foe, Otto Kerner.

◆ ◆ ◆

The intangible rights theory gave Woerheide critical and badly needed advantages against Kerner. It put the dubious extortion charge and the complicated and relatively minor income tax violations outlined by the CRIMP team firmly in the backseat. It permitted a more robust bribe conspiracy charge, one based on evidence of use of the mail, and a more convincing set of facts than the weak Travel Act evidence. The notion of defrauding citizens of their right to honest and faithful service by public officials, however vague, gave the case meaning and significance befitting the prosecution of a popular federal judge. When added to the Travel Act bribery charge, the mail fraud statute enabled the government to charge two "offenses against the United States" as predicates for an overarching bribe conspiracy allegation. And the conspiracy charge allowed prosecutors to present their circumstantial evidence and shield their principal witness, Marjorie Everett. The intricate construction of the indictment was debated by government lawyers throughout most of 1971 as Victor Woerheide, the Justice Department's warhorse, assembled documents and brought witnesses before grand jurors. The precise wording of the charges became a rigorous exercise in law, semantics, and courtroom strategy.

Taking up the work of Stufflebeam and Witkowski, IRS officials and tax experts in the Justice Department focused on a charge of conspiracy to evade taxes by Kerner and Isaacs. A June 28 memorandum by Thomas Fontecchio of the Justice Department's tax division reported that the IRS intelligence division intended to recommend an indictment based on a conspiracy to evade taxes and Travel Act bribery but made no mention of an intangible rights mail fraud charge.[37] Lawyers in the criminal division of the Justice Department, meanwhile, explored the mail fraud theory. Some found it inadequate to the task. Justice Department lawyer Thomas A. Kennelly endorsed the use of the intangible rights theory. In his August 20 review of the Kerner case, Kennelly cited the Louisiana levee board case and concluded, "Legally there is no problem with the theory of fraud on the State of Illinois."[38] But Jay C. Johnson, a Justice Department attorney in the fraud section of the criminal division, recommended that an intangible rights fraud charge be supplemented by a traditional and more understandable allegation of tangible loss to Illinois taxpayers—that "the State of Illinois was also deprived of the secret profits gained by the defendants through their official positions of trust."[39] John C. Keeney, chief of the fraud section and one of the lawyers who advised Lydon on the Zenith case, concurred in adding the "unjust enrichment" language, which, although no large sum of money was involved, would give a trial jury tangible evidence of a loss to the public and thereby reduce the government's reliance on the complex intangible rights theory. Keeney rejected mail fraud charges against Isaacs and Joseph Knight because "their official positions were immaterial to the fraud."[40]

The extensive deliberations over the wording of an indictment and the continuing inquiries of IRS agents into the affairs of Kerner and Isaacs eventually spawned leaks to the press, as the CRIMP team grew more restless about the fate of its biggest case. Walsh, Stufflebeam, and Witkowski acknowledged years later that they fraternized and shared information with reporters. In some cases the agents filtered information appearing in newspapers and on television through Sherman Skolnick, a self-employed legal researcher who had brought the initial charges that resulted in the resignations of Illinois Supreme Court Justices Klingbiel and Solfisburg in a scandal involving Theodore Isaacs. "Yes, I've met Skolnick," Stufflebeam said. "Every town needs one, but you wouldn't want two." Stufflebeam said Skolnick gained knowledge of the Kerner case through the questions IRS agents asked him on several occasions, "and knowing Sherman he was probably stirring the pot with the [news]paper," Stufflebeam said.[41] In a 1978 interview with journalist Jan Bone, Skolnick claimed he routinely leaked information he obtained from the IRS agents to Chicago newspapers and to television commentator Walter Jacobson. He said William Miller, who eventually subsidized Hank Messick's book on the case, fed information to the press as well.[42]

On July 29, when the indictment was still very much undecided, *Chicago Today,* an afternoon tabloid, published a copyrighted front-page exclusive: "$150,000 Kerner race stock profit: IRS probes income of former governor." Many details in the story were incorrect. The article reflected the IRS "bargain purchase" theory of the scheme. By then, however, the IRS view was not shared by Justice Department lawyers. Kerner was interviewed for the story and denied wrongdoing. He declined to discuss his personal financial affairs but said, falsely, "I have never used anybody in a trust or anything to hide my name." The scoop by *Today* reporters Sy Adelman and Robert Glass sparked a fierce competitive battle among Chicago's four major dailies. Reporters scrambled for fresh developments. Some of the stories entailed more journalistic effort than others. In addition to reporting on Kerner, reporters obtained shareholder lists of Illinois racing associations and revealed the widespread holdings of racetrack stock by Illinois politicians. They illuminated correctly the critical connection between the Kerner case and the Paul Powell scandal. Some of the reporting, however, often couched in crudely self-promotional language about newspaper "investigations," represented uncritical publishing of self-serving government leaks and differed hardly at all in terms of journalistic integrity and enterprise from the articles Everett's publicity writers handed to willing racetrack columnists.

As usual, no reporter jeopardized the flow of tips by exploring in print the motives of the leakers or the corrosive effects the leaks had on due process in the criminal justice system. For one thing, coverage of the scandal raised serious questions about the supposed sanctity of the secret grand jury system. The intense media coverage during the summer and early fall of 1971 yielded the government the strategic benefit of eroding Kerner's public esteem and facilitating the eventual introduction of the unfamiliar intangible rights theory to a jury. Ironically, Kerner's pronounced media identity as a "Mr. Clean" of Illinois politics made it virtually impossible that his complaints about harmful leaks would be taken up by the press. In addition, his unique position as a product of the Cook County Democratic organization who nonetheless was unwelcome in the bosom of the party meant that Mayor Richard Daley, who could have helped Kerner, would likely shun him.

Frank Sullivan, Daley's former press secretary, in his book about the mayor, *Legend,* wrote:

> The Mayor . . . separated himself from colleagues who got in trouble with the law. What is overlooked, of course, was that these so-called colleagues most often were rival politicians. The fact that Daley supported them politically did not necessarily mean he liked them. An example of this was the way Daley was totally unsympathetic to the fate which befell Federal Judge Otto Kerner. When the former governor was on his way to prison, Daley told me that he, too, had been offered "the same racetrack stock deal" that Kerner accepted but that he, the Mayor, had turned it down. He had no patience for Kerner and his troubles with the federal government.[43]

That may have been a short-sighted attitude. Daley and his advisers failed to realize that federal prosecutors unsheathing the novel intangible rights weapon against Kerner would continue the probe deep into their ranks, dramatically weakening Daley's power and prestige in his final years; forever tarnishing his legacy and damaging irreparably the Democratic organization he built.

Meanwhile in Washington, government lawyers wrestled to decide the precise nature of the bribes allegedly paid to Kerner and to agree on formal charges from the evidence Woerheide had developed in the grand jury room in Chicago. Questions persisted over when the bribes were supposed to have been made. Everett claimed that in November 1962 Miller coerced her to offer Kerner and Isaacs each twenty-five shares of Chicago Thoroughbred Enterprises stock at $1,000 per share. Everett took a capital loss on her 1966 taxes by claiming that the shares were actually sold to the two men in 1966. The IRS had disallowed the loss for that year, saying the shares were sold in 1962. The Chicago Thoroughbred Enterprises stock appeared to be the principal source of profit to Kerner and Isaacs and essential to the government's case. But prosecutors worried about statute of limitation problems dating back to 1962, as well as disputable assessments of 1962 share values. They resolved the timing problem by rejecting the IRS "bargain purchase" theory and the 1962 transaction date. The Woerheide team developed the notion that Kerner and Isaacs in effect never purchased stock from Everett at any price, in the normal sense of paying for an equity investment. Rather, the government reasoned, the two men collected a bribe in 1967, a bribe elaborately disguised as agreements to purchases, loans, exchanges, and sales of Chicago Thoroughbred Enterprises stock and Chicago Harness Racing stock beginning in 1962. It was, the government alleged, a complex, circular scheme in which a bribe was disguised as a fictitious gain on an investment that was never made.

Eldon F. Hawley, assistant chief of the tax section of the Justice Department's criminal division, in an August 19 memorandum reviewing the charges, wrote, "These are venal people, erudite, cunning and definitely not unsophisticated or naive." He said, "the evidence is replete with examples of deviousness and chicanery which should keep any jury awake."[44] Hawley urged prosecutors to call a bribe a bribe, not a bargain purchase, and recommended a charge of conspiracy to evade income taxes. He made no mention of the intangible rights mail fraud theory. He agreed that, based on her grand jury testimony, Everett would make an excellent witness to support the bribe allegation. With candor uncharacteristic of memorandums by government lawyers, Justice Department attorney Kennelly wrote: "They did it by a systematic cover-up so intricate and sophisticated that it boggles the mind. Having practiced to deceive, it was indeed a tangled web they weaved. All of which gives the case a great deal of jury appeal."[45]

But who was the deceiver? Woerheide essentially endorsed Everett's extortion allegation against Miller, as she had told the IRS more than eighteen months earlier. His August 2 analysis included a ten-paragraph description of the conspiracy. Each paragraph made former racing board chief Miller the principal actor, with such phrases as "Miller helped Everett," "With Miller's guidance Everett," "Miller also obtained from Mrs. Everett," "Miller extracted from Mrs. Everett," and "Miller caused Mrs. Everett."[46] These characterizations fit the government's plan to grant immunity to Everett. In a memorandum written after an indictment was drafted, however, Woerheide, Williamson, and Schaeffer declared "the actual makers of the bribe were Miller and Mrs. Everett."[47]

Woerheide's team also worked to establish evidence that Kerner did something in return for the bribes, evidence that was not required technically to prove a bribe conspiracy but that a jury surely would expect to hear. A quid pro quo could be suggested, he concluded, by Kerner's approval of several pro-Everett bills passed by the General Assembly, though many of them became law before the period of the alleged bribery; by Kerner's 1965 selection of then Everett ally Miller as chairman of a newly combined harness-racing and thoroughbred-racing board; by Kerner's appointment of other Everett-favored racing board members; and by testimony of several credible witnesses that Kerner interceded at least twice in awarding harness racing dates in a manner favorable to Everett's new harness-racing interests.

But Woerheide still lacked any direct evidence of a bribe offer to Kerner, which constituted a major gap in the case. Kerner insisted that he had dealt with Joseph Knight and Theodore Isaacs in making his racetrack stock investments, not with William Miller or Marjorie Everett. Knight and Isaacs were not racetrack entrepreneurs with a need to influence state government, and Miller and Everett would not acknowledge making bribes. In his August 20 memorandum Kennelly wrote: "Factually the evidence, at least as outlined in the memos and the indictment, looks pretty thin. . . . The evidence as outlined in the memos is strongest, of course, against Miller. . . . There is a particular problem regarding Isaacs in view of his departure from the public scene in 1963. But since Isaacs and Knight are lesser figures, I did not take time to analyze the evidence against them in detail. Kerner needs more work."[48] Kennelly said evidence that Kerner overruled a member of the harness-racing board assigning racing dates was not well founded and there was no evidence that Kerner had influenced thoroughbred-racing dates. "The problem with the evidence against Kerner is not merely that it is circumstantial, but that it has little probative value to establish that he took bribes to intervene in the allocation of favorable racing dates or assisted others in said allocation. [The evidence] shows merely that he was in a position to do so, and that he benefitted from his position. But I don't think that's enough against a circuit court judge," Kennelly wrote.[49]

By September, however, with the news media hot on the story, Everett was cooling off. On September 24 Everett contacted John Foy of the IRS intelligence division and said her notoriety in the Illinois racetrack stock scandal was prompting worrisome inquiries about her by California racing officials just when she was attempting to cement her shareholdings in Hollywood Park.

Darrell McGowen immediately relayed Foy's version of the conversation to his superiors in Washington. "Her friends are telling her nothing is going to happen to the people she has been testifying against and she is going to look foolish," McGowen wrote.

> Apparently she is having second thoughts about cooperating with the Government. I recommend, in an effort to preserve Mrs. Everett's potential as a cooperative witness, that I, or any other appropriate employee of the Department of Justice, be authorized to appear before the California Racing Commission [scheduled to meet September 28], not to recommend Mrs. Everett and not to disclose the results of any official investigation, but to assure the Commission that Mrs. Everett (1) is not the subject of an investigation (2) came forward voluntarily as a witness in our investigation of Illinois racing and (3) that she continues to be a willing, reliable and cooperative witness. I am advised by Mr. Foy that he made a similar recommendation to his superiors in the Internal Revenue Service.[50]

The case was in jeopardy, and there was still no consensus on the precise wording of an indictment. Two weeks later, on November 8, a formal document called a prosecution memorandum was drafted by assistant U.S. attorney Samuel Skinner and presented to William Bauer in Chicago and Henry Petersen in Washington. In it Skinner overruled the IRS and recommended that Kerner not be charged directly with tax evasion or filing a false 1967 tax return. "These are technical types of offenses with little or no jury appeal," Skinner said. "They lend themselves to an allegation of persecution. . . . I feel it is important to erase from the jury's mind that this may be a politically motivated indictment."[51] Moreover, Skinner urged that a charge of conspiracy to evade taxes and file a false tax return be avoided. He also said an indictment containing two conspiracies—one to violate the Travel Act and mail fraud statutes and another to violate the income tax code—would present "major legal problems which could lead to reversal on appeal." Skinner opposed perjury charges against Kerner. "Perjury cases tend to be difficult to prove and might tend to distract a jury from its true duty, the analysis of the bribe and mail fraud charges. I do not think the evidence is sufficient to convict a man of Kerner's stature for perjury and I do not recommend prosecution on perjury as to Kerner."

In that regard, Skinner noted Kerner's "excellent reputation in the State of Illinois" but added the following:

> The Internal Revenue Service is already beginning to canvass various persons who know Kerner in an attempt to find some adverse character testimony. It is not anticipated that we will locate a significant amount of this type of testimony but efforts are being made and it is possible we may find some slight help in this regard. It should be pointed out that because of an excessive amount of publicity

which this case has already achieved in all major news media in the Chicago area, the public has already become acclimated to the fact that their opinions as to Kerner's image and reputation is [sic] incorrect. . . . [Isaacs's] reputation is not excellent in this state and Kerner's association with him should be of benefit to the government in this regard.[52]

The indictment was being fine-tuned for presentation to Attorney General John N. Mitchell, a former municipal bond lawyer with little background in criminal law and a man known more for his cynicism than his intelligence. Mitchell, who held a great deal of power as a Nixon confidant, would have to sign off on the indictment of a federal judge. Before Mitchell made his decision, the *Chicago Tribune* on November 21 published a lengthy account of the proposed indictment in a story by reporter Ronald Koziol. Koziol's story, based on unnamed sources, correctly described certain details of the conspiracy allegations against Kerner still under review. The story went further to reveal evidence then being gathered by IRS agents concerning shareholdings by other state politicians in Washington Park Trotters Association, the entity Everett formed with the complicity of Paul Powell to run harness-racing meets at Washington Park. Powell had demanded control of 49 percent of the Washington Park Trotters stock. The Washington Park Trotters evidence had almost nothing to do with the Kerner case, but it was being actively pursued by the IRS and U.S. attorney's office as a separate matter.

Amid this new hail of publicity, Mitchell met in Washington on November 29 with Woerheide, Petersen, Deputy Attorney General Richard G. Kleindienst, and other senior Justice Department lawyers. According to a summary of the meeting written by Fred B. Ugast, deputy attorney general for the tax division, Petersen outlined the proposed charges and reviewed the evidence: "He indicated that the principal weakness in the case was the Government's dependence on a single key witness and the fact that Kerner was, in most cases, one step removed from the critical transactions. Mr. Petersen further pointed out that these factors, taken together with Judge Kerner's position in the community, in his opinion made our chances of obtaining a successful conviction about 50/50." Despite these misgivings, Mitchell "authorized going forward with the prosecution and urged that the matter proceed as quickly as possible," Ugast wrote.[53]

A nineteen-count indictment naming, in alphabetical order, Theodore Isaacs, Otto Kerner, Joseph Knight, Faith McInturf, and William Miller was signed December 15 by Harold H. Harmet, the investment banker and foreman of the May grand jury who had adopted his daughter in the court of Otto Kerner, and delivered by the new U.S. attorney in Chicago, James R. Thompson, who had first engaged Kerner in the public arena over the death sentence for Paul Crump. In the end the government threw most of the disputed issues into a sweeping indictment, including Travel Act charges and mail fraud charges—tangible and intangible—plus tax evasion against Kerner and Isaacs and perjury against Kerner. Secretary Leta Mogstad, who had worked in the U.S. attorney's office since the Capone era, typed the sixty-four pages of allegations against a former boss she admired.

Thompson and Skinner took the elevator to Kerner's chambers on the twenty-seventh floor of Chicago's Dirksen Federal Building shortly before joint press conferences were held in Washington and Chicago. "Judge, I'm very sorry to have to tell you this," Thompson recalled saying. "The grand jury will return an indictment charging you with offenses." According to Thompson, Kerner replied, "A fine Christmas present this is, gentlemen."[54]

Why did the government go forward with what Petersen called a fifty-fifty chance of convicting a federal appeals court judge? Kerner family members and friends believe the prosecution was a politically motivated, personal attack by Richard Nixon against Otto Kerner, the man who helped John Kennedy to carry Illinois against Nixon in 1960 and who helped to achieve a historic breakthrough in racial understanding through the Kerner Commission. A circumstantial case could be made for this point of view. By the second half of 1971 the Nixon White House was well into its game plan for the 1972 reelection campaign. Illinois, always a critical state in a national election, could be better acclimated to a Nixon candidacy if Richard Daley's Democratic machine was tarnished by a fresh corruption scandal, Nixon aides believed. With racial polarization the key to obtaining the votes of blue-collar northern whites, a scandal involving Kerner would overshadow the conciliatory message of the Kerner Commission and its chairman.

In 1976 Charles W. Colson, a Nixon White House troubleshooter who became infamous in the Watergate affair, related a story to Anton Kerner concerning a political strategy meeting he attended in Key Biscayne, Florida, four days after the 1970 midterm election. The story suggests that Nixon was aware of the political implications of the government's investigations in Illinois. Colson told Anton Kerner in the tape-recorded interview:

> During the meeting, at some point—and I'm not sure of the context in which it came up—the then attorney general, John Mitchell, said, "There's an investigation going on. There's a grand jury." We may have been talking about Illinois politics—particularly with Rumsfeld there. [Donald Rumsfeld was a close friend of Edgar D. Jannotta, an Illinois Republican activist and an investment banker at the Chicago firm William Blair and Company who represented Everett in the sale of Chicago Thoroughbred Enterprises to Gulf and Western.] That's possible—but he was saying, "There's an investigation going on," and he said "of the Daley organization." And he said words to the effect that "they may not be so powerful the next time around"—'72—"When this grand jury gets through with them, we might not

308 KERNER: THE CONFLICT OF INTANGIBLE RIGHTS

have to contend, we might not have to worry about the Daley organization being so powerful." We were talking back on how the stealing of votes and the iron grip of the Daley organization on the Cook County vote, and Mitchell made the point. He said, "There's an investigation going on, and they won't be so powerful when this grand jury gets through with them. . . ." There was a pause. Nixon didn't respond to it, I remember very distinctly. And then later on in the conversation, he came back to it and said, "By the way, John, talking about that thing in Chicago . . . , you know I have a lot of respect for Dick Daley. I don't care that he opposes me politically. I don't care that he's a Democrat. He's a patriot. He stood with me on the war issue. He's never attacked me personally, and whenever I've gone to Chicago he's been very decent to me. He's a great American, and a real patriot, and I don't want to do anything to hurt Dick Daley."

According to Colson, Mitchell looked rather smug in disclosing the investigation in Chicago. "I could swear under oath that Mr. Mitchell knew about it and was certainly discussing it in the context of the politics of the situation," Colson said. "There wasn't any question about that." But Colson added, "I don't ever remember your father's name coming up, per se. I don't remember his name ever coming up on any of the [enemies] lists that became so celebrated." Colson told Kerner's son he had never heard of Project CRIMP or Victor Woerheide.[55]

At the time that Mitchell stated his knowledge of the grand jury probe, federal prosecutors were busy presenting evidence to a grand jury about the Cook County assessor's office and other political corruption cases that were indeed assaults on "the Daley organization." But the Kerner case was not before a grand jury until the following spring. In a 1979 letter to newspaper editor Robert E. Hartley, cited in Hartley's biography of James Thompson, Mitchell said, "To the best of my recollection I never discussed the prosecution of Gov. Kerner with anyone outside the Justice Dept. If there was any political influence in the prosecution of Gov. Kerner I would not know where it might have come from. Such influence was not present in any of the discussions or decisions made while I was in the Department."[56] White House tapes released so far under the "abuse of power" disclosures about the Watergate affair, available documents, and interviews of participating government officials provide no evidence that the Kerner prosecution was ordered by the president.

A stronger argument can be made from available evidence that the voluminous findings and suspicions of political wrongdoing in Illinois created powerful incentives for the federal law-enforcement community, thoroughly embarrassed by its apparent lapse in the Paul Powell scandal, to undertake aggressive prosecutions of public corruption in Illinois. Kerner was the biggest target at hand. Thanks to Everett's war with Miller and the CRIMP investigators' diligence, evidence against him already existed at the time of Powell's death. It would not be unreasonable, in addition, to suggest that news coverage of the racetrack scandal during 1971, stimulated in large measure by leaks from government officials, not only generated a negative view of Kerner, as Skinner observed, but also pushed the government to act.

◆ ◆ ◆

There was another factor, however. Government officials involved in preparing the indictment were unanimous in their belief that Marjorie Everett was not the "single key witness" in the case. They expected another convincing witness to be Otto Kerner himself. The government chronicled in their dealings with Kerner an erratic pattern of dissembling and voluntary admissions which to the bemusement of even seasoned prosecutors seemed strangely self-destructive and remarkably inconsistent with Kerner's best interests. During the period of the alleged conspiracy—1961 through 1967—Kerner inexplicably and recklessly provided a roadmap to guilt. Several of his undisputed actions were clearly uncharacteristic of straightforward, legitimate investing and were tragically contrary to the expected behavior of an honest public official: he concealed or permitted to be concealed his racetrack stock ownership, which, if the stock was not a bribe, was perfectly permissible under state law at the time; he suggestively wrote checks payable to cash or to Theodore Isaacs in connection with the investments; he falsely declared in a 1964 Better Government Association candidate questionnaire that his financial interests in private companies included only listed securities; and he and Isaacs used identically cryptic and suspicious tax return entries in declaring racetrack stock transactions. And there was no question that his friend Theodore Isaacs broadened the aura of deceit around Kerner by his flair for gamesmanship in seeking to conceal Kerner's involvement in the racetrack investment scheme.

Whether Illinois residents held an "intangible right" that their governor would not behave in such an outwardly deceitful manner was a question of philosophic proportions that was never debated publicly or codified in law. But there is no question that over his career, Kerner both nurtured and justified a public belief that he would conduct himself in a manner above suspicion. The pattern casting doubts on that belief continued after the IRS investigation began. Kerner's initial interview with Stufflebeam and Campbell in July 1970, when he discussed Isidore Brown and an investment in "Chicago Company," was either witless or contrived. Whereas Miller shrewdly exercised his right to maintain silence before the grand jury, saying he feared a perjury charge, Kerner and Isaacs engaged in extensive banter with the curmudgeonly Victor Woerheide, whose experience in persuading twenty-three grand jurors was eons greater than theirs. Their grand jury colloquies severely damaged their cause. Kerner even volunteered to make a second appearance, which resulted in one of the perjury charges against him.

Certainly Kerner was justified in being frustrated and angry at the government's protracted probe of what he regarded as a legal investment in racetrack stock. Certainly he was entitled to believe his public stature required him not to stand mute. But why, government lawyers wondered, did the former U.S. attorney, governor, and current federal appeals court judge demonstrate so little practical skill as the target of a criminal investigation? His performance seemed directly opposite to the erudition and cunning that attorney Eldon Hawley had alleged in summarizing the conspiracy charge.

In his prosecution memorandum, Skinner, who was a relative newcomer to the case, noted that there was no evidence that Kerner attended key meetings involved in the alleged conspiracy. He even warned against relying too heavily on perjury allegations involving Kerner's meetings with IRS agents, including the fateful July 15, 1970, interview. "The reason Kerner lied to the agents is not clear and because of its boldness and obvious falsity is quite perplexing," Skinner wrote, adding that "efforts should be made to keep [witness] v. Kerner testimony contradictions to an absolute minimum to prevent the case from drifting into a [witness] v. Kerner posture that would not be healthy." Setting aside perjury controversies, however, Skinner found other evidence of intent that likely would play well before a trial jury: "His appearance of self-righteousness, indignance [sic] as well as his pompous attitude. . . . His pompous attitude and attitude of self-righteousness did not assist him before the Grand Jury. We have no assurance that his attitude and appearance will be the same at the trial but it is possible that he will create the same impression at the trial."[57] Skinner's assessment can be read as evidence of government bias against Kerner. More likely, it was an objective preindictment handicapping of a prospective defendant by a talented, cold-hearted prosecutor warming up for his biggest case.

Almost any experienced criminal lawyer would have restrained Kerner from his damaging displays during the investigation and grand jury proceedings. Well after the investigation began and Kerner was warned of his right against self-incrimination, he retained sixty-year-old Peyton Ford, a former Justice Department lawyer with whom he worked in the late 1940s when he was U.S. attorney in Chicago. Kerner may have believed that an indictment undertaken in Washington might best be curbed by a Washington lawyer, but Ford was unfit for the task. In July Ford wrote to Woerheide requesting that Kerner be given a second chance before the grand jury: "Judge Kerner believes, upon further reflection, that there are several items that should be stated in a clearer and more precise manner. In addition to this, and upon further mature and sincere consideration, he believes he can not only clear up the aforementioned matters, but that he may be able to make a contribution to assisting the Grand Jury during its deliberations."[58] This letter, signed by private attorney Ford but written on Kerner's appeals court stationery, was practically delusional in the context of Woerheide's record as a Justice Department prosecutor.

At a critical August meeting in Washington between Woerheide, McGowen, and Hawley for the government and Kerner, Ford, and Ford's associate Ralph Olson, Ford attempted to present Kerner's side. Hawley prefaced his extensive notes on Ford's commentary by recording that at several points "I could not understand him, even though I was only about three and one-half feet from him, as he speaks with a mumble and sometimes in a very low voice."[59] At this eleventh-hour meeting Ford permitted Kerner to commit additional self-inflicted injuries. Kerner acknowledged that he never before disguised his stock holdings through nominees until the racetrack stock transactions. He asserted repeatedly that Isaacs acted as his agent in most of the racetrack stock dealings. Far from exonerating Kerner, these admissions elevated his closest adviser from being a "lesser figure" in the case and sharpened the aim of the government's bribery and intangible rights conspiracy charges against Kerner.

Prosecutors could use Kerner's own words, uttered before prosecutors in his lawyer's presence, to demonstrate that Kerner was not "one step removed from the critical transactions," as Henry Petersen had warned. Rather, by both common sense and common law, Kerner, the governor of a great state, stood in the shoes of his agent, an otherwise minor-league lawyer and political crony, during calculated and arguably nefarious dealings over many years with big-league players Marjorie Everett, William Miller, and Mayor Daley's former law partners, George Schaller and William Lynch. Without his link to Kerner, the government easily could imply, Isaacs, a lawyer of great ambition but modest accomplishment, would have trouble getting a telephone call returned from these cagey and rich wheeler-dealers. Ford, who permitted his client to dig these deep holes, died on November 22.

✦ ✦ ✦

A week later, in a joint ceremony, William Bauer was sworn in as a federal district judge and James Thompson took the oath as the new U.S. attorney for the northern district of Illinois. It was a transition that doomed Otto Kerner. With Thompson and his first assistant, Samuel Skinner, now in charge, the prosecution of Kerner shifted from being a drawn-out investigation and legalistic debate about federal jurisdiction to become a highly charged campaign to win a conviction. Bauer, the federal prosecutor anxious for a judicial appointment who demanded courtesy for public officials in Chicago, was out of the picture. In his place was the man Illinois residents would come to know as "Big Jim."

In late 1969 James R. Thompson, thirty-three years old and eager for a political career, was unsure about a federal appointment. He demurred at first when Bauer invited him to join the U.S. attorney's office and become his heir apparent. Bauer wanted to anoint a successor and clear the way for his elevation to the federal court at the soonest opportunity. But Thompson knew the Hatch Act would bar him from active participation in politics, and he had his eye instead on running for Cook County sheriff.

Richard B. Ogilvie had used the unabashedly political post of sheriff as a stepping stone to the governor's office, and Thompson hoped to do the same. The U.S. attorney's office had served that purpose only once before in Illinois history, when Republican Dwight H. Green capitalized on his work on the Capone case to run for governor in 1940. (Kerner's tenure as U.S. attorney from 1947 to 1954 had little to do with his campaign for governor in 1960.) But Thompson found the work of the U.S. attorney's office engaging, apart from his political aspirations, and assembled around him a team of aggressive, smart young lawyers who would remain loyal to him for many years. Later, after leaving the governor's chair, he called his U.S. attorney post "the best job I ever had. . . . You can really focus. It's like being a football coach. You can focus on the goal, especially if you've got the resources in Washington and they keep their hands off."[60]

Whereas Dwight Green, a former IRS agent, had played an integral role in developing the income tax case against Capone, Thompson had the Kerner case handed to him at the point of indictment. Nonetheless, after months of headlines about the case drawn from anonymous sources inside the government, Thompson brought something new to the story: an imposing, dynamic prosecutor, born and educated in the community, who put an attractive public face on the federal government's claim of jurisdiction over wrongdoing by Illinois public officials. Regardless of the Hatch Act, no political debutante could have dreamed of a better coming out. The thin legal theory of intangible rights now had a tangible champion. And the career lawyers in Washington had their cover. Petersen "called me to tell me Justice had approved the indictment . . . but that it was my decision," Thompson said. "They, Washington, were not telling me to indict. I had gotten clearance to indict from the criminal division and the tax division." But Thompson said Petersen told him, "It was my decision and if I had the indictment returned, I had to try the case personally. The message was quite clear, this was on my head."[61] Thompson never hesitated at the opportunity to play and win.

Kerner's transition from federal prosecutor, Illinois governor, and federal appeals judge to criminal defendant was far less auspicious. At least two local lawyers—veteran criminal lawyer Harry J. Busch, who had represented Daley during Daley's interview with IRS intelligence agents, and high-profile corporate lawyer Don H. Reuben, whose clients included the *Chicago Tribune*—urged Kerner to quit helping the government make its case. At trial, they advised, Kerner should make a statement to the jury but decline to take the witness stand and be cross-examined. Kerner, who still appeared unaware of the magnitude of his difficulties, rejected that advice and declined to hire a Chicago criminal lawyer who understood Chicago juries.

Shortly after the indictment Kerner visited Ben W. Heineman, a nationally connected Chicago industrialist and a prominent liberal who had attended law school with Kerner and served in the Kerner administration for seven years as the first chairman of the new Illinois Board of Higher Education. The board was one of Kerner's most significant reforms, for the first time disrupting the cozy relationship between the state's universities and the legislature, and Heineman was proud of his service. "He came to me and he said he would like my help in finding good counsel," Heineman recalled. Heineman, who admired Kerner, suggested that Kerner retain nationally prominent criminal lawyer Edward Bennett Williams, whose Washington-based firm was employed by Heineman's company, Northwest Industries. "I said, I know Eddie Williams very well; I don't know the Chicago criminal bar. . . . I said, I'll arrange a meeting with Eddie but, I said to him, on one condition—that Eddie personally represents you." Kerner had met Williams socially months earlier when Williams was in town defending an associate of Ray Kroc, founder of McDonald's Corporation. Heineman invited Kerner to accompany him on his next trip to Washington in the Northwest Industries corporate jet. He reintroduced Kerner to Williams. "I said, Eddie I'm here purely as a friend of the governor . . . and there's only one thing I want—that if you and the governor agree that the firm should represent him I want your personal commitment that *you* will represent him. He said, 'Fine.'"[62]

As a result the initial lineup of lawyers in the case included Williams for Kerner; prominent Chicago lawyer Albert E. Jenner for Theodore Isaacs; nationally known F. Lee Bailey for Faith McInturf; and two skilled Chicago criminal lawyers, William Barnett for William Miller and George Callahan for Joseph Knight. Within weeks, however, the stage bill was missing the name of Edward Bennett Williams. He handed Kerner to his partner Paul R. Connolly, who had been Williams's student at Georgetown University Law Center. "To my total amazement, Paul Connolly was representing the governor," Heineman recalled. "I called Otto, and I said, 'Otto, you had heard my conversation with Eddie. Did you make this choice? Did you choose to have Paul represent you?' He said no. He said, 'The firm gave me him.' Well, Eddie and I had been very good friends. I called him up, and I said, 'Eddie, I have a wonderful memory. There is no need for either of us to repeat what we said. You in effect broke your word to me.' I said, 'We are no longer clients of yours' . . . and I said, 'I will no longer talk to you.' He really didn't say a goddamn thing. He offered no excuses."[63]

According to Joseph Califano, then a partner of Williams and Connolly, Williams had told Kerner the first thing he must do to clear his name was resign as a federal judge. Otherwise, Williams believed, the government would drill into the jury's mind the fact that he was the only defendant in the courtroom with any power over the man on the street.[64] Kerner flatly refused. Peyton Ford had even tried to claim that Kerner could not be indicted unless he was first impeached by the Congress. Williams, annoyed by Ford's disastrous performance and Kerner's intransigence, turned his attention to another case of state political corruption, a complex bank fraud indictment against Walter H. Jones, a former Republican Speaker of the New Jersey State Assembly. With Williams at his side, Jones won acquittal in 1974. Paul Connolly, a silver-haired lawyer of considerable skill but much in love with the sound of his own voice, and James Thompson, a lawyer who declared in high school that he wanted to be president, would carry Kerner's case to the trial jury.

✦ ✦ ✦

> Jan. 6, 1973. Sitting here in the Sheraton Inn looking out the picture window, facing west across Mannheim Rd. on a clear, sunny day seems like a nice thing to be doing. However, it would be nice if it were not for the fact that I am a ward of the Federal Court for the Northern District of Illinois and a prospective juror in the case of Otto Kerner, Jr., and Theodore Isaacs. Even that fact is not so bad if a body could get some rest from the monotonous whine of aircraft coming in low over the motel to land at O'Hare Airport. To add to the misery, one has the heavy traffic on Mannheim Rd. This sounds like I am bitching about my situation. Well, I am.[65]

Richard J. O'Brien, a night-shift commercial printer in Chicago, kept a journal of his service as a juror in the Kerner trial. He was born in Dublin, Ireland, and lived with his wife and three children on Chicago's North Side. He acknowledged during the jury selection process that he had read "quite a bit" about the case. He said, "I like to go to the track when I get the opportunity—mostly to Arlington." O'Brien said he had been audited by the IRS two years in a row in the late 1960s. It was "a little nerve-racking the first time." The first audit led to an additional payment of "a couple of hundred dollars;" the second, to a payment of less than forty dollars. "We call that chicken feed in Tennessee," said Judge Robert L. Taylor, a dedicated, introspective federal judge recruited from Tennessee to preside over the case. "I guess so, judge. You feed that to chickens?" replied O'Brien.[66]

Two years after Victor Woerheide was assigned to Chicago and more than a year after the grand jury he guided returned indictments, the trial of Otto Kerner and Theodore Isaacs was about to begin. Thompson and Skinner strengthened their case against Kerner and Isaacs significantly during 1972. In January Thompson flew to California to assure racing officials that Everett was a cooperative witness who was owed a debt of gratitude by the government. Soon afterward she won a license to be a director at Hollywood Park. During the summer Thompson and Skinner obtained the cooperation of Everett's enemy, William Miller, the man Woerheide believed was the king-pin of the conspiracy. "Flipping" Miller, as prosecutors called the final piece of the government's strategy, resulted from a series of interviews with Miller, Stufflebeam, and Thompson and many bottles of Scotch. "It was hard to keep up with the old man, I'll tell you," Thompson recalled. "These were long, arduous sessions for Stufflebeam and me."[67]

Thompson often rationalized leniency for Everett on the grounds that the first witness through the door of the prosecutor's office gets the best deal. In the end, however, he would pin his best chance for a conviction on the last witness through the door, William Miller. But it was a big risk. "Miller and Everett hated each other and would have done anything to destroy each other, even if it meant screwing up our case," Thompson recalled.[68] Miller, at the time a seventy-one-year-old downstate millionaire entrepreneur and long-time Democratic fund-raiser and influence peddler, was seeing his attempt to build his own racing empire crumble in 1972. The man the government once called "one of Governor Stevenson's closest friends and advisers"[69] and a dominant figure in Illinois racing for two decades was near the end of his rope. The "hell of a cantankerous guy," as Thompson called him, faced not only the criminal indictment but also an IRS assessment of $2.8 million for back taxes and penalties from his racetrack dealings. In August he agreed to testify for the government in return for a promise that the criminal charges against him would be dropped at the end of the trial if his testimony was deemed useful. Charges against his secretary, Faith McInturf, also were suspended. Miller's longtime political crony, Joseph Knight, was stricken from the case because of ill health.

Miller provided the government with what Henry Petersen knew the case lacked, a direct link between Kerner and a bribe. After reaching his deal with the government, Miller suddenly remembered that he had offered racetrack stock to Kerner on behalf of Everett at a meeting with Kerner and Isaacs in the governor's office on November 9, 1962. "That's very nice of Marje," Kerner replied, according to Miller's trial testimony.[70] Miller, the master extortionist in Everett's original plot, joined his adversary as a protected witness, although their stories clashed throughout the trial and they clearly impeached each other's testimony. Miller had new friends. "We became friends as only a prosecutor and a witness can become friends," Thompson said of Miller, adding that Miller nearly ruined things when he answered, "I don't remember" repeatedly during Connolly's cross-examination.[71] IRS special agent Stufflebeam, still looking for employment outside the government, drew close to Miller and discussed going into business with him after the trial. "He and I are good friends," Stufflebeam said in 1978. "And at one time . . . we talked about, you know, why don't we take a look at this deal or that deal, you know, go into business, but we never have."[72]

In his diary juror O'Brien sensed correctly that Everett and Miller "were using me and the other jurors to further their aims . . . to take vengeance on their enemies." He called Everett "vindictive." He called Miller "the homicidal witness," adding: "I have formed the opinion that he is lying or telling half-truths to save himself at the expense of Kerner and Isaacs. He is a 72-year-old windbag who was a wheeler-dealer all his life, living high on the hog, and even if his transactions were not all clear and above board he had not the guts to fight for his innocence and also to part with the money to pay for such a fight. He preferred to rat on the two men who were more or less patsies in the whole scheme."[73]

The contradictions between the Miller and Everett testimonies were left unresolved. Connolly pampered Everett on the stand, as he attempted to portray Miller as the villain. But he refused to ask Miller whether he had bribed Kerner. Connolly said later that, because Miller had become a government witness, he was unsure how Miller would answer the crucial question, which therefore was never asked in the trial. Connolly, who throughout the trial was enmeshed needlessly in the minutia of the government's case, abruptly made the November 9, 1962, meeting the cornerstone of his defense. In his summation to the jury at the end of the six-week trial, Connolly said:

> One of the most significant factual determinations you must make in this case, and I say to you with all the power and force at my command—if I am wrong about this, I think you are going to have to return a verdict against Otto Kerner—one of the most significant factual determinations that you will have to make is whether or not on November 9, 1962, William S. Miller discussed Marje Everett's stock offer with Governor Kerner, because you have a major conflict. Kerner says it did not happen. William Miller said it did happen.[74]

With that, reporters in the courtroom observed a noticeable sigh of relief emitted from the prosecution table. Connolly had simplified for the jury the government's complex bribe conspiracy allegations into a single event—take it or leave it. The meeting with Miller and Isaacs, which was recorded clearly in Kerner's daybook, provided jurors with their best tangible evidence. And, according to O'Brien, they needed it. "The thing that weighs on myself and [fellow juror] Dean McKinney is that the future of the two defendants lies in the hands of such a bunch of incompetents," he wrote about his fellow jurors. "For the life of me, I do not understand how the attorneys for either side could select us. . . . I know that it is virtually impossible for this jury to decipher or establish a true meaning of what either side is about. . . . Kerner and Isaacs do not know what a ding bat jury they are before."[75]

O'Brien had been a last-minute choice by the prosecutors, who selected him in place of a woman from Mayor Daley's ward. "I was of the firm belief that the Irishman was going to be trouble," recalled McGowen, the Justice Department's representative on the trial team. Applying a stereotype, McGowen feared O'Brien, a Catholic, "might know a thing or two about police states and would be anti-authoritarian."[76] In 1972 Britain had imposed direct rule in Northern Ireland to stem violence between Protestants and Catholics, but violence continued unabated.

"He was a real problem," Skinner agreed.[77] But "Thompson wasn't buying that; Thompson wanted the Irishman," McGowen said.[78] Years later Thompson did not recall a dispute about seating O'Brien but acknowledged that O'Brien was a loose cannon who hated the prosecutors. In the end, however, it did not matter. Unfortunately for Kerner and Isaacs, O'Brien's bitter alienation from his fellow jurors and the entire process of the case never made it into the jury deliberation room. A creative drinker who consumed mouthwash over ice when the U.S. marshals severely rationed the sequestered jury's alcohol consumption, O'Brien on the afternoon of February 2 pitched over in his chair in the jury box, vomited blood, and fell to the floor, unconscious from a bleeding ulcer. It was four days before the government was to complete its case. "There is a God," Thompson said later.[79] During his recuperation after he was excused from the jury, O'Brien wrote that "hell would have to freeze over" before he would have voted to convict either defendant.

On February 19, President's Day, the jury of six men and six women filed into the courtroom shortly before noon to deliver its verdict. William E. Michael, a brick mason who had served on a jury before and therefore was chosen foreman, handed an envelope to John Borris, a former grand jury clerk who had never handled a trial before. Borris struggled nervously to get the paper out of the envelope and the words out of his mouth. "Guilty as charged in the indictment," he read aloud.[80] A reporter scratched his right ear to signal a colleague watching through a sliver of glass in the rear door to the courtroom. The news would make the afternoon editions. The initial verdict was against Isaacs, and the next one was inevitable. Kerner's face lost its color. His hands were frozen on the defense table, pressed together, his fingers pointing upward as if in prayer. He looked sadly at the jury. Connolly reached grandly to shake Thompson's hand.

"Now, Mr. Foreman, 'guilty in the indictment'; does that mean as to each count?" asked Judge Taylor, a careful jurist who did not enjoy Chicago winters and who occasionally expressed agitation at the courtroom antics of lawyers for both sides. "Each count, your honor," said Michael.[81] Kerner and his lawyers exited one door of the courtroom. Isaacs and his lawyer, Warren D. Wolfson, left by another. The convicted men exchanged no words.

Three weeks later, at the sentencing hearing, Kerner and his lawyers appealed to Taylor, whose father had been governor of Tennessee, to consider Kerner's full tenure of public service and his accomplishments as Illinois governor over more than seven years. "I fear that the role of public servant is today regarded with such disdain and cynicism that it is difficult and at times virtually impossible for any man long in the public eye to receive fair treatment when accused of a crime and to enjoy the presumption of innocence which protects other citizens," Kerner said to Taylor.

> I was surely not the greatest chief executive of this state, but I did devote all of my heart and energies to be a good Governor. Yet, my energetic dedication to idealistic goals has ironically proven to be my downfall. . . . My entire life since leaving law school, almost forty years ago, has been devoted in large measure to civic and social responsibilities, with a wide range of many activities, from Scouting to the difficult and challenging problems of the aged and mental health. . . . In retrospect, one thing is clear to me: The burden and sacrifices of public service forced me to forsake my personal life, and I entrusted my personal and financial affairs to persons in whom I had long-time faith and confidence.[82]

But Thompson would not relent. Aside from his six-foot-six-inch frame, it was the conviction of Kerner under the intangible rights theory that put the "Big" into Big Jim Thompson. Like the skilled prosecutor he was, Thompson held no enmity toward Kerner, or any regard at all, except as an athlete might feel toward a competitor or a hunter toward prey. In his presentencing remarks to Judge Taylor, Thompson turned Kerner's plea against him and drove home the theme of betrayal that was the essence of the government's mail fraud prosecution strategy against Kerner and the basis of federal indictments of Chicago political figures that followed the Kerner conviction. Noting that one of Kerner's lawyers had called him "a builder" of public institutions and public welfare, Thompson said:

> One of the greatest things he built was a public reputation in this state, shared by well-nigh everyone, Republicans, Democrats, independents, the young, the old, the educated, the illiterate, that Otto Kerner was a rare breed of public servant and that he was living proof that a man could come out of patronage politics or orga-

nization politics, and rise above narrow partisan considerations, and be a public servant that everyone could look up to, and he built a reputation about which you heard testimony on the witness stand. But that building contained the fatal flaws or defects of corruption, arrogance, cynicism, as demonstrated by the evidence in this case, and so it came crashing down last February, in the verdict of the jury. In my view it would have been better for the people of the State of Illinois had that building not been built at all, because more than the career of Otto Kerner came tumbling down on verdict day—all the hopes and aspirations and longings of the citizens of the State of Illinois that somewhere in this field called politics, government service, that somewhere, on some occasions, there could be occasional rays of light, there could be people that the citizens could look to, could remove this dark cloud of cynicism that in these last years people have hung around the very notion of public service.[83]

In their appeals to Taylor, both Kerner and Thompson indirectly evoked—without naming it—the gathering public outrage over the Watergate scandal. The disdain, as Kerner put it, emerging toward Nixon created an unsympathetic context for him or any public official to seek leniency. Of "corruption, arrogance and cynicism," as Thompson put it, there would be no better example in U.S. history than Richard Nixon, Thompson's ultimate superior in the federal hierarchy. Taylor, emotionally wrought—at one point becoming confused and ordering Isaacs to serve time for counts in the conviction that concerned only Kerner—sentenced Kerner and Isaacs each to three years in a federal penitentiary. But Kerner would not incarcerate his pride. "Twelve jurors found that I betrayed the public trust," he told Taylor. "Twelve jurors that, among the millions of citizens whom I have served, chose to believe that I dishonored the high office of governor, and no matter what the ultimate outcome of this case may finally be, that verdict has deeply and irreparably tainted the good reputation which I cherished. Years of imprisonment can never compare in severity to that punishment which has already been meted to me, I think unjustly."[84]

12

Unfinished Work

In 1997 President Bill Clinton, seeking to fashion his place in history, announced that he wanted to "lead the American people in a great and unprecedented conversation about race." Speaking to a graduation ceremony at the University of California at San Diego, Clinton said: "I believe the greatest challenge we face . . . is also our greatest opportunity. Of all the questions of discrimination and prejudice that still exist in our society, the most perplexing one is the oldest, and in some ways the newest: the problem of race." Clinton invoked a previous American conversation about race: "At the high tide of the civil rights movement, the Kerner Commission said we were becoming two Americas, one white, one black, separate and unequal. Today, we face a different choice: Will we become not two but many Americas, separate, unequal and isolated? Or will we draw strength from all our people and our ancient faith in the quality of human dignity to become the world's first truly multi-racial democracy? That is the unfinished work of our time, to lift the burden of race and redeem the promise of America."[1]

Few Americans remember the Kerner of the 1968 Kerner Commission report. Fewer still remember how his dignity was stripped from him or how for him America's promise was extinguished by America's power. Kerner traveled far in public service, contributing along the way to many of the milestones Americans associate with progress. Yet none of it counted in the end. Looking behind history can be troubling in this way. Kerner's downfall marked a significant milestone on a regrettable journey into cynicism and coarseness in the system of public affairs. A clean judge found to be dirty, as his relentless pursuers in the IRS would say, must necessarily be humbled so that no one would doubt that the system works, but in response many people simply disengaged from a system that produced such disturbing and irreconcilable results.

In the crude lingo of politicians and journalists, it was not a system but rather a game that sent Kerner and Isaacs to federal prison. They played poorly and lost. U.S. Attorney James Thompson played well and won. He was elected Illinois governor four times and retired from public life to a lucrative law career. Completing the circle, President Gerald Ford appointed William Bauer, Thompson's mentor as U.S. attorney and a protégé of retired judge Winfred Knoch, to Kerner's seat on the U.S. Court of Appeals for the Seventh Circuit. The seat reverted to the domain of Du Page County Republicanism. But the system that incarcerated Kerner was not merely a game. Nor did he tragically fall away from the simple moral structure of his life that he had sought first in the military and later in politics. Rather, he was ensnared in a complex process of laws and law enforcement that responded with increasing convolutions over many decades to ever-changing social norms and the public's ambivalent demands for accountability and redress. The system that caught Kerner in its web became too remote and difficult for many ordinary people to understand. In the void left by public bewilderment, the system was captured by clever people to the exclusion of compassionate people.

✦ ✦ ✦

There was no better example of bewildering complexity in public affairs than the intangible rights doctrine of mail fraud. In April 1987 the U.S. Supreme Court, in the case of *McNally v. United States*, finally dealt with the theory and found it unconstitutional. Reversing political corruption convictions in Kentucky, the high court majority, in an opinion written by Kennedy appointee Justice Byron White, declared flatly, "The mail fraud statute clearly protects property rights, but does not refer to the intangible right of a citizenry to good government." Describing the indeterminate legislative history of the mail fraud statute, the majority ruled, "When there are two rational readings of a criminal statute, one harsher than the other, we are to choose the harsher only when Congress has spoken in clear and definite language."[2] White cited a 1926 Supreme Court ruling in another mail fraud case: "There are no constructive offenses; and before one can be punished, it must be shown that his case is plainly within the statute."[3] White concluded: "Rather than construe the statute in a manner that leaves its outer boundaries ambiguous and involves the Federal Government in setting standards of disclosure and good government for local and state officials, we read [the mail fraud statute] as limited in scope to protection of property rights. If Congress desires to go further, it must speak more clearly than it has."[4]

With this decision the court effectively voided the government's elaborate, expensive, and ruinous pursuit of Otto Kerner. Several other local political figures in Chicago and elsewhere convicted under the intangible rights doctrine won new hearings, although some whose misdeeds extended to quite tangible extortion did not escape their sentences entirely. Had he lived, Kerner almost certainly would have seen his conviction overturned, as did former Maryland governor Marvin Mandell in a 1977 corruption case also tried before federal judge Robert Taylor of Tennessee. Further prosecution of Kerner would have been unlikely, given the absence of significant federal charges beyond the intangible rights mail fraud offense. But the ruling came too late, eleven years after his death. In 1990 the seventh circuit appeals court denied a motion by Kerner's children to expunge his conviction. "That interest is personal to Otto Kerner Jr. and cannot survive his death," ruled Judge Daniel Manion.[5]

The McNally decision briefly spiked the most creative weapon of Chicago's newest generation of civic reformers. It disturbed, for a moment, the federal government's brute sway over Illinois and Chicago politics that was spawned during the crime-busting zeal of the Capone era, rekindled under Attorney General Robert Kennedy, and expanded by the Nixon administration. Expressing the post-Watergate mood of the country, Justice John Paul Stevens issued a stern dissent from the majority in the McNally case. Stevens, who as a private lawyer had exposed corrupt dealings between Theodore Isaacs and two Illinois Supreme Court justices and was well versed in Chicago politics, held a unique perspective from which to evaluate the intangible rights doctrine in the years after it was used to convict Kerner. When Kerner was indicted in December 1971, Stevens wrote to him: "I deeply regret this development and wish there were some meaningful way in which I could be of assistance to you. I am most grateful to you for your cordial welcome to the court and the many ways, both small and large, in which you have been helpful to me. I shall miss your valuable and honorable participation in our work, but am sure that temporary difficulties will not diminish our friendship."[6] After Kerner wrote from prison to congratulate Stevens on his Supreme Court appointment, Stevens wrote, "Dear Otto, Many thanks for your kind note. It is a little difficult to realize what seems to have happened. I trust and hope that the reports of your excellent health are accurate."[7] But Stevens's friendship toward Kerner did not extend to opposing the prosecution tactic that put Kerner in prison.

Political fraud, Stevens argued, is defined not by the tangibility of its loss to the public or reward to the corrupt officeholder but by the perniciousness of its method. The fundamental crime is deceit, an especially repugnant act by a public official who carries a broad fiduciary duty to his or her constituents. He scolded his fellow justices for overturning what he called consistent and sensible rulings by lower courts over many years that extended the mail fraud statute to schemes beyond the overt taking of money or property. Intangible fraud crimes are crimes nonetheless, especially when committed by public officials, Stevens argued. Lower courts rightly had affirmed Congress's intent to prevent the postal service from being used in commission of such crimes. "Can it be that Congress sought to purge the mails of schemes to defraud citizens of money but was willing to tolerate schemes to defraud citizens of their right to an honest government, or to unbiased public officials?" Stevens wrote.[8]

Stevens, who became one of the more liberal members of the Supreme Court, harshly rebuked his colleagues in the majority to the point of questioning their motives: "The possibilities that the decision's impact will be mitigated [by Congress] do not moderate my conviction that the Court has made a serious mistake. Nor do they erase my lingering questions about why a Court that has not been particularly receptive to the rights of criminal defendants in recent years has acted so dramatically to protect the elite class of powerful individuals who will benefit from this decision."[9]

Despite Stevens's criticism, his denunciation of official corruption was in no way at odds with the court majority, which was concerned principally with questions of federal jurisdiction and legislated congressional intent. The majority and minority opinions together prompted Congress to resolve those issues. In doing so Congress affirmed a history of judicial rulings throughout the 1980s that spun from the Kerner conviction. Before Kerner the oblique notion of a federally protected "right" to honest public servants was scarcely to be found in the law books. Afterward case after case and finally Congress itself established the theory, with no public criticism. In 1988 Congress, with little discussion, passed bipartisan legislation to restore the intangible rights doctrine by appending the words "intangible right of honest service" to the mail fraud statute. Late rather than never, the Kerner indictment was legitimized properly.

◆ ◆ ◆

As an introduction to his 1962 novel *Burn, Killer, Burn,* convicted murderer Paul Crump, writing from Cook County Jail, offered verse by Thomas Wolfe:

Which of us has known his brother?
Which of us has looked into his father's heart?
Which of us has not remained forever prison-pent?
Which of us is not forever a stranger and alone?[10]

On July 29, 1974, eleven days after resigning his judicial appointment in a letter to Nixon, Kerner began his incarceration in a minimum security prison in Kentucky's Fayette County, the heart of the Bluegrass. His seven months and one week as an inmate of the Federal Correctional Institution at Lexington had nothing to do with correction and rehabilitation, a process Kerner believed possible for Crump and other wrongdoers. He was, according to prison records, a model prisoner from start to finish. But his experiences since his indictment had changed him from a man of generous empathy to one who thought mostly of himself—a stranger and alone. He fought to retain his freedom, restore his reputation, and uphold his dignity. He had lost much: friends; memberships in social and fraternal organizations, including the Masons; the ability to practice law; and in October 1973 his wife of thirty-nine years.

Helena Irene Kerner died the night of October 10, 1973, in the kitchen of their retreat in Lake Geneva, Wisconsin. The couple was awaiting oral arguments later that month on Kerner's appeal. A chronic hematoma of the brain, a blood-filled swelling in the brain to which alcoholics are prone, caused her to choke to death on a piece of squash. Sixty-seven years old, she had undergone surgery in August to remove a blood clot in her brain but had not recovered fully. An autopsy revealed no trace of alcohol in her blood when she died. The youngest daughter of the powerful and immense Anton Cermak had been a difficult spouse. She was an acerbic but astute political observer and strategist. Were it not for her drinking addiction and its consequences, she might have asserted more effectively on behalf of her husband the pragmatic survival instincts that Kerner lacked. But she was spoiled as a youngster by her doting father and later in life developed childlike tendencies that caused many of Kerner's associates to marvel at his patience. Cermak's boisterous campaigns for the personal liberty to take a drink—the battle cry of his political career—rang hollow as the disease of alcoholism consumed Helena. For Kerner, she was a devoted companion nonetheless.

Kerner seemed to lose his compass after the jury's verdict and Helena's death. He refused to resign from the bench for more than a year after his conviction, a decision that eroded support in the Chicago legal community and among fellow progressive Democrats. Adlai Stevenson III, elected to the U.S. Senate in 1970, called for Kerner to be impeached after he was sentenced. An angry Anton Kerner wrote to Stevenson: "We are sons of fine, dedicated men. To our good fortune, however, is attached a responsibility for our actions not only as they reflect upon ourselves, but as they reflect upon our fathers. I believe that you have forgotten much for which your name has stood."[11] In a newspaper interview after his release from prison, Kerner scorned the working-class jury that convicted him. "I did not have a jury of my peers. . . . Peers means neighbors," Kerner told *Chicago Sun-Times* columnist Roger Simon as the two sat in Kerner's fashionable North Lake Shore Drive apartment.[12] It was a unseemly complaint that ill suited a champion of ordinary people.

Kerner, his family, and friends grasped vainly at the notion that he was a victim of the Nixon White House "dirty tricks" ethic. "I have reason to believe I was one of the victims of this overall plan," Kerner wrote in a May 1973 memorandum outlining his options after he was sentenced by Judge Taylor.[13] With the Senate Watergate hearings in full view on television that spring and summer, Kerner proposed that his conviction be fought on the grounds of "discriminatory prosecution" ordered by the White House of Watergate repute. His memorandum noted that many public officials named in newspapers as having owned Illinois racetrack stock, including William Lynch and George Schaller, both now judges, were not indicted. Thompson's vow in the days after Kerner's conviction that he would indict others in the racetrack stock scandal never materialized.

In pursuit of this theory, decorated World War II combat veteran Otto Kerner—for whom the leader of U.S. forces in Vietnam, General William Westmoreland, had testified as a character witness—found a strange affinity with a young Vietnam War protester named Jeffrey S. Falk. On April 19, 1973, the same day that Kerner's sentence was entered on the federal court record, Falk, a little-known draft resister in Chicago, won an extraordinary victory from Kerner's colleagues on the seventh circuit appeals court. The court, in an en banc decision, reversed Falk's conviction on charges of failing to carry his draft registration and Selective Service classification cards.

The four-to-three decision, which received almost no public attention, profoundly challenged the independence of federal prosecutors in general and specifically questioned the government's response to the antiwar movement. Chief Judge Luther M. Swygert and Judges Roger J. Kiley, Thomas E. Fairchild, and Robert A. Sprecher overturned Falk's conviction and three-year sentence for violating the draft card law. In an opinion written by Nixon appointee Sprecher, the majority held that Falk must be given a rare—perhaps unprecedented—opportunity to examine in court the purposes of his prosecutors; he would be allowed to call as witnesses officials of Thompson's office. The majority ruled that Falk was entitled to present to a judge his claim "that Falk was singled out for special prosecution," in violation of his free-speech rights, because he was an outspoken antiwar activist.[14]

During his trial Falk's attorney had said that more than 25,000 men mailed back or otherwise disposed of their draft cards, as Falk had done, without being indicted. There was a reasonable likelihood, the appeals court majority ruled, that Falk had been a victim of "invidious discrimination which cannot be reconciled with the principles of equal protection."[15] Falk's active war resistance, as a member of a draft counseling group called the Chicago Area Draft Resisters, could have inspired his indictment under the Selective Service law, the majority held.

"The particular circumstances of this case which we believe compelled the government to accept the burden of proving nondiscriminatory enforcement of law are several," Sprecher wrote. The court cited specific circumstances, including alleged remarks by assistant U.S. attorney Stephen Kadison (later a member of the Kerner prosecution team) to the effect that the government was pursuing Falk because of his draft-counseling activity. "The district court erred in refusing a hearing on the offer of proof" of these allegations, the majority declared.[16]

Judge Walter J. Cummings, a Johnson appointee writing for the minority, ridiculed the majority. "If they have not already done so, criminals would be well advised to criticize some policy of the government which may indict them," he wrote.

> If this unspecific and misleading allegation deserved a hearing to determine whether a defendant's prosecution violated equal protection, then it is practically inescapable that any defendant can precipitate such a hearing. . . . The "purpose" of the executive [branch], as Falk uses the term, is not a basis for declaring an otherwise valid prosecution unconstitutional. . . . It is the ultimate transgression of judicial authority to haul the executive to the witness stand for examination by a criminal defendant as to why it had chosen to indict him.[17]

This is exactly what Kerner proposed to do against Thompson and his associates. Kerner, a member of the seventh circuit on leave, contemplated a unique counteroffensive. He would file a habeas corpus petition on his own behalf, grounded in the *United States v. Falk* decision just issued by his fellow seventh circuit judges. Kerner sought to avail himself of the court's decidedly liberal temperament, which he had helped to engender. "In light of United States v. Falk . . . , it would appear that there are now solid grounds to file a Sec. 2255 [habeas corpus] petition," Kerner wrote. "It is my premise that I was prosecuted in violation of my civil rights because of past political offices that I have held and my prominence in the Democratic Party of the State of Illinois, and this motivated the improper and illegal use of the Department of Justice and IRS as a political arm of the Committee to Re-elect the President."[18] Kerner did not pursue the tactic, probably for the obvious reason that official bribe taking—the nub of the government's charges against Kerner and the jury's verdict—would be difficult to connect to a constitutionally protected right, such as free speech, without reducing the Falk ruling to the absurdity that Judge Cummings contemplated.

Kerner did appeal on grounds close to the Watergate case. In an argument not raised at the trial court level, Kerner asserted before the court of appeals and the U.S. Supreme Court that he could not be indicted until he had been impeached by the House and removed from office by the Senate, as implied in the impeachment clause of the Constitution. In its February 1974 opinion, the appeals panel—comprising three senior judges from appellate benches outside the seventh circuit—held that Kerner properly could wait until after he lost at the trial level to raise the risky issue of the impeachment priority. But the court cited Constitutional language that federal judges "hold their offices during good behavior" and ruled against Kerner: "The Constitution does not forbid the trial of a federal judge for criminal offenses committed either before or after the assumption of office. . . . Protection of [judicial lifetime tenure] is not a license to commit crime or forgiveness of crimes committed before taking office." Rejecting Kerner's separation of powers argument, the panel ruled, "We believe that the independence of the judiciary is better served when criminal charges against its members are tried in a court, rather than in Congress. With a court trial, a judge is assured of the protections given to all those charged with criminal conduct."[19]

In his partial dissent Senior Judge Harvey M. Johnsen, former chief judge of the eighth circuit in Omaha, advised fellow appellate panel members— J. Edward Lumbard, former chief judge of the second circuit in New York, and Jean S. Breitenstein, former chief judge of the tenth circuit in Denver— that they need not and should not stray into the sensitive issue of the Constitution's ambiguous impeachment clause while the Nixon drama was unfolding before the world. Without naming Nixon, Johnsen wrote: "It does not seem to me to be necessary or wise to undertake to make that determination [addressing the ambiguity of the impeachment clause] in the present situation. The question has been the subject of bitter agitation and heated dispute on both sides, and the majority's holding can open the door to consequences which it may be better for the nation not to have to experience in the turbulence of the present times."[20]

Four months later, while Nixon clung to office, the Supreme Court without comment declined to take up Kerner's appeal of the appellate panel's impeachment clause ruling. The *Washington Post* reported, "Like the President, Kerner contended that as an officer removable only by impeachment he was immune from criminal prosecution while still in office."[21] The *Post* noted that the Justice Department, reviewing the cases of Kerner and former Vice President Spiro Agnew, had ruled that only the president deserved immunity from criminal indictment before impeachment and removal from office. Shortly thereafter Kerner became prisoner number 00037-123 in Lexington, a man alone stepping with head held high into strange confinement.

✦ ✦ ✦

Justice Stevens was misinformed about Kerner's health, probably because of Kerner's own efforts to put the best face on his situation. According
to his prison medical records, Kerner, a heavy cigarette smoker, had been
hospitalized in May for heart failure and was taking medication for heart
disease as well as gout when he began his three-year sentence. He suffered
fainting spells before entering prison and afterward. He neither ate nor slept
well in the cramped room he shared with another prisoner, Jim Carr, who had
been convicted of transporting stolen property across state lines. After the
roommates were moved to a quieter, more spacious room, a prison doctor
prescribed for Kerner the antidepressant drug Elavil as a sleep aid. In October he complained of chest pains and thereafter took nitroglycerin four or
five times a week. Symptoms of depression intensified in January after a federal parole board denied his initial request for early release. In February a chest
X ray revealed for the first time evidence of a cancerous tumor in his right
lung. He was released on parole March 6, 1975, to undergo surgery, which
confirmed the presence of cancer.

On entering the Lexington prison Kerner at first wrote to friends that he
had undertaken his incarceration in the spirit of a fresh military recruit. "The
adjustment has not been too difficult," he wrote to Ralph and Pat Newman
a week after he arrived. "You must remember, I was a 'buck' private years
ago. The staff and those in my unit have been very helpful and thoughtful.
The medical facilities are really quite good and the concern and care excellent."[22]

Before its conversion to a minimum security prison earlier in the year, the
red-brick facility had been a drug rehabilitation center operated by the U.S.
Public Health Service. Set on a scenic hilltop in thoroughbred horse country,
the prison housed 350 nonviolent offenders. *Chicago Sun-Times* reporter Paul
Galloway, assigned to cover Kerner's incarceration, wrote that the facility was
"considered a model of modern penology. The regimen here is less restric-
tive than at the prisons and jails that house most of the persons convicted of
crimes in this country. There is an absence of punitive symbols. There are no
bars and few locks. The guards are unarmed, and Warden Lawrence Grossman sometimes has difficulty distinguishing the members of the staff from
the inmates, who are called residents. None wears a uniform."[23] One of his
fellow residents was James Stavros, the former Wheeling Township Democratic committeeman snagged in the early days of what became known as
Project CRIMP.

The day before Kerner arrived, Galloway watched prisoners tossing a Frisbee
"on the grass under giant oak trees while others sat at picnic tables writing

letters and talking to their families." One of Kerner's early visitors wrote to him how good he looked in a golf shirt. But the pastoral setting and relaxed appearances did not disguise for long the reality of Kerner's incapacitation. He soon became aware that he had been marked for special treatment, though not in the way he was accustomed. Nothing in Kerner's life, including his war-time service, had prepared him to be a prison inmate. He kept an occasional journal. At one point he wrote: "So frequently I sit here alone. I wonder of what use is our prison system—as I have often wondered when I was seeking an alternative to this inhuman manner of restraining those who have violated the law. The waste of man power—both by the restrainers and the one restrained. Removing the individual from the outside world really accomplishes nothing of a positive nature. The restraint builds up frustrations and a smothering of the will. It kills motivation and completely removes decision ability."[24]

In mid-November Kerner wrote of a meeting between prisoners and Warden Grossman in which Grossman urged prisoners to take advantage of escorted trips outside the facility because, Kerner wrote, "participation in these trips would aid in determining deportment when out of the institution and for parole consideration."[25] Later that day, Kerner said, he reminded his caseworker, Mary Moldestad, that when he had entered the prison, she had assured him he would be evaluated by a team of prison officials for possible furlough. "I stated I had not met with any team since my arrival and was not aware of any program or goals set for me in anticipation of parole," Kerner wrote. "She said there was none for me, that I was not here for rehabilitation and therefore needed no program. I then asked her whether I should apply for escorted trips so I might be tested for deportment out of the institution. She said no, that I would not be approved for any outside trips as are all others. I replied that any effort on my part then would be useless. She agreed."[26]

In other words, because he did not require rehabilitation, he was to be treated worse than the more incorrigible prisoners who did. Kerner wrote to his mother:

Because of a visit this week with the warden, I'm certain of one thing; now that I know, I can adjust myself to it. I've had confirmed what I suspected for some time. Unless there is a great emergency, I will not be allowed off the grounds until I'm released on parole board to go home. I will not even be allowed to go into town to purchase clothes, even though accompanied by a staff member. This type of trip is allowed everyone [else] in here. I am and will be completely restricted to the institution. . . . You can question, why me? Where they allow bank robbers, narcotic pushers, post office robbers and many others that have all sorts of privileges. The only answer I can give is that I am me. I've had too much recognition nationally and even internationally, while the others are unknown or would not be recognized by the public.[27]

Kerner's prison job assignment magnified his Kafkaesque circumstances. He worked in the prison's "research and evaluation" section and assisted in a "bureau-wide survey of current practices in the operation of the furlough program," according to prison records.[28] In that effort "Mr. Kerner designed a check sheet to insure complete and accurate reporting," wrote Emily S. Cottrell, a social science analyst who evaluated Kerner's work. "Mr. Kerner's tremendous store of knowledge and wide range of experience have been of great value in a research setting. His experience in all areas, including routine clerical assignments, has been given in a congenial, efficient manner. His association with staff and residents in the conduct of business has been most pleasant and a definite asset to the mission of the institution. His warmth and concern for others have made for a highly satisfactory working relationship."[29] None of this helped Kerner to obtain furloughs for himself. While reviewing furlough papers Kerner noted that "of the hundreds of forms that passed over [his] desk," only his contained orders against speaking to the news media while outside the prison, although the Bureau of Prisons issued several press releases about Kerner while he was in its custody.[30]

Kerner believed he had been designated a "special offender," a prisoner who had his privileges curtailed without a formal hearing or other due process because of one or more special features of his case. Litigation by prisoners in a federal correctional facility in Danbury, Connecticut, had brought the "special offender" designation to light, and a Bureau of Prisons memorandum written shortly before Kerner's release described the status, which apparently was imposed in cases of notoriety such as his. Though it did not use the term "special offender," the regional parole board, in refusing Kerner's initial request for parole, wrote in January, "Your offense behavior has been rated as high severity." Stating that the normal term before parole for similar convictions was sixteen to twenty months, the board concluded: "After careful consideration of all relevant factors and information presented, it is found that a decision outside the guidelines at this consideration does not appear warranted. Your release at this time would depreciate the seriousness of the offense committed and thus is incompatible with the welfare of society."[31] A confidential note signed by two parole board members after Kerner's hearing in October 1974 said Kerner's "high political position—Court of Appeals judge—creates a situation of national or unusual interest." The note said Kerner "gave a political speech" at the hearing.[32]

Despite the facility's minimum security regime, life at the prison was not an extended stay in a library or confinement on a cruise ship with few amenities. Prison personnel apparently had not been screened for sadistic tendencies, and some were all too willing to employ needless humiliation as a control technique. On one occasion Kerner challenged a guard to explain the excessively noisy manner in which prisoner head counts were conducted repeatedly throughout the night, a process that included shining flashlights in the face of "residents" trying to sleep. "I got up and asked the C.O. whether that was necessary," Kerner wrote in his journal. "He said, yes, he had to see a part of the body—and if I didn't like it I could sleep with my foot out of the door."[33]

As for the inmates, although none was a hard-core violent offender, many brought with them the aggressive, antisocial traits that had led them into the criminal judicial system. Kerner told a young prisoner who had butted ahead in a line to go to the end. The prisoner became belligerent. "He threatened to murder me," Kerner wrote. "I said we are all in this together—no one is any better or worse than another and to get into the line at the end." When the man refused again, "I asked him for his number—he refused—another person with him peeled him away and said, 'don't kill him'—'that would be cold-blooded murder.'" The next day the young prisoner apologized to Kerner through a prison officer, but the officer rebuked Kerner for asking for the man's prison number. "I wanted to know the number of the person who said he was going to murder me," Kerner wrote, proving his sense of humor had not been destroyed. "I didn't like to be murdered by an unknown."[34]

Kerner's health deteriorated. In mid-January he wrote in his typically correct, matter-of-fact manner to Dr. Thornton Scott, his prison physician: "Dear Dr. Scott, Saturday night I did not feel well. That night about 11:30 P.M. felt uneasy and developed diarrhea and nausea and felt a dizziness coming on and went into a faint in the bath-room. Do not know exactly how long I remained in that state. Fortunately, I was nauseous and on my knees at the time so did not fall from a sitting or standing position. Sunday did not feel too well or Monday. During the period stayed very much on liquids. Today, Tuesday, felt normal again and on regular diet. Very truly yours. Otto Kerner, 00037-123."[35]

✦ ✦ ✦

With his health failing, the bureaucratic inertia that held Kerner in its grasp quickly dissolved. But winning parole required Kerner to specify what occupation he planned to take up on release. At first he announced plans to accept a position with a Chicago-area concern called RDS Enterprises. Ross D. Siragusa, a contemporary of Kerner and the founder of home appliance manufacturer Admiral Corporation, had invited Kerner to work for him as a personal financial adviser. A wealthy patron of the Democratic Party and many civic organizations in Chicago, Siragusa had recently sold Admiral to Rockwell International Corporation and was busy redeploying part of the proceeds into new business ventures under the umbrella of his private investment company, RDS Enterprises. His offer to Kerner was a generous gesture to a man he admired. Kerner clearly lacked experience and credentials as a personal financial adviser, but the job would have given him a comfortable transition into private life. Later Kerner indicated in prison documents that he would work for Siragusa's philanthropic foundation. But Kerner ultimately declined Siragusa's offer. He did not want charity, recalled Mel Schneider, a long-time business associate of Siragusa.

While in prison Kerner had begun corresponding with Harry H. Woodward Jr., the executive director of an organization that sponsored self-motivation programs for prisoners nationwide. Woodward's Special Services Center for Correctional Programs was part of Lewis University, a tiny college in the Chicago suburb of Lockport. Lewis began in the 1930s as a home for wayward boys operated by the Catholic Christian Brothers order. Woodward met Kerner in Lexington in September 1974. According to Woodward's memorandum on the meeting, "[Kerner] has gone downhill pretty fast and is not making a good adjustment. I think this will be impossible for him to do. He does not want to be associated with the Law School [then being organized by Lewis University] because in his words he is 'too cynical about the law.' He did express interest in being involved in our program. Ross Siragusa and [Chicago industrialist] Henry Crown have offered him a job if he wishes it."[36]

After Kerner's initial request for parole was denied, Woodward wrote to Kerner, urging him

> to fight the parole board decision every inch of the way. My experience of working behind the walls for seven years is that you have to assert your rights continuously and without let-up or they will walk all over you. Unfortunately being a nice guy in prison is often equated by the staff with being a "patsy." You do not have to strike people physically or abuse them verbally in an emotional manner to let them know you will not stand for nonsense. You have thousands of friends on the outside who would like to help you. I could get a committee together in no time flat to stand behind you in an appeal if you so desire.[37]

Here was the spark of vigor Kerner sorely needed in the midst of his depression. Woodward's enthusiasm struck a chord. Kerner began to write about his prison experiences and to draw from them larger themes about the treatment of prisoners and inmate civil rights. He realized he had become a member of a distinct minority group, convicts, who virtually by definition and certainly by popular sentiment were oppressed and disadvantaged.

Kerner was looking for a way to make another contribution. He believed he had found it in the engaging Harry Woodward and agreed to become a consultant to the Special Services Center. Typical of Kerner's work for Woodward was a draft of a proposed speech he would make to a Special Services Center conference on prison conditions:

The completely autocratic manner in which rights of inmates are ignored is quite typical of our prisons and indicative of the "private preserve" attitude of many in authority. There are many beautifully written policy memoranda that when read exude fairness and equity but in the application are quite the opposite. For too many years the courts refused to hear matters filed by prisoners complaining of prison conditions. Prisoners having no lobby are without a voice until recent years when courts finally took jurisdiction. However, the "private preserve" atmosphere still exists. . . . If there is to be any hope of rehabilitation or retrieval of those imprisoned, there must be an improvement in the general atmosphere and attitude by staff. The "I am master, you are slave" feeling is much too pervasive. Under these circumstances, how can there be any hope of accountability, responsibility and integrity on the part of the inmate when his very word is doubted? Better communications must be established, rules and regulations must be positive and be capable of understanding by both staff and inmates. There is much misunderstanding. Cumulatively, these undermine confidence and develop frustrations and hasten the dehumanizing process.[38]

This point of view, born of personal experience, was the most quixotic of Kerner's public career. His advocacy of adoption rights for children, mental health reform, fair-housing laws, racial justice for urban blacks, and civil liberties for the underclass all had far larger constituencies. Moreover, his sentiments regarding prisoner rehabilitation were behind the public policy curve—a predicament shared in great measure by the Kerner Commission report. Support for convict rehabilitation, popular among progressive academics and practitioners of prison reform in the 1960s when Paul Crump had faced the electric chair, was eroding swiftly by the time Kerner reentered free society. California researchers Franklin E. Zimring and Gordon Hawkins, in their 1995 book *Incapacitation: Penal Confinement and the Restraint of Crime*, noted: "The normally warring ideologies that pervade the American criminal justice policy debate were united in hostility to rehabilitation by the mid-1970s just as they had been united in support of rehabilitation a few years earlier."[39]

On the other hand, Kerner was correct that in the 1960s courts had reversed their historical reluctance to interfere in the conduct of prisons. Until then judges had strictly followed the Thirteenth Amendment to the Constitution: "Neither slavery nor involuntary servitude, except as a punishment for crime whereof the party shall have been duly convicted, shall exist in the United States." Prisoners were said to exist in a state of "civil death." As the civil rights movement grew outside prison walls, however, courts throughout the country began to take up complaints that prisoners and prison welfare organizations made about conditions inside prisons. After the 1971 Attica prison rebellion in New York State, public attention favoring prison reform began to shift away from prisoner rehabilitation toward reforming the basic conditions of prisoners merely serving their time. Noted penologist John J.

DiIulio of Princeton University observed in his 1991 book *No Escape: The Future of American Corrections:* "Since 1970 . . . the doctrinal wall of separation between judges' chambers and prison walls has crumbled. The courts have intervened in a wide range of prison and jail issues, including crowding, food service, sanitation, health care, due process protection for inmates, and the constitutionality of prison and jail conditions in their totality. Federal judges in particular have abandoned the hands-off doctrine in favor of a hands-on doctrine."[40]

Kerner had much to say about toppling "the doctrinal wall of separation between judges' chambers and prison walls." He undertook the mission on his release from Lexington, after his initial cancer surgery in April. Lewis University's press release announcing its new association with the former governor quoted Woodward: "Mr. Kerner will initially provide research assistance for our upcoming National Congress for New Directions in Female Correctional Programming. . . . The Congress will pinpoint the vital issues relating to new directions in adult and juvenile corrections, and, as our consultant, Mr. Kerner will directly participate in the process of change: identifying and assessing trends. In addition, if his health permits, he will be assisting with programs in correctional institutions across the country."[41]

Kerner attempted to rekindle the can-do spirit he nearly lost in prison. At a United Auto Workers conference in Springfield shortly after his release, Kerner revisited liberal themes about the role of government that had animated his first days in Springfield fourteen years earlier. With economic conditions in the state deteriorating, he reminded a press conference of the report by the Cassell Committee, which in the early 1960s had studied unemployment in Illinois and become a national model for such inquiries.

"You don't overcome these problems by sitting and moaning about them and complaining," he said, his throat still raw after an operation on his cancerous lung. "You've got to be positive. . . . Perhaps there ought to be a second Cassell study, people from labor, industry, academia, just citizens . . . so we can overcome these problems instead of letting the economy take care of it, . . . to develop programs to put people back to work, and that really starts the economy moving. It's not a question of the egg or the chicken. You provide jobs, and the economy will move." Asked about the Kerner Commission report, he said, "The basis for the report, I think, is as valid today as the day we sent it to the government printing office." Asked about reports that James Thompson would run for governor, he said, "I think the primary is open to anyone who seeks to run. Of course, the position of governor is vastly different from that of being a prosecutor." He paused and added, "Vastly different."[42]

In December, with only five months left to live, Kerner appeared at a Chicago press conference sponsored by Woodward's group. Seated to his left was celebrated Vietnam war protester Jane Kennedy, a registered nurse from Chicago who was on furlough from a West Virginia prison serving a three-year sentence for draft card burning. Kerner called on Congress to transfer the responsibility for running federal prisons from the Justice Department to the Department of Health, Education, and Welfare. "There's a difference in philosophy," he said. "At HEW, they're concerned about individuals, but penologists are most interested in punishment." Kennedy spoke of the sub-standard quality of prison health care. Kerner agreed: "I was in a model in-stitution. Believe me, HEW could do better."[43]

This message was upbeat, genuine, and timely, but Kerner's choice of or-ganizations through which to express it was ironic, to say the least. Since 1971 Lewis University's College of Continuing Education had enrolled inmates in prisons at nearby Joliet and Pontiac. The university's president, Lester Carr, saw prison education, which he called "work behind the walls," as a key el-ement of the school's ambitious expansion plans. His patron in this effort was insurance magnate W. Clement Stone, one of the biggest contributors to Rich-ard Nixon's presidential campaigns in 1968 and 1972. In January 1974 Stone transferred to Lewis the operation of his nationwide Correctional Program, created in the 1960s by his private foundation to help the multimillionaire carry his "positive mental attitude" (PMA) motivational doctrine inside the nation's prisons. Stone had used PMA effectively for years to inspire the sales-people who made him rich selling insurance policies door to door. He gave Lewis a $233,500 grant to establish the Special Services Center. With the money came Harry Woodward, who had signed on with Stone years earlier as a prison educator.

In 1974 Woodward established an advisory board for the Special Services Center. One notable member was James R. Hoffa, the former president of the International Brotherhood of Teamsters union whose thirteen-year sen-tence on fraud, conspiracy, and jury tampering convictions had been com-muted by Nixon in 1971. On his release from the federal penitentiary in Lewisburg, Pennsylvania, Hoffa became an outspoken critic of prison con-ditions and advocate of jailhouse reform. Stone's daughter, Donna Stone Bradshaw, questioned Hoffa's presence on the advisory board, but Woodward assured her that Hoffa would be an effective fund-raiser. The day Hoffa dis-appeared forever—July 30, 1975—he had been scheduled to attend a meet-ing of the advisory board in Washington, recalled Ellis C. MacDougall, a nationally known authority on prison administration who served with Hoffa on the board. "Everybody arrived but Jimmy," MacDougall said.[44]

Another advisory board member was Thomas B. Evans Jr., a top national Republican Party official from Delaware. (Evans later won a seat in Congress but was retired by the voters after the news media exposed his affair with a female lobbyist who had posed nude in *Playboy* magazine.) The chairman of the advisory board was Jerris Leonard, a former Republican state legislator in Wisconsin who headed the civil rights division of the U.S. Justice Department in the first term of the Nixon administration and later ran the federal Law Enforcement Assistance Administration under Nixon. Victor Woerheide, the Justice Department lawyer who presented charges against Kerner to a grand jury in Chicago, had reported to Leonard when he investigated the Black Panther Party. In 1988 Leonard was an usher at the funeral of Nixon's attorney general, John Mitchell. He became a prominent lobbyist and Republican fund-raiser in Washington and in January 1997 joined the Washington office of the Chicago-based law firm Hopkins and Sutter.

The names of Stone, Hoffa, Leonard, and Evans all appeared on the Special Services Center letterhead in the uplifting correspondence Woodward had sent to Kerner in Lexington. In a report to the W. Clement Stone and Jessie V. Stone Foundation after Kerner's release, Woodward said: "Our chairman, Jerris Leonard, had a candid discussion with Mr. Kerner about his helping out in the fundraising area. Mr. Kerner is agreeable to doing this."[45] "We had Kerner; we had Hoffa," Leonard recalled in a 1997 interview. "Stone loved to pick up people like that who'd had problems and were good PR for him. I don't say that negatively. His theory was a good one—bring in people who had these kinds of problems who had high profiles because they helped us instill the philosophy of his program, which was getting people to think better of themselves." But Leonard said he could not recall meeting Kerner.[46]

Kerner must have known that in agreeing to work with Woodward he was aligning himself publicly with close associates of Nixon and Mitchell, the men he blamed for destroying his reputation and sending him to prison. But his biggest error in judgment concerned Woodward himself. According to Mac-Dougall, Stone and Woodward had a falling out in the late 1970s. An ex-convict and long-time PMA disciple who had worked in various prisons for Stone's Correctional Program for eight years wrote confidentially to Lewis University president Carr in the spring of 1975, just as Kerner was signing on, saying that the program was "going to die" because of Woodward's inattention and incompetence.[47] Stone also lost confidence in Lewis University, which defaulted on more than $3 million in bank loans that Stone had cosigned, according to university documents.

The following year Woodward became executive director of the well-known charitable organization Goodwill Industries in Chicago. Seven years later a federal organized crime task force targeted Woodward's activities at Goodwill. In 1987, at age fifty-four, he pleaded guilty to federal racketeering, mail fraud, and income tax charges relating to a scheme to loot the charity of nearly $500,000 in profits from real estate deals. Woodward was sentenced to eight years in prison and ordered to make restitution to Goodwill. The attorney for Woodward's accomplice in the scheme, pleading for leniency for his client, told a federal judge that Woodward was "a two-faced individual" and said his client "fell under Woodward's spell."[48]

✦ ✦ ✦

Kerner underwent cancer surgery a second time in the fall of 1975. "Now I can at least do a bit more than a slow walk—and that on occasion still causes a burning sensation if the atmosphere is heavy," he wrote to a staff member at Lexington in October.[49] He pursued unsuccessfully a petition for a presidential pardon from Gerald Ford. He attempted unsuccessfully to restore his state pension, which after extended court proceedings had been disallowed by the Illinois Appellate Court because of his conviction. In addition to working with Woodward, he resumed his decades-old association with the John Howard Association prison reform organization.

He enjoyed the marriage of his daughter. He nurtured a warm relationship with Lorraine Shomo, the widow of friend and former CBS executive Ernie Shomo. In September supporters in Springfield staged a rousing welcome-home reception where more than eleven hundred Springfield residents saluted the man from Chicago who was the best-loved governor in their town in recent memory. Kerner addressed the crowd in a good humor, joking with friends and remembering happier days. After his mother, Rose Kerner, ninety years old, thanked the crowd, Kerner said, "May I say she still drives a car and still drives it too fast for me." Seeing William C. Harris, the president of the Illinois Senate who in the 1950s had helped to enact adoption reform, Kerner said: "I gave [him] and his wife a couple of children. I made his wife a mother twice." Hearing the crowd's laughter, Kerner pulled out an old line: "I want you to know that as county judge I made more women mothers than any other man in Cook County." Only once did he refer to his recent past: "I would not wish on my worst enemy those things that have occurred to me in the last few years."[50] Edward J. Murphy, who had been Kerner's barber during his years as governor, was in the crowd. "I saw a real tired and worn-out man," he recalled. "The pin-striped suit that used to look so good on him was a little big."[51]

In January 1976 the National Association for the Advancement of Colored People honored Kerner in a Chicago dinner hosted by Theodore Jones. Kerner died of cancer on May 9, 1976, Mother's Day, in Chicago's Illinois Masonic Hospital.

Many journalists and pundits characterized him as a political Candide.

Mike Royko's remark that Kerner had been born with golden ballot in his mouth explained succinctly the conventional view of Kerner as a debonair passenger in a first-class compartment on the rough seas of midcentury politics. Kerner was not a skillful politician. But he was the kind of man politicians always say the public needs in politics—a dedicated, caring individual who could easily have exploited his father's reputation into a lucrative career in the private sector but who chose public service instead. Unlike the three greatest Democratic politicians from Illinois during Kerner's lifetime—Anton Cermak, Henry Horner, and Richard J. Daley—Kerner backed into politics after wartime military service nurtured his sense of duty. He was one of three men that Jacob Arvey in the late 1940s tapped from outside his organization to dress up the Democratic Party in the wake of public revulsion against the Kelly-Nash machine. Like the two other Arvey protégés, Paul Douglas and Adlai Stevenson, Kerner never paid traditional political dues early in life through street-level precinct work and unquestioning party loyalty. Douglas, an irascible product of the academic ivory tower; Stevenson, the aloof son of a wealthy downstate family; and Kerner, a proud icon of Chicago's ethnic community—all enjoyed the perquisites of political office and the acclaim of the party's liberal wing without having to fight to obtain them.

Of the three, however, Kerner most effectively used his public position for something besides a platform for cleverness and a well-endowed ego. Kerner's ego was no less inflated than those of Douglas and Stevenson, but his Bohemian tradition, ever-present in the person of his dynamic mother, Rose, kept him firmly grounded in healthy skepticism toward politics and focused on more tangible goals. Kerner was buried with full military honors in Arlington National Cemetery, a fitting resting place for a man who simply wanted a mission and an opportunity to accomplish it. His preference for tackling concrete public tasks rather than waging politics for its own sake placed him apart. Taking on unglamorous issues rather than merely fulfilling the transactional demands of party regulars and campaign supporters meant he would forever fail to be one of the boys. Speaking out for the right of African Americans to enjoy the same opportunities he had enjoyed separated him from the paternalism of the liberal establishment. Addressing the plight of underclass criminal defendants and finding common ground with prison inmates went much further than most progressive politicians cared to go. His quiet rebellions against political convention made this outwardly conventional man vulnerable, as defenders of the status quo and peddlers of cynicism soured the public mood toward public affairs.

Gwendolyn Brooks, now the poet laureate of Illinois, captured the essence of Kerner's downfall in a poem she wrote for his funeral:

He was a man extensive and extending.
But we do not love largeness very long.
We look with narrowing littleness on largeness.
He was a man of considerable Light.
Light frightens us. We squint. We cower.
We hurry forth the shadows of the hour.[52]

Almost a year to the day after he died, Kerner's children, Anton and Helena, dressed in formal attire, stood between the flags of the United States and Illinois on the stage of the Scottish Rite Cathedral in Peoria. They came to the ornate Masonic hall to accept on behalf of their late father the Order of Lincoln insignia conferred annually by the Lincoln Academy. Kerner, with inspiration and help from Michael Butler, had created the nonprofit, nonpartisan Lincoln Academy as an extension of Illinois's popular Lincoln commemoration at the 1964 New York World's Fair. Among the individuals who played roles in Kerner's career, Lincoln laureates inducted since 1965 included Adlai Stevenson II, Ben W. Heineman, Everett M. Dirksen, William C. Westmoreland, and Roy Wilkins. According to the program for the evening's lavish ceremony, the sole function of the academy was the annual selection of Lincoln laureates "to further, encourage and recognize the outstanding contributions made by Illinois citizens toward progress and the betterment of humanity."[53] While grateful for the academy's recognition of their father, Anton and Helena had to overcome deep reservations about accepting the award from James R. Thompson, who was just beginning his first term as Illinois governor and as such was the academy's presiding officer.

"Thompson was going to be the person who handed us the award," Anton Kerner recalled years later. "It was going to be a very strange and difficult situation for us because we esteemed the academy's work, but disdain Thompson's opportunistic dishonesty in prosecuting our father. We decided we would recognize Thompson as chief executive of the state and ignore him as a human being, which is basically what we did."[54] The next day, Mother's Day, the two presented the award to ninety-one-year-old Rose Kerner. Her son had intended the award to go to living individuals who could enjoy the acclaim. The girl who journeyed with her mother to Chicago from a tiny Bohemian village in 1889 was proud to do so in her son's memory.

Appendix:
Interviews

Many individuals, not just those quoted, contributed to this biography. The following individuals, whose personal or professional relationships to Otto Kerner (OK) are briefly described, were interviewed by Bill Barnhart (BB), Gene Schlickman (GS), or both during the course of researching Kerner's life and times.

Barnett, William A.—attorney for Shirley Kub and William S. Miller (BB, 9/28/95)

Barr, Jean—Judge Taylor's longtime secretary (GS, by phone, 7/20/93)

Bauer, William J.—DuPage County state's attorney; judge; U.S. attorney; U.S. district court judge; U.S. circuit court judge, seventh circuit (BB/GS, 1/21/93)

Becker, Raymond R.—chief, Division of Information and Publicity, Illinois Department of Business and Economic Development (BB/GS, 2/22/95)

Bennett, Robert W.—dean, Northwestern University Law School (BB, 6/2/93)

Berwick, Paul V.—IRS revenue agent (BB, by phone, 5/16/93)

Bonniwell, Donald R. —chair of Illinois Tollway Authority under OK (GS, 10/2/86)

Bowles, Clyde O., Jr.—Chicago attorney (BB, 10/3/95)

Bradley, Earl—Brown University alumnus (BB, 4/28/93)

Brennan, James—Judge Taylor's clerk (GS, by phone, 6/30/93)

Brickhouse, Jack—WGN reporter; sports announcer; OK character witness (BB, 12/16/92)

Brooks, William—early OK staff person, Springfield (BB, by phone, 6/9/93)

Bunn, Willard—Springfield banker; OK friend (BB/GS, 10/31/92)

Burke, Edward M.—Chicago alderman (GS, 3/21/93)

Burr, Edward—appeals attorney and Cook County circuit court judge (GS, 7/28/93)

Busch, Harry J.—attorney for Theodore J. Isaacs (BB, by phone, 7/15/93)

Bush, Robert—IRS supervisor (BB, 7/17/95)

Butler, Michael—OK friend; initiator of Lincoln Academy; producer of *Hair* (BB/GS, 2/15/92)

Butterfield (Reidy), Mary—OK aide (BB, 2/28/93)

Caetti, Ted—court buff; OK trial observer (GS, 4/10/86)

Califano, Joseph A., Jr.—top LBJ aide; secretary, U.S. Department of Health, Education, and Welfare; partner at Williams and Connolly (BB/GS, 8/22/94)

Callahan, Eugene J.—executive director, Chicago Council on Religion and Race (BB, 6/5/95)

Callahan, Gene—*Springfield Register* political reporter; aide for U.S. senator Alan Dixon (BB, 10/30/93)

Campbell, Robert F.—IRS special agent (BB, by phone, 5/14/93)

Carter, May Kerner—OK's sister (GS, 8/10/85; BB/GS, 4/4/92)

Cassell, Frank H.—OK consultant (BB, 2/13/93)

Cawley, Thomas—traffic and criminal judge (GS, 9/17/93)

Chapin, Samuel—Kerner family doctor in Springfield (BB, by phone, 6/28/93)

Chapman, Gerald—Illinois National Guard member; Chicago lawyer; husband of Democratic state representative (GS, 1/20/93)

Cicourel, Aaron—associate of Norton Long (BB, by phone, 3/11/93)

Clark, William G.—state representative; attorney general; Illinois Supreme Court justice (BB, 9/11/92)

Conlon, Denis J.—IRS attorney (BB, 1/26/93)

Cook, Robert—executive director of Illinois Association of Realtors (GS, 3/18/94; BB, by phone, 6/9/95)

Cooper, Stephen M.—OK appeals court clerk (BB, 6/10/93)

Corman, James C.—congressman; Kerner Commission member (BB/GS, 12/1/93)

Craven, James C.—Illinois Parole and Pardon Board member; Illinois appellate court judge (BB/GS, 6/26/93)

Cummings, Walter J., Jr.—U.S. circuit court judge, seventh circuit (BB/GS, 8/25/95)

Dammann, Peter—early OK campaign supporter (BB, by phone, 3/14/93)

Davis, Paul—WGN-TV news director (BB, 12/21/92)

Deutsch, Michael E.—OK's appeals court clerk (BB, by phone, 6/28/93)

Downing, Robert J.—assistant U.S. attorney under OK; Northfield Township committeeman; Illinois appellate court justice (GS, 5/27/87; BB/GS, 7/7/93)

Downs, Anthony—president, Real Estate Research Corporation (BB, by phone, 7/6/93)

Dunne, George W.—House Democratic majority leader; president, Cook County Board (BB, 6/2/92; BB, 7/7/92)

Dvorak, Joseph and Liberty—friends of Cermak and Kerner families (GS, 12/17/85)

Elward, Paul F.—state representative; Cook County circuit court judge (BB/GS, 2/4/93)

Engle, David—Judge Taylor's clerk; covered OK's trial (GS, by phone, 8/2/93)

Erdmann, E. Thomas, Jr.—OK 1971 federal grand jury member (BB, 2/23/93)

Erlenborn, John N.—state representative; congressman (BB, by phone, 8/15/94)

Feurer, William E.—assistant to Governor Kerner (GS, 3/13/86; BB/GS, 8/28/92)

Foy, John—IRS criminal investigator (BB, by phone, 10/11/95)

Fuesel, Robert—IRS criminal investigator (BB, 5/10/95)

Georgeff, Phil—Arlington racetrack announcer (BB, by phone, 9/13/94)

Gerty, Francis J.—first director of the Illinois Department of Mental Health (BB, 2/29/92; BB, 11/14/92)

Gertz, Elmer—First Amendment lawyer; author; Illinois Consitutional Convention delegate; attorney for Paul Crump (GS, 3/1/93)

Gianulis, John—chair, Rock Island County Democrats (BB, by phone, 6/16/93)

Ginsburg, David—executive director of the Kerner Commission (GS, 3/5/92; BB/GS, 11/30/93)

Glotzer, Martin—shareholder of Chicago Thoroughbred Enterprises (BB, by phone, 1/13/93)

Goldwasser, Edwin L.—deputy director of Fermi National Accelerator Laborator (BB, by phone, 4/19/95).

Gove, Samuel K.—director emeritus, Institute for Government and Public Affairs at the University of Illinois (BB/GS, 10/3/92)

Graebel, Dorothy—widow of the pastor of the First Presbyterian Church, Springfield (BB/GS, 7/10/93)

Graham, Richey, Jr.—OK's nephew-in-law (GS, 10/23/85)

Graves, Gene H.—OK's director of business and economic development (BB/GS, 2/22/92)

Gray, Milton H.—OK law school colleague (BB, by phone, 6/30/93)

Griesheimer, Ronald E.—state representative (GS, by phone, 8/13/93)

Haefele, Edward—associate of Norton Long (BB, by phone, 11/18/92)

Hanson, Henry—*Chicago Daily News* Springfield reporter (BB, 1/13/93)

Harmet, Harold H.—OK 1971 federal grand jury foreman (BB, 12/24/92)

Harris, William C.—Illinois state representative and senator; president of State Senate; Illinois bank commissioner (BB/GS, 10/5/95)

Heineke, Burnell—*Chicago Sun-Times* reporter (BB, 1/16/92)

Heineman, Ben W.—CEO, North Western Railway; chair, Illinois Board of Higher Education (BB, 10/6/93)

Herndon, Margaret Kolom—OK's county court secretary and mansion manager (BB/GS, 10/31/92; GS, 2/13/93)

Herring, Harry A.—OK's closest Springfield friend (GS, 6/5/92; BB/GS, 10/3/92)

Hogan, John—WGN-TV reporter at OK trial (BB, 1/12/93)

Holmquist, William—Helena Cermak Kerner's lawyer (GS, 1/23/86)

Inbau, Fred E.—professor at Northwestern University Law School (BB, 6/2/93)

Isaacs, Theodore J.—OK's long-time associate; Illinois National Guard member; OK's campaign manager; director, Illinois Department of Revenue (BB/GS, 1/14/95; BB/GS, 2/13/95)

Janis, Martin E.—OK public relations person (BB, 7/30/92)

Jannotta, Edgar D.—investment broker at William Blair and Company (BB, 11/10/94)

Johnson, Richard—OK intern, 1963 (BB, 10/15/92)

Jones, Theodore A.—president, NAACP's Chicago chapter; Illinois Parole and Pardon Board member; Illinois Public Aid Commission member; director, Illinois Department of Revenue; initial deputy executive director of the Kerner Commission (BB/GS, 11/9/93)

Joyce, Lou and Marty, Jr.—wife and son, respectively, of Marty Joyce Sr. (Chicago policeman and OK bodyguard) (GS, 4/3/93)

Katz, Harold A.—member of OK's veto force; state representative (BB/GS, 7/30/92)

Kay, Norton—*Chicago American* political editor; assistant to Governor Walker (BB/GS, 2/24/93)

Kerner, Anton C.—OK's son (GS, 9/4/85; BB/GS, 1/4/92; BB/GS, 1/25/92; BB, 6/5/93; BB/GS, by phone, 1/29/98)

Kinnaird, William R.—OK's Brown University fraternity roommate (BB, 6/13/92)

Klassen, Clarence W.—Long-time state sanitary engineer (BB/GS, 2/22/92)

Koziol, Ronald—*Chicago Tribune* reporter (BB, 1/8/95)

Kreml, Frank J., Jr.—OK boyhood chum (BB, 2/13/93)

Kriegel, Jay R.—aide to Mayor John Lindsay; CBS executive (BB, by phone, 11/4/93)

Landau, Eliot A.—OK appeals court clerk (BB, by phone, 6/23/93; BB, 7/2/93)

Lassers, Willard—Cook County circuit court judge (GS, 7/28/93)

Lawton, Samuel T., Jr.—OK military associate; OK friend; OK political acquaintance (GS, 2/6/86)

Leighton, George N.—federal district court judge; attorney for Paul Crump (BB, by phone, 7/8/93; BB, 7/12/93)

Leonard, Jerris—chair, Lewis University Special Services Center (BB, by phone, 8/6/97)

Lindsay, John V.—congressman; mayor of New York; vice chair of the Kerner Commission (BB/GS, 11/4/93)

Littlewood, Tom—*Chicago Sun-Times* Springfield correspondent; author of *Horner of Illinois* (BB/GS, 12/5/92)

Long, Norton E.—consultant to Governor Kerner (BB, 9/4/92)

Lorenz, Francis S.—director, Illinois Department of Public Works and Buildings; state treasurer; Illinois appellate court judge (BB/GS, 5/18/92)

Ludwig, Jerome—OK Illinois National Guard friend (BB, by phone, 12/21/92; BB, 6/4/93)

Lydon, Matthias—assistant U.S. attorney (BB, 1/15/97)

Lynk, David—Marge Everett's bodyguard; Arlington Park racetrack superintendent (GS, 1/29/92)

Mabley, Jack—newspaper columnist; advocate for the mentally handicapped; OK friend; mayor of Glenview, Ill. (OK's hometown) (BB, 12/12/91)

MacDougal, Ellis—board member, Lewis University Special Services Center (BB, by phone, 8/6/97)

Maher, Robert—state senator; OK assistant (BB/GS, 2/24/93)

Makarski, Richard—assistant U.S. attorney; chief, Justice Department's criminal division (BB/GS, 2/2/93)

Manary, Donald L.—clerk of Andalusia, Ill. (BB, 10/22/93)

Mandel, Richard—adoption lawyer (BB/GS, 10/12/95)

Marovitz, Abraham Lincoln—U.S. district court judge and OK eulogist (BB/GS, 8/11/92; BB/GS, 8/24/92)

Masica, Bill—OK's Springfield YMCA masseur (BB/GS, 1/13/92)

McGowen, Darrell—assistant U.S. attorney at OK trial (BB, 5/12/93)

McGuire, David—OK's caddy at the Illini Country Club (GS, 2/12/93)

Mikva, Abner J.—state representative; U.S. appeals court (D.C.) judge; counsel to president (BB, 4/13/92)

Morgan, Lewis V., Jr.—DuPage County state representative; judge (BB/GS, 12/6/94)

Morris, Virginia—OK's appointment secretary (BB/GS, 8/29/92)

Murphy, Ed—OK's Springfield barber (BB, 5/29/92)

Murrian, Robert—Judge Taylor's clerk (GS, by phone, 7/14/93)

Nachman, Norman H.—attorney for Tucker bankruptcy trustee (BB, 2/17/92)

Nathan, Richard—associate director of program research for the Kerner Commission (BB, by phone, 7/1/93; BB/GS, by phone, 7/1/93)

Nathan, Roger W.—chair, Committee on Human Relations (BB, 1/29/94)

Netsch, Dawn Clark—OK assistant; law professor; Illinois Constitutional Convention delegate; state senator; state comptroller (BB/GS, 11/13/92; BB/GS, 6/7/93)

Newman, M. W.—*Chicago Daily News* reporter (BB, 2/8/94)

Newman, Ralph—OK friend; appraiser; member and historian of Lincoln Academy (GS, 2/26/90)

Nimitz, Matthew—aide to Joseph Califano (BB/GS, 11/4/93)

O'Brien, Katherine Walsh—sister of OK girlfriend in early 1930s (BB, by phone, 9/21/92)

O'Connell, William—*Peoria Journal Star* Springfield correspondent (BB/GS, 1/23/93)

Otis, James T.—member of OK's veto force (BB, 1/19/93)

Palmieri, Victor H.—deputy executive director of the Kerner Commission (BB/GS, 11/5/93)

Parkhurst, John C.—state representative (BB/GS, 1/23/93)

Patton, Thomas E.—member of QK's defense team (GS, 3/6/92; BB/GS, by phone, 11/13/92; BB/GS, 11/29/93)

Pensoneau, Taylor—*St. Louis Post-Dispatch* reporter (BB, 1/15/92)

Percy, Charles H.—opposed OK for governor in 1964; elected U.S. senator in 1966 (GS, 3/5/92)

Pierce, Daniel M.—member of 1963 reapportionment committee; state representative; mayor of Highland Park, Ill. (BB/GS, 7/21/93)

Powers, Thomas—*Chicago Tribune* reporter (BB, 5/31/93)

Redmond, William A.—OK law school classmate; Illinois House Speaker; member of the Illinois Prison Review Board (BB/GS, 11/23/91)

Reidy, John—OK Springfield aide (BB, 2/28/93)

Reuben, Don H.—*Chicago Tribune* lawyer (BB, 11/20/96)

Reuss, Robert—Illinois Bell official; OK Springfield friend (BB, 11/3/92)

Rice, William—assistant to William Stratton and OK; University of Illinois lobbyist (BB/GS, 12/5/92)

Ringo, Miriam—assistant to OK; state personnel director (BB/GS, 11/15/93)

Roberton, Frederic—Illinois National Guard member (BB, 3/10/93)

Roberts, Walter—Cambridge University alumnus (BB, 6/16/93)

Rosenthal, Jacob—*New York Times* writer; Kerner Commission staff member (BB, by phone, 6/30/93)

Ross, Lawrence J.—former counsel to oversight committee, U.S. House Ways and Means Committee; associate of Oliver P. Stufflebeam (BB, 8/7/95)

Roth, Edwin C., Jr.—son of Edwin C. Roth, prominent Illinois horseman (BB, 9/10/94)

Rothschild, Donald—attorney for Paul Crump (BB, 10/22/93)

Routman, Melvin N.—House Speaker Paul Powell's parliamentarian; clerk of Court Claims (GS, 2/21/92)

Rubin, Joel D.—appeals court clerk under OK (BB, by phone, 6/23/93)

Sachnoff, Lowell E.—liberal Democrat; consultant in OK's first administration helping to reorganize the Illinois Department of Public Welfare (BB, 2/12/92; BB, 3/18/92)

Scariano, Anthony—assistant U.S. attorney under OK; state representative; chair, Illinois Racing Board; Illinois appellate court judge (GS, 10/15/86; BB/GS, 3/25/93)

Schaeffer, Paul J.—member of Justice Department's criminal division involved in OK prosecution (BB, by phone, 5/12/93; BB, by phone, 5/31/93; BB/GS, 11/29/93)

Schroeder, Robert—police chief in Andalusia, Ill. (BB, 10/22/93)

Scruggs, Donald Lee—author of Ph.D. dissertation on the Kerner Commission (BB, by phone, 10/13/93; BB, 2/5/94)

Seaborg, Glenn T.—chair, Atomic Energy Commission (BB, by phone, 4/14/95)

Seliger, Stephen G.—appeals court clerk under OK (BB, by phone, 6/14/93)

Sethness, Charles H., Jr., and Mary—OK's long-time devoted friends (BB/GS, 3/22/92)

Shellow, Robert—assistant deputy director of the Kerner Commission (BB, 10/30/93)

Shotke, Richard—director of the Youth Committee; Boy Scout leader (BB, 3/24/94)

Simon, Paul—newspaper publisher; state representative; state senator; lieutenant governor; U.S. senator; director of the Public Policy Institute at Southern Illinois University (BB/GS, 2/6/94)

Simon, Seymour—Chicago alderman; ward committeeman; president of Cook County Board; Illinois appellate court judge; state supreme court justice; partner at Rudnick and Wolfe (BB/GS, 6/29/94)

Skinner, Samuel K.—assistant U.S. attorney; chair, Rapid Transit Authority; secretary, U.S. Department of Transportation; White House chief of staff; president, Commonwealth Edison (BB/GS, 5/2/93)

Sowle, Claude—member of OK's veto force; observer of Crump hearing (BB, 6/17/93)

Spivak, Alan A.—press officer for Kerner Commission (BB, 10/30/93)

Starkman, Gary L.—assistant U.S. attorney (BB, 11/19/96)

Stein, Karl—Brown University, class of 1930 (BB, 9/26/92)

Stratton, William—congressman; state treasurer; governor (BB/GS, 7/8/92)

Suekoff, Raymond—OK's long-time professional acquaintance (GS, 5/15/92)

Suits, Maurice "Deke"—state trooper assigned to governor's mansion (BB/GS, 2/22/92)

Taylor, F. John—OK's assistant (BB/GS, 8/29/92; BB/GS, 1/22/93)

Taylor, Florence—widow of Robert Taylor, OK's trial judge (GS, by phone, 6/22/93)

Theriault, Arthur J.—mayor of Weston, Ill. (BB, 10/22/94)

Thomas, Evan—author of *The Man to See: Edward Bennett Williams* (GS, 3/5/92)

Thompson, James R.—Cook County assistant state's attorney; U.S. attorney; governor; attorney at Winston and Strawn (BB/GS, 7/8/93)

Thorne, Richard C.—OK public relations consultant (BB/GS, 11/5/92)

Visotsky, Harold M.—director of the Illinois Department of Mental Health under OK (GS, 9/27/91)

Vlahoplus, Christopher—OK's chief of staff; professor of journalism at Southern Carolina University (GS, 12/10/91; BB/GS, 10/5/92)

Walsh, John M.—IRS special agent and head of Project CRIMP (BB/GS, 5/8/93; BB, by phone, 7/31/95; BB, 10/12/95)

Warford, Rev. William—chair, Adams County Citizens for Kerner, 1960 (GS, by phone, 12/4/92)

Weinberger, Robert—Democratic activist (BB, by phone, 12/15/92)

Weiner, Robert—OK's pension attorney (GS, 6/5/92)

Welli, Stanley D.—IRS internal inspector (BB, by phone, 10/20/95)

Westmoreland, William C.—OK's World War II commander; OK character witness (GS, 6/13/86)

Wicker, Tom—*New York Times* writer and columnist, author (BB/GS, 10/31/94)

Willard, Joel—movie producer (election procedures, 1960 campaign, and European trade mission) (BB/GS, 10/20/91; BB/GS, 10/27/91)

Williams, Gordon—Cambridge University alumnus (BB, by phone, 6/15/93)

Witkowski, William—IRS special agent who investigated OK (BB/GS, 3/24/93; BB/GS, 5/5/93)

Witz, Charles—Cook County assistant state's attorney involved with mental health (BB, by phone, 10/29/93; BB/GS, 11/23/93)

Wolfson, Warren D.—Ted Isaacs's trial lawyer (GS, 6/13/86; BB/GS, 3/16/93)

Yung, R. Dale—legal assistant to Governor Kerner (GS, 2/27/86)

Notes

Introduction

1. Manary interview, October 22, 1993.
2. Klassen, oral history, "Illinois Statecraft," Sangamon State University, 87.
3. *Chicago Sun-Times,* August 5, 1959.
4. *Chicago Daily News,* December 16, 1971.
5. *Rock Island Argus,* July 28, 1967.
6. "Alleged Protest Demonstrations," Kerner FBI file, August 3, 1967.
7. *Rock Island Argus,* July 27, 1967.
8. National Advisory Commission on Civil Disorders, *Report,* 1–2.
9. Califano, *Triumph and Tragedy,* 260.
10. Ibid., 263.
11. In Schlesinger, *Robert Kennedy,* 908–9.
12. Pickney, "Professionals," *New York Review of Books,* April 20, 1995, p. 43.
13. "Remarks by Governor Otto Kerner, National Association for the Advancement of Colored People, Progressive Baptist Church, 3658 S. Wentworth Ave., Chicago, Monday, July 1, 1963," Anton C. Kerner collection.
14. Ibid.
15. *Chicago Daily News,* July 30, 1968.
16. *Chicago Tribune,* August 30, 1974.
17. Skinner interview, May 2, 1993.

Chapter 1: Schweiks No More

1. Hasek, *The Good Soldier Schweik.*
2. Kerner family history, Anton C. Kerner collection, 1.
3. Ibid., 2.

4. Rose Kerner taped interview, 1975, Anton C. Kerner collection.

5. Freund, *Watch Czechoslovakia!*, 11.

6. Kerner, *Czechoslovakia*, 6.

7. In Ludwig, *Defender of Democracy*, 31.

8. In Gottfried, *Boss Cermak*, 29.

9. In Ludwig, *Defender of Democracy*, 41.

10. Steiner, *On the Trail*, 10.

11. Ginsburg, "Czechs in Chicago Politics," 263–64.

12. Gottfried, *Boss Cermak*, 16.

13. Ibid., 10.

14. Barnard, *Anton the Martyr*, 32.

15. Helena Kerner interview, March 17, 1973, Anton C. Kerner collection.

16. Gottfried, *Boss Cermak*, 54–55.

17. In Peterson, *Barbarians in Our Midst*, 64.

18. Stead, *If Christ Came to Chicago!*, 305.

19. *Chicago Tribune*, December 23, 1912.

20. Dobyns, *Underworld of American Politics*, 172.

21. Merriam, *Chicago*, 51.

22. Dobyns, *Underworld of American Politics*, 37.

23. Rose Kerner taped interview, 1975; Rose Kerner written memoir, 1956, both in Anton C. Kerner collection.

24. Otto Kerner Sr., autobiographical sketch, undated, Anton C. Kerner collection.

25. *River Forest Optimist*, November 4, 1932.

26. Otto Kerner Sr., autobiographical sketch, undated, Anton C. Kerner collection.

27. Merriam, *Chicago*, 143.

28. Quoted in Kerner Sr. campaign material, Anton C. Kerner collection.

29. Merriam, *Chicago*, 226.

30. *Chicago Tribune*, June 26, 1917.

31. Lepawsky, *Judicial System of Chicago*, 150–51.

32. *New York Times*, February 2, 1933.

33. Rose Kerner taped interview, 1975, Anton C. Kerner collection.

34. Ibid.

35. Kreml interview, February 13, 1993.

Chapter 2: These Malicious Charges

1. *Chicago Tribune*, June 2, 1946.

2. *Chicago Tribune*, November 12, 1918.

3. State of Illinois, *Illinois Revised Statutes*, chapter 122, paragraphs 585–89, repealed 1945.

4. *Chicago Tribune*, May 8, 1926.

5. *Oak Leaves*, May 22, 1926.

6. *Chicago Tribune*, May 28, 1926.

7. Kerner, letter to William J. Lindsay, Otto Kerner Papers, Illinois State Historical Library, box 1357.

8. Merriam, *Chicago*, 214.

9. Ibid., 213.

10. *Chicago Tribune*, February 28, 1926; quoted in Hoffman, *Scarface Al*, 27.

11. *Chicago Herald and Examiner*, April 7, 1930.

12. Ruth, *Inventing the Public Enemy*, 35.

13. Martin, *Role of the Bar*, 14.

14. Kogan, *The First Century*, 145.

15. *Chicago Bar Record*, June, 1921.

16. *Chicago Bar Record*, May, 1927.

17. Ruth, *Inventing the Public Enemy*, 139.

18. "Report in re Investigation of Charges of the Chicago Crime Commission and Frank J. Loesch," Criminal Court of Cook County, July 3, 1928, p. 1.

19. *Chicago Daily News*, April 27, 1928.

20. Ibid.

21. Ibid.

22. *Chicago Tribune*, May 15, 1926.

23. *Chicago American*, May 22, 1928.

24. *Chicago Evening Post*, May 31, 1928.

25. "Report in re Investigation," 28.

26. *Chicago Herald and Examiner*, May 1, 1928.

27. Ibid.

28. Kinnaird interview, June 13, 1992.

29. "Report in re Investigation," 42.

30. *Chicago Tribune*, July 4, 1928.

31. Chicago Crime Commission, "Special Bulletin," July 18, 1928, Kerner Family Papers, Illinois State Historical Library, box 2.

32. Martin, *Role of the Bar*, 297.

33. *Chicago Daily News*, October 25, 1928.

34. *Chicago Tribune*, May 2, 1929.

35. *Chicago Times*, February 8, 1930.

36. *Chicago Herald and Examiner*, 1930.

37. Hoffman, *Scarface Al*, 164.

Chapter 3: This Job Is Much Better

1. "Sousa: The Complete Marches," booklet accompanying recordings of Sousa marches, Book-of-the-Month Records. See also Bierley, *The Works of John Philip Sousa*.

2. "History: Troops 'E' and 'F,' and Band, 106th Calvary Regiment, Chicago Black Horse Squadron and Mounted Band," *Armory Dedication Program*, February 17, 1940, pp. 13–16, Chicago Black Horse Troop Association file, Chicago Historical Society Reference Library.

3. Ibid.

4. Gray interview, June 30, 1993.

5. Rogers and Rickard, *Liber Brunensis*, 94.

6. Kinniard interview, June 13, 1992.

7. Otto Kerner Jr., student record, Brown University, February, 1927.

8. *Providence Journal,* May 30, 1929.

9. *Brown Daily Herald,* May 7, 1930.

10. Bradley interview, April 28, 1993.

11. Faunce, *Facing Life,* 158–59.

12. *Brown Daily Herald,* May 8, 1930.

13. *Brown Daily Herald,* April 17, 1930.

14. Rogers and Rickard, *Liber Brunensis,* 62.

15. David Williams, vice chancellor, University of Cambridge, letter to Bill Barnhart, July 13, 1993.

16. *Chicago Herald American,* November 26, 1943.

17. Gottfried, *Boss Cermak,* 198.

18. Biles, *Big City Boss,* 13.

19. Redmond interview, November 23, 1991.

20. Littlewood, *Horner of Illinois,* 54.

21. Kerner, "Recent Cases," 445–47.

22. Gottfried, *Boss Cermak,* 313–14.

23. Hallgren, "Chicago Goes Tammany," 445–47.

24. *Chicago Herald and Examiner,* October 31, 1932, in Gottfried, *Boss Cermak,* 281–82.

25. Bergreen, *Capone,* 424.

26. Stuart, *The Twenty Incredible Years,* 501–2.

27. Gottfried, *Boss Cermak,* 166, 213.

28. Death certificate, Anton Joseph Cermak, Florida State Board of Health, Bureau of Vital Statistics, March 6, 1933.

29. Gottfried, *Boss Cermak,* 330–31; see also Picchi, *The Five Weeks,* 131–40.

30. Dornfeld, *Behind the Front Page,* 118.

31. *Helena C. Kenlay v. Floyd M. Kenlay,* divorce decree, Circuit Court of Cook County, June 14, 1933.

32. May Carter interview, April 4, 1992; Rose Kerner interview, 1975, Anton C. Kerner collection.

33. Rose Kerner, letter to Helena Kerner, November, 11, 1934, Anton C. Kerner collection.

34. Rose Kerner, letter to Otto Kerner Jr., August 14, 1940, Anton C. Kerner collection.

35. Otto Kerner Sr., autobiographical sketch, undated, Anton C. Kerner collection.

36. Redmond interview, November 23, 1991.

37. Otto Kerner, letter to the adjutant general of Illinois, May 1, 1936, records of Illinois National Guard, Springfield, Illinois.

38. Otto Kerner Jr., letter to General Samuel T. Lawton, July 17, 1947, Otto Kerner Papers, Illinois State Historical Library, box 1357.

39. *Chicago Herald American,* November 26, 1943.

40. Rose Kerner memoir, October 1956, Anton C. Kerner collection.

41. Littlewood, *Horner of Illinois*, 218.

42. Rose Kerner memoir, October 1956, Anton C. Kerner collection.

43. Col. George I. Connolly Jr., letter to Gene Schlickman, October 6, 1994, in authors' possession.

44. Furgurson, *Westmoreland*, 96.

45. Otto Kerner Jr., letter to Helena Kerner, May 18, 1942, Anton C. Kerner collection.

46. Harry S. Truman, letter to Lt. General William Westmoreland, July 7, 1964, Harry S. Truman Library, post-president papers.

47. Furgurson, *Westmoreland*, 103.

48. Ibid., 103–4.

49. General William C. Westmoreland, letter to Gene Schlickman, June 1986.

50. Otto Kerner Jr., letter to Helena Kerner, March 2, 1943, Anton C. Kerner collection.

51. *Chicago Herald American*, November 27, 1943.

52. Ibid.

53. Otto Kerner Jr., letter to Helena Kerner, March 21, 1943, Anton C. Kerner collection.

54. Furgurson, *Westmoreland*, 125.

55. Leon R. Birum, letter to Gene Schlickman, September 13, 1994.

56. *Chicago Herald American*, November 27, 1943.

57. Helena Kerner, letter to Otto Kerner Jr., September 29, 1932, Anton C. Kerner collection.

58. Helena Kerner, letter to Otto Kerner Jr., October 11, 1943, Anton C. Kerner collection.

59. Otto Kerner Jr., letter to Helena Kerner, June 5, 1942, Anton C. Kerner collection.

60. Rose Kerner, letter to Helena Kerner, July 28, 1943, Anton C. Kerner collection.

61. Otto Kerner Jr., letter to Helena Kerner, October 27, 1945, Anton C. Kerner collection.

62. Furgurson, *Westmoreland*, 126.

Chapter 4: The Welfare of the Child

1. Littlewood, *Horner of Illinois*, 58.

2. Gottfried, *Boss Cermak*, 393.

3. Ibid., 178.

4. Rakove, *We Don't Want Nobody*, 8.

5. Douglas, *Fullness of Time*, 91.

6. Martin, *Adlai Stevenson*, 265.

7. Arvey, oral history, Adlai E. Stevenson Project, Columbia University, 4.

8. Royko, *Boss*, 55.

9. Biles, *Richard J. Daley*, 27–28.

10. Rakove, *We Don't Want Nobody,* 8.

11. Martin, *Adlai Stevenson,* 266.

12. Ickes, *Secret Diary,* 94.

13. Martin, *Adlai Stevenson,* 269.

14. Ibid.

15. Ibid.

16. Otto Kerner Jr., letter to John K. Knotz, August 19, 1947, Otto Kerner Papers, Illinois State Historical Library, box 1357.

17. Otto Kerner Jr., letter to Paul B. Musgrove, August 22, 1947, Otto Kerner Papers, Illinois State Historical Library, box 1357.

18. Otto Kerner Jr., letter to Ronald M. Kimball, July 17, 1947, Otto Kerner Papers, Illinois State Historical Library, box 1357.

19. Joseph S. Perry, letter to Democratic State Central Committee of Illinois, November 1, 1947, Otto Kerner Papers, Illinois State Historical Library, box 1357.

20. Otto Kerner Jr., letter to Joseph S. Perry, December 5, 1947, Otto Kerner Papers, Illinois State Historical Library, box 1357.

21. McCullough, *Truman,* 553.

22. Milton A. Jones, memorandum to Cartha DeLoach, January 3, 1961, Kerner FBI file, subject: Otto Kerner Jr.

23. Ibid.

24. Ibid.

25. Ibid.

26. Ibid.

27. Ibid.

28. Ibid.

29. *Chicago Tribune,* November 21, 1948.

30. Pearson, *The Indomitable Tin Goose,* 15.

31. Ibid., 32.

32. Ibid., 19.

33. *New York Times,* October 6, 1949.

34. *New York Times,* November 9, 1949.

35. *New York Times,* January 22, 1950.

36. *Chicago Tribune,* January 23, 1950.

37. *Chicago Tribune* "Arts," August 7, 1988, 6.

38. *New York Times,* December 6, 1949.

39. Harry A. Ash, letter to Otto Kerner Jr., December 19, 1947, Otto Kerner Papers, Illinois State Historical Library, box 1357.

40. Peyton Ford, letter to Otto Kerner Jr., August 16, 1951, Otto Kerner Papers, Illinois State Historical Library, box 1358.

41. Lindberg, *To Serve and Collect,* 233.

42. *Chicago Tribune,* October 29, 1941.

43. In O'Connor, *Clout,* 72.

44. Ibid.

45. Otto Kerner Jr., letter to Joseph S. Perry, December 5, 1947, Otto Kerner Papers, Illinois State Historical Library, box 1357.

46. The Girls Latin School of Chicago, *Vita Scholae*, 1947, Anton C. Kerner collection.

47. Otto Kerner Jr., letter to Mr. and Mrs. Neil Cox, May 7, 1948, Otto Kerner Papers, Illinois State Historical Library, box 1357.

48. *Chicago Tribune*, October 21, 1954.

49. Bukowski, "Judge Edmund K. Jarecki," 206–18.

50. In Bergreen, *Capone*, 107.

51. *Chicago Sun-Times*, August 5, 1959.

52. "Edmund Kaspar Jarecki, Judge of the County Court of Cook County, 1922–1954," Otto Kerner Papers, Illinois State Historical Library, box 1389.

53. *Chicago Tribune*, May 6, 1955.

54. *Chicago Daily News*, July 7, 1955.

55. *Chicago American*, June 14, 1955.

56. *Chicago Tribune*, July 28, 1955.

57. *Chicago Daily News*, February 14, 1957.

58. Otto Kerner testimony, *Hearings before the Subcommittee to Investigate Juvenile Delinquency*, 44.

59. Ibid., 39, 41.

60. "Report of the Commission on Adoption Laws to the Seventy-First General Assembly," 1.

61. Mandel interview, October 12, 1995.

62. *Chicago Sun-Times*, October 7, 1958.

63. *Chicago Tribune*, November 3, 1958.

64. *Chicago Herald American*, December 12, 1954.

65. Shotke interview, March 24, 1994.

66. *Chicago Tribune*, May 1, 1971.

67. Harmet interview, December 24, 1992.

Chapter 5: The Shame of It

1. Otto Kerner, interview with Anton C. Kerner, undated, Anton C. Kerner collection.

2. Ibid.

3. Richard J. Daley, interview with Anton C. Kerner, December 5, 1973, Anton C. Kerner collection.

4. O'Connor, *Clout*, 143–44.

5. Kallina, *Courthouse over White House*, 23.

6. Netsch interview, November 13, 1992.

7. Committee of Illinois Government, "A Democratic Challenge, 1958," preface, Otto Kerner Papers, Illinois State Historical Library, box 1385.

8. Tagge, oral history interview, "Illinois Statecraft," Sangamon State University, 18.

9. Ciconne, *Daley,* 63.

10. Littlewood interview, December 5, 1992.

11. *Tuscola Journal,* November 3, 1960.

12. Ciconne, *Daley,* 45.

13. Otto Kerner interview, with Anton C. Kerner, undated, Anton C. Kerner collection.

14. *Chicago Tribune,* August 27, 1959.

15. Skoff, ed., *Illinois Chess Bulletin,* 130.

16. Isaacs interview, January 14, 1995.

17. "Information Pamphlet, 3rd Pan-American Games, Chicago, 1959," City of Chicago, Pan-American Games files, *Chicago Tribune.*

18. Isaacs interview, January 14, 1995.

19. Oliver P. Stufflebeam, memorandum of interview with Otto Kerner, July 15, 1970, U.S. attorney's records, northern district of Illinois, RG 118, CR 71-1086, National Archives, Great Lakes Region.

20. Carter interview, April 4, 1992.

21. Theodore J. Isaacs, interview with Anton C. Kerner, November 15, 1973, Anton C. Kerner collection.

22. Otto Kerner Jr., letter to Theodore J. Isaacs, July 31, 1951, Otto Kerner Papers, Illinois State Historical Library, box 1358.

23. *United States v. Isaacs et al.,* trial transcript, February 8, 1973, records of the District Court of the United States, northern district of Illinois, RG 21, CR 71-1086, National Archives, Great Lakes Region.

24. Otto Kerner, interview with Anton C. Kerner, undated, Anton C. Kerner collection.

25. Mikva interview, April 13, 1992.

26. Downing interview, May 27, 1987.

27. Milton Rakove, interview with Anton C. Kerner, November 19, 1973, Anton C. Kerner collection.

28. Isaacs interview, January 14, 1995.

29. Long interview, September 4, 1992.

30. *Chicago Daily News,* February 20, 1973.

31. Messick, *Politics of Prosecution,* 50.

32. Otto Kerner, interview with Anton C. Kerner, undated, Anton C. Kerner collection.

33. Brickhouse interview, December 16, 1992.

34. Despres, "Corruption in Chicago," 220.

35. Ibid., 221.

36. Otto Kerner, interview with Anton C. Kerner, undated, Anton C. Kerner collection.

37. Clark interview, September 11, 1992.

38. Marvin W. Mindes, memorandum to T. J. Isaacs and Richard Thorne, June 22, 1960, Otto Kerner Papers, Illinois State Historical Library, box 1307.

39. Thorne interview, November 5, 1992.

40. Littlewood, letter to Bill Barnhart, December 5, 1996.

41. Katz interview, July 30, 1992.

42. Marvin W. Mindes, letter to Theodore Sorenson, June 16, 1960, Otto Kerner Papers, Illinois State Historical Library, box 1305.

43. James Q. Wilson, "Civil Rights in Illinois," memorandum, May 26, 1960, Otto Kerner Papers, Illinois State Historical Library, box 1298.

44. James Q. Wilson, "Campaigning in Negro Areas," memorandum, May 25, 1960, Otto Kerner Papers, Illinois State Historical Library, box 1298.

45. Otis interview, January 19, 1993.

46. Theodore J. Isaacs, interview with Anton C. Kerner, November 19, 1973, Anton C. Kerner collection.

47. Kenney, *A Political Passage,* 178.

48. Nixon, *RN: The Memoirs of Richard Nixon,* 224.

49. Steiner and Gove, "Governors, Issues and Styles," 47.

50. In Anton, *Politics of State Expenditure,* 120n.

51. Long, "After the Voting," 184–85, 187.

52. Anton, *Politics of State Expenditure,* 119.

53. Abner J. Mikva, letter to Otto Kerner, November 11, 1960, Otto Kerner Papers, Illinois State Historical Library, box 1328.

54. John F. Kennedy, telegram to Otto Kerner, February 15, 1961, Otto Kerner Papers, Illinois State Historical Library, box 980.

55. Otto Kerner, "Budget Message Submitted to the Seventy-Second General Assembly, April 19, 1961," Kerner Administration Records, Illinois State Archives.

56. Norton E. Long diary, February 26, 1961, in authors' possession.

57. Long diary, February 26, 1961.

58. Thorne interview, November 5, 1992.

59. Ibid.

60. Morris interview, August 29, 1992.

61. Long diary, February 24, 1961.

62. Long diary, February 26, 1961.

63. Ibid.

64. Gerty interview, February 29, 1992.

65. Ibid.

66. Otto Kerner, interview with Anton C. Kerner, undated, Anton C. Kerner collection.

67. Kerner campaign press release, October 22, 1958, Otto Kerner Papers, Illinois State Historical Library, box 1384.

68. *Chicago Sun-Times,* March 8, 1960.

69. Gerty interview, February 29, 1992.

70. Ibid.

71. Dr. Francis J. Gerty, speech to Welfare Council of Metropolitan Chicago, Health Division, April 16, 1958, quoted in Reidy, *Zone Mental Health Centers,* 14–15.

72. Gerty interview, February 29, 1992.

73. Sachnoff interview, February 12, 1992.

74. *Chicago Daily News,* July 15, 1961.

75. Dr. Robert H. Felix, quoted in Reidy, *Zone Mental Health Centers,* ix–x.

76. Littlewood, "Otto Kerner of Illinois," 19, 23.

77. Ibid.

78. Witz interview, November 23, 1993.

79. Long diary, August 9, 1962.

80. Long diary, July 17, 1962.

81. Kerner, "Incumbent Views the Office," 83–88.

Chapter 6: The Ultimate Decision

1. Butterfield interview, February 28, 1993.

2. The Reverend Dismas Clark, letter to Otto Kerner, quoted in *Chicago Tribune Sunday Magazine,* October 10, 1982.

3. Otto Kerner, letter to the Reverend Robert A. Edgar, August 3, 1962, Otto Kerner Papers, Illinois State Historical Library, box 651.

4. State Senator John Grotberg, quoted in *Chicago Sun-Times,* May 20, 1990.

5. Quoted in Baumann, *May God Have Mercy,* 417.

6. Mattick, *The Unexamined Death,* 1.

7. Ibid., 16.

8. *Chessman v. Teets,* 354 U.S. 156 (1957).

9. Daniel P. Ward, letter to Otto Kerner, March 16, 1962, Otto Kerner Papers, Illinois State Historical Library, box 595.

10. *Chicago Tribune,* July 30, 1954.

11. *Chicago Tribune,* August 5, 1954.

12. *Chicago Tribune,* July 30, 1954.

13. *Ciucci v. State of Illinois,* 78 S.Ct. 839.

14. Ibid.

15. *Chicago Tribune,* March 23, 1962.

16. *Chicago Tribune,* March 20, 1962.

17. *Chicago Tribune,* March 22, 1962.

18. Netsch interview, November 13, 1992.

19. Craven interview, June 26, 1993.

20. *Chicago Tribune,* March 23, 1962.

21. Baumann, *May God Have Mercy,* 7.

22. Lanier, "A Lifetime of Waiting," 192.

23. Crump, *Burn, Killer, Burn,* epigraph.

24. Bailey, "Facing Death," 26–29.

25. Segaloff, *Hurricane Billy,* 26.

26. Demaris, *Captive City,* 119.

27. In Friedken, *People versus Crump* (film), 1962.

28. Ibid.

29. Segaloff, *Hurricane Billy,* 35.

30. Donald Page Moore, "Application for Executive Clemency to the Honorable

Otto Kerner, Governor, and Petition for a Special Hearing by the Parole and Pardon Board," July 10, 1962, Otto Kerner Papers, Illinois State Historical Library, box 595.

31. In ibid.

32. Ibid.

33. Veronica Zukowski, letter to Otto Kerner, July 18, 1962, Kerner Administration Records, Illinois State Archives.

34. Otto Kerner, letter to Veronica Zubowski, July 23, 1962, Kerner Administration Records, Illinois State Archives.

35. Paul Crump, letter to Otto Kerner, July 27, 1962, Otto Kerner Papers, Illinois State Historical Library, box 595.

36. Nizer, *The Jury Returns*, 65.

37. Ibid., 66.

38. Ibid., 76.

39. The Reverend Billy Graham, letter to Otto Kerner, June 16, 1962, Otto Kerner Papers, Illinois State Historical Library, box 595.

40. Otto Kerner, letter to the Reverend Billy Graham, June 22, 1962, Otto Kerner Papers, Illinois State Historical Library, box 595.

41. Craven interview, June 26, 1993.

42. Nizer, *The Jury Returns*, 65.

43. Ibid., 87, 89.

44. Ibid., 87.

45. Ibid., 89.

46. In ibid., 126.

47. In ibid.

48. Statement, Illinois Parole and Pardon Board, August 1, 1962, Kerner Administration Records, Illinois State Archives.

49. Ibid.

50. Craven interview, June 26, 1993.

51. Otto Kerner, letter to Charles F. Carpentier, Illinois secretary of state, August 1, 1962, Otto Kerner Papers, Illinois State Historical Library, box 595.

52. Long diary, August 1, 1962.

53. *Newsweek*, August 13, 1962, p. 17.

54. Otto Kerner, letter to the Reverend Robert A. Edgar, August 3, 1962, Otto Kerner Papers, Illinois State Historical Library, box 651.

55. Craven interview, June 26, 1993.

56. James Dukes (Jesse Welsh), letter to Otto Kerner, August, 1962, Kerner Administration Records, Illinois State Archives.

57. Illinois Parole and Pardon Board, statement to Otto Kerner, August 22, 1962, Kerner Administration Records, Illinois State Archives.

58. Otto Kerner, press release, no. 1141-62, August 22, 1962, Kerner Administration Records, Illinois State Archives.

59. *Chicago Tribune*, July 15, 1972.

60. *Chicago Sun-Times*, August 24, 1962.

61. *Chicago Daily News*, August 22, 1962.

62. Mattick, *The Unexamined Death,* 14–15.

63. In Lanier, "A Lifetime of Waiting," 246.

Chapter 7: The Giant Ring

1. "Remarks of William G. Riley, President of Riley Management Corporation, January 7, 1964," National Accelerator Laboratory Historical Collection.

2. *Chicago Tribune,* January 8, 1964.

3. Theriault interview, October 22, 1994.

4. *Chicago Tribune,* September 28, 1967.

5. *Chicago Tribune,* November 27, 1964.

6. *Chicago Tribune,* September 28, 1967.

7. Cassell interview, February 13, 1993.

8. Graves interview, February 22, 1992.

9. Otto Kerner, prepared statement for U.S. Senate hearing, *Impact of Federal Research and Development Policies on Scientific and Technical Manpower: Hearings before the Subcommittee on Employment of the Committee on Labor and Public Welfare,* 89th Congress, First Session, 1965, quoted in Jachim, *Science Policy Making,* 80.

10. Jachim, *Science Policy Making,* 29.

11. Ibid., 180.

12. Matthew 13:12; Merton, "The Matthew Effect," 56–63.

13. Jachim, *Science Policy Making,* 86.

14. In ibid., 80.

15. Westfall, "First 'Truly National Laboratory,'" 165–66.

16. Graves interview, February 22, 1992.

17. Wilson, *Starting Fermilab,* 2.

18. Seaborg, "The Fermilab Story," 143.

19. Seaborg interview, April 14, 1995.

20. Theriault interview, October 22, 1994.

21. Ibid.

22. Arthur Theriault, letter to Paul W. McDaniel, June 7, 1965, papers of Arthur Theriault.

23. In Ralph, *Northern Protest,* 33.

24. Snow, *"The Two Cultures,"* 33.

25. Seaborg, "Science, the Humanities and the Federal Government—Partners in Progress," speech to American Philosophical Society, Philadelphia, Pennsylvania, April 22, 1966, National Accelerator Laboratory Historical Collection, 6.

26. Ibid., 14–15.

27. Village of Barrington, Board of Trustees, resolution, December 13, 1965, Otto Kerner Papers, Illinois State Historical Library, box 389.

28. *Journal of Glenn Seaborg,* March 29, 1966.

29. Ibid., March 31, 1966.

30. *Chicago Daily News,* April 2, 1966,

31. Becker interview, February 22, 1995.

32. *Journal of Glenn Seaborg,* April 7, 1966.

33. Ibid., 397.

34. Ibid., 398.

35. *Elmhurst Press,* April 20, 1967.

36. Eugene J. Callahan, letter to Otto Kerner, June 21, 1966, Otto Kerner Papers, Illinois State Historical Society, box 390.

37. In Jachim, *Science Policy Making,* 127.

38. *Chicago Daily News,* July 13, 1966.

39. Ibid.

40. Otto Kerner, letter to Glenn T. Seaborg, July 15, 1966, Otto Kerner Papers, Illinois State Historical Library, box 970.

41. *Chicago Weekly Defender,* July 23, 1966.

42. *Sunday Pantagraph,* July 17, 1966.

43. Christopher Vlahoplus, letter to editor, *Daily Pantagraph,* August 15, 1966, Otto Kerner Papers, Illinois State Historical Library, box 392.

44. Otto Kerner, letter to Julius W. Butler, August 15, 1966, Otto Kerner Papers, Illinois State Historical Society, box 390.

45. Ibid.

46. In Ralph, *Northern Protest,* 117.

47. Ibid., 235.

48. William L. Taylor, letter to Glenn T. Seaborg, in *Journal of Glenn Seaborg,* July 20, 1966.

49. "AEC Selections Site for 200-BEV Accelerator," Atomic Energy Commission press release, in *Journal of Glenn Seaborg,* December 16, 1966.

50. *Journal of Glenn Seaborg,* December 27, 1966.

51. *Journal of Glenn Seaborg,* January 21, 1967.

52. Jachim, *Science Policy Making,* 130.

53. David Judd, letter to Glenn Seaborg, February 10, 1967, in Westfall, "First 'Truly National Laboratory,'" 284.

54. "Weston Accelerator Fact Sheet," undated memorandum to "We in the Senate," Otto Kerner Papers, Illinois State Historical Library, box 405.

55. "Statement of Chairman Seaborg," in *Journal of Glenn Seaborg,* April 12, 1967.

56. Jachim, *Science Policy Making,* 140.

57. *Peoria Journal Star,* May 11, 1967.

58. Wilson, *Starting Fermilab,* 7.

59. *Chicago Tribune,* June 24, 1967.

60. Robert Rathbun Wilson, telegram to Martin Luther King, June 22, 1967, National Accelerator Laboratory Historical Collection.

61. Robert Rathbun Wilson, letter to Otto Kerner, June 23, 1967, National Accelerator Laboratory Historical Collection.

62. *New York Times,* July 16, 1967, in Westfall, "First 'Truly National Laboratory,'" 293.

63. *Chicago Tribune,* July 9, 1967.

64. Philip A. Hart, telegram to Otto Kerner, August 1, 1967, Otto Kerner Papers, Illinois State Historical Library, box 405.

65. Edwin L. Goldwasser, "The Scientist and the City—Pilot Projects at the National Accelerator Laboratory," January 27, 1970, National Accelerator Laboratory Historical Collection.

Chapter 8: The Sadness of Our Time

1. *Time,* August 4, 1967, p. 13.

2. Wicker, "Introduction," in National Advisory Commission on Civil Disorders (NACCD), *U.S. Riot Commission Report,* (Bantam ed.), v.

3. Ibid., v, ix.

4. NACCD, *Report,* 86.

5. Ibid., 87, 91.

6. Ibid., 92.

7. Shellow et al., "The Harvest of American Racism," Commission Research Studies, National Advisory Commission on Civil Disorders, Lyndon Baines Johnson Library, 10–11.

8. Johnson, *Vantage Point,* 168.

9. In Kearns, *Lyndon Johnson,* 305.

10. Califano, *Triumph and Tragedy,* 214.

11. Scruggs, "Lyndon Baines Johnson," 188.

12. In Johnson, *Vantage Point,* 170.

13. Califano, *Triumph and Tragedy,* 217.

14. In ibid.

15. NACCD, *Report,* 98.

16. Ibid., 102.

17. Ibid., 106.

18. *Newsweek,* August 7, 1967, p. 13.

19. In Kearns, *Lyndon Johnson,* 305.

20. Otto Kerner, statement to Hyde Park–Kenwood Community Organization, July 28, 1967, Otto Kerner Papers, Illinois State Historical Library, box 1392.

21. *New York Times,* August 11, 1967.

22. *Chicago Sun-Times,* July 29, 1967.

23. Kerner statement, July 28, 1967.

24. NACCD, *Report,* 536–37.

25. Ibid., 537.

26. Cassell interview, February 13, 1993.

27. Transcripts and agenda of hearings, NACCD, September 13, 1967, Lyndon Baines Johnson Library.

28. Ibid.

29. Scruggs, "Lyndon Baines Johnson," 287–88.

30. David Ginsburg, letter to Dawn Clark Netsch, September 10, 1967, papers of Dawn Clark Netsch.

31. Palmieri interview, November 5, 1993.

32. Joseph Califano, memorandum to Lyndon Johnson, August 7, 1967, NACCD files, Lyndon Baines Johnson Library.

33. Shellow interview, October 30, 1993.

34. Transcripts and agenda of hearings, NACCD, August 1, 1967, NACCD files, Lyndon Baines Johnson Library.

35. Shellow, "Social Scientists," 213.

36. In Platt, *Politics of Riot Commissions,* 386.

37. Transcripts and agenda of hearings, October 23, 1967, NACCD files, Lyndon Baines Johnson Library.

38. Shellow et al., "Harvest," 70–71.

39. Ibid., 36, 163.

40. Ibid., 115–16.

41. Ibid., 124.

42. Ibid., 150.

43. Ibid., 155.

44. Ibid., 168–69, 171.

45. Ibid., 171.

46. Ibid., 171, 172.

47. NACCD meeting transcript, September 21, NACCD files, Lyndon Baines Johnson Library.

48. Butler interview, February 15, 1992.

49. Scruggs, "Lyndon Baines Johnson," 291.

50. Isaac Hunt Jr., memorandum to NACCD staff, October 17, 1967, Otto Kerner Papers, Illinois State Historical Library, box 1392.

51. Ibid.

52. Klein, *Lindsay's Promise,* 1.

53. Lindsay, *Journey into Politics,* 135.

54. Ibid., 136.

55. *Chicago Tribune,* July 14, 1967.

56. Otto Kerner, letter to Murray S. Flander, July 24, 1968, Kerner Family Papers, Illinois State Historical Library, box 8.

57. Ibid.

58. John V. Lindsay, memorandum to commission members, January 9, 1968, NACCD files, Lyndon Baines Johnson Library.

59. James C. Corman, letter to Otto Kerner, January 13, 1968, NACCD files, Lyndon Baines Johnson Library.

60. Illinois Information Service press release, September 24, 1967, Kerner Administration Files, Illinois State Archives.

61. *Chicago Tribune,* September 25, 1967.

62. John Lindsay, "Summary Draft," February 18, 1968, NACCD Commission Reports and Drafts, Lyndon Baines Johnson Library.

63. Victor H. Palmieri, memorandum to commission, February 23, 1968, NACCD Commission Reports and Drafts, Lyndon Baines Johnson Library.

64. Ibid.

65. NACCD, *Report,* 203.

66. Ibid., 204–5.

67. Ibid., 23.

68. Johnson, *The Vantage Point,* 172–73.

69. Lyndon Johnson, telephone call to Harry McPherson, 4:20 P.M., March 13, 1968, White House Central Files, Harry McPherson, Lyndon Baines Johnson Library.

70. Roy Wilkins, oral history interview, April 1, 1969, Lyndon Baines Johnson Library.

71. Harry McPherson, oral history interview, March 24, 1969, Harry McPherson papers, Lyndon Baines Johnson Library.

72. Ibid.

73. NACCD, *The Kerner Report,* xiv.

74. *Wall Street Journal,* February 26, 1988.

75. *Chicago Tribune,* March 7, 1993.

76. *Chicago Daily News,* July 30, 1968.

77. Butler interview, February 15, 1992.

Chapter 9: Law and Order

1. "Nomination of Otto Kerner of Illinois to Be United States Circuit Court Judge for the Seventh Circuit," Report of Proceedings, Subcommittee on Nominations, Committee on the Judiciary, United States Senate, March 28, 1968, p. 2.

2. Ibid., 11.

3. Ibid., 40.

4. Ibid., 11.

5. Ibid., 4.

6. Ibid. The dialogue between Thurmond and Kerner is transcribed on 18–19, 27–28, and 36–37.

7. Coffin, *Ways of a Judge,* 4.

8. Otto Kerner, "A Judge's Eye View of Federal Appeals," undated speech, Anton C. Kerner collection.

9. McFeeley, *Appointment of Judges,* 4.

10. Ibid., 54–55.

11. *Chicago Tribune,* February 10, 1968.

12. Solomon, *History of the Seventh Circuit,* 149.

13. Ibid., 128–29.

14. Samuel Alschuler, letter to D. E. Ellis, December 30, 1914, in Solomon, *History of the Seventh Circuit,* 93.

15. Peter Grosscup, letter to Levy Mayer, in Solomon, *History of the Seventh Circuit,* 58.

16. "Memorial Ceremony for Judge Otto Kerner," *Proceedings of the U.S. Court of Appeals, Seventh Circuit,* April 7, 1953, pp. 25–26.

17. Ibid., 7.

18. Otto Kerner Sr., autobiographical sketch, undated, Anton C. Kerner collection.

19. "Memorial Ceremony," 4.

20. See Goulden, *The Benchwarmers,* 114–56.

21. *West Side News,* January 4, 1930.

22. *Waukegan News Sun,* January 21, 1935.

23. *Chicago Tribune,* December 10, 1944.

24. Otto Kerner Sr., untitled paper, Anton C. Kerner collection.

25. "Memorial Ceremony," 17–18.

26. Wright, "Observations," 1181.

27. Ibid., 1190–91.

28. Kerner, "A Judge's Eye View."

29. Cooper interview, June 10, 1993.

30. Rubin interview, June 23, 1993.

31. Kerner, "A Judge's Eye View."

32. Rubin interview, June 23, 1993.

33. Otto Kerner, letter to Melvin B. Yoken, June 22, 1971, Anton C. Kerner collection.

34. Landau interview, June 23, 1993.

35. *Davis v. Burke,* 408 F.2d 781.

36. Ibid.

37. Ibid., 782–83.

38. Ibid., 783.

39. In Hartley, *Big Jim Thompson,* 25.

40. Ibid.

41. Ibid., 30.

42. *Davis v. Burke,* 408 F.2d 783.

43. Ibid., 786.

44. Ibid., 787–88.

45. Ibid., 789.

46. *Rini v. Katzenbach,* 403 F.2d 701.

47. *United States ex rel. Pennington v. Pate,* 409 F.2d 762.

48. *United States ex rel. Worlow v. Pate,* 411 F.2d 975–76.

49. *United States ex rel. Townsend v. Twomey,* 452 F.2d 352.

50. Ibid., 365.

51. Ibid., 367.

52. Ibid., 369.

53. *Breen v. Kahl,* 419 F.2d 1035–38.

54. Ibid., 1039.

55. *United States v. Battaglia,* 394 F.2d 323–24, 325.

56. Ibid., 327.

57. *United States v. Amabile,* 395 F.2d 55.

58. Ibid., 52.

59. Ibid., 57.

60. *United States v. Palermo, Amabile, Neri, and Shababy,* 410 F.2d 470–71.

61. Ibid., 471.

62. Ibid., 472.
63. *Chicago Tribune*, April 5, 1969.

Chapter 10: To "CRIMP" Is to Hinder

1. Demaris, *Captive City*, 115.
2. Peterson, *Barbarians in Our Midst*, 189–90.
3. Ibid., 193.
4. *Chicago Tribune*, March 27, 1931.
5. *Chicago Tribune*, "Shirley Kub" file, January–February, 1931.
6. *Chicago Herald and Examiner*, March 7, 1931.
7. *Chicago American*, March 9, 1931.
8. *Chicago Tribune*, September 1, 1932.
9. *Chicago Tribune*, October 26, 1932.
10. *Chicago Herald and Examiner*, January 18, 1933.
11. Burnham, *A Law unto Itself*, 97.
12. Schlesinger, *Robert Kennedy*, 289.
13. In Navasky, *Kennedy Justice*, 56.
14. In Burnham, *A Law unto Itself*, 98.
15. Navasky, *Kennedy Justice*, 56.
16. Ibid., 49.
17. Schlesinger, *Robert Kennedy*, 304.
18. Navasky, *Kennedy Justice*, 53.
19. Hoover, *Memoirs of Herbert Hoover*, 276–77.
20. In Irey and Slocum, *The Tax Dodgers*, 35–36.
21. In Roemer, *Man against the Mob*, 299.
22. Surface, *Inside Internal Revenue*, 102.
23. Demaris, *Captive City*, 351.
24. *Kub v. Commissioner of Internal Revenue*, U.S. Tax Court (case no. 312-69), transcript of hearing, August 15, 1973, p. 309.
25. In Miller, *City of the Century*, 191.
26. Merriam, *Chicago*, 26.
27. Peterson, *Barbarians in Our Midst*, 348.
28. Scott, *Deep Politics*, 17.
29. Walsh interview, July 31, 1995.
30. Walsh interview, May 15, 1993.
31. *Kub v. Commissioner of Internal Revenue*, transcript of hearing, 311–13.
32. Walsh interview, May 15, 1993.
33. Papers of John M. Walsh, Cincinnati, Ohio.
34. John M. Walsh, memorandum to chief, intelligence division, Chicago district office, Internal Revenue Service, April 23, 1970, papers of John M. Walsh.
35. Bush interview, July 17, 1995.
36. Miller, *City of the Century*, 57.
37. Stead, *If Christ Came to Chicago!*, 232.

38. *Chicago Tribune*, June 14, 1971.

39. Auerbach, *Wild Ride*, 37.

40. Ibid., 44.

41. Ibid., 35.

42. "Benjamin Franklin Lindheimer," Arlington Park–Washington Park Jockey Club, *Chicago Tribune*, "Benjamin Lindheimer" files.

43. Ibid.

44. Littlewood, *Horner of Illinois*, 151.

45. In Ibid., 152–53.

46. *Chicago Tribune*, July 24, 1954.

47. Reuben interview, November 20, 1996.

48. Benjamin F. Lindheimer, letter to Colonel Jacob M. Arvey, October 31, 1950, Kerner Family Papers, Illinois State Historical Library, box 10.

49. *Chicago Tribune*, April 13, 1972.

50. Messick, *Politics of Prosecution*, 28–29.

51. Mikva interview, April 13, 1992.

52. Corman and Swanson, *Chicago Journalism Review*, November, 1971, 3.

53. Illinois Legislative Investigating Commission, "Illinois Horse Racing."

54. *Wall Street Journal*, June 1, 1972.

55. Illinois Legislative Investigating Commission, "Illinois Racing Board Controversy."

56. Witkowski interview, March 24, 1993.

57. Ibid.

58. Ibid.

59. Ibid.

60. Barnett interview, September 28, 1995.

61. Bush interview, July 17, 1995.

62. Messick, *Politics of Prosecution*, 98.

63. Walsh interview, May 15, 1993.

64. Ibid.

65. Bauer interview, January 21, 1993.

66. Walsh interview, May 15, 1993.

67. Ibid.

68. McGowen interview, May 12, 1993.

69. Schaeffer interview, November 29, 1993.

70. Witkowski interview, March 24, 1993.

71. Ibid.

72. *Chicago Sun-Times*, March 5, 1970.

73. Witkowski interview, March 24, 1993.

74. Walsh interview, May 15, 1993.

75. Ibid.

76. Ibid.

77. Ibid.

78. Stufflebeam, memorandum of interview with Otto Kerner, July 15, 1970, U.S.

attorney's records, northern district of Illinois, RG 118, CR 71-1086, National Archives, Great Lakes Region.

79. *Chicago Tribune,* July 15, 1970.

80. IRS background notes, Otto Kerner, card no. 1, sensitive case files, northern district of Illinois, RG 118, CR 71-1086, National Archives, Great Lakes Region.

81. Campbell interview, May 14, 1993.

82. Stufflebeam, memorandum of interview with Otto Kerner, July 15, 1970.

83. Campbell interview, May 14, 1993.

84. Ibid.

85. Stufflebeam, memorandum of interview with Otto Kerner, July 15, 1970.

86. Stufflebeam, memorandum of interview with Theodore Isaacs, July 15, 1970, northern district of Illinois, RG 118, CR 71-1086, National Archives, Great Lakes Region.

87. Campbell interview, May 14, 1993.

88. Witkowski interview, March 24, 1993.

89. Ibid.

90. Campbell interview, May 14, 1993.

91. Walsh interview, May 15, 1993.

Chapter 11: Intangible Rights

1. Schaeffer interview, November 29, 1993.

2. "Sustained Superior Performance Award" citation for Victor C. Woerheide, December 9, 1965, Federal Employment Records, United States Office of Personnel Management, St. Louis, Missouri.

3. Summers, *Secret Life of Hoover,* 442.

4. *Washington Post,* December 14, 1969.

5. *New York Times,* March 7, 1968.

6. *Washington Post,* April 4, 1970.

7. Victor C. Woerheide, "Personal Qualifications Statement," Form 171, U.S. Civil Service Commission, August 2, 1971, Federal Employment Records, United States Office of Personnel Management, St. Louis, Missouri.

8. Oliver P. Stufflebeam, interview with Jan Bone, July 24, 1978, Anton C. Kerner collection.

9. *New York Times,* January 15, 1971.

10. Ibid.

11. Martin, *Adlai Stevenson,* 362.

12. *New York Times,* January 15, 1971.

13. Vlahoplus profile of Paul Taylor Powell, United Press International, *Chicago Tribune* files.

14. *New York Times,* January 15, 1971.

15. Martin, *Adlai Stevenson,* 362.

16. In Vlahoplus profile of Paul Taylor Powell.

17. *New York Times,* January 15, 1971.

18. McGowen interview, May 12, 1993.

19. Makarski interview, February 2, 1993.

20. Ibid.

21. Undated, handwritten legal memorandum, northern district of Illinois, RG 118, CR 71-1086, National Archives, Great Lakes Region.

22. Isaacs et al., indictment, May 1971 grand jury, northern district of Illinois, RG 118, CR 71-1086, National Archives, Great Lakes Region.

23. Thomas A. Kennelly, memorandum to Edward T. Joyce, "Proposed Indictment of Otto Kerner and Others," August 20, 1971, northern district of Illinois, RG 118, CR 71-1086, National Archives, Great Lakes Region.

24. Gray, "Intangible-Rights Doctrine," 568.

25. *Shushman v. United States,* 117 F.2d 110, (fifth circuit, 1941).

26. *United States v. Procter and Gamble,* 47 F. Supp. 676 (district of Massachusetts, 1942).

27. *United States v. Faser,* 303 F. Supp. 380 (eastern district of Louisiana, 1969).

28. Lydon interview, January, 15, 1997; see also *Chicago Tribune,* July 9, 1987.

29. Hartley, *Big Jim Thompson,* 38.

30. Lydon interview, January 15, 1997.

31. Johnson, *The Vantage Point,* 165 (from Johnson's speech to a joint session of Congress on March 15, 1965).

32. Claude Pepper, in Loomis, "Federal Prosecution," 63.

33. *Shushman v. United States,* 117 F.2d 110.

34. Loomis, "Federal Prosecution," 68–69.

35. Gray, "Intangible-Rights Doctrine," 587.

36. Hoffman, *Scarface Al,* 26–27.

37. Thomas E. Fontecchio, memorandum to chief counsel, Internal Revenue Service, "Status Report on Otto Kerner, Theodore J. Isaacs, William S. Miller, Joseph Knight," June 24, 1971, northern district of Illinois, RG 118, CR 71-1086, National Archives, Great Lakes Region.

38. Kennelly, memorandum to Joyce, "Proposed Indictment of Otto Kerner and Others," August 20, 1971.

39. Jay C. Johnson, memorandum "to files," "United States of America v. Otto Kerner," August 23, 1971, U.S. Department of Justice Freedom of Information/Privacy Act Unit.

40. John C. Keeney, memorandum to Henry E. Petersen, "U.S. v. Kerner, et al.," November 30, 1971, northern district of Illinois, RG 118, CR 71-1086, National Archives, Great Lakes Region.

41. Oliver Stufflebeam, interview with Jan Bone, July 24, 1978, Anton C. Kerner collection.

42. Sherman Skolnick, interview with Jan Bone, May 16, 1978, Anton C. Kerner collection.

43. Sullivan, *Legend,* 221.

44. Eldon F. Hawley, "Review Memorandum, in re: Otto Kerner, et al.," August 19, 1971, northern district of Illinois, RG 118, CR 71-1086, National Archives, Great Lakes Region.

45. Kennelly, memorandum to Joyce, "Proposed Indictment of Otto Kerner and Others," August 20, 1971.

46. Victor C. Woerheide, memorandum to Will Wilson, "Recommendation of Prosecution," August 2, 1971, northern district of Illinois, RG 118, CR 71-1086, National Archives, Great Lakes Region.

47. Victor C. Woerheide, F. L. Williamson, and Paul Schaeffer, memorandum to Henry E. Petersen, "Kerner Investigation," undated, northern district of Illinois, RG 118, CR 71-1086, National Archives, Great Lakes Region.

48. Kennelly, memorandum to Joyce, "Proposed Indictment of Otto Kerner and Others," August 20, 1971.

49. Ibid.

50. Darrell McGowen, memorandum to Fred B. Ugast, September 24, 1971, northern district of Illinois, RG 118, CR 71-1086, National Archives, Great Lakes Region.

51. Samuel K. Skinner, memorandum to William J. Bauer and Henry Petersen, "Prosecution Memorandum—Otto Kerner," November 8, 1971, northern district of Illinois, RG 118, CR 71-1086, National Archives, Great Lakes Region.

52. Ibid.

53. Fred B. Ugast, "Memorandum for the File: Otto Kerner, Jr., Theodore Isaacs, et al.," November 30, 1971, northern district of Illinois, RG 118, CR 71-1086, National Archives, Great Lakes Region.

54. Thompson interview, July 8, 1993.

55. Charles Colson, interview with Anton C. Kerner, March 1, 1976, Anton C. Kerner collection.

56. In Hartley, *Big Jim Thompson*, 43.

57. Skinner, memorandum to Bauer and Petersen, "Prosecution Memorandum—Otto Kerner," November 8, 1971.

58. Peyton Ford, letter to Victor C. Woerheide, July 22, 1971, northern district of Illinois, RG 118, CR 71-1086, National Archives, Great Lakes Region.

59. Eldon F. Hawley, "Memorandum of Conference Re Otto Kerner, Jr.," August 23, 1971, northern district of Illinois, RG 118, CR 71-1086, National Archives, Great Lakes Region.

60. Thompson interview, July 8, 1993.

61. Ibid.

62. Heineman interview, October 6, 1993.

63. Ibid.

64. Califano interview, August 22, 1994.

65. Richard J. O'Brien diary, January 6, 1973, Anton C. Kerner collection.

66. *United States v. Isaacs et al.*, trial transcript, January 4, 1973, records of the District Court of the United States, northern district of Illinois, RG 21, 71-C-1086, National Archives, Great Lakes Region.

67. Thompson interview, July 8, 1993.

68. Ibid.

69. "Memorandum No. 2: Background Data on William S. Miller's Friendship and Association with Adlai E. Stevenson and Other Prominent Men in Business and Public Life Beginning with November, 1948," northern district of Illinois, RG 118, CR 71-1086, National Archives, Great Lakes Region.

70. *United States v. Isaacs et al.,* trial transcript, January 17, 1973.

71. Thompson interview, July 8, 1993.

72. Oliver P. Stufflebeam, interview with Jan Bone, July 24, 1978, Anton C. Kerner collection.

73. Richard J. O'Brien diary, January 17, 1973, and January 24, 1973, Anton C. Kerner collection.

74. *United States v. Isaacs et al.,* trial transcript, February 15, 1973.

75. Richard J. O'Brien diary, January 12, 1973, Anton C. Kerner collection.

76. McGowen interview, May 12, 1993.

77. Skinner interview, May 2, 1993.

78. McGowen interview, May 12, 1993.

79. Thompson interview, July 8, 1993.

80. *United States v. Isaacs et al.,* trial transcript, February 19, 1973.

81. Ibid.

82. *United States v. Isaacs et al,* sentencing hearing transcript, April 19, 1973, 71-C-1086, National Archives, Great Lakes Region.

83. Ibid.

84. Ibid.

Chapter 12: Unfinished Work

1. William J. Clinton, "Remarks by the President at University of California at San Diego Commencement," June 14, 1997, White House Office of the Press Secretary.

2. *McNally v. United States,* 107 S.Ct. 2875 (1987).

3. *Fasulo v. United States,* 272 U.S. 620, 629 (1926).

4. *McNally v. United States,* 107 S.Ct. 2875 (1987).

5. *United States v. Otto Kerner,* no. 88-2469.

6. John Paul Stevens, letter to Otto Kerner, December 5, 1971, Anton C. Kerner collection.

7. John Paul Stevens, letter to Otto Kerner, December 10, 1975, Anton C. Kerner collection.

8. *McNally v. United States,* 107 S.Ct. 2875 (1987).

9. Ibid.

10. Quoted in Crump, *Burn, Killer, Burn,* epigraph.

11. Anton C. Kerner, letter to Adlai E. Stevenson III, May 7, 1973, papers of Charles H. Sethness.

12. *Chicago Sun-Times,* December 21, 1975.

13. Otto Kerner, memorandum, May 31, 1975, papers of Charles H. Sethness.

14. *United States v. Falk,* 472 F.2d 1101 (1972).

15. Ibid.

16. Ibid.

17. Ibid.

18. Otto Kerner, memorandum, May 31, 1975, papers of Charles H. Sethness.

19. *United States v. Isaacs et al.*, 493 F.2d 1124 (1974)

20. Ibid.

21. *Washington Post,* June 18, 1974.

22. Otto Kerner, letter to Pat and Ralph Newman, August 7, 1974, Anton C. Kerner collection.

23. *Chicago Sun-Times,* July 30, 1974.

24. Kerner journal, undated handwritten page, Anton C. Kerner collection.

25. Kerner journal, November 14, 1974, Anton C. Kerner collection.

26. Ibid.

27. Otto Kerner, letter to Rose Kerner, November 11, 1974, Anton C. Kerner collection.

28. Emily S. Cottrell, memorandum to Mary Moldestad, "Otto Kerner Jr., 00037-123," September 30, 1974, Otto Kerner central file, U.S. Bureau of Prisons, Freedom of Information/Privacy Office.

29. Ibid.

30. Otto Kerner, undated handwritten draft, Anton C. Kerner collection.

31. U.S. Board of Parole, southeast region, "Notice of Action, January 15, 1975," Otto Kerner central file, U.S. Bureau of Prisons, Freedom of Information/Privacy Office.

32. U.S. Board of Parole members Bill Dawson and Steven Johnson, notes marked "Confidential—do not inform resident," October 8, 1974, Otto Kerner central file, U.S. Bureau of Prisons, Freedom of Information/Privacy Office.

33. Kerner journal, December 13, 1974, Anton C. Kerner collection.

34. Kerner journal, October 5 and 6, 1974, Anton C. Kerner collection.

35. Otto Kerner, letter to Dr. Thornton Scott, January 14, 1975, Anton C. Kerner collection.

36. Harry H. Woodward Jr., memorandum to Roland Breault, "Monthly Report—September, 1974," Lewis University archives.

37. Harry H. Woodward Jr., letter to Otto Kerner, January 21, 1975, Special Services Center, Lewis University archives.

38. Otto Kerner, draft speech prepared for Harry Woodward, undated, Anton C. Kerner collection.

39. Zimring and Hawkins, *Incapacitation,* 9.

40. DiIulio, *No Escape,* 148–49.

41. "Kerner Joins Lewis University," *The Candle,* June 1975, p. 2, Lewis University archives.

42. Courtesy of Richard Bradley, WUIS radio, Springfield.

43. *Chicago Sun-Times,* December 11, 1975.

44. MacDougall interview, August 6, 1997.

45. Lewis University Special Services Center, "Quarterly Report to W. Clement and Jessie V. Stone Foundation," undated, Lewis University archives.

46. Leonard interview, August 6, 1997.

47. Bob Heise, memorandum to Lester Carr, undated, Lewis University archives.

48. *Chicago Tribune*, March 10, 1989.

49. Otto Kerner, letter (name of recipient stricken), October 21, 1975, U.S. Bureau of Prisons.

50. Courtesy of Richard Bradley, WUIS radio, Springfield.

51. Murphy interview, May 29, 1992.

52. Gwendolyn Brooks, "Of Otto Kerner," from the program for the Otto Kerner memorial service, May 12, 1976, Anton C. Kerner collection, used by permission.

53. "Convocation and Investiture of Laureates of the Lincoln Academy of Illinois," May 7, 1977, files at the Office of Illinois Governor.

54. Anton Kerner interview, January 29, 1998.

Bibliography

Articles, Books, and Dissertations

Allswang, John M. *Bosses, Machines, and Urban Voters: An American Symbiosis.* Port Washington, N.Y.: National University Publications/Kennikat, 1977.

———. *A House for All Peoples: Ethnic Politics in Chicago, 1890–1936.* Lexington: University Press of Kentucky, 1971.

———. *The Political Behavior of Chicago's Ethnic Groups, 1918–1932.* New York: Arno, 1980.

Ambrose, Stephen E. *Nixon: The Education of a Politician 1913–1962.* New York: Simon and Schuster, 1987.

Anderson, Alan B., and George W. Pickering. *Confronting the Color Line: The Broken Promise of the Civil Rights Movement in Chicago.* Athens: University of Georgia Press, 1986.

Anton, Thomas J. *The Politics of State Expenditure in Illinois.* Urbana: University of Illinois Press, 1966.

Auerbach, Ann Hagedorn. *Wild Ride: The Rise and Tragic Fall of Calumet Farm, Inc., America's Premier Racing Dynasty.* New York: Henry Holt, 1994.

Baily, Ronald. "Facing Death, a New Life Perhaps Too Late." *Life,* July 27, 1962, pp. 26–29.

Baker, Jean H. *The Stevensons: A Biography of an American Family.* New York: Norton, 1996.

Baker, Nancy C. *Baby Selling: The Scandal of Black-Market Adoption.* New York: Vanguard, 1978.

Barnard, H. K. *Anton the Martyr.* Chicago: Marion, 1933.

Baumann, Edward. *May God Have Mercy on Your Soul: The Story of the Rope and the Thunderbolt.* Chicago: Bonus, 1993.

Bell, Griffin B. "Toward a More Efficient Federal Appeals System." *Judicature* 54, no. 6 (January 1971): 237–44.

Bergreen, Laurence. *Capone: The Man and the Era*. New York: Simon and Schuster, 1994.

Berkow, Ira. *Maxwell Street: Survival in a Bazaar*. New York: Vanguard, 1978.

Berman, Larry. *Lyndon Johnson's War: The Road to Stalemate in Vietnam*. New York: Norton, 1989.

Bierley, Paul E. *The Works of John Philip Sousa*. Columbus, Ohio: Integrity, 1984.

Biles, Roger. *Big City Boss in Depression and War: Mayor Edward J. Kelly of Chicago*. DeKalb: Northern Illinois University Press, 1984.

———. *Richard J. Daley: Politics, Race, and the Governing of Chicago*. DeKalb: Northern Illinois University Press, 1995.

Binkley, Wilfred E. *The American Political Parties: Their Natural History*. New York: Knopf, 1962.

Blum, Jerome, Rondon Cameron, and Thomas G. Barnes. *The European World: A History*. 2d ed. Boston: Little, Brown, 1970.

Blunden, Godfrey. *Eastern Europe: Czechoslovakia, Hungary, and Poland*. New York: Time, 1965.

Bone, Jan. *The Thompson Indictment*. Chicago: Public Interest, 1978.

Braden, George D., and Rubin G. Cohn. *The Illinois Constitution: An Annotated and Comparative Analysis*. Urbana, Ill.: Institute of Government and Public Affairs, University of Illinois, 1969.

Bremner, Robert H., ed. *Children and Youth in America: A Documentary History*. Cambridge, Mass.: Harvard University Press, 1974.

Breuer, William B. *Operation Torch: The Allied Gamble to Invade North Africa*. New York: St. Martin's, 1985.

Brinkley, David. *Washington Goes to War: The Extraordinary Story of the Transformation of a City and a Nation*. New York: Knopf, 1988.

Brodoes, Fawn M. *Richard Nixon: The Shaping of His Character*. Cambridge, Mass.: Harvard University Press, 1983.

Brooks, Gwendolyn, and Otto Kerner, Allan Nevins, Paul M. Angle, Mark Van Doren, Paul H. Douglas, Bruce Catton, and Adlai E. Stevenson, *A Portion of That Field: The Centennial of the Burial of Lincoln*. Urbana: University of Illinois Press, 1967.

Bryant, James R. "The Office of Master of Chancery—Development and Use in Illinois." *Northwestern University Law Review* 49 (1954): 458–79.

Bukowski, Douglas. "Judge Edmund K. Jarecki: A Rather Regular Independent." *Chicago History*, Winter 1979–80, pp. 206–18.

Burnham, David. *Above the Law: Secret Deals, Political Fixes, and Other Misadventures of the U.S. Department of Justice*. New York: Scribner's, 1996.

———. *A Law unto Itself: Power, Politics, and the IRS*. New York: Random House, 1989.

Califano, Joseph A., Jr. *The Triumph and Tragedy of Lyndon Johnson: The White House Years*. New York: Simon and Schuster, 1991.

Caro, Robert A. *The Years of Lyndon Johnson: The Path to Power*. New York: Knopf, 1982.

———. *The Years of Lyndon Johnson: Means of Ascent*. New York: Knopf, 1990.

Carpentier, Charles F. *Illinois Blue Book: 1961–1962*. Springfield: State of Illinois, 1963.

Chamberlain, William H. *Illinois Blue Book: 1963–1964*. Springfield: State of Illinois, 1965.

Chase, Harold W. "Federal Judges: The Appointment Process." *Minnesota Law Review* 51 (1966): 185–221.

Ciccone, F. Richard. *Daley: Power and Presidential Politics*. Chicago: Contemporary Books, 1996.

Clark, Kenneth B. *Dark Ghetto: Dilemmas of Social Power*. New York: Harper and Row, 1965.

Clayton, John. *The Illinois Fact Book and Historical Almanac, 1673–1968*. Carbondale: Southern Illinois University Press, 1970.

Coffin, Frank M. *The Ways of a Judge: Reflections from the Federal Appellate Bench*. Boston: Houghton Mifflin, 1980.

Commission on Adoption Laws. *Report of the Commission on Adoption Laws to the Seventy-first General Assembly*. Springfield: Illinois General Legislative Research Unit, n.d.

Corman, Steve, and Jack Swanson. "Cozy Times in the Press Box." *Chicago Journalism Review*, November 1971, pp. 3–6.

Cornelius, Janet. *Constitution Making in Illinois, 1818–1970*. Urbana: University of Illinois Press, 1972.

Crump, Paul. *Burn, Killer, Burn!* Chicago: Johnson, 1962.

Cutler, Irving. *Chicago: Metropolis of the Mid-Continent*. Dubuque, Iowa: Kendall-Hunt, 1976.

———. *The Jews of Chicago: From Shtetl to Suburb*. Urbana: University of Illinois Press, 1996.

Czechoslovak National Council of America. *Panorama: A Historical Review of Czechs and Slovaks in the United States of America*. Chicago: 1970.

Dallek, Robert. *Flawed Giant: Lyndon Johnson and His Times, 1961–1973*. New York: Oxford University Press, 1998.

Davis, Shelly L. *Unbridled Power: Inside the Secret Culture of the IRS*. New York: Harper Business, 1997.

Demaris, Ovid. *Captive City: Chicago in Chains*. New York: Lyle Stuart, 1969.

———. *The Director: An Oral Biography of J. Edgar Hoover*. New York: Harper's Magazine Press, 1975.

Derber, Milton. *Labor in Illinois: The Affluent Years*. Urbana: University of Illinois Press, 1989.

Despres, Leon M. "Corruption in Chicago: A City Ripe for Reform." *The Nation*, March 12, 1960, pp. 220–23.

DiIulio, John J., Jr. *No Escape: The Future of American Corrections*. New York: Basic Books, 1991.

Divine, Robert A. *The Johnson Years.* Volume 1: *Foreign Policy, the Great Society, and the White House.* Lawrence: University of Kansas Press, 1987.

———, ed. *Exploring the Johnson Years.* Austin: University of Texas Press, 1981.

Dobyns, Fletcher. *The Amazing Story of Repeal: An Exposé of the Power of Propaganda.* Chicago: Willett, Clark, 1940.

———. *The Underworld of American Politics.* New York: author, 1932.

Dornfeld, A. A. *Behind the Front Page.* Chicago: Academy Chicago, 1983.

Douglas, Paul H. *In the Fullness of Time: The Memoirs of Paul H. Douglas.* New York: Harcourt Brace Jovanovich, 1971.

Droba, Daniel D., ed. *Czech and Slovak Leaders in Metropolitan Chicago.* Chicago: Slavonic Club of the University of Chicago, 1934.

D'Souza, Dinesh. *The End of Racism.* New York: Free Press, 1995.

Ehrlichman, John. *Witness to Power: The Nixon Years.* New York: Simon and Schuster, 1982.

Erickson, Gladys A. *Warden Ragen of Joliet.* New York: E. P. Dutton, 1957.

Farago, Ladislas. *Patton: Ordeal and Triumph.* New York: Dell, 1965.

Farber, David. *Chicago '68.* Chicago: University of Chicago Press, 1988.

Faunce, W. H. P. *Facing Life.* New York: Macmillan, 1928.

Fiedler, George. *The Illinois Law Courts, 1673–1973: A Documentary History.* Berwyn, Ill.: Physicians' Record, 1973.

Fraser, David. *Knight's Cross: A Life of Field Marshal Erwin Rommel.* New York: HarperCollins, 1993.

Freund, Richard. *Watch Czechoslovakia!* London: Thomas Nelson and Sons, 1938.

Furgurson, Ernest B. *Westmoreland: The Inevitable General.* Boston: Little, Brown, 1968.

Gertz, Elmer, and Joseph. P. Pisciotte. *Charter for a New Age: An Inside View of the Sixth Illinois Constitutional Convention.* Urbana: University of Illinois Press, 1980.

———. *To Life: The Story of a Chicago Lawyer.* New York: McGraw-Hill, 1974.

Ginsburg, R. A. "Czechs in Chicago's Politics." In *Czech and Slovak Leaders in Metropolitan Chicago,* ed. Daniel D. Droba. Chicago: Slavonic Club of the University of Chicago, 1934.

Gitlin, Todd. *The Sixties: Years of Hope, Days of Rage.* New York: Bantam Books, 1987.

Gleason, Bill. *Daley of Chicago: The Man, the Mayor, and the Limits of Conventional Politics.* New York: Simon and Schuster, 1970.

Gold, Gerald, ed. *The Watergate Hearings: Break-in and Cover-up.* New York: Bantam Books, 1974.

Goldman. S. "Judicial Appointments to the United States Court of Appeals." *Wisconsin Law Review* (Winter 1967): 186–214.

Goldwater, Barry M., and Jack Casserly. *Goldwater.* New York: Bantam-Doubleday-Dell, 1988.

Goodwin, Richard N. *Remembering America: A Voice from the Sixties.* Boston: Little, Brown, 1988.

Gosnell, Harold F. *Machine Politics: Chicago Model*. Chicago: University of Chicago Press, 1937.

Gottfried, Alex. *Boss Cermak of Chicago: A Study of Political Leadership*. Seattle: University of Washington Press, 1962.

Goulden, Joseph C. *The Benchwarmers: The Private World of the Powerful Federal Judges*. New York: Weybright and Talley, 1974.

Gove, Samuel K. *Con-Con: Issues for the Illinois Constitutional Convention*. Urbana: University of Illinois Press, 1970.

Gove, Samuel K., and Louis H. Masotti. *After Daley: Chicago Politics in Transition*. Urbana: University of Illinois Press, 1982.

Gray, W. Robert. "The Intangible-Rights Doctrine and Political-Corruption Prosecutions under the Federal Mail Fraud Statute." *University of Chicago Law Review* 47 (1980): 562–87.

Green, Paul M., and Melvin G. Holli, eds. *The Mayors: The Chicago Political Tradition*. Rev. ed. Carbondale: Southern Illinois University Press, 1995.

The Grolier Society. *Lands and Peoples*. Vol. 2. New York: Grolier Society, 1954.

Halberstam, David. *The Fifties*. New York: Villard Books, 1993.

Haldeman, H. R., and Joseph DiMona. *The Ends of Power*. New York: New York Times Books, 1978.

———. *The Haldeman Diaries: Inside the Nixon White House*. New York: Putnam's, 1994.

———. *The Haldeman Diaries*. CD-ROM. New York: Sony Electronic Publishing, 1994.

Hall, Robert H. "The New President and the Selection of Judges." *Judicature* 52, no. 6 (January 1969): 249–60.

Hallgren, Mauritz A. "Chicago Goes Tammany." *The Nation*, April 22, 1931, pp. 445–47.

Halper, Albert, ed. *The Chicago Crime Book*. Cleveland: World, 1967.

Hamel, Helena. "History of Lawndale-Crawford." Unpublished manuscript. Lawndale Community Collection, Harold Washington Library, Chicago, 1951.

Hartley, Robert E. *Big Jim Thompson of Illinois*. Chicago: Rand McNally, 1979.

———. *Charles H. Percy: A Political Perspective*. Chicago: Rand McNally, 1975.

Hasek, Jaroslav. *The Good Soldier Svejk and His Fortunes in the World War*. New York: Thomas Y. Crowell, 1974.

Hoffman, Dennis E. *Scarface Al and the Crime Crusaders: Chicago's Private War against Capone*. Carbondale: Southern Illinois University Press, 1993.

Holli, Melvin G., and Peter Jones, eds. *Ethnic Chicago*. Grand Rapids, Mich.: Eerdmans, 1981.

Hoover, Herbert. *Memories of Herbert Hoover*. Volume 2: *The Cabinet and the Presidency*. New York: Macmillan, 1951.

Howard, Robert P. *Mostly Good and Competent Men: Illinois Governors 1818 to 1988*. Springfield: Sangamon State University and Illinois State Historical Society, 1988.

Howe, George F. *Northwest Africa: Seizing the Initiative in the West.* Washington, D.C.: U.S. Government Printing Office, 1993.

Howlett, Michael J. *Annual Report of the Auditor of Public Accounts, July 1, 1967– June 30, 1968.* Springfield: State of Illinois, 1968.

——. *Biennial Report of the Auditor of Public Accounts, July 1, 1960 and ending June 30, 1962.* Springfield: State of Illinois, 1962.

——. *Biennial Report of the Auditor of Public Accounts, July 1, 1962 and ending June 30, 1964.* Springfield: State of Illinois, 1964.

——. *Biennial Report of the Auditor of Public Accounts, July 1, 1964 and ending June 30, 1966.* Springfield: State of Illinois, 1966.

Ickes, Harold L. *The Secret Diary of Harold L. Ickes.* Vol. 3: *The Lowering Clouds.* New York: Simon and Schuster, 1954.

Illinois Commission on Revenue. *Report of the Commission on Revenue, State of Illinois.* Springfield: State of Illinois, 1963.

Illinois Legislative Investigating Commission. "Illinois Horse Racing: A Study of Legislation and Criminal Practices," 1974, Harold Washington Library, Chicago.

——. "The Illinois Racing Board Controversy: A Report to the Illinois General Assembly," March 1973, Harold Washington Library, Chicago.

Illinois Racing Board. *1961 Annual Report.* Springfield: State of Illinois, 1962.

——. *1962 Annual Report.* Springfield: State of Illinois, 1963.

——. *1963 Annual Report.* Springfield: State of Illinois, 1964.

——. *1964 Annual Report.* Springfield: State of Illinois, 1965.

——. *1965 Annual Report.* Springfield: State of Illinois, 1966.

——. *1966 Annual Report.* Springfield: State of Illinois, 1967.

——. *1967 Annual Report.* Springfield: State of Illinois, 1968.

——. *1968 Annual Report.* Springfield: State of Illinois, 1969.

Irey, Elmer L., and William J. Slocum. *The Tax Dodgers.* New York: Greenberg, 1948.

Jachim, Anton G. *Science Policy Making in the United States and the Batavia Accelerator.* Carbondale: Southern Illinois University Press, 1975.

Jacobs, James B. *Stateville: The Penitentiary in Mass Society.* Chicago: University of Chicago Press, 1977.

Jacobs, Paul. *Prelude to Riot: A View of Urban America from the Bottom.* New York: Vintage Books, 1968.

Jaeckel, Martin Theodor. "The Use of Social Science Knowledge and Research in a Presidential Commission: A Case Study in Utilization." Ph.D. diss., University of Pittsburgh, 1989.

Johnson, Lyndon Baines. *The Vantage Point: Perspectives on the Presidency, 1963– 1969.* New York: Holt, Rinehart, and Winston, 1971.

Kaiser, Charles. *1968 in America: Music, Politics, Chaos, Counterculture, and the Shaping of a Generation.* New York: Weidenfeld and Nicolson, 1988.

Kallina, Edmund F., Jr. *Courthouse over White House: Chicago and the Presidential Election of 1960.* Orlando: University of Central Florida Press, 1988.

Kearns, Doris. *Lyndon Johnson and the American Dream.* New York: Harper and Row, 1976.

Kennedy, Eugene. *Himself! The Life and Times of Mayor Richard J. Daley.* New York: Viking, 1978.

Kenney, David. *A Political Passage: The Career of Stratton of Illinois.* Carbondale: Southern Illinois University Press, 1990.

Kerner, Otto. *Attorney General's Opinions: For the Year 1937.* Springfield: State of Illinois, 1937.

———. *Attorney General's Report: For the Biennium 1933–1934 and Opinions for the Year 1934.* Springfield: State of Illinois, 1934.

———. *Attorney General's Report: For the Biennium 1935–1936 and Opinions for the Year 1936.* Springfield: State of Illinois, 1936.

———. *Attorney General's Report: For the Biennium 1937–1938 and Opinions for the Year 1938.* Springfield: State of Illinois, 1938.

Kerner, Otto, Jr. "The Incumbent Views the Office." In *The Office of Governor,* 83–88. Urbana: Institute of Government and Public Affairs, 1963.

———. "Recent Cases: Congressional Redistricting." *Illinois Law Review* 27 (December 1932): 445–47.

Kerner, Robert J., ed. *Czechoslovakia: Twenty Years of Independence.* Berkeley: University of California Press, 1949.

Kilian, Michael, Connie Fletcher, and F. Richard Ciccone. *Who Runs Chicago?* New York: St. Martin's, 1979.

Klein, Woody. *Lindsay's Promise: The Dream That Failed.* New York: Macmillan, 1970.

Kobler, John. *Capone: The Life and World of Al Capone.* New York: Putnam's, 1971.

Kogan, Herman. *The First Century: The Chicago Bar Association 1874–1974.* Chicago: Rand McNally, 1974.

Kolb, Adrienne, and Lillian Hoddeson. "A New Frontier in the Chicago Suburbs: Settling Fermilab, 1963–1972." *Illinois Historical Journal* 88, no. 1 (Spring 1995): 2–18.

Kopkind, Andrew, and James Ridgeway, eds. *Decade of Crisis: America in the '60s.* New York: World, 1972.

Kutler, Stanley I. *Abuse of Power: The New Nixon Tapes.* New York: Free Press, 1997.

Kutner, Luis. "The Illusion of Due Process in Commitment Proceedings." *Northwestern Law Review* 57 (1962): 383–99.

Lait, Jack, and Lee Mortimer. *Chicago: Confidential!* New York: Crown, 1950.

Lanier, Alfedo S. "A Lifetime of Waiting." *Chicago,* October 1983, pp. 191–92, 238–54.

Legislative Reference Bureau. *Final (#20) Legislative Synopsis and Digest of the Seventy-second General Assembly, State of Illinois: Action on All Bills and Resolutions Received through June 30, 1961.* Springfield: State of Illinois, 1961.

———. *Final (#23) Legislative Synopsis and Digest of the Seventy-third General Assembly, State of Illinois: Action on All Bills and Resolutions Received through June 30, 1963.* Springfield: State of Illinois, 1963.

———. *Final (#23) Legislative Synopsis and Digest of the Seventy-fourth General Assembly, State of Illinois: Action on All Bills and Resolutions Received through June 30, 1965.* Springfield: State of Illinois, 1965.

———. *Final (#25) Legislative Synopsis and Digest of the Seventy-fifth General Assembly, State of Illinois: Action on All Bills and Resolutions Received through October 19, 1967*. Springfield: State of Illinois, 1967.

Lepawsky, Albert. *The Judicial System of Metropolitan Chicago*. Chicago: University of Chicago Press, 1932.

Levinsohn, Florence Hamlish. *Harold Washington: A Political Biography*. Chicago: Chicago Review, 1983.

Lewis, Gavin. *Tomas Masaryk*. New York: Chelsea House, 1990.

Lindberg, Richard. *Ethnic Chicago*. Lincolnwood, Ill.: Passport Books/NTC, 1993.

———. "The Evolution of a Evil Business." *Chicago History*, July 1993, pp. 38–53.

———. *To Serve and Collect: Chicago Politics and Police Corruption from the Lager Beer Riot to the Summerdale Scandal*. New York: Praeger, 1991.

Lindsay, John V. *Journey into Politics*. New York: Dodd, Mead, 1967.

Lipsky, Michael, and David J. Olson. *Commission Politics: The Processing of Racial Crisis in America*. New Brunswick, N.J.: Transaction Books, 1977.

Littlewood, Thomas B. *Horner of Illinois*. Evanston, Ill.: Northwestern University Press, 1969.

———. "Otto Kerner of Illinois: The Problems of Being a Nice Guy." *Chicago Scene*, December 1962, pp. 19–23.

Loessberg, Richard Anthony. "An Analysis of the Kerner Report." Ph.D. diss., University of Texas, Austin, 1981.

Long, Norton E. "After the Voting Is Over." *Midwest Journal of Political Science* 6, no. 2 (May 1962): 183–200.

———. Diaries, February 1961–March 1963. Unpublished. In authors' possession.

———. *The Polity*. Chicago: Rand McNally, 1962.

Loomis, Frank E. "Federal Prosecutions of Elected State Officials for Mail Fraud: Creative Prosecution or an Afford to Federalism?" *The American University Law Review* 28 (1978): 63–85.

Louwennar, Karyl. "Where Have All the Farmers Gone?" Unpublished manuscript. National Accelerator Laboratory Historical Collection, Batavia, Ill., 1969.

Ludwig, Emil. *Defender of Democracy: Mazaryk of Czechoslovakia*. New York: Robert McBride, 1936.

Lutterbeck, Ann Goggin. "The Law in Illinois Pertaining to the Adoption of Children." *DePaul Law Review* 165 (1959): 165–212.

MacNeil, Neil. *Dirksen: Portrait of a Public Man*. New York: World, 1970.

Major, J. Earl. "Federal Judges as Political Patronage." *Chicago Bar Record* (1956): 7–11.

Martin, Edward M. *The Role of the Bar in Electing the Bench in Chicago*. Chicago: University of Chicago Press, 1936.

Martin, John Bartlow. *Adlai Stevenson of Illinois*. Garden City, N.Y.: Doubleday, 1976.

Martin, Pat, ed. *Czechoslovak Culture*. Monticello, Iowa: Penfield, 1989.

Martinek, Joseph. *One Hundred Years of the C.S.A.: The History of the Czechoslovak Society of America*. Cicero, Ill.: Czechoslovak Society of America, 1985.

Marx, Gary T. "Civil Disorder and the Agents of Social Control." *Journal of Social Issues* 26, no. 1 (Winter 1970): 19–57.

———. "A Document with a Difference." *Trans-Action*, September 1968, pp. 56–58.

Mattick, Hans W. *The Unexamined Death: An Analysis of Capital Punishment.* Chicago: John Howard Association, 1966.

Mayer, George H. *The Republican Party, 1854–1964.* New York: Oxford University Press, 1964.

McCullough, David. *Truman.* New York: Simon and Schuster, 1992.

McFeeley, Neil D. *Appointment of Judges: The Johnson Presidency.* Austin: University of Texas Press, 1987.

McGinniss, Joe. *Fatal Vision.* New York: Putnam's, 1983.

McKay, Robert B. *Reapportionment: The Law and Politics of Equal Representation.* New York: Simon and Schuster, 1965.

McKeever, Porter. *Adlai Stevenson: His Life and Legacy.* New York: William Morrow, 1989.

Meranto, Philip, ed. *The Kerner Report Revisited.* Urbana: Institute of Government and Public Affairs, University of Illinois, 1970.

Merriam, Charles E. *Chicago: A More Intimate View of Urban Politics.* New York: Macmillan, 1929.

Merritt, Anna J. *Redistricting: An Exercise in Prophecy.* Urbana: Institute of Government and Public Affairs and the Department of Journalism, University of Illinois, 1982.

Merton, Robert K. "The Matthew Effect in Science." *Science* 159 (January 1968): 56–63.

Messick, Hank. *John Edgar Hoover: A Critical Examination of the Director and of the Continuing Alliance between Crime, Business, and Politics.* New York: David McKay, 1972.

———. *The Politics of Prosecution: Jim Thompson, Richard Nixon, Marje Everett, and the Trial of Otto Kerner.* Ottawa, Ill.: Caroline House Books, 1978.

Miller, Donald L. *City of the Century: The Epic of Chicago and the Making of America.* New York: Simon and Schuster, 1996.

Mitford, Jessica. *Kind and Usual Punishment: The Prison Business.* New York: Vintage Books, 1974.

Morgan, Edward P. *The Sixties Experience: Hard Lessons about Modern America.* Philadelphia: Temple University Press, 1991.

Murray, David. *Charles Percy of Illinois.* New York: Harper and Row, 1968.

The National Advisory Commission on Civil Disorders. *The Kerner Report: The 1968 Report of the National Advisory Commission on Civil Disorders.* Introductions by Fred R. Harris and Tom Wicker. New York: Pantheon Books, 1988.

———. *The Report of the National Advisory Commission on Civil Disorders.* Washington, D.C.: U.S. Government Printing Office, 1968.

———. *Report of the National Advisory Commission on Civil Disorders.* Introduction by Tom Wicker. New York: Bantam Books, 1968.

———. *Supplemental Studies for the National Advisory Commission on Civil Disorders.* Washington, D.C.: U.S. Government Printing Office, 1968.

Navasky, Victor S. *Kennedy Justice.* New York: Atheneum, 1971.

Newman, Edward Polson. *Masaryk.* London: Campion, 1960.

Nixon, Richard M. *RN: Memoirs of Richard Nixon.* New York: Touchstone, 1990.

Nizer, Louis. *The Jury Returns.* Garden City, N.Y.: Doubleday, 1966.

Noonan, John T., Jr. *Bribes.* New York: Macmillan, 1984.

Oates, Stephen B. *Let the Trumpet Sound: The Life of Martin Luther King, Jr.* New York: Harper and Row, 1982.

O'Connor, John J. "McNally v. United States: Intangible Rights Mail Fraud Declared a Dead Letter." *Catholic University Law Review* 37 (1988): 851–79.

O'Connor, Len. *Clout: Mayor Daley and His City.* Chicago: Henry Regnery, 1975.

———. *Requiem: The Deline and Demise of Mayor Daley and His Era.* Chicago: Contemporary Books, 1977.

O'Neill, William L. *Coming Apart: An Informal History of America in the 1960s.* New York: Times Books/Random House, 1971.

Oudes, Bruce, ed. *From: The President—Richard Nixon's Secret Files.* New York: Harper and Row, 1989.

Oxman, Peter M. "The Federal Mail Fraud Statute after McNally v. United States, 107 S.Ct. 2875 (1987): The Remains of the Intangible Rights Doctrine and Its Proposed Congressional Restoration." *American Criminal Law Review* 25 (1988): 743–89.

Pack, Robert. *Edward Bennett Williams for the Defense.* New York: Harper and Row, 1983.

Parmet, Herbert S. *The Democrats: The Years after FDR.* New York: Macmillan, 1976.

———. *Richard Nixon and His America.* Boston: Little, Brown, 1990.

Pearson, Charles T. *The Indomitable Tin Goose: The True Story of Preston Tucker and His Car.* New York: Pocket Books, 1988.

Pensoneau, Taylor, and Bob Ellis. *Dan Walker: The Glory and the Tragedy.* Evansville, Ind.: Smith-Collins, 1993.

Peterson, Virgil W. *Barbarians in Our Midst: A History of Chicago Crime and Politics.* Boston: Little, Brown, 1952.

Philpott, Thomas Lee. *The Slum and the Ghetto: Neighborhood Deterioration and Middle-Class Reform, Chicago, 1880–1930.* New York: Oxford University Press, 1978.

Picchi, Blaise. *The Five Weeks of Giuseppe Zangara.* Chicago: Academy Chicago, 1998.

Pickney, Darryl. "Professionals." *New York Review of Books,* April 20, 1995, pp. 34, 43–49.

Platt, Anthony, ed. *The Politics of Riot Commissions 1917–1970: A Collection of Official Reports and Critical Essays.* New York: Macmillan, 1971.

Popper, Frank. *The President's Commissions.* New York: Twentieth Century Fund, 1970.

Potter, Jerry Allen, and Fred Bost. *Fatal Justice: Reinvestigating the MacDonald Murders.* New York: Norton, 1995.

Powell, Paul. *Illinois Blue Book: 1965–1966.* Springfield: State of Illinois, 1967.

———. *Illinois Blue Book: 1967–1968.* Springfield: State of Illinois, 1969.

Rakove, Milton. *Don't Make No Waves—Don't Back No Losers: An Insider's Analysis of the Daley Machine.* Bloomington: University of Indiana Press, 1975.

———. *We Don't Want Nobody Nobody Sent: An Oral History of the Daley Years.* Bloomington: University of Indiana Press, 1979.

Ralph, James R., Jr. *Northern Protest: Martin Luther King, Jr., Chicago, and the Civil Rights Movement.* Cambridge, Mass.: Harvard University Press, 1993.

Ramsey, Norman F. *The Early History of URA and Fermilab.* Batavia, Ill.: Fermi National Accelerator Laboratory, 1992.

Rather, Dan, and Gary Paul Gates. *The Palace Guard.* New York: Harper and Row, 1974.

Reeling, Kenneth. "The Story of the Village of Weston." Unpublished manuscript. National Accelerator Laboratory Historical Collection, Batavia, Ill., 1968.

Reeves, Thomas C. *A Question of Character: A Life of John F. Kennedy.* New York: Free Press, 1991.

Reidy, John P. *Zone Mental Health Centers: The Illinois Concept.* Springfield, Ill.: Charles C. Thomas, 1964.

Rentschler, Bill. *The Paper Sword of Bill Rentschler.* Chicago: Chicago Review Press, 1987.

Roberts, J. M. *History of the World.* New York: Oxford University Press, 1993.

Robles, Philip K. *United States Military Medals and Ribbons.* Rutland, Vt.: Charles E. Tuttle, 1971.

Roemer, William F., Jr. *Roemer: Man against the Mob.* New York: Donald I. Fine, 1989.

Rogers, LeRoy E., and Carroll H. Rickard, eds. *The Liber Brunensis for 1930.* Providence, R.I.: Brown University, 1930.

Royko, Mike. *Boss: Richard J. Daley of Chicago.* New York: E. P. Dutton, 1971.

Ruth, David E. *Inventing the Public Enemy: The Gangster in American Culture, 1918–1934.* Chicago: University of Chicago Press, 1996.

Sandburg, Carl. *The Chicago Race Riots July 1919.* New York: Harcourt, Brace and Howe, 1919.

Schapsmeier, Edward L., and Frederick H. Schapsmeier. *Dirksen of Illinois: Senatorial Statesman.* Urbana: University of Illinois Press, 1985.

Schlesinger, Arthur M., Jr. *Robert Kennedy and His Times.* New York: Houghton Mifflin, 1978.

Schmidt, John R. *The Mayor Who Cleaned up Chicago: A Political Biography of William E. Dever.* DeKalb: Northern Illinois University Press, 1989.

Schnepper, Jeff A. *Inside IRS: How Internal Revenue Works (You Over).* New York: Stein and Day, 1968.

Scott, Peter Dale. *Deep Politics and the Death of JFK.* Berkeley: University of California Press, 1993.

Scruggs, Donald Lee. "Lyndon Baines Johnson and the National Advisory Commission on Civil Disorders (The Kerner Commission): A Study of the Johnson Domestic Policy Making." Ph.D. diss., University of Oklahoma, Norman, 1980.

Seaborg, Glenn T. Journal. Unpublished. Seaborg Papers, Lawrence Berkeley Laboratory, Berkeley, Calif.

——. "The Fermilab Story." *Fermilab 1987*. Annual report of the Fermi National Accelerator Laboratory. NAL Historical Collection, Batavia, Ill.

Segaloff, Nat. *Hurricane Billy: The Stormy Life and Films of William Friedkin*. New York: William Morrow, 1990.

Shellow, Robert. "Social Scientists and Social Action from within the Establishment." *Journal of Social Issues* 26, no. 1 (Winter 1970): 207–20.

Sheresky, Norman. *On Trial: Masters of the Courtroom*. New York: Viking, 1977.

Shirer, William L. *The Rise and Fall of the Third Reich: A History of Nazi Germany*. New York: Simon and Schuster, 1960.

Skoff, Frank, ed. *Illinois Chess Bulletin* 4, no. 1 (May 1968): 128–30.

Sloan, Arthur A. *Hoffa*. Boston: MIT Press, 1991.

Snow, C. P. *"The Two Cultures" and "The Scientific Revolution."* New York: Cambridge University Press, 1962.

Solomon, Rayman L. *History of the Seventh Circuit 1891–1941*. Washington, D.C.: U.S. Government Printing Office, 1981.

Stanton, Fred, ed. *Fighting Racism in World Ward II: A Week-by-Week Account of the Struggle against Racism and Discrimination in the United States during 1939–45*. New York: Pathfinder, 1980.

Stanton, Shelby L. *Order of Battle: U.S. Army, World War II*. Novato, Calif.: Presidio, 1984.

Stead, William T. *If Christ Came to Chicago!* Chicago: Laird and Lee, 1894.

Steiner, Edward A. *On the Trail of the Immigrant*. New York: Arno, 1969.

Steiner, Gilbert Y., and Samuel K. Gove. "Governors, Issues, and Styles: 1933–1960." In *The Office of Governor*, 33–47. Urbana: Institute of Government and Public Affairs, University of Illinois, 1963.

——. *Legislative Politics in Illinois*. Urbana: University of Illinois Press, 1960.

Sterling, Claire. *The Masaryk Case*. New York: Harper and Row, 1969.

Stuart, William H. *The 20 Incredible Years*. Chicago: M. A. Donohue, 1935.

Sullivan, Frank. *Legend: The Only Inside Story about Mayor Richard J. Daley*. Chicago: Bonus Books, 1989.

Sulzberg, C. L. *World War II*. Boston: Houghton Mifflin, 1966.

Summers, Anthony. *The Secret Life of J. Edgar Hoover*. New York: Putnam's, 1993.

Surface, William. *Inside Internal Revenue: A Report to the Taxpayer*. New York: Coward-McCann, 1967.

Sutton, Robert P., ed. *The Prairie State: A Documentary History of Illinois, Civil War to the Present*. Grand Rapids, Mich.: Eerdmans, 1976.

Swygert, Luther M. "Bench and the Bar Work Together in the Seventh Circuit." *American Bar Association Journal* 61 (May 1975): 613–16.

——. "The State of the Judiciary of the Seventh Federal Circuit." *Chicago Bar Record* 56, no. 1 (July–August 1974): 8–15.

Theoharid, Athan. *J. Edgar Hoover, Sex, and Crime: A Historical Antidote*. Chicago: Ivan R. Dee, 1995.

Thomas, Evan. *The Man to See: Edward Bennett Williams: Ultimate Insider; Legendary Trial Lawyer.* New York: Simon and Schuster, 1991.

Thompson, Edward T. *Theodore H. White at Large.* New York: Pantheon Books, 1992.

Thompson, S. Harrison. *Czechoslovakia in European History.* Hamden Conn.: Archon Books, 1965.

Tine, Robert. *Tucker: The Man and His Dream.* New York: Pocket Books, 1988.

Tuttle, William M., Jr. *Race Riot: Chicago in the Red Summer of 1919.* New York: Atheneum, 1980.

United States Senate. Committee of the Judiciary. Subcommitee to Investigate Juvenile Delinquency. *Hearings before the Subcommitee to Investigate Juvenile Delinquency of the Committee of the Judiciary, United States Senate, July 15 and 16, 1955.* Washington, D.C.: U.S. Government Printing Office, 1956.

Van Der Slik, Jack R., and Kent D. Redfield. *Lawmaking in Illinois: Legislative Politics, People, and Processes.* Springfield, Ill.: Office of Public Affairs Communication, Sangamon State University, 1986.

Viorst, Milton. *Fire in the Streets: America in the 1960's.* New York: Simon and Schuster, 1979.

Vojan, J. E. S. *The Free English Version of J. J. Jelinek's Bohemian Historical Sketch.* Cicero, Ill.: Bohemian National Cemetery Association Semi-Centennial Jubilee, 1927.

Walker, Daniel. *Rights in Conflict: Convention Week in Chicago August 25–29, 1968.* New York: E. P. Dutton, 1968.

Wallace, William V. *Czechoslovakia.* Boulder, Colo.: Westview, 1976.

Ward, Baldwin H. *Crisis of Change: The Incredible Decade 1960–1970.* New York: Year, 1969.

Wendt, Lloyd, and Herman Kogan. *Big Bill of Chicago.* Indianapolis: Bobbs-Merrill, 1953.

———. *Bosses in Lusty Chicago: The Story of Bathhouse John and Hinky Dink.* Bloomington: Indiana University Press, 1943.

Westfall, Catherine Lee. "The First 'Truly National Laborabory': The Birth of Fermilab." Ph.D. diss., Michigan State University, East Lansing, 1988.

———. "The Site Contest for Fermilab." *Physics Today,* January 1989, pp. 44–52.

Westmoreland, William C. *A Soldier Reports.* Garden City, N.Y.: Doubleday, 1976.

White, Theodore H. *Breach of Faith: The Fall of Richard Nixon.* New York: Atheneum, 1975.

———. *The Making of the President 1960.* New York: Atheneum, 1961.

———. *The Making of the President 1964.* New York: Atheneum, 1965.

Wicker, Tom. *One of Us: Richard Nixon and the American Dream.* New York: Random House, 1991.

Wills, Garry. *Certain Trumpets: The Call of Leaders.* New York: Simon and Schuster, 1994.

Wilson, James Q. *The Amateur Democrat: Club Politics in Three Cities.* Chicago: University of Chicago Press, 1966.

Wilson, Robert Rathbun. *Starting Fermilab*. Batavia, Ill.: Fermi National Accelerator Laboratory, 1992.

Wofford, Harris. *Of Kennedys and Kings: Making Sense of the Sixties*. Pittsburgh: University of Pittsburgh Press, 1980.

Woodward, David E. "Governor Otto Kerner of Illinois and Civil Rights." *Transactions of the Illinois State Historical Society for the Years 1986–1987* (1989): 81–90.

Wright, Eugene A. "Observations of an Appellate Judge: The Use of Law Clerks." *Vanderbilt Law Review* 26 (1973): 1179–96.

Young, Desmond. *Rommel: The Desert Fox*. New York: Harper and Brothers, 1950.

Zaffiri, Samuel. *Westmoreland: A Biography of General William C. Westmoreland*. New York: William Morrow, 1994.

Zbynek, Zeman. *The Masaryks: The Making of Czechoslovakia*. New York: Barnes and Noble Books, 1976.

Zimring, Franklin E., and Gordon Hawkins. *Incapacitation: Penal Confinement and the Restraint of Crime*. New York: Oxford University Press, 1995.

Oral Histories

Columbia University Adlai E. Stevenson Project, New York
   Arvey, Jacob, by Kenneth S. Davis (1968)
Illinois General Assembly Oral History Program, Springfield, Oral History Office, Sangamon State University
   Burditt, George, by Horace Waggoner (2 vols., 1988)
   Burhans, Robert L., by Cullom Davis (1987)
   Clabaugh, Charles W., by Horace Waggoner (2 vols., 1982)
   Davis, Corneal A., by Horace Waggoner (2 vols., 1984)
   Dawson, Frances L., by Horace Waggoner (2 vols., 1982)
   Dunne, George W., by Horace Waggoner (1988)
   Katz, Harold A., by Horace Waggoner (2 vols., 1988)
   Kennedy, Leland J., by Horace Waggoner (2 vols., 1988)
   McCarthy, Robert W., by Horace Waggoner (2 vols., 1983)
   McGloon, Thomas A., by Horace Waggoner (2 vols., 1981)
   O'Brien, Donald, by Horace Waggoner (1988)
   Partee, Cecil A., by Horace Waggoner (2 vols., 1982)
   Rayson, Leland, by Horace Waggoner (1987)
   Redmond, William A., by Lee Nicholson (2 vols., 1986)
   Reum, Walter J., by Horace Waggoner (2 vols., 1980)
   Rowe, Harris, by Horace Waggoner (1988)
   Saltiel, Edward P., by Horace Waggoner (2 vols., 1985)
   Saperstein, Esther, by Horace Waggoner (2 vols., 1987)
   Scariano, Anthony, by Horace Waggoner and Cullom Davis (2 vols., 1988)
   Smith, Elbert S., by Horace Waggoner (2 vols., 1982)
   Van Der Vries, Bernice T., by Horace Waggoner (3 vols., 1980)

Williams, Gale, by Horace Waggoner (2 vols., 1986)
Illinois Statecraft: Memoirs of the Governors, Springfield, Oral History Office,
Sangamon State University
  Bradley, Ralph C., by Cullom Davis (1984)
  Day, William, by Nancy Huntley (1979)
  Downey, William "Smokey," by Marilyn H. Immel (1984)
  Howard, Robert P., by Cullom Davis (1982)
  Ice, Willard, by Cullom Davis (1977)
  Immel, Joseph, by Marilyn H. Immel (1984)
  Kanady, Johnson, by Marilyn H. Immel (1984)
  Klassen, Clarance W., by Ida Klassen (1984)
  McCarter, John W., Jr., by Cullom Davis (1984)
  Michaelson, Ron, by Cullom Davis (1984)
  Pisciotte, Joseph P., by Marilyn H. Immel (1984)
  Pree, Edward, by Marilyn H. Immel (1984)
  Scott, Maurice, by Marilyn H. Immel (1984)
  Selcke, Fred, by Lee Nickelson (1987)
  Tagge, George, by Cullom Davis (1986)
  Walker, Dan, by Marilyn H. Immel (1984)
National Archives and Records Administration, Lyndon Baines Johnson Library,
Austin, Texas
  Abel, I. W., by Joe B. Frantz (7/29/69)
  Cavanaugh, Jerome, by Joe B. Frantz (3/22/71)
  Clark, Ramsey, by Thomas H. Baker (3/21/69; 4/16/69; 6/3/69)
  Harris, Patricia, by Steve Godell (5/19/69)
  Jenkins, Herbert, by Thomas H. Baker (5/14/69)
  Kerner, Otto, by Paige E. Mulhollan (6/12/69)
  McPherson, Harry, by Thomas H. Baker (3/24/69)
  Peden, Katherine, by Joe B. Frantz (11/13/70)
  Wattenberg, Ben, by Thomas H. Baker (11/23/69)
  Wilkins, Roy, by Thomas H. Baker (4/1/69)
  Young, Whitney, by Thomas H. Baker (6/18/69)

Index

Bill Barnhart is the financial markets columnist for the *Chicago Tribune*. A Chicago-based journalist since 1970, he covered Illinois politics from 1970 through 1976. He resides in Chicago with his wife, Catherine A. Eaton.

✦ ✦ ✦

Gene Schlickman is a former Illinois state representative, having served from 1965 to 1981. He practiced law in Arlington Heights and now resides with his wife, Sherry, in Beverly Shores, Indiana. He has written a number of articles and reports covering labor relations and urban development, as well as political commentary.

Typeset in 10/13 Sabon
with Bodoni Poster Compressed display
Designed by Dennis Roberts
Composed by Jim Proefrock
at the University of Illinois Press
Manufactured by Thomson-Shore, Inc.

University of Illinois Press
1325 South Oak Street
Champaign, IL 61820-6903
www.press.uillinois.edu